A PEOPLE'S CHURCH

# A PEOPLE'S CHURCH

MEDIEVAL ITALY AND
CHRISTIANITY, 1050–1300

EDITED BY
AGOSTINO PARAVICINI BAGLIANI
AND NESLIHAN ŞENOCAK

CORNELL UNIVERSITY PRESS
*Ithaca and London*

Copyright © 2023 by Cornell University

All rights reserved. Except for brief quotations in a review, this book, or parts thereof, must not be reproduced in any form without permission in writing from the publisher. For information, address Cornell University Press, Sage House, 512 East State Street, Ithaca, New York 14850. Visit our website at cornellpress.cornell.edu.

First published 2023 by Cornell University Press

Librarians: A CIP catalog record for this book is available from the Library of Congress.

ISBN 978-1-5017-1676-8 (hardcover)
ISBN 978-1-5017-1677-5 (paperback)
ISBN 978-1-5017-1679-9 (pdf)
ISBN 978-1-5017-1678-2 (epub)

# Contents

*Preface* vii
*Acknowledgments* xi
*Note on Names* xiii

1. A View of the Historiography
   AGOSTINO PARAVICINI BAGLIANI AND
   NESLIHAN ŞENOCAK                                 1

2. The Papacy and Italian Politics
   AGOSTINO PARAVICINI BAGLIANI
   AND PIETRO SILANOS                              21

3. Bishops
   MAUREEN C. MILLER                               47

4. Pievi and the Care of Souls
   NESLIHAN ŞENOCAK                                71

5. Monasticism
   CÉCILE CABY                                     93

6. Lay Confraternities
   MARINA GAZZINI                                 128

7. Clerical Confraternities
   ANTONIO RIGON                                  161

8. Mendicants
   GIOVANNA CASAGRANDE                            189

9. Saints
   ANTONELLA DEGL'INNOCENTI                       222

10. Heresy
   MARIA PIA ALBERZONI                      257

11. Urban Religion
    FRANCES ANDREWS                         298

12. Case Study I: Florence
    GEORGE DAMERON                          335

13. Case Study II: Naples
    GIOVANNI VITOLO                         372

*Contributors  413*

*Index  417*

# Preface

The present volume was born out of a desire to insert Italy more firmly into the Anglophone historiography of medieval religious history. Medieval Italy has a very distinct history compared to other parts of Europe. North Italy during the High Middle Ages comprised numerous self-governing communes rather than being under the rule of a royal or aristocratic dynasty. The political system of communes was fairly sophisticated, with different socioeconomic classes such as magnates, *popolo grasso*, or *popolo minuto* being represented by different governing bodies, all of them working in collaboration, though at times not without sharp conflicts. Therefore, it would not be wrong to say that the ordinary folk were much more directly involved with the affairs of the state than anywhere else in Europe, and that habit demonstrated itself also in matters of religion. Civic pride was paramount, and urban life was especially vivid. As the city communes expanded their jurisdiction over the surrounding countryside, the *contado*, the divide between the rural and urban population became less sharp. The economic upheaval of the towns gave rise to a robust middle class, which was devoted to and able to support religious causes. That fact coupled with a warmer Mediterranean climate allowed a variety of eremitic, monastic, and mendicant movements, which relied on lay support, to flourish. The seat of the papacy in this period was in Rome, that is, right in the middle of the Italian peninsula; hence the papacy exerted a greater influence on medieval religious and political life in Italy than it did elsewhere. These are only a few of the factors that set Italy apart from the rest of Europe in the High Middle Ages and that allowed a very rich religious culture with a high variety of devotional expressions to flourish.

The purpose of this book is twofold: first, to provide, as much as possible, an even overview of the Christian institutional, devotional, and social history of one of the most vibrant and interesting regions of medieval Europe with marvelous archival riches; and second, to make the work of the prominent historians writing in Italian accessible to the English-speaking reader. The audience that the editors had especially in mind is graduate students and scholars who need a first introduction to the Christian culture and institutions in medieval Italy. Generally it has been assumed that the reader of this volume will have a basic familiarity with medieval religious history and its specific terminology. As editors, we made an effort to explain only those religious terms that are specific to Italy, but not others if a term signified a phenomenon found elsewhere in Europe.

Though it is customary in the edited volumes of collected articles to talk briefly about each and every chapter, here the topics are broadly conceived as essential aspects of Christian religious life. Therefore, the contents of the articles do not need an introduction; the short titles are meant to be self-explanatory. Instead, a brief outline of the editorial vision and choices might be pertinent and assist the reader in understanding the scope of this undertaking.

As editors, we bear the responsibility for fixing the list of subjects that made up the content of the chapters and inviting experts to write about them, but our choice was not without constraints. As a result, some of the topics that are prevalent in general Anglophone historiography of medieval religion, such as the Crusades, religious art, or materiality to give a few examples, have been left out. These constraints were the simple expedient of keeping the book within the length agreed with Cornell University Press, the current state of the Italian-language historiography that has had different priorities, interests, and focal points than its Anglophone counterpart, and the difficulty of securing an expert who would be able to deliver an article on a given topic within the given time frame. After all, the contributors did not have an easy task: they had to produce an essay giving an overview of their theme in a two-and-a-half-century period. We asked the contributors to produce fundamentally an introductory piece, presenting the essential historical knowledge in their assigned topic, not write an original research piece or develop a new theoretical perspective. We also requested that they focus more on the aspects of religious life that are distinctive to Italy.

The two case studies with their focus on a specific city, one from the north (Florence) and one from the south of Italy (Naples), stand out within the usual structure of this volume, where the other chapters are dedicated to a theme. This was a conscious choice from the beginning. There is a great deal of benefit in seeing how the various aspects of medieval religious life discussed in the theme-based chapters play out in a particular city to convey the sense of how the specific religious institutions, movements, and actors interact with and shape one another. These case studies help us to envision the religious landscape as a whole, while at the same time exemplifying how the religious life took on different forms in two different localities with distinct political and social heritage.

We also asked the contributors to use footnotes as sparingly as possible so as not to prolong the essays, confining the listing of essential works on subtopics to the selected bibliography section at the end of the chapters. These sections are meant to serve as a guideline for any scholar who would like to pursue deeper research into that topic.

Finally, although we set the time parameter of the book as 1050–1300, in certain cases the authors chose to go beyond this period. They saw value in expanding the time frame whenever their subject had an arc of historical development that did not match the periodical parameter of the book, and the earlier or later historical picture uniquely illuminated the distinctive history of the Christian religious culture in Italy. Exemplary in this respect is Antonio Rigon's chapter, where in his final section he talks of how the strong bonds between clerical confraternities and the laity prevented the Protestant Reformation from taking hold in Italy.

A last word on the translations: Italian academic prose has its own conventions and, being heavily stylized, does not lend itself easily to translation into English. The translators in this volume were often faced with the difficult choice of remaining faithful to the word choice and forms of expressions of the authors writing in Italian or French or rendering the text into English as colloquially as possible. All translated chapters have gone through numerous checks and retranslations, but our aim has not been to present them in English as if written by a native speaker of English. We did not want to altogether dismantle the authorial voice that is unique to each scholar. Moreover, certain terms that are prevalent in the Italian academic literature such as "associanismo" (to give but one example), which is used heavily in the Italian confraternal historiography, do not have colloquial equivalents in English. By translating them into English as close as possible to the original word, our hope was to introduce into the Anglophone scholarship new terms and concepts that might better explain the historical phenomena.

We sincerely hope that this volume will serve as a starting point for future research on the various religious aspects of medieval Christian culture and inspire more scholars to study the fascinating history of medieval Italy, as well as being a helpful reference resource not only for historians, but also historians of art, literary scholars, and scholars of religion. We also hope that such an undertaking will lead to comparative studies between Italy and other parts of Europe, in the spirit of Robert Brentano's work, which will allow us to understand why certain religious institutions or forms of worship took hold in certain parts of Europe and not in others. The ultimate judgment on whether the final product lived up to all these hopes we attached to it belongs no doubt to the reader.

# Acknowledgments

"Teamwork makes the dream work." This motto holds undeniably true for this particular occasion. To bring into life a historical enterprise of this kind, a great many people have brought in their labor, to all of whom we are grateful. We first discussed the idea for this book eight years ago over a dinner at an Indian restaurant in Florence. Sitting in the midst of the colorful and earthen colors of Haveli, we came up with the idea of editing a volume on the religious history of medieval Italy. We drew up a list of topics to be included in this book and paired them with the scholars whom we thought would deliver an excellent discussion of that topic.

We were not mistaken. We owe tremendous thanks and gratitude to the marvelous team of contributors to this book, all of them distinguished scholars in their field. It was not an easy task we asked them to do, which was to give an overview of the important historical and historiographical points on these vast topics complete with a bibliography for further reading. They all generously agreed and delivered their chapters in due time. We would like to thank them all not just for their contributions, but also for their patience as the work proceeded over the years slowly amid teaching and administrative duties and family obligations, with a big disruption during the years of the pandemic.

The next round of thanks, no doubt, goes to translators. Among them, scholars of medieval history will recognize the names of William North and George Ferzoco, both of them exemplary scholars and persons. We can never repay their kindness and diligence, and their willingness to be involved in this project. Carolyn Quijano, whom I (Nesli) am very proud to call my PhD student, contributed two translations. Hilary Siddons has been an example of kindness and professional prowess, translating two chapters and lending her expert knowledge of Italian in other chapters as well. We would also like to thank to Lochlin Brouilliard, who translated the only chapter written in French.

Laura Napran deserves much praise for her professionalism and sheer bravura as a copy editor and indexer.

Brette L. Jackson and David Mayernik deserve our gratitude for gifting us the wonderful cover. Together, they traveled to the site of the medieval Pieve of Romena in Tuscany, and David, an amazingly talented artist, painted it en plein air just for this book.

Cornell University Press has been for many years the home of so many essential books on medieval history. We would also like to thank very much Mahinder Kingra, Karen Hwa, and the entire team at Cornell for their enthusiasm for, support of, and meticulous work on this project.

A number of institutions also need to be warmly acknowledged here. Among these are the Villa I Tatti, the Harvard Center for Italian Renaissance Studies, the National Humanities Center, and the Shelby Cullom Davis Center for Historical Studies at Princeton University. We owe tremendous gratitude to Fredrick C. Harris, dean emeritus of Social Science at Columbia University, who provided the funds necessary for the translations.

## Note on Names

A medieval person's name that originates from Italy has been left in Italian unless that person is well known in Anglophone scholarship, in which case we use the anglicized name, such as Francis of Assisi instead of Francesco d'Assisi. For saints, if the name is Italian we use the Italian "san" or "santa" but "Saint" with anglicized names. In Italian, these markers of holiness are used without being capitalized when they signify the person but are capitalized when that saint's name is used to designate an ecclesiastical institution, such as a church or a monastery— "santa Verdiana" but the "church of Santa Verdiana."

CHAPTER 1

# A View of the Historiography

*Agostino Paravicini Bagliani and Neslihan Şenocak*

If only for the age and number of its dioceses, and for the presence of the pope, nowhere in medieval Europe did the Church have such an omnipresent role as in Italy. In its various branches—secular and monastic, episcopal and canonical—the Church had extremely complex relations with the enormous quantity and vast array of political, economic, and cultural/social entities there. This explains why, despite the richness of recent historiography of medieval Italy, works of synthesis and breadth dealing with premodern Italian religious and ecclesiastical history are rare. A notable exception is to be found in "La storia religiosa," the large and fundamental work published half a century ago (1974) by Giovanni Miccoli (1933-2017) for the *Storia d'Italia* published by Einaudi, an extremely innovative study that even now remains at the root of many historiographical studies.[1] For the first time within the sphere of Italian historiography, the religious realities of the entire medieval period were presented in a broad

---

1. Giovanni Miccoli, "La storia religiosa," in *Storia d'Italia*, vol. 2, *Dalla caduta dell'Impero romano al secolo XVIII*, ed. Ruggero Romano and Corrado Vivanti (Turin: Einaudi, 1974), bk. 1:431-1079. Roberto Rusconi, "Un profilo della vita religiosa in Italia," in *Una storiografia inattuale? Giovanni Miccoli e la funzione civile della ricerca storica* (Rome: Viella, 2005), 103-50. See also the acts of a seminar organized in Turin by Franco Bolgiani, published in *Rivista di storia e letteratura religiosa* 32 (1996): 333-433 (with a contribution by Giovanni Miccoli himself).

field of observations including the economy, politics, and culture. Inspired in part by the work of Delio Cantimori (1904-66),[2] the author of a foundational study on sixteenth-century Italian heretics, Giovanni Miccoli based his historical research upon the conviction that religion has to be understood on its own terms but within a broader historical process, without ideological presuppositions. He was mindful of the fact that from the time of Pope Gregory VII (1073-85) onward (see his important 1966 study on the Gregorian Church), the religious evolution of medieval Christendom was deeply influenced not only by the affirmation of the monarchic power of the papacy over the religious life of the faithful, but also by attempts at renewal and reform, or rather by religious expectations aimed at recovering "the primitive form of the Church" (recalling the title of another of Miccoli's important works, this one from 1960).[3] These are themes to which Miccoli returned in the last years of his life with important studies on Fra Dolcino and Francis of Assisi.[4]

A reply to Miccoli's historical synthesis for Einaudi's *Storia d'Italia* was attempted by Gregorio Penco (1926-2013), a monk of the abbey of S. Maria di Finalpia (Finale Ligure, Savona) and professor of medieval history at Rome's Pontificio Ateneo Sant'Anselmo. The first volume of Penco's *Storia della Chiesa in Italia* covers the entire period from "the origins" to the Council of Trent.[5] This work—the only one with this title to appear during the twentieth century—was not welcomed by scholars on account of its antiquated approach (as Giorgio Cracco put it), as Penco provided at once a "history and nonhistory of the Church."[6]

---

2. Delio Cantimori, *Eretici italiani del Cinquecento e altri scritti* (Turin: Einaudi, 1992). On Delio Cantimori, see Giovanni Miccoli, *Delio Cantimori: La ricerca di una nuova critica storiografica; in appendice, l'elenco ei corsi e dei seminari, e la bibliografia degli scritti* (Turin: Einaudi, 1970).

3. Giovanni Miccoli, *Chiesa Gregoriana: Ricerche sulla Riforma del secolo XI* (Florence: La Nuova Italia, 1966; new ed., Rome: Herder, 1979). Giovanni Miccoli, "Ecclesiae primitivae forma," *Studi medievali*, 3rd series, 1 (1960): 470-98.

4. Giovanni Miccoli, "Fra Dolcino," in *Arnaldo da Brescia*, ed. Grado Giovanni Merlo and Francesco Mores, Variazioni 34 (Pisa: Edizioni della Normale, 2017), 79-81; Miccoli, *Francesco d'Assisi e l'Ordine dei minori* (Milan: Edizioni Biblioteca Franciscana, 1999); Miccoli, *Francesco d'Assisi: Memoria, storia e storiografia* (Milan: Edizioni Biblioteca Franciscana, 2010).

5. Gregorio Penco, *Storia della Chiesa in Italia*, vol. 1, *Dalle origini al Concilio di Trento* (Milan: Jaca Book, 1978).

6. Giorgio Cracco, "La 'Storia della Chiesa in Italia' di padre Gregorio Penco, 1. Storia e non storia della Chiesa," *Ricerche di storia sociale e religiosa* 21-22 (1982): 56-67. See also the critical reflections of Giacomo Martina, "La 'Storia della Chiesa in Italia' di Gregorio Penco," *Gregorianum* 62 (1981): 115-34.

# 1. A VIEW OF THE HISTORIOGRAPHY

Original in its aim to highlight the institutional differences of the Churches of England and Italy in the thirteenth century, *Two Churches: England and Italy in the Thirteenth Century* by Robert Brentano (1926–2002) was very quickly and positively received in Italy, thanks to its (perhaps overly) speedy translation into Italian.[7] The author had not set out to write a history of the two Churches, and his comparison often relied on intuitive insights based on his extraordinary capacity to gather often neglected (and even hitherto unknown) essential pieces, arising from textual sources, institutional aspects, and biographical information. Previously, Brentano had made his reputation through a profound study of the metropolitan jurisdiction of the Church of York in its relations with papal judicial delegates.[8]

In more recent times, problems relating to Italian ecclesiastical and religious history have found the attention they deserve in general historical syntheses on medieval Italy. Examples include articles by Paolo Cammarosano (born 1943) and by Ovidio Capitani (1930–2012) on the early and late medieval periods respectively;[9] others can be found in books of collected articles dealing with, for example, the communal period, particular regions (such as Puglia), the Latin Church in Norman Italy or the hills near Treviso and Verona, or, indeed, particular chronological periods (such as the twelfth century).[10] A scholar of diverse historiographical interests, Ovidio Capitani made important contributions to the study of the so-called Gregorian Reform, paying special attention to the recent scholarly literature.[11]

---

7. Robert Brentano, *Two Churches: England and Italy in the Thirteenth Century* (Berkeley: University of California Press, 1968; new ed., 1988); Brentano, *Due chiese: Italia e Inghilterra nel XIII secolo* (Bologna: Il Mulino, 1972).

8. Robert Brentano, *York Metropolitan Jurisdiction and Papal Judges Delegate, 1279–1296* (Berkeley: University of California Press, 1959).

9. Paolo Cammarosano, *Storia dell'Italia medievale: Dal VI all'XI secolo* (Bari: Editori Laterza, 2008); Ovidio Capitani, *Storia dell'Italia medievale, 410–1216* (Bari: Editori Laterza, 2009).

10. Giuliano Milani, *I comuni italiani: Secoli XII–XIV* (Bari: Editori Laterza, 2005); F. Menant, *L'Italia dei comuni (1100–1350)* (Rome: Viella, 2011); Jean-Marie Martin, *La Pouille du VI$^e$ au XII$^e$ siècle* (Rome: École française de Rome, 1993); G. A. Loud, *The Latin Church in Norman Italy* (Cambridge: Cambridge University Press, 2007); Giuseppina De Sandre Gasparini, *La vita religiosa nella Marca veronese-trevigiana tra XII e XIV secolo* (Verona: Libreria Universitaria Editrice, 1993); Maureen C. Miller, "Italy in the Long Twelfth Century: Ecclesiastical Reform and the Legitimization of a New Political Order, 1059-1183," in *European Transformations: The Long Twelfth Century*, ed. Thomas F. X. Noble and John Van Engen (Notre Dame, IN: University of Notre Dame Press, 2012), 117–31.

11. Ovidio Capitani, "Gregorio VII, papa, santo," in *Dizionario biografico degli Italiani*, vol. 59 (Rome: Istituto della Enciclopedia Italiana, 2002), 146-60; Capitani, "La riforma della

The near or total absence of comprehensive studies on the history of the Church in Italy contrasts with the extraordinary historiographical output in Italy on particular themes of religious and ecclesiastical history published in the journals and editorial collections (the highest number among the European nations), in addition to many long-standing series of international conferences dealing with problems of religious and ecclesiastical history.

In Italy, before the end of World War II, there were few journals devoted to religious history (apart from ones dealing with specific religious orders or geographical areas), and some of these originated in marginal religious movements. One example is the *Bulletin de la Société d'histoire vaudoise*, founded in 1881 in Torre Pellice (Turin), which was published under the title *Bollettino della Società di storia valdese* from 1931 to 1940, when the title again changed, this time to *Bollettino della Società di studi valdesi: Rivista di studi e ricerche concernenti il valdismo e i movimenti di riforma religiosa in Italia*. Another is *Bilychnis: Rivista mensile di studi religiosi*, published by the Scuola Teologica Battista di Roma from 1912 to 1931. There was at least one religious history journal inspired by the *histoire des religions*, which was at that time highly dominant north of the Alps: *Studi e materiali di storia delle religioni*, founded in 1925 by Raffaele Pettazzoni at the University of Rome. Paolo Guerrini (1880-1960), future director of the Archivio Storico Cittadino, had already founded in 1910 a journal of historical-ecclesiastical studies of the diocese of Brescia, *Brixia Sacra*, which remains one of the most active journals of Church history of Italian cities, edited by the Associazione per la storia della Chiesa bresciana.

In 1944, while Rome was under Nazi occupation, in a meeting at the Vatican the decision was made to establish a journal of religious history. It was born with the support not only of the pontifical universities but also of the Vatican Library, the Archivio Apostolico Vaticano, and the secretary of state; notable was the role of Giovanni Battista Montini, then substitute for general affairs in the Vatican Secretariat of State and later Pope Paul VI (1963-78). Following this decision, Michele

---

Chiesa e la lotta per le investiture," in *Storia della società italiana*, vol. 5, *L'Italia dell'Alto Medioevo*, ed. Giovanni Cherubini (Milan: Sandro Teti Editore, 1984), 279-344; Capitani, "Storiografia e riforma della Chiesa in Italia," in *La storiografia altomedievale* (Spoleto: Centro italiano di studi per l'alto medioevo, 1970), 557-630; Capitani, "Gregoriana: Impressioni di lettura e note in margine a 'Studi Gregoriani,'" *Rivista di storia della Chiesa in Italia* 18 (1964): 467-94; Capitani, *L'Italia medievale nei secoli di trapasso: La riforma della Chiesa (1012-1122)* (Bologna: Patròn, 1984).

# 1. A VIEW OF THE HISTORIOGRAPHY

Maccarrone (1910–93), then a young professor of ecclesiastical history, finalized the project inspired by the initiatives that had developed at the turn of the twentieth century as well as more recent ones (especially *Zeitschrift für Kirchengeschichte*, 1877–; *Revue d'histoire de l'Église de France*, 1910–). The inaugural issue of the first Italian journal dedicated to the history of the Church in Italy—*Rivista di storia della Chiesa in Italia*—was published in 1947. At that time, Maccarrone was teaching Church history at the Pontificia Università Lateranense and was already a recognized authority on papal history, particularly Pope Innocent III (1198–1216),[12] and was being supported in his efforts by two great scholars. One was Hubert Jedin (1900–80), author of fundamental studies on the Council of Trent; the other was Pio Paschini (1878–1962), rector from 1932 to 1957 of the Lateranense and among the most important historians, in the ecclesiastical sphere, of the Church in Italy. The final two words of the journal's title, "in Italia," were suggested by Giovanni Mercati (1866–1957; cardinal and librarian and archivist of the Holy See from 1936). By this, Mercati intended to evoke the many traditions within the history of the nation, convinced of the absence of a single or homogeneous Italian Church.[13] Inspired by the *Revue d'histoire ecclésiastique*, founded in 1900 by Professor Alfred Henri Joseph Cauchie of the Catholic University of Louvain, the *Rivista di storia della Chiesa in Italia* devoted considerable attention to bibliographical notices. Thus was born a systematic annotated bibliography, subdivided into historical periods and sociopolitical regions, that remains to this day one of the focal points of the *Rivista*.

Four years later (1951), the priest Giuseppe De Luca (1898–1962) established a journal, *Archivio italiano per la storia della pietà*, notable in the Italian and international editorial panorama not only for its title but for its aim to examine expressions of interior religiosity that De

---

12. Michele Maccarrone, "Innocenzo III prima del pontificato," *Archivio della Società romana di storia patria* 66 (1943): 59–134.

13. Paolo Vian, "Le origini e il programma della 'Rivista di storia della Chiesa in Italia' (1938–1947)," in *Cinquant'anni di vita della "Rivista di storia della Chiesa in Italia": Atti del convegno di studio (Roma, 8–10 September 1999)*, ed. Pietro Zerbi (Rome: Herder, 2003), 15–99; Maria Lupi, "Italian Historical Periodicals on the Church and Christianity since the End of the Second World War," in *Religious Studies in the 20th Century: A Survey on Disciplines, Cultures and Questions. Proceedings of the International Colloquium, Assisi 2003*, ed. M. Faggioli and A. Melloni (Münster: LIT Verlag, 2006), 275–80. See also Giovanni Miccoli, "La storia della Chiesa di fronte agli studi storici positivi: Dalla *Revue d'histoire ecclésiastique* alla *Rivista di storia della Chiesa in Italia*," in *Introduzione all'uso delle riviste storiche*, ed. Nino Recupero and Giacomo Todeschini (Trieste: EUT Edizioni Università di Trieste, 1994), 127–38.

Luca himself sought passionately within poems, prayers, songs, and devout celebrations that emanate from popular social environments—a far cry from the institutional framework found within the *Rivista di storia della Chiesa in Italia*. De Luca had for years expressed damning judgments of religious studies in Italy, which had suffered particularly due to (as he put it) "the overly rigid, often repressive and occasionally destructive measures" taken against modernism.[14] The *Archivio italiano per la storia della pietà* became a focal point of Edizioni di Storia e Letteratura, founded earlier by De Luca in collaboration with the noted philologist and Italianist Alfred Schiaffini (1895-1971), which (guided by De Luca's sister, Nuccia) became in the second half of the twentieth century one of the most important editorial enterprises of high erudition in all of Europe.

In 1954 the journal *Ricerche di storia religiosa* was launched, directed by a committee based mainly at Rome's Università La Sapienza. The journal did not last long—only four annual issues were produced—but its birth was the result of profound changes in the Italian historiographical panorama. Following on from foreign (and especially French) approaches, interest in religious themes increased, partly due to the influence of the institutional Church in Italy over the years, but perhaps even more in relation to the religious aspects of Italian society.

The *Rivista di storia e letteratura religiosa* was founded in 1965, its title echoing the *Revue d'histoire et littérature religieuses* that had been founded in 1896 by Alfred Loisy (1857-1940). The new journal's approach was outlined in its first issue, and taken up repeatedly by its main editor, Franco Bolgiani (1922-2012).[15] This new religious studies journal underlined the "distinction between theological analysis and historical analysis," taking on "an open and dynamic conception of the history of Christianity." Thematic areas would not be limited (for example, by geography) and would be open to other religions.[16]

The outlooks of the two other most important journals, at a national level, founded around the same time were broadly similar in regard to their historiographical outlooks, particularly in their explicit

---

14. Giuseppe De Luca-Giuseppe Prezzolini, *Carteggio (1925–1962)* (Roma: Edizioni di Storia e Letteratura, 1975), 51.

15. *Rivista di storia e letteratura religiosa: Periodico quadrimestrale redatto presso la Biblioteca interdipartimentale di scienze religiose Erik Peterson dell'Università di Torino* (Florence: Olschki, 1965). See "Franco Bolgiani (1922-2012): Autoritratto," *Rivista di storia e letteratura religiosa* 48 (2012): 487-91.

16. Cf. Lupi, "Italian Historical Periodicals on the Church and Christianity," 290-92.

## 1. A VIEW OF THE HISTORIOGRAPHY

contrasts with the ecclesiastical historiographical tradition. These journals are *Ricerche di storia sociale e religiosa*, founded in 1972 by Gabriele De Rosa (1917-2009), and *Cristianesimo nella storia*, founded in 1980 by Giuseppe Alberigo (1926-2007).[17] They reflect the vitality of two research centers: Vicenza's Istituto per le ricerche di storia sociale e di storia religiosa, and Bologna's Istituto per le scienze religiose. They explicitly declare an independence in historical research and apply it to the entire historical period of Christianity. *Cristianesimo nella storia* set itself the goal of following a "commitment to critical historical research worthy of global understanding of the Christian reality," beyond the "traditional limits of 'Church history'" and institutional denominations more generally—not only geographically but, beyond institutions and historical events, to include "doctrines, traditions, spiritualities, the lived experiences of Christians in community, Christianity that is to be seen outside established churches... with careful attention to the historical-cultural contexts with which Christians are in contact with one another."[18] *Cristianesimo nella storia* intended to be open to "critical analyses of theological considerations," not only within the history of theology, such that there would be an increased awareness of "the distinction [between] a historical understanding of Christianity and theological reflection."

Beyond the systematic bibliography on the history of the Church in Italy to be found in each volume of the *Rivista di storia della Chiesa in Italia*, a section dealing with Italian cities as well as with the papacy has been maintained since annual publication began in 1980 of *Medioevo latino*, founded by Claudio Leonardi (1926-2010). This annotated bibliography on themes relative to the Latin culture of the Middle Ages is now accessible online via the site *Mirabile* (www.mirabileweb.it) of the Società internazionale per lo studio del Medioevo latino (SISMEL), based in Florence. The bibliography of the *Archivum Historiae Pontificiae* (founded in 1963), brilliantly edited for its first thirty years by Pál Arató (1914-93), is important in relation to the infinite links between the papacy and the Church in Italy.[19]

---

17. *Ricerche di storia sociale e religiosa* (Rome: Edizioni di storia e letteratura, 1972- ). *Cristianesimo nella storia* (Bologna: EDB, 1980-).

18. *Cristianesimo nella storia*, 1 (2008), 1-2.

19. *Archivum Historiae Pontificiae* (Rome: Pontificia Universitas Gregoriana Facultas Historiae Ecclesiasticae, 1963-); see M. S. Boari, "L'Archivum Historiae Pontificiae e la sua bibliografia," *Archivum Historiae Pontificiae* 51 (2013): 197-220.

Leafing through the indexes of some of these journals up to the 1990s, some prevalent thematic interests clearly emerge. The time period that is least represented is antiquity; although it is to be found easily in *Rivista di storia e letteratura religiosa* (39.5 percent) and *Cristianesimo nella storia* (23 percent), its presence in the other journals is well below 10 percent. The medieval period is most prevalent in *Archivum Historiae Pontificiae* (44 percent), *Rivista di storia della Chiesa in Italia* (40 percent up to 1976, but 34 percent from 1977 to 1991), and the first series of the *Archivio italiano per la storia della pietà* (51 percent), but is also easily found in *Rivista di storia e letteratura religiosa* (20 percent) and *Cristianesimo nella storia* (19 percent). In *Ricerche di storia sociale e religiosa* there appears instead a clear emphasis on the modern and contemporary periods (46 percent modern and 46.5 percent contemporary), which is understandable, given the sources favored by most authors who publish in the journal.[20]

In 1961, thanks to Michele Maccarrone, the *Rivista di storia della Chiesa in Italia* gave rise to a series of international conferences on aspects of ecclesiastical and religious history. The success of these conferences, and their influence on historiography, surpassed the hopes of the organizers. The theme of the second conference, dealing with bishops and dioceses in medieval Italy, confirmed the historical-institutional line privileged by the *Rivista* since its creation.[21] These years witnessed particularly intensive collaborations in areas relative to historiography. Parallel to the second conference of the *Rivista di storia della Chiesa in Italia*, Paolo Sambin (1913–2003) founded a new series of studies, with the notable title "Italia Sacra," that has become the most important in the world relative to aspects of Italian religious and ecclesiastical history.[22]

---

20. Maria Lupi, "Italian Historical Periodicals on the Church and Christianity since the End of the Second World War," in *Religious Studies in the Twentieth Century: A Survey on Disciplines, Cultures, and Questions. Proceedings of the Assisi Conference, December 11–13, 2003*, ed. Massimo Faggioli and Alberto Melloni, Christianity and History 2, (Münster: LIT Verlag, 2006) 298–99.

21. *Vescovi e diocesi in Italia nel medioevo (sec. IX–XIII): Atti del II Convegno di Storia della Chiesa in Italia (Roma, 5–9 sett. 1961)* (Padua: Editrice Antenore, 1964). Almost thirty years later, a second conference was held on the same theme, but restricted to the fourteenth through the sixteenth centuries: Giuseppina De Sandre Gasparini et al., eds., *Vescovi e diocesi in Italia dal 14. alla metà del 16. secolo: Atti del 7. convegno di storia della Chiesa in Italia, Brescia, 21–25 settembre 1987* (Rome: Herder, 1990).

22. Paolo Sambin, "Nuove iniziative di pubblicazioni di storia della Chiesa in Italia," *Archiva Ecclesiae* 2 (1979): 179–88. Volumes 1–22 were published in Padua by Editrice Antenore; volumes 23–84 in Rome by Herder Editrice e Libreria; from volume 85 onward, publishing is by the Istituto Storico Italiano per il Medio Evo (Rome).

# 1. A VIEW OF THE HISTORIOGRAPHY

Through the University of Padua, Sambin gave life to a lively workshop, unique in Italy, dealing with the ecclesiastical history of the areas of Padua and Venice. In 1976, Sambin and two other editors of the series (including Germano Guardo of the Vatican Apostolic Archive) withdrew from the committee of the Rivista after the journal's director, Monsignor Maccarrone, suspended Paolo Brezzi, deemed culpable for having run for political office as a member of the Independent Left group.[23]

Even before the aforementioned conference on Italian bishops and dioceses, the Centro italiano di studi sul Basso Medioevo–Accademia Tudertina had in 1957 organized the first of a lengthy (and still operative) series of conferences, the first one dedicated to the first great religious poet in the Italian vernacular, Iacopone da Todi.[24] Two years later saw the first of the "Convegni della Mendola," organized by the Catholic University of Milan, with the theme of the little-explored common life of clerics.[25] In the decades to follow, the "Mendola" conferences became a highlight of international meetings dedicated to historiography, often concentrating on themes that broke away from a primarily institutional perspective, such as the religious life of laypeople in the eleventh and twelfth centuries.[26] Many themes of religious history in international conferences drew their origin from concepts relative to Italy—for example, the 1993 conference organized by André Vauchez of the École française de Rome on civic religion, or that of the medieval parish organized in Lausanne in 1991.[27]

That the second conference of the *Rivista di storia della Chiesa in Italia* was dedicated to bishops and dioceses confirms their fundamental

---

23. Antonio Rigon, "Paolo Sambin e la 'Rivista di storia della Chiesa in Italia,'" *Rivista di storia della Chiesa in Italia* 58 (2004): 381–89.

24. *Iacopone da Todi e il suo tempo: Atti del I Convegno storico internazionale Todi, 13–15 ottobre 1957* (Spoleto: Centro italiano di studi sull'alto medioevo, 1959).

25. *La vita comune del clero nei secoli XI e XII: Atti della Settimana di studio, Mendola, settembre 1959*, 2 vols. (Milan: Vita e Pensiero, 1962).

26. *I laici nella Societas christiana dei secoli XI e XII: Atti della terza Settimana internazionale di studio, Mendola 1965* (Milan: Vita e Pensiero, 1968). At least two other conferences of the "Mendola" concern problems of Italian ecclesiastical history, in concert with medieval Christianity: *Le istituzioni ecclesiastiche della "Societas christiana" dei secoli XI–XII: Papato, cardinalato ed episcopate. Atti della quinta settimana internazioanale di studio, Mendola, 26–31 agosto 1971* (Milan: Vita e Pensiero, 1974); Giancarlo Andenna, ed., *Sperimentazioni istituzionali nella societas Christiana (1046–1250): Atti della sedicesima Settimana internazionale di studio, Mendola, 26–31 agosto 2004* (Milan: Vita e Pensiero, 2007).

27. André Vauchez, ed., *La religion civique à l'époque médiévale et moderne (chrétienté et islam): Actes du colloque de Nanterre (21–23 juin 1993)* (Rome: École française de Rome, 1995); Agostino Paravicini Bagliani and Véronique Pasche, eds., *La parrocchia nel Medio Evo: Economia, scambi, solidarietà* (Rome: Herder, 1995).

historical importance, in a country that had known the greatest number of dioceses from the earliest Christian centuries to the present day. It is useful to recall that the oldest historiographical attempt at an episcopal prosopography for an entire nation dates back to 1644, through the efforts of the monk Ferdinando Ughelli (1595-1670).[28] Since then there have been only two large-scale prosopographical enterprises, both the work of German scholars, dealing with Italian bishops on a regional basis. Gerhard Schwartz has concentrated on Italian bishops of regions belonging to the Holy Roman Empire from 951 to 1122, and Norbert Kamp (1927-99) dedicated his work to the bishops of the Kingdom of Sicily under the Hohenstaufen (1194-1266).[29] Although Francesco Lanzoni a century ago rigorously reconstructed the history of Italian dioceses up to Gregory the Great (590-604), scholars still lack comprehensive studies of Italian dioceses similar to what is available in France through the series Histoire des diocèses de France.[30]

As is the case for many other aspects of Italian history, the historiography relative to individual cities is the space in which one finds the best historical research. This field is so rich and ample that it is impossible to give its worth in this brief overview, as can be seen from just a number of studies dealing with the cities of Lucca, Orvieto, Florence, Rieti, Piemonte, Pisa, or Asti,[31] or volumes containing analyses of the relations between bishops and holders of political power, especially

---

28. Ferdinando Ughelli and Niccolò Coleti, *Italia Sacra sive de episcopis Italiae et insularum adjacentium: Rebusque ab iis præclare gestis, deducta serie ad nostram usque ætatem*, 9 vols. (Rome, 1644-62; 2nd ed., 10 vols., Venice, 1717-22).

29. Gerhard Schwartz, *Die Besetzung der Bistümer Reichsitaliens unter den sächsischen und salischen Kaisern mit den Listen der Bischöfe, 951-1122* (Leipzig: B.G. Teubner, 1913); Norbert Kamp, *Kirche und Monarchie im staufischen Königreich Sizilien*, vol. 1, *Prosopographische Grundlegung: Bistümer und Bischöfe des Königreichs 1194-1266*, 4 vols. (Munich: Fink, 1973-82).

30. Francesco Lanzoni, *Le diocesi d'Italia dalle origini al principio del secolo VII (a. 604): Studio critico*, 2 vols. (Faenza: Istituto Grafico F. Lega, 1927), then reprinted in the series Studi e Testi by the Biblioteca Apostolica Vaticana (1963). Histoire des diocèses de France (Paris: Leteouzey et Ané, 1967-).

31. Duane J. Osheim, *An Italian Lordship: The Bishopric of Lucca in the Late Middle Ages* (Berkeley: University of California Press, 1977); David Foote, *Lordship, Reform, and the Development of Civil Society in Medieval Italy: The Bishopric of Orvieto, 1100-1250* (Notre Dame, IN: University of Notre Dame Press, 2004); George W. Dameron, *Florence and Its Church in the Age of Dante* (Philadelphia: University of Pennsylvania Press, 2005); Robert Brentano, *A New World in a Small Place: Church and Religion in the Diocese of Rieti, 1188-1378* (Berkeley: University of California Press, 1994); Caterina Ciccopiedi, *Diocesi e riforme nel Medioevo: Orientamenti ecclesiastici e religiosi dei vescovi nel Piemonte dei secoli X e XI*, Studia taurinensia 39 (Turin: Effatà, 2012); Mauro Ronzani, "La chiesa cittadina pisana tra Due e Trecento," in *Genova, Pisa e il Mediterraneo tra due e trecento: Per il 7 centenario della battaglia della Meloria, Genova, 24-27 ottobre 1984*, Atti della società ligure di storia patria 24 (Genoa: Società Ligure di storia patria, 1984), 283-348; Ezio

## 1. A VIEW OF THE HISTORIOGRAPHY

from the viewpoint of family strategies.³² The undeniable connection of the bishop's pastoral function and his political power is at the center of particularly innovative studies on the bishop's palace, examined in cultural terms alongside important analyses of thirteenth-century Roman pontifical residences.³³ Nicolangelo D'Acunto contributed greatly to the understanding of the political and institutional function of bishops.³⁴

The importance of bishops in medieval Italian society is witnessed by a large number of studies over the years of the many bishops who left a hagiographical footprint.³⁵ Episcopal elections often gave rise to local conflicts that went beyond mere personal disagreements with cathedral canons, involving questions of an institutional or political nature; indeed, these were often occasions when the papacy would impose itself

---

C. Pio, *La giustizia del vescovo: Società, economia e Chiesa cittadina ad Asti tra 13 e 14 secolo* (Rome: Viella, 2014).

32. Gian Maria Varanini, "Signorie cittadine, vescovi e diocesi nel Veneto: L'esempio scaligero," in De Sandre Gasparini et al., *Vescovi e diocesi in Italia dal 14. alla metà del 16. secolo*, 2:860-921; Carlo Guido Mor and Heinrich Schmidinger, eds., *I poteri temporali dei Vescovi in Italia e in Germania nel Medioevo: Atti della Settimana di studio, 13–18 settembre 1976* (Bologna: Il Mulino, 1979); Gerardo Sangermano, *Poteri vescovili e signorie politiche nella Campania medievale* (Galatina: Congedo, 2000); Michele Pellegrini, *Vescovo e città: Una relazione nel Medioevo italiano, secolo II–XIV* (Milan: Mondadori Bruno, 2009); Nicolangelo D'Acunto, *Cum anulo et baculo: Vescovi dell'Italia medievale dal protagonismo politico alla complementarietà istituzionale* (Spoleto: Fondazione Centro italiano di studi sull'alto medioevo, 2019); Gian Maria Varanini, "Strategie familiari per la carriera ecclesiastica (Italia, sec. XIII-XIV)," in *La mobilità sociale nel Medioevo italiano*, vol. 3, *Il mondo ecclesiastico*, ed. S. Carocci and A. De Vincentiis (Rome: Viella, 2017), 362-97.

33. Maureen C. Miller, *The Bishop's Palace: Architecture and Authority in Medieval Italy* (Ithaca, NY: Cornell University Press, 2000); Miller, "The Political and Cultural Significance of the Bishop's Palace in Medieval Italy," in *Princes of the Church: Bishops and Their Palaces. Proceedings of the International Conference at Auckland Castle (30 June–4 July 2015)*, ed. David W. Rollason (London: Routledge, 2017), 34-54; Pierre-Yves Le Pogam, *De la "cité de dieu" au "palais du pape": Les résidences pontificales dans la seconde moitié du XIIIᵉ siècle (1254-1304)* (Paris: École française de Rome, 2005); Alessio Monciatti, *Il Palazzo Vaticano nel Medioevo* (Florence: Olschki, 2005).

34. His collected articles have been published in D'Acunto, *Cum anulo et baculo*.

35. In addition to the fundamental study of André Vauchez, *La santità nel Medioevo*, trans. Alfonso Prandi (Bologna: Il Mulino, 1989), originally published as *La sainteté en Occident aux derniers siècles du Moyen Âge d'après les proces de canonisation et les documents hagiographiques* (Rome: École française de Rome, 1981), see also Anna Benvenuti Papi, *Pastori di popolo: Storie e leggende di vescovi e di città nell'Italia medievale* (Florence: Arnaud, 1988); Amalia Galdi, *Santi, territori, poteri e uomini nella Campania medievale (secc. XI–XII)*, Schola Sallernitana Studi e Testi 9 (Salerno: Laveglia, 2004); Umberto Longo, *Come angeli in terra: Pier Damiani, la santità e la riforma del secolo XI* (Rome: Viella, 2012); Edoardo D'Angelo, "Bibliotheca Hagiographica Umbriae (1130-1500)," in *Hagiographies: Histoire internationale de la littérature hagiographique latine et vernaculaire en Occident des origines à 1550*, ed. Guy Philippart, vol. 6 (Turnhout: Brepols, 2014), 107-234; Luca Demontis, "Perfetta pazienza e miles celestis nella Vita di San Lanfranco, vecovo di Pavia († 1198)," *Antonianum* 90 (2015): 145-52.

on the local scene, especially from the twelfth century onward.[36] There has been renewed scholarly interest in pastoral visits, among them studies demonstrating the difficulty of organizing systematic research due to the quantity and complexity of historical problems faced in the vast number and variety of primary sources linked to this field.[37]

Prosopographical research on the late medieval Italian ecclesiastical sphere is necessarily alert to the innumerable personal affairs linking Italian dioceses and the Roman curia. One example may suffice: of the ecclesiastical collaborators in the service of the twenty-five cardinals created by Gregory IX and Innocent IV, about fifty became bishops, many of them in Italian dioceses. This phenomenon is also notable when approached chronologically, as this is the first time in the history of the Roman curia and the medieval papacy that we face such intensive personal interweavings between Rome and the dioceses of Christianity in countries and areas such as England, France, and northern Italy, not to mention the Latin East and the dioceses of the Papal States or the Kingdom of Sicily. Some of these dioceses are very important, such as Milan, Pisa, or Sens, as are personages such as Federico or Otto Visconti, not to mention others like Pietro Caetani (Anagni and Todi) or Ruggero da Torre (Split) who all left notable marks on the history of their respective dioceses.[38]

Federico Visconti's episcopal activity was intense in many areas, not least his pastoral visits and his preaching.[39] Federico descended from one of the most important families of Pisa. He was chaplain to Sinibaldo Fieschi, even after the latter became pope as Innocent IV, and

---

36. See for example Antonio Rigon, "Le elezioni vescovili nel processo di sviluppo delle istituzioni ecclesiastiche a Padova," *Mélanges de l'École française de Rome: Moyen Âge, Temps modernes* 89, no. 1 (1977): 371–409; Maria Clara Rossi, "Le elezioni vescovili: Il caso di Verona scaligera," in *Gli Scaligeri (1277–1387)*, ed. Gian Maria Varanini (Verona: Arnoldo Mondadori, 1988), 405–11; Giulio Silano, "The Apostolic See and the Elections of the Bishops of Perugia in the Duecento and Trecento," *Mediaeval Studies* 50 (1988): 488–511; Blake Beattie, "Local Reality and Papal Policy: Papal Provision and the Church of Arezzo, 1248-1327," *Mediaeval Studies* 57 (1995): 131–53; Nicolangelo D'Acunto, "Le elezioni vescovili nel *Regnum Italiae* tra contesti locali e sistemi a vocazione universalistica (secoli X–XI)," in *Chiese locali e chiese regionali nell'alto medioevo*, Settimane di studio della Fondazione Centro italiano di studi sull'alto medioevo 61 (Spoleto: Fondazione Centro italiano di studi sull'alto medioevo, 2014), 649–87.

37. Umberto Mazzone and Angelo Turchini, eds., *Le visite pastorali: Analisi di una fonte* (Bologna: Il Mulino, 1985).

38. Agostino Paravicini Bagliani, *Cardinali di Curia e "familiae" cardinalizie dal 1227 al 1254*, Italia Sacra: Studi e documenti di storia ecclesiastica 18 (Padua: Editrice Antenore, 1972), 2:513.

39. *Les sermons et la visite pastorale de Federico Visconti, archevêque de Pise (1253–1277): Edition critique*, ed. Nicole Bériou et al. (Rome: École française de Rome, 2001).

was with him at the canonization of Peter Martyr. He accompanied the pope to Lyon and went on to Paris to continue his studies. Elected archbishop of Pisa in 1255, Federico established a major hospital, started the building of the famous Camposanto, oversaw a synod, and undertook a lengthy, complex, and carefully organized pastoral visitation that Robert Brentano declared as the "best of all Italian visitations" after those of the bishops of Città del Castello.[40] Federico, representing a doctrinal culture obtained in Paris and enriched during his lengthy curial career, was a deeply religious man taking inspiration from Francis of Assisi, whom Federico had actually seen in the main piazza of Bologna. Indeed, many years later, Federico preached a sermon in which he remembered his profound emotion in touching Francis: "I saw him, and with my own hand I touched him, in a heavy press of people in the great piazza at Bologna."[41]

Historical research on the relationship between liturgical life and civic identity is attracting increasing attention from scholars,[42] in large part due to the richness of available Italian primary source material, whether newly published or in manuscript form. The recently published *Liber ordinarius* of Padua permits detailed observations of the processional rituals celebrated outside the cathedral, underlining the alliances between the cathedral clergy and various civic realities.[43]

Recently there has been renewed and expanded interest for a greater understanding of confraternal networks, whether lay or clerical.[44] Lay confraternities continue to draw scholarly attention, thanks in part to the 1977 three-volume collection of Gilles Gérard Meersseman's articles.[45] This scholar's influence substantially follows his twofold outlook

---

40. Robert Brentano, *Two Churches: England and Italy in the Thirteenth Century* (Berkeley: University of California Press, 1968; new ed., 1988), 202.

41. Brentano, *Two Churches*, 195.

42. Guido Cariboni, "Il culto, la festa e la processione del Corpus Domini a Milano presso i primi Visconti," in *Il "Corpus Domini": Teologia, antropologia e politica*, ed. Laura Andreani and Agostino Paravicini Bagliani (Florence: SISMEL-Edizioni del Galluzzo, 2015), 259–73; Alberto Cadili, "Le magnificenze di Giovanni Visconti vescovo di Novara: Arte e celebrazhione nell'inserimento della Chiesa milanese nell'orbita viscontea (1331–1342)," *Nuova Rivista Storica* 99 (2015): 23–76.

43. Giulio Cattin and Anna Vildera, eds., *Il "Liber ordinarius" della Chiesa di Padova: Padova Biblioteca Capitolare, ms. E 57, sec. XIII* (Padua: Istituto per la storia ecclesiastica padovana, 2002).

44. Gilles Gérard Meersseman, "Bibliografia di G.G. Meersseman," in *Miscellanea Gilles Gérard Meersseman*, 2 vols. (Padua: Editrice Antenore, 1970), 1:xvii–xxix.

45. Gilles Gérard Meersseman, in collaboration with Gian Piero Pacini, *Ordo fraternitatis: Confraternite e pietà dei laici nel Medioevo*, 3 vols. (Rome: Herder, 1977). See also Marco Rainini, "Il frate predicatore e la storia: Gilles Gérard Meersseman," in *Studi e fonti del Medioevo Vicentino*

evidenced in his lifelong attention to this area of study, through the discovering of hitherto inaccessible manuscripts and his editions of them, and through an increasingly well-informed connection with various historical and social contexts. The publications of this great Dominican historian were characterized by rigorous *Quellenforschung* with an acute sensitivity to the social and spiritual components of the confraternal movement over the entire chronological span from the Carolingian period to the late Middle Ages. His work in this area was preceded by his research on the works of Albert the Great (at the Thomas-Institut of Cologne) and on the writings of Dominican figures of the past (at Rome's Istituto storico-domenicano).[46]

After many years of studies inspired by Meersseman's research,[47] the 1987 conference on the *movement confraternel* marked the arrival point of past research and pointed to future areas of exploration.[48] More recently, there has been an understanding of the need for updating research methodology, with general reflections as well as specific links to pastoral care and preaching, to social order, or to links between

---

*e Veneto*, vol. 3, ed. Antonio Morsoletto and Tarcisio Bellò (Vicenza: Accademia Olimpica, 2007), 19-28.

46. Gilles Gérard Meersseman, *Introduction in opera omnia B. Alberti Magni O.P.* (Bruges: Apud Carolum Beyaert, 1931); Meersseman, "Les manuscrits du cours inédit d'Albert le Grand sur la Morale à Nicomaque, recueilli et rédigé par Saint Thomas d'Aquin," *Revue néo-scolastique de philosophie* 38 (1935): 64-83; *Laurentii Pignon Catalogi accedunt Catalogi Stamsensis et Upsalensis Scriptorum O.O.*, ed. Gilles Gérard Meersseman (Rome: Institutum Historicum Fratrum Praedicatorum, 1936). The first studies on confraternities appear after the Second World War, around 1950. Gilles Gérard Meersseman, "Études sur les anciennes confréries dominicaines," *Archivum Fratrum Praedicatorum* 20 (1950): 5-113; 21 (1951): 51-196.

47. Lia Sbriziolo, *Le confraternite veneziane di devozione: Saggio bibliografico e premesse storiografiche (dal particolare esame dello statuto della Scuola mestrina di San Rocco)* (Rome: Herder, 1968); Giuseppina De Sandre Gasparini, ed., *Statuti di confraternite religiose di Padova nel Medio Evo / testi, studio introduttivo e cenni storici* (Padua: Istituto per la storia ecclesiastica padovana, 1974); Giovanni Vitolo, "Confraternite dell'Italia centro-meridionale," in "Le confraternite in Italia fra Medioevo e Rinascimento: Atti della tavola rotonda, Vicenza, 3-4 novembre 1979," ed. Gabriele De Rosa, special issue, *Ricerche di storia sociale e religiosa* 17-18 (1980): 64-70; Vitolo, *Istituzioni ecclesiastiche e vita religiosa dei laici nel Mezzogiorno medievale: Il codice della confraternita di S. Maria di Montefusco (sec. XII)* (Rome: Herder, 1982); Lester K. Little, *Libertà, carità, fraternità: Confraternite laiche a Bergamo nell'età del Comune*, edition of the statutes by Sandro Buzzetti, codicological research by Giulio Orazio Bravi (Bergamo: Lubrina, 1988); M. Zangarini, ed., *Il buon fedele: Le confraternite tra medioevo e prima età moderna*, Quaderni di storia religiosa 5 (Verona: Cierre, 1998).

48. *Le mouvement confraternel au Moyen Âge: France, Italie, Suisse. Actes de la table ronde organisée par l'Université de Lausanne avec le concours de l'École française de Rome et de l'Unité associée 1011 du CNRS "L'institution ecclésiale à la fin du Moyen Âge," Lausanne, 9-11 mai 1985* (Rome: École française de Rome, 1987).

# 1. A VIEW OF THE HISTORIOGRAPHY

confraternities and schools or hospitals.[49] More systematic analyses have been attempted in regard to Bologna and the Papal States, as well as the banners of Italian confraternities up to Renaissance times.[50]

One of Meersseman's first studies on confraternities had taken into account clerical congregations from the Carolingian period to the time of Innocent III.[51] However, it was only from the 1980s onward that one observes a renewed interest in urban confraternities or congregations, especially in the Veneto and more recently in other Italian areas,[52] including the publication of hitherto unedited source material.[53] Lay confraternities continue to attract greater interest, especially in a country whose religious life and civic identity has experienced, from the age of the *comuni* onward, continual and profound interaction.

In the area of intense research on lay confraternities, the role of women has given rise in some cases to systematic and independent studies, especially in regard to local or regional scenes such as Tuscany, Umbria, or Bergamo, with reference to more general problems.[54]

---

49. Marina Gazzini, ed., *Studi confraternali: Orientamenti, problemi, testimonianze*, Reti medievali E-book 12 (Florence: Firenze University Press, 2009); Gazzini, *Confraternite e società cittadina nel Medioevo italiano* (Bologna: Clueb, 2006); Gazzini, "Costruire la comunità: L'apporto delle confraternite fra Due e Trecento. Alcuni esempi dal Nord e Centro Italia," *Rivista di storia della Chiesa in Italia* 68 (2014): 331–48; Neslihan Şenocak, "Twelfth-Century Italian Confraternities as Institutions of Pastoral Care," *Journal of Medieval History* 42 (2016): 202–25; Nicholas Terpstra, *The Politics of Ritual Kinship: Confraternities and Social Order in Early Modern Italy* (Cambridge: Cambridge University Press, 2000); Antonio Rigon, "Schole, confraternite e ospedali," in *Pensiero e sperimentazioni istituzionali nella "Societas Christiana" (1046–1250)*, ed. Giancarlo Andenna (Milan: Vita e Pensiero, 2007), 407–27.

50. Mario Fanti, *Confraternite e città a Bologna nel Medioevo e nell'età moderna* (Rome: Herder, 2001); Thomas Frank, *Bruderschaften im spätmittelalterlichen Kirchenstaat: Viterbo, Orvieto, Assisi* (Tübingen: de Gruyter, 2002); Andreas Dehmer, *Italienische Bruderschaftsbanner des Mittelalters und der Renaissance* (Munich: Deutscher Kunstverlag, 2004).

51. Gilles Gérard Meersseman, "Die Klerikervereine von Karl dem Grossen bis Innocenz III," *Zeitschrift für schweizerische Kirchengeschichte* 46 (1952): 1–42, 81–112.

52. Bianca Betto, *Le nove congregazioni del clero di Venezia (sec. XI–XV): Ricerche storiche, matricole e documenti vari* (Padua: Editrice Antenore, 1984); Antonio Rigon, "Le congregazioni del clero urbano in area veneta (XII–XV sec.)," in *Le mouvement confraternel au Moyen Âge*, 343–60; Jean-Loup Lemaître, "Le consorce du clergé de Lodi et son Missel, XIIe–XIVe siècle," in *Le mouvement confraternel au Moyen Âge*, 185–209; Antonio Rigon, *Clero e città: "Fratalea cappellanorun," parroci, cura d'anime in Padova dal XII al XV secolo* (Padua: Istituto di storia ecclesiastica padovana, 1988); Rigon, "Congregazioni del clero cittadino e storia della parrocchia nell'Italia settentrionale: Il problema delle fonti," in Paravicini Bagliani and Pasche, *La parrocchia nel Medio Evo*, 3–25; Cosimo Damiano Fonseca, "Riforma ecclesiastica e collegialità del clero: Il caso di Aversa," in *Preti nel medioevo*, Quaderni di storia religiosa 4 (Verona: Cierre, 1997), 9–25.

53. Andrea Maiarelli, *La Congregatio clericorum Perusinae Ecclesiae: Edizione e studio del codice 39.20 della Biblioteca Capitular di Toledo*, with an essay byPietro Messa (Rome: Herder, 2007).

54. Anna Benvenuti Papi, *"In castro poenitentiae": Santità e società femminile nell'Italia medievale* (Rome: Herder, 1990); Giovanna Casagrande, "Confraternities and Lay Female Religiosity

These studies thus demonstrate how the rich documentation available in Italy can offer interesting research prospects in this field, starting from those put forward a half century ago by Giovanni Miccoli, who posited that religious and ecclesiastical realities can never be examined in isolation. Rather, scholars must always be conscious of the presence of the historical, political, social, and cultural aspects of the Middle Ages.

While religious history has been the dominant field within the Italian-language medieval historiography, catalyzed in part by the great number of clergy functioning in this field, the same cannot be said for the historiography produced outside of Italy. In the English-language historiography of the Middle Ages, Italy has been a bit of an outlier when it comes to religious history. The great majority of scholars working in this field have focused traditionally on the parts of Europe that correspond to modern-day England, France, Germany, and the Low Countries. The great attraction of Italy to Anglophone scholars has primarily been due to its economic and mercantile vibrancy, unparalleled in Europe, and the "civic" culture of the Italian communal republics, which set a marked difference from the royal and imperial rules elsewhere in Europe. In fact, the studies on religion in Italy have often been inextricably linked to the civic and urban culture.

The study of Renaissance Italy has in great part overshadowed the study of medieval Italy. The Anglophone publications on aspects of Renaissance Italy by far outnumber those on medieval Italy, where the thirteenth and fourteenth centuries witnessing the rise of economically robust city-states leading to the high Renaissance have been privileged. A cursory overview of this historiography would reveal that cities like Florence, Venice, and Rome, which are enormous touristic attractions, closely followed by Siena, Bologna, Lucca, and Genoa, have been the main focus of scholarly interest rather than the lesser-visited towns, such as Novara, Modena, Vercelli, or Piacenza—even though these latter cities have rich episcopal and/or capitular archives. In the United States, an auxiliary reason for the relative lack of study of medieval Italy

---

in Late Medieval and Renaissance Umbria," in *The Politics of Ritual Kinship: Confraternities and Social Order in Early Modern Italy*, ed. Nicholas Terpstra (Cambridge: Cambridge University Press, 2000), 48–66; Maria Teresa Brolis and Giovanni Brembilla, "Mille e più donne in confraternita: Il *consorcium Misericordiae* di Bergamo nel Duecento," in Zangarini, *Il buon fedele*, 107–34; Daniel Bornstein and Roberto Rusconi, eds., *Women and Religion in Medieval and Renaissance Italy* (Chicago: Chicago University Press, 1996), 91.

## 1. A VIEW OF THE HISTORIOGRAPHY

has been the language requirements for graduate students in PhD programs, which in universities like Columbia, Yale, or Harvard prioritize French and German over Italian.

A mixture of the elements mentioned above has shaped the major publications on the religious landscape of medieval Italy. Robert Brentano's *Two Churches* made scholars aware of how different the religious institutions looked in Italy and England, and how much the local customs and politics shaped them. His meticulous archival work and unearthing of previously unused material opened up new venues of research.[55]

David Herlihy, who was a student of Robert Lopez, a highly influential scholar of trade and the economy of medieval Italy, opened up the field of medieval social history of Italy through his research on family, urban, and rural communities.[56] In the final chapter in his 1967 book on the social history of Pistoia, he included a section on "Civic Christianity," which (as his student Sam K. Cohn Jr. has noted) influenced a number of eminent historians including Robert Brentano, Philip Gavitt, and Cohn himself, along with Maureen Miller.[57] Indeed, Herlihy's students, well trained in his practice of archival research and social understanding of religion, have dominated the historiography of medieval Italy in recent decades. Early in their careers, both Steven Epstein and Sam K. Cohn Jr. studied wills, of Genoa and Siena respectively, which not only revealed the richness of information in this particular type of record, but alerted the scholars to the undeniable importance of piety, afterlife, and penance by revealing the sheer numbers and sophistication of the pious bequests.[58] Maureen Miller started her career with the study of the Veronese Church and the effects of the reform movement on its clergy.[59] Her second book, *The Bishop's Palace*, has significantly combined

---

55. Robert Brentano, *Rome before Avignon: A Social History of Thirteenth-Century Rome* (London: Longman, 1974); Brentano, *A New World in a Small Place*.

56. For a bibliography of Herlihy prepared by Maureen Miller, see Samuel K. Cohn Jr., Steven Epstein, and David Herlihy, eds. *Portraits of Medieval and Renaissance Living: Essays in Memory of David Herlihy* (Ann Arbor: University of Michigan Press, 1995), 455–63.

57. David Herlihy, *Medieval and Renaissance Pistoia: The Social History of an Italian Town, 1200–1430* (New Haven, CT: Yale University Press, 1967). On Herlihy's influence, see Samuel K. Cohn Jr., "David Herlihy: A Student's View," *History Teacher* 27 (1993): 53–61.

58. Steven Epstein, *Wills and Wealth in Medieval Genoa, 1150–1250* (Cambridge, MA: Harvard University Press, 1984); Samuel K. Cohn, *Death and Property in Siena, 1205–1800: Strategies for the Afterlife* (Baltimore, MD: Johns Hopkins University Press, 1988).

59. Maureen C. Miller, *The Formation of a Medieval Church: Ecclesiastical Change in Verona, 950–1150* (Ithaca, NY: Cornell University Press, 1993).

the then emerging subfields of materiality and space, civic religion, and Church reform, and has drawn attention to what she called "cultural expressions of claims to power."[60] Miller's latest book continued in this vein of the study of materiality and clerical power, this time turning to the vestments of the clergy as signifiers of changing scales of clerical authority.[61] As such, Miller's work is part of a particularly strong trend in the Anglophone religious history that has turned to examining material objects, not only as mere nondocumentary evidence but as things that medieval people consciously crafted and used to express their own understanding of religiosity, religious authority, and piety.[62] Another eminent scholar trained by Herlihy is George Dameron, whose books on the episcopacy and religious culture of Florence have been models for many students and scholars, combining rigorous archival evidence with a wide reading of secondary sources in Italian, often unknown or not easily accessible for Anglophone scholars.[63]

The interest in civic Christianity, in particular the exchange between the religious movements, devotional forms, and Church reform on the one side, and the growing civic consciousness and urban culture on the other, has shaped the scholarly output of many prominent scholars. William Bowsky, a very well-known figure to many Italian scholars, began with a communal study of Siena but later in his career turned his attention to the powerhouse canonry of San Lorenzo in Florence.[64] Duane Osheim's two books—one on the bishopric of Lucca, and another as a detailed social study of the local and communal connections and interactions with the laity of a Luccan monastery—published within the famous Italia Sacra series have been rare contributions to the field.[65] Lester K. Little's *Religious Poverty and the Profit Economy*, with

---

60. Miller, *The Bishop's Palace*, 253.

61. Maureen C. Miller, *Clothing the Clergy: Virtue and Power in Medieval Europe, c. 800–1200* (Ithaca, NY: Cornell University Press, 2014).

62. It is impossible not to mention here the pathbreaking work of Caroline Bynum, especially her *Holy Feast and Holy Fast: The Religious Significance of Food to Medieval Women* (Berkeley: University of California Press, 1987) and *Christian Materiality: An Essay on Religion in Late Medieval Europe* (Cambridge, MA: MIT Press, 2011).

63. Dameron, *Florence and Its Church*; and George W. Dameron, *Episcopal Power and Florentine Society, 1000–1320* (Cambridge, MA: Harvard University Press, 1991).

64. William M. Bowsky, *A Medieval Italian Commune: Siena under the Nine, 1287–1355* (Berkeley: University of California Press, 1981); Bowsky, *Piety and Property in Medieval Florence: A House in San Lorenzo* (Milan: A. Giuffrè, 1990).

65. Osheim, *An Italian Lordship*; and Duane J. Osheim, *A Tuscan Monastery and Its Social World: San Michele of Guamo (1156–1348)*, Italia Sacra: Studi e documenti di storia ecclesiastica 40 (Rome: Herder, 1989).

# 1. A VIEW OF THE HISTORIOGRAPHY

its thesis on the effect of the popular reaction to the growing urban economy in the Italian city-states leading to the rise of mendicants, has been a standard inclusion in the syllabi of religious history courses.[66] His subsequent study of the confraternities of Bergamo was one of the pioneers in the Anglophone study of medieval Italian confraternities.[67] Another prominent historian of urban religious culture is Frances Andrews, whose research began with the study of the Humiliati and mendicant orders. She has been instrumental in raising the awareness of how much these new religious contributed not only to religious culture but also to the governing of the cities by taking up official positions of authority within the communes. This culminated in a volume of collected articles she edited with Maria Agata Pincelli.[68] Her other publications have cemented her place in the field as a historian of both lay devotional forms and clerical practices, in particular within the urban setting of the Italian city-states.[69] Katherine L. Jansen has been another influential scholar on religious culture in Italian communes.[70] Jansen and Andrews' 2009 edition of primary source texts for the study of medieval Italy with Joanna Drell has become a classroom staple.[71] Augustine Thompson's *Cities of God*, where he presented the city as a sacred space, and David Foote's study of the episcopal reform in Orvieto are other important contributions to the field of urban religious culture.[72]

Saints, especially woman saints in medieval Italy have been a particularly fruitful subject of study, as explored by, among others, Diana

---

66. Lester K. Little, *Religious Poverty and the Profit Economy in Medieval Europe* (Ithaca, NY: Cornell University Press, 1978).

67. Lester K. Little, *Liberty, Charity, Fraternity: Lay Religious Confraternities at Bergamo in the Age of the Commune* (Northampton, MA: Smith College Publications, 1988).

68. Frances Andrews, ed., with Maria Agata Pincelli, *Churchmen and Urban Government in Late Medieval Italy, c.1200–c.1450: Cases and Contexts* (Cambridge: Cambridge University Press, 2013).

69. In particular Andrews's seminal article "Living Like the Laity? The Negotiation of Religious Status in the Cities of Late Medieval Italy," *Transactions of the Royal Historical Society* 20 (2010): 27–55.

70. Katherine Ludwig Jansen, *The Making of the Magdalen: Preaching and Popular Devotion in the Later Middle Ages* (Princeton, NJ: Princeton University Press, 2001); and *Peace and Penance in Late Medieval Italy* (Princeton, NJ: Princeton University Press, 2018).

71. Katherine L. Jansen, Joanna H. Drell, and Frances Andrews, eds., *Medieval Italy: Texts in Translation* (Philadelphia: University of Pennsylvania Press, 2009).

72. Augustine Thompson, *Cities of God: The Religion of the Italian Communes, 1125–1325* (University Park: Pennsylvania State University Press, 2005); David Foote, *Lordship, Reform, and the Development of Civil Society in Medieval Italy: The Bishopric of Orvieto, 1100–1250* (Notre Dame, IN: University of Notre Dame Press, 2004).

Webb, Mary H. Doyno, and E. Ann Matter.[73] The numerous Italian heresies have been explored by Carol Lansing, Jerry Pierce, and Janine L. Peterson.[74] For the understanding of the religious culture of South Italy, we are indebted to Graham A. Loud, Valerie Ramseyer, and Paul Oldfield.[75]

The contribution of the historians of art such as Caroline Bruzelius, Dorothy Glass, and Julian Gardner, among others, to the understanding of Italian religious landscape cannot be disputed.[76]

The books and scholars mentioned here are in no way an exhaustive list of scholars who work on religious culture of medieval Italy. And once we move beyond the 1300s, the list of Anglophone scholars working on Italian religious history grows rapidly, where there are many prominent scholars such as Daniel E. Bornstein, John Henderson, and Nicholas Terpstra to name a few. The religious history of medieval Italy is becoming a vibrant field, and more interregional studies in the spirit of Brentano's work will lead to a better understanding of the religious culture in medieval Europe as a whole.

---

73. Diana Webb, *Patrons and Defenders: The Saints in Italian City-States* (New York, NY: Tauris, 1996), and her collection of primary sources, *Saint and Cities in Medieval Italy* (Manchester, UK: Palgrave, 2007); Mary Harvey Doyno, *The Lay Saint: Charity and Charismatic Authority in Medieval Italy, 1150–1350* (Ithaca, NY: Cornell University Press 2019); John W. Coakley, *Women, Men, and Spiritual Power: Female Saints and Their Male Collaborators* (New York: Columbia University Press, 2006); E. Ann Matter, "Italian Holy Women: A Survey," in *Creative Women in Medieval and Early Modern Italy: A Religious and Artistic Renaissance*, ed. E. Ann Matter and John Coakley (Philadelphia, PA: University of Pennsylvania Press, 1994).

74. Carol Lansing, *Power and Purity: Cathar Heresy in Medieval Italy* (Oxford: Oxford University Press, 2001); Jerry B. Pierce, *Poverty, Heresy, and the Apocalypse: The Order of Apostles and Social Change in Medieval Italy 1260–1307* (London: Continuum, 2012); Janine Larmon Peterson, *Suspect Saints and Holy Heretics: Disputed Sanctity and Communal Identity in Late Medieval Italy* (Ithaca, NY: Cornell University Press, 2019).

75. Loud, *Latin Church in Norman Italy*; Valerie Ramseyer, *The Transformation of a Religious Landscape: Medieval Southern Italy, 850–1150* (Ithaca, NY: Cornell University Press, 2006); Paul Oldfield, *Sanctity and Pilgrimage in Medieval Southern Italy, 1000–1200* (New York: Cambridge University Press, 2014).

76. Caroline Bruzelius, *Preaching, Building, and Burying: Friars and the Medieval City* (New Haven, CT: Yale University Press, 2014); Dorothy F. Glass, *Portals, Pilgrimage and Crusade in Western Tuscany* (Princeton, NJ: Princeton University Press, 1997) and *The Sculpture of Reform in North Italy, ca 1095–1130: History and Patronage of Romanesque Façades* (Aldershot: Ashgate, 2010); Julian Gardner, *The Roman Crucible: The Artistic Patronage of the Papacy 1198–1304* (Munich: Hirmer Verlag, 2013).

CHAPTER 2

# The Papacy and Italian Politics

*Agostino Paravicini Bagliani and Pietro Silanos*

The link between the papacy and the Italian peninsula is one that dates back to the very dawn of Christianity. Rome, the capital of the empire, was the seat of an ancient Christian community. According to tradition, the eternal city was where Peter and Paul were martyred, and it was on the relics of these two pillars of Christianity that the primacy of the Roman see was built. Despite the ecclesiastical and jurisdictional primacy recognized by those who presided over the patriarchal see of Rome from the first centuries of the Christian era, it was only from the eleventh century that the popes fully assumed the role of monarch, exercising an increasingly decisive role not only in the ecclesiastical but also in the political affairs of Latin Christendom, and of the Italian peninsula in particular. We cannot, therefore, understand the ecclesiological evolution of the Roman papacy and the influence it exercised over religious life without also taking into consideration its political role. In the Middle Ages the processes that concerned spiritual and temporal affairs influenced each other in a reciprocal way and must therefore be considered as closely linked to one another.[1]

---

This chapter was translated by Hilary Siddons.

1. For an overall treatment of these topics, see Ovidio Capitani, *Storia dell'Italia medievale, 410–1216* (Bari: Editori Laterza, 2009), 277–470, and Giovanni Miccoli, "La storia religiosa," in *Storia*

From the eleventh century the Roman papacy played an increasingly pervasive role in the Italian peninsula thanks above all to the action of the German emperor Henry III (1016–56), who attempted to set in motion a process with two precise and intrinsically interconnected aims: to remove the ministry of St. Peter from the internecine struggles of the most influential Roman families, restoring the spiritual and moral stature that should have distinguished it, and consequently, mediating the collaboration with it, to reestablish those prerequisites needed to exert a greater influence in the *Regnum italiae*. After the death of Leo IX in 1054, to render the moderating force of the papacy more effective (in central Italy above all), the emperor granted the Duchy of Spoleto, the March of Fermo, and numerous other territories in the Marche to the newly elected Victor II. The death of pope and emperor in midcentury—and especially that of the emperor who left his heir Henry IV as a minor—had a lasting effect on the political situation of the peninsula, however, where three actors in particular seemed to dominate: the Normans,[2] the papacy, and Godfrey the Bearded, originally from Lorraine, who had become margrave of Tuscany by marrying the widow of Boniface III of Canossa, one of the most powerful lay barons of the peninsula.

The newly elected pope was Godfrey's brother, the abbot of Montecassino Frederick of Lorraine, who took the name of Stephen IX (1057–58); in the election a major role was played by one of the principal exponents of the so-called reform party,[3] the Roman subdeacon Hildebrand of Sovana, the future Gregory VII. This was an important turning point in the action of the papacy on Italian soil because it created an initial alliance between the group of reformers and the family of the margraves

---

*d'Italia*, vol. 2, *Dalla caduta dell'Impero romano al secolo XVIII*, ed. Ruggero Romano and Corrado Vivanti (Turin: Einaudi, 1974), bk. 1:431–1079. On the individual popes quoted, see the relevant biographies in the *Enciclopedia dei papi* (Rome: Istituto della Enciclopedia Italiana, 2000). The political role of the papacy in the Italian peninsula must be contextualized in the broader political and social history of this geographical area. For this, see the analysis over a long span of time by Giovanni Tabacco, "La storia politica e sociale: Dal tramonto dell'Impero alle prime formazioni di Stati regionali," in *Storia d'Italia*, vol. 2, bk. 1:3–274. For a brief documented history of the papacy between the eleventh and thirteenth centuries, see Agostino Paravicini Bagliani, *Il trono di Pietro: L'universalità del papato da Alessandro III a Bonifacio VIII* (Rome: Carocci, 2001) and Bernhard Schimmelpfennig, *Il papato: Antichità, medioevo, rinascimento* (Rome: Viella, 2006).

2. Hubert Houben, *I Normanni* (Bologna: Il Mulino, 2015); Donald Matthew, *I normanni in Italia* (Bari: Editori Laterza, 2008).

3. This term usually refers to a group of ecclesiastics—whether they belonged to the secular clergy or the *ordo monasticus*—who worked within the highest levels of the Church to promote and in some way to guide the process of reform in the eleventh century. It must be noted that it was not a monolithic group, either geographically or as to the sensibility of its members concerning the resolution of the spiritual and legal problems that emerged in this historical moment.

of Tuscany, which was to have important consequences in the course of the subsequent decades, from both a political and an ecclesiastical point of view. In order to seal the coalition, Godfrey was granted the rights over the Duchy of Spoleto and the counties of the Marche that he had previously received from Victor II, thus transforming the margrave of Tuscany into the most important lay potentate of the peninsula.

The history of Italy in the eleventh century and the role played there by the papacy is subject to moments of acceleration and moments of sudden stalling. An example is the situation that was created immediately after the death of Stephen IX in 1058. The absence of Hildebrand of Sovana from Rome and the apparent lack of interest in the papal succession by the German court, together with the attempt by the Roman families to regain control of the papal election, led to a schism that saw the election of Benedict X by the Roman nobles headed by the family of the Tuscolani, and Nicholas II (1058-61), chosen by Peter Damian and other exponents of the reform party as legitimate successor. The end of this brief schism in 1060, which was reached thanks in part to the military support given to Nicholas II by the Normans, clearly showed the political weight of the group of reformers, in particular Hildebrand of Sovana, Peter Damian, and Humbert of Silva Candida. Indeed these figures, who were among the most influential churchmen not only in Italy by also in Europe, contributed to defining the agenda of the ecclesiastical and religious reform of the Church of the time, supporting some of what were to become the guidelines of the eleventh-century reform, in particular, strong criticism of married priests and the sale of ecclesiastical offices.

Hildebrand of Sovana (1015-85) was educated in Rome, even though he was not born there. His family, of Tuscan origin, was probably not of a high social standing. When he was still young, he was entrusted to the abbot of the monastery of St. Mary on the Aventine in Rome. By the time he was an adolescent, he expressed the desire to become a monk, but he only took the habit after the death of Gregory VI in 1046. Under Leo IX he became one of the main collaborators of the first reforming pope of the eleventh century, who appointed him cardinal of the Roman Church and granted him the office of rector of the abbey of St. Paul.

Peter Damian was born into a very poor family and was trained in the liberal arts in the cathedral schools of Ravenna, Parma, and Faenza. In 1035 he retired from the world to become a monk in the Camaldolese hermitage of Fonte Avellana, where he became prior in 1043. His fame as an ascetic and educated man spread, and this allowed him not only to make contact with numerous monastic cultural centers in the peninsula but also, in 1057, to become part of the inner circle of the pope as the cardinal bishop of Ostia.

Humbert of Silva Candida became a monk in the Lorraine abbey of Moyenmoutier in France, but he was called to Rome by Pope Leo IX in 1049, who made him cardinal bishop of Porto and Santa Rufina during the Roman synod. He had an important role in the negotiations that led to the excommunication of the patriarch of Constantinople Michael Cerularius in 1054 and the definitive failure to heal the schism with the Greek Church.

These and other figures of the so-called reform party set the papacy on a new course, the most peculiar characteristic of which was a tendency to undertake independent political action in the context of central and southern Italy above all, and with respect to the influence of the German court in particular.

The first consequence of this new direction, and partly a result of the newly resolved schism, was the attempt to isolate the choice of pope from possible outside interference, which took the form of the decree on papal election defined by the Lateran synod of 1059 convened by Nicholas II.[4] It stated that it was in the first place the canonical task of the cardinal bishops to elect the pope; that the person designated could be chosen from among the Roman clergy but also from outside it; that the election could take place, if need be, even outside Rome; and that the choice of candidate had to respect imperial *honor* and *reverentia*.

Nicholas II attempted to put into practice the aspiration, which had first been expressed by Henry III, for a papacy that could act to guarantee the balance of political and ecclesiastical power above all in central and southern Italy. To do this he convened a synod in Melfi in 1059 in which, besides condemning simony and clerical marriage, he managed to obtain from the Normans Robert Guiscard and Richard of Aversa an oath of fealty to the Church of Rome and the promise to respect the principles of the decree on papal election. The second front that Nicholas II had to tackle was the delicate relationship with the dioceses of

---

4. On the decree of 1059 and its complex textual tradition, see Hans-Georg Krause, *Das Papstwahldekret von 1059 und seine Rolle im Investiturstreit* (Rome: Abbazia di San Paolo, 1960); Detlev Jasper, *Das Papstwahldekret von 1059: Überlieferung und Textgestalt* (Sigmaringen: Thorbecke, 1986). More recently Agostino Paravicini Bagliani, *Morte e elezione del papa: Norme, riti e conflitti* (Rome: Viella, 2013), 19–22.

northern Italy, institutions that were placed within a system of power relations that were difficult to square with the plan for centralization that the acts of papal reform were preparing and beginning to put into practice.

In this context it is worth mentioning the archdiocese of Milan, whose internal situation seemed complex yet at the same time well suited to the intervention of Rome. In the years preceding the pontificate of Nicholas II, in fact, the phenomenon of the Pataria of the deacon Arialdo had begun to establish itself.[5] This experience originated in exponents of the lower Milanese clergy and members of the city *popolo*, and it managed to give form to various aspirations of a spiritual, social, and political nature. The preaching of Arialdo, characterized by his harsh criticism of simony and clerical marriage, in fact, undermined the bases of the system that Cinzio Violante has defined as the "feudal Church," linked as it was to ecclesiastical territorial lordship and the cultural world connected to it.[6] For this reason, the Pataria movement had alarmed the leaders of the Church of Milan, and others besides, forcing them to react strongly. The apostolic legates in Milan, Hildebrand of Savona and Anselmo da Baggio first (1057) and Peter Damian later (1059-60), who attempted to form a truce between the archbishop and clergy of Milan and the *patarini*, represented a first attempt to carry out that form of mediation from above in the affairs of the local churches that was to become increasingly characteristic in the following decades.

After the death of Nicholas II, the cardinal bishops and a part of the Romans, with the support of the Normans, elected Anselmo da Baggio, bishop of Lucca, as pope, under the name of Alexander II (1061-73). All of this happened in contravention of the canon rules established in 1059, in particular without Henry IV (1056-1105) and the German court being informed. This initiative was met by a parallel one involving part of the Roman clergy and the bishops of Lombardy, with the backing of the German court, who elected as pope the bishop of Parma, Cadalo, under the name of Honorius II. After only a few years,

---

5. On the phenomenon of the Pataria in Milan, see Cinzio Violante, *La pataria milanese e la riforma ecclesiastica*, vol. 1, *Le premesse (1045–1057)* (Rome: Istituto Storico Italiano per il Medio Evo, 1955); Paolo Golinelli, *La pataria: Lotte religiose e sociali nella Milano dell'XI secolo* (Milan: Jaca Book, 1984). More recently, see Olaf Zumhagen, *Religiöse Konflikte und kommunale Entwicklung: Mailand, Cremona, Piacenza und Florenz zur Zeit der Pataria* (Cologne: Bohlau, 2002).

6. Cinzio Violante, *"Chiesa feudale" e riforme in Occidente (secc. X–XII): Introduzione a un tema storiografico* (Spoleto: Centro italiano di studi sull'alto medioevo, 1999).

therefore, another schism had opened up, this time, however, coinciding with the unforeseen rupture between the German king and the group of reformers.

The situation in the south of the peninsula represented another challenge for the eleventh-century popes. The Norman domination of southern Italy, and Sicily in particular, was one of the most delicate topics on the political and ecclesiastical agenda of the Apostolic See. Investiture by the papal Curia that had been agreed in Melfi in 1059, in fact, only concerned the power held by Robert Guiscard and not the other Norman territorial lords in the south of Italy, in particular in Sicily, which was invested to Robert's brother, Roger I of Altavilla, by Guiscard himself.[7] As Ovidio Capitani has pointed out, "the connection of the Norman conquests . . . with the Church of Rome . . . contributed decisively to giving a much broader European scope to the papacy" and to its political action in the peninsula.[8]

It was precisely in this historical context, indeed, that the Italian peninsula became the space in which the papacy affirmed itself as one of the principal protagonists of the history of the region—and not only that. The Church exploited the absence of the empire in the south and the progressive expansion of the Normans in this area not only to activate a process of Latinization of the local dioceses that had been established in the previous centuries by the Church of Constantinople on the coasts of Calabria and Puglia, but also to favor the creation of new dioceses, at the request of the Normans themselves. In this way, the ecclesiastical geography of southern Italy began to change noticeably, bringing consequences of a cultural nature as well.[9]

The other pole of interest, as we have mentioned above, were the dioceses of northern Italy, and that of Milan in particular, where tensions broke out again on the death of Archbishop Guido da Velate (d. 1071)

---

7. Salvatore Fodale, *L'apostolica legazia e altri studi su Stato e Chiesa* (Messina: Sicania, 1991).
8. Capitani, *Storia dell'Italia medievale*, 299.
9. On the ecclesiastical institutions of southern Italy and their relationship with the Normans, see the important works by Cosimo Damiano Fonseca: "Gli assetti metropolitici del mezzogiorno tra Bisanzio e Roma," in *Nel IX centenario della metropoli ecclesiastica di Pisa: Atti del convegno di studi (7–8 maggio 1992)*, ed. Maria Luisa Ceccarelli Lemut and Stefano Sodi (Ospedaletto: Pacini, 1995), 27–44; "Le istituzioni ecclesiastiche dell'Italia meridionale e Ruggero il Gran Conte," in *Ruggero il Gran Conte e l'inizio dello Stato normanno: Atti delle seconde giornate normanno-sveve* (Bari: Dedalo, 1991), 43–66; and "Le istituzioni ecclesiastiche legate alla conquista: Gli episcopati e le cattedrali," in *I caratteri originari della conquista normanna: Diversità e identità nel Mezzogiorno, 1030–1130. Atti delle sedicesime giornate normanno-sveve, Bari, 5–8 ottobre 2004*, ed. Raffaele Licinio and Francesco Violante (Bari: Dedalo, 2006), 335–48.

and the election of his successor. Gotofredo da Castiglione, the candidate chosen and invested by Henry IV, was rejected by the *patarini*, and an alternative, "Roman" candidate, Attone, received the support of the apostolic legate Bernardo and the reformers. What was beginning to be challenged was the control over the major and minor churches by lay barons. It was not a question of limiting the various prevarications, which did exist and were at times violent, by the laity in the administration of ecclesiastical offices. Rather, what was beginning to reach critical point was the very system of the post-Carolingian age with its social, cultural, and religious foundations, which had led to the patrimonialization of power, including that of the bishops, abbots, and the minor clergy. As Giovanni Grado Merlo has aptly summarized, "if everything is patrimony, everything can be subject to hereditary transmission or to being bought and sold,"[10] even the churches and the abbeys with their benefices. This characteristic of the Carolingian and post-Carolingian Church was the source of a "disorder" that created not only reactions from below such as that of the *patarini* of Milan, or the hermits of the area of Tuscany, which led to a decisive spiritual renewal, but also reactions from the leading clerical structures (part of the Roman Curia and the papacy), which attempted to model the Latin Church according to a hierarchical system with the Apostolic See at its apex.

The decades following on from the schism of Cadalo saw an exacerbation of these phenomena; but they were above all the theater for the great struggle between the two universal powers, the papacy and the empire, that dominated the scene and had as their principal actors Gregory VII (1073–85) and Henry IV. The choice of Hildebrand of Sovana in 1073 as pope must be viewed in the context of the serious problems presented by the general political situation of the Italian peninsula; it has been rightly defined by historiography as a "political" election, not only because, once again, the canon rules established in 1059 were disregarded, but also because resolving these problems required a strong personality who was able to resist the force of circumstances. Within the group of reformers, Hildebrand seemed, if not the only, then certainly the ideal candidate.

The dramatic events of Gregory's papacy became unexpectedly more intense between 1074 and 1085. In the space of only ten years

---

10. Giovanni Grado Merlo, "Il papato e le istituzioni ecclesiastiche della cristianità latina," in *Storia del cristianesimo*, vol. 2, *L'età medievale (secoli VIII–XV)*, ed. Marina Benedetti (Rome: Carocci, 2015), 141.

the Western world was to undergo one of the most significant turning points in its history, which was to mark it for centuries. The so-called papal revolution, in fact—whose ideological manifesto was represented by *Dictatus papae* (a series of twenty-seven propositions of a political and ecclesiological nature transcribed into the register of letters of Gregory VII)[11]—activated that process of "disenchantment of the world," as Max Weber put it, that gradually dissolved the early medieval symbiosis between the sacred and the temporal order, opening up new political, social, and religious horizons for the constitutional development of the West.[12]

The crucial point in the struggle with the empire specifically concerned the ordination of bishops and the attribution to the elected bishop of the benefices (lands, immunities, and jurisdictions) connected to his episcopal church, granted by the emperor or the lay sovereign by means of an investiture. By the term "investiture" historians mean that practice that developed from the Carolingian age of the transfer of possession of land or political or ecclesiastical office and the benefices connected to it, carried out by the lord to the advantage of his vassal, and the ceremony that symbolically sanctioned this transfer, binding the parties to reciprocal fealty.[13] Gregory VII wanted to reform this system, at least insofar as it concerned ecclesiastical institutions, and in order to carry out his plan he set in motion a profound and wide-ranging synodal operation (1074, 1075, 1078), intending to make, with the collaboration of bishops mainly from northern and central Italy, important decisions to reform the clergy. In the Lenten synod of 1075 he began to undermine the system of the lay investiture of ecclesiastical goods and functions from a theoretical as well as a practical and

---

11. For the text of the *Dictatus papae* contained in the register of letters of Gregory VII, see the edition in *Das Register Gregors VII.*, ed. Erich Caspar, Monumenta Germaniae Historica, Epistolae selectae 2 (Berlin: Weidmannsche Buchhandlung, 1920), 1:201–8. See here the observations by Horst Furhmann, *Papst Gregor VII. und das Zeitalter der Reform: Annäherungen an eine europäische Wende. Ausgewählte Aufsätze*, ed. Martina Hartmann (Wiesbaden: Harrassowitz, 2016), 59–89 and 90–119.

12. Paolo Prodi, *Il sacramento del potere* (Bologna: Il Mulino, 1992), 105–60. Along the same lines, see also Ovidio Capitani, *L'Italia medievale nei secoli di trapasso: La riforma della Chiesa (1012–1122)* (Bologna: Patròn, 1984), and finally Stefan Weinfurter, *Canossa: Il disincanto del mondo* (Bologna: Il Mulino, 2014). These works take up in part the well-known theory of the German constitutionalist, "Böckenförde's dilemma," that sees the "investiture struggle" as the beginning of the process of the desacralization of power in the West and its consequent secularization: Ernst-Wolfgang Böckenförde, *La formazione dello Stato come processo di secolarizzazione* (Brescia: Morcelliana, 2006), 34–45.

13. Giuseppe Albertoni, *Vassalli, feudi, feudalesimo* (Rome: Carocci, 2015).

## 2. THE PAPACY AND ITALIAN POLITICS

political point of view, defining for the first time a close link between obedience to the Apostolic See and the office of bishop and comparing investiture in practice to an act of simony.

The year 1076 was marked by a series of reciprocal excommunications between pope and emperor. The tensions within the Kingdom of Germany were all that allowed the pope to reach a position of apparent superiority, which manifested itself in the famous episode of Canossa of January 1077, when the excommunicated Henry IV was "forced" to humble himself at the castle of Canossa and be pardoned by the pope, who then allowed him to go back and take part again in the game that had been created between them.[14] The pope could count on the unconditional support of the house of the margraves of Tuscany, in the person of Matilda of Canossa, who symbolically donated to St. Peter, and hence in practice to the Apostolic See, all her possessions, providing the papacy with a base for its territorial power that had been unimaginable before.[15]

Gregory's victory over Henry, however, turned out to be only apparent. The end of his life—besieged in Rome in 1081 by the imperial army and forced to flee to Salerno where he died in 1085—is proof. What is certain, however, is that the Church, the empire itself, and all of western Europe could no longer claim to be the same as it was before this pontificate: the ideal of unity between the two universal powers, which had marked the history of the continent from the Carolingians to Henry III, had been definitively compromised. The struggle between papacy and empire, moreover, accelerated the process of rendering the individual dioceses within the Italian peninsula uniform to the Roman model, which was possible thanks also to the development of canon law.

The tensions that had been created during Gregory's pontificate could certainly not be maintained for much longer. For this reason, the attitudes of Popes Victor III (1086-87) and Urban II (1088-99) were marked by a realpolitik that took into account above all the military forces deployed in the Italian peninsula: Henry IV in northern and

---

14. Weinfurter, *Canossa*, 9-23.
15. On the controversial donation of Matilda's goods, see Paolo Golinelli, "L'Italia dopo la lotta per le investiture: La questione dell'eredità matildica," *Studi medievali*, 3rd series, 42 (2001): 509-28. Golinelli believes that the first donation by Matilda of Canossa (albeit in the absence of the original document, which has probably been lost) is true, unlike the second donation of 1102, made in the hands of the cardinal legate Bernardo degli Uberti, which is considered false. Of the opposite opinion is Werner Goez, "Über die Mathildischen Schenkungen an die Römische Kirche," *Frühmittelalterliche Studien* 31 (1997): 158-96.

central Italy and the Normans in the south. The success of Urban's politics—which found the crusade to be a formidable ideological and strategic tool to coalesce different forces from all over the continent—was possible precisely because of its ability to create within the Italian political context a special link between the Apostolic See and Norman Sicily. Urban held one of his first councils in Melfi in 1089, in the course of which Roger, the son of Robert Guiscard, received the Duchy of Puglia and Calabria from the hands of the pope himself, in exchange for an oath of fealty to the Apostolic See. A veritable relationship of vassalage was therefore created in southern Italy toward the Roman pope. This allowed Urban to appoint the bishop of Messina in 1096-97 as permanent legate of the Apostolic See in Sicily and in all of the Norman domains.

In the final years of the eleventh century as in the first years of the following century the conflict between the papacy and the German court seemed destined to remain unresolved, however. In February 1111 in Sutri, in the present-day region of Lazio, Paschal II (1099-1118) reached a first agreement that established that if the emperor—then Henry V (1111-25), son of Henry IV, as the king of Germany—gave up episcopal investiture, the bishops promised not to administer the *regalia* (jurisdictional rights over cities, duchies, etc.), on pain of excommunication. Despite this agreement, only a few months later in Ponte Mammolo, just outside Rome, the popes and the cardinals in the presence of the future emperor were "forced" to accept a new agreement that stipulated the explicit recognition of the investiture of the *regalia* by the emperor before episcopal consecration. Rigidly pursuing Gregorian principles could have involved not only the risk of a new rupture with the German court, but also destabilizing the entire ecclesiastical apparatus still jealously guarding the prerogatives that the feudal world had granted. The line chosen was one of compromise, therefore, and it led to the well-known Concordat of Worms of 1122 (also known as the *Henricianum* and the *Callixtinum*), reached between Calixtus II (1119-24) and Henry V.[16] The pope granted Henry V the possibility for the election of bishops and abbots in the kingdom of Germany to take place in his presence and the granting of the *regalia* to take place before the rite of consecration. In Italy and Burgundy, on the other hand, the *regalia* could only be bestowed six months after consecration. It was a deliberately

---

16. Ernst Werner, *Zwischen Canossa und Worms: Staat und Kirche 1077–1122* (Berlin: Akademie Verlag, 1978).

ambiguous solution that in reality left numerous problems, which the Gregorian period had brought up for consideration unresolved.

The background to these events in the Italian peninsula was also characterized by the development of a phenomenon that though it was not exclusively Italian, was certainly one of the most peculiar features of this region: the progressive advance of the communes.[17] Population increase, the economic growth of the cities, and the emergence of new social classes in the shadow of the episcopal authorities that increasingly demanded a voice in the administration of the *res publica* considerably modified the ecclesiastical and political context, of the *Regnum italiae* in particular, thus contributing to the crisis of the power of the lay barons and the bishops, as it had taken shape in post-Carolingian Italy.[18]

The Apostolic See was equally marked by a schism, with the election of Innocent II (1130–43) and Anacletus II, both candidates from noble Roman families. The actors on the Italian political stage took sides in this contest: the Normans supported Anacletus; the king of Germany, Lothar of Supplingenburg, Innocent. Thanks to military aid from Lothar, Innocent managed to prevail, and in 1133 he returned to take possession of Rome. The schism of 1130 was resolved in a context of political allegiances that were no longer merely governed by the papacy-empire divide, but was one in which, besides other European sovereigns and the Normans of southern Italy, the Italian communes also began to play a considerable role.

In March 1152, the son of Frederick of Swabia, of the same name but better known as Barbarossa, was elected king of Germany.[19] The pope, Eugene III (1145–54), was interested in resolving the unstable situation in Rome, where a commune had been created and a political and religious controversy was under way thanks to the preaching of Arnaldo da Brescia (d. 1155). A pupil of Peter Abelard, the famous master of theology, Arnaldo managed to involve the popular classes of Rome in a movement that was both religious and political at the same

---

17. For a brief overview, see François Menant, *L'Italia dei comuni (1100–1350)* (Rome: Viella, 2011), 9–42, for the first phase of this phenomenon, at least up until the end of the twelfth century. See also Chris Wickham, *Sonnambuli verso un nuovo mondo: L'affermazione dei comuni italiani nel XII secolo* (Rome: Viella, 2017).

18. Giovanni Tabacco, *Egemonie sociali e strutture del potere nel medioevo italiano* (Turin: Einaudi, 1979), 397–427. On the relationship between the bishops, communal authorities, and the papacy, and the most recent research on the subject, see also Maria Pia Alberzoni, *Città, vescovi e papato nella Lombardia dei comuni* (Novara: Interlinea, 2001), 7–26.

19. For the life of the German emperor, see the historical biography by Knut Görich, *Friedrich Barbarossa: Eine Biographie* (Munich: Beck, 2011).

time, just as Arialdo had done in Milan with the Pataria. His preaching, in fact, which was ascetic in nature, was characterized by the radical words he aimed not only at the clergy for its simony, but also at the papacy itself.[20]

The uncertain social and political situation of the Roman commune and the fragile relationship with the German court induced the papacy to forge stronger ties with the Normans. In 1154, in fact, the Roman Curia began to negotiate with William I of Altavilla, the king of Sicily. Hadrian IV signed a treaty in Benevento in 1156, which stipulated that the Norman king should pay feudal homage for the territories with which he had been invested by the pope and give military aid in order to help him reenter Rome. If we remember that in the kingdom of Germany at the same time Frederick I was preparing a military expedition against the Normans to reconquer lands that he believed rightfully belonged to the empire, then we can begin to see not only how difficult it was to put in place a single plan that could reconcile empire and papacy, but also how the papacy intended to play its cards on several fronts, looking to gain the maximum advantage in every situation.

The breaking point between the two universal powers came with the diet of Besançon (1157), when two cardinal legates, Rolando and Bernardo, brought a letter from Hadrian to the emperor that implicitly referred to the superiority of the papacy over the empire. As the letter stated, the *beneficium*—a term that meant the goods (lands, moveable goods, and offices) that a lord granted his vassal—of the imperial crown that had just been granted to Barbarossa could be interpreted as a feudalization of the empire to the Roman Church. In this way, on a political level, the emperor could be equated, for example, with the king of Sicily. The break between empire and papacy was imminent, and it took the form of a schism that opened up on the death of Hadrian in 1159 when the choice was made for his successor. The largest group of cardinals chose Rolando Bandinelli (the cardinal legate who had taken part in the diet of Besançon), who took the name Alexander III (1159-81); another part of the college of cardinals, on the other hand, supported by the Vatican clergy, the Roman *popolo*, and the imperial legates, chose the cardinal of St. Cecilia, Ottaviano Monticelli, who took the name of Victor IV (1159-64).

---

20. Arsenio Frugoni, *Arnaldo da Brescia nelle fonti del secolo XII* (Turin: Einaudi, 1989).

In this schism an important role was played by the common Italian citizens. During the diet—the general assembly that the emperor normally convened in the month of May to discuss the interests of the empire (war, peace, laws, etc.), with the participation of the aristocrats and the most important churchmen of the kingdom—held in Roncaglia (1158), near Piacenza, the emperor presented an overall plan to reaffirm his authority in the *Regnum italiae*, advocating for himself the *regalia* that were his by right. This plan was to have been implemented in two ways in particular: by the exercise of justice; and by the exaction of the *fodro*, the right of the sovereign when on a journey to demand fodder for his horses, which by twelfth century had been transformed into a monetary tax. In this way, Frederick I intended to set himself up as the authority controlling the composite Italian political panorama, made up of overlapping powers (the *signori*, the bishops, the communes). The emperor, moreover, wanted to govern the situation in the peninsula by placing himself as arbiter between the two pretenders to the papacy; he thus convened a council in Pavia in 1160 to resolve the question. The cities all took sides: Lodi, Como, and Cremona took the part of the emperor and Victor IV; Milan and its allies, Alexander III. At the same time, however, a widespread awareness was gaining ground in the cities of the center and the north of the limits that the imperial plan in the *Regnum italiae* would, in the long term, place on the freedom that these cities had gradually achieved.

Barbarossa's refusal to listen to the communes and his strong reaction to the "perfid" Milan, which he razed to the ground in 1162, mobilized the communal forces into a league (*Societas Lombardiae*) created in 1167, which defeated Frederick militarily and forced him to abandon the *Regnum*.[21] The ideal point of reference and common policy for the cities that made up the *Societas Lombardiae*, which were very different from one another, was their link to Pope Alexander III, who legitimized their armed resistance to an emperor whom he had excommunicated because of his support for Victor. The pope used the communes against

---

21. On the destruction of Milan in 1162 and the way that this event remained in the collective cultural memory of Milan, and more generally of Italy in the long term, see Pietro Silanos and Kai-Michael Sprenger, eds., *La distruzione di Milano (1162): Un luogo di memorie* (Milan: Vita e Pensiero, 2015). On Barbarossa's wars in the Italian peninsula, see the overview by Paolo Grillo, *Le guerre del Barbarossa. I comuni contro l'imperatore* (Bari: Editori Laterza, 2018).

Frederick, and this also gave him greater bargaining power compared to Barbarossa in any future negotiations.

The only way out of the impasse for the emperor was to attempt to divide the front between the papacy and the communes by trying to deal directly with Alexander. Nevertheless, the negotiations in Veroli soon came to naught, and so Frederick opted for a military solution by descending on Italy for the last time in 1174. He was defeated, however, in the famous Battle of Legnano that in practice marked the end of hostilities.[22] Negotiations were reopened in Anagni, with the emperor's representatives. All the topics present on the political agenda of all the actors in play (pope, emperor, communes, and Normans) were discussed. The following conditions were imposed on Frederick: he would recognize Alexander as the only legitimate pope, restore the *Patrimonium beati Petri* to how it had been in the time of Conrad III, and make peace with the communes and William II of Altavilla. In exchange, the safety of the antipope and the churchmen who had supported him would be granted.

Thus, in Chioggia, near Venice, in 1177, the emperor reached a truce with the communes and the king of Sicily, and finally, in Constance in 1183 he signed a peace that recognized the Lombard League and the rights and customs gained by the cities in the course of the previous decades, in exchange for the swearing of an oath of fealty to the emperor and the acceptance that he would invest the city consuls, that is to say, the representatives of the first communal magistracies. Though he had placed the cities and their governments in a hierarchy of a feudal nature, which culminated in the king, Frederick did not manage, however, to limit the institutional dynamism of the communes, thus failing in his objective to carry out a plan of coherent domination of the Italian peninsula.[23] This outcome was also due to the growing awareness of the papacy that it played an important role in the governing not only of the spiritual sphere but also of the political one, in Italy and the entire *societas Christiana*.[24]

---

22. Paolo Grillo, *Legnano 1176. Una battaglia per la libertà* (Bari: Editori Laterza, 2010).

23. On the development of the Lombard League in the years from the end of hostilities with Barbarossa to the first decades of the thirteenth century, see Gianluca Raccagni, *The Lombard League, 1167–1225* (Oxford: Oxford University Press, 2010).

24. Enlightening from this point of view are the considerations by Pietro Costa, *Iurisdictio: Semantica del potere politico nella pubblicistica medievale* (Milan: Giuffrè, 2001), 262–363, who also goes back over the canonical and theological theory and its effects on the practical application of papal *iurisdictio* in temporal affairs. For the events that marked the papacy after the death of

## 2. THE PAPACY AND ITALIAN POLITICS

The twelfth century, however, was not only a period in which the papacy managed to impose itself—not without difficulty—as one of the principal political actors in the Italian political scene, but also a period in which it attempted to define and systematize the process of religious and ecclesiastical uniformity of the Latin Church. In this sense we must remember in the first place the development of canon law as a tool for placing local ecclesiastical experiences within a common normative framework and for identifying legal references to bring about the reform of the clergy, the monastic orders, and the laity. Of particular importance was the work of the Camaldolese monk Gratian (ca. 1075-ca. 1147), the most famous master of the twelfth-century school of law of Bologna, who was an obligatory point of reference for the centuries to come. Indeed between 1140 and 1142 he wrote his *Concordia discordantium canonum*, better known as the *Decretum Gratiani*, which attempted to gather together and harmonize the canon legislation of the Church that had accumulated over the centuries, thus serving as a basis for further collections of canon law and as a tool for its teaching in the new universities.[25] Besides the elaboration of canon law in the schools, we must also remember the conciliar legislation of the twelfth century. After the rupture with the Greek Church and the turning point brought about by Gregory VII, in fact, the papacy began to convene a series of councils—ecclesiastical assemblies that brought together archbishops, bishops, abbots, exponents of local churches, and laymen to tackle the principal tasks facing the life of the Church—that for the first time in centuries began to define themselves as "general."

It was not by chance that the seat of these councils was the Lateran Basilica in Rome, the ancient residence of the Roman emperors that, according to tradition, Constantine had given to Pope Silvester I. Three councils were convened in the twelfth century (1123, 1139, 1179), which had the principal aims of preparing the crusade to combat the Saracen enemy and reforming the customs of the clergy and the laity.

---

Barbarossa up until the end of the twelfth century, see Piero Zerbi, *Papato, impero e "respublica christiana" dal 1187 al 1198* (Milan: Vita e Pensiero, 1980). On the development of the symbolic communication of papal *potestas*, which from the twelfth century in particular was enriched by new language and contents in line with the process of *imitatio imperii*, see the work of Gerhart Burian Ladner, *Die Papstbildnisse des Altertums und des Mittelalters*, 5 vols. (Vatican City: Pontificio Istituto di archeologia cristiana, 1941-84) and the more recent Agostino Paravicini Bagliani, *Le chiavi e la tiara: Immagini e simboli del papato medievale* (Rome: Viella, 2005).

25. Wilfried Hartmann and Kenneth Pennington, eds., *The History of Medieval Canon Law in the Classical Period, 1140–1234: From Gratian to the Decretals of Pope Gregory IX* (Washington, DC: Catholic University of America Press, 2008).

Legislation of these conciliar assemblies reached its peak in the Fourth Lateran Council, convened by Innocent III in 1215, probably one of the most important councils in the history of the Church.[26]

On January 8, 1198, Lothar of Segni was elected pope and took the name of Innocent III (1198–1216). As scholars have recently pointed out, this pontificate marked an important break in the relationship between the papacy and the political and ecclesiastical space of the Italian peninsula. In particular, what changed was the vision and the form of the relationship between the Apostolic See and the local dioceses and, consequently, between the papacy and the political institutions of the cities.[27] This did not happen by chance. Innocent is probably, in fact, the only pope to have used the word "Italy" in his letters, with expressions that reveal more than "a clear awareness of the unity of the nation,"[28] but a vision of the world that presupposed a central position for the Italian peninsula in a universal perspective. He revealed himself in this way to be a master in referring to a clear ideal of nationality and the *patria* that he then placed within the horizon of divine Providence. The pope attributed to Italy what Leo the Great and the early medieval tradition had attributed to Rome, as a reason for its glory among all the cities of the world, that is, the privilege of being the seat of the "princedom" of the Church and the empire. This was not an exclusively political move; or rather, it placed a specifically political action within the theology of history. Starting from the biblical metaphor of the sun and the moon,[29] Innocent justified his temporal action in Tuscany by stating that Italy had been chosen as the foundation of the Christian religion and the seat of the princedom of the priesthood and the kingdom. Divine Providence and political action had a profound effect

---

26. The critical edition of the council canons can now be found in Antonio García y García et al., eds., *Conciliorum oecumenicorum generaliumque decreta. Editio critica*, vol. 2, bk. 1, *The General Councils of Latin Christendom: From Constantinople IV to Pavia-Siena (869–1424)*, Corpus Christianorum (Turnhout: Brepols, 2013). An overview of the history of the Lateran councils can be found in Raymonde Foreville, *Lateranense I, II, III, e Lateranense IV*, ed. Ottorino Pasquato, trans. M. G. Fornaci (Vatican City: Libreria Editrice Vaticana, 2001).

27. See the work quoted above by Alberzoni, *Città, vescovi e papato*. See also Laura Baietto, *Il papa e le città: Papato e comuni in Italia centro-settentrionale durante la prima metà del secolo XIII* (Spoleto: Centro italiano di studi sull'alto medioevo, 2007), 3–167 for the age of Innocent III.

28. Michele Maccarrone, *Chiesa e Stato nella dottrina di papa Innocenzo III* (Rome: Facultas theologica P. Athenaei Lateranensis 1940), 148–53; Michele Maccarrone, *Studi su Innocenzo III* (Padua: Editrice Antenore, 1972), 16.

29. On this, see the studies by Othmar Hageneder collected in *Il sole e la luna: Papato, impero e regni nella teoria e nella prassi dei secoli XII e XIII*, ed. Maria Pia Alberzoni (Milan: Vita e Pensiero, 2000).

because, thanks to the government of the Church, the people subject to it in these regions could "enjoy the benefits proper to ecclesiastical government and at times" be elevated "to the level of special children of the Roman Church, a title reserved for sovereigns and a sign of honor for those who receive it."[30]

Even the social composition of the Roman Curia in the period between the schism of 1159 and the end of Innocent's pontificate reflects a close link to the Italian peninsula. All the popes of the second half of the twelfth century were Italian, just like the overwhelming majority of the cardinals, coming above all from the region of Lazio. Under Clement III the number of cardinals from Rome or the surrounding area was extremely high: seventeen. Most of the other Italian cardinals came from the communes of the north and the center. Cities like Genoa and Venice, as well as the Kingdom of Sicily, on the other hand, were strongly underrepresented, a sign that the social configuration of the Roman Curia was defined not only by the relationships of its leaders but also by the sphere of influence of the popes. The presence in the college of cardinals of monks of the abbots of Montecassino, for example, began to decline during the pontificates of Calixtus II and Honorius II. Only when the criteria governing the entry of new members to the college of cardinals changed did geographical provenance become less important and the college opened itself to figures from outside Italy. Alexander III, for example, requested capable clerics who had had a particular training in the *scientia letterarum*. Of the thirty-four cardinals that he created many had the title of *magister* or had studied in a theological or legal *studium*. Some were masters who enjoyed great fame, such as Robert Pullus, Odo of Ourscamp, Henry of Marcy, Nicholas Breakspear, Albert of Morra, or Conrad of Wittelsbach. Most of them were jurists, and their proportion increased further under Lucius III (nine *magistri* out of fifteen new cardinals). Despite this, the connection of the college to Rome and Italy remained strong throughout the thirteenth century.[31]

---

30. *Die Register Innozenz' III.*, vol. 1, *Pontifikatsjahr, 1198/99: Texte*, ed. Othmar Hageneder and Anton Haidacher (Graz: Böhlaus, 1964), 568–69.

31. On the biographical profiles of the cardinals, from the pontificate of Celestine III to that of Innocent III, see Werner Maleczek, *Papst und Kardinalskolleg von 1191 bis 1216: Die Kardinäle unter Coelestin III. und Innocenz III* (Vienna: Verlag der Österreichischen Akademie der Wissenschaften, 1984). On the biographical profiles of the cardinals during the subsequent pontificates up to that of Innocent IV, see Agostino Paravicini Bagliani, *Cardinali di curia e "familiae" cardinalizie dal 1227 al 1254*, 2 vols. (Padua: Editrice Antenore, 1972). For the second half of the thirteenth century, see Andreas Fischer, *Kardinäle im Konklave. Die lange Sedisvakantz der Jahre 1268 bis 1271* (Tübingen: Niemeyer, 2008). The social picture of the thirteenth-century

Innocent III's link with Italy is also documented by the position taken by the recovery of the *Patrimonium beati Petri*, or in other words, the "apostolic patrimony" understood in a much broader sense than in the past, in Innocent's political and ecclesiastical agenda. Tuscany, Umbria, and the lands on the southern border of Lazio and Campagna were subject to particular attention by the papal court—as testified by a letter sent by the pope in April 1198 to the rectors of the Tuscan League, which refers to the protection offered by the papacy to the cities of the league as if they were ecclesiastical bodies[32]—according to a plan that Innocent aimed to carry out in the territory of the peninsula, thanks also to the absence of the emperor: a form of control similar to that which Frederick Barbarossa had imagined only a few years earlier.

The confines of papal jurisdiction were thus being enlarged following a theocratic design that saw the progressive enlargement of the temporal functions of the papacy in a veritable process of *imitatio imperii*.[33] To justify a coherent political and territorial entity, Innocent III had recourse to the famous Donation of Constantine[34]—the act by which Constantine the Great allegedly offered Pope Silvester I landholdings in Rome and in the surrounding region that had belonged to the empire—and to the will of Christ himself, whose vicar on earth the pope described himself to be. In a sermon of February 22, 1199, using the metaphor of the sacrament of marriage to describe the intimate relationship between a bishop and his church, the pope stated that the Roman Church, his bride, had brought him "a priceless dowry": the *plenitudo potestatis* (the fullness of power) and the *latitudo temporalium* (the breadth of temporal power). As a "symbol of the spiritual things she has given me a miter, as a symbol of temporal things she has given

---

Curia, and of the chancellery in particular, is outlined in the study by Gerd Friedrich Nüske, "Untersuchungen über das Personal der päpstlichen Kanzlei 1254-1304," *Archiv für Diplomatik* 20 (1974): 39–240, 250–431. Centered more on the pontificate of Boniface VIII, on the other hand, is the work of Thérèse Boespflug, *La curie au temps de Boniface VIII: Étude prosopographique* (Rome: Istituto Storico Italiano per il Medio Evo, 2005).

32. *Die Register Innozenz' III.*, 1:127–28.

33. Horst Furhmann, "'Il vero imperatore è il papa': Il potere temporale nel medioevo," *Bullettino dell'Istituto storico italiano per il Medio Evo e Archivio Muratoriano* 92 (1985–86): 367–79. See also Hageneder, *Il sole e la luna*, quoted above.

34. On the Donation of Constantine in general, see Giovanni Maria Vian, *La donazione di Costantino* (Bologna: Il Mulino, 2004). On the use of the Donation by the popes in the course of the twelfth and thirteenth centuries it is useful to refer to Jürgen Miethke, "Costantino e il potere papale post-gregoriano," in *Enciclopedia Costantiniana* (Rome: Istituto della Enciclopedia Italiana, 2013), 57–595.

me a crown; the miter for the priesthood, the crown for the kingdom."[35] The pope went much further than Constantine, however: it was from Christ himself, in the imagination of Innocent, that the Roman Church had received its dominion, as he explained in a letter sent to the bishop of Fermo on January 13, 1206.[36] In the famous decretal *Per Venerabilem* of December 1202, the pope had also explained that he possessed "plenitudo potestatis in temporalibus" above all in the Patrimony of Saint Peter, thus presenting himself as both the true head of Christendom and justifying the papacy's possession of a veritable "State."

Innocent's policy of recovery, however, only enjoyed partial success and this above all to the north of Rome and in Tuscany. The Patrimony of Saint Peter was thus becoming a series of provinces: the Patrimony, the Duchy of Spoleto, the March of Ancona, Campagna, and Marittima, joined by Romagna at the end of the century. The organization of the Papal State had at the head of its administrative hierarchy a new figure, the *rector*, who undertook important tasks of arbitration and administration such as the census, the confirmation of magistrates in the small communes, or military authority over the castellans. The appointment of rectors had two objectives: to affirm papal sovereignty in the territories of the Patrimony and to exercise spiritual control, especially against heretics.

Besides the Patrimony, Innocent also sought to exercise his influence in the political affairs of the cities of central and northern Italy. This took place by following several constants: an ever-increasing control over the episcopate, which became in practice the element connecting the center and the periphery and the principal defender of the *libertas ecclesiastica* conceived of as the material and jurisdictional patrimony of the Roman Church; the dispatching to local churches of figures charged with carrying out papal jurisdiction delegated by the vicar of Christ (*visitatores et provisores*, judges, delegates, and apostolic legates);[37] the involvement of trusted collaborators recruited from among the local clergy (papal subdeacons) or the religious orders capable of maintaining an active connection between the Apostolic See and the local

---

35. Innocenzo III, *I sermoni*, ed. Stanislao Fioramonti (Vatican City: Libreria Editrice Vaticana, 2006), 630-31.
36. Maccarrone, *Chiesa e Stato*, 48-50.
37. Maccarrone, *Chiesa e Stato*, 79-110, and Baietto, *Il papa e le città*, 101-39. On the use of the institution of the apostolic legates and papal justice, see the articles contained in Maria Pia Alberzoni and Claudia Zey, eds., *Legati e delegati papali: Profili, ambiti d'azione e tipologie di intervento nei secoli XII–XIII* (Milan: Vita e Pensiero, 2012).

churches; the pacification of cities; and the definition of alliances with those factions in the cities that showed themselves open to implementing papal intentions.

Among Innocent's achievements we must also include his convening of the Fourth Lateran Council in 1215. The plan to hold a general council of Christendom preoccupied the pope throughout his pontificate, but he was not to carry it out until seventeen years after his election. The council was part of an overall strategy, aimed at presenting to the outside world the political and military plan that would allow the crusaders to recover what they had lost, and presenting to the Christian world a vast program of reform under the guidance of the Roman Church. The only one of the councils celebrated in the Lateran Basilica to be designated as a *generale Concilium* by the thirteenth-century canonists, the Fourth Lateran Council, inaugurated on November 11, 1215, with an important sermon by the pope, was meant to imitate the great councils of the ancient Church. The official list of members included more than four hundred cardinals, patriarchs, archbishops or bishops, and representatives from eighty ecclesiastical provinces (against the sixty-two of the Lateran council of 1179), more than half of which were of Italian origin, as well as eight hundred lower prelates (abbots, priors, provosts, and deans). The legislation that the pope himself had drawn up for promulgation included constitutions concerning the discipline of the clergy and the spiritual life of the faithful; and it introduced novelties from a sacramental point of view such as the requirement to confess at least once a year (at Easter). The council strongly desired to extend pastoral and religious practices that had been established in many areas of Christendom, like Italy, to the West in its entirety.[38]

One of the principal problems dealt with by the council was the regulation of the religious life. It was the point of arrival of a tendency to uniformity that the papacy and the Roman Curia had already begun to adopt several decades earlier, especially with those experiences of religious life that distinguished themselves from traditional monastic or canonical rules, above all because they mostly originated among the laity. The new religious impulses in the life of the Church that arose

---

38. On the Fourth Lateran Council, see in particular: *Il lateranense IV: Le ragioni di un concilio. Atti del LIII Convegno storico internazionale, Todi, 9–12 ottobre 2016* (Spoleto: Centro italiano di studi sull'alto medioevo, 2017) and Gert Melville and Johannes Helmrath, eds., *The Fourth Lateran Council: Institutional Reform and Spiritual Renewal. Proceedings of the Conference Marking the Eight Hundredth Anniversary of the Council Organized by the Pontificio Comitato di Scienze Storiche (Rome, 15–17 October 2015)* (Affalterbach: Didymos-Verlag, 2017).

from the laity forced the Roman Curia to rethink traditional models and experiment with new solutions that were partly influenced by the theology elaborated in the schools of Paris, where many of the cardinals themselves had been educated.[39] Part of these new experiences, such as those of the Humiliati, the first brotherhood of Francis of Assisi, or the canons of St. Mark, originated in an Italian context; others, like those of the Waldensians or the Friars Preachers of Dominic of Guzman, although arising outside Italy, nevertheless found the Italian cities to be a fertile environment in which to develop. The popes of the first half of the thirteenth century succeeded in channeling this new religious ferment and using it to consolidate their own ecclesiastical and political vision.

On the death of Innocent III "the fundamental features of the forms of government, the territorial terms to be reached . . . , the ideological requirements for the effective transformation of the primitive *Patrimonium beati Petri* into a much more complex papal state had been set down for papal successors,"[40] as had the means for administering relations with the cities of central and northern Italy and with their bishops, and the guidelines for the whole of Christendom. The picture, however, was complicated by the advent to the imperial throne of Frederick II (1220-50), the son of Henry VI and grandson of Barbarossa, which opened up a new phase. From 1226, in fact, Frederick attempted to reestablish his authority in northern Italy by trying to obtain the obedience of the communal cities. Two opposing fronts came to constitute themselves: Milan and its allies revived the Lombard League, while Cremona and the cities that were enemies of Milan took the side of the emperor, including Ezzelino da Romano, *signore* of the March of Treviso.

The pontificates of Honorius III (1216-27), Gregory IX (1227-41), and Innocent IV (1243-54), which marked the decades up to midcentury, saw papal temporal policy adapt itself to the various contingent situations, and to the struggle with the emperor in particular, which was becoming increasingly intractable. The principle at the basis of the

---

39. Pietro Silanos, "'In sede apostolica specula constituti': Procedure curiali per l'approvazione di regole e testi normativi all'alba del IV concilio lateranense," *Quellen und Forschungen aus italienischen Archiven und Bibliotheken* 94 (2014): 33–93. On the evolution of the monastic rules in this historical moment, see the overall view presented in Gert Melville, *The World of Medieval Monasticism: Its History and Forms of Life* (Collegeville, MN: Cistercian Publications Liturgical Press, 2016).

40. Capitani, *Storia dell'Italia medievale*, 444.

temporal action of the Apostolic See in the different historical situations was to defend the *libertas ecclesiastica*, a value that was as old as the Church itself, but that from the eleventh century onward, became subject to a theoretical reelaboration that enlarged its semantic value, making it suitable for legitimating the various forms of political action undertaken by the papacy.[41] If Innocent's plan to make the Church the principal organizer and regulator of the entire *societas Christiana*—and of the political context of the Italian peninsula in particular—had been threatened by the attacks brought by the communal institutions at the end of the twelfth century and the beginning of the thirteenth, which aimed primarily to undermine its economic bases, then during the pontificates of Gregory IX and Innocent IV it was the policy of Frederick II that constituted an even graver threat to the papal theocratic vision. For the actors in the Italian political space, therefore, defending the *libertas ecclesiastica* from Frederick's attacks meant adhering to the side of the papacy, thus supporting the pope in a war against the emperor that took on apocalyptic tones in the narratives that were elaborated by the respective sides.

In the years in which the struggle between pope and empire became more intractable, the terms "Guelph" and "Ghibelline" started to spread in the Italian cities. These words derived from the names of the sides in the struggle for the German crown in the kingdom of Germany, which were headed by the Welfen (Guelph) and the Waiblingen (Ghibelline) families. Cremona, Pavia, and Siena formed the axis of the imperial Ghibelline party, while Florence, Milan, Genoa, Bologna, and Parma (at least until 1245) were on the papal Guelph side. This terminology was to mark the political history of the peninsula later too when, after the death of Frederick II in 1250, it lost the sense for which it had been created and took on other meanings linked to the factional strife within or between the various cities. Once again, the presence and the action of the papacy in Italy and its ambition to become the regulating force of the political space had characterized not only the effective relations between the actors in play but the very vocabulary of politics.

---

41. On the evolution of this concept in the time period under investigation here, see Brigitte Szabó-Bechstein, "'Libertas ecclesiae' vom 12. bis zur Mitte des 13. Jahrhunderts: Verbreitung und Wandel des Begriffs seit seiner Prägung durch Gregor VII.," in *Die abendländische Freiheit vom 10. zum 14. Jahrhundert: Der Wirkungszusammenhang von Idee und Wirklichkeit im europäischen Vergleich*, ed. Johannes Fried (Sigmaringen: Thorbecke, 1991), 147–75. The theme is also dealt with in Baietto, *Il papa e le città*, 437–47.

## 2. THE PAPACY AND ITALIAN POLITICS

The close link between the papacy and the Italian peninsula can also be observed in the biographies of the individual popes. Once the great ecclesiological and political disputes of the twelfth century had been left behind, in fact, the papacy became even more "Roman" in the geographical sense of the word, with the ascent to the throne of Saint Peter of three popes who came from Rome or Lazio: Innocent III, Honorius III, and Gregory IX. This series of Roman popes was interrupted in 1241 by the election of prelates who came from other areas of the Italian peninsula, whose families were intimately linked to the ruling classes of important cities of the north: Goffredo Castiglioni (Celestine IV) of Milan and, particularly, Sinibaldo Fieschi (Innocent IV) from Genoa. The interruption was brief. In 1261 a new cardinal from Lazio, Reginaldo di Jenne, became Pope Alexander IV. The advent of Urban IV, the first French pope after Urban II (1088-99), and even more that of Clement IV, reflected the upheaval brought about by the death of Frederick II and the creation of a new important political tie between Rome and the French court (and the count of Provence, Charles I of Anjou). The longest conclave in history (1268-71) created the only pope of this period—Gregory X—who had not belonged to the college of cardinals. He was also Italian and, like Celestine IV and Innocent IV, came from a city in the north, Piacenza.

Until the death of Gregory X all the popes of the thirteenth century belonged to the secular clergy. The traditional monastic orders only had sporadic representatives in the college of cardinals. The movement that had begun in the second half of the twelfth century in favor of the secular clergy also impeded the regular canons from acceding to the papal throne. It was therefore the biographical elements of each individual (intellectual training, personality, career in the Curia, geographical origin) more than family or membership of a monastic order that determined the choice of candidate for the highest role in the Roman Church of this century. The roots many had in the Italian political, social, and religious tissue was one of these elements, if not the most decisive.

## Selected Bibliography

Alberzoni, Maria Pia. *Città, vescovi e papato nella Lombardia dei comuni*. Novara: Interlinea, 2001.
Alberzoni, Maria Pia, and Claudia Zey, eds. *Legati e delegati papali: Profili, ambiti d'azione e tipologie di intervento nei secoli XII–XIII*. Milan: Vita e Pensiero, 2012.

Baietto, Laura. *Il papa e le città: Papato e comuni in Italia centro-settentrionale durante la prima metà del secolo XIII*. Spoleto: Centro italiano di studi sull'alto medioevo, 2007.

Boespflug, Thérèse. *La curie au temps de Boniface VIII: Étude prosopographique*. Rome: Istituto Storico Italiano per il Medio Evo, 2005.

Brentano, Robert. *Due chiese: Italia e Inghilterra nel XIII secolo*. Bologna: Il Mulino, 1972; orig. ed. Princeton, NJ: Princeton University Press, 1968.

Cantarella, Glauco Maria. *Gregorio VII*. Rome: Salerno, 2018.

Capitani, Ovidio. *Storia dell'Italia medievale*. Bari: Editori Laterza, 2009.

Costa, Pietro. *Iurisdictio: Semantica del potere politico nella pubblicistica medievale*. Milan: Giuffrè, 2001.

D'Acunto, Nicolangelo. *Cum anulo et baculo: Vescovi dell'Italia medievale dal protagonismo politico alla complementarietà istituzionale*. Spoleto: Fondazione Centro italiano di studi sull'alto medioevo, 2019.

———. *La lotta per le investiture: Una rivoluzione medievale (998–1122)*. Rome: Carocci, 2020.

*Enciclopedia dei papi*. Rome: Istituto della Enciclopedia italiana, 2000.

Fischer, Andreas. *Kardinäle im Konklave: Die lange Sedisvakantz der Jahre 1268 bis 1271*. Tübingen: Niemeyer, 2008.

Fodale, Salvatore. *L'apostolica legazia e altri studi su Stato e Chiesa*. Messina: Sicania, 1991.

Foreville, Raymonde. *Lateranense I, II, III, e Lateranense IV*. Edited by Ottorino Pasquato, translated by M. G. Fornaci. Vatican City: Libreria Editrice Vaticana, 2001.

Frugoni, Arsenio. *Arnaldo da Brescia nelle fonti del secolo XII*. Turin: Einaudi, 1989.

Furhmann, Horst. *Papst Gregor VII. und das Zeitalter der Reform: Annäherungen an eine europäische Wende. Ausgewählte Aufsätze*, edited by Martina Hartmann. Wiesbaden: Harrassowitz, 2016.

García y García, Antonio, et al., eds. *Conciliorum oecumenicorum generaliumque decreta. Editio critica*. Vol. 2, bk. 1, *The General Councils of Latin Christendom: From Constantinople IV to Pavia-Siena (869–1424)*. Corpus Christianorum. Turnhout: Brepols, 2013.

Golinelli, Paolo. *La pataria: Lotte religiose e sociali nella Milano dell'XI secolo*. Milan: Jaca Book, 1984.

Guardo, Marco. *Titulus e tumulus: Epitafi di pontefici e cardinali alla corte dei papi del XIII secolo*. Rome: Viella, 2008.

Hageneder, Othmar. *Il sole e la luna: Papato, impero e regni nella teoria e nella prassi dei secoli XII e XIII*, edited by Maria Pia Alberzoni. Milan: Vita e Pensiero, 2000.

Hartmann, Wilfried, and Kenneth Pennington, eds. *The History of Medieval Canon Law in the Classical Period, 1140–1234: From Gratian to the Decretals of Pope Gregory IX*. Washington, DC: Catholic University of America Press, 2008.

Johrendt, Jochen, and H. Müller, eds. *Römisches Zentrum und kirchliche Peripherie: Das universale Papsttum als Bezugspunkt der Kirchen von den Reformpäpsten bis zu Innozenz III*. Berlin: de Gruyter, 2008.

## 2. THE PAPACY AND ITALIAN POLITICS 45

Johrendt, Jochen, and H. Müller, eds. *Rom und die Regionen: Studien zur Homogenisierung der lateinischen Kirche im Hochmittelalter*. Berlin: de Gruyter, 2012.
Ladner, Gerhart Burian. *Die Papstbildnisse des Altertums und des Mittelalters*. 5 vols. Vatican City: Pontificio Istituto di archeologia cristiana, 1941-84.
*Il lateranense IV: Le ragioni di un concilio*. Atti del LIII Convegno storico internazionale. Spoleto: CISAM, 2017.
Maccarrone, Michele. *Studi su Innocenzo III*. Padua: Antenore, 1972.
Maleczek, Werner. *Papst und Kardinalskolleg von 1191 bis 1216: Die Kardinäle unter Coelestin III. und Innocenz III*. Vienna: Verlag der Österreichischen Akademie der Wissenschaften, 1984.
———. *Pietro Capuano patrizio Amalfitano, cardinale, legato alla quarta crociata, teologo († 1215)*. Amalfi: Centro di cultura e storia amalfitana, 1997; orig. ed. Wien, 1988.
Melville, Gert. *The World of Medieval Monasticism: Its History and Forms of Life*. Collegeville, MN: Cistercian Publications Liturgical Press, 2016; orig. ed. Munich, 2012; ital. ed. Brescia, 2020.
Melville, Gert, and Johannes Helmrath, eds. *The Fourth Lateran Council: Institutional Reform and Spiritual Renewal. Proceedings of the Conference Marking the Eight Hundredth Anniversary of the Council Organized by the Pontificio Comitato di Scienze Storiche (Rome, 15-17 October 2015)*. Affalterbach: Didymos-Verlag, 2017.
Merlo, Giovanni Grado. "Il papato e le istituzioni ecclesiastiche della cristianità latina." In *Storia del cristianesimo*, vol. 2, *L'età medievale (secoli VIII-XV)*, edited by Marina Benedetti, 133-62. Rome: Carocci, 2015.
Miccoli, Giovanni. "La storia religiosa." In *Storia d'Italia*, vol. 2, *Dalla caduta dell'Impero romano al secolo XVIII*, edited by Ruggero Romano and Corrado Vivanti, bk. 1:431-1079. Turin: Einaudi, 1974.
Paravicini Bagliani, Agostino. *Cardinali di curia e "familiae" cardinalizie dal 1227 al 1254*. 2 vols. Padua: Editrice Antenore, 1972.
———. *Le chiavi e la tiara: Immagini e simboli del papato medievale*. Rome: Viella, 2005.
———. *Morte e elezione del papa: Norme, riti e conflitti*. Rome: Viella, 2013.
———. *Il papato nel secolo XIII: Cent'anni di bibliografia (1875-2009)*. Florence: SISMEL-Edizioni del Galluzzo, 2010.
———. *Il trono di Pietro: L'universalità del papato da Alessandro III a Bonifacio VIII*. Rome: Carocci, 2001.
———. *La vita quotidiana alla corte dei papi del Duecento*. Bari: Editori Laterza, 1996.
Prodi, Paolo. *Il sacramento del potere*. Bologna: Il Mulino, 1992.
Raccagni, Gianluca. *The Lombard League, 1167-1225*. Oxford: Oxford University Press, 2010.
Schimmelpfennig, Bernhard. *Il papato: Antichità, medioevo, rinascimento*. Rome: Viella 2006; orig. ed. Darmstadt, 1996.
Silanos, Pietro. *Gerardo Bianchi da Parma († 1302): La biografia di un cardinale-legato duecentesco*. Rome: Herder, 2010.

———. "'In sede apostolica specula constituti': Procedure curiali per l'approvazione di regole e testi normativi all'alba del IV concilio lateranense." *Quellen und Forschungen aus italienischen Archiven und Bibliotheken* 94 (2014): 33–93.

Vian, Giovanni Maria. *La donazione di Costantino*. Bologna: Il Mulino, 2004.

Violante, Cinzio. *"Chiesa feudale" e riforme in Occidente (secc. X–XII): Introduzione a un tema storiografico*. Spoleto: Centro italiano di studi sull'alto medioevo, 1999.

———. *La pataria milanese e la riforma ecclesiastica*. Vol. 1, *Le premesse (1045–1057)*. Rome: Istituto Storico Italiano per il Medio Evo, 1955.

Weinfurter, Stefan. *Canossa: Il disincanto del mondo*. Bologna: Il Mulino, 2014; orig. ed. Munich, 2007.

Werner, Ernst. *Zwischen Canossa und Worms: Staat und Kirche, 1077–1122*. Berlin: Akademie Verlag, 1978.

Zerbi, Piero. *Papato, impero e "respublica christiana" dal 1187 al 1198*. Milan: Vita e Pensiero, 1980.

Zumhagen, Olaf. *Religiöse Konflikte und kommunale Entwicklung: Mailand, Cremona, Piacenza und Florenz zur Zeit der Pataria*. Cologne: Bohlau, 2002.

CHAPTER 3

# Bishops
*Maureen C. Miller*

Medieval Italy was teeming with bishops. This distinctive characteristic of Christianity in medieval Italy was dramatically visualized in map 1 of Robert Brentano's *Two Churches: England and Italy in the Thirteenth Century*: the boot and its islands are speckled in a riot of dots while comparatively England appears nearly blank.[1] A less impressionistic comparison, taking into consideration comparability of geographical areas, is between Italy (its area 116,303 square miles) and England, Wales, Scotland, and Ireland (with a combined area of 113,346 square miles). Using Denys Hay's figures for 1400, the latter had only 67 sees while Italy had 263, nearly four times as many.[2] Another distinctive feature of this large community of pastors is the disparities among them. Although sees throughout Europe varied in status and resources, these variations among Italian bishoprics were extreme. To be the bishop of Cremona on the Po River in Lombardy was to be a great feudal lord with numerous vassals, several residences, and a substantial income from lucrative rights and estates, while to be

---

1. Robert Brentano, *Two Churches: England and Italy in the Thirteenth Century* (Berkeley: University of California Press, 1988), 65.
2. Denys Hay, *The Church in Italy in the Fifteenth Century: The Birkbeck Lectures, 1971* (Cambridge: Cambridge University Press, 1977), 10.

the bishop of Aquino in Campania near Capua was to be proprietor of a few farms, five mills, and some fishing rights on the local lake.³ All of these bishops, moreover, were geographically closer to Rome, the undisputed center of Western Christianity, than were other European prelates. These three characteristics of the episcopate in Italy from 1050 to 1300—the large number of sees, extreme disparities in their status and resources, and proximity to the Holy See—shaped the experience of Christianity and the institutional character of the medieval Italian Church.

## Numbers and Their Implications

The large number of bishops in the Italian peninsula was chiefly due to its dense urbanization, a heritage from Etruscan, Greek, and Roman antiquity. In the fourth century, when synodal *acta* begin to list the names of bishops attending and affirming the decrees issued, these local heads of Christian communities were identified with urban centers: Lucius of Verona, Fortunatianus of Aquileia, Severus of Ravenna, Ursacius of Brescia, and Protasius of Milan, for example, subscribed at the Council of Serdica (modern Sofia) in 343.⁴ While in Asia Minor there were references to bishops in cities and then "country bishops" (*chorepiskopoi*) in rural areas, in Italy episcopal sees were resolutely urban even if what counted as a city varied widely.

Various upheavals from late antiquity through the early Middle Ages did take their toll, with the Lombard incursions having the most devastating effects on the number of Italian sees. The steepest reductions were in the south: of the fifteen early Christian sees documented in Puglia only six survived into the eighth century, and Campania suffered similar losses.⁵ So too in the mountainous interior of Abruzzo, the seven sees documented in the fifth century were reduced to three by the ninth.⁶ In the north, many bishops were forced to abandon

---

3. G. A. Loud, *The Latin Church in Norman Italy* (Cambridge: Cambridge University Press, 2007), 391.

4. Mark Humphries, *Communities of the Blessed: Social Environment and Religious Change in Northern Italy, AD 200–400*, Oxford Early Christian Studies (Oxford: Oxford University Press, 1999), 48.

5. Jean-Marie Martin, "L'ambiente longobardo, greco, islamico e normanno nel Mezzogiorno," in *Storia dell'Italia religiosa*, vol. 1, *L'antichità e il medioevo*, ed. André Vauchez (Bari: Editori Laterza, 1993), 197.

6. Laurent Feller, *Les Abruzzes médiévales: Territoire, économie et société en Italie centrale du IXᵉ au XIIᵉ siècle* (Rome: École française de Rome, 1998), 118.

their sees for a period—Milan's to Genoa, for example, and Aquileia's to Grado—but only one, Brescello, disappeared permanently.⁷ Over the central Middle Ages, however, new sees continued to be established. One need only think of the new Piedmontese city and see of Alessandria, founded in the late twelfth century, and the numerous foundations that emerged over the eleventh and twelfth centuries with the Norman conquest of the south. Indeed, the conquest, with its expansion of Latin Christianity in Muslim Sicily and in the Byzantine areas of the mainland, led to a significant reconfiguration of dioceses with bishops installed at new centers of Norman settlement such as Aversa, Mileto, and Melfi.⁸ The number of sees in Italy, in sum, was not stable over the entire millennial-long arc of the Middle Ages, but it was always high in comparison to northern Europe.

One corollary of the large number of bishops on the peninsula was that most Italian dioceses were considerably smaller than those north of the Alps. Certainly, some northern Italian sees approached or even slightly exceeded the dimensions of some of their northern European counterparts. The bishop of the large Italian see of Brescia, for example, had a journey of roughly 108 miles ahead of him to traverse the distance from the northernmost edge of his diocese at the origins of the Oglio River in the Val Camonica to its southernmost along the Oglio as it meanders southeast across the Po plain. These dimensions exceeded those of the bishop of Auxerre's diocese, which measured seventy-three miles from Pontigny in its northeast to La Charité sur Loire on its southwestern border.⁹ But many northern European dioceses far exceeded even a large Italian see in size. The bishop of Lincoln had a trip of 162 miles across his diocese, which ran from the Humber to the Thames along England's east coast, and the bishop of Constance had a trek of 214 miles from the Saint Gotthard pass at the southern extreme of his diocese to Stuttgart in its north.¹⁰

---

7. Louis Duchesne, "Les évêchés d'Italia et l'invasion lombarde," *Mélanges d'archéologie et d'histoire* 23 (1903): 86–88.

8. See especially Loud, *The Latin Church*, 118–27.

9. *Enciclopedia dell'arte medievale*, 12 vols. (Rome: Istituto della Enciclopedia Italiana fondata da Giovanni Treccani, 1991–2001), s.v. Brescia; François Menant, *Campagnes lombardes du moyen âge: L'Économie et la société rurales dans la région de Bergame, de Crémone et de Brescia du Xᵉ au XIIIᵉ siècle* (Rome: École française de Rome, 1993), 913, carte 1; Constance Brittain Bouchard, *Spirituality and Administration: The Role of the Bishop in Twelfth-Century Auxerre* (Cambridge, MA: Medieval Academy of America, 1979), 7.

10. F. Donald Logan, *University Education of the Parochial Clergy in Medieval England: The Lincoln Diocese, c. 1300–c. 1350* (Toronto: Pontifical Institute of Mediaeval Studies, 2014), 2:

Italy's smallest dioceses were in the south. The microdiocese of Bitetto, a less than five-mile-wide spot carved out of the see of Bari, may have been the smallest: it was "a tiny hill town with a single parish based on the cathedral" with an equally miniscule annual income.[11] Less extreme examples are the nearby diocese of Molfetta, first documented in 1136, that covered an area of only roughly sixteen square miles and the diocese of Calvi in the Terra di Lavoro that was a mere ten miles wide. More average might be a see like Nola, where the bishop could still reach the farthest communities under his pastoral care—those on the coast—in a roughly five-hour walk.[12] This is, of course, the most important measure, and a factor in the small size of many southern sees is the mountainous character of much of this part of the peninsula. Bishops of the larger Po valley sees could move through much of their dioceses on the many tributaries of the Po that laced the plain. The bishops of Cremona, for example, had two rural residences in the northernmost zone of their diocese, one at Fornovo on the west bank of the River Serio and another at Genivolta on a navigable canal linking the Oglio and the Delma Rivers.[13] Bishops of Apennine dioceses traversed their territories on foot or beast.

While the energy and pastoral commitment of bishops played a large part in the degree of contact the members of their flocks had with them, the modest territorial dimensions of Italian dioceses certainly increased the likelihood that individuals received episcopal ministrations directly. The archpriest of the village of Isola della Scala on the plain south of Verona, for example, witnessed the provision of sacraments by his bishop: he recalled of Bishop Tebaldus (1135–57), "I always saw him confirm the children of Saint Romanus and Ostiglia at Ostiglia."[14] Another scroll of witness testimony, this time from Cremona in 1163,

---

Lincoln was the largest of the medieval dioceses of England and Wales, including eight counties and 1,928 parishes; Stefan Weinfurter, *The Salian Century: Main Currents in an Age of Transition*, trans. Barbara M. Bowlus (Philadelphia: University of Pennsylvania Press, 1999), 23.

11. Loud, *The Latin Church*, 271.

12. Loud, *The Latin Church*, xv–xvii; Jean-Marie Martin, *La Pouille du VI$^e$ au XII$^e$ siècle* (Rome: École française de Rome, 1993), carte 17, "Les évêchés de Pouille (X$^e$–XII$^e$ siècles)."

13. Maureen C. Miller, "The Political and Cultural Significance of the Bishop's Palace in Medieval Italy," in *Princes of the Church: Bishops and Their Palaces. Proceedings of the International Conference at Auckland Castle (30 June–4 July 2015)*, ed. David W. Rollason (London: Routledge, 2017), 49–50.

14. "Semper vidi eum confermare pueros sancti romani et ostilie in ostiglia," Archivio di Stato, Verona, Ospitale Civico no. 1 app.; Maureen C. Miller, *The Formation of a Medieval Church: Ecclesiastical Change in Verona, 950–1150* (Ithaca, NY: Cornell University Press, 1993), 171.

recorded the attestations of those who saw Bishop Oberto ordain clerics as well as baptize and confirm children in Morengo, roughly thirty-seven miles northeast of the city.[15] In 1126, a baron of Aversa sent for his bishop as he lay dying, and Bishop Robert came directly and administered last rites to him.[16] Visitation records in the thirteenth century reveal bishops moving through their territories, being received in local churches, and inquiring into the state of both persons and property. We see Matteo, bishop of Città di Castello (1229-34), working his way through the baptismal churches (*plebes*) in his diocese between 1229 and 1231, usually visiting a few on each foray into the countryside and avoiding travel during the heat of the summer. On November 26, 1229, he visited Canoscio and the next day Falzano, eight miles to the southwest toward Cortona. In March and April of 1230 Matteo visited two more *plebes*, Appecchio and San Cipriano, and in the fall he was back on the road to Sant'Antimo, Cagnano, and Monte Santa Maria. Over the winter and spring of 1231 the bishop visited Morra and Ronti in January, Callione and Pratolungo (Prato) in February, Rubbiano and Comunaglia in March, and Saddi and Montone in April.[17] The effects of such direct contact with the bishop were certainly variable, but this more intimate character of episcopal care of souls seems a significant intangible to ponder in understanding the character of Christianity in medieval Italy.

The relatively small size of medieval Italian dioceses had other effects: it tended to flatten their internal administrative hierarchies. Northern European dioceses were usually divided up territorially into regional archdeaconries, each headed by an archdeacon who on behalf of the bishop visited the baptismal churches in his territory, supervising and disciplining its clergy, as well as collecting ecclesiastical dues. As we saw in the diocese of Città di Castello above, the Italian bishop directly handled such duties. There were officials called archdeacons within Italian cathedral chapters, who sometimes can be seen in documents

---

15. S. A. Anninskii, ed., *Akty Kremony X–XIII vedov v sobranii Akademii nauk SSSR* (Moscow: zd-vo Akademii Nauk SSSR, 1937), 125-28, 137-41; see also Miller, "The Political and Cultural Significance of the Bishop's Palace," 48, 52.

16. Loud, *The Latin Church*, 363-64.

17. Archivio Storico della Diocesi di Città di Castello, Registri della Cancelleria vescovile Archivio Vescovile, I, fols. 124v-131r. Matteo died in 1234 before he could visit all twenty-eight of the *plebes* listed in a bull of Honorius II to Bishop Ranieri dated February 6, 1126: Giovanni Muzi, *Memorie ecclesiastiche e civili di Città di Castello*, 6 vols. in 3 (Città di Castello: Presso Francesco Donati, 1842), 2:46-48 (the list of *plebes* on 47).

acting on behalf of the bishop, but they appear mainly as chapter dignitaries. They were not the intermediaries between the bishop and his rural churches that the archdeacons of northern Europe were: the medieval Italian diocese lacked an entire tier of ecclesiastical administration common north of the Alps.[18]

From the early Middle Ages, the rural territories of northern Italian dioceses were divided into discrete areas served by a baptismal church (*plebs*) headed by an archpriest. The circumscription, or *plebatus*, included other churches, oratories, and chapels, but all children born within it had to be baptized at the *plebs* and the clergy serving these other churches were under the authority of the baptismal church's archpriest, who "exercised the powers of a petty bishop throughout the baptismal area."[19] These *plebes* were the churches bishops visited; when Bishop Matteo of Città di Castello arrived at the baptismal church of Montone on April 22, 1231, the archpriest Ugolino had assembled all the chaplains of his *plebs* for inspection: the priests Bono and Gilio, who served in the *plebs* itself, plus twelve other priests and one cleric serving named churches and communities in its territory, all of whom swore obedience to the bishop.[20] The urban *plebs* was, of course, the bishop's cathedral where all children born within the city walls and immediate suburbs received baptism and the major feasts of the Christian year were celebrated. Over the eleventh and twelfth centuries this urban space was usually divided into discrete parishes staffed by priests who assisted the bishop in the care of souls, but the cathedral's dominance was maintained.[21]

This system of organizing the rural territories of a see into baptismal churches headed by archpriests was largely absent in southern Italian dioceses until the twelfth century, and even then was not ubiquitous.

---

18. Brentano, *Two Churches*, 66–68; Duane J. Osheim, *An Italian Lordship: The Bishopric of Lucca in the Late Middle Ages*, Publications of the Center for Medieval and Renaissance Studies (Berkeley: University of California Press, 1977), 31. On the development of the office in one important diocese, see Lorenzo Paolini, "L'evoluzione di una funzione ecclesiastica: L'arcidiacono e lo Studio a Bologna nel XIII secolo," *Studi medievali*, 3rd series, 29 (1988): 129–72.

19. Catherine E. Boyd, *Tithes and Parishes in Medieval Italy: The Historical Roots of a Modern Problem* (Ithaca, NY: Cornell University Press, 1952), 52–64, 159(quote)–160.

20. Archivio Storico della Diocesi di Città di Castello, Registri della Cancelleria vescovile Archivio Vescovile, I, fol. 129r.

21. Paolo Sambin, *L'ordinamento parrochiale di Padova nel medioevo* (Padua: CEDAM, 1941); Miller, *Formation of a Medieval Church*, 59–60; Augustine Thompson, *Cities of God: The Religion of the Italian Communes, 1125–1325* (University Park: Pennsylvania State University Press, 2005), 16–18.

The evidence for its emergence is strongest and earliest for Salerno: two twelfth-century papal bulls (1169 and 1182) list "archpresbyteries" subject to the bishop, indicating that the diocese was divided into districts centered on a baptismal church led by an archpriest. Similar evidence indicates systems of baptismal churches in the dioceses of Isernia and Chieti (and here the bulls use the term *plebes*) during the twelfth century and in Apulian dioceses in the thirteenth century. But for other southern dioceses both papal privileges and local charters give no indication of *plebes* or archpresbyteries.[22] In much of the south, therefore, there was not even the flattened administrative hierarchy of bishop–plebanal archpriest–local clerics, but simply direct supervision of local diocesan churches by the bishop.

Southern Italy's many small dioceses also yielded more archbishoprics than the north. In the late twelfth century, most of the 144 dioceses of the Norman-Hohenstaufen kingdom were grouped into twenty provinces led by an archbishop (with the exception of twenty exempt sees directly dependent on Rome). Some of these archbishops had only one or two suffragan dioceses: Brindisi and Siponto in Puglia, Cosenza in Calabria had one each, while Trani and Taranto in Puglia, and Messina and Monreale in Sicily had two each. On the other extreme, the archbishop of Benevento had twenty-four subject sees.[23] Northern Italy had only six archdioceses and a less skewed distribution of suffragans. The two competing maritime republic metropolitans, Pisa and Genoa, had the fewest suffragans—four for Pisa and eight for Genoa—and even the ancient and immensely powerful archbishops of Milan and Ravenna had fewer subject dioceses (nineteen and thirteen, respectively) than did Benevento.[24]

These provincial groupings in Italy seem not to have developed the kind of strong regional solidarities achieved in many northern European archbishoprics. Provincial councils in the archdiocese of Reims, for example, were annual events in the late eleventh and twelfth centuries, and these regular gatherings of bishops made ecclesiastical governance a collaborative exercise.[25] Metropolitan synods in Italy never quite achieved this regularity. There were synods in Benevento in 1061,

---

22. Loud, *The Latin Church*, 46–47, 412–16.
23. Loud, *The Latin Church*, 525–26.
24. Hay, *The Church in Italy*, 110–17.
25. John S. Ott, *Bishops, Authority and Community in Northwestern Europe, c. 1050–1150* (Cambridge: Cambridge University Press, 2015), 120–30.

1075, and 1119, for example, and in the archdiocese of Milan in 1266, 1287, and 1291. The archbishops of Ravenna in the early fourteenth century attained greater frequency—holding provincial synods in 1307, 1309, 1311, 1314, and 1317—as did the patriarchs of Aquileia, who convened synods in 1307, 1310, 1311, 1335, and 1339. Andrea Tilatti, on the basis of the Aquileian case, has argued that provincial synods coordinated episcopal actions in defense of ecclesiastical liberties and created relations and solidarities among the suffragans.[26] Could this have been the case more broadly in medieval Italy? Graham Loud's conclusions on the role of provincial gatherings in the south, grounded in a thorough evaluation of the surviving evidence for the central Middle Ages, would suggest not. But for the north, particularly in the later Middle Ages, further archival work may erode some of the pessimism in Denys Hay's assertion that the "the provinces of Italy were of little meaning in normal circumstances."[27]

As far as our documentation reveals, moreover, the huge number of sees on the peninsula tended to produce more friction than solidarity. More dioceses meant more borders of dioceses to dispute. From the 1120s through at least the early 1150s, for example, the bishops of Ferrara and Verona, each backed by the consuls of their respective urban communes, fought over Ostiglia and its baptismal church of San Lorenzo. This was not just a legal tussle. In 1123 Bishop Bernardo of Verona had a Ferrarese priest thrown out of the church, only later to have Bishop Grifo of Ferrara show up in Ostiglia and demand the hospitality of the clergy at San Lorenzo for his entourage (threatening to have the Veronese official who refused seized by the throat, dragged aboard the bishop's boat, and taken to Ferrara). A border conflict between the bishops of Orvieto and Savona over jurisdiction in Grotte lasted close to a century: it was brought four times before papal judges, and the records from the 1194 inquest include witnesses recounting an armed attack by Bishop Ildibrando of Orvieto's knights on people going to a *plebs* of the bishop of Savona a short distance from the castle at Grotte. Border disputes also abounded in the south with its many new or renewed dioceses in the eleventh and twelfth centuries. One

---

26. Loud, *The Latin Church*, 378–79; Andrea Tilatti, "Sinodi diocesane e concili provinciali in Italia nord-orientale fra Due e Trecento: Qualche riflessione," *Mélanges d'archéologie et d'histoire: Moyen Âge* 112, no. 1 (2000): 289 n. 68, and 292–304.

27. Loud, *The Latin Church*, 378–81; Hay, *The Church in Italy*, 12; Hay's pessimism was shared by Brentano, *Two Churches*, 88–97.

between the archbishop of Benevento and the bishop of Troia began in the 1080s and, mainly due to the delaying tactics of the Beneventan prelate, was not resolved until 1113. While it is not clear whether the bishop of Troia's allegation that Bishop Roffredo of Benevento had "violently seized" the disputed territory or simply the zone's greater proximity to Troia was more persuasive, Urban II ruled for Troia against the procrastinating archbishop. Disputes over metropolitan status and rights also frequently brought southern bishops into conflict.[28]

## Status and Resources

The best measure of the wealth of medieval Italian dioceses is the papal assessment of "common services" in the late Middle Ages. These papal taxes were assessed at roughly a third of the estimated gross annual income of the see. Although excluding the islands, appendix I in Denys Hay's *The Church in Italy in the Fifteenth Century* offers the most accessible overview of the relative wealth of Italian dioceses using these assessments. The gap between the wealthiest see, the patriarchate of Aquileia assessed at ten thousand florins, and the poorest, the Calabrian hill town of Rossano assessed at twenty-five florins, is staggering: the northern patriarchate's estimated annual income was four hundred times that of Rossano's. Only six of the twenty-two sees with assessments of one thousand florins or more are in the south, four of these in Campania (Naples, Capua, Salerno, Cava) and two in Puglia (Bari and Trani). Of the thirty-two sees with assessments of less than fifty florins, only four were in northern (Caorle, Jesolo) and central (Segni, Orte) Italy: 87.5 percent of the peninsula's poorest sees were in the south.

Some of the disparities in the resources bishops enjoyed in medieval Italy resulted from variations in the extent and fertility of agricultural lands, which were the enduring foundations of wealth across the Middle Ages. The largest zone of rich arable was in the Po valley with less extensive plains in Puglia, in Sicily, and around Naples. The poorest parts of Italy, still today, are the most mountainous, and most of these are in the south: the Molise, Basilicata, Abruzzo, and Calabria. The south

---

28. Andrea Castagnetti, *Società e politica a Ferrara dall'età postcarolingia alla signoria estense (Sec. X–XIII)* (Bologna: Pàtron Editore, 1985), 66–75; David Foote, *Lordship, Reform, and the Development of Civil Society in Medieval Italy: The Bishopric of Orvieto, 1100–1250* (Notre Dame, IN: University of Notre Dame Press, 2004), 50–57; Loud, *The Latin Church*, 195, 182–88. Witness testimony from a dispute in the 1170s between the sees of Cremona and Piacenza over the church of San Lorenzo de Ripalta may be found in Anninskii, *Akty Kremony X–XIII*, 137–41.

also has less water: of the peninsula's six major rivers, only one, the Volturno, is in the south. Commerce and both the direct and indirect revenues it generated tended to magnify the agricultural disparities. Although southern cities like Amalfi profited from trade with Byzantium and the Arab world before the northern Genoese and Venetian maritime republics became dominant in the central Middle Ages, there was little commerce inland. The Po valley was the heart of medieval Italy's commercial as well as agricultural wealth.

The needs and goals of rulers, however, further shaped these disparities. The Carolingian rulers who incorporated northern Italy into their empire collaborated with bishops to rule as Christian monarchs and provide for the salvation of their subjects, and their Ottonian heirs to imperial sovereignty in the Kingdom of Italy intensified these ties. To facilitate access across the Alps to their Italian kingdom and especially to the Holy See, rulers particularly wanted reliable allies in the dioceses along key Alpine passes and routes. These political aims had several effects on northern Italian sees. Particularly in the ecclesiastical provinces of Aquileia and Ravenna, the Ottonian and early Salian emperors appointed many German bishops: of the 109 bishops in these two provinces between 950 and 1080, 35 percent were Germans, most from Bavaria.[29] More significantly for the northern Italian episcopate in the central Middle Ages, however, these rulers also cultivated episcopal allies by donating lands and public rights to their sees. A number of bishops in the Po valley—such those at Reggio, Novara, Cremona, and Piacenza—even gained the powers of counts (chiefly *districtus*, judicial authority) within their cities and immediate suburbs, some even throughout the entire county (Vercelli, Parma). But even some northern Italian bishops who did not receive comital powers were accorded estates and rights that significantly enriched their sees: imperial diplomas ceded numerous estates along Lake Garda to the bishops of Verona in addition to minting rights, river tolls, and fees at the city's two busiest gates. All of these grants of lands and rights, nonetheless, were conditioned primarily by the political strategies of monarchs rather than by the needs of Christian communities or the merits of their bishops.[30]

---

29. Romuald Bauerreiss, "Vescovi bavaresi nell'Italia settentrionale tra la fine del X secolo e l'inizio dell'XI," in *Vescovi e diocesi in Italia nel medioevo (sec. IX–XIII): Atti del II Convegno di Storia della Chiesa in Italia (Roma, 5–9 sett. 1961)* (Padua: Editrice Antenore, 1964), 158; Miller, *Formation of a Medieval Church*, 144–46.

30. Cesare Manaresi, "Alle origini del potere dei vescovi sul territorio esterno delle città," *Bullettino dell'Istituto storico italiano per il Medio Evo e Archivio Muratoriano* 58 (1944): esp. 228–59,

## 3. BISHOPS 57

The Norman conquest of the south also constructed a new set of relations between sees and temporal authority as it altered ecclesiastical organization. Dioceses, as in the north, usually had some landed wealth from donations made across the early Middle Ages. To these assets the Norman conquerors, in contrast to their imperial counterparts in the north, tended not to add more real property in the form of estates. Their gifts were of fiscal rights, most commonly portions of the taxes collected on the sale or transport of goods or on specific commercial activities, such as dyers and butchers (these sectors often dominated by Jews), but sometimes also judicial fees. Over time these royal subsidies of ecclesiastical institutions, including monasteries, came to be known collectively as *decimae* (but note that these royal "tithes" were distinct from those that individual Christians owed their church). They were not, as far as our sources indicate, uniformly distributed: only about two-thirds of southern dioceses received these royal subsidies, and the amounts varied. The entire annual incomes of the archdioceses of Palermo and Trani, for example, came from the crown in the late thirteenth and early fourteenth centuries, whereas royal subsidies provided less than 10 percent of the episcopal incomes of sees like Melfi, Bari, Monopoli, and Amalfi.[31]

While we only have some basis for comparing diocesan resources from the late Middle Ages, various kinds of evidence suggest that Italian dioceses were wealthier in the preceding centuries. In the south, state subsidies underwent considerable change from the 1230s after Frederick II returned from the Holy Land, reconquered the areas that papal troops had seized during his absence, and faced new military challenges from the revived Lombard League. Among the financial reforms he instituted in many sees was a substitution of fixed sums for the earlier percentages of revenues from royal taxes and fees. Although we do not have figures for the incomes generated under the original percentage-based grants, two things suggest that the new fixed-figure

---

263-72, 282-313; Andrea Gamberini, "Vescovo e conte: La fortuna di un titolo nell'Italia centrosettentrionale (secoli XI-XV)," *Quaderni storici* 46, no. 138 (2011): 671-95; Vito Fumagalli, "Il potere civile dei vescovi italiani al tempo di Ottone I," in *I poteri temporali dei Vescovi in Italia e in Germania nel Medioevo: Atti della Settimana di studio, 13–18 settembre 1976*, ed. Carlo Guido Mor and Heinrich Schmidinger (Bologna: Il Mulino, 1979), 77-86; Miller, *Formation of a Medieval Church*, 149-50.

31. Kristjan Toomaspoeg, ed., *Decimae: Il sostegno economico dei sovrani alla Chiesa del Mezzogiorno nel XIII secolo dai lasciti di Eduard Sthamer e Norbert Kamp* (Rome: Viella/Istituto Storico Germanico di Roma, 2009), 45-52, 59-66, 75-79, 69, and tavola n. 3, 536-39.

system limited and reduced episcopal incomes even as they made those incomes more predictable. First, the change was often accompanied by other changes in the royal taxes that were drawn upon to provide ecclesiastical support with the most lucrative sources being returned fully to the royal fisc. Second, Frederick's reforms were implemented in a period of military challenges and soaring political aspirations that were likely generating huge outlays of royal resources.[32]

Different, but still political, pressures reduced episcopal resources in northern Italy. The communal governments that emerged in the late eleventh and twelfth centuries, especially in cities where bishops had exercised public authority and been ceded comital or other royal rights, seized control of these prerogatives outright or progressively diminished episcopal patrimonies. Florence provides a particularly well-documented case. In the early thirteenth century, as rural communes emerged on episcopal lands and challenged the bishop's lordship, the urban commune interceded to adjudicate these disputes and in the process extended its own dominion in these areas of the *contado*. Military threats from neighboring cities in the early fourteenth century provided a pretext for the commune to declare protectorates over zones once ruled directly by Florentine bishops, further diminishing the see's control over vast parts of its patrimony and access to the revenues they produced. Finally, during the War of the Eight Saints (1375-78) between Pope Gregory XI and an alliance of several city-states led by Florence, the city's communal government seized and sold off ecclesiastical property to support its war effort. The bishop's patrimony was decimated, and decades of efforts to get properties restored yielded little but shares in the communal debt.[33] Florence may be an extreme example, but other studies have also documented a pattern of diminishing episcopal rights and resources, especially within urban centers. The see of Arezzo, for example, having lost lands to both its vassals and cultivators had to sell its public rights to the commune and tax its clergy to pay its debts, and Bishop Tiso of Treviso in 1218 finally ceded the see's control over mercantile taxes and tolls in both city and countryside to that city's commune after years of litigation. Over the twelfth and

---

32. Toomaspoeg, *Decimae*, 46-47.
33. George W. Dameron, *Florence and Its Church in the Age of Dante* (Philadelphia: University of Pennsylvania Press, 2005), 235-39; David S. Peterson, "The War of the Eight Saints in Florentine Memory and Oblivion," in *Society and Individual in Renaissance Florence*, ed. William J. Connell (Berkeley: University of California Press, 2002), 173-214.

thirteenth centuries the sees of Milan, Como, and Asti lost jurisdictional and administrative rights and revenues within their cities.[34]

Did the varied resources of sees and the different polities on the peninsula influence the kinds of men who became bishops? The only broad and systematic prosopographical study of the medieval Italian episcopate accomplished to date treats the south in the Norman-Hohenstaufen era. Norbert Kamp's observations are epistemologically sobering: we can draw conclusions or make plausible hypotheses about the social origins and educational backgrounds of less than 15 percent of the episcopate. For some of the poorer dioceses, particularly in Calabria, we know virtually nothing. Still, his results and Graham Loud's judicious assessment of them reveal some interesting patterns and provide a set of observations that can at least be compared to the work on sees that has been accomplished for northern Italy.[35]

Before exploring the character of the episcopate north and south, however, the question of the influence of different polities on who became a bishop ought to be addressed. In the south, the heyday of the influence of local powers and of the papacy was the eleventh and early twelfth centuries, before the consolidation of the Norman kingdom.

---

34. Giovanni Cherubini, "Aspetti della proprietà fondiaria nell'aretino durante il XIII secolo," *Archivio Storico Italiano* 121 (1963): 9; Augusto Lizier, *Storia del comune di Treviso* (Treviso: Tipografia editrice trevigiana, 1979), 61–65; Cinzio Violante, "Eresie nelle città e nel contado in Italia dall'undicesimo al dodicesimo secolo," in *Studi sulla cristianità medievale*, ed. Piero Zerbi (Milan: Vita e Pensiero, 1972), 349–79; for losses suffered by the sees of Como and Asti, see Maureen C. Miller, *The Bishop's Palace: Architecture and Authority in Medieval Italy* (Ithaca, NY: Cornell University Press, 2000), 98–99; in 1253 Volrico de Portis, bishop of Trieste, had to cede to the commune all his temporal powers in the city to pay off debts incurred supporting Frederick II, Giuseppe Cuscito, "Chiese e organizzazione religiosa a Trieste," in *Medioevo a Trieste: Istituzioni, arte, società nel Trecento*, ed. Paolo Cammarosano (Rome: Viella, 2009), 103.

35. Norbert Kamp, *Kirche und Monarchie im staufischen Königreich Sizilien*, vol. 1, *Prosopographische Grundlegung: Bistümer und Bischöfe des Königreichs 1194–1266*, 4 vols. (Munich: Fink, 1973–82); the most accessible summary of his results is "The Bishops of Southern Italy in the Norman and Staufen Periods," in *The Society of Norman Italy*, ed. G. A. Loud and A. Metcalfe, The Medieval Mediterranean 38 (Leiden: Brill, 2002), 185–209; for Loud's assessment, see *The Latin Church*, 364–72. In 1964, Cinzio Violante declared "l'origine sociale dei vescovi tema ancora quasi del tutto inesplorato per i secoli XI e XII," and a decade later Gabriella Rossetti offered only a few opening observations, mainly that social origins were chiefly a question of concern only to us today and that to men of the time it was not considered an issue: "l'acesso all'episcopato, con qualche variante regionale tuttavia assimilabile, è retaggio dei maggiori ceti feudali." Cinzio Violante, "I vescovi dell'Italia centro-settentrionale e lo sviluppo dell'economia monetaria," originally published in *Vescovi e diocesi in Italia nel medioevo (sec. IX–XIII)*, 193–217, republished in Zerbi, *Studi sulla cristianità medievale*, 345; Gabriella Rossetti, "Origine sociale e formazione dei vescovi del 'Regnum Italiae' nei secoli XI e XII," in *Le istituzioni ecclesiastiche della "Societas christiana" dei secoli XI–XII: Diocesi, pievi e parrocchie. Atti della sesta Settimana internazionale di studio Milano, 1–7 settembre 1974* (Milan: Vita e Pensiero, 1977), 57.

In this period, for example, the Lombard and Neapolitan duchies as well as the principalities of Capua, Benevento, and Salerno held sway over appointments with bishops drawn often from the princely families themselves. In Abruzzo the influence of the counts of Marsi predominated. After Urban II's synod at Melfi in 1089, the papacy intervened to appoint several cardinals to southern sees. In 1090, for example, Urban II consecrated the cardinal priest of Santa Susanna Rangerio, a Burgundian monk of Marmoutier, to the archbishopric of Reggio Calabria, and in 1100 Paschal II appointed Alberto, cardinal priest of Santa Sabina and a monk of San Savino in Piacenza, to be archbishop of Siponto. From the consolidation of the Norman kingdom under Roger II, however, and for the rest of the *Regno*'s medieval history, the monarchy exerted considerable influence through its power of confirming (or overriding) local nominations. Royal interest, however, was uneven, concentrated on the metropolitan sees of the mainland and the Sicilian bishoprics.[36]

In the north the chronological pattern of political influence was exactly the opposite: in the eleventh and early twelfth centuries Ottonian and Salian monarchs dominated episcopal appointments, and then in the following centuries local powers and the papacy shaped the episcopate. Royal interests here too came to bear most directly on powerful and strategically situated sees—Pavia, Como, Ravenna—but ties with regional powers also influenced how directly monarchical rights of appointment were exercised. The influence of the *Reichskirche* was most pervasive under Conrad II (1024–39) and Henry III (1039–56).[37] After the investiture contest, however, the local elections sought by reformers succeeded in selecting bishops in northern Italian cities for much of the twelfth century and into the thirteenth. But contested elections frequently sparked appeals to Rome, and these opened the way for papal influence. By the mid-thirteenth century, such discord and other factors produced Clement IV's encyclical *Licet ecclesiarum* (1265) articulating a papal right to dispose of all ecclesiastical benefices. A Paduan case explicated by Antonio Rigon details how local election gave way to papal provision over the thirteenth century. Contestation after the

---

36. Kamp, "The Bishops of Southern Italy," 189, 195–96; Loud, *The Latin Church*, 271.
37. Nicolangelo D'Acunto, "Le elezioni vescovili nel *Regnum Italiae* tra contesti locali e sistemi a vocazione universalistica (secoli X–XI)," in *Chiese locali e chiese regionali nell'alto medioevo*, Settimane di studio della Fondazione Centro italiano di studi sull'alto medioevo 61 (Spoleto: Fondazione Centro italiano di studi sull'alto medioevo, 2014), 668, 672–75.

death of Bishop Giordano in 1228 over who had the right to participate in the election of his successor first led to a negotiated settlement at the papal court and the election of Giacomo Corrado, archpriest of the cathedral chapter. The death of this bishop in 1239, however, and the complex politics both of Ezzelino da Romano's domination of the city and of the papacy's conflict with Frederick II resulted in the direct papal provision of Giovanni Forzatè as the see's new leader. At this prelate's demise in 1283 the right to appoint passed definitively to the Holy See.[38] While in many cases papal appointments advanced the needs and temporal ambitions of the Holy See in central Italy, in some instances the papacy's involvement upheld local ecclesiastical interests and autonomy against local elites with signorial aspirations. At Ravenna, for example, clerical electors gathered in the cathedral to choose a successor to Archbishop Simeone (1217-28) found themselves surrounded by armed supporters of the counts of Bagnocavallo and of Paolo Traversari (who eventually became *signore* of the city in 1240). The armed men tried to provoke fights in order to defer the proceedings until the *podestà* intervened with his forces to ensure the safety of the electors, expelling the armed intruders and securing the doors of the cathedral. At first suspicious of the outcome of the election under these circumstances, Pope Gregory IX intervened; but after calling witnesses to Rome he confirmed the electors' choice of Tederico, provost of the cantors of the cathedral chapter of Ravenna.[39]

These different political forces influenced the character of the men who became bishops in medieval Italy, but each see's resources did too. In the south, the meager resources of most sees resulted in the bishops

---

38. Antonio Rigon, "Le elezioni vescovili nel processo di sviluppo delle istituzioni ecclesiastiche a Padova," *Mélanges de l'École française de Rome: Moyen-Age, Temps modernes* 89, no. 1 (1977): 393-409. On the transition from election to provision in Rieti, see Robert Brentano, *A New World in a Small Place: Church and Religion in the Diocese of Rieti, 1188-1378* (Berkeley: University of California Press, 1994), 146-51; on the system of provisions generally, Kenneth Pennington, *Popes and Bishops: The Papal Monarchy in the Twelfth and Thirteenth Centuries* (Philadelphia: University of Pennsylvania Press, 1984), 115-53, and Thomas W. Smith, "The Development of Papal Provisions in Medieval Europe," *History Compass* 13, no. 3 (2015): 110-21.

39. Augusto Vasina, "L'elezione degli arcivescovi ravennati del sec. XIII nei rapporti con la Santa Sede," *Rivista di storia della Chiesa in Italia* 10 (1956): 65-66; other case studies are G. Pochettino, "L'elezione dei Vescovi di Parma nell'età feudale," *Archivio storico per le province parmensi*, n.s., 22bis (1922): 419-40; Martino Giusti, "Le elezioni dei vescovi di Lucca specialmente nel secolo XIII," *Rivista di storia della Chiesa in Italia* 6 (1952): 205-30; Giulio Silano, "The Apostolic See and the Elections of the Bishops of Perugia in the Duecento and Trecento," *Mediaeval Studies* 50 (1988): 488-511; Blake Beattie, "Local Reality and Papal Policy: Papal Provision and the Church of Arezzo, 1248-1327," *Mediaeval Studies* 57 (1995): 131-53.

being overwhelmingly from the local families dominating the cathedral chapter: they were sons from the knightly families of the *contado* or from the urban patriciate of judges and notaries, not those of the highest aristocracy. The poorer dioceses probably offered the greatest prospects for achieving social mobility through an episcopal career, but a socially elevated background was generally the rule. Papal influence in the late eleventh and early twelfth centuries brought Benedictine monks—from Montecassino, Cava de' Tirreni, and the Norman abbey of Sant'Eufemia in Calabria—to several sees and at least some of them from afar: Gerard, appointed archbishop of Siponto in 1064 by Alexander II, was a German monk of Montecassino, while the see of Troia had a whole succession of foreign prelates (Bishop Walter described as *francigenus*, his successor Gerard from Piacenza, then Hubert from Maine and William from Bigorre). But monastic appointees could also be locals. Both Peter of Naples (1094–1100) and Alfanus I of Salerno came to their sees via Montecassino but had deep roots in Campania. After the reform era, however, monk-bishops were mainly evident only in Calabria and in the sees of Sicily with monastic chapters; the kings of the *Regno* favored secular clerics. Kamp estimated that the proportion of prelates from local cathedral chapters increased from the late twelfth century and that "the secular and ecclesiastical ruling classes of the kingdom became intertwined," with royal administrators recruited from local lineages and individuals passing from royal service to key sees.[40]

For the sees of northern Italy, as Gabriella Rossetti in her 1974 *lezione* at the Spoleto Settimana di Studio has remarked, the only expressions used in the sources of the eleventh and twelfth centuries to describe the social origins of bishops were "nobili genere natus" and "nobili progenie ortus."[41] Indeed, when it is possible to know more of their backgrounds, bishops appear to come from noble families, some from the most elite. Most of the eleventh-century bishops of Parma, for example, had been imperial chancellors before their promotions to the see, with the exception of Cadalo (1045–71; antipope Honorius II, 1061–64) who was from a wealthy Veronese castellan family with imperial ties. In her study of the bishops throughout the Piedmont in the tenth and eleventh centuries, Caterina Ciccopiedi found too that

---

40. Kamp, "The Bishops of Southern Italy," 191–209, quote on 202; Loud, *The Latin Church*, 364–69.

41. Rossetti, "Origine sociale e formazione dei vescovi," 57.

whether they had been trained in the imperial chapel and chancery or had risen in their local church, "membership in an aristocratic family with vast landed holdings is attested for just about all." Some could be from the greatest families: Tedaldo, bishop of Arezzo (1023-1036), was the son of Tedaldo, marquis of Canossa (d. 1012), and the brother of the ruling marquis, Boniface (father of the famous countess, Matilda of Canossa). Florence provides evidence that elite status remained the norm for holders of the see even as the sources of aristocratic wealth changed. The eleventh-century bishop Pietro Mezzabarba came from a noble Pavian family supposedly wealthy enough to buy the office at the imperial court. Two centuries later the see's prelates were still scions of ruling lineages, some from those proscribed as magnates: Andrea de' Mozzi (1286-95) was from a wealthy banking family that had achieved knightly status, Lottieri Tosinghi (1302-09) from a magnate lineage holding extensive rural and urban properties, and Antonio degli Orsi (1309-21) from a family of the mercantile elite. The same holds for Rieti where many of its thirteenth- and fourteenth-century bishops were from "baronial and patrician families."[42] The increasing numbers of bishops from the mendicant orders in the thirteenth and fourteenth centuries likely made little dent in the overall aristocratic character of the episcopate in northern Italy: many if not most of the members of these orders were from families of means by the second half of the thirteenth century.[43]

Some bishops, both north and south, achieved the status of saints, and this dignity, at least, was not determined by the material resources of their sees. Their *vitae* trace the evolution of different models of episcopal sanctity. Peter Damian's life of Saint Radulfo, bishop of Gubbio (d. ca. 1066), praised his ascetic life as a Benedictine monk before becoming

---

42. Pochettino, "L'elezione dei Vescovi di Parma," 428-36; Miller, *Formation of a Medieval Church*, 74; Caterina Ciccopiedi, *Diocesi e riforme nel Medioevo: Orientamenti ecclesiastici e religiosi dei vescovi nel Piemonte dei secoli X e XI*, Studia taurinensia 39 (Turin: Effatà, 2012), 15-16, quote at 16: "Per quasi tutti è attestata l'appartenza a una famiglia aristocratica con vasti possedimenti fondiari"; Jean Pierre Delumeau, *Arezzo: Espace et sociétés, 715-1230. Recherches sur Arezzo et son contado du VIIIe au début du XIIIe siècle*, 2 vols., Collection de l'École française de Rome 219 (Rome: École française de Rome, 1996), 1:498-504, 508-14; George W. Dameron, *Episcopal Power and Florentine Society, 1000-1320* (Cambridge, MA: Harvard University Press, 1991), 51, 152; Brentano, *A New World in a Small Place*, 181.

43. The only detailed study of the social origins of the medieval mendicants is John B. Freed's excellent *The Friars and German Society in the Thirteenth Century* (Cambridge, MA: Medieval Academy of America, 1977), especially 109-34, and he concludes that few mendicants were from social orders lower than the urban patriciate, and mendicants from nonelite backgrounds who became bishops were very rare indeed.

bishop more than his pastoral ministrations in his see, and such virtues also dominated the anonymous *vita* of the great reforming bishop of Lucca, Saint Anselm II (d. 1086). For the holy pastors Bernardo degli Uberti, bishop of Parma (1108-33), and Giovanni Cacciafronte, bishop of Vicenza (1179-84), monastic rigors were depicted as the prelude to their episcopal careers, but their virtues were strongly pastoral. Like Saint Ubaldo, bishop of Gubbio (1129-60), Saint Galdino della Sala, archbishop of Milan (1166-76), and Saint Lanfranco, bishop of Pavia (1180-98), they corrected both clergy and people, protected their cities, preached and taught, cared for the poor, and valiantly defended their churches.[44] Similar saintly reforming bishops are found in the south: Peter, bishop of Anagni (1062-1105); Bruno, bishop of Segni (1079-1123); and Berardo, bishop of Marsi (ca. 1110-30). Unique to the south in this period, when the Norman conquest was remaking the ecclesiastical landscape, were bishops venerated chiefly as founders of their sees: Saints Amato of Nusco (d. 1093?), Giovanni of Montemarano (d. 1095), Gerardo of Potenza (d. 1119), and Alberto of Montecorvino (d. 1137). They were portrayed as exemplifying more monastic values—asceticism, eremitic interludes, manual labor—along with pastoral care, much of it miraculous assistance to the poor and afflicted in fortified hill towns.[45] The emergence of the papal canonization process in the thirteenth century notably reduced the number of new episcopal cults: between 1198 and 1431, only the martyred bishop of Vicenza, Giovanni Cacciafronte (d. 1184, beatified 1824), and Ranieri, bishop of Forcona (d. 1077, beatified?), merited processes, and neither resulted in canonization.[46]

Many aspects of the stark income inequalities among medieval Italian sees merit further systematic and comparative research. Did radically unequal episcopal incomes influence the material culture of the local church? We know, for example, a good deal about the funding mechanisms that enabled northern Italian cities to build new cathedrals

---

44. Miller, *The Bishop's Palace*, 125, 136, 157-63, 239-41; Paolo Golinelli, "Indiscreta Sanctitas," in *Indiscreta Sanctitas: Studi sui rapporti tra culti, poteri e società nel pieno medioevo* (Rome: Istituto Storico Italiano per il Medio Evo, 1988), 168-69; Anna Benvenuti Papi, *Pastori di popolo: Storie e leggende di vescovi e di città nell'Italia medievale* (Florence: Arnaud, 1988), 179-203.

45. Pierre Toubert, *Les structures du Latium médiéval: Le Latium méridional et la Sabine du IX$^e$ siècle à la fin du XII$^e$ siècle*, 2 vols. (Rome: École française de Rome, 1973), 807-29; Paul Oldfield, *Sanctity and Pilgrimage in Medieval Southern Italy, 1000-1200* (Cambridge: Cambridge University Press, 2014), 77-81; Amalia Galdi, *Santi, territori, poteri e uomini nella Campania medievale (secc. XI-XII)*, Schola Sallernitana Studi e Testi 9 (Salerno: Pietro Laveglia, 2004), 95-182.

46. André Vauchez, *Sainthood in the Later Middle Ages*, trans. Jean Birrell (Cambridge: Cambridge University Press, 1997), 249-60, 285-310.

over the central Middle Ages, most initially involving collaborations between bishops and their flocks with lay *opere* becoming major partners, and in some cities the dominant forces, from the late thirteenth century. One might, for example, hypothesize that cathedrals would be smaller or less ornate in the poorer sees of the south. But then the Romanesque cathedral of Taranto (with a common papal services assessment of 400 florins) has a nave as long as that of Verona (with an assessment of 900), and even the small see of Vieste in Puglia (with the meager assessment of 66 2/3) still built a cathedral in the eleventh century with an aisled nave of six bays and carved capitals.[47] Of course the sacraments were equally valid regardless of the size and decoration of the church, but did the inequalities in episcopal resources across the peninsula affect the quality of pastoral care? Since the wealth of some sees attracted the ambitious, and in the later Middle Ages the papacy itself used the incomes of leading northern sees to support largely non-resident legates, one might explore whether medieval Italian Christians received more consistent pastoral care in the smaller dioceses of the south where clerics from leading local families were advanced to the episcopate. And what of poor relief and hospitals? From Late Antiquity, bishops were expected to be *amatores pauperum*, "lovers of the poor," and a good bit of scholarly attention has been devoted to the institutions that developed in northern Italian cities to care for the poor and sick.[48] But beyond the Roman hospital of Santo Spirito in Sassia and the activities of the Knights Hospitaller of Saint John, poor relief in southern Italy and the episcopal role in it remains a history yet to be written.

---

47. Andrea Giorgi and Stefano Moscadelli, "*Quod omnes cerei ad Opus deveniant*: Il finanziamento dell'Opera del duomo di Siena nei secoli XIII e XIV," and Gigliola Soldi Rondinini, "*In Fabrica artis*: Il Duomo di Milano. Partecipazione di popolo (e favore di principi?)," both in *Nuova Rivista Storica* 85 (2001): 489-584 and 585-98, respectively; *Enciclopedia dell'arte medievale*, s.v. Puglia, giving greatest agency to bishops in the reconstruction of cathedrals, and s.v. Salerno, citing both Bishop Alfano and Duke Robert Guiscard as the "principali animatori" of the rebuilding of the cathedral of Salerno; Pina Belli D'Elia, ed., *Alle sorgenti del Romanico: Puglia XI secolo* (Bari: Pinoteca Provinciale, 1975), 27-30, 143-51, 268, 274 (Vieste and Taranto); Pierpaolo Brugnoli, ed., *La Cattedrale di Verona nelle sue vicende edilizie dal secolo IV al secolo XVI* (Verona: Editoriale Bortolazzi-Stei, 1987), 47.

48. Vasina, "L'elezione degli arcivescovi ravennati," 65-84; Hay, *The Church in Italy*, 16-20; on hospitals, see the useful overview of sources and studies by Marina Grazzini, "Ospedali nell'Italia medievale," *Reti Medievali Rivista* 13, no. 1 (2012): 211-37, https://doi.org/10.6092/1593-2214/338, and Giuliana Albini, *Città e ospedali nella Lombardia medievale* (Bologna: Clueb, 1993).

## Proximity to the Holy See

Any and every diocese in Italy is closer to Rome and its bishop than other sees. Before 1309, when the papal court relocated to Avignon, this geographical proximity came with few advantages and many disadvantages. Proximity did mean that Italian bishops dominated the reforming papal synods of the late eleventh and early twelfth centuries—Gregory VII's held in Rome, the majority of Urban II's and Paschal II's in Italy—and they were likely still the largest contingent of participants in the four Lateran councils.[49] But power in the Church at large was increasingly in the hands of popes and cardinals, most of whom were Italians in our period, but not Italian bishops. Of the fifty-five popes from 1000 to 1350, for example, thirty-four were Italians, but only two had held an Italian see before becoming bishop of Rome: Anselmo da Baggio, bishop of Lucca, as Alexander II (1061-73), and Umberto Crivelli, archbishop of Milan, as Urban III (1185-87). At least 80 percent of the cardinals of the twelfth and thirteenth centuries whose backgrounds can be known were Italian, and some of these of course held the seven suburbicarian sees around Rome, but the usual paths to these dignities were through curial service, religious orders, and (increasingly from the twelfth century) the universities, not through diocesan leadership.

The chief disadvantage of proximity to Rome was papal territorial ambitions; they affected sees both north and south. As I have argued elsewhere in greater detail, the emergence of a powerful, monarchical papacy in the eleventh and twelfth centuries in the context of movements for reform was an important development in Western political history, and its significance within the peninsula was even greater.[50]

---

49. All of Gregory VII's synods were in Rome, while Urban II's were three times in Rome and then in Melfi (1089), Benevento (1091), Troia (1093), Piacenza (1095), Clermont (1095), Tours (1096), Nimes (1096), and Bari (1097); Paschal II's were at the Lateran five times (1102, 1105, 1110, 1112, 1116), Benevento three times (1108, 1113, 1117), Melfi (1100), Guastalla (1106), Florence (1106), Troyes (1107): I. S. Robinson, *The Papacy, 1073–1198: Continuity and Innovation* (Cambridge: Cambridge University Press, 1990), 121-45; Raymonde Foreville, "Procédure et débats dans les conciles médiévaux du Latran (1123-1215)," *Rivista di storia della Chiesa in Italia* 19 (1965): 24; J. Werner, "Die Teilnehmer des Laterankonzils, v. J. 1215," *Neues Archiv Gesellschaft für ältere deutsche Geschichtskunde* 31 (1906): 584-92, revealing 190 Italian bishops in attendance at Lateran IV in comparison to 77 from sees in France (including Provence and Burgundy), 23 from German sees, 23 from those in the Iberian peninsula, 11 from sees in England.

50. Maureen C. Miller, "Italy in the Long Twelfth Century: Ecclesiastical Reform and the Legitimization of a New Political Order, 1059-1183," in *European Transformations: The Long Twelfth Century*, ed. Thomas F. X. Noble and John Van Engen (Notre Dame, IN: University of Notre Dame Press, 2012), 117-31.

## 3. BISHOPS 67

Papal claims in Italy to temporal as well as spiritual authority shaped interactions between medieval Italian bishops and the Holy See.

Within the Patrimony of Saint Peter and in the south, bishops frequently had to host the pontiff and papal Curia. While such visits could be a boon to the local economy, they tended to displace the city's bishop and subordinate his leadership to that of the heir of Saint Peter. During Pope Urban IV's stay in Orvieto from October 1262 to September 1264, for example, Bishop Giacomo ceded his palace to the pontiff and moved his own household to lodgings at a much less central location. The major liturgies usually performed by the bishop were instead celebrated by the pope and his magnificently arrayed entourage. Pope Urban II (1088-99) spent fully a third of his pontificate in southern Italy (chiefly because the antipope Clement III held Rome), and although not all stops on his itineraries can be securely identified, he likely enjoyed a great deal of episcopal hospitality during his sojourns. He held councils in Melfi (September 1089), Benevento (March 1091), Troia (March 1093), and Bari (October 1098). Paschal II visited Benevento eight times.[51] Papal claims to suzerainty over the Norman-Hohenstaufen kingdom also resulted in bouts of violent conflict and direct military intervention in the south, especially during the reign of Frederick II and its immediate aftermath. While the emperor was in the east on crusade, papal forces engaged an imperial army in the Marches and the Duchy of Spoleto and invaded the kingdom in 1228. Hostilities were renewed from 1239 and continued after Frederick's death in 1250 with his heirs Conrad, Manfred, and Conradin. Needless to say, during such periods of conflict bishops faced difficult political choices that had consequences: Pope Gregory IX in 1240, for example, removed the episcopal dignity from Osimo because it supported Frederick II.[52]

---

51. Maureen C. Miller, "The Bishops of Orvieto and Their Culture," in *Il "Corpus Domini": Teologia, antropologia e politica*, ed. Laura Andreani and Agostino Paravicini Bagliani (Florence: SISMEL-Edizioni del Galluzzo, 2015), 281; Loud, *The Latin Church*, 143; Urban was in Troina, Sicily in 1088 and again in 1089, and after leaving Rome early in 1090, for example, he headed south stopping at Capua, Salerno, Benevento, and then through Apulia to Taranto and on to Sicily. Alfons Becker, *Papst Urban II. (1088–1099)*, 3 vols., Schriften der Monumenta Germaniae Historica 19 (Stuttgart: Anton Hiersemann, 1964), 1:128-29; 2:66-70.

52. G. A. Loud, "The Papal 'Crusade' against Frederick II in 1228-1230," in *La Papauté et les croisades: Actes du VIIe Congrès de la Society for the Study of the Crusades and the Latin East / The Papacy and the Crusades: Proceedings of the VIIth Conference of the Society for the Study of the Crusades and the Latin East*, ed. Michel Balard (Farnham: Ashgate, 2011), 91-103; Peter Partner, *The Lands of St. Peter: The Papal State in the Middle Ages and the Early Renaissance* (Berkeley: University of California Press, 1972), 246-68; Brentano, *Two Churches*, 84-85.

Similar quandaries faced bishops in the north. As the papacy intervened both within cities and in struggles among them, some bishops always had tricky political choices to make. In the eleventh and twelfth centuries popes and their allies, such as Matilda of Canossa, aided the emergence of some communes in order to place reforming bishops in sees, and if you were one of those bishops, as was Landulfo, bishop of Ferrara, the support of the pope was surely welcome. But for bishops, such as those of Pavia and Como, who remained faithful to Emperor Frederick Barbarossa, the active support of Popes Adrian IV and Alexander III for the Lombard League was rather more challenging.[53] In the thirteenth and early fourteenth centuries the politics of papal interventions became even more complex: bishops might be aided by papal coercion of communal governments trampling on episcopal rights and property but then undercut by legates on peacemaking or other missions, who could overrule them. The shifting fortunes within cities of contestation between propapal (Guelph) and proimperial (Ghibelline) parties for dominance of the commune, and papal responses to these shifts, undermined the bishop's autonomy and capacity to be pastor to all citizens. As Augusto Vasina remarked on the state of the Bolognese see on the eve of the city's incorporation into the papal state, "bishop and church seemed to be in a state of suffering and uncertainty, hemmed in between repeated papal initiatives and the exuberant but still disordered religious life of the new orders and of the more recent spontaneous forms, individual and associative, of lay spirituality." Even bishops not in the path of territorial expansion found the increasing presence and power of the papacy reducing their own jurisdiction and autonomy.[54]

While the proximity of the papal court likely facilitated the process of obtaining privileges and accessing papal justice, this worked both for and against bishops. On the one hand, Italian bishops did obtain numerous bulls confirming the privileges of their sees and frequently brought cases to the Curia defending their rights and patrimonies. On the other hand, ecclesiastical institutions within their dioceses also had ready access to the Curia, often petitioning for and gaining exemptions

---

53. Miller, "Italy in the Long Twelfth Century," 123–26; Giuliano Milani, *I comuni italiani: Secoli XII–XIV* (Bari: Editori Laterza, 2005), 94–103.

54. Partner, *The Lands of St. Peter*, 255–60, 268–77; Augusto Vasina, "Chiesa e comunità dei fedeli nella diocesi di Bologna dal XII al XV secolo," in *Storia della Chiesa di Bologna*, ed. Paolo Prodi and Lorenzo Paolini, 2 vols. (Bologna: Istituto per la storia della chiesa di Bologna, 1997), 1:137; Dameron, *Florence and Its Church*, 74–77.

from episcopal jurisdiction: not only major orders such as the Cistercians and mendicants but even modest women's religious communities were able to achieve and defend independence from their bishop's authority. On the whole, the detrimental effects of exemptions and papal dispensations on diocesan authority outweighed episcopal gains. Evaluating the effect of Rome's role as *mater ecclesiae* on Italian dioceses, Robert Brentano lamented the "crushing quality of this Roman motherhood" in the thirteenth century "through the relatively easy access to appeal of the papal curia."[55]

Was the embrace of this papal monarch really worse, however, than that of the peninsula's secular royal or urban rulers? A fundamental issued raised by this overview of the Italian episcopate during the central Middle Ages is the degree to which pastoral care and the spiritual well-being of the peninsula's Christians actually depended upon bishops. The Church's hierarchy broadcast that it did, even as it was taxing sees and undercutting episcopal authority, but believers then and now appear both resourceful and enterprising in finding the spiritual sustenance they need. Certainly bishops mattered—to reformers, popes, and rulers—in policing orthodoxy and enforcing increasingly uniform practice and belief. And undoubtedly many bishops were dedicated and caring pastors amidst the constraints of time and resources as well as the challenges of disasters of both human and environmental origins. One might be tempted to hypothesize that bishops mattered more before the rise of the mendicant orders, lay confraternities, and what André Vauchez called the "emergence of the laity within the church (11th to 13th centuries)," but the laity had been there all along, and the kind of critique John Howe accomplished in his important article on "The Nobility's Reform of the Medieval Church" might profitably be applied more broadly, socially and chronologically.[56] The large number of bishops in Italy meant that they were prominent figures in the ecclesiastical landscape shaping what the local church was, but they had partners, not just flocks. Those, however, are the subjects of other chapters.

---

55. On exemption generally, see Robinson, *The Papacy*, 209–43, and Pennington, *Popes and Bishops*, 154–89; Sherri Franks Johnson, *Monastic Women and Religious Orders in Late Medieval Bologna* (Cambridge: Cambridge University Press, 2014), 99–104; Brentano, *Two Churches*, 87–88.

56. André Vauchez, *The Laity in the Middle Ages: Religious Beliefs and Devotional Practices*, ed. Daniel E. Bornstein, trans. Margery J. Schneider (Notre Dame, IN: University of Notre Dame Press, 1993), v, 1; John Howe, "The Nobility's Reform of the Medieval Church," *American Historical Review* 93, no. 2 (1988): 317–39.

## Selected Bibliography

Brentano, Robert. *A New World in a Small Place: Church and Religion in the Diocese of Rieti, 1188–1378*. Berkeley: University of California Press, 1994.

———. *Two Churches: England and Italy in the Thirteenth Century*. Berkeley: University of California Press, 1988.

Dameron, George W. *Episcopal Power and Florentine Society, 1000–1320*. Cambridge, MA: Harvard University Press, 1991.

———. *Florence and Its Church in the Age of Dante*. Philadelphia: University of Pennsylvania Press, 2005.

Foote, David. *Lordship, Reform, and the Development of Civil Society in Medieval Italy: The Bishopric of Orvieto, 1100–1250*. Notre Dame, IN: University of Notre Dame Press, 2004.

Gamberini, Andrea. "Vescovo e conte: La fortuna di un titolo nell'Italia centro-settentrionale (secoli XI–XV)." *Quaderni storici* 46, no. 138 (2011): 671–95.

Hay, Denys. *The Church in Italy in the Fifteenth Century: The Birkbeck Lectures, 1971*. Cambridge: Cambridge University Press, 1977.

*Le istituzioni ecclesiastiche della "Societas christiana" dei secoli XI–XII: Diocesi, pievi e parrocchie. Atti della sesta Settimana internazionale di studio Milano, 1–7 settembre 1974*. Milan: Vita e Pensiero, 1977.

Kamp, Norbert. "The Bishops of Southern Italy in the Norman and Staufen Periods." In *The Society of Norman Italy*, edited by G. A. Loud and A. Metcalfe, 185–209. The Medieval Mediterranean 38. Leiden: Brill, 2002.

Loud, G. A. *The Latin Church in Norman Italy*. Cambridge: Cambridge University Press, 2007.

Miller, Maureen C. *The Bishop's Palace: Architecture and Authority in Medieval Italy*. Ithaca, NY: Cornell University Press, 2000.

———. *The Formation of a Medieval Church: Ecclesiastical Change in Verona, 950–1150*. Ithaca, NY: Cornell University Press, 1993.

———. "Italy in the Long Twelfth Century: Ecclesiastical Reform and the Legitimization of a New Political Order, 1059–1183." In *European Transformations: The Long Twelfth Century*, edited by Thomas F. X. Noble and John Van Engen, 117–31. Notre Dame, IN: University of Notre Dame Press, 2012.

Osheim, Duane J. *An Italian Lordship: The Bishopric of Lucca in the Late Middle Ages*. Publications of the Center for Medieval and Renaissance Studies. Berkeley: University of California Press, 1977.

Toomaspoeg, Kristjan, ed. *Decimae: Il sostegno economico dei sovrani alla Chiesa del Mezzogiorno nel XIII secolo dai lasciti di Eduard Sthamer e Norbert Kamp*. Rome: Viella/Istituto Storico Germanico di Roma, 2009.

*Vescovi e diocesi in Italia nel medioevo (sec. IX–XIII): Atti del II Convegno di Storia della Chiesa in Italia (Roma, 5–9 sett. 1961)*. Padua: Editrice Antenore, 1964.

CHAPTER 4

# Pievi and the Care of Souls

*Neslihan Şenocak*

*In memory of Cadoc D. A. Leighton, O. Praem.*

In a volume such as this that focuses on the aspects of Christian religious life in medieval Italy, it would be unthinkable not to devote an entire chapter to the pieve. Despite its undisputable prominence in Italian history, the term is still unfamiliar or not entirely clear to many historians not specializing in Italy, hence the necessity to begin here with its definition. Starting from as early as the fifth century, the rural territories of all central and northern Italian dioceses were further subdivided into smaller administrative districts. Each of these districts was governed by a collegiate baptismal church (lat. *ecclesia baptismalis*) later called pieve (lat. *plebs*), exercising jurisdiction over smaller churches in its territory (it. *piviere*, lat. *plebium* or *plebatum*). According to Cinzio Violante, the term *plebs* used in this way first appears at the end of the seventh century in Tuscany and then diffuses slowly into all of central and northern Italy in the course of the ninth and tenth centuries, often used to mean both the church and the territory of its jurisdiction.[1] In fact, the term "piviere" seems to have become the nomenclature for the area of jurisdiction of any baptismal church, including the cathedral, which is sometimes referred to in the

---

1. Cinzio Violante, "Che cos'erano le pievi?," *Critica Storia* 26 (1989): 430.

medieval Italian documents as the urban pieve.[2] In contrast, elsewhere in Europe starting from the Carolingian period, we observe the mushrooming of private churches founded by the nobility, which offered pastoral care to the inhabitants subject to the landowning nobility. In Italy, the particular nature of the rural settlements, where households were scattered throughout the countryside and where one household could serve more than one lord, did not allow the private churches or chapels that were often established by the landlord to assume the function of care of souls.[3] When they did acquire some pastoral functions, it only happened gradually and piecemeal, starting with the right to public Mass, private penance, and the establishment of a cemetery and burial rights, leading eventually to the formation of parishes from the twelfth century onward. The other pastoral functions, such as baptism, and the consecration of the chrism and holy oil remained exclusively the right of the pieve.[4]

There were three important characteristics of the Italian pieve that distinguished it from the baptismal churches found elsewhere in Europe: first, the pieve was served by a college of priests, sometimes living together in a domus adjacent to the pieve and following a rule; second, the pieve had jurisdiction over the lesser churches (called *cappellae, ecclesiae, oratoria, cellae*, etc. depending on their status) in its piviere; and third, the pieve had the right to collect tithes over the ecclesiastical patrimony in its piviere.[5] The churches dependent on the pieve had no parochial rights: they could not baptize, have a cemetery, or collect tithes, unless by way of a special dispensation.[6] This meant that, for most of the Middle Ages, the pieve was the main institution providing pastoral care in Italy, with the dependent churches reserved solely for the Mass, taking the communion to the sick, blessings, and prayer. The pieve was, therefore, the heart of religious life in the rural Italy of the Middle Ages. As an institution, it fulfilled a great number of social, political, and economic functions. It was at once a place of worship, a

---

2. On this, see Mauro Ronzani, "Aspetti e problemi delle pievi e delle parrocchie cittadine nell' Italia centro-settentrionale," in *Pievi e parrocchie in Italia nel basso medioevo (Sec. XIII–XV): Atti del VI convegno di storia della chiesa in Italia (Firenze, 21–25 Sett., 1981)*, 2 vols. (Rome: Herder, 1984), 1:307–39.

3. Violante, "Che cos'erano le pievi?," 433–34.

4. Violante, "Che cos'erano le pievi?," 435.

5. Giuseppe Forchielli, *La pieve rurale: Ricerche sulla storia della costituzione della Chiesa in Italia e particolarmente nel Veronese* (Bologna: N. Zanichelli, 1938), 105.

6. Forchielli, *La pieve rurale*, 107.

hospital, a hospice, and a school, that is, an institution "to satisfy the spiritual and material needs of the people," as Forchielli has put it.[7]

From the pastoral point of view, the relation of the pieve to the faithful in its plebanal district is akin to the relation of the cathedral to the urban population. Just as the cathedral had the monopoly for baptism within the city, the pieve had the monopoly on baptism and the cemetery in its district. The archpriest of the pieve, also known as the pievano (lat. *plebanus*), was expected to preach on holy days and Sundays just as the bishop did in his cathedral. The smaller churches in the plebanal district would receive the chrism and holy oil from the pieve. Finally, the pievano was expected to go on regular visitations of the smaller churches, even as the bishop carried out visitations of the pievi in his diocese. This appears to be a unique structure in Italy, which was understood to be so by its contemporaries. The canonist Stephen of Tournai, in his commentary on Gratian's *Decretum*, goes so far as to state that it was among the customs of the Italian Church (*consuetudines ecclesiae italicae*) that by "diocese" one would understand the territory of a baptismal church, while "parish" is the word used for the smaller churches subject to the baptismal church.[8]

As such, the organization of pastoral care in Italy was distinctly different from other parts of Europe, such as England, France, or Germany, where the parish churches, often evolving from the proprietary churches, exercised full pastoral service and were directly under the jurisdiction of the bishop or a lay lord. All these abovementioned characteristics make the pieve a key institution within the religious life of the Christian inhabitants of medieval central and northern Italy.

## Jurisdictional Framework of the Pieve

In his seminal work on the parishes of medieval Lucca, Luigi Nanni reminds us that, given the feudal organization and relations of the medieval institutions, the churches operated in various dependencies. They

---

7. Forchielli, *La pieve rurale*, 106.
8. *Die Summa des Stephanus Tornacensis über da Decretum Gratiani*, ed. J. F. von Schulte (Vienna: Verlag von Emil Roth, 1891), 218. "Aliquando diocesis et parochia pro eodem ponitur, scilicet pro baptismali ecclesia; alioquin diocesis illa baptismalem tantum significat, parochiae vero cappellas sub illa quasi maiori constitutas. Quod melius intelligunt, qui consuetudines ecclesiae italicae norunt. Sunt enim quaedam, quas vocant plebes et in eis archipresbyteri sedent, et ipsae baptismales dicuntur habentque sub se alias minores, quas cappellas sive parochias vocant."

could be under the jurisdiction of the papacy, the bishop, the cathedral chapter, another church, a monastery, or a hospital, or they could be proprietary church.[9] In practice, many churches operated in a combination of these dependencies. Looking at the churches under the jurisdiction of the bishop, Nanni suggests two categories of dependency: one with respect to the origin (*iure nativo*), and the second with respect to the mode of dependence (direct or indirect dependence). The churches that were dependent on a bishop were those that were placed under the authority of the bishop at the time of their foundation or donated to him by the lay founders. Pievi belonged to this category, as they were normally placed under the jurisdiction of the bishop. With respect to the second mode, we talk of direct dependency when a church was located on the land of a lay or ecclesiastical landlord, while an indirect dependency meant that the church would be in possession of a governing entity that was under the jurisdiction of another.[10]

Although pievi in the early Middle Ages were almost always under the jurisdiction of a bishop, in the later centuries they were assigned to other ecclesiastical landholders. Twelfth-century popes seem to have been diligent in issuing bulls confirming the authority of bishops over the pievi and monasteries in their dioceses. Such bulls serve as important documents to show the number and location of the pievi and the churches subject to each pieve in a given diocese. They are also important in reminding us that most but not all pievi were under the jurisdiction of a bishop. One example is the 1132 bull of Innocent II addressed to Litifredo, bishop of Novara, where the bull contains names of the twenty-six pievi (including the pieve matrix, i.e., the cathedral of Novara) and its dependent churches (*cum capellis suis*) confirmed to be under the jurisdiction of the bishop.[11] However, this list does not contain the names of six further pievi that were known to be in existence by 1032, suggesting the possibility that some of the pievi in the diocese may not have been under the jurisdiction of the bishop, but perhaps

---

9. Luigi Nanni, *La parrocchia studiata nei documenti lucchesi dei secoli VIII–XIII* (Rome: Apud Aedes Universitatis Gregorianae, 1948), 31.

10. Nanni, *La parrocchia studiata*, 35.

11. G. Andenna, "Le pievi della diocese di Novara: Lineamenti metodologici e primi risultati di ricercar," in *Le istituzioni ecclesiastiche della "Societas christiana" dei secoli XI–XII: Papato, cardinalato ed episcopato. Atti della quinta settimana internazionale di studio, Mendola, 26–31 agosto 1971* (Milan: Vita e Pensiero, 1974), 492.

were under the cathedral chapter or lay nobility.[12] At least one pieve in Novara was placed under the jurisdiction of the cathedral chapter by Bishop Pietro III of Novara "for the remedy of his soul" sometime between 1027 and 1030 through an act of donation. This act of donation mentions all that was pertaining to a pieve: "cum capellis, titulis, decimis, mansis, terris, vineis, campis, silvis, pratis, pascuis, aquis earumque decursibus et cum universis apendicibus suis et omnibus reditibus."[13] Starting with the twelfth century, it seems not unusual for the bishops to give a pieve to the cathedral chapter, sometimes as an incentive to make the canons live together. In 1210, the pieve of Gruaro in the diocese of Concordia was conceded to the cathedral chapter of Concordia by the bishop. This transfer carried the condition that the canons would receive one-fourth of the income of the territory of the pieve, that is, a *quartese*, which was formally destined for the sacristy of Concordia, but it also came with the obligation for the canons to provide the plebanal services, essentially the care of souls.[14]

Similarly, the pieve of Santa Maria a Fine in Pisa is not mentioned in the 1137 bull of Innocent II among the pievi conceded to the authority of the archbishop of Pisa, but it is mentioned in the 1154 bull of Anastasius IV.[15] It is missing in the *Rationes Decimarum* of 1260, but in 1271 it reappears in a document as being dependent to the Cistercian monastery Santa Maria di Mirtelo.[16]

The number of pievi in a diocese was obviously not standard and changed according to the size and importance of a diocese. In the province of Tuscia, the biggest diocese was that of Florence with a total

---

12. "Oppure, ed è un'altra ipotesi, poiché la bolla di Innocenzo II confermava solo le pievi del vescovo, si può pensare che quelle ivi non menzionate appartenessero alla cattedrale o ad altri enti ecclesiastici, o fossero imbeneficiate a signori laici": Andenna, "Le pievi della diocese di Novara," 497-98.

13. Andenna, "Le pievi della diocese di Novara," 501.

14. Eugenio Marin, "La pieve di San Giusto di Gruaro e i suoi rettori," *Atti dell'Accademia "San Marco" di Pordenone* 7/8 (2005-6): 46-47. The use of the term *quartese* appears to be specific to the provinces of the Venetian Republic, denoting one-fourth of the tithe assigned to the parish priest. See Catherine E. Boyd, *Tithes and Parishes in Medieval Italy: The Historical Roots of a Modern Problem* (Ithaca, NY: Cornell University Press for the American Historical Association, 1952), 4, 20.

15. Antonino Mastruzzo and Maria Christina Rossi, "Le più antiche fondazioni di canoniche regolari a Pisa tra XI e XII secolo: Vicende storiche e rappresentazione documentaria," *Scrineum Rivista* 12 (2015): 88.

16. Maria Luisa Ceccarelli Lemut and Stefano Sodi, "Il sistema pievano nella diocesi di Pisa dall'età carolingia all'inizio del XIII secolo," *Rivista di storia della Chiesa in Italia* 58 (2004): 408.

of fifty-nine pieve noted in the *Rationes Decimarum Italiae* of 1274–80. The second largest diocese of Arezzo had sixty-eight pievi. In the same province, however, the smallest diocese of Sovana had seventeen pievi, followed by Grosseto with twenty pievi.[17]

The pieve, being in effect the only real parish church in a large area, had the right and the duty to collect the tithes of all the faithful living in its plebanal district. Along with the tithes, the pievi also had the right to collect burial fees, oblations, and first fruits, as well as the income from the land and its properties like mills, waterways, etc. This was a duty imposed on the pievi by the bishop, who would indeed inquire during his visitations to the pievi whether all laymen in the plebanal district had paid their tithes.[18] There could be, however, certain churches (often those founded by nobles) that by way of special privilege granted to them by the bishop, were entitled to the collection of the tithes in their district.

Collection of tithes was a closely guarded privilege but also opened the pievi to conflicts and contentions with other patrons who claimed ancient privilege of the churches in its district. A case in point was the dispute between the pieve of Riperbella and the monastery of San Felice di Vada in the diocese of Pisa concerning the tithes in 1125. The archpriest of the pieve, Lamberto, complained to Ruggero, archbishop of Pisa, that the monastery was driving his church to ruin by appropriating the tithes and burial fees. The archbishop responded by sending an archpriest, Ugo, to the villagers to instruct them to pay their tithes and burial fees not to the monastery, but to the pieve by invoking the ancient tradition that the faithful should be buried where they had received baptism, and as such had been born to the faith. Only those who have become *conversi* of the monastery, or who for a spiritual rather than temporal reason wanted to be buried in the monastery, were allowed to do so after receiving permission from the pieve and having paid their dues.[19]

---

17. Pietro Guidi, *Rationes decimarum Italiae nei secoli XIII e XIV: Tuscia*, vol. 1, *La Decima degli anni 1274–1280* (Vatican City: Biblioteca Apostolica Vaticana, 1932), xl.

18. Antonio Olivieri, "Un inedito statuto per il plebanato di Castrum Turris emanato dal visitatore Eusebio da Tronzano, vicario del vescovo di Vercelli Uberto Avogadro (luglio 1319)," *Bollettino Storico-Bibliografico Subalpino* 113 (2015): 187.

19. Ceccarelli Lemut and Sodi, "Il sistema pievano," 418.

## The Relation between the Pievano and the Rectors of the Dependent Churches

Similarly, it is impossible to standardize the number of churches that a pieve would have under its jurisdiction. This number changed greatly depending on the size of the diocese, and on the number of churches and pieve in a given diocese. A pieve like Santa Maria di Pescia with its confraternity had sixteen dependent churches, whereas the pieve of Padule in the same diocese had only one dependent church. Whenever earlier documentation is missing, the thirteenth- and fourteenth-century papal survey of tithes, *Rationes Decimarum Italiae*, usually serves as the main source of information for the boundaries of a pieve and which churches were its dependents.[20]

A Lucca manuscript dating from 1260, prepared for the collections of tithes in the diocese, gives us the entire list of churches, abbeys, and large collegiate churches in the diocese of Lucca together with their monetary worth.[21] The entire diocese is largely composed of two parts: the territory within the walls (urban) and outside of the walls (suburban). First the urban area is divided into four districts, each designated with its *porta*, that is, the corresponding city gate. Under the first porta, Saint Gervase's gate, the bishopric (*episcopatus*) and the chapter of the cathedral of Saint Martin (*canonica sancti Martini*) are listed as two distinct entities. It is noteworthy that while the bishopric is assessed at 3,500 pounds, the chapter's worth reaches the noble sum of 4,200 pounds. The hospital of the cathedral is assessed as a separate entity (as are all other hospitals) at a worth of 1,200 pounds. The other gates are those of Saint Peter, San Donato, and San Frediano. After the urban district comes the section entitled "sub urbani." The title is followed by a list of thirty-one ecclesiastical institutions, including churches, hospitals, and monasteries. The rest of the diocese is divided into pievi. Each district (whose list is separated from the following district list by a blank line) is headed by a pieve. The list of religious institutions under each pieve include not only the churches, but also the hospitals, monasteries, hermitages, other collegiate churches, and even cells of anchors of holy persons.

---

20. *Rationes decimarum Italiae nei secoli XIII e XIV* is published by the Studi e Testi series of the Vatican Library, one volume for each province of Italy. The volumes span 1936 to 2005.

21. Lucca, Biblioteca Statale, MS 135.

The subjection of a church to a pieve meant that the tithes collected in the territory of each church would go to the pieve, and its rector would be elected by the pievano and was subordinated to him. The pievano was for all intents and purposes an overlord for all the rectors of the churches in its plebanal district. He was responsible for the pastoral care not only of the laity, but also of the priests assigned to the dependent churches, who were to be chosen by him and the bishop together. The investiture, the essential medieval act of forging hierarchical bonds between persons and between institutions, was also present in the relation between pievi and dependent churches. Many surviving documents attest that the pievano would formally invest the chaplain (lat. *cappellanus*), the priest assigned to a dependent church, reminding him that the pieve has full jurisdiction over pastoral services and tithes of all churches in the piviere.

This was an important incentive for the pieve to assert periodically its patronage over the churches in its plebanal district, particularly when faced with other contenders, and especially in cases where the church was an ancient foundation. This was the case with the church of Saint Christopher in Colignòla in the diocese of Pisa. Between March 25 and September 23, 1155, Villano, the archbishop of Pisa, was called to adjudicate a dispute between the pieve of Santa Giulia, on which the church of Colignòla was dependent, and the monastery of San Michele in Borgo. The abbot of the monastery claimed that the church was erected on the land of the monastery, and that the rectors had been nominated for the last fifty years and were subject to abbatial jurisdiction. Furthermore, he asserted that when the church of Mezzana was destroyed, his predecessors had transferred the relics and other precious things to the church of Colignòla, considering it as their own. The archpriest of the pieve, on the other hand, claimed that his predecessors with the consent of the people of Colignòla had elected the rector of this church, and that the rector, like other priests in the plebanal district, was subordinated to the archpriest. The archbishop's solution to the dispute was to let the abbot select the rector and present him to the pievano, who, if he had no canonical objections, was to instate him as rector. The temporal goods of the church were to go to the monastery, but the spiritual goods (oblations of the living and the dead, tithes, and first fruits) belonged to the pieve.[22]

---

22. Ceccarelli Lemut and Sodi, "Il Sistema pievano," 414.

## 4. PIEVI AND THE CARE OF SOULS

Since the pievano was such a powerful figure, wielding considerable authority, his election was a matter of great importance to all clergy in the piviere. The Council of Pavia in 850 ordained that rectors of the dependent churches would be canonically assigned to the chapter of the pieve, and the chapter and the clergy had to choose the pievano with the consent of the lay faithful.[23] The common legal understanding was that the right to elect the pievano belonged to the chapter of the pieve and the rectors of the churches subject to it. This was something commonly invoked in the disputes concerning the election of an archpriest. In 1287, during such a contended election of the pievano of San Pancrazio in Pistoia, one of the candidates, Bandino del fu Ammannato, declared that the *ius eligendi* belonged to "the rectors of the subject churches and the chapter of the canons of the pieve."[24] We also have the surviving medieval records of such an election for the pieve of Fosciana in the diocese of Lucca. In 1236, at the invitation of Dolce, a priest and primicerius of the cathedral of Lucca, the rectors of the dependent churches of the pieve of Fosciana (Ubaldo, a canon of the pieve, and Orso, his subdeacon) came together in the pieve with the rectors of the twenty dependent churches. They followed a precise procedure. The rectors first chose a "grand elector," a sort of elector of electors (*elector eligentium*), Stefano, rector of the church of Castelnuovo. He in his turn chose four electors among the clergy present.[25] The four electors then came up with a nomination, in this case a certain Manfredino, rector of the church of Ottavo in the pieve of Diecimo. This church of Ottavo was the richest church in that piviere, coming only second after the pieve itself with respect to the tithes collected in 1260.[26] The election concluded with the acceptance of the post by Manfredino.

In fact, the rectors of the subject churches could assert their right not only in the election of the pievano but also for the second dignity

---

23. Cinzio Violante, "Le strutture organizzative della cura d'anime nelle campagne dell'Italia centrosettentrionale (Secoli V–X)," in *Cristianizzazione ed organizzazione ecclesiastica delle campagne nell'alto Medioevo: Espansione e resistenze, 10–16 aprile 1980*, 2 vols. (Spoleto: Centro italiano di studi sull'alto medioevo, 1982), 2:1061–62.

24. Mauro Ronzani, "Come lavorare con le rationes decimarum? Riflessioni sul rapporto fra l'insediamento e le forme d'inquadramento civile ed ecclesiastico in Toscana fra Due e Trecento," in *Paesaggi, comunità, villaggi medievali: Atti del Convegno internazionale di studio Bologna, 14–16 gennaio 2010*, ed. Paola Galetti (Spoleto: Fondazione centro italiano di studi sull'alto medioevo, 2012), 527.

25. Lorenzo Angelini, *Una pieve toscana nel medioevo* (Lucca: Maria Pacini Fazzi, 1979), 64–65.

26. Lucca, Biblioteca Statale, MS 135, fol. 13r.

of *prepositus*. In 1308, during the election of the prepositus of the pieve of San Stefano in Prato (the Pistoian pieve that in the fifteenth century became the cathedral of the newly created diocese of Prato), the pievano Bartolomeo clashed with the rectors of the dependent churches on this point. The pievano stated that the rectors should not have any say in the election of the prepositus, but the rectors replied that they, "de iure et antiqua consuetudine," had the right to participate in the election.[27]

In 1290, in another contended election in the same diocese, Cante di Baldo, pievano-elect of the pieve of Carmignano, based his case on the legal point that Sighibuldo, who opposed his election, was no longer a canon of Carmignano and therefore did not have the right to oppose the election.[28]

Some rectors were resident in the territory of the dependent church and some could be residing at the pieve, but regardless of their residency they were often considered to be a member of the chapter of the pieve and therefore obliged to come to the chapter meetings. In the diocese of Vercelli, the rectors, along with all priests and clergy of the plebanal district, were expected to come to the pieve during scrutinies of Lent and for the blessings of the fonts on both Saturdays of the Resurrection and the Pentecost.[29]

These obligations can be observed in the assignment of the churches San Pietro in Fenestrella and San Stefano in Maconeto to the monastery of Santa Maria in Vezzolano (a monastery of regular canons) by Bishop Ugo of Vercelli in 1235. From the investiture document we learn that these two churches were lacking spiritual and temporal goods ("sint satis destitute in spiritualibus et temporalibus rebus"), and since the town of Albugnano, in whose domain the two churches were located, was under the jurisdiction of the monastery, the bishop assigned the churches to the canons. The conditions attached to the investiture were these: A canon of the monastery was to officiate at the two churches and take residence at the church of Fenestrella. The prepositus and the canons were to present this canon to the pievano Pino who was to invest and confirm him, while the canon was to give him obedience for the said churches. He was expected to obey the bishop and the canons

---

27. The charter of this dispute is edited in Sabatino Ferrali, "Pievi e clero plebano in diocesi di Pistoia," *Bollettino storico pistoiese*, 3rd series, 8 (1973): 61.

28. Giuliano Pinto, "Clero e chiese rurali nel Pistoiese alla fine del Duecento," in *Pistoia e la Toscana nel Medioevo: Studi per Natale Rauty*, ed. Elena Vannucchi (Pistoia: Società pistoiese di storia patria, 1997), 119.

29. Olivieri, "Un inedito statuto," 182.

of the chapter of the pieve, to come to the chapter meetings like all the other *titulani*, to take part in the episcopal synods and every meeting of the lord bishop and the cathedral of Vercelli, to observe its *interdictum* as well as general and special excommunications, and to contribute five pounds of wax to the bishop and the cathedral of Vercelli on the feast of Saint George.[30]

## Visitations of the Dependent Churches by the Pievano

At least once a year, the pievano, accompanied by one or two of the rectors of dependent churches, had to make visitations to all the churches in the piviere.[31] He was to inquire into the condition of the liturgical *paramenta*, altar ornaments, clerical vestments, and books, as to whether they were clean and orderly and kept in a venerated way and were appropriate for worship. He was to inquire concerning the life and status of the clergy, that they were resident in their churches and celebrated the Mass and the Divine Office regularly and devoutly, whether the synodal and provincial constitutions were observed, whether there were any heretics, excommunicated, publicly known usurers, adulterers, or any couple living together against the rules of consanguinity.[32] The pievano was then to inform the bishop of any such known public sinners, but it was the bishop's duty to reconcile them.[33] In identifying the sick and ensuring that they would receive the sacrament of extreme unction, the priests posted in the daughter churches, who would have a better chance of knowing who is sick and reaching them in time, would collaborate with the archpriest. The visitations of the pievano in Italy are in some way reminiscent of the visitations in France, where each cathedral featured a number of archdeacons, each responsible for a part of the territory also called archidiaconate, and every archdeacon had to visit his territory once a year.[34] The difference here is that the pievani

---

30. Domenico Arnoldi, ed., *Le carte dello Archivio arcivescovile di Vercelli* (Pinerolo: Brignolo, 1917), 285–86.
31. Violante, "Le strutture organizzative della cura d'anime," 1062–63, 1067. Olivieri, "Un inedito statuto," 181.
32. Olivieri, "Un inedito statuto," 182.
33. Olivieri, "Un inedito statuto," 181.
34. This is attested by the Paris theologian Gerard d'Abbeville in his quodlibetal question no. 5. Paris, Bibliothèque nationale de France, MS Lat. 16405, fol. 55v: "Respondio dicendum quod archidiaconus tenetur singulis annis visitare suum archidiaconatum aut plebies."

often were not members of the cathedral and were often resident in their plebanal district, at least before the thirteenth century.

Until the early thirteenth century, it was customary for the Italian bishops to visit only the pievi but not the dependent churches. The rectors of the dependent churches would all be present at the pieve on the days of the visitations, but it was the pievano who would primarily answer the questions of the bishop or his vicar based on the visitations he himself did.[35]

## Pieve as a Collegiate Church

From its very beginnings, a pieve was a collegiate church served by multiple clergy, whose presence was necessary for the proper administration of pastoral-liturgical functions, above all the chanting of the Divine Office. In the pievi, the priests lived in the residential building attached to the church, referred to in the Latin documents and in Italian as *canonica*. The origin of this word goes back to the ninth century and was often used to mean not just the residence but the community itself, another word used in the same meaning being *schola*.[36] Clergy who were formally attached to that pieve would be called "canons,"[37] although in general the canons in the pievi did not have individual prebends like cathedral canons in the High Middle Ages. Instead, the patrimony of a pieve was one and held in common, of which the canons would have a share.[38]

The clergy who served at the pieve would be of various levels of the orders: priests, deacons, and subdeacons. In addition to the pievano, there could also be a prior or prepositus as a second dignity, who would have a privileged position in the liturgy and could substitute the pievano when needed.[39]

With the reform movement of the eleventh century, the plebanal clergy were encouraged to live together and follow a Rule for the canons. A document in the episcopal archives of Pisa relates an act of

---

35. See, for example, the visitations done by Matteo, bishop of Città di Castello. Sonia Merli, "Qui seminat spiritualia debet recipere temporalia: L'episcopato di Città di Castello nella prima metà del Duecento," *Melanges de l'École française de Rome: Moyen-Âge* 109, no. 2 (1997): 269–301.
36. Forchielli, *La pieve rurale*, 157–58.
37. Ferrali, "Pievi e clero plebano," 40–41.
38. Ferrali, "Pievi e clero plebano," 44.
39. Ferrali, "Pievi e clero plebano," 46–47.

donation to the pieve of Santa Maria a Fine by the layman Andrea del fu Teuperto, in which it is stipulated that a canonica at the pieve will be constructed where clergy will live according to the rule of canons.[40] To live together rather than individually was probably something not desirable for many canons, who often came from important local families. In 1113 in Novara, a group of laymen in Gozzano donated a mill with all its pertaining rights to the canonica of the pieve, provided that the canons would live in common during the first four days of Lent.[41] A pieve where the canons lived together and regularly chanted the Divine Office was a source of encouragement for lay donations.[42] The common regulated life of the canons was important from a pastoral point of view in more than one way.[43] In the visitation formula from Lucca (possibly dating to 1260) one of the questions for the pievi was whether all canons, chaplains, and clergy ate and slept at the church and *in communi*.[44]

In its spatial structure, the pieve was in many ways not that different from a monastery,[45] having a cloister, a refectory, and a dormitory. Historically, therefore, the difference between the monks and the secular canons living a communal life was not that evident.[46] However, in the later Middle Ages the living together entered an irreversible decline for a number of reasons as listed by Ferrali: the loss of religious fervor combined with an increasing worldliness of the clergy; the dispersion of the pievi's patrimony; the lack of efficient leadership; and the slow but steady increase of the benefices *sine cura* among the canons of the pievi, where the holder could enjoy all the economic advantages of a benefice

---

40. Ceccarelli Lemut and Sodi, "Il sistema pievano," 407.
41. Andenna, "Le pievi della diocese di Novara," 516.
42. Mastruzzo and Rossi, "Le più antiche fondazioni di canoniche regolari," 87.
43. The two volumes of the proceedings of a 1959 conference in Mendola are the best reference source for the common life of the canons. *La vita comune del clero nei secoli XI et XII: Atti della Settimana di studio, Mendola, settembre 1959*, 2 vols. (Milan: Vita e Pensiero, 1962).
44. Lucca, Biblioteca Statale, MS 135, fols. 24r–27r.
45. In fact, in the Italian documents, it is not uncommon to see the term *monasterium* used for churches where canons resided. Forchielli, *La pieve rurale*, 159 n. 1, gives a list of medieval documents employing the term to refer to a pieve. See also Nanni, *La parrocchia studiata*, 11–13, who finds *monasterium* in the document of Lucca to refer to simple churches from the eighth century onward.
46. William D. Carpe, "The Vita Canonica in the Regula Canonicorum of Chrodegang of Metz" (PhD diss., University of Chicago, 1975), 9–42; Martin A. Claussen, *The Reform of the Frankish Church: Chrodegang of Metz and the Regula Canonicorum in the Eighth Century* (Cambridge: Cambridge University Press, 2004), 60–62. See also J. Schneider, ed., *Saint Chrodegang, communications présentées au Colloque tenu à Metz à l'occasion du douzième centenaire de sa mort* (Metz: Editions Le Lorrain, 1967).

without providing any ecclesiastical or spiritual labor, and thus a lack of presence of canons actually in the pievi, who resided instead in other places.[47]

## Pastoral Work of the Pieve

In Italian historiography, the study of the pieve has been dominated by its institutional aspects rather than pastoral-religious aspects. The themes most widely studied are the connections of the pievi to the nascent communes, the links between the pieve and the Roman pagus, the collection of tithes along with other economic aspects, and juridical aspects of the pieve such as its relation to bishops and to its daughter churches. To a great extent, the nature of the surviving records is responsible for this, as most medieval records on the pieve concern its jurisdictional status. What is much less studied is the actual pastoral work.

As mentioned above, one of the most distinguishing elements of the pieve with respect to other churches was that it alone had the right to baptize. Everyone who is baptized in a pieve would constitute its flock. "Until the thirteenth century, if a private church would acquire baptismal function, that would in effect mean that this church would assume the title and the institutional character of a pieve."[48] Many of the pieve are believed to have had a baptistery adjacent to the church, though it is difficult to determine the exact number, as in many cases these have fallen out of use over the intervening centuries.[49] With respect to changes in baptism, Cattaneo remarks that having the baptistery as a separate building starts to decline after the twelfth century. While in the earlier centuries baptisteries had a large hollow built into the floor in the center of the baptistery to accommodate full-body immersion, from the twelfth century onwards there is an increasingly common tradition of building baptismal fonts as relatively small octagonal structures to the left of the church doors.[50]

Apart from baptism, the faithful had to come to the pieve for the Masses of feast days to hear the sermon and for communion. The liturgy

---

47. Ferrali, "Pievi e clero plebano," 42.
48. Violante, "Che cos'erano le pievi?," 434.
49. For a list of the known pieve with baptisteries, see Enrico Cattaneo, "Il Battistero in Italia dopo il Mille," in *Miscellanea Gilles Gérard Meersseman*, 2 vols. (Padua: Editrice Antenore, 1970), 1:177–80.
50. Cattaneo, "Il Battistero in Italia dopo il Mille," 181.

## 4. PIEVI AND THE CARE OF SOULS

of the Mass and Divine Office in a pieve had to conform to the liturgy of the matrix church, that is, the cathedral. They were required to keep all the priestly vestments and other *paramenta* used in the services in a clean condition, employing honest women to wash and clean them if necessary.[51] Priests in a plebanal district were expected to celebrate the Mass for both the living and the dead every day.

As part of the care of souls, the plebanal clergy were to take the consecrated host to the sick. In the reform statutes made for the pieve of Castrum Turris by the bishop of Vercelli, it was decreed that the host for the sick should not be kept more than a month, but remade every month and kept locked inside the church in a clean and well-lit place, and the same should be done with the chrism and holy oil for the catechumens and the sick. The priests should take these to the sick with a viaticum, while chanting the penitential psalms or litanies.[52]

All rectors of the dependent churches, priests, and clergy in the plebanal district were obliged to confess at least once a year to the pievano. The pievano, if he chose to do so, could choose confessors among his clergy who would have the authority to absolve, in order to facilitate more frequent confession.

Preaching was another part of the pastoral care that was offered solely by the pieve. In fact, in the Council of Pavia, it is mentioned that the elites often had a chapel attached to their homes where they went to hear the Divine Office, only rarely coming to the *ecclesias maiores* (i.e., the pieve and the cathedral) for Mass and to hear preaching. The clergy were admonished to encourage the elites to come to the pieve so that they could hear the sermon. If they did come to the pieve, the preaching should instruct them not to exploit and oppress the poor, to abstain from hoarding wealth, and to redeem their sins with alms.[53] Obviously, there must have been the legitimate concern that if the elites hired their own clergy, even without any episcopal approval, and if such clergy celebrated Mass and preached in the proprietary churches, the preaching

---

51. Olivieri, "Un inedito statuto," 180.
52. Olivieri, "Un inedito statuto," 181.
53. "Si autem divites, qui pauperibus iniuriam facere soliti sunt, venire non rennuerent, illis omnino praedicandum esset, ut a rapinis se compescerent utque, dum possunt, elemosynis peccata sua redimerent, ut a fluxu rerum temporalium se abstinerent. Admonendi sunt igitur potentes, ut ad maiores ecclesias, ubi praedicationem audire possint, sepius conveniant, et quantum dono omnipotentis Dei divitiis et honoribus caeteros antecedunt, tanto ad audienda praecepta conditoris sui alacrius festinent." Alfredus Boretius and Victor Krause, eds., *Capitularia regum Francorum*, 2 vols., Monumenta Germaniae Historica (Hannover: Hahnsche Buchhandlung, 1883-97), 2:81.

they would do, if any, would tend to avoid any theme that could be perceived as a criticism of the lifestyle of the wealthy.[54]

Violante has argued that the faithful were most concerned about burial rites. The multiplication of private churches with cemeteries led the baptismal churches to reassert their exclusive right to bury the faithful, often in connection with the canonicality that the faithful should be buried where they had received baptism.[55]

One of the lesser known aspects of the pieve is its schools. Long before Lateran III's ordaining that cathedrals must offer schooling, the Roman council of 826 had ordered that not only in the episcopal seats but also in all pievi and in other places where there is a need, schools must be established for the teaching of Latin and liberal arts.[56] Forchielli mentions the presence in the pieve of clergy called "magistri," who would most likely be teaching the young children.[57]

It needs to be mentioned here that there were instances, mostly starting in the thirteenth century, in which a pieve did not have fixed clergy but was instead appointed temporary curates by its ecclesiastical patron. In the case of the donation of a pieve to the canons of Concordia by the bishop, mentioned above, the canons of Concordia would assign to the pieve not a proper pievano, but rather *vicari curati*, hired priests who were usually assigned for the duration of three years and would receive one-fourth of the income of a single village called Boldara and fruits from one other territory.[58] As such, the income received by the vicars was only a fraction of the actual income that the canons received as holders of the pieve. Another example is from 1297, when the pieve of Tricesimo in the diocese of Aquiela (province of Udine) officially

---

54. Hiring of priests to celebrate the Mass in the chapels of the wealthy without episcopal license seems to be an ongoing practice that the Council of Pavia warned against in the same decree. "Quidam autem comites et vassi dominici presbyteros et caeteros clericos nostros, quod nec episcopis facere licet, absque nostra licentia recipiunt, insuper etiam ubicumque ordinatos et quosdam, de quibus dubium est, utrum consecrati sint, in parroechiis nostris absque nostra examinatione missas sibi celebrare faciunt quod, ne ulterius fiat, omnimodis est inhibendum." Boretius and Krause, *Capitularia regum Francorum*, 2:81.

55. Violante, "Che cos'erano le pievi?," 430–31.

56. Boretius and Krause, *Capitularia regum Francorum*, 1:376. "De scolis reparandis pro studio litterarum. De quibusdam locis ad nos refertur, non magistros neque curam inveniri pro studio litterarum. Idcirco in universis episcopiis subiectisque plebibus et aliis locis, in quibus neeessitas occurrerit, omnino cura et diligentia adhibeatur, ut magistri et doctores constituantur, qui studia litterarum liberaliumque artium habentes dogmata, assidue doceant, quia in his maxime divina manifestantur atque declarantur mandata."

57. Forchielli, *La pieve rurale*, 168.

58. Marin, "La pieve di San Giusto di Gruaro e i suoi rettori," 46–47.

## 4. PIEVI AND THE CARE OF SOULS

established a vicariate. The pievani would receive the benefice allocated to them *in commenda*, but they would often reside far away from Tricesimo. The care of the souls of the plebanal flock would be subcontracted to a viceregent of the pievano and a vicar as his helper. These two would be selected by the pievano alone and could be deposed any time at his will.[59]

Another episode of the absence of a pievano shows us the degree to which the situation of nonresidence could lead to a breakdown in pastoral services and the resulting anger of the faithful. This episode concerns the pieve of Fosciana in Lucca (mentioned above). In April 1243, a priest named Paolo, belonging to one of the noble families of the region and a canon of Lucca cathedral, becomes the new pievano. It is most likely that Paolo continued to reside in Lucca instead of Fosciana after the election, as his name appears in the documents of the chapter of the cathedral in the subsequent years. Nine months later, in January 1244, Paolo appoints to the pieve a priest named Armanno di Mignardo to take care of the pastoral services. Armanno had to be resident in the pieve and would receive twenty denari lucchesi as the annual stipend.[60] However, on April 9, 1246, a few days after Easter, a crisis erupted in the piviere. The rectors of the two dependent churches of the pieve, who were at the same time canons of the pieve of Fosciana, appeared before the vicars of the bishop of Lucca to inform them that no solemn baptism celebration had taken place in the pieve on the Holy Saturday, and there were a few infants who had died without receiving baptism. As a result, the people were up in revolt, threatening to turn out all the clergy of the piviere and take over their property. The rectors therefore asked the bishop's vicars for a license to celebrate the solemn baptismal rites. The vicars seemed at a loss in the face of such an unusual request. The account of the rectors regarding the revolt of the people was corroborated by another witness: one of the layfolk of the piviere arrived at the bishop's palace with the same request, speaking on behalf of the others who could not come to Lucca because of the disruption on the roads leading to the city (*propter discrimina viarum*). It appears in fact that the people of the piviere had already made good their threat, since in another document of the same date (April 9, 1246), a vicar of the bishop and a canon of the cathedral of Baliante received twenty-five

---

59. Luisa Villotta, *L'archivio storio della pieve di Tricesimo* (Tricesimo: Comune di Tricesimo, 2008), 93.
60. Angelini, *Una pieve toscana*, 65.

solidos from the rector of the Hospital of San Pietro Maggiore to help the clergy of Garfagnana (the locality of the pieve of Fosciana) who have been driven out of their churches ("pro subsidio clericorum Garfagnane expulsorum de suis ecclesiis").[61] This is a rare account testifying to the power of the lay faithful over the clergy, and to how much they were concerned with the regularity of the pastoral services.

Apart from baptism, the Mass, penance, and burial, which technically make up what is called *cura animarum*, pievi were also instrumental in establishing and supporting what might be called "parapastoral" activities. An important one in this respect is the local confraternities of prayer and burial that emerged around a pieve. A fragment of a twelfth-century *recordatio* from the pieve of San Giuliano in Gazzano in the province of Novara contains the statutes of a confraternity that included the clergy of the pieve: The members were to congregate four times a year to celebrate the Mass and vigils for the brothers and for all the deceased faithful; those who could not attend had to give money to the poor. If one of them became ill, the others had to attend to his needs, and if he should die the pievano and the canons of the pieve had to be notified. All members of the confraternity were expected to attend the funeral. If the deceased were a layperson, the priests had to celebrate five Masses and chant two psalteria. If the deceased were a priest, then the laymen had to arrange for three Masses to be celebrated.[62]

Since all churches in a plebanal district were under the jurisdiction of the pieve, any religious community that would have the use of a church, be it a confraternity or a community of *conversi*, would have obligations toward the pieve. In a document dating from 1141, the bishop of Novara, Litifredo, in the presence of leading clergy and laymen, assigns the church of San Lorenzo (a dependent church of the pieve) to a certain Alberto and his companions. Understood to be *conversi*, this lay community was responsible for the restoration of the church while being allowed the living there, presumably with the income of the land that belonged to the church, and they were placed by the bishop under the obedience of the pieve.[63] The plebanal clergy, however, had no right to alienate any land or goods pertaining to the church of San Lorenzo.

---

61. Angelini, *Una pieve toscana*, 66.

62. M. Bori, *Le carte del Capitolo di Gozzano (1002–1300)* (Pinerolo: G. Cantone, 1913), 59–60.

63. Simone Caldano, "Chiese amministrate da laici: San Lorenzo e Santa Maria de Bozolo di Gozzano nei secoli xii–xiii," in *Borghi nuovi, castelli e chiese nel Piemonte medieval: Studi in onore di Angelo Marzi*, ed. Simone Caldano and Aldo A. Settia (Turin: Nuova Trauben, 2017), 306.

In 1174, the community received a donation from a laywoman that they invested by buying more land.[64] Another charter of the same pieve, dated February 14, 1208, reveals an agreement between the pieve and the community at San Lorenzo. Prandus, leader of the community, and his companions would have to provide a meal to the canons of the pieve on the feast of San Lorenzo or give five imperial *solidos* and oblations; they could not sell or alienate the land or goods.[65]

Similarly, the pieve of Santa Maria di Pescia, which in the twelfth century was part of the diocese of Lucca, was the center of another mixed lay-clerical confraternity including the clergy of the pieve. Its statutes made very similar provisions to that of Gozzano, although in the case of Pescia we have the entire confraternity book, including sermons, an obituary, confraternity statutes, and liturgy of the Mass for the dead and for the Virgin.[66]

## The Gradual Erosion of the Pieve

The transference of the pastoral service from the pieve to the dependent churches was very gradual and not complete in Italy until the nineteenth century. In time, an increasing number of dependent churches acquired the privilege to become parish churches in their own right, in part due to the fact that from the thirteenth century onward pievani were increasingly absent.[67] Nevertheless, this was not a complete independence. Until modern times, such churches were not given a baptismal font, and hence the faithful would still have to be baptized in the pieve. The parish rector might have the privilege of hearing private confessions, but it was still the pievano who had to present the public penitents to the bishop at the beginning and end of the penitential cycle. The rectors were still required to come to the pieve on certain feast days and for solemn processions, especially the rogations and the Corpus Domini. The episcopal visitations to a plebanal district would revolve around the pieve. The bishop or episcopal visitator would first

---

64. Caldano, "Chiese amministrate da laici," 307.

65. Bori, *Le carte del Capitolo*, 61–62. Caldano, "Chiese amministrate da laici," 307. Caldano presents the documentary evidence regarding the demise of these *conversi*, as the pieve during the course of the thirteenth century manages the land and goods of the church of San Lorenzo.

66. A. Spiccani, "Una confraternita rurale nella Lucchesia del secolo XII: Appunti per una ricerca," *Confraternitas* 2 (1991): 10.

67. Angelini, *Una pieve toscana*, 72.

visit the pieve and take up residence there, meeting with the rectors of the churches in that district either at the pieve or by making daily visits from the pieve to the churches.[68]

Until the twelfth century, the pieve was the only church that could be called a parish church. After the twelfth century, certain changes to this system, or rather the slow and gradual decline of the pieve system, started as an increasing number of churches subject to the pieve gained the rights for full pastoral service, thus becoming parishes in their own right and collecting their own tithes. In practice the process would play out gradually, by a church perhaps acquiring partial privileges regarding certain pastoral services, then expanding them to others. This development can be well observed from many records of litigation that took place between a pieve and its dependency. To give an example, the pieve of Santa Maria in Biandrate in the diocese of Vercelli entered into a dispute with the church of Colombano. In typical fashion, San Colombano was founded by a noble family, the counts of Biandrate, in their castle. Being a noble establishment, it was given certain privileges at the beginning: it had a baptismal font to be used only by the members of the noble family, and it had the rights to the tithes of the seigneurial lands. But gradually, it started to participate in the pieve's right of burial, administration of the sacraments, and collection of tithes from areas under the jurisdiction of the pieve. At first, the approval of the pievano was sought, but soon it became a jurisdictional trespass, "contra ius."[69]

Similarly, Boyd's study of the Genoese documents has found that in the twelfth century, the pieve's parish would no longer be equal to the entire plebanal district. The churches in the plebanal district would now have their own parishes. At least one pieve in Genoa is said to have all the tithes from its parish, which constituted one-fourth of its *plebium*.[70]

The pieve is a highly complex institution showing great changes over time, particularly as the dependent churches start acquiring rights to certain pastoral services and the collection of their tithes. As well, in various dioceses, the pievi and its structure and obligations play out quite differently. Since the publication of the seminal conference

---

68. Ferrali, "Pievi e clero plebano," 47–48.
69. Aldo A. Settia, "Crisi e adeguamento dell'organizzazione ecclesiastica nel Piemonte bassomedievale," in *Pievi e parrochie in Italia nel basso medioevo*, 2:611.
70. Boyd, *Tithes and Parishes*, 156 n. 2.

proceedings *Pievi e parrocchie*, there has been no work that attempts a synthesis of the pieve as a distinct ecclesiastical institution. A better understanding of this institution can pave the way for comparisons with the institution of the "minster" in England and the archidiaconate in France.

## Selected Bibliography

Andenna, Giancarlo. "Le pievi della diocese di Novara: Lineamenti metodologici e primi risultati di ricercar." In *Le istituzioni ecclesiastiche della "Societas christiana" dei secoli XI–XII: Papato, cardinalato ed episcopato. Atti della quinta settimana internazionale di studio, Mendola, 26–31 agosto 1971*, 487–516. Milan: Vita e Pensiero, 1974.

Boyd, Catherine E. *Tithes and Parishes in Medieval Italy: The Historical Roots of a Modern Problem*. Ithaca, NY: Cornell University Press for the American Historical Association, 1952.

Castagnetti, Andrea. *L'organizzazione del territorio rurale nel Medioevo: Circoscrizioni ecclesiastiche e civili nella Langobardia e nella Romania*. Turin: G. Giappichelli, 1979.

———. *Una pieve rurale nell'Italia padana: Territorio, organizzazione patrimoniale e vicende della pieve veronese di San Pietro di Tillida dall'alto Medioevo al secolo XIII*. Rome: Herder, 1976.

Ceccarelli Lemut, Maria Luisa, and Stefano Sodi. "Il sistema pievano nella diocesi di Pisa dall'età carolingia all'inizio del XIII secolo." *Rivista di storia della Chiesa in Italia* 58 (2004): 391–432.

Coradazzi, G. *La Pieve: L'antica istituzione alto medievale della Chiesa, nella storia, nell'archeologia, nel diritto, nell'arte (Vecchie e nuove prospettive)*. Mantua: Polesini, 1980.

Ferrali, Sabatino. "Pievi e clero plebano in diocesi di Pistoia." *Bollettino storico pistoiese*, 3rd series, 8 (1973): 39–62.

Forchielli, Giuseppe. *La pieve rurale: Ricerche sulla storia della costituzione della Chiesa in Italia e particolarmente nel Veronese*. Bologna: N. Zanichelli, 1938.

Foschi, Paola, Edoardo Penoncini, and Renzo Zagnoni. *Ecclesiae baptismales: Le pievi della montagna fra Bologna, Pistoia e Modena nel Medioevo*. Pistoia: Società pistoiese di storia patria, 1999.

*Le istituzioni ecclesiastiche della "Societas christiana" dei secoli XI–XII: Diocesi, pievi e parrocchie. Atti della sesta Settimana internazionale di studio, Milano, 1–7 settembre 1974*. Milan: Vita e Pensiero, 1977.

Nanni, Luigi. *La parrocchia studiata nei documenti lucchesi dei secoli VIII–XIII*. Rome: Apud Aedes Universitatis Gregorianae, 1948.

*Pievi e parrocchie in Italia nel basso medioevo (Sec. XIII–XV): Atti del VI convegno di storia della chiesa in Italia (Firenze, 21–25 Sett., 1981)*. 2 vols. Rome: Herder, 1984.

Santini, Giovanni. *I comuni di pieve nel Medioevo italiano: Contributo alla storia dei comuni rurali*. Milan: Giuffrè, 1964.

Violante, Cinzio. "Che cos'erano le pievi?," *Critica Storia* 26 (1989): 429–39.

——. "Le strutture organizzative della cura d'anime nelle campagne dell'Italia centrosettentrionale (Secoli V–X)." In *Cristianizzazione ed organizzazione ecclesiastica delle campagne nell'alto Medioevo: Espansione e resistenze, 10–16 aprile 1980*, 2:963–1158. Spoleto: Centro italiano di studi sull'alto medioevo, 1982.

CHAPTER 5

# Monasticism
*Cécile Caby*

Around the millennium, the Italian peninsula was characterized by a network of abbeys, in part inherited from the Lombard and Carolingian periods and in part renewed in the context of the reorganization of powers during the tenth century. Already in the seventh century, and after a significant push in the subsequent century, the entire peninsula had become the soil for the blossoming of monastic foundations, among them many female institutions. Establishing monastic sites appears to have been a favored practice for kings and Lombard elites, especially since these foundations functioned as a meeting point between different populations: the Italians, the Lombards, and even the Irish as in the case of Bobbio. In this context, the Rule written in the second quarter of the sixth century, probably by Benedict of Nursia, spread quickly, often alongside other normative texts. The Frankish conquest (774) consolidated this state of affairs, and it is no coincidence that the first diploma emanating from Charlemagne after the conquest of Pavia specifically addresses the confirmation of the property of Bobbio. Farfa, Montecassino, and San Vincenzo al Volturno would follow soon after, while new foundations, supported by bishops, were added to this system, which entailed a strong connection between monastic institutions and imperial power.

As an internal struggle threw the public powers and the Carolingian balance of power into turmoil, the sporadic raids of the Hungarians (in 899 at Nonantola) and of the Saracens (in 906 at Nonantola again, in 881 at San Vincenzo al Volturno, in 883 at Montecassino, in 898 at Farfa) precipitated a crisis, which struck right at the very function of monasticism within society at the end of the ninth century. This crisis involved, among other things, a rapid redefinition of the status of monastic establishments in relation to new territorial powers, whether lay or religious.

## Restructuring of Powers and Monastic Reorganization

Countless case studies, which vary depending on the geographical area and generation, reflect this shifting landscape. This is especially evident between the ninth and the eleventh centuries, as monastic reforms were almost always tied to the personal initiative of certain monks or abbeys, and strongly connected to the local aristocracy. Between the end of the ninth century and the mid-tenth century, episcopal power underwent a growth closely linked to the developing urban renaissance, characteristic of Italy, that allowed bishops to reinforce their control over monastic lands. In Verona, for instance, toward the end of the tenth century, Bishop Raterio's favorable attitude toward monastic life combined with his interventionist zeal provided the impetus for—among other works—restorations such as that of San Zeno, but also the suppressions of establishments considered to have been tainted by irreparable scandal, such as Maguzzano (966).[1] In many cases, we can see how the resurgence of the alliance between monks and elites in power is to the benefit of new players. Indeed, some of the new familial groups increased their influence by relying upon the land reserves of monasteries and by developing ties with them. Other groups chose to bank on their territorial power and claim public authority by founding new monasteries. At times, they endowed these new foundations with lands whose possession (regardless of their sometimes dubious origins) was legitimized by donations, and retained the prerogative of nominating the abbot and monastic officers, thereby preserving control over these houses over generations. In Umbria, not far from Foligno, the abbey

---

This chapter was translated by Lochlin Brouillard.

1. Maureen C. Miller, *The Formation of a Medieval Church: Ecclesiastical Change in Verona, 950–1150* (Ithaca, NY: Cornell University Press, 1993), 65–70.

of Sassovivo was founded and developed in this manner until the end of the eleventh century, thanks to the donations of the descendants of Count Monaldo, who extended their patronage over Sassovivo, promised never to harass it, and guaranteed its protection and support (*tuitio*). The direct dependence that Sassovivo acquired from the papacy in 1138, during the reign of Innocent II, stabilized the network of dependencies and the patrimony of the abbey, while also providing the popes with an entry point into this region in the vicinity of Rome.[2]

In general, the close relationship between the papacy and reformed monasticism started growing from the mid-eleventh century, taking various forms. At Montecassino, under Abbot Teobaldo (1022-35), the monastery found a new calling in the reforming ambitions of the papal Curia, which expanded at the time of Abbot Desiderius (from 1058), who became Pope Victor III (1086-87). In this period, a new church was consecrated by Pope Alexander II (in 1071), the scriptorium of the monastery was very active, and the patrimony was reorganized in the *terra sancti Benedicti*.[3] At Farfa, which adopted the Cluniac customs in the eleventh century, a characteristic of the network resulted from the exemption claimed and flaunted with pride as the "complete freedom of the monastery, conceded by the pontiffs, the kings, and the emperors, and always preserved and defended in the past," as Gregorio da Catino's *Liber Floriger* says.[4] However, at neither Montecassino nor Farfa in the same period did reform imply the slightest break with the system of the imperial Church or indeed with the relationships with the emperor and local aristocracy.

Different types of founders and reformers succeeded one another, comprised of great lay figures, newly in charge of public offices, or of bishops driven by a desire to exert their authority over cities and by the slow territorialization of their power over the space of their diocese. Gradually urban groups also joined their ranks. In any case, monasteries, as professional prayer houses, were by far the principal recipients of

---

2. Stefania Zucchini, "S. Pietro di Perugia e Sassovivo," in *Dinamiche istituzionali delle reti monastiche e canonicali nell'Italia dei secoli X–XII (Fonte Avellana, 29–31 agosto 2006)*, ed. Nicolangelo D'Acunto (Negarine di S. Pietro in Cariano [Verona]: Il segno dei Gabrieli editori, 2007), 157-74.

3. Amalia Galdi, "Alle origini dell'*Aureum Saeculum* desideriano: Montecassino tra i secoli X–XI," *Mélanges de l'École française de Rome: Moyen Âge* 129, no. 2 (2017), http://journals.openedition.org/mefrm/3705.

4. *Il Chronicon farfense di Gregorio di Catino; precedono la Constructio farfensis e gli scritti di Ugo di Farfa*, ed. U. Balzani (Rome: Istituto Storico Italiano per il Medio Evo, 1903), 121.

land donations from aristocratic groups (acting as founders but not exclusively so), who expected prayers and the cultivation of their dynastic memory in return. These donations, understood in a very broad sense and sometimes coming with temporary retrocessions, fostered an intensive circulation of estates and wealth, and thus in the mid-eleventh century monasteries found themselves at the head of vast landed estates and in possession of equally impressive rights over the inhabitants of these same estates. Alongside the efforts of the Gregorian Reform to affirm the unalienable nature of ecclesiastical property, many monastic houses regrouped their landholdings—which used to be organized in a system of great domains—into more compact units constituting proper lordships, which gave monks power over the land and its *homines*. It is in this context that between the tenth and the twelfth centuries, and especially in central Italy, we see a proliferation of fortified habitat centers, located on previously vacant high areas (the *castrum* or *castellum*), overlooking the village below. This phenomenon has been called *incastellamento* in scholarly literature (initially by Pierre Toubert) and was first identified in territories controlled by the abbey of Farfa in Sabina, north of Rome.

## Cluniac Monasticism and Reform of the Italian Church

Beyond the native monastic foundations, Italian monasticism around the year 1000 was also in touch with forms of religious life coming from elsewhere/abroad. From the tenth century, Cluniac monasticism played a part in the establishment of a seigneurial society in the plain of the Po. Its expansion in Italy, although limited, was steered by the aristocratic networks to which the abbots of Cluny were attached. For instance, Odo (d. 942) opened Cluny to the Bosonids, who were represented in Italy by Hugh of Arles and his son Lothar. Hugh and Lothar thus facilitated the access of the *ecclesia Cluniacensis* to the Theophylact clan, an aristocratic family based in nearby *Tusculum*, who controlled the papacy. By a multiabbatiate system (i.e., the takeover of several monastic establishments simultaneously as a result of reforms), Cluny entered Rome and Montecassino at the time of Abbot Balduino.[5] Polirone Abbey, founded by

---

5. Isabelle Rosé, "La présence 'clunisienne' à Rome et dans sa région au Xe siècle: Réformes et ecclésiologie monastiques d'Odon à Maïeul," in *Il monachesimo italiano dall'età longobarda all'età ottoniana (secc. VIII–X)*, ed. Giovanni Spinelli (Cesena: Badia di Santa Maria del Monte, 2006), 231–71.

the Canossa family in 1007, was first endowed and then given to the pope by Matilda in 1077, and temporarily came under Cluniac influence thanks to this papal connection. This Cluniac expansion was in the end short-lived since it was already declining toward the 1140s on account of Cluny's financial difficulties as well as competition coming from new networks like the Cistercians or the Vallombrosians, who were already present in Lombardy in the 1120s.

Nonetheless, if we look for Cluniac influence in the Italian peninsula, we have to take into account the different paths it could follow, including local adaptations. This is what we see with the monastery of Cava, founded in the diocese of Salerno by a certain Alferio (d. 1050), who had gone to Cluny to complete his novitiate out of admiration for Abbot Odilo. Under the abbacy of Hugh of Cluny, the influence of Cluny returned to Cava through the efforts of Cava's third abbot, Pietro Pappacarbone (d. 1123), and it probably impacted the writing of the *consuetudines Cavenses*, the specific liturgical and daily/life customs addressed to the monastery of the Holy Trinity of Cava and its dependencies.[6] We also observe the same situation with William of Volpiano (d. 1031) and Fruttuaria in the diocese of Ivrea, the monastery founded on his family's domains by his relatives, his brothers in particular. William first made his monastic profession at Lucedio. After having met Maiolus of Cluny (987), he became involved in a vigorous movement of foundation and reform inspired by the customs of Cluny, which guided the practices of the first monks of Fruttuaria. The two men who took up the leadership in the first half of the eleventh century were direct disciples of William, and they slowly elaborated a cenobitic style specific to Fruttuaria, which long remained transmitted orally. Fruttuaria's observance drew the praise of even the most demanding reformers, such as Peter Damian in 1065, and was the basis of an expansion that ultimately led to the birth of an *ordo Fruttuariensis*, unified by its set of customaries and its privileged relationship with the papacy.[7]

---

6. Giovanni Lunardi, "I cavensi," in *Regulae-Consuetudines-Statuta: Studi sulle fonti normative degli ordini religiosi nei secoli centrali del Medioevo*, ed. Cristina Andenna and Gert Melville, Vita Regularis 25 (Münster: LIT Verlag, 2005), 141–55; Valerie Ramseyer, "Questions of Monastic Identity in Medieval Southern Italy and Sicily (c. 500-1200)," in *The Cambridge History of Medieval Monasticism in the Latin West*, ed. Alison I. Beach and Isabelle Cochelin (Cambridge: Cambridge University Press, 2020), 411.

7. Alfredo Lucioni, "L'abbazia, l'episcopato, il papato e la formazione della rete monastica di S. Benigno di Fruttuaria nel secolo XI," in *Il monachesimo del secolo XI nell'Italia nord-occidentale*, ed. Alfredo Lucioni (Cesena: Badia di Santa Maria del Monte, 2010), 237–308.

Besides Cluny, the papacy, within the framework of a larger movement of ecclesiastical reform, often turned to the strictest form of monasticism in order to impose reform. In Sardinia, for example, monks from Saint-Victor of Marseille, which had spearheaded the Gregorian reform in Provence, were sent to colonize the former insular foundations toward the end of the eleventh century.[8]

## Eremitic Movements and the Emergence of a New Italian Monasticism

It is undeniable that cenobitic monasticism around the year 1000, even in its most reforming guise, was strongly integrated into the social fabric and closely linked to the sphere of the lay aristocracy: aristocrats frequently visited monasteries where they were received as guests, and their children were educated in monastic schools. However, from the turn of the millennium, eremitic or markedly ascetic movements came to muddy these waters and instigated an Italian version of new monasticism. These movements started out as experiments around a charismatic figure, often that of a hermit, who was able to gather around him a critical number of disciples and donors.

### Charismatic Leaders

Such figures include Romuald of Ravenna, the embodiment of the new Latin eremitic spirituality of the millennium, who, after a brief stay at Sant'Apollinare in Classe, roamed around the Pyrenees and then, from 988, around central and northern Italy, from the Adriatic Plain to the Apennines. Although he was fleeing the world, Romuald was seldom alone: either he would choose to settle close to a monastery, from which he could receive necessities for his survival, or he would, though remote from everything, attract disciples, even crowds. Romuald's reforming spirit compelled him to embrace the Church at large. In common with Emperor Otto III he shared the aspiration to spread Christianity to the East. With the support of Holy Roman Emperor Henry II, he addressed

---

8. Michel Lauwers, "Réforme, romanisation, colonisation? Les moines de Saint-Victor de Marseille en Sardaigne (seconde moitié XI$^e$–première moitié XII$^e$ siècle)," in *La réforme "Grégorienne" dans le Midi, milieu XIe–début XIII$^e$*, Cahiers de Fanjeaux 48 (Toulouse: Privat, 2013), 257–310.

## 5. MONASTICISM

the problems of the restitution of churches, the violence of those who held power, and the oppression of the poor.

After all his wandering, Romuald is believed to have died on June 19, possibly in 1027, in a cell at the hermitage of Valdicastro, which he had founded a few years earlier. One of his disciples, Bruno of Querfurt, asserted that his master was "the father of the organized hermits who live according to a rule" (*pater rationabilium heremitarum qui cum lege vivunt*).[9] Indeed, while he never wrote down an eremitic rule, Romuald offered a model to the hermits who wished to live according to a *ratio* or a *lex*. One of the innovations of his model appears to have been the association between a community of hermits and a community of cenobites, with the hermits taking up the spiritual direction of both groups, and the cenobites acting as protectors and providers of material necessities. It is such a model that Romuald put to the test, although without enduring success, in various locations like Valdicastro (in the Marches), Sitria (located at the borders of Perugia, Pesaro, and Ancona), Pereo (an isle of the Po delta), and Biforco (now San Benedetto in Alpe, in an Apennine valley toward Ravenna), which would outlast Camaldoli—founded a few years before his death, thanks to the patronage of the bishops of Arezzo.

The life of Romuald is attested by two main sources, both of them hagiographical: the most complete and widely circulated is the *Vita beati Romualdi*, written by Peter Damian (1007–72). Peter Damian, converted in his youth through the fame of the hermit of Ravenna, wrote Romuald's *Vita* in around 1042, about fifteen years after the death of the saint. At this time, Peter Damian was living in the Apennines between the Marches and Umbria, at the hermitage of Santa Croce di Fonte Avellana, where he had first withdrawn ten years previously. He reformed this same community on the basis of Romuald's teachings, which he reinterpreted and systematized into an "eremitic rule" laid down in a letter addressed to his brothers. He also founded or reformed various eremitic communities in the vicinity of Fonte Avellana. However, after the invasion of Emperor Henry III into Italy in December 1046, Peter Damian's activity widened its scope as he abandoned his local monastic terrain and dedicated himself to reforming the institution of the Church at its core. It was indeed in this period that he came into conflict with other movements, which were supportive of a collective

---

9. Bruno of Querfurt, *Vita quinque fratrum*, ed. Reinhard Kade, Monumenta Germaniae Historica, Scriptores, 15.2 (Hannover: Monumenta Germaniae Historica, 1888), 718.

effort toward reform—involving both laypeople and hermits—including the group comprised of Giovanni Gualberto's disciples. In the midst of this polemic, Peter Damian relentlessly produced writings defining his deeply heroic and penitential conception of eremitic asceticism and its key role in ecclesial reform.

Giovanni Gualberto, who came from a family of the middling Chianti aristocracy, made his monastic profession in his youth at San Miniato al Monte, close to Florence. He is said to have rejected this hub of the local aristocracy due to his antisimoniac convictions, and then to have begun his fight against the prelates perceived to be guilty of this sin, starting with Bishop Attone of Florence (1032–46). Looking for a place conforming to his desire for moral rigor and his faithfulness to the *Rule of Saint Benedict*, Giovanni Gualberto settled on Vallombrosa, on the Tuscan side of the Apennines, with a small but growing group of disciples in the mid-1030s. The prestige of his new foundation quickly spread: other new foundations blossomed, and many preexisting monasteries passed into the hands of Gualberto's disciples. It is in such a successful context that we can situate the conflict, occurring in the 1060s, with the Florentine bishop Pietro Mezzabarba and his ally, Marquis Goffredo, that greatly shaped the identity of Vallombrosian monasticism and launched its monks onto the scene of radical reform.[10]

## Italo-Greek Monasticism

We cannot conclude this portrait of the Italian eremitic movements without touching upon the situation in the south of the peninsula, that is, upon the existence of a number of small Italo-Greek monastic foundations, which saw a renewed scholarly attention, claiming the primacy of asceticism over any form of structural organization. In spite of the presence of an increasingly dominant Latin monasticism, promoted by the Normans, followed by the Swabians and the Angevins, monastic life regulated by traditional Eastern normative sources (*typika*) endured into the thirteenth century in the south of the peninsula,

---

10. Nicolangelo D'Acunto, *I laici nella Chiesa e nella società secondo Pier Damiani: Ceti dominanti e riforma ecclesiastica nel secolo XI* (Rome: Istituto storico italiano per il Medio Evo, 1999), 168–80; Nicolangelo D'Acunto, *L'età dell'obbedienza: Papato, Impero e poteri locali nel secolo XI* (Naples: Liguori, 2007), 101–10, 147–56; Francesco Salvestrini, "Conflicts and Continuity in the Eleventh-Century Religious Reform: The Traditions of San Miniato al Monte in Florence and the Origins of the Benedictine Vallombrosan Order," *Journal of Ecclesiastical History* 72 (2021): 491–508.

in locales where the Greek population was concentrated—like southern Calabria, Sila, Salento, and other regions with strong Greek minorities. In general we are dealing here with small familial foundations, which were somewhat precarious and which followed various kinds of observances, from total eremitism to *lauras* (a cluster of cells of hermits with a common church) and cenobitism. Their founder was usually the landowner, while leadership was granted to a hegumen (i.e., abbot) who acted as the teacher and supervisor of the community. Some of these hegumens gained fame beyond their own community, such as Nil of Rossano (910–1005), the epitome of the virtuous ascetic, who founded monasteries while yet refusing to be at their head, instead entrusting their care to one of his disciples, as he himself withdrew increasingly from his foundations, exerting spiritual guidance over his community based on the model of his own life.

Far from disappearing or being forced to assimilate to Latin monasticism, this Italo-Greek monasticism was encouraged by the Norman rulers, who made it part of their campaign toward the control of ecclesiastical affairs and ensured the wealth of certain establishments like Santissimo Salvatore in Messina. Contrary to some common assumptions, the intervention of the papacy in Calabria and Sicily, enabled by Frederick II's nonage and lasting until his return from the German lands (1198–1220), cultivated this Italo-Greek monasticism. Such an intervention served as a means for the papacy to signal its policy of plurality in terms of rites, languages, and ecclesial organization. It is in this context of the integration of Byzantine monasticism into the Western Church that we should understand the admission of the "Rule of Saint Basil" into the limited number of monastic rules permitted by the Fourth Lateran Council, as well as the emergence, in the forms of the papal chancery, of the notion of the "Order of Saint Basil" in reference to the Italo-Greek monasteries, which had until then operated without these concepts of monastic rule and monastic order.[11]

Quite apart from the actual (yet elusive) situation on the ground, Greek monasticism in southern Italy was the focus of an imaginary representation of Eastern monasticism. This is attested by the many examples of wandering hermits who, between the eleventh and the twelfth centuries, travelled to these regions, which were considered (rightly or

---

11. Annick Peters-Custot, "Bessarion et le monachisme italo-grec: L'Orient en Italie du Sud?," *Cahiers d'études italiennes* 25 (2017), https://journals.openedition.org/cei/3616; Ramseyer, "Questions of Monastic Identity," 411–12.

wrongly) as a place where one could live out the ideal monastic life of the Desert Fathers, at the crossroads between Eastern cenobitism and eremitism, instead of risking a venture to distant Sinai, Constantinople, or Syria.

### Three Trajectories of the New Italian Monasticism

As a reflection of the individual journeys of Romuald, Peter Damian, and Giovanni Gualberto, reformed monasticism followed different trajectories as it emerged in the eleventh and twelfth centuries at the monasteries of Camaldoli, Fonte Avellana, and Vallombrosa, and in their dependancies. Indeed, the three movements diverged when it came to essential aspects such as the evaluation of the relationship between eremitism and cenobitism, the conception of ecclesiastical reform and the role played by monks within this same reform, and finally, the institutional shape that these experiences were supposed to take.

Though they were driven by a common desire to renovate the ecclesial institution and a shared resistance against certain practices linked to the system of the imperial Church, the reformers and their disciples did not adopt the same means to fight these ills. In Milan (within the framework of the movement of the Pataria) or in Florence, Giovanni Gualberto and his disciples had recourse to an extreme form of activism: monks were directly invested in the struggle against simony, which they conceived as a perfect cause to espouse. In contrast to this approach, Peter Damian directed his efforts, especially in the second part of his life, according to the will of the pope, the bishops, and the synods, and condemned the direct action of monks (and particularly of hermits) in the secular world, even for such issues as simony and the promotion of reform. The figure of the Florentine hermit Teuzone focuses these radically different approaches: Peter Damian accused him of being an impostor, since Teuzone was preaching in an urban environment and displaying his ascetic life to all, while in contrast Andrea da Strumi, one of Giovanni Gualberto's hagiographers, cited Teuzone as a model for Giovanni Gualberto.[12] As for the Camaldolese, they were less openly involved in the antisimony cause, except for one occasion,

---

12. Umberto Longo, "Pier Damiani 'versus' Teuzone: Due concezioni sull'eremitismo a confronto," in *Monaci, ebrei, santi: Studi per Sofia Boesch Gajano*, ed. Antonio Volpato (Rome: Viella, 2008), 63–77.

around 1091, when they opposed Daimberto, bishop of Pisa—a gesture that was vehemently condemned by Pope Urban II.

While the first disciples of Giovanni Gualberto, founder of Vallombrosa, supported the dismantling of the present ecclesiastical structure in the marquisate of Tuscany, which depended on a *consortium* between the pope and the margrave, they were not, however, entirely opposed to a monastic model based upon landholding. Like Romuald or Peter Damian, the Vallombrosans did not completely renounce—especially not under the pontificate of Urban II—an alliance with the great seigneurial families for the good of the revival of monasticism, nor did they fundamentally challenge the traditional relationship between monasticism and the local aristocracy.

As for the *propositum vitae*, the first monks of Fonte Avellana again observed practices quite different from those of Vallombrosa or Camaldoli. This is clear in respect to their attitude toward communal life and solitary life, as well as toward normative models. The experiences of Romuald and Giovanni Gualberto were characterized by a plurality of models: among them, one may count Benedict, of course, but also the apostles, Basil, and the Desert Fathers. Moreover, their *vitae*, composed as veritable fighting texts by their hagiographers (a young Peter Damian in the case of Romuald's life), were meant to fulfill an obvious normative function. It is only in the course of the second generation, under the aegis of Pope Urban II and the prior Bernardo degli Uberti, that the Vallombrosans were normalized according to the *Rule of Saint Benedict*, which led to the institutionalization of the congregation and the end of the monks' direct involvement within the reform. On the other hand, at Camaldoli, eremitism remained an essential characteristic, which defined the identity of the community as it developed into a full-fledged network and competed against other movements, like the neighboring Vallombrosa. Camaldoli's situation is explained by the clauses enshrined in the 1027 act of donation by Teodaldo, bishop of Arezzo, which irredeemably bound the original *fundus* to the faithfulness of the Camaldolese to their eremitic vocation.[13] In spite of this emphasis on eremitism, Romuald's disciples eventually assimilated

---

13. Edited in Giuseppe Vedovato, *Camaldoli e la sua congregazione dalle origini al 1184: Storia e Documentazione*, Italia Benedettina 13 (Cesena: Badia di Santa Maria del Monte, 1994), 279–85; French translation and commentary in Cécile Caby, "Les voies de l'érémitisme en Italie, X$^e$–XI$^e$ siècles," in *Le christianisme en Occident du début du VII$^e$ au milieu du XI$^e$ siècle*: Textes et documents réunis par François Bougard (Paris: SEDES, 1997), 319–33.

into their network not only eremitic communities, but also cenobitic monasteries, *hospitia*, and churches, often with the approval of bishops and the local aristocracy. While the Camaldolese absorbed such diverse communities, charismatic eremitism retained its revered status and attracted patronage in a way that would determine the structure of the Camaldolese congregation, centered around the hermitage of Camaldoli.

## From the Network to the Order

Throughout the eleventh century, the monastic networks we have discussed remained fluid and lacked structure. Their success or decline across time and, in particular, across space depended upon their ability to organize into religious orders in the course of the twelfth century.

While he was still alive, Peter Damian's Umbrian and Marchesian foundations remained communities institutionally distinct from Fonte Avellana, and were only related to one another and with the hermitage of Mount Catria by the figure of their founder. As such, in 1139, when Pope Innocent II confirmed the goods and dependencies of Fonte Avellana, and in doing so sketched the contours of the congregation, he made no mention of Peter Damian's personal foundations. This fluidity of the ties between the foundations and the ambiguity of their status between cenobitism and eremitism also characterized the foundations of Romuald of Ravenna. Indeed Romuald, with the help of the local powers in the areas he was wandering through, continued to establishing hermitages as well as male and female monasteries but never formally structured the relationships and the hierarchy between these foundations. A small number of them ended up part of the order that gradually grew around Camaldoli in the first decades of the twelfth century. In this regard, it is striking that Valdicastro, the place where Romuald ended his days and where his body lay, did not join the Camaldolese until the beginning of the fifteenth century. As for the houses that gravitated toward Vallombrosa—there were nine of them at the death of their founder—they were at first united only by links of a spiritual and moral nature, which did not entail anything concrete in institutional terms: they are mentioned in Giovanni Gualberto's last will or *testamentum* as links of charity and union (*vinculum caritatis* and *unio*). Yet the fact that these houses shared a common form of life (*conversatio*) constituted the first step, already at the end of the eleventh century, toward the formalization of the Vallombrosian family. At

Vallombrosa, such a process occurred at the time of the recording of the first customs of the community in the years 1095-1101. At Camaldoli, we witness the same phenomenon with the customary charter of Rodolfo I (1076-81/82), who insisted above all on the definition of the hierarchical relationship, in both legal and spiritual terms, between the hermitage and its *hospitium* (Fontebuono, located below the hermitage), which was transitioning towards cenobitism.[14]

Overall, it is not until the very end of the eleventh century, or even the beginning of the twelfth century, that these monastic networks acquired centralized structures of governance and control, which set them on the course toward becoming an order. In this context, the relationships to bishops, which had previously been similar to those we can observe in autonomous monasteries from central Italy, tended to change: the *libertas romana*—in its various forms and degrees—became a central element in the construction of the orders. Thus, at San Benigno de Fruttuaria, the establishment of written customs from the end of the eleventh century went hand in hand with the battle for securing exemption from the powers of the local bishop. Such a battle was endorsed by the privileges granted by Urban II (1096) and Paschal II (1101) and facilitated the process of transforming Fruttuaria from an abbey owning scattered land possessions to a centralized network with dozens of dependent priories.[15] At Camaldoli, Paschal II's bull of 1113 (called *Gratias Deo*) was a landmark toward the construction of the "order of the hermitage of Camaldoli and its *hospitium*," which would be overseen by a single governing body, constituted of the general prior, elected by the abbots, priors, and hermits of the congregation. The increasingly frequent conflicts with the bishops of Arezzo along with the rebellions of subordinate communities provided the opportunity for the ecclesiastical hierarchy, especially the papacy, to increase its authority at the expense of the order's autonomy. In spite of the countless concessions relinquished to the congregation, notably outside of the diocese of Arezzo, Camaldolese legislation failed to keep pace with these changes. For example, far from instituting a legal milestone, the book of customs called *Liber eremitice regule* (1158-76) and the brief

---

14. Pierluigi Licciardello, ed., *Consuetudo Camaldulensis, Rodulphi Constitutiones, Liber Eremiticae Regulae*, Edizione Nazionale dei Testi Mediolatini 8 (Florence: SISMEL-Edizioni del Galluzzo, 2004), xxi-lxxi.

15. Alfredo Lucioni, "L'evoluzione del monachesimo fruttuariense tra la fine dell'XI e la metà del XIII secolo: Dalla 'ecclesia' all''ordo,'" in *Il monachesimo italiano nell'età comunale*, ed. Francesco G. B. Trolese (Cesena: Centro Storico Benedettino Italiano, 1998), 97-138.

constitutions of Prior Placido (1180-88) discussed the definition of the relationships between eremitism and cenobitism in spiritual terms, oscillating between an origin narrative and a spiritual exegesis.[16] At Vallombrosa, on the other hand, institutionalization was well under way beginning with the abbacy of Bernardo degli Uberti (1099-1106) and continued by his immediate successors. The formalization of the Vallombrosian *conventus abbatum* and its role in recording written and prescriptive norms—already quite distinct from the earlier customs—laid the foundations for the organization of the order.[17]

At a later stage in the organizational normativization of these new orders, a common legislation is diffused to all the members of the congregation in order to regulate uniformity in spiritual matters (liturgy, habit, diet) and temporal ones (autonomous management, exclusion of certain sources of revenue, contribution to a joint fund), but also to set up a collegial government in charge of collectively elaborating the order's norms. Before the fourteenth century, such tools to ensure the smooth functioning of an order were absent from Peter Damian's network of foundations, but they developed quite early at Camaldoli and Vallombrosa. In order to understand this evolution, we need to take into account the influence of Cistercian monasticism in Italy. The influence of the Cistercian model of organization manifested itself either directly through the foundations affiliated to the order, or indirectly through its promotion by the papacy, starting with Innocent III, among the monastic networks of the eleventh and twelfth centuries and any new forms of religious life.

## Cistercians and Cistercian Models in Italy

Cistercian monasticism only began its spread in the Italian peninsula in the second generation of the order (1120-30). This first foray onto Italian soil was for the most part the product of Bernard of Clairvaux's trip to Italy in the context of his commitment to the cause of Pope Innocent II against his rival, the so-called antipope Anacletus. The first foundations in northern Italy were therefore direct dependents of Clairvaux,

---

16. Cécile Caby, *De l'érémitisme rural au monachisme urbain: Les Camaldules en Italie à la fin du Moyen Âge*, Bibliothèque des Écoles françaises d'Athènes et de Rome 305 (Rome: École française de Rome, 1999), 81-98, 151-72; Pierluigi Licciardello, ed., "Le Costituzioni di Placido, priore di Camaldoli (1180-1189/1190)," *Revue Bénédictine* 118 (2008): 69-88.

17. Francesco Salvestrini, *"Disciplina caritatis": Il monachesimo vallombrosano tra medioevo e prima età moderna* (Rome: Viella, 2008), 230-34.

as their names indicate: Chiaravalle Milanese (1135), a few kilometers south of Milan, and Chiaravalla della Colomba (1136), south of the Via Emilia between Piacenza and Parma. In 1139, Pope Innocent II entrusted the Cistercians of Milan with the task of reforming the monastery of San Pietro in Cerreto in the diocese of Lodi. The first abbot, Bruno, one of Bernard's close disciples, was abbot of both Cerreto and the Milanese foundation for a period of five years (1139–44). It is he who ought to be credited with the reform of the monastery of Santa Maria di Follina (Belluno) and the foundation of Chiaravalle di Fiastra in the Marches toward the end of the 1140s.

But Bernard's influence should not be overestimated, insofar as his presence in Italy was in the end quite brief and his success was limited to certain regions. Thus in southern Italy, the long postponed agreement between Roger II and Pope Innocent II (1139) did not result in an immediate entry of Clairvaux into the Kingdom of Sicily, where the Cistercian presence remained sporadic under the Hautevilles. Besides Bernard, we must turn to other actors: first of all (at least in chronological order) the feudal and imperial aristocracy. The filiation of La Ferté Abbey (the first daughter house of Cîteaux, some miles south), which was very present in Liguria, owed its swift expansion to these families. Before Bernard could even exert his influence, the Aleramici (a powerful aristocratic family later known as the del Bosco and di Ponzone) had founded Tiglieto, close to Genoa, in 1120, and some of their members later established the abbey of Lucedio in the diocese of Vercelli. From Lucedio, in 1180, a small group of monks founded Rivalta Scrivia near Tortona. As for the margraves of Vasto and their descendants, the counts of Saluzzo, they founded two daughter houses of Tiglieto: Staffarda (1135) and Casanova (1142).[18]

As for the Cistercian monastic presence in the *Regnum Siciliae*, if it was indeed the fruit of Clairvaux's network, it developed under the Hohenstaufen by way of the filiations of the abbeys in southern Latium (Fossanova or Casamari) or the Roman abbey of Tre Fontane, which was intimately connected to Innocent III and his interventionist policy in the south of the peninsula during Frederick II's minority. However,

---

18. Cécile Caby, "Les cisterciens dans l'espace italien médiéval," in *Unanimité et diversité cisterciennes: Filiations, réseaux, relectures du XII<sup>e</sup> au XVII<sup>e</sup> siècle* (Saint-Étienne: Publications de l'Université, 2000), 175–91; Guido Cariboni, "Der Zisterzienserorden in Italien: Ausbreitung und institutionelle Bindungen," in *Norm und Realität: Kontinuität und Wandel der Zisterzienser im Mittelalter*, ed. Franz J. Felten and Werner Rösener (Berlin: LIT Verlag, 2009), 411–40.

the abbeys of the Cistercian houses of the *Regnum*, which often arose out of the transformation of preexisting Latin or even Greek monasteries, seemed chiefly motivated by a sense of belonging to the Sicilian Church, in other words, a Church dominated by the monarch. In spite of being affiliated to the Cistercian order, which was very closely connected to the papacy, these abbeys did not become papal agents, at least not until the geopolitical conditions shifted after the death of Frederick II in 1250 and the establishment of the Angevin dynasty. At that time the Cistercian monasteries, like the other ecclesial structures of southern Italy, underwent a normativization resulting in a strengthening of their relationship to the papacy. It is, moreover, in the second half of the thirteenth century that a new phase of the Cistercian expansion into Sicily was inaugurated. This phase was initiated by the papacy, which handed over to the Cistercian abbeys control over small establishments as well as significant Italo-Greek monasteries.[19]

### Specific Characteristics and Local Interactions

Unlike the Burgundian ideal of foundation and dissemination through filiation, the expansion of the Cistercian *propositum* in Italy often operated through the affiliation of more or less ancient abbeys entrusted to the Cistercians' care by the pope, but also by bishops and members of the ruling urban elite, as was also the case with the new Italian monasticism. In this context, the number of incorporations relative to the number of foundations in the Cistercian diffusion in Italy is such that it determined the import of specific characteristics inherited from the local setting on monastic observance. The phenomenon is especially conspicuous in the abbeys of Latium, whose affiliation to the Cistercian order was mostly due to the policy of the popes in this region. Thus, the incorporation of the three abbeys of Sant'Anastasio alle Tre Fontane, Fossanova, and Casamari between 1135–40 and 1152 raised various questions about the management of their patrimony, which clashed with the prohibitions of Cistercian legislation regarding certain sources of income, such as churches or tithes, rents from mills or ovens, vills or villeins. A petition from the three abbeys was even submitted to the general chapter in order to earn a dispensation, which would allow

---

19. Annick Peters-Custot, *Les Grecs de l'Italie méridionale post-byzantine (IX$^e$-XIV$^e$ siècle)*: Une acculturation en douceur (Rome: École française de Rome, 2009), 530–32.

the Italian abbeys to preserve the entirety of their patrimony, including several churches and the right to collect tithes.[20]

In its campaign of regularization of the *vita religiosa*, the papacy in the thirteenth century often turned to the Cistercian normative model, though it did not always enforce complete integration into the order, especially in the cases of small communities of nuns or hermits. For instance, the Guglielmiti or Williamites, the heirs of the mysterious and potentially legendary William of Maleval (d. 1157, beatified in 1202) united by their shared observance, were spared assimilation into the order of the Hermits of St. Augustine in 1256 and managed to retain their juridical independence. In fact, from 1237 the institutionalization of the Williamites had been stalled by the process of regularization according to the Benedictine *Rule* and the Cistercian institutes. With papal support, the Williamites were recognized as an *ordo monasticus* ruled by a general chapter and expanded energetically, even in north Europe, although lacking administrative unity.[21]

Finally, Cistercian monasticism in Italy—or to be more precise, the specific Cistercian form we find in Sicily and southern Italy—gave rise to, despite itself, an exceptional if modest case of dissidence, in the network that developed around the monastery of Fiore and its famous abbot, Joachim. Fiore was thus regularized as an autonomous monastic order, ruled by the Rule of Benedict and the *institutio Florensium fratrum*, in the time of Celestine III and Innocent III. It all began in 1188-89 when Abbot Joachim left his abbey of Santa Maria di Corazzo along with his faithful disciple Rainerio of Ponza. Though it had been incorporated into the Cistercian order, the Calabrese abbey of Corazzo had for the most part continued living according to the model of the great abbeys in the Kingdom of Sicily. Joachim's arrival and his reforming ambitions were a source of tension, which ended with Joachim's abandonment of Corazzo, as he found himself unable to enact the strict Cistercian ideal he was seeking. Instead Joachim carried out his vision at his new foundation of Fiore in the mountainous plateau of La Sila. In the meantime, since he had neglected to present himself at the

---

20. Rinaldo Comba, "Aspects économiques de la vie des abbayes cisterciennes de l'Italie du Nord-Ouest (XII$^e$-XIV$^e$ siècle)," in *L'économie cistercienne: Géographie-Mutations du Moyen Âge aux temps modernes* (Auch: Abbey of Flaran, 1983), 119-33.

21. Frances Andrews, *The Other Friars: Carmelite, Augustinian, Sack and Pied Friars in the Middle Ages* (Woodbridge: Boydell, 2006), 76-77.

convocation of the chapter, he was condemned as a fugitive and apostate by the general chapter in 1195. Before his death in March 1202, a second monastery had been given to Joachim, and seven of them can be counted at the moment of the 1196 pontifical approval. Thanks to the patronage of Gregory IX, the order spread even beyond Calabria and penetrated into southern Latium (Ninfa and Anagni) and the region of Lucca.[22]

## The Papacy and the Institutionalization of the New Italian Monasticism

Cistercian monasticism fell short of fulfilling the demand for reformation of the monastic life across Italy. In many cases, it came into competition or was replaced by local initiatives, which were themselves adapting to some of the institutional characteristics of the Cistercian model. In the Latin parts of the *Regnum Siciliae*, the local demand for monastic renewal was channeled by regional networks revolving around Santa Maria di Pulsano, located on Mount Gargano in Apulia, a foundation of Giovanni da Matera (d. 1139); Santa Maria di Montevergine, northwest of Avellino, founded by Guglielmo da Vercelli (d. 1142) after a life of wandering and making foundations between Irpinia, Apulia, and Calabria; and Santa Maria di Gualdo Mazzoca. All of these networks synthesized, in various shapes and forms, the ascetic desire of eremitism and institutional renovation true to the cenobitism of the Benedictine *Rule*.[23]

In general, it is in such conditions of complementarity, if not of competition, that we can interpret the late and small-scale diffusion of the Cistercians in some parts of the Italian peninsula like Tuscany, which was already crisscrossed by Camaldolese and Vallombrosian foundations, two monastic families that from the end of the twelfth century, had moved toward centralized governance. It is indeed no coincidence that Pope Innocent III, in his project of reforming monasticism in central Italy, first relied upon the heads of these homegrown orders, namely the prior of Camaldoli (also general prior of the Camaldolese order), the prior of Vallombrosa, and a representative of the regular canons, also much praised by Innocent. From the first months of his

---

22. Valeria De Fraja, *Oltre Cîteaux: Gioacchino da Fiore e l'ordine florense* (Rome: Viella, 2006), chaps. 4–5.
23. Francesco Panarelli, "Reti monastiche in Italia meridionale tra X e XII secolo," in D'Acunto, *Dinamiche istituzionali delle reti monastiche e canonicali nell'Italia dei secoli X–XII*, 337–55.

pontificate, the two main vectors of Innocent III's policy, which would later be taken up by his successors, were on the one hand to galvanize the development of extant monastic congregations (like the Cistercians, who received the care of important abbeys) and of orders providing a local alternative to the Cistercian model, and on the other hand to encourage the unification of autonomous monasteries within structures akin to orders. This second aspect of his policy was carried out in 1203, through the instauration of general chapters for the abbeys directly subject to the *libertas romana*, which Innocent III interpreted in a novel manner as a form of protection entailing a duty of reform and control. As a matter of fact, the abbots of various regions were convoked to these chapters for the purpose of developing a common program of reform and supervision. In Italy, beyond the direct interventions of the pope in certain monasteries close to Rome (Subiaco, Farfa, San Martino al Cimino, and Montecassino), these chapters were organized at Perugia and Piacenza. We still have the letter of convocation of the first of these chapters, as well as a report written by the abbot of Rimini who participated in the chapter inaugurated on October 2, 1203, at Perugia, presided over by the bishop of Città di Castello, the prior of Camaldoli, and the prior of San Frediano of Lucca. Within the extensive list of abbots and autonomous monasteries, the report clearly values the abbots who represented, in addition to their own monastery, a network already on the way to becoming structured. Such is the case with Abbot Nicola of Santa Croce di Sassovivo and Abbot Benigno of Vallombrosa, under whose rule the Vallombrosian network was beginning to take a sharp turn toward institutionalization. In 1208, Pope Innocent III attempted once again to establish his control over the monasteries of Tuscany and its southern margins, by sending on a wide-scale visitation agents who had been present at the chapter of Perugia in 1203, such as the bishop of Florence (who had presided over the chapter when he was still prior of San Frediano), the prior of Camaldoli, and the abbot of Sassovivo.[24]

The concrete results of these measures were not immediate, although the constitution *In singulis regnis* of the Fourth Lateran Council had extended to the whole of Christendom the obligation for the superiors of monasteries of monks and canons regular, which were not constituted in an order, to meet in triennial chapters, prepared for and preceded by triennial visits organized by the monks and canons (and distinct

---

24. Michele Maccarrone, *Studi su Innocenzo III* (Padua: Editrice Antenore, 1972), 226–46.

from those of the bishops). Nonetheless, it is likely that small Italian congregations, like those of Vallombrosa or Camaldoli, benefited from the support that the papacy brought to the new structure they were introducing (such as visitations and the general chapter) and that they consolidated in the early decades of the thirteenth century. At Vallombrosa, the turning point came with the decision by Abbot Benigno, starting in 1206, to record the statutory legislation of the community, which implemented the holding of annual general chapters and instituted visitations. At Camaldoli, we preserve an important documentation on a long trial, which in 1216 opposed the hermitage as a *caput ordinis* to the bishop of Arezzo who claimed authority over the order. The debates were used by the Camaldolese as a platform to promote the institutionalization of the order. The testimonies collected by the inquiry (*inquisitio*) paint a picture of an order unified by its geographical space (in part legendary) centered around Camaldoli, but also by the regular meetings of the general chapter that held elective and deliberative functions, by its system of visitations, and by the centralizing role of the prior of Camaldoli, who was able to appoint and transfer monks and officers within the congregation. Apart from these exceptional documents and a handful of others, produced under Priors Martino II (1189–1205) and Guido II (1206–48), both of them very close to Innocent III, we must wait until the mid-thirteenth century to find the written evidence of a legislative shift, already discernible at the end of the twelfth century. Indeed in 1253, Martino III promulgated three books *de moribus* and a liturgical *ordo*, which formalized a set of practices constituting the basis for the *ius proprium* of the Camaldolese order.[25]

Once this statutory shift had occurred, the Camaldolese and Vallombrosian orders, as well as the small Sylvestrine order—which emerged out of the abbey of San Benedetto di Montefano (Marches of Ancona), founded in 1231 by Silvestro Guzzolini (ca. 1177–1267) and institutionalized according to the *Rule of Saint Benedict* by Innocent IV (1247)—tended to conform to the legislative processes of other Western religious orders in this period, including the mendicants. These legislative processes involved a constant revision of the *ius proprium* and the adoption of the innovations circulating in the monastic world: the role

---

25. Cécile Caby, "Règle, coutumes et statuts dans l'ordre camaldule (XI$^e$–XIV$^e$ siècle)," in Andenna and Melville, *Regulae-Consuetudines-Statuta*, 195–221; Martino III priore di Camaldoli, *Libri tres de moribus*, ed. and trans. Pierluigi Licciardello (Florence: Sismel–Edizioni del Galluzzo, 2013), 1–45.

of the definitors, the cardinal-protectors, etc. The evolution of the Sylvestrines, but also that of the disciples of Pietro da Morrone (1209-96), later Pope Celestine V, highlight the fact that from the Fourth Lateran Council and the Second Council of Lyon onward, the adoption of a written constitution was no longer a prerequisite toward papal approval, but was rather a step on the path toward approval. From 1263, the hermits of San Spirito di Maiella, not yet associated with the observance of any order ("qui nullius ordinis observantiis sunt adscripti"), were regularized by Urban IV into the so-called Benedictine order (*ordo sancti Benedicti*). Later on, in the aftermath of the Second Council of Lyon, the disciples of Pietro da Morrone were subject to this same observance by Pope Gregory X. It is only after his trip to Lyon and the approval of Gregory X that, in June 1275, Pietro da Morrone called the general chapter of the priors for the first time and decided to determine the constitutions that would state the specific vocation of his group within the *ordo sancti Benedicti*, to which it had just been incorporated, laying out the *doctrina* that he had until then only taught by *verbo et exemplo*.[26]

### The Status of Women?

Within the legislative compilations of these new orders, some statutes—whether isolated or collected in thematic subsections—concerned the religious life of women. Indeed, like the Cistercians, many monastic networks and orders in Italy somehow integrated female communities or double communities, such as San Salvatore di Goleto (Lucania, southern Italy), which was part of the Montevergine movement.[27] We are still far from a widespread understanding of this phenomenon, but all indications seem to suggest that the papacy and the bishops, overwhelmed with their pastoral role toward these *mulieres religiosae*, asked these networks and orders, and then beginning in the thirteenth century the mendicant orders, to act as instruments for regularizing the female experience of the *vita religiosa*. We should therefore not overlook the initiative of orders, or at least of certain communities, in their

---

26. Cécile Caby, "*Finis eremitarum*? Les formes régulières et communautaires de l'érémitisme," in *Ermites de France et d'Italie (XI$^e$-XV$^e$ siècles)*, ed. by André Vauchez (Rome: École française de Rome, 2003), 71-73.

27. Cristina Andenna, "Female Religious Life in the Twelfth and Thirteenth Centuries," in Beach and Cochelin, *The Cambridge History of Medieval Monasticism in the Latin West*, 2:1041.

desire to integrate female communities. For instance, the foundation of the female monastery of San Pietro di Luco (Mugello, Tuscany) was explicitly conceived in 1086 by the prior of Camaldoli in order to grant women—in particular those of the middling rural aristocracy, who were the patrons of their foundations—a religious outlet away from the promiscuity (*indiscretia comunio*) of men. Furthermore, from this monastery and thanks to the donations of the family supporting Luco, the monastery of Santa Cristina de Stifonte (in the rural hinterland of Bologna) was founded, probably before 1090. Its abbess turned out to be the daughter of the founder and first abbess of Luco. A century later (1186–87), a group of nuns of Stifonte in turn left the monastery and established the community of Santa Cristina de Quinto al Tiveron, in the Trevigiano. Adding another link to this chain of foundations, Santa Maria di Betleem, in the area of Bologna, sprouted out of Santa Cristina de Quinto al Tiveron. It was subjected by the family that founded it to the hermitage of Camaldoli and to the specific model of observance of Santa Cristina. We see here that the landowning strategies of seigneurial families and the expansion of the rising Camaldolese order worked together to constitute a female branch of the order.[28]

The institutional details and the daily concrete expression of the submission of female communities under the wing of an order remain understudied and require a case-by-case approach. Indeed, the solutions are very diverse and seem to have been elaborated through sporadic crises (economic hardships, moral scandal, conflict with the local clergy) that required the intervention of a representative of the order or from the pope, rather than through the *ius proprium* of the order. We can nevertheless enumerate some common characteristics that signaled a community's belonging to an order, like the contribution to the joint fund of the order (and thus the payment of taxes), the hosting of male superiors of the order, among them the general or the visitors, the dispatching of representatives to the general chapters, and at times the adoption of liturgical practices (like a shared sanctoral) and a habit. The third book of statutes of the Camaldolese prior Martino III thus devotes eight chapters (VII to XIV) to the nuns of the order, which are inserted after the chapters on the uniformity of the order (*De*

---

28. Caby, *De l'érémitisme rural au monachisme urbain*, 108–10; Isabella Gagliardi, "Il monastero di Luco nel contesto locale (XI–XII secolo)," in *I Camaldolesi nell'Appennino nel Medioevo*, ed. Andrea Barlucchi and Pierluigi Licciardello (Spoleto: Fondazione Centro italiano di studi sull'alto medioevo, 2015), 209–41.

*uniformitate ordinis*) and end with an invitation for the nuns to observe the constitutions in the books *de moribus*, as they are observed in male monasteries.[29] We should underscore that these chapters, like those of the Vallombrosian order directed at nuns, often copy the Cistercian statutes word for word, which highlights the role of the Cistercians if not in the uniformization of practices, then at least in the modeling of their legal formulation.

## Monks and Lay Men and Women in Medieval Italy

Italian monasticism, whether it was the fruit of the reform of the eleventh and twelfth centuries or heir to a more ancient monasticism, was primarily a monasticism of landowners. Defining the features of a specifically Italian type of monastic land management is probably impossible. The new Italian monasticism did not diverge much from its predecessor on this front. Even if Giovanni Gualberto was, according to his hagiographers, burning with such a desire for poverty that he discouraged his disciples from acquiring churches (*accipere capellas*), this tendency does not seem to have lasted long. Indeed, relying upon the seigneurial families for the building of their landed estates, none of the religious groups that developed in the twelfth century took it upon themselves, as the Cistercians or the hermits of Grandmont had, to decline certain types of possessions like churches, the income from altars, tithes, and the rights tied to the practice of the *cura animarum*.

### Lay Brothers and Sisters

While not completely dismissing a seigneurial form of exploitation of the land (which implied the involvement of dependent peasants), nor restricting themselves to a direct use of their lands, the new forms of Italian monasticism early on devised a distinct type of association between laypeople and the religious life. This took the form of a category of converts (*conversi, conversae*) different from previous models of lay conversion.[30] This category is especially well known in historiography

---

29. Martino III priore di Camaldoli, *Libri tres de moribus*, 260–67.
30. Cécile Caby, "Conversi, commissi, oblati et devoti: Les laïcs dans les établissements camaldules (XIII$^e$–XV$^e$ s.)," in *Les mouvances laïques des ordres religieux* (Saint-Étienne: Publications de l'Université, 1996), 51–65; Duane J. Osheim, "Conversion, Conversi, and the Christian Life in Late Medieval Tuscany," *Speculum* 58 (1983): 368–90; Francesco Salvestrini, "Natura e ruolo

on account of its adoption from the 1110s by the Cistercians, who defined its status and practices very rigorously in the *Usus conversorum* (1120s), which were regularly updated by the general chapter. Beyond this regularization, which certainly influenced other Italian orders (the statutes of the Camaldolese converts, covered in the three books *de moribus* mentioned above, are largely inspired by the Cistercian *Usus*), it is through the documents of practice that we can sketch a better picture of these *conversi* or lay brothers and sisters.

The function of the lay brothers and sisters in the new Italian monasticism went far beyond agricultural work. Most of them were in charge of the mediation (which was often made official by acts of procuration, recorded in the presence of a notary) between cloistered communities dedicated to prayer and the society around them. In rural environments, the *conversi* often acted as rural officers (*ministeriales*) and representatives of the monastic lordships, for instance in the *castra*. In urban milieus, they dealt with all kinds of transactions and acted on behalf of the communities in legal matters like civil or ecclesiastical trials. Finally, it is they who were tasked by the high-ranking officers of the order with carrying circular letters and other communications among the houses of the order. This is all in addition to the many priest-converts who oversaw the churches, especially the parish churches, belonging to the orders, and in doing so ensured that monks did not infringe canonical norms regarding enclosure and the pastoral care they ought to provide to the parishes under their authority. One thing is clear: these functions precluded that all *conversi* would be totally illiterate.

These lay brothers and sisters lived in religious establishments, in spaces—like the dormitory or the refectory—reserved for them, and the most elitist forms of monastic life were potentially open to them (such as reclusion at the hermitage of Camaldoli or eremitism at Celle in the Vallombrosian order). Aside from these lay brothers and sisters, we see the emergence around monasteries, especially urban ones, of groups of laypeople with diverse statuses and designations (*donati, commissi*), who bound themselves to the community in a more or less stable and dedicated way. While the *conversi* made a profession and lived apart but in the monastery, these *commissi* of both genders were linked by what appears to be a contract. This contract stipulated that the *commissi* would hand over their property to the community and adopt some monastic

---

dei conversi nel monachesimo vallombrosano (secoli XI-XV): Da alcuni esempi d'area toscana," *Archivio Storico Italiano* 159 (2001): 49-105.

obligations (chastity, obedience) in exchange for the usufruct of the property they had given up, which guaranteed them lodging and food for their lifetime, and sometimes monastic burial. Some of them even benefited from clerical privileges like the exemption from secular taxes, which did not fail to rile civil powers, particularly in an urban, communal context, where the number of these semireligious people was increasing.[31]

### Italian Monasticism and Attraction of the City

The Italian monasticism of the twelfth and thirteenth centuries was affected by the consequences of the marked urban development of the peninsula, as much on account of the competition caused by the territorial claims of the communes as on account of the strong pull exerted by the towns.[32]

The reorganization of religious life between the mid-eleventh and mid-twelfth centuries and the foundation of new churches in cities or their periphery on their way toward urbanization often prompted calls (on the part of bishops and/or the communities) for monks who would provide liturgical services and supervise these foundations. This reflects the idea that monks (or those they chose to assume the pastoral office) were deemed, in the eyes of the partisans of this reorganization, the religious personnel with the most experience and competence. Before the arrival of the mendicant orders in the thirteenth century, the new Italian monasticism thus took a significant part in the urban religious landscape. Nonetheless, we should not forget the role played by great monastic centers of the early Middle Ages, such as Nonantola, which possessed a dependency in Florence from the tenth century onward and which received the church of San Leonardo of Padua, which functioned as an urban parish served by monks beginning at the end of the

---

31. For instance Francesco Salvestrini, "Forme della presenza benedettina nelle città comunali italiane," *Mélanges de l'École française de Rome: Moyen Âge* 124, no. 1 (2012), https://journals.openedition.org/mefrm/327; Francesco Salvestrini, "Religious Orders and Cities in Medieval Tuscany (10th to 14th Centuries)," in *Life and Religion in the Middle Ages*, ed. Flocel Sabaté (Newcastle-upon-Tyne: Cambridge Scholars Publishing, 2015), 202–21.

32. Cécile Caby, "Les implantations urbaines des ordres religieux dans l'Italie médiévale: Bilan et propositions de recherche," *Rivista di storia e letteratura religiosa* 35 (1999): 151–79; Cécile Caby, ed., "Espaces monastiques et espaces urbains de l'Antiquité tardive à la fin du Moyen Âge," special issue, *Mélanges de l'École française de Rome: Moyen Âge* 124, no. 1 (2012), https://journals.openedition.org/mefrm/343.

century.³³ Likewise, foundations by counts or bishops were significant players, including the Badia Florentina, the project of Hugh, margrave of Tuscany. We should also add to this portrait the transfers of rural monasteries to the city (*inurbamento*), which were sometimes operated under coercion and duress by the communes who were seeking to eliminate any competition against their conquest of rural territory. Thus, at the turn of the twelfth and thirteenth centuries, the Commune of Arezzo, deeply concerned with the control of the local clergy, moved the cathedral, which used to be located in the periphery, to its center and imposed in the same period a compulsory *inurbamento* on the powerful abbey of Santa Fiora.³⁴

The distribution of obediences varied according to the individual towns, among which arose certain preferences for monastic families. Hence, while Pisa and Arezzo (the diocese in which Camaldoli was born) hosted most of the Camaldolese foundations, Florence was the chief urban site for the Vallombrosian family (eight establishments, including two female foundations and four churches and hospitals). For its part, Siena presented a more balanced monastic scene, probably because of the Cistercian presence at San Galgano.

Certain orders, like the Vallombrosians, had from their very origins a clear development in an urban setting. Other orders, like the Camaldolese, did so later on, and not without contradictions, given the defining role of charismatic eremitism within the order. Certain original experiments grew out of this context, such as urban hermitages like the *romitorio* of Santa Maria degli Angeli, founded in Florence at the very end of the thirteenth century, at the request of the poet Guittone d'Arezzo.³⁵ We can also cite the creation of the *ordo sancti Benedicti de Padua* as a symbol of this Italian symbiosis between certain forms of new monasticism and urban growth, but also of the pontifical orthodoxy defined by the Fourth Lateran Council. The center of the *ordo sancti Benedicti de Padua* was located in the monastery of San Benedetto, founded in

---

33. Giannino Carraro, "La parrocchia di S. Leonardo di Padova dipendenza Nonantolana (secc. XII-XVIII): Fondazione, sviluppo, soppressione," *Benedictina* 50 (2003): 35-88; Domenico Cerami, "I monasteri femminili dipendenti dall'abbazia di Nonantola (secc. IX-XIV)," *I quaderni del m.æ.s.: Journal of Mediæ Ætatis Sodalicium* 16 (2018): 117-20.

34. Jean Pierre Delumeau, *Arezzo: Espace et sociétés, 715-1230. Recherches sur Arezzo et son contado du VIIIᵉ au début du XIIIᵉ siècle*, 2 vols., Collection de l'École française de Rome 219 (Rome: École française de Rome, 1996), 1:641-88.

35. Cécile Caby, "Erémitisme et *inurbamento* dans l'ordre camaldule à la fin du Moyen Âge," *Médiévales* 28 (1995): 79-92.

1195 just outside the walls of the city of Padua. Other monastic groups (male, female, or even double communities) gravitated around this center, whether in the town itself or on its territory, and were looking for regularization. This explains why these groups were gathered into a congregation, approved by the papacy on May 30, 1224, and bestowed, ten years later, with the title of "white monks." This *ordo* was equally characterized by its local context and by its collegial structure, emphasized by the adoption of a general chapter and of regular visitations, as well as by the fostering of an organic relationship with the bishops, who presided over the annual capitulary meetings laid down by the *ordo*'s statutes from 1239.[36]

Far from being always idyllic, the relationships between the secular clergy and monks could be compared to what we know (often in more depth) about the conflictual relationships between the mendicants and the secular clergy in towns. At Forlì, Bishop Alessandro (1160-90) set up the Vallombrosians in his city from 1160, entrusting them with the care of two parishes (including the monastery of San Mercuriale). In contrast, his successor tried to impose control over the *cura animarum* of the whole town, which precipitated an endless legal controversy with the Vallombrosians, carrying over to his own successors and lasting through the 1230s. In this period, bishops, often with the support of communal authorities, were almost uniformly attempting to reclaim the parishes over which their episcopal seat had progressively lost any form of control. Such a phenomenon varied from town to town, but nonetheless fit a global pattern in favor of bishops, which culminated at the Council of Vienna and the *Constitutiones Clementinae* of 1311-14.[37] This episcopal restoration moreover reacted to the fact that many monastic families, who had come early on into possession of these parish churches, had in the meanwhile received wide-ranging exemptions from the papacy. Thus, in Florence, a few years after the synodal statutes of 1310, the bishop prohibited monks from living outside of their houses. In the same way, two rubrics of the urban statutes of 1322-25 and 1355 tried to reinforce the jurisdiction of the commune over the monks of the Vallombrosian order and to restrict the rights of the *conversi*, whose

---

36. Antonio Rigon, "Ricerche sull'Ordo sancti Benedicti de Padua' nel XIII secolo," *Rivista di storia della Chiesa in Italia* 29 (1975): 511-35; Antonio Rigon, "Monasteri doppi e problemi di vita religiosa femminile a Padova nel Due e Trecento," in "Uomini e donne in comunità," special issue, *Quaderni di storia religiosa* 1 (1994): 221-57.

37. Giuseppe Alberigo et al., eds., *Conciliorum oecumenicorum decreta* (Bologna: Edizioni Dehoniane, 1991), 4:362-63.

status in between the boundaries of lay and religious life required clarification on the side of the law.[38]

From an economic perspective, the monastic presence in towns took two main forms. It derived first of all from the practice of monasteries of the *contado* of founding urban dependencies, whether they were granaries or hostelries, which slowly turned into proper monastic establishments. This is what we see with Sant'Urbano of Padua, which was created in order to serve as the *procuratoria* of the monastery of Praglia in town, at a time when Padua itself was undergoing an economic, political, and cultural boom between the twelfth and thirteenth centuries. The church was founded and quickly erected in the very heart of the city (1185-86), not far from the cathedral and the communal palace, which were themselves in the process of being built. The *domus Sancti Urbani*, whose multiple functions (prayers, hospitality, business) came after, was soon taking an active part in the cultural flourishing of the town. It is there (*in claustro Sancti Urbani*) that in April 1262, the notary Rolandino read out loud his *Chronicle of the Facts of the March of Treviso*—an account of the Paduan struggle against Ezzelino da Romano—in front of an audience of doctors and masters, and of the association of arts students and graduates of the fledgling university.[39] Far from being an isolated case, the close links between the *domus* of Sant'Urbano and the university recalls the custom, practiced by monastic families, of sending their members to study in towns, or to organize actual colleges or houses for their students in some cities boasting a university *studium*. This state of affairs even preceded the papacy's enforcement of common rules for the collective organization of university studies among the orders. Thus starting from the end of the thirteenth century, the Camaldolese used the monasteries of Bologna to host the students of the order who were attending classes.[40] Because of the wars that devastated the territories of various Italian cities in the fourteenth century, these urban houses turned into safe houses. In April 1314, the chapter of the monastery of Praglia, which had been destroyed by the fighting, convened at its *domus* in Padua.[41] First used as a temporary

---

38. Salvestrini, "Forme della presenza benedettina," 1.
39. Antonio Rigon, "S. Urbano di Padova 'procuratoria' del monastero di Praglia," in *L'abbazia di Santa Maria di Praglia*, ed. Callisto Carpanese and Francesco Trolese (Milan: Silvana editoriale, 1985), 56–62.
40. Caby, *De l'érémitisme rural au monachisme urbain*, 276–77.
41. Rigon, "S. Urbano di Padova 'procuratoria' del monastero di Praglia."

place of respite and reclusion, these *domus* ended up becoming, in some cases, the most important element of the rural monastery/urban house combination.

Secondly, if we consider the patrimony of urban monasteries, we come to the conclusion that these urban monasteries invested more into towns than did the great rural monasteries overseeing agricultural landed lordships. These investments can be divided into two types of goods: on the one hand, real estate in towns (houses or building lots); on the other hand, treasury bills, as credit developed as a means for financing communal life, especially from the fourteenth century onward. The control of urban real estate by Italian monks deserves our attention because of its consequences for the fabric of urban space at the turn of the twelfth and thirteenth centuries. In Florence, the discrepancy in value between rural lots and building lots located in towns or close to towns pushed the monks of Florence toward urban investments from the second half of the twelfth century. But this phenomenon of subdividing the land into parallel lots, offering the possibility of erecting one or many buildings, all under the jurisdiction of the monks-property developers, was especially forceful in other cities, like Brescia around Santa Giulia, Bologna around Santo Stefano, Genoa around the female monastery of Sant'Andrea della Porta, or Venice around San Zaccaria, to name only a few examples.[42]

In central Italy, these monks, accustomed to urban life, often performed technical or high-level tasks within communal administrations, including in the fields of engineering, accounting, recording and documenting, and even diplomacy as they acted as ambassadors on behalf of their town. The office of the *Biccherna* (the leading financial magistracy) of the commune of Siena was therefore often placed under the supervision of a treasurer who came from a religious order, like the Cistercians of San Galgano. It is one of them, a certain brother Ugo, who is depicted upon the painted cover of the accounting ledger of the year 1258, the first of a rich series of 254 painted wood tablets.[43]

---

42. Étienne Hubert, "Propriété ecclésiastique et croissance urbaine (à propos de l'Italie centro-septentrionale, XII$^e$–début du XIV$^e$ siècle)," in *Gli spazi economici della Chiesa nell'Occidente mediterraneo (secoli XII–metà XIV)* (Pistoia: Centro italiano di studi e storia d'arte, 1999), 125–55.

43. Frances Andrews, ed., with Maria Agata Pincelli, *Churchmen and Urban Government in Late Medieval Italy, c.1200–c.1450: Cases and Contexts* (Cambridge: Cambridge University Press, 2013), 237–50, 277–78.

## Toward a New Monastic Phase in Italy?

While it did not entirely disappear from the religious landscape of the Italian peninsula, it is undeniable that Italian monasticism, in the various forms it took, suffered from the political and economic transformations that shook the peninsula, but also from the competition of other players, like the mendicant orders. Thus, in the domain of cultural practices, while some monks attended the great urban *studia*—first as individuals but later increasingly within a collective framework set by their orders—and contributed to the scholastic disciplines, they no longer acted as pioneering figures of innovation. In the same vein, the crisis of the land rents, the struggle of new urban powers over rural lordships, and the rise of tax collections of all kinds all had a negative impact upon the finances of the landowning monks and their power over their estates and their inhabitants.

In this context, we can observe that it is the most ascetic forms of religious life, inclined toward solitude, that were best able to attract the patronage of laypeople. The mendicant orders themselves were not safe from this fascination for the ideal of the Desert Fathers. This is the ideal to which a number of Camaldolese foundations adhered, such as the hermitage of Santa Maria degli Angeli in Florence (1293) or San Mattia of Murano, in the Venetian lagoon, which founded and reformed many monasteries of strict observance—often called hermitages in our sources—in Venetia and around the Via Emilia throughout the fourteenth century.[44] The same phenomenon occurred with the second wave of diffusion of the Carthusian order in Italy, which initially remained limited to a few specific locations. We may recall that the trip to Calabria that Bruno of Cologne (ca. 1024/31–1101), founder of the Grande Chartreuse, had made upon the invitation of Pope Urban II did not result in a foundation like the one Bruno had left behind him in the diocese of Grenoble. The house he founded—Santa Maria *de Turri* or *de Heremo*, close to the *castrum* of Stilo—was quickly turned into a Cistercian establishment (at end of the twelfth century) and did not return to the Carthusians before 1514.[45] It is thus only in the subalpine region that we can find Carthusian foundations between the years 1170 and 1250, clearly on account of the geographical proximity to the first

---

44. Caby, *De l'érémitisme rural au monachisme urbain*, 193–95, 227–34.
45. Annick Peters-Custot, *Bruno en Calabre: Histoire d'une fondation monastique dans l'Italie normande. S. Maria de Turri et S. Stefano del Bosco* (Rome: École française de Rome, 2014), 57–177.

foundations of the order. The few exceptions came about thanks to the intervention of the papacy, like the affiliation of the Carthusian house of Trisulti, which emerged from the reform of a Benedictine community initiated by the pope in 1204. It is between 1301 and 1455 that the number of Italian foundations increased—twenty-eight between 1285 and the end of the fourteenth century—and the Chartreuse extended its spatial influence. This was the work of great figures like Niccolò Acciaiuoli, founder of the Carthusian house of Galluzo close to Florence (1342), or the dukes of Milan, Gian Galeazzo and Filippo Maria Visconti, patrons of the Chartreuse of Pavia, or bishops like the bishop of Siena, in whose diocese three Carthusian houses were founded between 1314 and 1345.[46]

Finally, the fascination for solitude and asceticism was the cause of the foundation of new monastic branches, mostly attached to the order of Saint Benedict, as stipulated by conciliar injunctions: the Sylvestrines, the Celestines, or in the middle of the fourteenth century, the Olivetans. The abbey of Monteoliveto arose around 1313-19 from the withdrawal of some of the members of the great families of Siena, among them Bernardo Tolomei, to their rural domain of Acona in order to live the ideals of solitude and poverty—in part forgotten by the Franciscans of the Sienese convent—while respecting ecclesiastical norms, in contrast to some contemporary Tuscan groups of *Fraticelli* or Spirituals. The form of life of Monteoliveto was canonically approved by the papacy in 1324 and spread rapidly in central and northern Italy. While it synthesized the chief institutional characteristics of monasticism, as had been defined by the conciliar injunctions of the thirteenth century, the order of Monteoliveto introduced various innovations, like the rotation of abbatial duties, as a response to the pressures exerted upon monastic communities by the new curial practices of beneficial appointments. In this way, it announced and anticipated the monastic observances of the end of the fourteenth and the fifteenth centuries.[47]

---

46. Franco Dal Pino, "Il secolo delle certose italiane: Inizi Trecento-metà Quattrocento," *Annali di Storia Pavese* 25 (1997): 37-48.

47. Cécile Caby, "La papauté d'Avignon et le monachisme italien: Camaldules et Olivétains," in *Il monachesimo italiano nel secolo della grande crisi*, ed. Giorgio Picasso and Mauro Tagliabue (Cesena: Centro Storico Benedettino Italiano, 2004), 23-41; Michele Pellegrini, "La conversione di frate Bernardo: Realtà e memoria delle origini olivetane nella Toscana del primo Trecento," in *Bernardo Tolomei e le origini di Monte Oliveto*, ed. Giancarlo Andenna and Mauro Tagliabue (Cesena: Badia di Santa Maria del Monte, 2020), 29-70.

## Selected Bibliography

### Primary Sources

*Alle fonti della spiritualità Silvestrina*. Fabriano: Monastero di S. Silvestro Abbate, 1983–2002: vol. 1, *Regola e Vita di S. Benedetto*, edited by L. Sena and V. Fattorini; vol. 2, *Vita di san Silvestro, beato Giovanni dal Bastone, beato Ugo, san Bonfilio*, edited by Ugo Paoli; vol. 3, *Costituzioni dell'ordine di S. Benedetto di Montefano*, edited by L. Bux and V. Fattorini.

Bruno of Querfurt. *Vita quinque fratrum*. Edited by Reinhard Kade. Monumenta Germaniae Historica Scriptores 15.2. Hannover: Monumenta Germaniae Historica, 1888.

Licciardello, Pierluigi, ed. *Consuetudo Camaldulensis, Rodulphi Constitutiones, Liber Eremiticae Regulae*. Edizione Nazionale dei Testi Mediolatini 8. Florence: SISMEL-Edizioni del Galluzzo, 2004.

———, ed. "Le Costituzioni di Placido, priore di Camaldoli (1180–1189/1190)." *Revue Bénédictine* 118 (2008): 69–88.

Martino III priore di Camaldoli. *Libri tres de moribus*. Edited and translated by Pierluigi Licciardello. Florence: Sismel-Edizioni del Galluzzo, 2013.

Monks of the Abbaye Notre-Dame de Maylis, eds. and trans. *Regardez le rocher d'où l'on vous a taillés: Documents primitifs de la Congrégation Bénédictine de Sainte-Marie de Mont-Olivet*. Maylis: Abbaye Notre-Dame de Maylis, 1996.

Peter Damian. *Die Briefe des Petrus Damiani*. Edited by Kurt Reindel. 4 vols. Monumenta Germaniae Historica, Die Briefe der deutschen Kaiserzeit 4. Munich: Monumenta Germaniae Historica, 1983–93.

Petri Damiani. *Vita beati Romualdi*. Edited by Giovanni Tabacco. Roma: Istituto Storico Italiano per il Medio Evo, 1957.

Spätling, Luchesius G., and Peter Dinter, eds. *Consuetudines Fructuarienses-Sanblasianae*. Corpus consuetudinum monasticarum 12. Siegburg: F. Schmitt, 1985–87.

Vasaturo, Nicola R., ed. *Acta capitulorum generalium Congregationis Vallis Umbrosae*. Vol. 1, *Institutiones abbatum (1095–1310)*. Rome: Edizioni di Storia e Letteratura, 1985.

### Secondary Sources

Andenna, Cristina, and Gert Melville, eds., *Regulae-Consuetudines-Statuta: Studi sulle fonti normative degli ordini religiosi nei secoli centrali del Medioevo*. Vita Regularis 25. Münster: LIT Verlag, 2005.

Andenna, Giancarlo, ed. *Dove va la storiografia monastica in Europa? Temi e metodi di ricerca per lo studio della vita monastica e regolare in età medievale alle soglie del terzo millennio. Atti del Convegno internazionale (Brescia-Rodengo, 23–25 marzo 2000)*. Milan: Vita e Pensiero, 2001.

———. "Guglielmo da Vercelli e Montevergine: Note per l'interpretazione di una esperienza religiosa del XII secolo nell'Italia meridionale." In *L'Esperienza Monastica Benedettina e la Puglia*, edited by Cosimo Damiano Fonseca, 1:87–118. Galatina: Lecce, 1983.

———. "I priorati cluniacensi in Italia in et. comunale (secoli XI–XIII)." In *Die Cluniazenser in ihrem politisch-sozialen Umfeld*, edited by Giles Constable, 485–521. Münster: Lit, 1998.

Avarucci, Giuseppe, Rosa Marisa Borraccini Verducci, and Gianmario Borri, eds. *Libro, scrittura, documento della civiltà monastica e conventuale nel Basso Medioevo (secoli XIII–XV)*. Spoleto: Centro italiano di studi sull'alto medioevo, 1999.

Beach, Alison I., and Isabelle Cochelin, eds. *The Cambridge History of Medieval Monasticism in the Latin West*. 2 vols. Cambridge: Cambridge University Press, 2020.

Caby, Cécile. *De l'érémitisme rural au monachisme urbain: Les Camaldules en Italie à la fin du Moyen Âge*. Bibliothèque des Écoles françaises d'Athènes et de Rome 305. Rome: École française de Rome, 1999.

———, ed. "Espaces monastiques et espaces urbains de l'Antiquité tardive à la fin du Moyen Âge." Special issue, *Mélanges de l'École française de Rome: Moyen Âge* 124, no. 1 (2012). https://journals.openedition.org/mefrm/343.

Caby, Cécile, and Pierluigi Licciardelli, eds. *Camaldoli e l'ordine camaldolese dalle origini alla fine del XV secolo*. Cesena: Centro storico benedettino, 2014.

Cariboni, Guido. "Cistercian Nuns in Northern Italy: Variety of Foundations and Construction of an Identity." In *Women in the Medieval Monastic World*, edited by Janet E. Burton and Karen Stöber, 53–74. Medieval Monastic Studies 1. Turnhout: Brepols, 2015.

Cariboni, Guido, and Nicolangelo D'Acunto, eds. *Costruzione identitaria e spazi sociali: Nuovi studi sul monachesimo cistercense nel Medioevo*. Spoleto: Centro italiano di studi sull'alto medioevo, 2017.

Carrara, Valerio. *Reti monastiche nell'Italia padana: Le chiese di San Silvestro di Nonantola tra Pavia, Piacenza e Cremona, secc. IX–XIII*. Modena: Aedes Muratoriana, 1998.

Carraro, Silvia. *La laguna delle donne: Il monachesimo femminile a Venezia tra IX e XIV secolo*. Pisa: Pisa University Press, 2015.

Comba, Rinaldo Merlo, and Giovanni Grado, eds. *Certosini e Cistercensi in Italia (secoli XII–XV)*. Cuneo: Società per gli Studi Storici, Archeologici ed Artistici della Provincia di Cuneo, 2000.

D'Acunto, Nicolangelo, ed. *Dinamiche istituzionali delle reti monastiche e canonicali nell'Italia dei secoli X–XII (Fonte Avellana, 29–31 agosto 2006)*. Negarine di S. Pietro in Cariano (Verona): Il segno dei Gabrieli editori, 2007.

———. *L'età dell'obbedienza: Papato, Impero e poteri locali nel secolo XI*. Naples: Liguori, 2007.

———. *I laici nella Chiesa e nella società secondo Pier Damiani: Ceti dominanti e riforma ecclesiastica nel secolo XI*. Rome: Istituto storico italiano per il Medio Evo, 1999.

———, ed. *Papato e monachesimo "esente" nei secoli centrali del Medioevo*. Florence: Reti Medievali-Firenze University Press, 2003.

Dal Pino, Franco. "Il secolo delle certose italiane: Inizi Trecento–metà Quattrocento." *Annali di Storia Pavese* 25 (1997): 37–48.

De Fraja, Valeria. *Oltre Cîteaux: Gioacchino da Fiore e l'ordine florense*. Rome: Viella, 2006.

Grillo, Paolo. *Monaci e città: Comuni urbani e abbazie cistercensi nell'Italia nord-occidentale (sec. 12.–14.)*. Milan: Edizioni Biblioteca francescana, 2008.

Guerrieri, Elisabetta. *Clavis degli autori camaldolesi (secoli XII–XVI)*. Florence: SISMEL-Edizioni del Galluzzo, 2012.

Longo, Umberto. *Come angeli in terra: Pier Damiani, la santità e la riforma del secolo XI*. Rome: Viella, 2012.

Lucioni, Alfredo. "Percorsi di istituzionalizzazione negli 'ordines' monastici benedettini tra XI e XIII secolo." In *Pensiero e sperimentazioni istituzionali nella "Societas Christiana" (1046–1250)*, edited by Giancarlo Andenna, 429–61. Milan: Vita e Pensiero, 2007.

Merlo Grado, Giovanni. "Le riforme monastiche e la 'vita apostolica.'" In *Storia dell'Italia religiosa*, vol. 1, *L'antichità e il medioevo*, edited by André Vauchez, 271–91. Bari: Editori Laterza, 1993.

Monzio Compagnoni, Giordano, ed. *L'"Ordo Vallisumbrosae" tra XII e XIII sec.: Gli sviluppi istituzionali e culturali e l'espansione geografica (1101–1293)*. Vallombrosa: Edizioni Vallombrosa, 1999.

Panarelli, Francesco. *Dal Gargano alla Toscana: Il monachesimo riformato latino dei Pulsanesi (secoli XII–XIV)*. Rome: Istituto Storico Italiano per il Medio Evo, 1997.

Paoli, Ugo, ed. *Silvestro Guzzolini e la sua congregazione monastica*. Fabriano: Monastero di S. Silvestro Abbate, 2001.

Pellegrini, Luigi. *"Che sono queste novità?": Le Religiones novae in Italia meridionale (secoli XIII e XIV)*. Naples: Liguori, 2000.

Peters-Custot, Annick. *Bruno en Calabre: Histoire d'une fondation monastique dans l'Italie normande. S. Maria de Turri et S. Stefano del Bosco*. Rome: École française de Rome, 2014.

———. *Les Grecs de l'Italie méridionale post-byzantine (IX$^e$–XIV$^e$ siècles): Une acculturation en douceur*. Rome: École française de Rome, 2009.

Picasso, Giorgio, and Mauro Tagliabue, eds. *Il monachesimo italiano nel secolo della grande crisi*. Cesena: Centro Storico Benedettino Italiano, 2004.

Polonio, Valeria. "Il monachesimo nel Medioevo italico." In *Chiesa, chiese, movimenti religiosi*, edited by Glauco Maria Cantarella, Valeria Polonio, and Roberto Rusconi, 84–187. Bari: Editori Laterza, 2001.

Ramseyer, Valerie. "Questions of Monastic Identity in Medieval Southern Italy and Sicily (c. 500–1200)." In *The Cambridge History of Medieval Monasticism in the Latin West*, edited by Alison I. Beach and Isabelle Cochelin, 1:399–414. Cambridge: Cambridge University Press, 2020.

Salvestrini, Francesco. *"Disciplina caritatis": Il monachesimo vallombrosano tra medioevo e prima età moderna*. Rome: Viella, 2008.

———. "Per un bilancio della più recente storiografia sul monachesimo italico d'età medievale." *Quaderni di storia religiosa medievale* 22, no. 2 (2019): 307–61.

———. *Santa Maria di Vallombrosa: Patrimonio e vita economica di un grande monastero medievale*. Florence: Olschki, 1998.

Spinelli, Giovanni, ed. *Il monachesimo italiano dall'età longobarda all'età ottoniana (secc. VIII–X)*. Cesena: Badia di Santa Maria del Monte, 2006.

Toubert, Pierre. *Les structures du Latium médiéval: Le Latium méridional et la Sabine du IX$^e$ siècle à la fin du XII$^e$ siècle*. 2 vols. Rome: École française de Rome, 1973.

Trolese, Francesco G.-B., ed. *Il monachesimo italiano nell'età comunale*. Cesena: Centro Storico Benedettino Italiano, 1998.

Vauchez, André, ed. *Ermites de France et d'Italie (XI$^e$–XV$^e$ siècles)*. Rome: École française de Rome, 2003.

Vedovato, Giuseppe. *Camaldoli e la sua congregazione dalle origini al 1184: Storia e documentazione*. Italia Benedettina 13. Cesena: Badia di Santa Maria del Monte, 1994.

Violante, Cinzio, Amleto Spicciani, and Giovanni Spinelli, eds. *L'Italia nel quadro dell'espansione del monachesimo cluniacense*. Cesena: Centro Storico Benedettino Italiano, 1985.

*Vita religiosa al femminile (secoli XIII–XIV): Atti del Ventiseiesimo Convegno Internazionale di Studi del Centro italiano di studi di storia e d'arte (Pistoia, 19–21 maggio 2017)*. Rome: Viella, 2019.

Vitolo, Giovanni. "Il monachesimo benedettino nel Mezzogiorno angioino: Tra crisi e nuove esperienze religiose." In *L'état angevin: Pouvoir, culture et société entre XIII$^e$ et XIV$^e$ siècle*, 205–20. Rome: École française de Rome, 1998.

West-Harling, Veronica, ed. "Il Monachesimo femminile in Italia nei secoli VIII–XI: Famiglia, potere, memoria." Monographic section in *Reti Medievali Rivista* 20, no. 1 (2019): 327–578. https://doi.org/10.6092/1593-2214/6073.

Zarri, Gabriella, ed. *Il monachesimo femminile in Italia dall'alto medioevo al secolo XVII a confronto con l'oggi*. Negarine di San Pietro in Cariano: Il segno dei Gabrieli editori, 1997.

CHAPTER 6

# Lay Confraternities
*Marina Gazzini*

Confraternities are an associative experience common to all human civilizations, in the lay as well as the religious sphere. Ubiquitous in space and transversal in time, the historical object "confraternity" defies any precise definition. Responding to the question, "What is a confraternity?" is difficult, even when we confine the question to a period, like the Middle Ages, and to an area, Italy, and even to a *societas*, such as the Christians. A broad definition could be the following: a group variously composed of the laity and clerics, men and women, associated in cities as well as in the countryside for purposes of religious edification, devotional solidarity, liturgical activity, penitential and charitable practice, socialization, pedagogical growth, and mutual support. There are, however, forms of *fraternitates* that do not all fit into the category of confraternity even if they are strictly similar. These range from the *scholae* of Byzantine Italy, which were not always easily distinguishable as professional or devotional associations, to the colleges of clerics, each responsible for one church, and the prayer unions that included the laity in a spiritual brotherhood not affiliated with religious communities.

On the other hand, the Middle Ages was a golden age for the development of associationism in general, whether it was for devotional reasons, or whether it derived from the need for professional organization, political distinction, the defense of identity, or social protection. In the Middle Ages, to an even greater extent than today, it was difficult to imagine existing without codified social relations within a group organized in a more or less stable manner. Being part of an association meant entering into a context that protected and conferred an accepted and recognized identity, that of a fellow citizen, a confrere, a colleague, or a good neighbor. If there were no important blood relations, remaining outside these contexts could mean, above all, the exclusion from the sphere of civil rights and the impossibility of accessing any network of economic, legal, and spiritual support.

## Terminology and Definition of the Phenomenon

As the confraternity is a difficult phenomenon to circumscribe, historians have often resorted to circumlocutions to try to capture the essence of these formations in order to indicate what type of group and organization they had in mind. For example, Gioacchino Volpe defined confraternities effectively as "the formation of a group on a religious, or at least religiously motivated basis," because he rightly placed them within the broader framework of religious movements of the Middle Ages.[1] Gabriel Le Bras grasped the important function of social protection carried out by these groups, by understanding them as "artificial families."[2] Finally, Edoardo Grendi spoke of "associative and religious phenomena" to underline the inseparable nature of the two aspects—one relating to associative dynamics and the other pertaining to the sphere of religiosity—that constituted the morphology of the medieval confraternities.[3]

Even in the past, the question did not have a clear answer. In sources from the Middle Ages, the associations that in the major European languages are called by a variety of terms today (for example, *confraternita, confraternity, gild/guild, confrérie, confradía, confraria, Bruderschaft,*

---

This chapter was translated by Carolyn Quijano.

1. Gioacchino Volpe, *Movimenti religiosi e sette ereticali nella società medievale italiana: Secoli XI–XIV* (Florence: Vallecchi, 1922), 170.

2. Gabriel Le Bras, "Les confréries chrétiennes: Problèmes et propositions," *Revue historique de droit français et étranger* 19–20 (1940–41): 311.

3. Edoardo Grendi, "Le confraternite come fenomeno associativo e religioso," in *Società, Chiesa e vita religiosa nell' "ancien régime,"* ed. Carla Russo (Naples: Guida, 1976), 115–86.

*Gilde, Broederschap*) were known by other terms, which stood for diversified associative realities that only partly coincided with modern confraternities. Some of these were *schola, consortium, confraternitas, fraternitas, congregatio, societas, universitas,* and *gilda.* There were also innumerable vernacular variations that have perceptible semantic differences depending on the diverse geographic areas and are too numerous to examine in detail here, but we need to bear them in mind as they have provided historians with a lively field of discussion. On this question of terminology, classic debates have focused on the relationship between confraternities and corporations, and on the continuity between the associationism of the Roman period and that of the Middle Ages (for example, on the basis of the survival of the word *schola*). More recently, attempts have been made to identify elements common to the different forms of community that characterized all of medieval Europe, with interesting proposals on the use of the term *Gilde* for the Germanic world, and *universitas* for the Latin world.[4]

## Legal Profile and Legislation

Not even the law can help us to resolve every element of uncertainty. Medieval legal doctrine regarded the confraternities as *collegia licita causa religionis*, without jurisdictional powers, and within the system of the *ius civile commune*, but at the same time it included them, together with hospitals and *fabricae*, bodies in charge of church maintenance, among the *pia loca*. *Pia loca* was a generic term that, at the time, indicated those bodies that had pious aims, namely the religious activities of worship and charity, and came to be considered as integral to the ecclesiastical order. Through their activities of worship, and assistance to the impoverished, weak, or needy, the confraternities inevitably entered into relations with ecclesiastical institutions and the bishop (who was traditionally presented as the "father of the poor"). At the same time, because of their charitable work and their contribution to the creation of a social framework for the laity, the confraternities also fell under the jurisdiction of the public authorities.[5]

---

4. Otto Gerhard Oexle, "Die mittelalterlichen Gilden: Ihre Selbstdeutung und ihr Beitrag zur Formung sozialer Strukturen," in *Soziale Ordnungen im Selbstverständnis des Mittelalters*, ed. Albert Zimmermann (Berlin: de Gruyter, 1979), 203–26; Pierre Michaud-Quantin, *Universitas: Expression du mouvement communautaire dans le Moyen Âge latin* (Paris: Vrin, 1970).

5. Luigi Prosdocimi, *Il diritto ecclesiastico dello stato di Milano dall'inizio della signoria viscontea al periodo tridentino (sec. XIII–XVI)* (Milan: Cisalpino Goliardica, 1941), chap. 4, 221–38.

Therefore, in the Middle Ages, the law remained unclear as to whether confraternal affiliation fell under ecclesiastical or civil jurisdiction, and uncertain concerning the basis on which these types of associations should be founded. Canon law did not closely examine the details of this matter until 1604, when in the constitution of Clement VIII, the Roman Curia mandated how a confraternity should be founded and outlined its relations with the diocesan bishop.[6] Nevertheless, medieval jurists focused on several particular issues of great importance. For example, in the first half of the thirteenth century, Pope Innocent IV, a prominent jurist, permitted the existence of the *universitates* (associations or corporations), with the purposes of piety and devotion. However, he recommended that the *universitates* be subject to ecclesiastical authorities, who would retain the right to dissolve them if they were to cause any problems. Around that time, Raymond of Peñafort, a prominent Catalan jurist belonging to the Dominican order, questioned the lawfulness of the confraternal custom of charging a fee to those who wanted to join a confraternity and, more generally, the problem of establishing community patrimony and the relative administrative and financial operations.[7] In fact, many confraternities accumulated huge real estate assets and landholdings thanks to wills and donations, which they managed productively entering the contemporaneous economic circuits. The honesty and administrative skills of the almonry associations managed by the laity came to be recognized and praised, for example in Milan, as opposed to the difficulties in managing the hospitals. Consequently, when the local authorities implemented a drastic administrative reform of the institutions managing hospitals—conforming to a trend common to many other Italian and European cities—they turned to the almonry associations to find new lay administrators who would replace the previous religious ministers at the head of the new centralized hospital.[8]

The difficulty of defining confraternities, their wide lexical range, and their ambiguous legal position are undoubtedly consequences of their protean nature. We should not imagine a single type of confraternal

---

6. Gilles Gérard Meersseman and Gian Piero Pacini, "Le confraternite laicali in Italia dal Quattrocento al Seicento," in *Problemi di storia della chiesa nei secoli XV–XVII* (Naples: Edizioni Dehoniane, 1979), 114.

7. Michaud-Quantin, *Universitas*, 185.

8. Marina Gazzini and Antonio Olivieri, eds., "L'ospedale, il denaro e altre ricchezze: Scritture e pratiche economiche dell'assistenza in Italia nel tardo Medioevo," monographic section in *Reti Medievali Rivista* 17, no. 1 (2016): 105–366, https://doi.org/10.6092/1593-2214/501.

association, indifferent to the passage of time. In the Middle Ages, local devotional brotherhoods containing a dozen members, large associations with wider recruitment that encompassed the entire urban territory, local branches of widespread movements (above all that of the *disciplinati* [flagellants], also called the *battuti* or *scovati*), and finally groups with memberships limited by age (the confraternities of young people) or *nationes* (the confraternities of foreigners) all coexisted. Some confraternities presented more markedly religious features—because of their connection to an ecclesiastical institution, their primarily devotional aims, or through subjection to directives of the clergy—while others had a more secular character because they were independent from religious institutions, because they were subject to public jurisdiction, or because they were made up exclusively of laypeople or practiced only welfare assistance (in the broadest sense that the term "assistance" assumes when we refer to the Middle Ages). However, it is important not to presuppose the existence of an opposition between the sacred and the profane in the world of confraternities. Even the secular brotherhoods never disregarded religious reference points, as they were the expression of a single conception of *fraternitas*, both Christian and civic.

If it is difficult to define confraternities as general institutions, it is equally impossible to frame them as realities unchanging in time. We must take a chronological and evolutionary approach to the phenomenon and not neglect the possible problem of false continuity. On the one hand, we must bear in mind the change of functions within the same confraternal structure, and therefore investigate what needs and interests confraternities fulfilled, depending on the time and place. On the other, we must grasp the permanence of the functions in the changing forms of the confraternities, and therefore research which groups or institutions discharged tasks necessary for the organization of urban life (i.e., defense, aid, collective identity, etc.) at certain times and places.[9]

## Local Variants and the Circulation of Models

The specific Italian situation depends upon the variable of geographical location. In some centers and in some territories, the confraternal

---

9. For a broad thematic and chronological approach to the subject of confraternities, see Konrad Eisenbichler, ed., *A Companion to Medieval and Early Modern Confraternities* (Leiden: Brill, 2019).

phenomenon appears to have been more developed and pervasive, capable of signifying to a greater extent religious observance, the organization of the society, and artistic, literary, and musical production. Traditionally, the historians of the confraternal movements in Italy have underlined the substantial difference between the central-northern and southern parts of the peninsula. Out of the five Italian confraternities with the oldest surviving sources (i.e., a corpus of statutes, sermons, and liturgical texts dating back to the eleventh and twelfth centuries), four were in fact built in central-northern Italy (two in Tuscany, in Sant'Appiano in Valdelsa and Pescia, one in Emilia-Romagna, in Imola, one in Piedmont, in Gozzano) and only one in the south (the confraternity of Montefusco, in Campania).[10] The southern confraternities also appear to show less diversity in their typologies, even though they were equally capable of expressing themselves in original forms, such as in the case of the Annunziate of the Kingdom of Naples.[11] In the historiography, the southern religious context has been characterized by a subordinate and fundamentally passive laity in comparison to the clergy and its organizations, in contrast to the religious dynamism of the laypeople in central-northern Italy, who were often locked in a struggle against clergy concerning heresy, simony, and concubinage. This discrepancy between two parts of the peninsula was also attributed to a lesser commitment by the mendicant orders in the south to the work of the religious education of the laity.[12]

As the recent research shows, this interpretation depends in large part on historiographical stereotyping and the problems of documentary conservation.[13] The records of the southern Italian medieval confraternities have long remained obscure in many areas.[14] They have consequently received less scholarly attention than the records of the

---

10. Giovanni Vitolo, *Istituzioni ecclesiastiche e vita religiosa dei laici nel Mezzogiorno medievale: Il codice della confraternita di S. Maria di Montefusco (sec. XII)* (Rome: Herder, 1982); Neslihan Şenocak, "Twelfth-Century Italian Confraternities as Institutions of Pastoral Care," *Journal of Medieval History* 42 (2016): 202-25, http://dx.doi.org/10.1080/03044181.2016.1141702.

11. Salvatore Marino, *Ospedali e città nel Regno di Napoli: Le Annunziate, istituzioni, archivi e fonti (secc. XIV–XIX)* (Florence: Olschki, 2014).

12. Giovanni Vitolo, "Confraternite dell'Italia centro-meridionale," in "Le confraternite in Italia fra Medioevo e Rinascimento: Atti della tavola rotonda, Vicenza, 3-4 novembre 1979," ed. Gabriele De Rosa, special issue, *Ricerche di storia sociale e religiosa* 17-18 (1980): 64-70.

13. See the introduction of David D'Andrea and Salvatore Marino, eds., *Confraternities in Southern Italy: Art, Politics, and Religion (1100–1800)* (Toronto: Centre for Renaissance and Reformation Studies, 2022).

14. Hubert Houben, "Le confraternite nel Mezzogiorno medioevale (sec. XII-XV): Status quaestionis e prospettive di ricerca," in *Tra Nord e Sud: Gli allievi per Cosimo Damiano Fonseca*

confraternities of central and northern Italy, with most studies focusing on Tuscany and Veneto, followed by Lombardy and Umbria. Historians have explained the lack of development of southern associations by linking this to the different economic, political, and social fate of the Italian Mezzogiorno compared to other areas of the peninsula. The more robust development of confraternities in northern and central Italy was linked to the successful development of neighborhood and parish communities, as well as *societates* of arms and crafts, which was observed mainly in areas with a strong communal presence.[15] But also on this point, recent studies have revised our impression of a weakness in the development of the southern Italian cities during the period in which the communal autonomy emerged in the north.[16] A case in point is the extraordinary proliferation of the churches, parishes, and confraternities in the town of Benevento between the eleventh and thirteenth centuries. This is highly remarkable and requires further study, as this papal enclave was in a strategic location in terms of the military, diplomatic, and commercial routes that connected it to Rome, Naples, and Puglia.[17]

We must, therefore, be careful not to relate the geographical diffusion of confraternities exclusively to the confines of communal Italy's political framework, and remember that even in North Italy there were strong disparities. For example, the Florentine and Venetian cases appear to be unusual for their diffusion, their articulation (the Florentine youth confraternities have no equal elsewhere), the public authorities' interest, and fundamentally the abundance of documentation, with sources that can be effectively interwoven with others of nonstrictly confraternal production. The Florentine land register of 1427 is a good example, as it allows us to identify with great precision the age, economic condition, and family origin of the members of the confraternities in

---

*nel sessantesimo genetliaco*, ed. Giancarlo Andenna, Hubert Houben, and Benedetto Vetere (Galatina: Congedo, 1993), 171–90.

15. Dylan Reid, "Measuring the Impact of Brotherhood: Robert Putnam's Making Democracy Work and Confraternal Studies," *Confraternitas* 14 (2003): 3–12.

16. Christopher Black, "The Putnam Thesis and Problems on the Early Modern Transition Period," in *Sociability and Its Discontents: Civil Society, Social Capital, and Their Alternatives in Late Medieval and Early Modern Europe*, ed. Nicholas Terpstra and Nicholas Eckstein (Turnhout: Brepols, 2009), 227–45; Paul Oldfield, *City and Community in Norman Italy* (Cambridge: Cambridge University Press, 2009); Joanna H. Drell and Paul Oldfield, eds., *Rethinking Norman Italy: Studies in Honour of Graham A. Loud* (Manchester: Manchester University Press 2021).

17. Gemma T. Colesanti and Eleni Sakellariou, "Confraternities in Medieval Benevento", in D'Andrea and Marino, *Confraternities in Southern Italy*, 203–29.

Florence.[18] On the other hand, the confraternities of another great commune of northern Italy, Milan, seem to have experienced a limited development despite the undeniable social, religious, political, and economic dynamism that characterized central Lombardy throughout the entirety of the Middle Ages. The same circumstances that especially between the thirteenth and fourteenth centuries, facilitated the stronger affirmation of the associative movement in other places (economic wealth, social articulation, the diffusion of religious movements with a popular and often heretical background, dialogue between political parties) did not leave the same imprint on the associative fabric of medieval Milan, at least according to surviving evidence. It is not clear whether the limitation of testimonies is based upon an actual deficit in the development of the Milanese associations, or if it is a consequence of the often-random processes that always intervene in the production, selection, and conservation of these sources.[19]

Regional and local particularities do not signify the existence of rigid local categories. Thanks to the circulation of men, texts, and models of devotion and welfare, there was instead a great permeability between the associative experiences of different areas. In fact, scholars have documented the existence of interregional confraternal networks that involved individuals in different centers of the Italian territory in the same spiritual and material community. This is the case with many religious orders that in their initial phase (before being officially recognized by the papacy), passed through a sort of confraternal embryonic period. Some of them remained anchored to this primitive phase, like the order of the Consortium of the Holy Spirit, also known as the Consortium of the Holy Spirit of Blessed Facio, or Colombetta, founded in Cremona in the mid-thirteenth century and subsequently spread to numerous centers of the Po valley (Emilia-Romagna, Veneto, and Lombardy).[20] The creation of a network turned out to be useful for more than the dissemination of religious messages—the brothers and the sisters of the Consortium, which initially recruited within the professional and artisanal

---

18. David Herlihy and Christiane Klapisch-Zuber, eds., *Tuscans and Their Families: A Study of the Florentine Catasto of 1427* (New Haven, CT: Yale University Press, 1985). For a digital edition of the source, see http://cds.library.brown.edu/projects/catasto/.

19. Marina Gazzini, *Confraternite e società cittadina nel Medioevo italiano* (Bologna: Clueb, 2006), chap. 5.

20. Marina Gazzini, "Donne e uomini in confraternita: La matricola del Consorzio dello Spirito Santo di Piacenza (1268)," *Archivio Storico per le province parmensi*, 4th series, 52 (2000): 253-74.

classes close to the political parties of Guelphs and the Popolo, were involved in fighting heresy. By the thirteenth century, heresy had also assumed a political meaning of opposition to the *pars Ecclesiae* (party of the Church). They also helped pilgrims, prisoners, destitute poor, and the sick, and usually also managed hospitals. In the case of the Consortium of the Holy Spirit, there was a good deal of internal circulation as the brothers moved from one branch to the other. Other confraternal networks were that of the Società o Fraternità della Frusta dei Raccomandati della beata Vergine Maria (the Penitential Brotherhood of the Favorites of the Virgin), which originated in Rome and then spread throughout Italy, or that of the Annunziate, which arose in the fourteenth century in the kingdom of Naples.

It was the models that circulated rather than people. However, in the case of the Raccomandati della beata Vergine Maria a spiritual rather than a devotional model set on penance came to be exported through branches aggregated to the same "order" (a term that at the time, also indicated an informal adherence to a religious form of life). The network of the Annunziate of the Kingdom of Naples, although it also originated in the context of penitence, was centered upon circulating a model of hospital assistance with a lay template. It would have been precisely the house of the Annunziata of Naples that directed the southern process of administrative and health centralization in the fifteenth century, which would have included the welfare institutions of the city and nearby localities. This same process of reform in the center and north of the peninsula also involved hospitals, in which the secular alms consortiums played an important role.[21]

However, one should not make clear distinctions between the penitential, devotional, or charitable and assistance-based nature of the confraternities, because it was the places—and therefore their religious and civic traditions—that gave widespread movements particular features. For example, the movement of the *disciplinati*, which began in Perugia in 1260 and soon spread along the roads of the peninsula, took on different connotations according to time and place: political (as in Bologna or in the Po valley where it was rejected by the Ghibelline governments), in the form of hospitals (coming to monopolize the management of assistance in some areas, such as Veneto), or pastoral (competing and

---

21. Marina Gazzini, "Ospedali e reti: Il medioevo," in *Redes Hospitalarias: Historia, economía y sociología de la sanidad*, ed. Conceptión Villanueva Morte, Antoni Conejo da Pena, and Raúl Villagrasa-Elías (Zaragoza: Excma. Diputación de Zaragoza, 2018), 13-30.

often in conflict with the parish clergy both for spiritual care and the burial of those who were helped, especially when it came to those condemned to death).[22]

## Community Memory

We must also ask ourselves about the absence of evidence, in addition to its presence. Every single confraternity must be studied while keeping one eye on the general evolution of the phenomenon and the other on local particularities, such as different approaches to documentary production and archival conservation.

The numerous confraternities that made up the fabric of medieval society, together with other forms of community and corporation, produced abundant documentation aimed at fulfilling internal management needs and mediating relations with external institutions. Confraternities had internal regulations (which came to be known as "statutes," for convenience rather than from an entirely legal point of view), matriculations, account books and other records of asset management, chapter orders, lists of those who received assistance, obituaries, inventories of goods, and in later centuries, maps of landholdings. A good part of this documentation has been lost, both because it was often written on loose pieces of paper not collected within a codex, and due to the dissolution of the associations, policies of suppression, and negligence. Only later, from the end of the thirteenth century onwards, was there any systematic conservation of documentary material in precise places. Confraternal attachment to an ecclesiastical, monastic, conventual, or hospital institution often played a decisive role in the development of this new tendency to preserve documents.

However, the sources that allow us to reconstruct the active experience of confraternal organizations are obviously not only those written within the confraternity itself, but often above all those produced externally, such as pontifical and episcopal privileges (approvals of rules, foundations and reforms, concessions of indulgences,

---

22. *Il movimento dei Disciplinati nel settimo centenario del suo inizio (Perugia 1260)* (Perugia: Deputazione di Storia Patria per l'Umbria, 1962); *Risultati e prospettive della ricerca sul movimento dei disciplinati* (Perugia: Deputazione di Storia Patria per l'Umbria, 1972); Giuseppina De Sandre Gasparini, "Movimento dei disciplinati, confraternite e ordini mendicanti," in *I Frati Minori e il Terzo Ordine: Problemi e discussioni storiografiche* (Todi: Accademia Tudertina, 1985), 79–114.

authentications of relics, consecrations of altars and oratories) and decrees by the public authority (communal, seignorial, royal, and princely) concerning exemptions and privileges of various kinds. There are also documents prohibiting assembly so as to avoid the danger of conspiracies, and then municipal statutes, council deliberations, pastoral visits (starting from the fifteenth century), land registers, notarial acts (wills, donations, patrimonial management negotiations), and historical writings. Some of these external sources were also kept in the confraternal archives (for example, this is the case with episcopal and papal privileges), while others remained external through their archival classification and are to be found outside the confraternal archives (for example, the records of public deliberations were and are in the state archives). In addition to this documentation, there are also sources in libraries (such as liturgical and prayer books, catechisms, sermon collections, *laudari*) and artistic representations of religious themes and iconographic sources (decorated miniatures in statutes and manuscripts, paintings, and other works of art commissioned by the confraternities). Often the documents relating to the life of the confraternity—statutes and lists of the members, but also diary entries with records of official elections, building works, sacred performances, or copies of ecclesiastical confirmations and privileges, of notarial acts proving property rights—were bound together into a single codex, which in some cases left the original site of conservation and ended up in different collections, in public and private libraries. Such sources preserved in the libraries have their own independent codicological tradition.

The conservation of confraternal records called for their preservation in caskets, trunks, and armoires. These were located in the seat of the confraternity itself, or in churches or hospitals to which the confraternity was attached. The archival tasks were assigned to treasurers and custodians, that is, personnel with various managerial and administrative duties. Rarely documented, but very interesting, is the conservation open to the public that particularly concerns bulls of indulgence, authentications of relics, lists of bequests, and miracle narratives. A good example of this form of conservation can be observed in the Valtellina archive of the Blessed Virgin of the Assumption of Morbegno, in the diocese of Como, which preserves a series of parchments destined for hanging in the church of the confraternity. These documents in Latin and the vernacular date back to the last decade of the fifteenth century and are displayed in both the original and as copies, and often within *narrationes* that explain the documents themselves.[23] Having been designed for exhibition, these writings also had strict graphic criteria. They exemplify a form of written communication with particular oral and visual characteristics. The different modes of conserving confraternal documents responded to different needs. On the one hand, it was necessary to guarantee the verifiability of certain documents, such as authentications of relics or pious bequests. On the other hand, the display of documents for communal use was useful for the construction of the confraternity's memory. In fact, the invention of miracles and their narration did not have a merely internal function, but served to affirm the confraternal group and accredit it with the local community.

Of course, not all confraternities enjoyed such a wealth of testimonies; indeed we often know nothing more than a name, a date, or a significant event of a confraternity. However, to varying degrees, the confraternities in Italy, especially in the central and northern regions, boasted much more abundant and precocious archival documentation than in the rest of Europe.

## Continuity and Discontinuity, Parallelism and Contiguity

The first attestations of the Italian confraternities occur in the early Middle Ages. The term *confraternitas* itself has early medieval origins and was coined to indicate those communities of prayer made up of monks, clerics, and the laity who, united around religious establishments (above all monasteries), participated in the same spiritual benefits. The term *schola*, perhaps most widespread in the Middle Ages, has even older origins. Of clear Greek derivation (from σχολή = free time) and already used in Roman times to mean a building in which "conveniunt plurimi eiusdem negotii causa,"[24] the term later extended its semantic reach from the simple meaning of "meeting place" to the more complex "association of individuals having common interests." One therefore usually spoke of *schola cantorum, schola militum, schola tabellionum,* and

---

23. Rita Pezzola, *"Et in arca posui": Scritture della confraternita della Beata Vergine Assunta di Morbegno diocesi di Como* (Morbegno: Confraternita della Beata Vergine Assunta della Parrocchia di San Giovanni Battista di Morbegno, 2003).

24. Charles Du Fresne Du Cange, ed., *Glossarium mediae et infimae latinitatis*, 10 vols. (Niort: Léopold Favre, 1863–87), 7:349.

so forth. The survival of this term from the ancient era to the Middle Ages, and its spread even outside the lands of the Exarchate, has raised questions not only concerning the persistence of connections between Byzantine and Lombard Italy after the sixth century, but also about the original nexus between trade and devotional associations. Debates on the issue of continuity or discontinuity between ancient, early medieval, and late medieval associationism have also been very heated, and the issue has not been resolved in an unequivocal manner.[25]

Given its ambiguity—as it can mean any association of people practicing the same profession, clerics assigned to a particular church, lay associates for secular and religious purposes, as well as the seat of their respective associations—the term *schola* was well adapted to act as the equivalent to "society," "corporation," and "confraternity": indeed the *Corpus Iuris Civilis* indicated *schola, corpus, officium,* and *universitas* as synonyms.[26] The most significant examples of this semantic polyvalence can be found in Venice, where the word *schola* had a long tradition and was widely used in the field of devotional associations and, from the twelfth century at least, also in the associations of artisans.[27] There were frequent moments of intersection and overlap, even if they were never completely identical, between large *scholae* (which recruited from the whole city and all the professions, with an internal bond for the purposes of worship as it was made up of penitents), *communes scholae* (the minor confraternities of devotion), *scholae d'arte* (with subscription quickly becoming obligatory for anyone wishing to practice an artisanal profession), and *scholae nationales* (each uniting foreigners of the same ethnic provenance). Within a *schola d'arte* one could, for example, create a subcategory made up of the tradesmen of the same *natio* who in turn could give life to an additional school of devotion: thus the

---

25. Gennaro Maria Monti, *Le confraternite medievali dell'alta e media Italia*, 2 vols. (Venice: La Nuova Italia, 1927); Gazzini, *Confraternite e società cittadina*, chap. 1.

26. *Corpus Iuris Civilis* (I, 23, 7).

27. Giovanni Monticolo, ed., *I capitolari delle arti veneziane sottoposte alla Giustizia e poi alla Giustizia vecchia, dalle origini al MCCCCXXX*, 3 vols. (Rome: Istituto Storico Italiano per il Medio Evo, 1896-1914); Lia Sbriziolo, "Per la storia delle confraternite veneziane: Dalle deliberazioni miste (1310-1476) del Consiglio dei Dieci. 'Scolae comunes,' artigiane e nazionali," *Atti dell'Istituto veneto di scienze, lettere ed arti* 126 (1967-68): 405-42; Lia Sbriziolo, "Per la storia delle confraternite veneziane: Dalle deliberazioni miste (1310-1476) del Consiglio dei Dieci. Le scuole dei battuti," in *Miscellanea Gilles Gérard Meersseman*, 2 vols. (Padua: Antenore, 1970), 2:715-63; Brian Pullan, *Rich and Poor in Renaissance Venice: The Social Institutions of a Catholic State, to 1620* (Oxford: Blackwell, 1971); Richard S. Mackenney, *Tradesmen and Traders: The World of the Guilds in Venice and Europe, c. 1250–c. 1650* (London: Croom Helm, 1987).

three elements—national, artisanal, and devotional—are intertwined. For example, these elements interweave in the foundation by the *ligadori* (porters and workers in the packaging of goods) of the Fondaco dei Tedeschi (Fondaco of the Germans) who, although they already had their own *schola* by 1418 with many statutes, obtained a license in 1423 from the Venetian Council of Ten to found another *schola*, this time with a devotional aim.[28] In the sphere of artisanal associations, artisanal guilds and *schola*, despite remaining distinct on a theoretical level, came to coincide in practice with the identities of the members as adherence to the artisanal guild became obligatory. The Venetian *scholae*, in their various forms, are without a doubt exemplary of the relationship between the associations of artisans and the confraternities, even if they constitute a unique case, given the particular institutional reality of Venice imbued by a strong statism. Both trade guilds and *scholae* were in fact strictly subject to the control of the authorities.

Less controversial, but equally important to consider, is the question of the evolution of confraternities at the end of the Middle Ages, and therefore their continuity or discontinuity in the modern era. Each area experienced chronologies. If significant structural changes were observed at the end of the Middle Ages in the Veneto area, greater continuity is recorded in the Roman area, where a break occurred with the Council of Trent. Meanwhile, in the Lombard area it is possible to affirm that the forms of lay associationism with a religious background not only lack major changes before the Tridentine age, but in fact only with the process of secularization in the eighteenth century were they to undergo any real form of critique, also in the Catholic sphere.[29]

Beyond the chronological continuity and discontinuity, historians have questioned the typological contiguity between the different associative forms. For example, scholars have often emphasized the devotional and charitable characteristics when discussing the origins of confraternities and their consequent close relationship with the bishop as well as the public authorities, yet they aligned the associations that in time became trade guilds more with economic and political objectives rather than solidaristic. Characterized by an articulate associative

---

28. Sbriziolo, "Per la storia delle confraternite veneziane: 'Scolae comunes,' artigiane e nazionali," 415.

29. Marina Gazzini, "Confraternite tra medioevo ed età moderna: Confini e contaminazioni (a mo' di post-fazione)," in *Confraternite in Trentino e a Riva del Garda*, ed. Emanuele Curzel, Maria Clara Rossi, and Marina Garbellotti (Verona: Cierre Edizioni, 2018), 195–200.

presence, the devotional origin of the *schola* seems evident both in Venice and in Milan. However, in Milan, despite the early economic and social development of the city, not all trades formed themselves into guilds—for example, the goldsmiths and the *agugiari* (manufacturers of needles) always remained at the level of *schola*—nor did they rise to the summit of political life, as happened in neighboring Piacenza and Parma, and particularly in Florence and Bologna where the Arts came to power between the thirteenth and fourteenth centuries.[30] In Bologna, the case of the spiritual brotherhoods of penitents is particularly significant: the Congregatio devotorum civitatis Bononie reflects a particular type of civic consciousness in its very title, which animated it and linked it to the city institutions, rather than having only a religious purpose. Together with the trade guilds and the Società d'Armi, the Congregatio devotorum constituted the third pillar of support for the commune of the Popolo. Although maintenance of the town's peace was among its institutional duties, this certainly did not mean that they would assume a neutral attitude. Rather, it was to be actively supportive of the Popolo party, which guaranteed order against the claims and threats of disorder by the magnates.[31]

The relationship between confraternities and corporations is the aspect that most attracted the attention of historians. However, recent studies have shown that the confraternal *schola* may have constituted the original nucleus, or at least the contemporary and analogous counterpart, with respect to the claim of managerial and jurisdictional autonomy of other associations destined to develop much greater institutional importance. In some Italian and transalpine situations—Rome and Marseilles—scholars have identified significant evolutionary parallels between the confraternal associations of the laity or the clergy and the commune, which was also born as an association of cocitizens (*concives*).[32] This connection cannot be hypothesized for all cities, but nevertheless we can also see elsewhere a common relational and institutional model in the internal organization of these communities of

---

30. Gazzini, *Confraternite e società cittadina*, chap. 2.

31. Marina Gazzini, "I Disciplinati, la milizia dei frati Gaudenti, il comune di Bologna e la pace cittadina: Statuti a confronto (1261-1265)," *Bollettino della Deputazione di storia patria per l'Umbria* 101 (2004): 419-37.

32. Tommaso Di Carpegna Falconieri, *Il clero di Roma nel Medioevo: Istituzioni e politica cittadina (secoli VIII–XIII)* (Rome: Viella, 2002); Antonio Rigon, "Schole, confraternite e ospedali," in *Pensiero e sperimentazioni istituzionali nella "Societas Christiana" (1046–1250)*, ed. Giancarlo Andenna (Milan: Vita e Pensiero, 2007), 407-27.

*confratres* and *concives*, which envisaged similar organizational methods through the convocation of assembly meetings, the establishment of specific offices, the appointment of officials and representatives, and the consequent similar documentary production of statutes, council acts, collections of privileges, and administrative documents.

One example of this overlap between civil and confraternal perimeters happened in Arezzo, where public authorities in the fourteenth century arranged that every newborn in the city should be registered in the Fraternita dei Laici (Fraternity of the Laity) at the time of their baptism.[33] This was a confraternity founded in the thirteenth century in a mendicant context, and it was subsequently identified by the commune as an organizational center of collective services of great utility and was therefore subject to public control. To be a member of the Fraternity of the Laity was to be a citizen of Arezzo. This total overlap actually seems to be a quite exceptional case, while it was more common to see a case of shared identity and representation between the inhabitants in a certain district of a city and a confraternity established in that district. For example, in Aosta at the end of the thirteenth century, a confraternity of clerics and the laity named after the Holy Spirit was formed by the *burgenses* and *habitatores* of Porta Sant'Orso, one of the three distinct districts of the city. The confraternity represented an institutional support for the inhabitants of the *burgus de Porta Sancti Ursi*. The inhabitants of the neighborhood preferred to turn to the officers of the confraternity as their representatives in negotiations that involved collective action, instead of to the clerics of the church of Sant'Orso or the noble Porta Sant'Orso family, vassals of the bishop of Aosta and House of Savoy.[34] On the other hand, a city is made up not only of districts, but also of places where people gather, where events take place, and the spirit of the city is elaborated.

## The Confines of Solidarity and Spaces of Sharing

In the confraternal statutes and sermons there are repeated references to peace and solidarity. This solidarity had a universal aim, as in the

---

33. Anna Benvenuti, "Ad procurationem caritatis et amoris et concordiae ad invicem: La Fraternita dei Laici di Arezzo tra sistema di solidarietà e solidarietà di sistema," *Annali Aretini* 1 (1993): 79–104.
34. Elena Corniolo, "La confraternita del Santo Spirito della Porta Sant'Orso (Aosta, secoli XII–XIV)," *Reti Medievali Rivista* 15, no. 2 (2014): 3–39, https://doi.org/10.6092/1593-2214/437.

ecumenical appeal that appears at the beginning of the fourteenth-century statutes of the confraternity of *disciplinati* of Parma and Piacenza. The confreres were invited to pray for the holy mother Church, for the pope and his cardinals, archbishops, bishops, priests, and friars, and even for the emperor and all of his vicars, princes, and barons, and then for every creature endowed with reason, such as Jews, pagans, and Muslims, and so for every Christian soul, for pilgrims, for merchants and travelers by sea and by land, for peace, for the fruits of the earth, for the souls of fathers and mothers, brothers and sisters, and for the confreres of the flagellant congregation.[35]

In reality, rather than places of integration, the medieval confraternities were the places of confrontation between different groups, often confirming hierarchies and social divisions. Confrontation first occurred within the association itself. Here, individuals formed a body by sharing religious practices, community rites, and Christian and civic ideals. This sharing led to a temporary equality: the robes of the *disciplinati* with the hoods ensured an anonymity that among other things, also included the momentary guarantee of equality among the members. By joining together, individuals became qualitatively something other than what they had been before, but they could not forget who they were. External reality, with its social and partisan subdivisions, continued to be reflected within the confraternal group. The members were distinguished by different roles (rector, estate manager, treasurer, and simple confrere), and this led to a hierarchy of tasks and offices, elective and time-limited, that did not disregard the social status (from age, gender, family, and wealth) of those who held them.

The presence of women, for example, must be considered not only in terms of quantity, but also of quality. Female participation in medieval confraternities presented important variations according to geographical context and period. In some areas, such as Veneto, female participation went through a progressive expansion, in contrast to Bologna, where it underwent a major reduction in the fifteenth century. In Florence, the female presence does not seem to have ever reached particularly significant dimensions, while around Bergamo, Emilia, and Umbria in the thirteenth through fourteenth centuries, women are attested in numerically dominant proportions—to be precise, within the consortium of the Misericordia of Bergamo, in the consortium of the

---

35. Candido Mesini, "Statuti piacentini-parmensi dei Disciplinati," *Archivio Storico per le province parmensi*, 4th series, 12 (1960): 66–68.

Spirito Santo in Piacenza, and the fraternity of Santa Maria del Mercato of Gubbio. In any case, however few or many there were, the participation of women qualitatively conformed to the existing gender roles within the contemporary society that excluded women from positions of governance and gave them little power in decision-making. "Being part" did not automatically translate into "being important."[36]

Moreover, the membership of confraternities was not open to anyone. Most confraternity statutes had some constants in their criteria for exclusion, for example, on the basis of faith (heretics and those considered enemies of the Church were excluded) and on the basis of behavior (from gambling to immorality). To these one could add variable exclusions, those depending on residence (in the case of the parish confraternities), on age (some associations discriminated in favor of youth, for example, the Florentine youth confraternities did not admit members who were more than twenty-five years old, while others were selective in the other direction, imposing a minimum age of entry at thirty years old), by sex (some flagellant confraternities were reluctant to admit women, even if the most recent scholarship raises doubt about the exclusion of women not only from adherence to penitential spirituality, but also from the practice of the discipline itself), by profession (like the Venetian schools of craft and of devotion), and by physical disability (the confraternities of the blind, crippled, and deformed).

However, the logic of some exclusions is not always comprehensible. The fourteenth-century statutes of the consortium of San Giacomo di Galizia of Parma, a confraternity that brought together the pilgrims from Parma who had traveled to Santiago de Compostela, allowed for the registration of residents of only three of the four quarters of the city—the inhabitants of Porta Parma, Porta Nuova, and Porta Santa Cristina—while explicitly forbidding entry to the residents of Porta Benedetta. It is not clear if this was a polemical exclusion, for reasons unknown to us, or if it was a division of zones of influence within the

---

36. Maria Teresa Brolis and Giovanni Brembilla, "Mille e più donne in confraternita: Il *consorcium Misericordiae* di Bergamo nel Duecento," in *Il buon fedele: Le confraternite tra medioevo e prima età moderna*, ed. M. Zangarini, Quaderni di storia religiosa 5 (Verona: Cierre, 1998), 107–34; Giovanna Casagrande, "Confraternities and Lay Female Religiosity in Late Medieval and Renaissance Umbria," in *The Politics of Ritual Kinship: Confraternities and Social Order in Early Modern Italy*, ed. Nicholas Terpstra (Cambridge: Cambridge University Press, 2000), 48–66; Anna Esposito, "Donne e confraternite," in *Studi confraternali: Orientamenti, problemi, testimonianze*, ed. Marina Gazzini, Reti medievali E-book 12 (Florence: Firenze University Press, 2009), 53–78, http://www.rm.unina.it/rmebook/index.php?mod=none_Gazzini_Studi.

city. The Benedictine monastery of San Giovanni Evangelista, upon which the confraternity of San Giacomo along with its church and hospital were dependent, was located in the neighborhood of Porta Benedetta that was excluded by the consortium in the statutes. The monastery had its own hospital at its headquarters, which might have created competition with the hospital of the confraternity.[37]

In the late Middle Ages, the confraternities developed new barriers, while continuing to promote traditional solidarity. Constraints were imposed on the individual freedom to choose whether or not to join a group and then which to join, even within the limits indicated above. In Venice, as we have seen, enrollment in some *scholae* became obligatory when one belonged to a trade.[38] On the other hand, in Milan some enlarged associations were dissolved and transformed into new, more exclusive societies. This resulted in the loss of membership in the older confraternity, along with the loss of spiritual and material benefits ranging from access to social assets, to the prospect of receiving subsidies and assistance in the event of an illness, to the Masses and prayers for the salvation of their souls. Such were the cases of the large brotherhood of the Raccomandati della Beata Vergine Maria, which was reduced into the almoner association of the Quattro Marie and of the consortium of the Third Order Franciscans to become the elite Consorzio della Carità.[39]

Barriers were also erected in external relations, as the recipients of the resources charitably disbursed became subject to strict conditions. Toward the late Middle Ages, the range of people assisted became increasingly restricted. In cities as in the countryside, as time progressed, confraternities and other forms of associative solidarity (such as the *charitates* and the *elemosinae*) passed from the fundamental function of solidarity based on the social integration of the poor—who were the figure of Christ and as such a mediator of salvation, as well as an individual to be integrated into the community—to a function of assistance based on the identification of the "real" poor. The poor seem to be considered passive recipients of charity, not necessarily subjects to be

---

37. Marina Gazzini, "Confraternite e assistenza tra devozione e civismo," in *Storia di Parma*, vol. 3, bk. 2, *Parma medievale*, ed. Roberto Greci (Parma: Monte Università Parma, 2011), 207.
38. See note 28, above.
39. Gazzini, *Confraternite e società cittadina*, chap. 5.

integrated or to be associated with.[40] New almoner consortia and hospitals went through a management and administrative reform in the fifteenth century that distanced them from their religious background, but allowed them to better provide for the poor (to be assisted but not integrated) than the traditional confraternal communities.[41]

The spaces most open to social hybridization were found in the confraternities of the foreigners, which were founded to act as a contact point for the various needs of the people living outside of their homeland. These brotherhoods offered their members assistance, protection, linguistic and intercultural mediation, and opportunity for socialization, but they also acted a filter and connection between the foreign community and the local society. Some of these *scholae* accepted only members of a specific ethnic group, while others, despite their title indicating a specific ethnic community, were nevertheless open to outsiders. From both a social and political point of view, the national *scholae* represented a moment of negotiation between the communities of foreigners and the city's government and inhabitants.[42]

National *scholae* with significant influence developed, unsurprisingly, in those cities where there was the consistent presence of foreigners, who were sometimes pilgrims but more often economic migrants. In Rome, associations of *forenses* (Frisians, Lombards, Franks, Saxons), which aided their compatriots, have been attested since the Carolingian era.[43] In Palermo, from the end of the eleventh century onward, the presence of *exteri* (foreigners) from North and Central Italy and later from Catalonia marks distinctly the social topography, with the creation of different urban districts developing around the churches, *fondaci*, and confraternities of national character.[44] In Venice, the first

---

40. Giuseppina De Sandre Gasparini, "Confraternite e campagna nell'Italia settentrionale del basso medioevo: Ricerche sul territorio veneto," in Gazzini, *Studi confraternali*, 19-51.

41. Giuliana Albini, "La gestione dell'Ospedale Maggiore nel Quattrocento: Un esempio di concentrazione ospedaliera," in Giuliana Albini, *Carità e governo delle povertà (secoli XII–XV)* (Milan: Unicopli, 2002), 267-81.

42. Ermanno Orlando, *Migrazioni mediterranee: Migranti, minoranze e matrimoni a Venezia nel basso Medioevo* (Bologna: Il Mulino, 2014).

43. Marina Gazzini, "Aiutare il forestiero: L'assistenza di ospedali e confraternite nel medioevo (Italia centro-settentrionale)," in "Hospitalité de l'étranger au Moyen Âge et à l'époque moderne: Entre charité, contrôle et utilité sociale. Italie Europe," ed. Ilaria Taddei and Naïma Ghermani, special issue, *Mélanges de l'École française de Rome: Moyen Âge* 131, no. 2 (2019): 407-16, http://journals.openedition.org/mefrm/5756.

44. Vita Russo and Daniela Santoro, "Medieval Confraternities in Palermo", in D'Andrea and Marino, *Confraternities in Southern Italy*, 449-75.

aggregations of foreigners appeared in the fourteenth century. These were the Lucchesi (from Lucca), then the Milanese, and in the fifteenth century, the Florentines, Germans, Albanians, Dalmatians (or Schiavoni), and Greeks. We see the establishment of confraternities of foreigners also in border territories. In northeastern Italy, geographical proximity combined with the local economies' need for skilled workers was favorable to German immigration, leading to the emergence of the confraternities of the Alemanni. We have already mentioned the German confraternity in Venice, but those of Trento were founded earlier. There is evidence of a *Hauerbruderschaft* (brotherhood of the *zappatori*) from the middle of the thirteenth century. *Hauer* can mean both winemaker and, more probably, miner, whom the city and its prince-bishop, wealthy thanks to mining, needed. Later, the brotherhood also opened itself up to other categories of workers, such as artisans and merchants, to become the point of contact for the entire German community in Trento.[45] This also happened in Bassano del Grappa, where the Germans established their own religious brotherhood, with the society's tomb and headquarters at the altar of San Pietro in the church of San Francesco. For work activities they joined the local trade guilds, which were mixed (i.e., open to both locals and foreigners). In this way, immigrants had more support networks available: in addition to their own natural family, there was the confraternal family, made up of fellow artisans and fellow countrymen, with whom they shared the urban space. All these families, natural and artificial, were equally important and formative in shaping the professional and emotional experiences of the immigrants' lives.[46]

## Private Activities and Public Functions between Protection and Control

At first, the confraternity emerged as a closed space, which determined its characteristics: "the particularism, the team spirit, the rivalry for prestige, and competition, all these come from the exclusivity of

---

45. Serena Luzzi, "La confraternita alemanna degli zappatori: Lineamenti per una storia della comunità tedesca a Trento fra tardo medioevo e prima età moderna," *Studi Trentini di Scienze Storiche* 73 (1994): 231–76, 331–63; 74 (1995): 47–92.

46. Marina Gazzini, "I giovani tra famiglia naturale e famiglie artificiali," in *I giovani nel medioevo: Ideali e pratiche di vita*, ed. Isa Lori Sanfilippo and Antonio Rigon (Rome: Istituto Storico Italiano per il Medio Evo, 2014), 54–55.

space."⁴⁷ However, the confraternities stepped into the space outside at times when, with sacred representations and ritual processions for example, they crossed the whole city and parts of the countryside, and when they acted as suppliers of goods and services, spiritual and material, to the neighborhood and the parish.

In some contexts, the close ties between the confraternities on the one side and the neighborhoods and parishes on the other meant that the confraternities, to some extent, replaced the parish churches in the sphere of the care of souls, as happened in Verona in the fifteenth century, or in the discharge of administrative duties for a portion of urban territory, as happened in Florence and Rome. For Florence, it has been suggested that the social control assumed by confraternal institutions was fostered by the crises of the neighborhood/parish in the phase of social and demographic expansion in the city, and by the consequent lesser grip of the parochial organization on the territory of its own jurisdiction. For Rome, scholars have found that one of the most important confraternities in the city, the Società dei Raccomandati del Salvatori *ad Sancta Sanctorum*, which also ran a hospital, was given the secular jurisdiction over an entire district "for the safety and protection of the men and those coming to these places" (pro securitate et tuitione hominum et venentium per dicta loca) and with the "power to reprimand, condemn and punish" (arbitrium castigandi, condempnandi et puniendi) the inhabitants of the neighborhood, except for the crimes of theft, murder, and lèse-majesté that remained the responsibility of the city government.⁴⁸

The assignment of confraternities to important public tasks usually took place by way of incorporating them into the implementation of policies aimed at mitigating pauperism, begging, or regarding health and justice issues, since the confraternities provided alms, ran hospitals, guaranteed social aid for disadvantaged persons, such as widows and the elderly, prisoners and those sentenced to death. In an age lacking social welfare, confraternities (and guilds) functioned as institutions of social security and insurance. Through the payment of fees during registration and its annual renewals, through the donation or bequest of a part of their property, and finally through the lending of their labor in the form of material and spiritual assistance, the members were protecting themselves and their families from the uncertainties of the

---

47. Grendi, "Le confraternite come fenomeno associativo e religioso," 176.
48. Archivio di Stato di Roma, Sancta Sanctorum, cass. 407, 16 (anno 1418).

future by ensuring they would receive the same kind of assistance in case of need. The confraternity statutes contained clauses for general assistance in case of sickness, injury, death, or other problems (such as falling into difficulty in foreign lands or imprisonment).[49]

However, confraternities could also be asked to turn their attention to other areas. In Assisi in 1367, the commune entrusted the priors of the confraternal brotherhoods with the task of evaluating the extent of the damage to the mills on the Chiascio River in Bastia, which had been devastated by the passage of condottieri Giovanni Acuto and Ambrogio Visconti's troops from Milan.[50] From 1433 in Bologna, the Confraternity of Santa Maria della Morte (of thirteenth-century origins), in addition to its welfare activities, had also begun to subsidize the hospital, which had for some time already managed the city's devotional practices regarding the principle civic cult, that of the Virgin of Saint Luke. Furthermore, some fifteenth-century confraternities, such as the Opera dei Poveri Prigionieri (Foundation for Poor Prisoners) in Bologna, played an informal role as extrajudicial negotiators in cases involving the disputes or debts of prisoners.[51] The Società dei Protettori dei Carcerati (Society of the Protectors of Prisoners), founded with ducal approval in Milan in 1466 by people of great political importance and social prestige, both lay and ecclesiastic and including esteemed jurists and notaries, had the purpose of providing legal assistance to Milanese prisoners. They also initiated the review of trials for individuals considered imprisoned unjustly.[52]

Both secular and ecclesiastical authorities were very eager to make use of lay associations that could support projects of social or anti-heretical intervention. At the same time, they kept the confraternities in close check in case of a possibility of an adverse effect to the existing order. The fear of potential dangers inherent in the lay associations, as places where dissent could develop and conspiracies could be

---

49. Marina Gazzini, "Guilds and Mutual Support in Medieval Italy," in *Professional Guilds and the History of Insurance: A Comparative Analysis*, ed. Phillip Hellwege (Berlin: Dunkler & Humblot, 2020), 166–217.

50. Marina Gazzini, "Costruire la comunità: L'apporto delle confraternite fra Due e Trecento. Alcuni esempi dal Nord e Centro Italia," *Rivista di storia della Chiesa in Italia* 68 (2014): 331-48.

51. Mario Fanti, *Confraternite e città a Bologna nel Medioevo e nell'età moderna* (Rome: Herder, 2001).

52. Marina Gazzini, *Storie di vita e di malavita: Criminali, poveri e altri miserabili nelle carceri di Milano alla fine del medioevo*, Reti medievali E-book 30 (Florence: Firenze University Press, 2017), http://www.rm.unina.it/rmebook/index.php?mod=none_Gazzini_Carceri.

organized, caused numerous interventions by the public authorities over the centuries, even though they showed little interest in issues of internal management of the confraternities. The Carolingian capitulars already contained provisions for controlling the *gildoniae*, a term that as we read in Hincmar of Rheims, also included confraternal associations.[53] The authorities' attitude of suspicion did not change as time passed. The Ghibelline governments of thirteenth-century Italy showed great hostility against the flagellant movement, which began in Perugia in 1260 and spread to numerous areas of the peninsula. In the fifteenth century, the governments of Florence, Milan, and Mantua carried out repeated interferences and suppressions of the confraternities in their territories.[54] And even where the confraternities experienced extraordinary development in terms of number and type, as in Venice, the authorities were able to implement limitations. This was the case of the Albanian national *schola* in Venice that in the fifteenth century functioned illegally for several years because it was not recognized by public authorities.[55]

If secular powers feared conspiracies and controlled associations, whenever they suspected disturbance to the existing order, the Church feared the spread of heterodox doctrines. Therefore, in some instances, the Church rewarded and encouraged the activity of some groups of laymen, such as the Società della Fede, which arose in Florence and Milan on the initiative of the Dominican Peter of Verona.[56] In other instances, it punished and dissuaded the most elusive congregations that could plunge into heresy. This eventuality was amplified by the fact that since the thirteenth century after the dispositions of Innocent III, heresy and politics were often juxtaposed. For the Roman Church, a heretic was also a political enemy, and a political enemy was also a heretic.[57] For example, in 1322 the Visconti, Ghibelline lords of Milan, were themselves banished by a crusade against heresy. However, already in the thirteenth century, Milan had been called a "lair of heretics," and

---

53. Alfredus Boretius, ed., *Capitularia regum Francorum*, Monumenta Germaniae Historica, Karoli Magni Capitularia, 2 vols. (Hannover: Hahnsche Buchhandlung, 1883), vol. 1, no. 20, c. 16 (779). Rudolf Pokorny and Martina Stratmann, eds., *Capitula Episcoporum*, vol. 2, Monumenta Germaniae Historica (Hannover: Hahnsche Buchhandlung, 1995), Kirchenprovinz Reims, Hinkmar von Reims, I, c. XVI, 43–44.

54. Gazzini, *Confraternite e società cittadina*, chap. 5.

55. Orlando, *Migrazioni mediterranee*.

56. Gazzini, *Confraternite e società cittadina*, chap. 3, 88.

57. Grado Giovanni Merlo, *Contro gli eretici: La coercizione all'ortodossia prima dell'Inquisizione* (Bologna: Il Mulino, 1996), 64, 102.

therefore the papacy's watch over local events had always been high. Thus, the Inquisition judged it to be a "heretical conventicle" and severely repressed the *congregatio* of women and men who had gathered around the figure of a devotee named Guglielma, also called Boema, in the last years of the thirteenth century. In reality, this group does not seem to have done anything other than share a rituality, external and internal, "of a broadly confraternal type," coming together in the household of Guglielma herself in the parish of San Pietro all'Orto at Porta Orientale to hear her sermons. After her death, they met at the Humiliati monastery of Biassono and the Cistercian monastery of Chiaravalle, reading passages from the holy scriptures, feasting together, organizing processions, adopting a common habit, and iconographically promoting the cult of saints of Catherine of Alexandria and Margaret. Guglielma's devotees of both sexes, who appear to have been of different social origins (in some cases including high social classes), were branding themselves as the children of the Holy Spirit. Their devotion inclined toward the feminine (Guglielma would have been the incarnation of the Holy Spirit). This form of devotion might be linked to other similar experiences elsewhere, always smelling of heresy, that would have reached from England to Milan, where in 1301 an English woman "who said she was the Holy Spirit" died.[58] The link may also have passed through the Flanders of Marguerite Porete, a contemporary Beguine author of the *Mirror of Simple Souls*, who was burned at the stake in Paris in 1310. It probably would have also been connected with the later Milanese *cenacoli*, which may have welcomed theories inspired by the lay movements of the brothers and sisters of the Free Spirit.[59]

Those who respected the rules were in any case rewarded. Popes, archbishops, and communal and seignorial powers were fairly solicitous in favor of those institutions—confraternities, alms consortia, and hospitals—that occupied themselves with assisting the poor spiritually and materially, as evidenced by the numerous concessions of privileges of indulgence and tax exemptions. The ability to obtain indulgences and exemptions, as well as donations, made many confraternities' fortunes. The wealth of these institutions was reflected in their economic and

---

58. Marina Benedetti, *Io non sono Dio: Guglielma di Milano e i Figli dello Spirito Santo* (Milan: Edizioni Biblioteca francescana, 1998).

59. Robert E. Lerner, *The Heresy of the Free Spirit in the Later Middle Ages* (Berkeley: University of California Press, 1972).

social role. The confraternities were money collectors and administrators of real estate and land assets. Agricultural products, food products, and money were invested in a socially useful way. Together with hospitals, they developed into an important part of social security cushions.

## The Legacy of Medieval Growth

From the late Middle Ages to the early modern era, a gap opened up between institutions that insisted on charitable aspects, often greatly indebted to the themes of economic ethics preached by the friars of the mendicant orders, and others that instead concentrated on devotional purposes. This was the case of the confraternities of the *disciplinati*, a legacy of the mid-thirteenth-century movement, that were widespread in churches and neighborhood oratories until the end of the eighteenth century, where they continued to insist on moments of penance and prayer as a cathartic bond of the community. Likewise, one can observe the spread of new societies linked to religious orders, such as the confraternities of the Holy Rosary, for example, founded from the mid-fifteenth century in Dominican churches and later also promoted by the secular clergy.[60] Other devotional associations had more peculiar characteristics: they did not fit into the same matrix as the flagellant confraternities or those of the rosary, but this did not mean that they were destined for a lesser degree of success, as they focused on both the more intimate, erudite, and elite aspects of the religious sensibility, and on the most visible, popular, and easily shared manifestations.

These associations continued to evolve thanks to their intrinsic ability to reinvent themselves on the basis of the various impulses they were subjected to. There were indeed many stimuli to adapt to between the fifteenth and sixteenth centuries, deriving from a turbulent political framework, which led to the establishment of new foreign dominations over parts of Italy (first in the south, then in the north). These foreign governments upset the structures of social, economic, and religious life. There was also great pressure from an ecclesiastical order in a defensive position, but also on a proactive counterattack against political and

---

60. Danilo Zardin, "Beyond Crisis: Confraternities in Modern Italy between the Church and Lay Society," in *Faith's Boundaries: Laity and Clergy in Early Modern Confraternities*, ed. Nicholas Terpstra, Adriano Prosperi, and Stefania Pastore, Europa Sacra 6 (Turnhout: Brepols, 2012), 331-51.

pontifical interference on the one hand, and the criticism of reformers on the other. Indeed, as we know, the reformers took the confraternities themselves, their corporate spirit, their worldly apparatus (made up of banquets, images, relics), and not least the indulgences they promised, as a symbol of religion deviated and suffocated by the weight of material and particularistic interests.

With the transition to the new political and social structures of the modern age, that long phase of corporate proliferation that had characterized the Middle Ages appeared to be definitively waning. That phase had manifested itself in new or at least renewed forms compared to the past and was liable to a deep degree of permeability, confirming how this historical period represented a unique moment of community and institutional experimentation and innovation.

This change, however, does not translate to the disappearance of confraternities. On the contrary, in many Roman Catholic contexts their number increases. Not even the Council of Trent, which is often regarded as a watershed between a "before" and an "after" in the world of Catholic associationism for its strong disciplinary stand toward the associations of the lay religious, reduced access to the devotional confraternities. In fact, the confraternities, though regulated and sanctioned, continued to be a foundational model of the "good life" for the laity. The real change only arrived in the eighteenth century when, for the first time, questions were raised in the Catholic milieu concerning the formal and ritual aspects of the confraternities that were deemed to be too archaic and old-fashioned, even before in some territories, such as those subject to the Habsburg Empire or later to Napoleon, the ax of secularizing policies struck down.[61]

## Selected Bibliography

Here I include only the principal historiography for useful reference. Sources cited are referenced directly next to the corresponding text.

### Overview of the Documentary Heritage of Medieval Lay Solidarity

Cammarosano, Paolo. *Italia medievale: Struttura e geografia delle fonti scritte*. Rome: Carocci, 1991.
Gazzini, Marina. "Gli archivi delle confraternite: Documentazione, prassi conservative, memoria comunitaria." In *Studi confraternali: Orientamenti,*

---

61. Gazzini, "Confraternite tra medioevo ed età moderna."

*problemi, testimonianze*, edited by Marina Gazzini, 369-89. Reti medievali E-book 12. Florence: Firenze University Press, 2009. http://www.rm.unina.it/rmebook/index.php?mod=none_Gazzini_Studi.

## Medieval Community Movements

*Cofradías, gremios, solidaridades en la Europa Medieval*. Pamplona: Gobierno de Navarra, Departamento de Educación y Cultura, 1993.
Eisenbichler, Konrad, ed. *A Companion to Medieval and Early Modern Confraternities*. Leiden: Brill, 2019.
Escher-Apsner, Monika, ed. *Mittelalterliche Bruderschaften in europäischen Städten: Funktionen, Formen, Akteure/Medieval Confraternities in European Towns: Functions, Forms, Protagonists*. Frankfurt am Main: Peter Lang, 2009.
Michaud-Quantin, Pierre. *Universitas: Expression du mouvement communautaire dans le Moyen Âge latin*. Paris: Vrin, 1970.
*Le mouvement confraternel au Moyen Âge: France, Italie, Suisse. Actes de la table ronde organisée par l'Université de Lausanne avec le concours de l'École française de Rome et de l'Unité associée 1011 du CNRS "L'institution ecclésiale à la fin du Moyen Âge," Lausanne, 9–11 mai 1985*. Rome: École française de Rome, 1987.
Oexle, Otto Gerhard. "Die mittelalterlichen Gilden: Ihre Selbstdeutung und ihr Beitrag zur Formung sozialer Strukturen." In *Soziale Ordnungen im Selbstverständnis des Mittelalters*, edited by Albert Zimmermann, 203-26. Berlin: de Gruyter, 1979.
Zardin, Danilo, ed. *Corpi, "fraternità," mestieri nella storia della società europea*. Rome: Bulzoni, 1998.

## Italian Confraternities in General

Casagrande, Giovanna. *Religiosità penitenziale e città al tempo dei comuni*. Rome: Istituto Storico dei Cappuccini, 1995.
D'Andrea, David, and Salvatore Marino, eds. *Confraternities in Southern Italy: Art, Politics, and Religion (1100–1800)*. Toronto: Centre for Renaissance and Reformation Studies, 2022.
De Sandre Gasparini, Giuseppina. "Movimento dei disciplinati, confraternite e ordini mendicanti." In *I Frati Minori e il Terzo Ordine: Problemi e discussioni storiografiche*, 79-114. Todi: Accademia Tudertina, 1985.
Gazzini, Marina. *Confraternite e società cittadina nel Medioevo italiano*. Bologna: Clueb, 2006.
———. "Confraternite religiose laiche." In *Reti medievali Repertorio*. Florence: Reti medievali—Firenze University Press, 2007. http://www.rm.unina.it/repertorio/confrater.html.
———, ed. *Studi confraternali: Orientamenti, problemi, testimonianze*. Reti medievali E-book 12. Florence: Firenze University Press, 2009. http://www.rm.unina.it/rmebook/index.php?mod=none_Gazzini_Studi.
Meersseman, Gilles Gérard, in collaboration with Gian Piero Pacini. *Ordo fraternitatis: Confraternite e pietà dei laici nel Medioevo*. 3 vols. Rome: Herder, 1977.

Meersseman, Gilles Gérard, and Gian Piero Pacini. "Le confraternite laicali in Italia dal Quattrocento al Seicento." In *Problemi di storia della chiesa nei secoli XV–XVII*, 109–36. Naples: Edizioni Dehoniane, 1979.

Monti, Gennaro Maria. *Le confraternite medievali dell'alta e media Italia*. 2 vols. Venice: La Nuova Italia, 1927.

*Il movimento dei Disciplinati nel settimo centenario del suo inizio (Perugia 1260)*. Perugia: Deputazione di Storia Patria per l'Umbria, 1962.

Pastore, Stefania, Adriano Prosperi, and Nicholas Terpstra, eds. *Brotherhood and Boundaries/Fraternità e barriere*. Pisa: Edizioni della Normale, 2011.

Rigon, Antonio. "Schole, confraternite e ospedali." In *Pensiero e sperimentazioni istituzionali nella "Societas Christiana" (1046–1250)*, edited by Giancarlo Andenna, 407–27. Milan: Vita e Pensiero, 2007.

*Risultati e prospettive della ricerca sul movimento dei disciplinati*. Perugia: Deputazione di Storia Patria per l'Umbria, 1972.

Terpstra, Nicholas, ed. *The Politics of Ritual Kinship: Confraternities and Social Order in Early Modern Italy*. Cambridge: Cambridge University Press, 2000.

Vauchez, André. *Les laïcs au Moyen Âge: Pratiques et expériences religieuses*. Paris: Cerf, 1987.

Zangarini, M., ed. *Il buon fedele: Le confraternite tra medioevo e prima età moderna*. Quaderni di storia religiosa 5. Verona: Cierre, 1998.

## Specific Issues

Albini, Giuliana. "La gestione dell'Ospedale Maggiore nel Quattrocento: Un esempio di concentrazione ospedaliera." In Giuliana Albini, *Carità e governo delle povertà (secoli XII–XV)*, 267–81. Milan: Unicopli, 2002.

Artifoni, Enrico. "Corporazioni e società di 'popolo': Un problema della politica comunale nel secolo XIII." *Quaderni storici* 25, no. 74 (1990): 387–404.

Banker, James R. *Death in the Community: Memorialization and Confraternities in an Italian Commune in the Late Middle Ages*. Athens: University of Georgia Press, 1988.

Benedetti, Marina. *Io non sono Dio: Guglielma di Milano e i Figli dello Spirito Santo*. Milan: Edizioni Biblioteca francescana, 1998.

Benvenuti, Anna. "Ad procurationem caritatis et amoris et concordiae ad invicem: La Fraternita dei Laici di Arezzo tra sistema di solidarietà e solidarietà di sistema." *Annali aretini* 1 (1993): 79–104.

Bianchi, Francesco. "L'associazionismo nel medioevo." In *"Custode di mio fratello": Associazionismo e volontariato in Veneto dal medioevo a oggi*, edited by Francesco Bianchi, 25–131. Venice: Marsilio, 2010.

Black, Christopher. "The Putnam Thesis and Problems on the Early Modern Transition Period." In *Sociability and Its Discontents: Civil Society, Social Capital, and Their Alternatives in Late Medieval and Early Modern Europe*, edited by Nicholas Terpstra and Nicholas Eckstein, 227–45. Turnhout: Brepols, 2009.

Braunstein, Philippe. *Les Allemands à Venise (1380–1520)*. Rome: École française de Rome, 2016.

## 6. LAY CONFRATERNITIES

Brolis, Maria Teresa, and Giovanni Brembilla. "Mille e più donne in confraternita: Il *consorcium Misericordiae* di Bergamo nel Duecento." In *Il buon fedele: Le confraternite tra medioevo e prima età moderna*, ed. M. Zangarini, 107-34. Quaderni di storia religiosa 5. Verona: Cierre, 1998.

Casagrande, Giovanna. "Confraternities and Lay Female Religiosity in Late Medieval and Renaissance Umbria." In *The Politics of Ritual Kinship: Confraternities and Social Order in Early Modern Italy*, edited by Nicholas Terpstra, 48-66. Cambridge: Cambridge University Press, 2000.

Cattaneo, Enrico. "La corporazione dei muratori e la chiesa di S. Maria dei Ceppis." *Ricerche Storiche sulla Chiesa Ambrosiana* 10 (1981): 163-74.

Corniolo, Elena. "La confraternita del Santo Spirito della Porta Sant'Orso (Aosta, secoli XII-XIV)." *Reti Medievali Rivista* 15, no. 2 (2014): 3-39. https://doi.org/10.6092/1593-2214/437.

De Sandre Gasparini, Giuseppina. "Confraternite e campagna nell'Italia settentrionale del basso medioevo: Ricerche sul territorio veneto." In *Studi confraternali: Orientamenti, problemi, testimonianze*, edited by Marina Gazzini, 19-51. Reti medievali E-book 12. Florence: Firenze University Press, 2009. http://www.rm.unina.it/rmebook/index.php?mod=none_Gazzini_Studi.

———. *La vita religiosa nella Marca veronese-trevigiana tra XII e XIV secolo*. Verona: Libreria Universitaria Editrice, 1993.

Di Carpegna Falconieri, Tommaso. *Il clero di Roma nel Medioevo: Istituzioni e politica cittadina (secoli VIII-XIII)*. Rome: Viella, 2002.

Drell, Joanna H., and Paul Oldfield, eds. *Rethinking Norman Italy: Studies in Honour of Graham A. Loud*. Manchester: Manchester University Press, 2021.

Du Cange, Charles Du Fresne, ed. *Glossarium mediae et infimae latinitatis*. 10 vols. Niort: Léopold Favre, 1863-87.

Esposito, Anna. "Donne e confraternite." In *Studi confraternali: Orientamenti, problemi, testimonianze*, edited by Marina Gazzini, 53-78. Reti medievali E-book 12. Florence: Firenze University Press, 2009. http://www.rm.unina.it/rmebook/index.php?mod=none_Gazzini_Studi.

———. "Le minoranze indesiderate (corsi, slavi e albanesi) e il processo di integrazione nella società romana nel corso del Quattrocento." In *Cittadinanza e mestieri: Radicamento urbano e integrazione*, edited by Beatrice Del Bo, 283-98. Rome: Viella, 2014.

Fanti, Mario. *Confraternite e città a Bologna nel Medioevo e nell'età moderna*. Rome: Herder, 2001.

Gazzini, Marina. "Aiutare il forestiero: L'assistenza di ospedali e confraternite nel medioevo (Italia centro-settentrionale)." In "Hospitalité de l'étranger au Moyen Âge et à l'époque moderne: Entre charité, contrôle et utilité sociale. Italie Europe," edited by Ilaria Taddei and Naïma Ghermani, special issue, *Mélanges de l'École française de Rome: Moyen Âge* 131, no. 2 (2019): 407-16. http://journals.openedition.org/mefrm/5756.

———. "L'associazionismo religioso laicale a Milano dalla tradizione medievale all'età di Carlo Borromeo." In *Prima di Carlo Borromeo: Istituzioni, religione e società a Milano agli inizi del Cinquecento*, edited by Alberto Rocca and Paola Vismara, 269-89. Milan: Bulzoni, 2012.

———. "Confraternite e assistenza tra devozione e civismo." In *Storia di Parma*, vol. 3, bk. 2, *Parma medievale*, edited by Roberto Greci, 189–213. Parma: Monte Università Parma, 2011.

———. "Confraternite tra medioevo ed età moderna: Confini e contaminazioni (a mo' di post-fazione)." In *Confraternite in Trentino e a Riva del Garda*, edited by Emanuele Curzel, Maria Clara Rossi, and Marina Garbellotti, 195–200. Verona: Cierre edizioni, 2018.

———. "Costruire la comunità: L'apporto delle confraternite fra Due e Trecento. Alcuni esempi dal Nord e Centro Italia." *Rivista di storia della Chiesa in Italia* 68 (2014): 331–48.

———. "I Disciplinati, la milizia dei frati Gaudenti, il comune di Bologna e la pace cittadina: Statuti a confronto (1261–1265)." *Bollettino della Deputazione di storia patria per l'Umbria* 101 (2004): 419–37.

———. "Donne e uomini in confraternita: La matricola del Consorzio dello Spirito Santo di Piacenza (1268)." *Archivio Storico per le province parmensi*, 4th series, 52 (2000): 253–74.

———. "La fraternita come luogo di economia: Osservazioni sulla gestione delle attività e dei beni di ospedali e confraternite nell'Italia tardo-medievale." In *Assistenza e solidarietà in Europa: Secc. XIII–XVIII / Social Assistance and Solidarity in Europe from the 13th to the 18th Centuries*, edited by Francesco Ammannati, 261–76. Florence: Firenze University Press, 2013.

———. "I giovani tra famiglia naturale e famiglie artificiali." In *I giovani nel medioevo: Ideali e pratiche di vita*, edited by Isa Lori Sanfilippo and Antonio Rigon, 39–55. Rome: Istituto Storico Italiano per il Medio Evo, 2014.

———. "Guilds and Mutual Support in Medieval Italy." In *Professional Guilds and the History of Insurance: A Comparative Analysis*, edited by Phillip Hellwege, 166–217. Berlin: Dunkler & Humblot, 2020.

———. "Ospedali e reti: Il medioevo." In *Redes Hospitalarias: Historia, economía y sociología de la sanidad*, edited by Conceptión Villanueva Morte, Antoni Conejo da Pena, and Raúl Villagrasa-Elías, 13–30. Zaragoza: Excma. Diputación de Zaragoza, 2018.

———. "Solidarity and Brotherhood in Medieval Italian Confraternities: A Way of Inclusion or Exclusion?" *Reti Medievali Rivista* 13, no. 2 (2012): 109–20. https://doi.org/10.6092/1593-2214/359.

———. *Storie di vita e di malavita: Criminali, poveri e altri miserabili nelle carceri di Milano alla fine del medioevo*. Reti medievali E-book 30. Florence: Firenze University Press, 2017. http://www.rm.unina.it/rmebook/index.php?mod=none_Gazzini_Carceri.

Gazzini, Marina, and Antonio Olivieri, eds. "L'ospedale, il denaro e altre ricchezze: Scritture e pratiche economiche dell'assistenza in Italia nel tardo Medioevo." Monographic section in *Reti Medievali Rivista* 17, no. 1 (2016): 105–366. https://doi.org/10.6092/1593-2214/501.

Greci, Roberto. *Corporazioni e mondo del lavoro nell'Italia padana medievale*. Bologna: Clueb, 1988.

Grendi, Edoardo. "Le confraternite come fenomeno associativo e religioso." In *Società, Chiesa e vita religiosa nell' "ancien régime,"* edited by Carla Russo, 115–86. Naples: Guida, 1976.

Henderson, John. *Piety and Charity in Late Medieval Florence*. Oxford: Clarendon Press, 1994.
Houben, Hubert. "Le confraternite nel Mezzogiorno medioevale (sec. XII–XV): Status quaestionis e prospettive di ricerca." In *Tra Nord e Sud: Gli allievi per Cosimo Damiano Fonseca nel sessantesimo genetliaco*, edited by Giancarlo Andenna, Hubert Houben, and Benedetto Vetere, 171-90. Galatina: Congedo, 1993.
Le Bras, Gabriel. "Les confréries chrétiennes: Problèmes et propositions." *Revue historique de droit français et étranger* 19-20 (1940-41): 311-63.
Lerner, Robert E. *The Heresy of the Free Spirit in the Later Middle Ages*. Berkeley: University of California Press, 1972.
Luzzi, Serena. "La confraternita alemanna degli zappatori: Lineamenti per una storia della comunità tedesca a Trento fra tardo medioevo e prima età moderna." *Studi Trentini di Scienze Storiche* 73 (1994): 231-76, 331-63; 74 (1995): 47-92.
Mackenney, Richard S. *Tradesmen and Traders: The World of the Guilds in Venice and Europe, c. 1250–c. 1650*. London: Croom Helm, 1987.
Marino, Salvatore. *Ospedali e città nel Regno di Napoli: Le Annunziate, istituzioni, archivi e fonti (secc. XIV–XIX)*. Florence: Olschki, 2014.
Merlo, Grado Giovanni. *Contro gli eretici: La coercizione all'ortodossia prima dell'Inquisizione*. Bologna: Il Mulino, 1996.
Mesini, Candido. "Statuti piacentini-parmensi dei Disciplinati." *Archivio Storico per le province parmensi*, 4th series, 12 (1960): 43-70.
Monticolo, Giovanni, ed. *I capitolari delle arti veneziane sottoposte alla Giustizia e poi alla Giustizia vecchia, dalle origini al MCCCCXXX*. 3 vols. Rome: Istituto Storico Italiano per il Medio Evo, 1896-1914.
Natalini, Cecilia. "Appunti sui *collegia religionis causa* nella dottrina civilistica tra Glossa e Commento." In *Studi confraternali: Orientamenti, problemi, testimonianze*, edited by Marina Gazzini, 97-124. Reti medievali E-book 12. Florence: Firenze University Press, 2009. http://www.rm.unina.it/rmebook/index.php?mod=none_Gazzini_Studi.
Oldfield, Paul. *City and Community in Norman Italy*. Cambridge: Cambridge University Press, 2009.
Orlando, Ermanno. *Migrazioni mediterranee: Migranti, minoranze e matrimoni a Venezia nel basso Medioevo*. Bologna: Il Mulino, 2014.
Pezzola, Rita. *"Et in arca posui": Scritture della confraternita della Beata Vergine Assunta di Morbegno diocesi di Como*. Morbegno: Confraternita della Beata Vergine Assunta della Parrocchia di San Giovanni Battista di Morbegno, 2003.
Pini, Antonio Ivan. "In tema di corporazioni medievali: La 'Schola piscatorum' e la 'Casa Matha' di Ravenna." *Nuova Rivista Storica* 76 (1992): 729-76.
Prosdocimi, Luigi. *Il diritto ecclesiastico dello stato di Milano dall'inizio della signoria viscontea al periodo tridentino (sec. XIII–XVI)*. Milan: Cisalpino Goliardica, 1941.
Prosperi, Adriano, ed. *Misericordie: Conversioni sotto il patibolo tra Medioevo ed età moderna*. Pisa: Edizioni della Normale, 2007.
———. "Parrocchie e confraternite tra Cinquecento e Seicento." In *Per una storia dell'Emilia Romagna*, edited by Roberto Finzi, 174-86. Ancona: Il lavoro editoriale, 1985.

———. "Il sangue e l'anima: Ricerche sulle Compagnie di giustizia in Italia." In "I vivi e i morti," special issue, *Quaderni storici* 17, no. 50 (1982): 959-99.

Pullan, Brian. *Rich and Poor in Renaissance Venice: The Social Institutions of a Catholic State, to 1620*. Oxford: Blackwell, 1971.

Reid, Dylan. "Measuring the Impact of Brotherhood: Robert Putnam's Making Democracy Work and Confraternal Studies." *Confraternitas* 14 (2003): 3-12.

Russo, Vita, and Daniela Santoro. "Medieval Confraternities in Palermo." In *Confraternities in Southern Italy: Art, Politics, and Religion (1100–1800)*, edited by David D'Andrea and Salvatore Marino, 449-75. Toronto: Centre for Renaissance and Reformation Studies, 2022.

Sbriziolo, Lia. "Per la storia delle confraternite veneziane: Dalle deliberazioni miste (1310-1476) del Consiglio dei Dieci. 'Scolae comunes,' artigiane e nazionali." *Atti dell'Istituto veneto di scienze, lettere ed arti* 126 (1967-68): 405-42.

———. "Per la storia delle confraternite veneziane: Dalle deliberazioni miste (1310-1476) del Consiglio dei Dieci. Le scuole dei battuti." In *Miscellanea Gilles Gérard Meersseman*, 2:715-63. Padua: Editrice Antenore, 1970.

Şenocak, Neslihan. "Twelfth-Century Italian Confraternities as Institutions of Pastoral Care." *Journal of Medieval History* 42 (2016): 202-25, http://dx.doi.org/10.1080/03044181.2016.1141702.

Taddei, Ilaria. *Fanciulli e giovani: Crescere a Firenze nel Rinascimento*. Florence: Olschki, 2001.

Terpstra, Nicholas. *Lay Confraternities and Civic Religion in Renaissance Bologna*. Cambridge: Cambridge University Press, 1995.

Verga, Ettore. *La Camera dei Mercanti di Milano nei secoli passati*. Milan: Camera di Commercio e Industria di Milano, 1914.

Vitolo, Giovanni. "Confraternite dell'Italia centro-meridionale." In "Le confraternite in Italia fra Medioevo e Rinascimento: Atti della tavola rotonda, Vicenza, 3-4 novembre 1979," edited by Gabriele De Rosa. Special issue, *Ricerche di storia sociale e religiosa* 17-18 (1980): 64-70.

———. *Istituzioni ecclesiastiche e vita religiosa dei laici nel Mezzogiorno medievale: Il codice della confraternita di S. Maria di Montefusco (sec. XII)*. Rome: Herder, 1982.

Volpe, Gioacchino. *Movimenti religiosi e sette ereticali nella società medievale italiana: Secoli XI–XIV*. Florence: Vallecchi, 1922.

Weissman, Ronald F. E. *Ritual Brotherhood in Renaissance Florence*. New York: Academic Press, 1982.

Zardin, Danilo. "Beyond Crisis: Confraternities in Modern Italy between the Church and Lay Society." In *Faith's Boundaries: Laity and Clergy in Early Modern Confraternities*, edited by Nicholas Terpstra, Adriano Prosperi, and Stefania Pastore, 331-51. Europa Sacra 6. Turnhout: Brepols, 2012.

# Chapter 7

## Clerical Confraternities

*Antonio Rigon*

The confraternities or congregations of the clergy are among the most widespread yet least known realities in the history of the Church and the religious life of medieval Italy.[1] It was only thanks to the studies of Meersseman in the second half of the last century that the subject started to attract the attention of scholars and go beyond the purely erudite or localistic dimension of the research conducted up to that point.[2]

In the context of the many studies on medieval priests that have characterized Italian and international historiography from the 1980s onward, some works of a general and local nature have revealed the great richness of the archives of the clerical congregations in Italy, the opportunity they offer us to improve our knowledge of the fundamental structures of the care of souls and its protagonists, the importance

---

This chapter was translated by Hilary Siddons.

1. Gilles Gérard Meersseman, in collaboration with Gian Piero Pacini, *Ordo fraternitatis: Confraternite e pietà dei laici nel Medioevo*, 3 vols. (Rome: Herder, 1997), 1:113-35, 150-87.

2. Gennaro Maria Monti's *Le confraternite medievali dell'alta e media Italia* (Venice: La Nuova Italia, 1927) is an exception; in the context of wide-ranging research into the confraternity movement in central and northern Italy, it also pays some attention to the congregations of the clergy, but the work did not give rise to further significant research or create reflection on this topic.

of the confraternities of the clergy within the framework of medieval associations, and the particularity of the clerical confraternities compared to other forms of lay and clerical association.

The congregations of the clergy under discussion here should not be confused with the clerical colleges of individual churches, such as the collegiate churches or cathedral chapters. They are also different from the associations that sometimes formed in the late Middle Ages (here understood as the period corresponding to roughly 1250–1400) under the name of "Unions" predominantly for the purpose of taxation. The congregations of clergy, on the other hand, were free pious confraternities established for the purposes of prayer, worship, Masses for the souls of the dead, and mutual assistance, which brought together those members of the clergy serving different churches in the same city who wished to participate (and which generally admitted the laity under certain conditions as well).

Some of them, while maintaining the character of associations dedicated to prayer for the souls of the dead, mutual aid of their members, and the promotion of charitable initiatives, also took on the form of veritable corporations to protect and represent the clergy in the care of souls and the defense of the rights and privileges associated with this function. Even though they were present in other parts of Europe, where for the late Middle Ages at least, models of association that were extremely diverse are often lumped together indistinctly,[3] the clerical associations that went by a variety of names (*fratalea, fraternitas, congregatio, conventus, consortium*) were present throughout the whole of Italy, from north to south,[4] and were closely linked to the world of the city; in fact it would not be wrong to say that they were one of its characteristic features.

When it comes to rural clerical confraternities, we know very little; even in those places where we know they were present, such as the case of the congregation of the *clero estrinseco* of Verona,[5] the lack of records

---

3. Tommaso di Carpegna Falconieri, "Il clero secolare nel basso medioevo: Acquisizioni e proposte di ricerca," *Archivio della Società romana di storia patria* 132 (2009): 35–40; and cf. Antonio Rigon, "Le congregazioni del clero in Italia: Bilancio di studi e prospettive di ricerca," in *Realtà archivistiche a confronto: Le associazioni dei parroci. Atti del Convegno di Ravenna (24 settembre 2010)*, ed. Gilberto Zacchi (Modena: Mucchi, 2011), 10, 12.

4. See the data collected by Giancarlo Rocca, "Per un primo censimento delle associazioni sacerdotali in Italia dal medioevo a oggi," *Rivista di storia della Chiesa in Italia* 64 (2010): 397–517.

5. For which see Maria Clara Rossi, "Forme associative del clero medievale: La Congregatio cleri extrinseci di Verona," in *"Arbor ramosa": Studi per Antonio Rigon da allievi amici colleghi*, ed. Luciano Bertazzo et al. (Padua: Centro studi antoniani, 2011), 415–30.

limits the possibility of further study. As for the urban congregations of the clergy, however, it must be pointed out that they were not only very widespread but they also lasted for a long time, some even surviving up to the present day in various forms. In Venice, many priests, for example, take part in the processions for the feast of the Redeemer, the Madonna della Salute, and the feast of Saint Anthony, dressed in precious garments of varying colors, which indicate their membership of one of the nine ancient congregations of the clergy.[6] These Venetian congregations continue to exist even today as a lively aspect of the urban and religious life. Similarly, in Piacenza, the congregation of the urban parish priests is still today a vital part of worship, Masses for the souls of the dead, and mutual assistance for its members.[7]

## The Problem of the Origins

Local historians have often indicated that the first evidence of the life of the congregations dates to the tenth century. This is true of Venice and Piacenza as mentioned above, of Treviso, Ferrara, Faenza, and other cities.[8] There is no doubt that in the Carolingian period there was already enthusiastic support for the ideals and forms of communal life for the secular clergy.[9] It must be said, however, that placing the origins of clerical congregations in Italy in the tenth century tends to be in general vague and cannot be attested on the basis of reliable documentary evidence. In Rome, however, epigraphical evidence dating to 984 would

---

6. Cf. Diego Sartorelli and Manuela Barausse, "Le nove congregazioni del clero di Venezia e i loro archivi," in Zacchi, *Realtà archivistiche a confronto*, 47.

7. Ugo Bruschi, "Le carte e i silenzi: La Congregazione dei parroci di Piacenza, un millennio vissuto tra luci della ribalta e ritiri nell'ombra," in Zacchi, *Realtà archivistiche a confronto*, 163.

8. On the problem of the origins of the nine congregations of the clergy of Venice and the difficulties of dating the beginnings of these associations, see Bianca Betto, *Le nove congregazioni del clero di Venezia (sec. XI–XV): Ricerche storiche, matricole e documenti vari* (Padua: Antenore, 1984), 9–24. Bruschi, "Le carte e i silenzi," 155–57 (on Piacenza). Antonio Rigon, "La congregazione dei parroci di Treviso nel medioevo (secoli XII–XIV)," in *Studi e fonti del Medioevo Vicentino e Veneto*, vol. 2, ed. Antonio Morsoletto (Vicenza: Accademia Olimpica, 2003), 92–93. Antonio Samaritani, "Il 'conventus' e le congregazioni chiericali di Ferrara tra analoghe istituzioni ecclesiastiche nei secoli X–XV," *Ravennatensia* 7 (1979): 159–202. Marco Mazzotti, "Notizie sul collegio dei parroci di Faenza e il suo archivio," in Zacchi, *Realtà archivistiche a confronto*, 122.

9. Gilles Gérard Meersseman, "Die Klerikervereine von Karl dem Grossen bis Innocenz III," *Zeitschrift für schweizerische Kirchengeschichte* 46 (1952): 22–32.

seem to indicate the existence at this date of the *Romana fraternitas*, that is, the principal medieval association of the city's clergy.[10]

In reality, some doubts remain as to the relationship between the inscription dated to that year and the clerical association in Rome; another three epigraphs dating to the end of the tenth century and the beginning of the eleventh century would seem to confirm the existence of the *fraternitas*, however. What needs to be stressed is that it was established primarily for funerary services, that is to say, to celebrate the funerals of the members of the confraternity. Regardless of the particular problems that an association born in a city like Rome, the seat of papacy, faced, and the difficulty of making it a paradigm for the other Italian cities, the reason for its establishment was of a liturgical nature, not unlike that of other similar associations in other cities, for which we begin to find records in the centuries that followed.[11]

Celebrating funerals, prayers for the dead, the liturgical exercise of charity to the poor, the meetings on the first day of the month (calends) with a communal banquet, the chanting of the Divine Office, and the communal celebration of the Mass were the principal activities that congregations had in common in the early phase of their life, when their liturgical vocation prevailed. It is not a coincidence that the traces of these ancient rituals can still be found in the late medieval statutes of some confraternities that, as we will discuss later, refer to the common meal according to a tradition that goes back to the calends of the Carolingian age or are a reminder of charity to the poor as practiced in prayer meetings.

In the course of the eleventh and twelfth centuries, when the evidence for the existence of clerical confraternities starts to appear with increasing frequency, the promotion of forms of aggregation of priests and clerics seems also to be linked to episcopal plans for reform along lines that had already been shaped in the Carolingian age and were experimented with during the Gregorian period. The presence of passages from the works of Bruno of Segni (bishop, theologian, and advisor to Pope Gregory VII), as well as liturgical texts and statutes in a register of the congregation of the chaplains of Lucca has rightly made scholars hypothesize a link between the promotion of the communal life of clergy by Gregorian reformers and the development in the Italian

---

10. Tommaso di Carpegna Falconieri, *Il clero di Roma nel Medioevo: Istituzioni e politica cittadina (secoli VIII–XIII)* (Rome: Viella, 2002), 242–47.

11. Cf. Meersseman, *Ordo fraternitatis*, 1:182.

cities of congregations of urban clergy, who were expected to revive and consolidate the identity of the parish priest during a period of profound change in the Church and rapid transformation of society.[12]

In the same way, the fact that the statutes of the congregation of the clergy of Perugia included a chapter of the so-called Rule of Aachen, written for the canon regulars, shows a connection with the lifestyles that had led to the development of the common life of the clergy as the qualifying element of the reform of the eleventh century.[13] In the case of the congregation of the clergy of Aversa in the south of Italy too, scholars have pointed out the connection between the strong role it had in creating clerical aggregation under the hierarchical and disciplinary control of the bishop in the twelfth century and plans for reform of a Gregorian nature that had been accepted by the First Lateran Council in 1123.[14]

## Expansion and Change

Up until the end of the eleventh century, we have little certain evidence of clerical associations. Only in the next century do we enter a period in which there is solid documentary evidence of clerical congregations with features that were destined to become consolidated and to last. These also reveal changes, however, compared to the exclusively liturgical contents of previous experiences, at least for those few examples we know about. It is as if, with the congregations, the clergy too was discovering associationism as a force for creating new realities: a force that in Italy above all, was giving rise in the political field to the emergence of the communes, in the field of labor and economic and social organization to the guilds, and in the religious field to the confraternities of laypeople and clergy or laypeople only.

The associations of the clergy were born from the bottom up, freely and spontaneously, sometimes with the explicit support of the bishops and popes who favored their development. In Padua, the first evidence of the *fratalea cappellanorum* dates back to the bishopric of Saint Bellino (1128–47), who was committed to turning around the fortunes of the

---

12. Raffaele Savigni, "L'archivio della congregazione dei cappellani lucchesi," in Zacchi, *Realtà archivistiche a confronto*, 78.
13. Andrea Maiarelli, *La Congregatio clericorum Perusinae Ecclesiae: Edizione e studio del codice 39.20 della Biblioteca Capitular di Toledo* (Rome: Herder, 2007), 53–65, 92–98.
14. Cosimo Damiano Fonseca, "Riforma ecclesiastica e collegialità del clero: Il caso di Aversa," in *Preti nel medioevo*, Quaderni di storia religiosa 4 (Verona: Cierre, 1997), 12.

Paduan Church, which had been shaken by the long crisis during the investiture conflict. After him, Bishop Gerardo Offreducci, who led the diocese from 1165 to 1213, made a long series of interventions to define the proper duties and the organizational structure of the association, which also enjoyed papal backing.[15]

In Verona, during the period in which the papal Curia was present, the so-called congregation of the *clero intrinseco* (the urban clergy), mentioned for the first time in 1102, received recognition of their goods and rights from Popes Lucius III (1184) and Urban III (1186).[16] From the twelfth century onward, the bishops, popes, and other organs of the Roman Curia intervened in favor of the convent of the chaplains of Lucca, which probably originated in the context of the process of reconstruction of the diocese initiated by Bishop Rangerio (1096–ca. 1112).[17] In Piacenza, a privilege from Pope Alexander III dating to June 15, 1163, with which the pope took the congregation of urban parish priests under his protection, records the foundation or perhaps more probably the restructuring of the association by the late Bishop Sigifredo.[18]

The examples could easily be multiplied, but what should be stressed now is that the birth of the clerical confraternities in the twelfth century was not an isolated phenomenon; indeed, it was very often related to that of the urban parishes, which, in turn, paralleled urban development and the increase in the city population. This is a phenomenon that can be observed in various cities, which favored above all that part of the clergy linked to the popular classes locked in a battle for representation and power within the commune. While the canons of the cathedral belonged mostly to the aristocracy of blood and money, the priests and the clergy of the parishes generally had more humble origins.

Even though there were no clerical associations like those in other cities, in Milan the conflict between the nobles and the *popolo* that was taking place in civic society in the twelfth and thirteenth centuries for access to the principal communal magistracies was intertwined and had a clear effect on the conflict that was taking place in an ecclesiastical context between the higher clergy (*ordinario*) from the military classes

---

15. Antonio Rigon, *Clero e città: "Fratalea cappellanorum," parroci, cura d'anime in Padova dal XII al XV secolo* (Padua: Istituto per la storia ecclesiastica padovana, 1988), 22–24.

16. Maureen C. Miller, *Chiesa e società in Verona medievale*, ed. Paolo Golinelli (Verona: Cierre, 1998), 84–86. Rossi, "Forme associative del clero medievale," 422–23.

17. Savigni, "L'archivio della congregazione dei cappellani lucchesi," 67, 71–72.

18. Bruschi, "Le carte e i silenzi," 157.

of the *capitanei* and the *valvassores* and the lower clergy (*decumano*)—numerous and underpaid, generally from families who had acquired their wealth more recently and who claimed the right to the immunity to taxation enjoyed by the higher clergy and the possibility of access to the more important and prestigious ecclesiastical positions.[19]

In Rome, the process that allowed the urban clergy to establish itself in an institutionally defined association under the name of *Romana fraternitas* corresponds to the evolutionary process that led the lay citizens of Rome to establish themselves as a commune.[20] Indeed, the tendency for the clerical confraternities to take a corporate form developed during a period of leadership of the urban clergy in both the religious life (between the incipient decline of traditional monasticism and the emergence of mendicant orders) and civic life, with significant points of contact and exchange with the social context and the new urban political realities.

It is worth noting that in a city like Lucca, the *conventus cappellanorum* normally met in churches that also hosted the judicial courts of the city or associations like those of the merchants.[21] In Padua, the meetings of the *fratalea cappellanorum* and the communal *concio*, assemblies of new political and ecclesiastical organisms, were held initially, at least on some occasions, in the same church of Saint Martin, whose parish priest also officiated at the church of the communal *palazzo* dedicated to the bishop San Prosdocimo, patron of the city.[22]

These are clues to a real link between the new organisms of the clergy, the city, and the communal governments. It also should be pointed out that in southern Italy, when the political organisms fell under the structures of the Regno, congregations of the clergy very similar to those of central and northern Italy were created. An emblematic case is that of Benevento, where in the twelfth century as many as three clerical congregations emerged (Santo Spirito, San Bartolomeo, and Sant'Eufemia) in the decades during which the establishment of new parishes reached a peak, and in a period full of experimentation at the height of local power that took on forms that tended to be very similar

---

19. Cf. Antonio Rigon, "Il ruolo delle chiese locali nelle lotte tra magnati e popolani," in *Magnati e popolani nell'Italia comunale: Quindicesimo convegno di studi, Pistoia 15–18 maggio 1995* (Pistoia: Centro italiano di studi di storia e d'arte, 1997), 118–21.
20. Di Carpegna Falconieri, *Il clero di Roma*, 86, 97.
21. Savigni, "L'archivio della congregazione dei cappellani lucchesi," 72–73.
22. Rigon, *Clero e città*, 36–37.

to those of the communal regimes of central and northern Italy.[23] Moreover, it is perhaps not devoid of significance that Benevento constituted an extraterritorial enclave with respect to the Regno, from which it had been separated during the course of the eleventh century, submitting itself to papal power and developing a strong spirit of autonomy and a strong civic consciousness not unlike that of the communal cities of central and northern Italy.[24]

In reality, with the formation of clerical confraternities, especially those that without abandoning their liturgical vocation, assumed a more markedly corporate structure, the clergy showed a clearer awareness of itself and its role in the Church and in urban society. Its relationship with the political and social contexts of the city should not be understood, however, merely as a parallel development of organizational systems in an associative sense and a resemblance to the evolution of institutional organisms, urban planning, and social structures, but also as conflict and participation in the internal struggles of the communes.

We know, for example, that in Brescia in the second decade of the thirteenth century, a *colligatio* of the clergy formed against the bishop, perhaps in protest against the taxation imposed to finance the Crusades. Honorius III condemned the initiative, however, accusing the priests of having given rise to a *conspiratio* and not a *fraternitas*.[25] In the cities of Padua, Verona, and Treviso, the associations of parish priests demanded a precise institutional role, claiming the right to participate in the election of the bishop with their own representation.[26]

And if, even in the course of the thirteenth century, in Padua this prerogative was not effectively recognized *de facto* if not *de iure*, in the other two cities the representatives of the pastoral clergy were taking part in the appointment of the bishop in the fourteenth century too. It is on these and other similar occasions (for example, in the repeated contrasts with the canons of the cathedral churches on the most varied subjects) that the pastoral clergy reveals an associative awareness and

---

23. Giovanni Araldi, *Vita religiosa e dinamiche politico-sociali: Le congregazioni del clero a Benevento (secoli XII–XIV)* (Naples: Società napoletana di storia patria, 2016), 11, 198 n. 39.
24. Araldi, *Vita religiosa e dinamiche politico-sociali*, 305–6.
25. Rigon, "Il ruolo delle chiese locali," 122.
26. For Padua, see Rigon, *Clero e città*, 65–67; for Verona, see Maria Clara Rossi, "Le elezioni vescovili: Il caso di Verona scaligera," in *Gli Scaligeri (1277–1387)*, ed. Gian Maria Varanini (Verona: Arnoldo Mondadori, 1988), 405–11; for Treviso, see Rigon, "La congregazione dei parroci di Treviso," 95–96.

an esprit de corps, a consciousness of their own identity, and a perception of the dignity of their mission. These aspects also manifest themselves in the rules contained in the statutes of their associations, in religious and charitable practices, and in the rites fixed in the registers and in the books kept in the archives of the congregations.

## Statutes and Other Confraternity Books: Typology and Contents

Like other political, religious, economic, or social bodies, the twelfth- and thirteenth-century confraternities of the urban clergy elaborated normative texts regulating their members' lives and activities, establishing their rights and obligations, admission requirements, internal hierarchies, and ways of managing the common patrimony. Traces of ancient rules can already be found in the eleventh century in the confraternities of cities like Treviso and Perugia.[27] Subsequently, the development of more or less organic statutory legislation can be seen in all clerical associations. Alongside the statutes, there are accounting books and notarial acts, the registers of the enrolled members, and registers of attendance and absences in order to document the administrative functioning and the social dimension of the life of clerical associations; obituaries, registers of the dead, calendars, and liturgical codes attest instead to their religious activity. In some cases, as with the congregations of Lodi, Treviso, Perugia, Viterbo, and Santo Spirito in Benevento, the main materials needed to ensure their proper functioning were collected together with the regulatory corpus in a single manuscript that ended up becoming a veritable archive-manuscript.[28] Although

---

27. Rigon, "La congregazione dei parroci di Treviso," 93. The *constitutio* of the *congregatio clericorum* of Perugia, contained in Codice 39.20 of the Biblioteca capitular of Toledo, "un 'fossile' normativo, assai ben conservato, della prima metà dell'XI secolo," "si presenta come il risultato di una revisione condotta dal vescovo Andrea su un testo precedente, risalente almeno al secolo X e non necessariamente di origine locale" (Maiarelli, *La Congregatio clericorum*, 42, 69, and 70–76 for information on Bishop Andrea who ruled the diocese of Perugia from at least 1036).

28. For Lodi the obligatory reference is to Jean-Loup Lemaître, "Le consorce du clergé de Lodi et son Missel, XII<sup>e</sup>–XIV<sup>e</sup> siècle," in *Le mouvement confraternel au Moyen Âge: France, Italie, Suisse. Actes de la table ronde organiseé par l'Université de Lausanne avec le concours de l'École française de Rome et de l'Unité associée 1011 du CNRS "L'institution ecclésiale à la fin du Moyen Âge," Lausanne, 9–11 mai 1985* (Rome: École française de Rome, 1987), 185–220; for Treviso, see Antonio Rigon, "Messaletto, sec XIV," in *Treviso cristiana: 2000 anni di fede. Percorso storico, iconografico, artistico della diocesi*, ed. Lucio Bonora, Eugenio Manzato, and Ivano Sartor (Treviso: Diocesi di Treviso, 2000), 225; for Perugia, see Maiarelli, *La Congregatio clericorum*, 39–43; for Viterbo,

differences can be detected on a case-by-case basis, these manuscripts have many similar features, and hence they could be identified as a specific typology of historical source for congregational books. However, no systematic research has been carried out with a comparative method that could allow us to come to a conclusion on this subject.

Likewise, from the point of view of the contents, we have no studies that address the problem of whether or not any common liturgical and normative models existed and how they were transmitted to different and sometimes distant dioceses.[29] Certainly, the ideal inspiration and aims of the associations were very similar. As we can read in the statutes, documents, and liturgical books, the mission of priests and clerics can only be the salvation of the souls of the living and the dead. The doctrine of the communion of the saints, defined with increasing clarity by the scholastics, was the theological foundation of this mandate, and the clerical associations provided a suitable structure for carrying out such a task.[30] In particular, however, the congregations were responsible for the *cura animarum defunctorum*. As Christ had cared for all infirmities, so he had conferred on his servants the power to care for the souls of the dead through prayers and orations offered to the poor deceased. This is stated in the constitutions of the *clero intrinseco* of Verona dating back to around 1323.[31]

Prayer, however, did not represent all the activities carried out in the sphere of the care of souls. Salvation could also be achieved by means of works such as alms, charitable initiatives, assistance in the case of illness, and funeral services, which primarily concerned members of the congregations. Charitable works were extended, however, in various more or less ritualized forms to outsiders too, and therefore may have included (as in Padua) visiting prisoners or (as in Benevento) the management of a hospital.[32]

As for the recruitment of its members, in the cities where there was a single congregation, the tendency was to bring all the clergy of the

---

see Corrado Buzzi, ed., *La "Margarita iurium cleri Viterbensis"* (Rome: Società romana di storia patria, 1993); and for Benevento, Alfredo Zazo, ed., *L'"Obituarium S. Spiritus" della Biblioteca Capitolare di Benevento (secc. XII–XIV)* (Naples: Fausto Fiorentino, 1963) and cf. Araldi, *Vita religiosa e dinamiche politico-sociali*, 89-127.

29. Cf. Savigni, "L'archivio della congregazione dei cappellani lucchesi," 77.

30. Antonio Rigon, "Le congregazioni del clero urbano in area veneta (XII–XV sec.)," in *Le mouvement confraternel au Moyen Âge*, 353.

31. Rigon, "Le congregazioni del clero urbano," 353.

32. For Padua, see Rigon, *Clero e città*, 174. For Benevento, Araldi, *Vita religiosa e dinamiche politico-sociali*, 246-49.

parishes of the towns and villages together. Where there was more than one congregation, such as in Venice and Benevento, recruiting was equally open to clerics of the whole city. But the forms of orientation could be very different. In Benevento it seems that most of the members of the confraternity of Santo Spirito were not the titulars of the parish churches, who were often absent, but their substitutes who were in a very precarious situation.[33]

From the beginning, we also find laypeople in most of the clerical associations, men and women. Although excluded from any involvement in the management and administration of the confraternity and the enjoyment and management of its goods, laypeople could, however, associate with it and thus participate in the spiritual benefits that derived from it, acquired by the congregation thanks to the way of life of its members, the exercise of the works of mercy, intense liturgical activity, and almsgiving. Structurally included in the congregations, the laity participated in the associated life of clerics in their own ways.

According to the constitutions of the *clero intrinseco* of Verona of 1323, for example, laypeople had to take part in Mass and the procession on the first Friday of the month, reciting prayers aloud; they were obliged to attend the funerals of the members; they had to say prayers once a month—albeit different ones depending on their ability to read—for the souls of the deceased benefactors and members, and for the salvation of the living persons and the whole city.[34] In Padua the statutes of 1400 prescribe that on the death of a confrere, be he a cleric or a layman, the laypeople, men or women, should pray for him, saying daily, until the thirtieth day, twenty-five paternosters for his soul.[35]

The lay confreres, however, had no decision-making role within the associations nor did they occupy any positions, which remained the exclusive prerogative of the clergy members. At the top there were one or more priests who held their position for life or, more often, were elected for a certain period of time. Variously named (*abbas, prior, major, primicerius, archipresbiter, rector, praepositus*), they were assisted by collaborators (*decani, conciliatores*), administrators (*camerarii, sindici, procuratores*), nuncios, and sometimes other officials according to local customs. These people were charged with the leadership, the administration, and the economic management of the congregations.

---

33. Araldi, *Vita religiosa e dinamiche politico-sociali*, 146–48.
34. Rigon, "Le congregazioni del clero urbano," 350, n. 21.
35. Rigon, "Le congregazioni del clero urbano," 350, n. 21.

## An Economy of the Casual

Each confraternity possessed more or less extensive real estate property in lands and houses, the income from which was shared between its members or used for their charitable activities. In Padua the *fratalea cappellanorum* also received revenues from the collection of the *quartese* tithes of the parish churches of the city.[36] The congregation of the *clero intrinseco* of Verona even possessed a village, donated to it by Bishop Norandino in 1220.[37] But at the present state of research we do not know to what extent this situation can be generalized. It is certain, however, that the congregations received donations, testamentary bequests, enrollment fees from the laity, and sums of money for the celebrations of funerals and anniversaries, which were distributed among the confreres as a payment for participating in the activities of the confraternity. Everything was punctually paid: the attendance at periodical meetings, funerals and anniversaries, ceremonies and processions, or holding positions within the association. Significant in this respect, and an indication of a widespread mentality, is a statement made in 1328 by a Paduan parish priest in his will: each confrere of the *fratalea cappellanorum* who had taken part in the anniversary Mass to commemorate his death had to be paid a salary for his work (*stipendia sui laboris offerre*), and therefore his fatigue had to be rewarded with the fruits from a piece of land he had left the association for this purpose in his will.[38]

It was thanks to this kind of legacy and other donations that the congregations started to own and to increase their possession of real estate and land, although, as far as we know, with some exceptions like that of the *clero intrinseco* of Verona, the amount possessed never seems to have reached great proportions. While not neglecting the traditional forms of economy linked to the possession of land and houses and rights on land (*quartese* and *decime dominicali* tithes), the confraternities of the clergy, which had developed throughout the Italian peninsula in the age of urban rebirth and were closely connected to the social, political, and religious contexts of the city, became part of the urban world from an economic point of view as well. Mobile and dynamic, they adapted themselves to the growing monetarization of the economy and to a new

---

36. Rigon, *Clero e città*, 41–61, 191–96.
37. Rossi, "Forme associative del clero medievale," 426.
38. Rigon, *Clero e città*, 218.

way of procuring and using resources, thanks to which, what mattered most were the human relations and the social network to which the associations referred and were connected, rather than property and the possession of titles.

Enrollment fees for new lay members, bequests from wills, occasional donations, sums of money related to funeral services and funeral rites, and pecuniary remuneration in exchange for prayers for the dead were the most widespread source of revenue, more casual than stable. In order to secure these revenues, it was crucial to keep the prestige of the associations high and to broaden their network of relations with the urban society as far as possible.

## Confraternities of the Clergy and City Society

As we can see, even a rule like that contained in the statutes of the congregation of the chaplains of Lucca of 1295—which stipulated that each member, if he so desired, could have an anniversary Mass for the souls of his relatives celebrated in his own church or in another[39]—went in the direction of enlarging and strengthening the bonds of association with the urban society. Albeit in a limited way, extending liturgical services in favor of the deceased to the relatives of its members allowed the congregations to go beyond the restricted circle of its mere members. Commemorating the dead and, with it, family memories, domestic piety, and private religious traditions, all intertwined and were inevitably present in funeral celebrations, converging in the liturgical activity carried out by the associations of the clergy, which in most cases welcomed the priests and clerics of all or most of the parish churches and opened their doors to the lay faithful from the whole city.

In urban contexts deeply divided and disturbed by factional struggles, individual churches were often a reference point for groups fighting among themselves (particularly in the most intense phases of internal conflict within the communes between the *magnati* and the *popolo*).[40] On the contrary, the clerical confraternities, overcoming the purely local dimensionality of the parish and the *contrada* through the union

---

39. "*De anniversario faciendo pro animabus parentum nostrorum*. Item quod quilibet de nostra congregatione faciat fieri, si vult, aniversarium annuatim pro animabus parentum suorum in ecclesia sua vel alibi ut sibi placuerit" (Savigni, "L'archivio della congregazione dei cappellani lucchesi," 89, no. 20).

40. Cf. Rigon, "Il ruolo delle chiese locali," 124–28.

of the clergy and laity of several churches in their work in the care of souls, could also play a role in balancing and pacifying the different factions.

Indeed, in documents and statutes of the associations, concord between the members is indicated as a fundamental requirement when joining or belonging to the association, and it was obligatory for those who were the leaders of the association to settle possible conflicts, even by using penalties against those who may have fostered fights. "No one will be accepted unless he is at peace with the others and no one may be removed without knowing the cause and after having heard the opinion of all or most of them."[41] This request, introduced in 1192 by two priests in a controversy with the priors of the chaplains of Lucca, clearly summarizes what more or less detailed legislation required in the statutes of many congregations.

It is true, however, that the presence in the statutes of many norms aimed at repressing and, in any case, controlling disagreements among members demonstrates that there was a high degree of conflict within the associations. The documents preserved in the congregation archives give extensive proof of this. In Lucca there were disputes about how to accept and remove members, the election of priors, and removing benefits from members who had moved elsewhere;[42] in Padua there were disputes over the collection of the *quartese*;[43] and in Faenza the association intervened in the case of disputes between parish priests and parishioners.[44]

And we could easily add more examples. Even more important was the conflict between the members and other ecclesiastical authorities. Conflict with the canons, antagonists of the parish priests in urban pastoral life, in the management of legacies and benefits, and in the demand for greater dignity within the local ecclesiastical world, were frequent more or less everywhere. In Padua, a very high proportion of the earliest records of the *fratalea cappellanorum* deal with disputes with

---

41. "Nullus recipiatur nisi in pace et . . . nullus amoveatur nisi cognita causa et cognito consilio omnium vel maioris partis" (Savigni, "L'archivio della congregazione dei cappellani lucchesi," 81).

42. Savigni, "L'archivio della congregazione dei cappellani lucchesi," 80–81.

43. Rigon, *Clero e città*, 81–83.

44. Antonio Rigon, "Congregazioni del clero cittadino e storia della parrocchia nell'Italia settentrionale: Il problema delle fonti," in *La parrocchia nel Medio Evo: Economia, scambi, solidarietà*, ed. Agostino Paravicini Bagliani and Véronique Pasche (Rome: Herder, 1995), 16.

the chapter of the cathedral, with churches that were not part of the confraternity, and with monasteries for the right to collect tithes and *quartesi*.[45] The succession of contrasts also arose due to an uncertainty over boundaries and the need to make a precise division and an exact delimitation of the new cultivated spaces on which the mobile boundary of the city territory was enlarging in the twelfth and thirteenth centuries.[46]

It should also be added that the resolution of these conflicts was also strongly affected by the commune, in whose courts the cases that set the *fratalea* against the lay landowners located within the *territorium civitatis* were discussed. In Padua again, regardless of the outcome of the cases, which normally favored the associations of the parish priests, the repeated disputes debated in the *palazzo* of the commune in front of the judge of the *podestà* clearly show the political power's desire to control matters concerning the *quartese*.[47]

But not everything was contended. There was a strong symbiosis between the clergy and the city, which was explicit in the names of the congregations that referred to the city to which they belonged and its suburbs, in the recruitment of members that excluded members of the clergy who did not belong to the city parishes, and in the sense of belonging to a wider urban community—the divine protection of which was invoked in the statutes and to the honor of which the congregations declared they were constituted.[48] The congregations operated in an urban space, a theater of rites, processions, and funeral cortèges, and they acted at a time that was urban, marked by the sound of the bells of the churches and the civic *palazzi*.[49]

---

45. Rigon, *Clero e città*, 53–61.
46. Rigon, *Clero e città*, 53.
47. Rigon, *Clero e città*, 60–61.
48. See here the *proemio* of the fifteenth-century statutes of the *fratalea cappellanorum* of Padua, in which the *rettori* of the churches who were part of it, having paid homage to the heavenly beings and the earthy institutions, declared that the association was constituted "ad laudem Redemptoris nostri eiusdemque matris Virginis gloriose tociusque curie celestis nec non ad honorem et reverenciam sacrosancte Romane Ecclesie dominique episcopi et capituli Paduani dominorumque primicerii et rectorum presentis congregacionis et tocius cleri Paduani, ad honorem et bonum statum civitatis Padue et tocius eiudem populi, ad utilitatem et proficuum animarum omnium fidelium et potissime descriptorum in hac congregacione fratalee" (Rigon, *Clero e città*, 303).
49. For interesting evidence relating to Verona and Venice, see Rigon, "Le congregazioni del clero urbano," 357–58.

## Death, the Body, and Rites

Although they were involved on several fronts, funeral liturgy in all its parts and aspects was still at the center of the activities of the clerical confraternities. Taking on the responsibility for serving in everything related to the management of death and the *cura animarum defunctorum* allowed the secular clergy involved in the parishes to play a key role in controlling funeral rites, increasingly putting themselves forward in the late Middle Ages as a specialized body delegated to carry out the primary function of mediation between the living and the dead.

By creating special associations, the clergy thus increased the chances of dealing with the growing demand for Masses for the dead, which the monks traditionally designated to this office were no longer able to satisfy fully.[50] In addition, clerics associated with confraternities were guaranteed additional economic benefits as well as those that came from the ordinary daily care of souls in the parish churches. The constant presence in the statutes of the associations of instructions concerning funeral celebrations and the commemoration of the deceased, both clerical and lay, confirms the specific funerary function these associations carried out and, for the late Middle Ages, was an important sign of change in religious sensitivity and new mental attitudes toward death.

It is well known in fact that after much uncertainty, clearly visible in the perplexities of Saint Augustine, for whom burial was not destined to have any influence on the resurrection of the dead, in the Christian religion the practices of piety toward the deceased began to be considered a devout work, and from the twelfth century burial of the dead was added to the six works of mercy indicated in Matthew 25:6. This turning point was also influenced by a renewed interest in the body and the respect due to it after death, stimulated by theological, philosophical, and scientific debates on resurrection and the new sensibility for the human body that developed in the thirteenth and fourteenth centuries.[51] It is thus that the congregations of the clergy intercepted the demands and pressing requests of the faithful.

Assistance to the dying and the ceremonies over the bodies of the dead were indeed the focus of much attention. The regulations contained in the *Constitutiones et ordinamenta congregationis antique* of the

---

50. Cf. Rigon, "Le congregazioni del clero urbano," 353.
51. Cf. Araldi, *Vita religiosa e dinamiche politico-sociali*, 244–45.

priests of Lucca of March 4, 1295, with the additions of 1308 and 1345, are among the most detailed and clear on the subject. The salient moments and aspects of the practices and funeral rites described there, which in a more or less detailed way are found in the statutes of many other congregations, are recommending the soul of the dying on the point of death, washing and dressing the body, convening the confreres for the funeral, a Mass celebrated by a prior or one of his delegates with the assistance of a deacon and a subdeacon, incensing the body of the deceased to the singing of the responsory, and then burial. The behavior of the participants was strictly regulated. Priests had to go to the funeral, chanting psalms and proceeding in twos in a dignified and orderly manner; clothes, gestures, and attitudes had to induce the attendants to tears and not to laughter; everyone was also obliged to take part in the Mass celebrated seven days after the death (*settima*), wearing a cowl, surplice, and cap.[52]

Besides funeral ceremonies and death rites, which were still the most important part of the activities of the clerical congregations in Lucca as in other cities, and which made the congregations highly visible in a religious and civic context, the statutes of the Lucca congregation also reflect in their terminology a new attention to the human body and the tendency to qualify it in detail in its lifeless reality. In the constitutions of 1295 the term *corpus* alternates with the term *cadaver*—indeed it is the presence of the dead body that gives a name and a meaning to the funeral rite: "Volumus quod nullus prior possit aliquem licentiare quod non intersint dictis cadaveribus et septimis" (We do not want any prior to authorize anyone not to attend funeral duties [*cadaveribus*] and Masses for the dead on the seventh day after death).[53] The identification of rite and the dead body is evident: the corpse is the rite and the rite is the corpse. It is the presence of the body of the deceased that qualifies the rite; when it is absent the definition refers instead to time: *septimis*, seven days after death. And in another part of the statutes it states that each confrere is obliged to go "ad corpora mortuorum et ad septima,"[54] using the word *corpus* instead of *cadaver*, but the reality to which it refers remains the same.

Smell was also part of the corporeality and materiality of the rite. Beyond the symbolic value, it is significant that in the statutes of Lucca

---

52. Cf. Savigni, "L'archivio della congregazione dei cappellani lucchesi," 83-95.
53. Savigni, "L'archivio della congregazione dei cappellani lucchesi," 88/11.
54. Savigni, "L'archivio della congregazione dei cappellani lucchesi," 88/12.

of 1295, it states that priests had to prepare the altar for the celebration of the anniversary Masses in the parishes by preparing clean priestly garments and procuring incense to spread on the altar during the sacrifice of the Mass, so that even the priests and the people present could smell it.[55]

Created with essentially liturgical aims, the congregations maintained a high degree of rituality in their activities. Ancient practices are reflected and kept alive in many associations throughout the Middle Ages: regular meetings, especially those of the monthly calends; the common banquet, held with variable frequency and observing monastic procedures (sobriety, silence, listening to a reading);[56] and the liturgical practice of charity toward the poor, exercised on various ritual occasions.[57] The celebration of All Saints, celebrating the communion of living believers with the dead,[58] was also ancient and was remembered in many statutes as an occasion for members to meet at Masses and other sacred ceremonies.

Complex procedures and entrance rites accompanied the admission of clerics and laymen to the associations. As stated in the constitutions of 1471, in Lucca anyone who wanted to be part of the *conventus cappellanorum* had to be put forward by two of its members after a survey of the will of the associates, and be approved by two-thirds of the assembly, once all dissent had been overcome. Only then could the postulant make the solemn profession of obedience in the hands of the prior and

---

55. "Item quod sacerdotes in quorum ecclesiis celebrantur anniversaria teneantur preparare altare et vestimenta sacerdotalia nitida et munda et etiam incensum ad incensandum sacrificium super altare appositum, quod etiam tribuatur odorandum sacerdotibus et populo circumstantibus" (Savigni, "L'archivio della congregazione dei cappellani lucchesi," 88/13).

56. In Treviso, for example, the communal meal, which had to be held fifteen days before the feast of All Saints, must take place in silence while one of those present read the statutes *in modum lectionum* (Rigon, "La congregazione dei parroci di Treviso," 100); in Lucca in the month of May, thanks to the bequest of a priest, a lunch was held during which each member of the confraternity was obliged to eat in a sedate fashion without any muttering, and listening to a sermon: "in quo prandio quilibet discrete et sine murmuratione edat et librarii legant ad mensam de sermonibus consuetis" (Savigni, "L'archivio della congregazione dei cappellani lucchesi," 86/9).

57. In Piacenza, for example, alms were distributed to the poor by the congregation of parish priests at the end of the calends (Bruschi, "Le carte e i silenzi," 167); in Padua the general alms of bread, wine, meat, and other food to prisoners took place in relation to the feast of All Saints, the most important feast in the life of the *fratalea cappellanorum* (Rigon, *Clero e città*, 174).

58. Cf. Henri Leclercq, "Toussaint et Trépassés," in *Smyrne-Zraia*, ed. Henri Marrou, vol. 15, bk. 2 of *Dictionnaire d'archéologie chrétienne et de liturgie*, ed. Fernand Cabrol and Henri Leclercq (Paris: Letouzey et Ané, 1953), 2677–82.

promise to observe the statutes.[59] More or less similar procedures were necessary to join the groups of the clergy in other cities.

The entrance of laypeople was also characterized by a high degree of ritualization. The statutes of the Faenza College of Parish Priests briefly determined that if a layman, moved by devotion, asked to be part of the college in order to enjoy the spiritual benefits that enrollment ensured, he had to address his parish priest who, according to traditional usage, would welcome him into the association *cum stola et libro* and the kiss of peace.[60] An analogous rite with a stole and a book was held to admit laypeople into the congregation of Santo Spirito in Benevento. In this case we also have a testimony of extraordinary interest. The rite is in fact represented by a series of miniatures, alternating with writing, contained in MS Beneventano 28 of the Biblioteca Capitolare of Benevento from the late twelfth century, which belonged to the Santo Spirito confraternity. The miniatures illustrate the arrival of laypeople eager to be admitted to enjoying the spiritual benefits of the *fraternitas*, their welcome by the *abbas* (leader of the association), seated in liturgical dress with a book open on his knees, and the celebration of the rite, included in the *Ordo*, which describes its content and performance in writing.[61] A miniature depicts the enrollment of the new affiliate by the abbot who collects the established fee and writes the affiliate's name in the association's book. Everything ends with a miniature that takes up a full page depicting a crucified Christ with the Madonna and Saint John the Baptist beneath the arms of the Cross. Above this are the heads of a man and a woman within medallions, allegorically representing the sun and the light, perhaps depicting the sanctifying effect of the members' recommendation to prayers (*commendatio in orationibus*).[62]

If the rituals in use among the congregations of the clergy often had ancient origins, in any case prior to the thirteenth century, others were introduced in later periods, testifying to a liturgical orientation that had never disappeared. Even in the case of associations in which the

---

59. These conditions are found in the 1471 statutes (approved by the bishop in 1475), Savigni, "L'archivio della congregazione dei cappellani lucchesi," 99–100.

60. Antonio Guerra, ed., *Le costituzioni del collegio dei parrochi di Faenza dal 1300 al 1600: Con appendice di documenti* (Faenza: Società tipografica faentina, 1924), 9–10, and see Rigon, "Congregazioni del clero cittadino," 18, n. 68.

61. Cf. Araldi, *Vita religiosa e dinamiche politico-sociali*, 107–10, to which we refer for a description of the miniatures that are briefly described here.

62. Thomas Frank, *Studien zu Italienischen Memorialzeugnissen des XI und XII Jahrhunderts* (Berlin: de Gruyter, 1991), 168.

corporate character was more prominent, the tendency was to give a religious value to facts that were devoid of any spiritual connotations in themselves. The case of Padua is an example. Here the frequent quarrels between the *fratalea cappellanorum* and its members over the rights to collect the *quartese*, which were resolved in the mid-thirteenth century with a simple agreement between the parties documented by a notarial act that put an end to the dispute, progressively took on a different nature from the end of that century, ending with a penitential religious rite. The single brother, who in practice always lost in similar cases, was excluded from communion with the *fratalea*. In order to be readmitted, he had to acknowledge that he was wrong and ask for forgiveness before the other members gathered in chapter. The resolution of a dispute according to normal legal methods was thus transformed into a confraternity rite of redemption, at the end of which the *primicerius*, having accepted the humble and devout plea of the guilty acknowledged as such, readmitted him into the confraternity.[63]

## The Age of the Restrictions

During the fourteenth century, a new phase in the history of the confraternities of the clergy began, partly linked to the crisis and the changes in the Church and society that were taking place in that century. The economic difficulties that were beginning to be felt in many cities, reducing their resources, facilitated the interruption of new recruits and the corporate closure of clerical associations. Indeed, the strengthening of the bureaucratic structures of the Church and the development of bishoprics as centers of administration and regulation led to a greater desire to control the life and customs of the clergy on the part of bishops and local ecclesiastical authorities. In some cities, both in the north (like Ferrara) and the south (like Benevento), the number of members of the congregations was reduced, and the prohibition against admitting members of the regular clergy became stricter.[64]

In Benevento, the decline in members of the congregation of Santo Spirito became dramatic due to a loss of economic resources, also

---

63. Cf. Rigon, *Clero e città*, 80–85.
64. In Ferrara an initial opening to all priests and clergy of the city changed in the thirteenth and fourteenth centuries to a restriction to parish priests, still without any obligation to membership (Samaritani, "Il 'conventus' e le congregazioni chiericali," 171–76, 189–90); for Benevento see the text that follows here.

linked to the political turmoil in the city. In 1331, the number was set at forty; between 1331 and 1358 it fell to twenty-five; in the same year, 1358, at the request of the members of the congregation themselves, the archbishop of Benevento reduced them to twelve, thus creating the conditions for its definitive crisis.[65] While we lose all trace of the clerical confraternity of Santa Eufemia after the first decades of the thirteenth century, the confraternities of Santo Spirito and San Bartolomeo were transformed into collegiate associations made up only of the clergy of their respective churches.[66] The *congregatio clericorum* of Perugia also disappeared in the course of the fourteenth century,[67] while the *Romana fraternitas*, even though it did not dissolve on an institutional level, changed its physiognomy. It was no longer characterized as a collegiate institution of the clergy of Rome, autonomous and directly dependent only on the pope, but as a college of parish priests led by a *camerlengo* that had very limited powers compared to its predecessors.[68]

Apart from a few cases like Benevento or Perugia where they disappeared, the congregations continued to live and sometimes to prosper, even though they had to face reorganization and a reform of their statutes more or less everywhere. Apart from a few exceptions, from the late thirteenth century onward, collections of legislation were elaborated that replaced the older constitutions, which rarely remained in their entirety, and these new collections updated previous legislation by adapting it to new needs. Grafted onto the ancient liturgical system, or becoming more explicit, were rules regarding the control and discipline of the clergy, often in perfect harmony with the more general conciliar and synodal norms.

The intent to discipline the lifestyle and the behavior of their associates strongly and put them under the control of their superiors was a common denominator of the rules of the associations of the parish clergy elaborated in the late Middle Ages. At the basis of many regulations were the constitutions of the Fourth Lateran Council, in particular the sixteenth, which prohibited clerics in the first place from intervening in secular affairs and trades and from paying attention to mimes, jugglers, and actors, banning gambling and the frequenting of

---

65. Araldi, *Vita religiosa e dinamiche politico-sociali*, 267, 271–72.
66. Araldi, *Vita religiosa e dinamiche politico-sociali*, 276–78.
67. Maiarelli, *La Congregatio clericorum*, 170–79.
68. Cf. Tommaso di Carpegna Falconieri, "Le congregazioni del clero secolare a Roma e la loro documentazione (secoli X–XVI)," in Zacchi, *Realtà archivistiche a confronto*, 25.

taverns, making the tonsure obligatory, and recalling the duty to wear clothing suited to the dignity of the clergy.[69]

Detailed instructions were subsequently introduced relating to the obligation to reside, often neglected by the clergy.[70] Closely related on this issue to the conciliar and synodal legislation on which they depended or to which they conformed, the statutes of the congregations present a body of norms designed to give the clergy a code of conduct, insofar as the clergy was an essential component of the Church and a social category distinct from other categories and from the *genus laicorum* in general. For this reason, these norms started to attract the attention of the city governments, and not by chance, in moments of tension with the local churches, these norms, established in conciliar decrees and synodal constitutions and the normative codes of the clerical associations, were often included in peace treaties and were accepted into the city statutes. This happened in Siena, Florence, Padua, Bologna, and other cities, where the rulers felt the need to have a system of rules capable of giving the clergy a clear identity.[71] If the purpose of ecclesiastical legislation was to ensure that the clerics lived *clericaliter*, it was equally important for the city governments to have accepted criteria on the basis of which they could identify those persons who possessed the requisites needed to be able to benefit from the exemptions and the privileges of the clergy.

## Toward the Modern Age

As local realities that were subject to the problems of the Church and the society of their time, the congregations of the clergy felt the tensions and conflicts caused by the schisms of the fourteenth and fifteenth centuries and the spread of conciliarist ideas in ways that were not univocal and whose true significance still has to be clarified. At the

---

69. Giuseppe Alberigo et al., eds., *Conciliorum oecumenicorum decreta*, 3rd ed. (Bologna: Istituto per le scienze religiose, 1973), cost. 16, p. 243.

70. There are examples relating to the congregations of parish priests in the cities of the Veneto in Rigon, "Congregazioni del clero cittadino," 14, to compare, for example, with the fourteenth-century statutory norms of the confraternity of Santo Spirito in Benevento, Araldi, *Vita religiosa e dinamiche politico-sociali*, 269.

71. On this see Antonio Rigon, "Il clero curato," in *Ceti, modelli, comportamenti nella società medievale, secoli XIII–metà XIV: Diciassettesimo convegno internazionale di studi, Pistoia, 14–17 maggio 1991* (Pistoia: Centro italiano di studi di storia e d'arte, 2001), 68–70.

present state of research, the events related to the clerical associations in the cities of Florence and Venice look particularly interesting.

In Florence, in response to the pressure of taxation by the pope and the commune, synodal constitutions of the clergy were promulgated in which the clergy itself established self-governing rules in their own defense that tended to reduce the authority of the bishop and propose collective leadership in the government of the diocese, entrusted to the clergy itself. At the basis of these rules, in addition to conciliarist ecclesiology and the traditions of republicanism in Florence, were also the experiences of associationism and solidarity of the Florentine clergy and of the associations constituted for the purposes of taxation. Collegiality experienced in the life of clerics who had formed into confraternities and groups, together with other factors, promoted initiatives in Florence that were in line with the conciliarist ideas applied to the government of the local church.[72]

By changing their vocation as devout associations exclusively dedicated to prayer and to the works of mercy, the nine congregations of the clergy of Venice took on a role representing the clerical community of the city, participating with their own representatives at the Council of Basel (1431-37). Their participation was not, however, due to the need for a democratic enlargement of the conciliar assembly, but was at the request of the Venetian pope Eugene IV, who hoped in this way to ensure that there would be a majority in his favor at the council, which was questioning papal primacy.[73] It is true, in fact, that by changing their physiognomy as associations with the purpose of prayer, the nine congregations took a stand in favor of the clergy in the disputes with the patriarch on the taxation of the clergy, and ended up by assuming the role of a corporate body opposed to the patriarch's excessive power, with the tacit support of the state magistratures.[74]

These aspects deserve detailed study, along with other issues, such as the part that the associations may have had in the formation and culture of the parish priests and more generally in the city culture. Archives such as that of the congregation of chaplains of Lucca contain musical

---

72. For all this see the important articles by David S. Peterson, "Florence's 'universitas cleri' in the Early Fifteenth Century," *Renaissance Studies* 2 (1988): 185-96; David S. Peterson, "Conciliarism, Republicanism and Corporatism: The 1415-1420 Constitution of the Florentine Clergy," *Renaissance Quarterly* 42 (1989): 183-225.

73. Sartorelli and Barausse, "Le nove congregazioni," 53.

74. Sartorelli and Barausse, "Le nove congregazioni," 53.

texts, catalogs of books, liturgical manuscripts, and grammars.[75] It is worth noting that at the beginning of the fourteenth century the *Romana fraternitas* also chose the *magistri* of the *Studium Urbis*.[76] This was certainly an exceptional case.

One can not fail to observe indeed that in other contexts, alongside claims for and the expansion of their functions, there also appeared signs of the weakness and inadequacy of the parish priests in the face of their mission. In Verona in 1323 the congregation of the *clero intrinseco* hired someone *de ordinibus praedicancium* (preaching orders) to preach the sermon on the first Friday of the month, thus giving up direct responsibility for an important task in the care of souls.[77] In Vicenza, the *Ordinationes* of the Congregation of the Seven Chaplains (Congregatio septem capellanorum) of 1400 recognized a sort of moral and spiritual superiority of the canons of the chapter of the cathedral.[78] In Faenza in December 1497, in the time of plague, fearing the spread of the disease among their churches, the parish priests delegated the care of souls and the task of administering the sacraments to and caring for the sick to a Camaldolese monk.[79] These are symptoms of the awareness of the parish priests of their own fragility and subordination to other protagonists of religious life and components of the ecclesiastical community, a subordination that was not just hierarchical. It is important to remember, however, that with their associations, clerics in the care of souls played an important role in the Italian cities of the late Middle Ages, maintaining a strong bond with the city society and developing a sense of belonging that are still largely to be investigated for their cultural aspects and long-term consequences in particular.

As has been emphasized in a recent work devoted to the *Romana fraternitas*, something that deserves further investigation, for example, is the theme of the culture of the clergy, not only with reference to the *Studium Urbis*, but in relation to *romanitas*—that is, the sense of belonging to the *Urbe* that can be seen in the writings of many exponents of the clergy, who created veritable monuments to the greatness of Rome with their works.[80] By extending our investigation to other Italian cities, we would discover that a significant part of local erudition that

---

75. Savigni, "L'archivio della congregazione dei cappellani lucchesi," 68-69.
76. Di Carpegna Falconieri, "Le congregazioni del clero secolare," 25.
77. Rigon, "Congregazioni del clero cittadino," 16.
78. Rigon, "Le congregazioni del clero in Italia," 19-20.
79. Mazzotti, "Notizie," 123.
80. Di Carpegna Falconieri, "Le congregazioni del clero secolare," 29-30.

aimed at celebrating the city's glories was written by the clergy, not infrequently parish priests, and probably members of the congregations of the clergy. Moreover, it is not a coincidence that, as has already been observed, in statutes such as those of Padua's *fratalea cappellanorum* of the fifteenth century, it states that the association had been constituted for the honor and for the good state of the city of Padua and all its people.[81]

In reality, in the Italian cities, thanks to the clerical confraternities, there was no separation between clergy and cities as there was in other European countries. Clerical associations facilitated cohesion between clerics and laypeople. The great number of laypeople's names (especially women, and in the north as in the south of Italy) that we find in the registers of members, obituaries, and necrologies of the associations of the secular clergy of many congregations,[82] demonstrates the strong and tenacious bond that continued to exist in urban society between the ecclesiastical component and the laity, without irreparable fractures. The laypeople who were members of the clerical groups were not just passive beneficiaries of the spiritual treasure of the associations they had joined.

Although they were excluded from office and had no rights of presence and representation in the confraternity assemblies, laypeople shared in the experience of prayer with the clergy in their own way: they participated in weekly and monthly liturgies of their confraternity, contributed to the works of mercy of their members, and played a significant role in funerals and in the commemoration of the deceased. By sharing a faith in the doctrine of the communion of saints that united the living and the dead and belief in the effectiveness of the Masses for the souls of the dead, clerics and laity also shared pious and devout practices and charitable commitments for many years that exceeded normal participation in the religious life of the parishes.

Bonds were inevitably formed and a wealth of experiences and common memories were created that went beyond the family and the parish circle, through the clerical confraternities, and opened up to the city. In this regard, by avoiding irreparable ruptures and separations between

---

81. Rigon, *Clero e città*, 264.

82. In the list of the dead of the *fraternitas* of Santo Spirito in Benevento there are thousands of names (Araldi, *Vita religiosa e dinamiche politico-sociali*, 233); in the registers of members of the congregation of parish priests of Treviso more than two thousand people were registered as members throughout the whole of the fourteenth century, most of them laypeople (Rigon, "La congregazione dei parroci di Treviso," 105).

clerics and laity, continuing to preserve the liturgical memory of the departed and the hope of contributing to their eternal salvation with their prayer for the souls of the dead and works of mercy, the congregations of the clergy constituted a point of reference deeply rooted in local realities, in the religious tissue and the popular sensibility of the cities, the supporting columns of Italian history. They are perhaps a marginal element, but they still deserve to be remembered, alongside others, in assessing the reasons for the failure of the Reformation in Italy.

## Selected Bibliography

### Primary Sources

Alberigo, Giuseppe, et al., eds. *Conciliorum oecumenicorum decreta*. 3rd ed. Bologna: Istituto per le scienze religiose, 1973.

Buzzi, Corrado, ed. *La "Margarita iurium cleri Viterbensis."* Rome: Società romana di storia patria, 1993.

Guerra, Antonio, ed. *Le costituzioni del collegio dei parrochi di Faenza dal 1300 al 1600: Con appendice di documenti*. Faenza: Società tipografica faentina, 1924.

Zazo, Alfredo, ed. *L'"Obituarium S. Spiritus" della Biblioteca Capitolare di Benevento (secc. XII–XIV)*. Naples: Fausto Fiorentino, 1963.

### Secondary Sources

NB: Those studies that contain editions of texts and appendices of documents concerning the confraternities of the clergy are marked by an asterisk.

Araldi, Giovanni. *Vita religiosa e dinamiche politico-sociali: Le congregazioni del clero a Benevento (secoli XII–XIV)*. Naples: Società napoletana di storia patria, 2016.*

Betto, Bianca. *Le nove congregazioni del clero di Venezia (sec. XI–XV): Ricerche storiche, matricole e documenti vari*. Padua: Editrice Antenore, 1984.*

Bruschi, Ugo. "Le carte e i silenzi: La Congregazione dei parroci di Piacenza, un millennio vissuto tra luci della ribalta e ritiri nell'ombra." In *Realtà archivistiche a confronto: Le associazioni dei parroci. Atti del Convegno di Ravenna (24 settembre 2010)*, edited by Gilberto Zacchi, 155-95. Modena: Mucchi, 2011.

Di Carpegna Falconieri, Tommaso. *Il clero di Roma nel medioevo: Istituzioni e politica cittadina (secoli VIII–XIII)*. Rome: Viella, 2002.

———. "Il clero secolare nel basso medioevo: Acquisizioni e proposte di ricerca." *Archivio della Società romana di storia patria* 132 (2009): 23-40.

———. "Le congregazioni del clero secolare a Roma e la loro documentazione (secoli X–XVI)." In *Realtà archivistiche a confronto: Le associazioni dei parroci.*

*Atti del Convegno di Ravenna (24 settembre 2010)*, edited by Gilberto Zacchi, 23–30. Modena: Mucchi, 2011.

Fonseca, Cosimo Damiano. "Riforma ecclesiastica e collegialità del clero: Il caso di Aversa." In *Preti nel medioevo*, 9–25. Quaderni di storia religiosa 4. Verona: Cierre, 1997.

Frank, Thomas. *Studien zu Italienischen Memorialzeugnissen des XI und XII Jahrhunderts*. Berlin: de Gruyter, 1991.

Leclercq, Henri, "Toussaint et Trépassés." In *Smyrne-Zraia*, edited by Henri Marrou, vol. 15, bk. 2 of *Dictionnaire d'archéologie chrétienne et de liturgie*, edited by Fernand Cabrol and Henri Leclercq, 2677–82. Paris: Letouzey et Ané, 1953.

Lemaître, Jean-Loup. "Le consorce du clergé de Lodi et son Missel, XII$^e$–XIV$^e$ siècle." In *Le mouvement confraternel au Moyen Âge: France, Italie, Suisse. Actes de la table ronde organiseé par l'Université de Lausanne avec le concours de l'École française de Rome et de l'Unité associée 1011 du CNRS "L'institution ecclésiale à la fin du Moyen Âge," Lausanne, 9–11 mai 1985*, 185–220. Rome: École française de Rome, 1987.*

Maiarelli, Andrea. *La Congregatio clericorum Perusinae Ecclesiae: Edizione e studio del codice 39.20 della Biblioteca Capitular di Toledo*. Rome: Herder, 2007.*

Mazzotti, Marco. "Notizie sul collegio dei parroci di Faenza e il suo archivio." In *Realtà archivistiche a confronto: Le associazioni dei parroci. Atti del Convegno di Ravenna (24 settembre 2010)*, edited by Gilberto Zacchi, 121–30. Modena: Mucchi, 2011.

Meersseman, Gilles Gérard. "Die Klerikervereine von Karl dem Grossen bis Innocenz III." *Zeitschrift für schweizerische Kirchengeschichte* 46 (1952): 1–42, 81–112.

Meersseman, Gilles Gérard, in collaboration with Gian Piero Pacini. *Ordo fraternitatis: Confraternite e pietà dei laici nel Medioevo*. 3 vols. Rome: Herder, 1977.*

Miller, Maureen C. *Chiesa e società in Verona medievale*, edited by Paolo Golinelli. Verona: Cierre Edizioni, 1998.

Monti, Gennaro Maria. *Le confraternite medievali dell'alta e media Italia*. Venice: La Nuova Italia, 1927.*

*Le mouvement confraternel au Moyen Âge: France, Italie, Suisse. Actes de la table ronde organiseé par l'Université de Lausanne avec le concours de l'École française de Rome et de l'Unité associée 1011 du CNRS "L'institution ecclésiale à la fin du Moyen Âge," Lausanne, 9–11 mai 1985*. Rome: École française de Rome, 1987.

Peterson, David S. "Conciliarism, Republicanism and Corporatism: The 1415–1420 Constitution of the Florentine Clergy." *Renaissance Quarterly* 42 (1989): 183–225.

———. "Florence's 'universitas cleri' in the Early Fifteenth Century." *Renaissance Studies* 2 (1988): 185–96.

Rigon, Antonio. "Il clero curato." In *Ceti, modelli, comportamenti nella società medievale, secoli XIII–metà XIV: Diciassettesimo convegno internazionale di studi, Pistoia, 14–17 maggio 1991*, 59–74. Pistoia: Centro italiano di studi di storia e d'arte, 2001.

———. *Clero e città: "Fratalea cappellanorum," parroci, cura d'anime in Padova dal XII al XV secolo*. Padua: Istituto per la storia ecclesiastica padovana, 1988.*

———, "La congregazione dei parroci di Treviso nel medioevo (secoli XII–XIV)." In *Studi e fonti del Medioevo Vicentino e Veneto*, vol. 2, edited by Antonio Morsoletto, 91–111. Vicenza: Accademia Olimpica, 2003.

———. "Congregazioni del clero cittadino e storia della parrocchia nell'Italia settentrionale: Il problema delle fonti." In *La parrocchia nel Medio Evo: Economia, scambi, solidarietà*, edited by Agostino Paravicini Bagliani and Véronique Pasche, 3–25. Rome: Herder, 1995.

———. "Le congregazioni del clero in Italia: Bilancio di studi e prospettive di ricerca." In *Realtà archivistiche a confronto: Le associazioni dei parroci. Atti del Convegno di Ravenna (24 settembre 2010)*, edited by Gilberto Zacchi, 9–21. Modena: Mucchi, 2011.

———. "Le congregazioni del clero urbano in area veneta (XII–XV sec.)." In *Le mouvement confraternel au Moyen Âge: France, Italie, Suisse. Actes de la table ronde organisée par l'Université de Lausanne avec le concours de l'École française de Rome et de l'Unité associée 1011 du CNRS "L'institution ecclésiale à la fin du Moyen Âge,"* Lausanne, 9–11 mai 1985, 343–60. Rome: École française de Rome, 1987.

———. "Messaletto, sec. XIV." In *Treviso cristiana: 2000 anni di fede. Percorso storico, iconografico, artistico della diocesi*, edited by Lucio Bonora, Eugenio Manzato, and Ivano Sartor, 225. Treviso: Diocesi di Treviso, 2000.

———. "Il ruolo delle chiese locali nelle lotte tra magnati e popolani." In *Magnati e popolani nell'Italia comunale: Quindicesimo convegno di studi, Pistoia 15–18 maggio 1995*, 117–35. Pistoia: Centro italiano di studi di storia e d'arte, 1997.

Rocca, Giancarlo. "Per un primo censimento delle associazioni sacerdotali in Italia dal medioevo a oggi." *Rivista di storia della Chiesa in Italia* 64 (2010): 397–517.

Rossi, Maria Clara. "Le elezioni vescovili: Il caso di Verona scaligera." In *Gli Scaligeri (1277–1387)*, edited by Gian Maria Varanini, 405–11. Verona: Arnoldo Mondadori, 1988.

———. "Forme associative del clero medievale: La Congregatio cleri extrinseci di Verona." In *"Arbor ramosa": Studi per Antonio Rigon da allievi amici colleghi*, edited by Luciano Bertazzo, Donato Gallo, Raimondo Michetti, and Andrea Tilatti, 415–30. Padua: Centro studi antoniani, 2011.

Samaritani, Antonio. "Il 'conventus' e le congregazioni chiericali di Ferrara tra analoghe istituzioni ecclesiastiche nei secoli X–XV." *Ravennatensia* 7 (1979): 159–202.

Sartorelli, Diego, and Manuela Barausse. "Le nove congregazioni del clero di Venezia e i loro archivi." In *Realtà archivistiche a confronto: Le associazioni dei parroci. Atti del Convegno di Ravenna (24 settembre 2010)*, edited by Gilberto Zacchi, 47–63. Modena: Mucchi, 2011.

Savigni, Raffaele. "L'archivio della congregazione dei cappellani lucchesi." In *Realtà archivistiche a confronto: Le associazioni dei parroci. Atti del Convegno di Ravenna (24 settembre 2010)*, edited by Gilberto Zacchi, 65–109. Modena: Mucchi, 2011.*

Zacchi, Gilberto, ed. *Realtà archivistiche a confronto: Le associazioni dei parroci. Atti del Convegno di Ravenna (24 settembre 2010)*. Modena: Mucchi, 2011.*

CHAPTER 8

# Mendicants

*Giovanna Casagrande*

Marcel Pacaut wrote: "Without the mendicant brothers, the thirteenth century would not have been what it really was: an age of profound faith."[1] In fact, the mendicants burst forth, in Italy and elsewhere, within a well-established framework of ecclesiastical and religious institutions: bishoprics, *pievi*, parishes, communities of canons, and monastic settlements connected through the network of Benedictinism. The mendicants inserted themselves into a preexisting and already consolidated structure, and although they did not destroy it, they imposed themselves on it in an impressive way.

Italy presents an infinite variety of political, institutional, and socioeconomic contexts, with territories of distinctive geomorphologies and diverse regions of settlement: inland cities, coastal cities, some small, medium, and large cities, castles, neighborhoods, valleys, plains, mountains, hills, etc. Indeed, it is impossible to speak of Italy as a single, more or less homogeneous and/or cohesive, entity. We must keep at least "two Italies" in mind: the communal Italy of the central and northern part, and that of the *Regno* (Kingdom) in the south.[2] At the same time,

---

This chapter was translated by William North.

1. Marcel Pacaut, *Monaci e religiosi nel Medioevo* (Bologna: Il Mulino, 1989), 272.
2. Giuseppe Galasso, "Due Italie nel Medioevo?," *Mediterranea: Ricerche Storiche* 8 (2011): 217–36.

we must be careful, as we cannot speak about these regions as two coherent blocks because reality was much more complicated in the north, the center, and the south.

## A Disruptive Novelty

Mendicants settled everywhere, in some places earlier, in some later, according to a more or less developed rate of evolution and/or speed of the orders' own development. Everywhere they found diverse forms of support, from civic and communal authorities to the sovereigns of the Regno to the mass of the faithful drawn from various socioeconomic conditions: nobles, merchants, professionals, and artisans. Each order had its own way of inserting itself: some initially approached the city from protected positions on the periphery of the city before integrating themselves into it with larger, more substantial buildings, often located at specific distances from one another; it was a kind of urban destiny that no mendicant order could escape, not even those of an eremitic nature.

The rivalry with the secular clergy came into play to the extent that the mendicant orders acquired, with papal support, prerogatives relating to the *cura animarum*: preaching, confession, administration of the sacraments, as well as burial rights. How disturbing this must have been is shown by the fact that in the middle of the thirteenth century (1255), Humbert of Romans, master general of the Preachers, sent an encyclical letter to all the convents with which he admonished the brethren not to inflict injury on the rectors of parish churches, that is, by diminishing the alms due to rectors through civic preaching, by inducing laypeople to choose burial in the friars' convents without conferring the canonically decreed portion of the burial fee to the parish priests, and by inserting themselves into the drafting of wills.[3]

The importance of the *novitas* represented by the mendicants was immediately perceived by contemporaries in the first decades of the thirteenth century. In a famous passage from his *Historia Occidentalis*, Jacques de Vitry comments:

> For a long while there have been three religious orders: hermits, monks, and canons. But the Lord willed that those who live according to a Rule be firmly on a solid foundation and therefore

---

3. Michele Bacci, *Investimenti per l'aldilà: Arte e raccomandazione dell'anima nel Medioevo* (Bari: Editori Laterza, 2003), 113.

he added in these days a religious institution, the beauty of a new order, the holiness of a new Rule. Yet if we attentively observe the way of the life of the primitive Church, we must conclude that he did not so much add a new Rule as renew that ancient one, he raised up again what lay upon the ground, and he revived the religion that was almost dead, in this evening of the world drawing near to dusk, while the time of the son of perdition presses. And thus did he prepare new athletes for the conflict with the times of the Antichrist that shall be full of dangers, fortifying and reinforcing his Church in advance.[4]

In another famous passage from the *Chronicon* of the Premonstratensian Burchard of Ursperg, we read: "The world at that time was already showing signs of old age, but God aroused in the Church two new orders to renew its youthfulness, like an eagle; and the Apostolic See has approved them. They are the Friars Minor and the Preachers."[5] There was, therefore, the sense of an innovation that reawakens the world. This reawakened world itself produces and/or requires new religious forces and energies.

The twelfth and thirteenth centuries present a lively ferment of manifestations and forms of religious life that are embedded in a dynamic social, political, and economic context: the rebirth of cities, the so-called urban revolution; the revitalization and expansion of commerce; the appearance and growing power of new emerging classes (mercantile, artisan, and professional); increasing mobility within which the cities became axes of growth, development, and encounter. It is in the cities that an active and hardworking laity moves and acts, a laity that is even critical of a rich and powerful Church and clergy. It is in this crucible of the urban world that heretical movements spread, such as the Cathars and their anti-Church beliefs. There is a new emphasis on the rediscovery of the Gospel, which should be understood literally and points toward the imitation of the apostolic or evangelical life: a typical example of this is the Waldensian movement (Waldo and the Poor of Lyon), while the Humiliati exemplify a style of apostolic life that is centered upon labor. The Church was at risk of losing elements of connection with the world of the faithful. Innocent III (1198–1216) acted

---

4. *Fonti Francescane* (Padua: Editrici Francescane, 2011), 1464.
5. *Fonti Francescane*, 1476.

harshly with regard to heretics but rehabilitated the Humiliati and reconciled the orthodox Waldensians.

Nonetheless, it was necessary to go further and to do more. "A link between the aspirations of a society animated by the urban faithful, and a pastoral practice without monastic renunciation of the world" was necessary.[6] At the outset, the new mendicant orders clearly differentiated themselves from the earlier tradition established by Benedictine monasticism through their profession of poverty in the name of the Gospel and through their fundamental renunciation of every kind of property, real estate, and especially agricultural lands. Hence, they are called mendicants as, in the absence of a landed endowment, it was necessary to resort to work and/or mendicancy. They were the defenders of orthodoxy, obedient to the ecclesiastical hierarchy and, above all, linked directly to the papacy. Charged with the Inquisition and continuously supported by the papacy despite conflicts with bishops and the secular clergy, the mendicant orders were the great innovation in the religious life of the thirteenth century. They were capable of positioning themselves in the midst of the people through their preaching fortified by new instruments such as the *sermones ad status* and the confession manuals, as well as being effective at increasing the associative forms of the faithful such as confraternities, groups of penitents, and devout laypeople, reinvigorating devotion to Christ and the Virgin, creating new saints (with a civic meaning as well), and setting forth the example of a life coherently organized around poverty and the Gospel.

## Mendicant Orders Present and Active in Italy

Francis of Assisi (1181/82–1226)—layman, hermit-penitent who moved between wilderness (*Rule for the Hermits*)[7] and city, and preacher of "penance" as an invitation to conversion, that is, to the transformation of one's way of life—gathered around himself a *fraternitas* that grew tremendously and acquired a regular structure with its approved rule and hierarchy of governance. Francis expressed its great religious and spiritual ideals in the *The First Rule* (1221), *The Second Rule* (1223), and

---

6. Stanislao da Campagnola, "I fedeli e i frati Minori," in *I Frati Minori e il Terzo Ordine: Problemi e discussioni storiografiche* (Todi: Accademia Tudertina, 1985), 22.

7. "Regola di vita degli eremi," in *Fonti Francescane*, 3rd ed. (Padua: Editrici Francescane, 2011), 104–5. This was a Rule written by Francis for the friars who preferred an eremitic life, which was very common in central Italy and along the Apennines.

the *Testament* (1226). Living according to the model set by the holy Gospel, absolute poverty (that is to say, private as well as common or the "highest poverty"), friars rejected money, sought work, and took recourse to mendicancy whenever work was insufficient for the survival of the brethren. Such great ideals gave rise to an order rich in spiritual resources but also complex and riven by strong tensions that would produce two currents already in the thirteenth century, the rigorist current (Spirituals, or *Fraticelli*) and the moderate one of the Community, while retaining the eremitical soul that was part of the essential nature of the Franciscan experience. Originally, the order received both lay and clerical brothers but then moved toward the clericalization and sacerdotalization of the order.

Dominic of Guzman (1170–1221) was a regular canon (of the cathedral of Osma) who followed the Rule of Saint Augustine. And while Francis acted out of profound episodes of repentance and conversion, Dominic was guided by the strong need to oppose the Cathar heresy that was widespread through the south of France. To fight against the Cathar opposition and to gain back the world of the faithful, it was fitting not only to preach but also to make oneself credible through a renewed way of life, that is, an apostolic life that was itinerant, without any visible property, and relying on alms for sustenance.

Having been first formed in Toulouse and approved by Honorius III in 1216, assuming the Rule of Saint Augustine, the Friars Preachers launched themselves into a universal mission with locations such as Paris, Bologna, and Oxford, all university cities. This speaks volumes on the intention of the Preachers to insert themselves into these cities to become integrated with the university cultures. Study of theology was absolutely fundamental for this new religious order (an example followed by the Franciscans), while manual labor was put aside.

Each mendicant order has its own specific history and its own dynamic and evolution. The Carmelites and the Augustinians emerged from an eremitic background. The Order of our Lady of Mount Carmel appeared toward the end of the twelfth century when groups of hermits from Palestine returned to the West. These groups of hermits had a Rule of their own given to them by the Latin patriarch of Jerusalem, Alberto da Vercelli, after 1206. This Rule was approved by Honorius III in 1226. It provided for settlements in deserted places, occupation of separate cells, assembly for daily Mass and feasts, and manual labor.

The transformation of the Carmelites into a mendicant order was a gradual process over time. In 1242, Pope Innocent IV granted the

Carmelites their mendicant status and modified their rule in the direction of urban pastoral care, a role also to be carried out by these friars. The call of eremitic life remained strong in the heart of this order, which had been transformed from an eremitic-contemplative one to a mendicant-contemplative one. Emblematic of this change is the lament of Nicholas Gallo, general of the order, in 1270:

> Perhaps they will answer, "it was never our intent to resist the divine will, but rather to follow it. For we desire to build up the people of God by preaching his Word, hearing confessions and counselling, so that we can be useful to ourselves and our neighbours. For this reason, a most just one, we fled the solitude of the desert to settle among the people in the cities, so as to perform these tasks." O foolish men! I will show you that in the city you accomplish none of this, but that in time past in the solitude you accomplished it all.... What is this new religion discovered in the cities?... Tour the provinces, go to and fro among superiors, and tell me, how many have been found in the order who are fit and sufficient to preach, to hear confessions and counsel the people, as is proper for those who dwell in towns?[8]

The Order of the Augustinians, that is, of the Hermits of Saint Augustine, was a formation directed and constructed by the Apostolic See itself. In central Italy, a region filled with eremitic vocations, there were many groups of hermits, including those of San Agostino of Tuscia, Giovanni Bono (Cesena) (*Giamboniti*), and Brettino (*Brettinesi*). The unification (*magna unio*) of these different groups eventually occurred in 1256, approved by Pope Alexander IV.

Both the Carmelites and the Augustinian Friars came into being as groups of monks who pursued the eremitical life and were transformed into orders of friars in response to the powerful call exercised by the mendicant idea that found its first strong expression in the Franciscans and the Dominicans. The ideal of imitating Christ and therefore the apostolic and evangelical life implied a ministry of active preaching as well as the practice of voluntary poverty. The cities were without question the suitable place to carry out a more intense program of pastoral activity, to gain a livelihood, and to dedicate oneself to study. The movement into the cities, however, did not eliminate certain eremitical

---

8. Clifford Hugh Lawrence, *Medieval Monasticism: Forms of Religious Life in Western Europe in the Middle Ages*, 4th ed. (London: Routledge, 2015), 250.

impulses; these remained alive and reemerged, for example, among the Franciscans themselves. But the enthusiasm for eremitism of early Franciscanism nonetheless grew weaker over the course of the later thirteenth century.

The Franciscans, Dominicans, Carmelites, and Augustinians were the recognized mendicant orders over the course of the thirteenth century, while the Servants of Mary had to wait a little longer. The order of the Servants of Mary drew its origin from a small group of Florentine lay penitents who withdrew around 1233 to a hermitage at the gates of Florence (Cafaggio) and then on Monte Senario. Initially this new group, which retired to pursue the religious life, was approved by the bishop of Florence, the papal legate, and, in 1256, by Pope Alexander IV himself, and during the 1250s we know of sites in Florence, Città di Castello, and Sansepolcro. From their initial focus on penance, contemplation, and a dedication to poverty, the order developed in the direction of apostolic mendicancy, and new convents arose over time in central Italy and beyond. It was the last of the five great mendicant orders to be officially and definitively approved in 1304 by Pope Benedict XI.

Meanwhile, the Second Council of Lyon (1274) forbid the emergence of new forms of religious life. The Servants of Mary, having moderated their eremitic-cenobitic form, altered their attitude toward radical poverty, and adopted the Rule of Saint Augustine, could at this point merit definitive recognition. The Friars Minor, Preachers, Carmelites, Augustinian Hermits, and Servants of Mary as well as the Brethren of Penitence of Jesus Christ (the Sack Friars), the Servants of the Blessed Mary Mother of Christ (Brothers of the Valle Verde), and the Apostolic Brethren of Gerardo Segarelli were all active. While the Sack Friars, in particular, were noted in various cities of central and northern Italy, the Council of Lyon in 1274 also introduced uncertainty among the Augustinians and Carmelites and ushered in, for example, the extinction of the Sack Friars. Not all of the mendicant orders had the same fate, so to speak.

The success and affirmation of these orders, however, did not happen without encountering obstacles introduced by a secular clergy that saw itself outmatched and outpaced by the mendicants' actions. The friars carried out preaching, received confessions, performed burials, attracted bequests and donations, acted independently of the parish clergy and diocesan ordinaries, and taught without remuneration at the university. At issue was a conflict of interests, a conflict of authorities, but also and more profoundly a conflict over the ecclesiological order. The ecclesiastical order, of divine origin, was founded upon bishops and parishes; the mendicant orders broke this system. The question that occupied Thomas Aquinas and Bonaventure of Bagnoregio was certainly not an easy one. The mendicants relied on papal authority from whom they had received their apostolic mission, but it was not always easy to overcome the hostility of the secular clergy. Behind the well-known constitution *Religionum diversitatem* of the Second Council of Lyon (1274) can be read the desire of the bishops to hold back the expansion of the mendicant orders. However, the Friars Minor and the Preachers remained firm, unharmed, and ever more privileged (the 1281 bull *Ad fructus uberes* of Martin IV).[9] The Carmelites and the Hermits of Saint Augustine were left in suspense, and all the other orders were suppressed, which rendered the recognition of the Servants of Mary extremely difficult and led to the disappearance of the Sack Friars, the friars of Val Verde, and the Apostolic Brethren.

### Mendicancy's Diffusion or Urban Destiny

The pairing "mendicant orders–cities" was irreversible. For these orders we can in fact speak of an urban destiny: the city as an area of apostolic activity, the city as the possibility of resources for survival, the city as a center of study, the city as the exercise of Inquisition. The context of the city became a privileged space on account of the exercise of preaching, its possibilities of subsistence, and the protection that it could offer.[10] Cities became populated by convents, and the orders formulated their own style of administration in the surrounding territories. Franciscans, for example, divided their provinces into "custodies," and Dominicans into zones of preaching, indicating the thrust of their action within a territory.

The Dominicans were the civic order par excellence. From the very beginning, they preferred the big cities. The Franciscans and Augustinians did not overlook settlements of more modest significance, and in the case of the Franciscans, the call to the eremitic life would remain strong—this was true for the more radical and dissident fringe

---

9. With this bull, Martin IV conceded to the Friars Minor the right of preaching and confessing wherever they like, without the need to ask permission from the bishop or the parish priests. G. G. Merlo, *Nel nome di san Francesco: Storia dei frati Minori e del francescanesimo sino agli inizi del XVI secolo* (Padua: Editrici Francescane, 2003), 240.

10. Pacaut, *Monaci e religiosi*, 247–48.

(Spirituals, or *Fraticelli*) but also, later, for the Observant strand of the order.

The establishment of convents of the mendicant orders in the cities can be seen as a reflection of the importance and dimensions assumed by the cities themselves. One city that would be able to count the presence of four or even five or more mendicant orders was without doubt a large city; a center with a lower number of mendicant orders was a settlement of lesser importance. Beginning in the 1980s, the study of the mendicant orders and the city became the imperative, and Italy was second to none in becoming involved in this line of research: one thinks of Pellegrini's study of Franciscan settlements and a myriad of scholars who have focused on the history of religious settlement in individual cities and regions.[11] We can say that the mendicant orders achieved the goal assigned to them by the Church, that is, that of evangelizing urban society and recuperating and framing urban society within the web of the Roman Church (under papal guidance).

The friars would have been active in various forms of pastoral care, in political interventions at moments of particular tension and difficulty, in providing support and technical consulting for the realization of urban infrastructure, in welcoming into their own environments civic assemblies of different levels, and in assuming offices of public trust. In exchange the urban community guaranteed the friars sustenance and a place to live. The mendicant communities required an extensive and articulated space for their work and demanded resources for sustenance suitable to the group's number, their activities, and their prestige. The natural environment for the new mendicant orders became the city, which would have become more demographically consistent and economically robust according to the greater number of mendicant communities they hosted and the higher the number of constituent elements in them.[12] Next to the settlements of Friars Minor and Preachers that were located in major urban centers, there arose those of the Augustinians in the second half of the thirteenth century as if

---

11. Luigi Pellegrini, *Insediamenti francescani nell'Italia del Duecento* (Rome: Laurentianum, 1984).

12. Luigi Pellegrini, "Territorio e città nell'organizzazione insediativa degli Ordini Mendicanti in Campania," *Rassegna storica salernitana* 5 (1986): 11; Luigi Pellegrini, "Dalla fraternità all'Ordine: Origini e primi sviluppi del francescanesimo nella società del secolo XIII," in *Francescanesimo nelle Marche, secoli XIII–XVI* (Cinisello Balsamo [Milan]: Edizioni San Paolo, 2000), 22.

to bear clear witness as to which population centers, aside from any official designation, were understood at the time to be large cities.[13]

We speak of the mendicant orders as innovations that generated and fostered other innovations: the third orders that were yet to come were one of the innovations; another were the female followers that they, willingly or unwillingly, attracted. Here I do not wish to speak about the female religious movement—another argument of great historiographical importance—but I cannot avoid recalling female Franciscanism, that of Clare and her *pauperes dominae*. Clare of Assisi is the first woman who composed a Rule for other women: a Rule for women animated by the demanding ideal of absolute poverty. However, we may wish to interpret the figure of Clare (her relation to Francis, to the popes, and to the Friars Minor) as something truly new because of the Rule of 1253, which over time has been imposed and reproposed, and today is the point of reference for many communities of Clarisse.[14] On the Dominican front, female institutions were not lacking in Rome and Bologna.[15] Next to the male mendicant orders the so-called second orders formed, contributing in every city and various centers to the impressive flowering of female religious sites between the thirteenth and fourteenth centuries. The third orders were attaching themselves to the first orders (those of men) and to the second orders (those of women), allowing the laypeople to be instructed on their Rule and/or constitutions, and these became streams of involvement broadly open to women.

We speak of the *novitas* represented by the mendicant orders and of the *novitates* that they themselves set in motion, but the thirteenth century also witnessed the affirmation and diffusion (in northern Italy and elsewhere) of the Humiliati. The documents granted to them by Pope Innocent III in 1201 were a sign of their great innovation with regard to traditional monasticism. The characteristic tripartite division into First, Second, and Third Orders was an absolutely novel development,

---

13. Pellegrini, "Territorio e città," 12.

14. Amid the vast sea of historical scholarship on this topic, I note the trilogy published by the Federazione S. Chiara di Assisi delle Clarisse di Umbria e Sardegna, *Chiara di Assisi e le sue fonti legislative*; *Chiara di Assisi: Una vita prende forma*; *Il Vangelo come forma di vita* (Padua: Edizioni Messaggero, 2003, 2005, 2007).

15. Marco Rainini, "La fondazione e i primi anni del monastero di San Sisto: Ugolino di Ostia e Domenico di Caleruega," in *Il velo, la penna e la parola*, ed. Gabriella Zarri-Giovanni Festa (Florence: Nerbini, 2009), 49–70; and Angelita Roncelli, "Domenico, Diana, Giordano: Nascita del monastero di S. Agnese di Bologna," in Zarri-Giovanni Festa, *Il velo, la penna e la parola*, 71–86.

but the Third Order of the Humiliati preceded all the other third orders linked to the mendicants.[16]

## An Italy of Mendicants

As for the mendicant orders, their diffusion was swift. "In less than a century, the Dominicans established more than seven hundred convents located in cities throughout Latin Christendom, while the Franciscans founded almost twice that number."[17] Within Italy it was the Franciscans who achieved a wide diffusion. In the course of the thirteenth century, the Friars Minor came to number almost six hundred settlements, with a very tight net of convents concentrated especially in the territory of Umbria and Le Marche where the friars had settled from the very beginning.[18] The distribution of the Dominicans was very unequal, with an extreme concentration in the region of the Po and a strong diffusion in the south and the islands.[19] Around 1300, the Hermits of Saint Augustine controlled around 165 sites distributed for the most part in central Italy and in particular in the area of Tuscany-Siena, Umbria-Marches of Ancona, and Lazio.[20] The diffusion of the Carmelites and the Servants of Mary was more circumscribed. The former began their expansion from Messina before subsequently expanding into central and northern Italy.[21] The latter had central Italy as their natural and immediate zone of diffusion, along with various eremitical options.[22]

Catalogues compiled in the first decades of the fourteenth century by Bernard Gui (on the Dominican side) and by Paolo da Venezia (on

---

16. Maria Pia Alberzoni, Annamaria Ambrosioni, and Alfredo Lucioni, eds., *Sulle tracce degli Umiliati*, Bibliotheca erudita: Studi e documenti di storia e filologia 13 (Milan: Vita e Pensiero, 1997).

17. Lester K. Little, "Monaci e religiosi," in *Dizionario dell'Occidente medievale* (Turin: Einaudi, 2011), 764.

18. Roberto Rusconi, "La vita religiosa nel tardo Medioevo fra istituzione e devozione," in *Chiesa, chiese, movimenti religiosi*, edited by Glauco Maria Cantarella, Valeria Polonio, and Roberto Rusconi (Bari: Editori Laterza, 2001), 207.

19. Rusconi, "La vita religiosa," 206.

20. Rusconi, "La vita religiosa," 208; Frances Andrews, *The Other Friars: Carmelite, Augustinian, Sack and Pied Friars in the Middle Ages* (Woodbridge: Boydell, 2006), 100; Pellegrini, *Insediamenti francescani*, 163.

21. Rusconi, "La vita religiosa," 206.

22. Franco Andrea Dal Pino, *I frati Servi di S. Maria dalle origini all'approvazione (1233 ca.–1304)* (Louvain: UCL Presses, Universitaires de Louvain, 1972); Andrea Czortek, *A servizio dell'altissimo Creatore: Aspetti di vita eremitica tra Umbria e Toscana nei secoli XIII–XIV* (Assisi: Edizioni Porziuncola, 2010).

the Franciscan side) indicated that there were around 120 Dominican convents and 572 Franciscan convents, while the Augustinians, who had a more gradual diffusion than the Dominicans, "did not reach two hundred locations before the middle of the fourteenth century."[23] The map of Franciscan communities in thirteenth- and fourteenth-century Italy, developed by Luigi Pellegrini, shows their diffusion throughout the peninsula but also highlights their concentration in a host of centers of middling and small size in the Apennine part of Umbria and the Marches of Ancona, as well as on the Adriatic side of Abruzzo and the Marches. It offers a good idea, on the one hand, of the gradual manner of diffusion that was suited to the order's calling and, on the other, of the settled nature of those areas that teemed with vital collectivities.

In Italy, following Pellegrini's research, great emphasis was placed on the Franciscans, but we must nonetheless be careful as the picture is much more diverse, complex, and refined than that, since the other mendicant orders also found spaces there. In this way, the model of the Umbrian region whence Franciscanism took its impetus could be significant.[24] Aside from the special case of Assisi, in the great Umbrian cities, which were ancient episcopal sees, at least three other new orders—in addition to the Friars Minor—found space: the Preachers, the Augustinian Hermits, and the Servants of Mary. While it is true that in some smaller centers the Franciscan presence seems to have been exclusive, it is also true that there were plenty of other centers where more than one type of mendicant order was present (Bevagna, Cascia, Corciano, Montefalco, Norcia), generally Friars Minor and Augustinian Hermits. The "quasi-city" of Sansepolcro, then in the diocese of Città di Castello, hosted Friars Minor, Servites, and Hermits, while only the Hermits were found at Castel Ritaldi, Cerqueto, and Gualdo Cattaneo.

## The First Settlements of Mendicants and Cities in Umbria

As can be seen in table 1, Friars Minor, Friars Preachers, Augustinian Hermits, and Servants of Mary (or Servites) are present in seven cities; the Carmelites entered late into Orvieto and Perugia. Among smaller towns, Narni received the Friars Minor, the Preachers, and the

---

23. Pellegrini, *Insediamenti francescani*, 163.
24. Giovanna Casagrande, "Monaci e Ordini Mendicanti nell'Umbria del secolo XIII," in *L'Umbria nel XIII secolo*, ed. Enrico Menestò (Spoleto: Centro italiano di studi sull'alto medioevo, 2011), 55-60.

*Table 1* The first settlements of mendicants and cities in Umbria

| CITIES (IN ALPHABETICAL ORDER) | FRANCIS- CANS | DOMINI- CANS | HERMITS | SERVANTS OF MARY | CARMEL- ITES |
|---|---|---|---|---|---|
| Città di Castello | 1228-55 | *before* 1270 | 1256 | 1249-51/52 | – |
| Foligno | The time of St. Francis | 1285 | *after* 1245/58 | 1273 | – |
| Gubbio | The time of St. Francis-1240 | 1280s | 1256 (Brettinesi ca. 1245) | – | – |
| Orvieto | ca. 1227 | ca. 1230 | 1253 (*before the great union*) (Brettinesi) | 1258/59 | 1308 |
| Perugia | 1236 | 1234 | 1256-60 | ca. 1260 | End of the 13th– beginning of the 14th c. |
| Spoleto | 1226 | 1247 | 1250 (Brettinesi) | 1273 | – |
| Todi | 1230s | *before* 1236 | 1256 | 1283 | – |

Augustinian Hermits; Amelia hosted Friars Minor and Augustinian Hermits; Terni the Preachers and the Friars Minors; and Nocera only the Friars Minor. The region of Umbria, included within the province of Saint Francis, was subdivided into nine custodianships, including the *Custodia Regni*, a sign of the capillary presence of the Friars Minor. In addition to these major friars' orders, the rather short-lived Sack Friars (it. *Saccati*) also established small centers in Spoleto, Todi, and Perugia.

The settlements of the new mendicant orders engendered everywhere a profound transformation in the social and religious reality of the city but also in its architecture and urban design.[25] Their churches and convents became poles of attraction and organization of the city's population. After an initial, precarious, and provisional phase in preexisting buildings, modest churches, and suburban sites, they constructed convents suited to their needs as the thirteenth century progressed. Regarding the Franciscans, Pellegrini has profiled the distinction in urban, rural, and eremitic settlements.[26] The Franciscan custody of

---

25. Gabriella Villetti, *Studi sull'edilizia degli ordini Mendicanti* (Rome: Gangemi, 2003); Wolfgang Schenkluhn, *Architettura degli ordini Mendicanti: Lo stile architettonico dei Domenicani e dei Francescani in Europa* (Padua: Editrici Francescane, 2003).

26. Luigi Pellegrini, "Gli insediamenti degli Ordini Mendicanti e la loro tipologia: Considerazioni metodologiche e piste di ricerca," *Mélanges de l'École française de Rome: Moyen Âge, Temps modernes* 89, no. 2 (1977): 570.

Arezzo was in this sense paradigmatic: there was an urban settlement, Cortona (in the custody of Arezzo), that was almost the size of a town; rural settlements in Castiglion Fiorentino, Lucignano, Ganghereto, and Poppi; and hermitages such as la Verna and le Celle.[27] The custody of Tivoli was marked by the presence of diverse hermitages located in the open countryside outside of inhabited centers.[28] The diffusion of settlements of the mendicant orders in urban areas was in a direct relationship with their demographic character because the subsistence of the religious depended on offerings of the faithful. As mentioned above, the larger cities could support one convent for every mendicant order, while smaller centers could sometimes support only one.

All the Tuscan cities teemed with mendicants. The six orders present in Florence—Augustinian Hermits, Carmelites, Dominicans, Servites, Friars Minor, and Sack Friars—situated themselves along vectors of urban expansion, and we should note that the settlement of the Franciscans (Santa Croce) and that of the Dominicans (Santa Maria Novella) represent opposite geographical poles of the city. How deeply the mendicants cut into this city in central Italy is shown by the fact that in the fourfold division of thirteenth-century Florence, the city dedicated one of its quarters to the city's patron, Saint John the Baptist, but three were named after the three great mendicant centers: Santa Maria Novella (Dominicans), Santa Croce (Franciscans), and Santo Spirito (Augustinian Hermits).[29]

In Pisa there were four orders—Dominicans, Carmelites, Augustinians, and Franciscans—that settled, and although there were some conflicts with the local clergy, Bishop Federico Visconti (ca. 1200-1277) favored the friars.[30] Lucca also had a presence of multiple mendicant orders with Friars Minor and Dominicans (both favored by the Republican government just as they were in Venice and Perugia), Carmelites with their characteristic tendency to move in from outside the city, and the Augustinian Hermits who were marked by a strong eremitical

---

27. Maria Grazia Nico Ottaviani, *Francesco d'Assisi e francescanesimo nel territorio aretino (secc. XIII–XIV)* (Arezzo: Biblioteca della città di Arezzo, 1983), 47–61.

28. Mariano D'Alatri, "I più antichi insediamenti francescani della custodia tiburtina," *Atti e memorie della Società Tiburtina di Storia e Arte* 53 (1980): 65–78.

29. Anna Benvenuti Papi, "L'impianto Mendicante in Firenze, un problema aperto," *Mélanges de l'École française de Rome: Moyen Âge, Temps modernes* 89, no. 2 (1977): 597–608.

30. Mauro Ronzani, "Gli Ordini Mendicanti e le istituzioni ecclesiastiche preesistenti a Pisa," *Mélanges de l'École française de Rome: Moyen Âge, Temps modernes* 89, no. 2 (1977): 667–77; Mauro Ronzani, "Il francescanesimo a Pisa fino alla metà del Trecento," *Bollettino storico pisano* 54 (1985): 30–33.

structure before and after the grand union, when the five eremitic congregations (the Guglielmiti, the Order of Saint Augustine, and the communities of the Brothers of Giovanni Bono, Favale, and Brettino) united under the papal bull of April 9, 1256, *Licet Ecclesiae catholicae* during the reign of Pope Alexander IV.[31] Cortona, a Franciscan city— which had been visited by Francis, and in which the famous Brother Elias (companion of Francis and one of the first minister generals of the order) was a citizen—was also settled by Dominicans, Augustinians, and Servants of Mary. In Siena, there were five mendicant orders— Franciscans, Dominicans, Augustinians, Carmelites, and Servants of Mary—who were well distributed within the city, sustained in various ways by the commune, and used by it for many purposes.[32]

In the situation where we can determine the presence of various mendicant settlements in a comparable urban center, each of the orders is placed at a specific distance from the others. This is true not only in larger cities such as Florence and Venice but also in those of middling size like Arezzo, where every single quarter had a mendicant order: Friars Minor, Friars Preacher, Servants of Mary, and Augustinians.[33] In Rieti, which appears to be a nice case of tripartition, the churches of Saint Agustine, Saint Dominic, and Saint Francis are placed on the city's periphery between the old and new walls.[34] The situation in Perugia is typical: there the five mendicant orders are spread out in the five neighborhoods.[35]

In the Veneto, Venice forms a pendant with Florence with the same six mendicant orders. The areas obtained by the Friars Minor and the Friars Preachers for the construction of their centers, in the first decades of the thirteenth century, were located in zones opposite each other. The Friars Minor obtained theirs through donations, while the Dominicans received theirs through a public concession.[36] Fairly soon

---

31. Pierantonio Piatti, "Gli Ordini Mendicanti a Lucca: Prospettive di ricerca," in *Il patrimonio documentario della Chiesa di Lucca* (Florence: Sismel-Edizioni del Galluzzo, 2010), 421–49.

32. Brigitte Szabò Bechstein, "Sul carattere dei legami tra gli Ordini Mendicanti, la confraternita laica dei Penitenti ed il Comune di Siena nel Duecento," *Mélanges de l'École française de Rome: Moyen Âge, Temps modernes* 89, no. 2 (1977): 743–47.

33. Nico Ottaviani, *Francesco d'Assisi e francescanesimo*, 33.

34. Robert Brentano, *A New World in a Small Place: Church and Religion in the Diocese of Rieti, 1188–1378* (Berkeley: University of California Press, 1994), 18–21.

35. Anna Imelde Galletti, "Insediamenti degli Ordini Mendicanti nella città di Perugia," *Mélanges de l'École française de Rome: Moyen Âge, Temps modernes* 89, no. 2 (1977): 587–94.

36. Fernanda Sorelli, "Gli ordini Mendicanti," in *Storia di Venezia: L'età del comune* (Rome: Istituto della Enciclopedia Italiana, 1995), n. 16, online at http://www.treccani.it/enciclopedia/gli-ordini-mendicanti_%28Storia-di-Venezia%29/.

thereafter, the Augustinian Hermits arrived; both the Hermits and the Franciscans had more locations within the city, with the Hermits, after the Dominicans and the Franciscans, assuming the most noteworthy position there. Venice did not lack the Sack Friars and the Carmelites either, while the Servants of Mary arrived in the second decade of the fourteenth century. From wills it appears that the Franciscans and Dominicans above all, followed by the Augustinians, and finally the Sack Friars and Carmelites (the Servants appeared later) were almost always the beneficiaries of individual bequests but more often of collective ones.[37]

In various cities on the Venetian mainland, that is, Treviso, Verona, Padua, and Vicenza, groups of Augustinian Hermits (Giamboniti, Brettinesi, Guglielmiti/Toscani) were present even before the union of 1256. Between 1260 and 1270 in the cities of the Venetian mainland, and the 1290s in Venice, they shared fully in the triumph of the mendicants and placed themselves, along with the Franciscans and Dominicans, as a third axis of religious presence with churches of considerable importance. Thus, the church of Saint Michael in Vicenza arose along with that of Saint Anthony of Padua, as a sacred site of memory and communal representation.[38]

Among the Venetian cities, Padua had a reputation for Franciscanism—one may think of Saint Anthony—but Dominicans, Carmelites, and Hermits were also present. In Vicenza and its district the presence of the Franciscans was developed and widespread, but this did not stop the settlement of the Dominicans;[39] in Treviso, a city animated by penitential presences, Franciscans and Dominicans competed in attracting the attention of the faithful as the wills here—as elsewhere—demonstrate.[40] In Verona, Dominicans and Franciscans appear to have been in a completely dynamic and fluid situation, a picture also populated

---

37. Sorelli, "Gli ordini Mendicanti," 905–27.
38. Franco Dal Pino, "Formazione degli Eremiti di Sant'Agostino e loro insediamenti nella Terraferma Veneta e a Venezia," in *Gli Agostiniani a Venezia e la chiesa di S. Stefano* (Venice: Istituto Veneto di Scienze, Lettere ed Arti, 1997), 27–85.
39. Francesca Lomastro, "Appunti sulla fortuna dei Minori a Vicenza nel Duecento," *Civis* 7 (1983): 41–62.
40. Daniela Rando, "Minori e vita religiosa nella Treviso nel Duecento," *Civis* 7 (1983): 63–91.

by *sorores minores*, Humiliati, large and small hospitals, the sick, lepers, hermits, and Augustinian Hermits.[41]

In the heart of northern Italy, in the middle of Lombardy, Brescia, torn apart by urban strife and pervaded by heretical elements, took in the Dominicans in 1221 when they received the grant of a preexisting church directly from cardinal and papal legate Ugolino of Ostia. Starting in 1234, the Commune of Brescia undertook acquisitions in the suburb of san Lorenzo in order to endow the Dominicans with an area where they might be able to build their convent and church. In the third decade of the thirteenth century Franciscans were also present who, thanks to the favor of the commune and the faithful, had their own stable settlement at the time. Around the middle of that century, alongside the Franciscans and Dominicans, the Hermits inserted themselves, also with the favor of the commune and the faithful. A statute of 1313 placed on the same level Dominicans, Franciscans, and Hermits regarding the offering coming from the commune on the occasion of the principal liturgical feasts. Already in the second half of the thirteenth century, the entire area south of the city, which was born out of an enlargement of the walls, ended up being divided into three zones, each the focus of activity and influence of one of the three mendicant orders, almost as if to signal to the mendicants the obligation to collaborate with the commune's government.[42] In the 1340s, Carmelites also joined in.

Milan was a melting pot of religious experiences. Franciscans and Dominicans arrived there in the 1220s. The Friars Minor came in 1224 to the area of san Vittore all'Olmo, a suburban area on the periphery, and from there passed into the basilica of San Nabore in the 1250s. The Dominicans possessed Sant'Eustorgio from the 1220s onward, and already in 1228 they were working with the commune and the archbishop to persecute the heretics of the city and territory. The Augustinian Hermits settled in the 1250s near the church of San Marco. Bonvesin da la Riva, in his *De Magnalibus* from the 1280s, referred to the flowing of the mendicant orders into Milan. He was in contact with the brethren of

---

41. Gian Maria Varanini, "Per la storia dei Minori a Verona nel Duecento," *Civis* 7 (1983): 92-125.

42. Gianmarco Cossandi, "Gli insediamenti degli ordini Mendicanti e i nuovi aspetti della vita religiosa tra XIII e XIV secolo," in *A servizio del Vangelo: Il cammino storico dell'evangelizzazione a Brescia*, ed. Giancarlo Andenna (Brescia: Editrice La Scuola, 2010), 435-82.

Sant' Eustorgio and bears witness to the preeminence of this convent among the houses of the four mendicant orders (Dominicans, Franciscans, Augustinians, and Carmelites) that were present in Milan in the last decades of the thirteenth century, and it was also the Lombard headquarters of the important office of the Inquisition.[43]

In the middle of central Italy, the case of the Marches of Ancona offers an emblematic example of the distribution of mendicant houses in relation to a hierarchy of cities by order of size. The *Descriptio Marchiae*, ordered by Cardinal Egidio di Albornoz in the middle of the fourteenth century, classified cities of the territory of the Marches as *maiores* (largest), *magne* (large), *mediocres* (middling), and *parve* (small). Among the largest cities (Urbino, Ancona, Fermo, Camarino, Ascoli) and in some of the large cities (Fano, Iesi) were located three centers of mendicant orders; in the middling ones (Cingoli, Osimo, Matleica, Tolentino, Rocca Contrada, Sanginesio) there were at least two mendicant orders (Franciscans and Augustinians); and in the small cities only the Franciscans were present. The locations of the mendicant orders reproduced the scale of cities envisioned in the *Descriptio*, which is not only formulated on the basis of political importance, but also attends to the socioeconomic situation of the individual urban centers. Only in the centers that were socially more vibrant could diverse religious communities engaged in pastoral care flow together, and only the economically more robust urban centers were in a position to sustain the burden of maintaining two or three churches and the convents of the mendicants who, because they did not have their own incomes, weighed heavily on the resources of the citizenry.[44]

Campania—which corresponded to the Franciscan province of the Terra di Lavoro and in the Dominican context was included in the large province of the *Regnum*—can also be taken as an example of the distribution of mendicant centers. The principal centers of activity were Salerno, Amalfi, Naples, Capua, Benevento, and Gaeta. The Dominican presence was advanced in Naples and in Gaeta (in the 1220s); the Dominicans pursued a pattern of settlement characterized by a rather slow diffusion of their centers through a more loosely structured network, with an absolute preference for major centers of cultural and economic

---

43. Maria Pia Alberzoni, *Francescanesimo a Milano nel Duecento* (Milan: Edizioni Biblioteca francescana, 1991).
44. Pellegrini, "Dalla fraternità all'Ordine."

life.⁴⁵ Franciscans did not occupy only the great cities but many other centers of various sizes, reaching a total of fifty-six sites at the beginning of the Trecento.⁴⁶ The entry of the Augustinians into Campania began in 1271 from Naples, the city that designed itself to be the principal axis of the region. In Naples, there was room for everyone: Franciscans and Dominicans with more than one location, and then the Augustinians and Carmelites.⁴⁷

Nothing stopped the advance of mendicant settlements, not even political conflicts like that between Frederick II and Gregory IX. Around 1240, in the territory of the *Regnum*, there were six Franciscan provinces (Sicily, Calabria, Terra di Lavoro, Apulia, San Angelo, and the Abruzzo or Pennese). At the end of the Swabian era and in the first years of the reign of Charles of Anjou, these six provinces were divided into twenty-three custodies for a total of more than one hundred settlements. Regarding the Dominicans, it appears that we can attribute with certainty to the era of Frederick II the foundations in Naples, Gaeta, Benevento, Brindisi, and Trani, to which should be added the Sicilian cities of Messina, Piazza Armerina, Palermo, and Trapani. The Kingdom of Sicily, barely touched by the currents of heresy active in communal environments and devoid of major centers of study, occupied a marginal place among the Dominican provinces.⁴⁸ Regarding the province of Sicily, it is clear that already in the years between 1263 and 1270, it had been broken up into four custodies of the Friars Minor; in time it would rise to five. Following the argument of Jacques Le Goff, which was confirmed by Pellegrini, there emerges a picture of the urban centers in Sicily during the thirteenth and fourteenth centuries that establishes a hierarchy of importance. In first place was Palermo, followed by Messina, Catania, and Trapani—cities that show both the religious receptivity and economic potential to host three mendicant communities.⁴⁹

---

45. Pellegrini, "Territorio e città."
46. Pellegrini, *Insediamenti francescani*, 305–6.
47. Pellegrini, "Territorio e città"; Rosalba Di Meglio, *Gli ordini Mendicanti nella Napoli dei secoli XIII–XV* (Naples: ECI, 2005).
48. Giulia Barone, "Federico II di Svevia e gli ordini Mendicanti," *Melanges de l'École française de Rome: Moyen Âge, Temps modernes* 90, no. 2 (1978): 607–26.
49. Luigi Pellegrini, "Impianto insediativo e organizzazione territoriale dei francescani nella Sicilia dei secoli XIII-XIV," in *Francescanesimo e cultura in Sicilia* (Palermo: Officina di Studi Medievali, 1987), 306. For Le Goff's argument Pellegrini cites Jacques Le Goff, "Ordres mediants et urbanisation dans la France médiévale," *Annales E.S.C.* 25 (1970): 924–46.

## Integration of Mendicants into Urban Societies

Although not without conflicts and competition, the mendicant revolution had the task of renewing the relationship with the faithful. If the phrase "mendicant orders–city" had become a catch phrase, another very successful catch phrase was "mendicant orders–laity." In the cities, the mendicant orders came into contact with an active and hardworking laity. To this laity it was necessary to give correct guidance not only through preaching, confession, etc., but also, and even better, through formations leading to better social integration by means of normative texts that regulated every moment of the life of the faithful. In a society that needed to gather together, unite, congregate, and become a body, the mendicant orders encouraged and promoted the formation of confraternal associations under a variety of guises: Marian-*laudesi* brotherhoods; Raccomandati of the Virgin; *disciplinati*; and societies for the defense of the faith. These associations succeeded in capturing devout laypeople in various ways, among which that of the "penitents" of the Order of Penitence were transformed into tertiaries, as the Franciscans had done in the first place.

The integration of the mendicants into the associations is attested by a vast quantity and variety of documentary sources: notarial acts, statutes, papal letters, urban annals, conciliar deliberations, and administrative or accounting registers present the mendicants as trustworthy men, to be called upon as witnesses for both public acts and private. At their convents various contracts were penned: brothers were named executors of wills, guarantors of agreements, and advisors to individuals and communities.

Of the tight network of relationships between the mendicants and the laity the infinite testamentary bequests offer the best proof. Indeed, among the notarial acts, wills, in which the Italian archives abound, are the most suitable means by which to understand the radical and profound penetration of the mendicant orders into the heart of the varied universe of the faithful. These documents appear as milestones and "encyclopedias" of the religious sites within a city and its territory (diocese and *contado*). In them, mendicant monasteries and convents and charitable and service institutions often take up a great amount of space, and the realities kept in mind by the testators are often so many and varied that they do not omit the cells of male and female recluses. The significance of individual bequests reflects the consideration that the testator accorded to various institutions. Sometimes

*Table 2* The place of the mendicants in the hierarchy of consideration from the faithful testators

|  | # WILLS | # BEQUESTS |
|---|---|---|
| Franciscans | 173 | 192 |
| Dominicans | 172 | 182 |
| Hermits | 152 | 163 |
| Carmelites | 126 | 132 |
| Sack Friars | 8 | 8 |

some are placed on equal footing, while at other times one encounters real hierarchies. Wills are not only a sign of the hold of the mendicants on the religious and spiritual sensibilities of individual believers but also of the relationships between them. The case of Pisa, with 568 wills between 1240 and 1320, allows us to arrive at the overview in table 2 that nicely demonstrates the place of the mendicants in the hierarchy of consideration from the point of view of the faithful testators.[50]

Wills are a privileged source of evidence because they allow us to understand the orientation and interests of the faithful. For example, the 1238 will of Buffono di Bertoloto, a magnate from Padua, allows us to gain a picture of his world of the religious settlements, churches, communities, brotherhoods, and more.[51] In Perugia, the will of Paolo d'Angelo (1305) devoted attention to the Franciscans, Dominicans, Augustinians, and Servants of Mary, and desired that his palace become a site for religious persons under the guidance of the Franciscan friars. That of the illuminator Angelo di Bencivenne (1322) is typically encyclopedic, rich in bequests to mendicant places and others.[52] Well developed in the thirteenth century, this testamentary practice grew even more solid in the fourteenth. In Padua, for example, it would seem that in the course of the century the bequests to religious communities tended to be concentrated on the mendicant orders.[53] This also holds true for all the localities of greater or lesser demographic importance.

---

50. Eleonora Rava, *"Volens intestatus vivere": Testamenti a Pisa, 1240–1320* (Rome: Istituto Storico Italiano per il Medio Evo, 2016), 176.

51. Antonio Rigon, "Francescanesimo e società a Padova nel Duecento," *Civis* 7 (1983): 22–26.

52. Giovanna Casagrande, "Dallo spazio topico a quello devozionale: Perugia," in *Francesco d'Assisi: Storia e Arte* (Milan: Electa, 1982), 83–90.

53. Antonio Rigon, "Orientamenti religiosi e pratica testamentaria a Padova nei secoli XII–XIV," in *Nolens intestatus decedere* (Perugia: Regione dell'Umbria, 1985), 62.

In Brescia, too, wills offer proof of the amalgamation between the friars and society. As Gianmarco Cossandi, who studied the mendicant settlements in this city notes,

> Although there seems to emerge from the bequests a certain preponderance toward the Dominicans—perhaps because of their greater involvement in the care of souls that rendered them more deserving in the eyes of the testators—between the end of the thirteenth and the beginning of the fourteenth century, the Friars Minor also earned a central position in social and religious life, as the numerous cases of burial in their church particularly demonstrate. One has the impression of a broad civic consensus that bears witness to the capacity of the friars to relate to urban society in both a vertical and horizontal manner, overcoming even the different political factions.[54]

For Milan, Maria Pia Alberzoni has focused on the figure of Paxius de Ossona, a brother of Penance and likely a wealthy merchant, who conferred importance in his 1296 will on specific religious houses: Saint Francis of the Friars Minor, Sant'Eustorgio of the Friars Preachers, Saint Mark of the Augustinian Hermits, and the church of the Servants of Mary who took the place of the Sack Friars in the church of Santa Maria del Sacco, and Santa Maria del Carmine of the Carmelites. Alberzoni also places great importance on the testamentary source as one that shows the network of relations between the friars and the faithful. Bonvesin de la Riva chose to be buried in the church of the Friars Minor even though he was a member of the Third Order of Humiliati, a fact that attests to the religious vitality that could be directed—here as elsewhere—in very different ways in a climate of absolutely fluid relationships and encounters. The multiplicity of the mendicant orders present in the city, along with other orders of a more ancient tradition, suggests a variety of forms of "convivenza."[55]

The mendicant orders immediately identified in the confraternities an effective instrument for acting in the lay world. They favored the Marian-*laudesi* confraternities, which were widespread in the thirteenth century when the cult of the Virgin was being strengthened in opposition to the Cathar doctrine that denied Mary the role of the Mother of God. But there were other factors for their popularity linked to a

---

54. Cossandi, "Gli insediamenti degli ordini Mendicanti," 481.
55. Alberzoni, *Francescanesimo a Milano*.

comprehensive mutation in sensibilities and in the perception of the divine made human. Meersseman's work shows the broad diffusion of brotherhoods named after the Virgin that were linked to the Dominicans and appeared precociously in numerous cities: from Bologna to Spoleto, from Mantova to Arezzo, from Vercelli to Viterbo, from Padua to Siena, from Venice to Bergamo, from Lucca to Cremona, and so on.[56] As Daniela Rando remarks,

> We know that some congregations of laypeople dedicated to the Madonna existed already in the twelfth century, but that in the thirteenth century they assumed a new purpose thanks to the work of Peter of Verona, that of spreading and promoting devotion to the Virgin, thereby opposing the propaganda of the heretics. Among the first Marian confraternities of this type, Meersseman recalls the Society of the Virgin in Milan which was founded in 1232; and the Florentine and Bolognese confraternities that already existed in 1245 and 1252, respectively.[57]

Famous in Perugia, the brotherhood of Saint Mary took its origins from the Dominicans already in the middle of the thirteenth century. In Orvieto there were three Marian brotherhoods, one belonging to the Friars Minor, another to the Dominicans, and one to the Servants of Mary; at Montefalco a similar brotherhood is attested in the mid-twelfth century linked to the Friars Minor.[58] Indeed, at the request of the Franciscan order, between the 1250s and 1260s, there appeared a network of brotherhoods named solely after the Virgin and Saint Francis.[59] Nevertheless, the Marian-*laudesi* brotherhoods were not always nor necessarily connected with the mendicants. The movement of the Raccomandati di Maria, although it gave life to a system of confraternities, does not seem particularly bound to the new orders, even if it was strengthened by them. This is proven by the text of the *forma vitae* attached to the letters of spiritual affiliation by Bonaventure, minister general of the Franciscans; by Sinibaldo da Alma, prior of the Roman

---

56. Cf. Gilles Gérard MEERSSEMAN, IN COLLABORATION WITH GIAN PIERO PACINI, ORDO FRATERNITATIS: CONFRATERNITE E PIETÀ DEI LAICI NEL MEDIOEVO, 3 vols. (Rome: Herder, 1977), 921–1117.

57. Rando, "Minori e vita religiosa," 75.

58. Giovanna Casagrande, *Religiosità penitenziale e città al tempo dei comuni* (Rome: Istituto Storico dei Cappuccini, 1995), 391–92.

59. Servus Gieben, "Confraternite e penitenti dell'area francescana," in *Francescanesimo e vita religiosa dei laici nel '200* (Assisi: Università degli Studi di Perugia, 1981), 183–84.

Province of the Preachers; and by Clement of Osimo, prior general of the Hermits of Saint Augustine. Nor is the vast phenomenon of voluntary reclusion particularly connected with the mendicants. In the thirteenth and fourteenth centuries, it flourished throughout central Italy and other places; individuals autonomously and freely attached themselves to various religious institutions.[60] Strongly connected with the mendicants—Dominicans and Franciscans—was the politico-religious movement of peacemaking known as the Alleluia, which in 1233 involved the cities of Lombardy.[61] This was a sign of the impact of the friars of the new orders on the political and social realities of the cities in times of ferment and evolution.

As a fruit of the mendicants' actions there were also several militia groups that placed themselves in defense of the faith. In Parma, the Knighthood of the Blessed Glorious Virgin, a new associative formation, was approved by the pope in 1261 thanks to the Franciscan Ruffino Gorgone da Piacenza. Earlier in Parma, in 1233, the Dominican Bartolomeo da Braganze promoted the Knighthood of Jesus Christ, which later joined with the Knighthood of the Blessed Mary Glorious Virgin that had been established in Bologna, supported by the aforementioned Ruffino Gorgone da Piacenza, and approved by the pope in 1261. It portrayed itself as a kind of religious chivalric order (Cavalieri Gaudenti). This new order, having been founded in Bologna with the general necessity of curbing heresy, spread to Modena, Reggio, and Parma, and the aforementioned Rufino Gorgone da Piacenza played a role in the composition of the Rule. The order spread through various Italian cities and was distinctive for welcoming among its members those belonging to the high aristocracy. In Bologna, which was the organizational center of the Dominican order, the friars became promoters and supervisors of various societies of the faith such as the Society of the Blessed Virgin Mary, the Society of Saint Dominic, and the Society of the Cross.[62]

The famous movement of the *Disciplinati* (1260) in its first appearance does not show any specific links with the mendicant orders. It is only later, when the confraternities focused on penitential discipline

---

60. Casagrande, *Religiosità penitenziale*, 17–74.
61. André Vauchez, *Ordini Mendicanti e società italiana* (Milan: Mondadori, 1990), 119–61.
62. Marina Gazzini, *Confraternite e società cittadina nel Medioevo italiano* (Bologna: Clueb, 2006), 85–155; Marina Gazzini, "Costruire la comunità: L'apporto delle confraternite fra Due e Trecento. Alcuni esempi dal Nord e Centro Italia," *Rivista di storia della Chiesa in Italia* 68 (2014): 331–48.

began to spread rapidly, that brotherhoods emerged following the mendicant settlements, with Perugia and Florence being examples of this.[63] Although the penitential brotherhoods were for the most part autonomous and free in relation to the mendicants, their civic dimension, their pursuit of peace and of a well-defined moral code governed by the sacrament of confession, their ritual and prayerful reevocation of the passion of Christ, and their devotion to the Mother of God were nevertheless all elements of mendicant pastoral care.

Among the various examples that can be adduced concerning the relationships between the mendicants and the confraternities, in Parma in 1295 the Franciscan Rainerio da Genova inspired the ordinances for a society dedicated to the Virgin and to Saint Francis; these statutes would have been read to all the citizens of Parma who had attended the Franciscan convent around the time of the feast of the Conception of the Virgin. In Mantua, at the outset of the fourteenth century, the statute of the penitential confraternity of Santa Maria della Misericordia was inspired by the city's bishop, Giacomo Benfatti who was a Dominican, and he used the statutes almost as a homily to give adequate direction to the life of the members of the confraternity.[64] In Pisa, Dominicans combined three confraternities into one with a statute to that effect in 1312: a Marian confraternity of *laudesi*; another confraternity of the Raccomandati di Maria; and that of the *disciplinati* of the Cross.[65] Decisively connected to the convent of Saint Francis were the brothers of the *Congregatio beatissime virginis Marie ac beatissimo confessoris Francisci, apud fratres Minores de Brixia*. This brotherhood, bringing together men and women, obtained spiritual benefits from the Friars Minor thanks to Saint Bonaventure in 1274. Moreover, it obtained other letters of spiritual favor from Clement of Osimo, prior general of the Augustinian Hermits, and from Raimondo Goffredi, minister general of the Franciscans.[66]

Florence is a splendid example of confraternal gatherings (*laudesi*, brotherhoods of Misericordia, and *disciplinati*) around the mendicants.[67]

---

63. Giovanna Casagrande, "Penitenti e Disciplinati a Perugia," *Mélanges de l'École française de Rome: Moyen Âge, Temps modernes* 89, no. 2 (1977): 711-21; Massimo Papi, "Confraternite e ordini Mendicanti a Firenze," *Mélanges de l'École française de Rome: Moyen Âge, Temps modernes* 89, no. 2 (1977): 723-32.
64. Gazzini, "Costruire la comunità."
65. Meersseman, *Ordo fraternitatis*, 1:1049-54.
66. Cossandi, "Gli insediamenti degli ordini Mendicanti," 465-66.
67. Papi, "Confraternite e ordini Mendicanti a Firenze."

Here the zones of greater density of the confraternities are traceable to the conventual areas of the mendicants, with pride of place going to the Dominicans. It was not only Florence, the great metropolis, that teemed with all kinds of brotherhoods,[68] but we also know of the *laudesi* penitential brotherhoods in more modest centers like Sansepolcro: one linked to the church of Saint Francis, another to the church of Saint Agustine. The confraternity of San Bartolomeo in Sansepolcro distinguished itself as a civic institution, and its members received spiritual benefits from both the Franciscans and the Augustinians, while among its members were Augustinian and Dominican friars.[69]

In Padua, the Franciscans must have influenced the composition of the fourteenth-century statutes of the brotherhood of Saint Anthony. The visitator to this brotherhood was selected from among Franciscans, which evidences the link between the brotherhood and the convent; the brotherhood of San Nicola da Tolentino was linked to the Hermits.[70] Perugia is a typical case of the correspondence of penitential confraternities to individual settlements of the mendicant orders.[71] Here, the brotherhood of the Disciplinati of Saint Francis found a "long-distance spiritual director" in the Franciscan Alvaro Pais.[72]

In Milan, on the one hand, the church of the Friars Minor offered patronage to at least three confraternities named after, respectively, Saint Francis, Saint Anthony, and the Virgin. On the other, at the church of the Dominicans two societies of the devout are found starting in the 1230s, which, according to the tradition, were established by Peter of Verona during his stay in Milan: a *societas fidelium*, named after Peter Martyr, and the Congregation of the Virgin.[73]

In Bergamo, the comprehensive Confraternity della Misericordia arose under the aegis of the Dominican bishop, Erbord, with the blessing of the city's prelates:

> And with the counsel and approval of the Friars Preachers, Friars Minor and other lay faithful. And with the labor of friar

---

68. The flagellant confraternities praised God, the Virgin, and the saints; those of the *disciplinati* did indeed praise the divinity but with penitential intent in imitation of Christ's humility and suffering.

69. Andrea Czortek, *Eremo, convento, città* (Assisi: Edizioni Porziuncola, 2007), 55-131.

70. Giuseppina De Sandre Gasparini, *Statuti di confraternite religiose di Padova nel Medioevo* (Padua: Istituto per la storia ecclesiastica padovana, 1974).

71. Casagrande, "Penitenti e Disciplinati a Perugia."

72. Mariano D'Alatri, "I Minori e la 'cura animarum' di fraternite e congregazioni," in *I Frati Minori e il Terzo Ordine*, 145-70.

73. Alberzoni, *Francescanesimo a Milano*, 36.

Pinamonte da Brembate of the Order of Preachers, who composed these statutes for the remedy of his soul and remission of his sins and that everyone is obliged and should pray for him, since he is a member of this confraternity and is faithful and supportive of all the actions of this confraternity.[74]

This is a significant proof of the full involvement of Dominicans in the making of this confraternity.

If the massive phenomenon of confraternities can offer a privileged perspective on how much mendicants rooted themselves in the heart of individual urban societies, other aspects such as the bonds between the friars—for example, the Franciscans—and the noble and mercantile classes have also been shown. In Perugia the case of the blessed Egidius, third companion of Saint Francis, is a case that epitomizes how the Friars Minor found support in members of a family at the pinnacle of the city's hierarchy, the Coppoli, who hosted him in a house of their own at the gate of Perugia.[75]

The integration between the mendicant orders and the citizen body is also demonstrated by the support that public entities gave to each of the mendicant establishments in various cities (Siena, Perugia, Lucca, Venice, Brescia, etc.). All the communes were generous and made systematic donations in cash and in kind. In Naples, it was the rulers themselves who made regular as well as occasional subsidies.[76]

Another reality that demonstrates the social and political integration of the mendicants are the services carried out by the friars for the cities. Important books for the commune (Padua, Perugia, Siena) were deposited at mendicant convents. Friars were entrusted with diplomatic duties, the mediation of peace, the responsibility of neutral referees (*super partes*) for the selection of public officials, counting of the votes, the control of the operations of authorities and administrators, as well as the distribution of alms and visitations to prisoners. They could be used as experts (in building and many other things),

---

74. "Et cum consilio et assensu fratrum Predicatorum et fratrum Minorum et aliorum fidelium laicorum. Et cum labore fratris Pinamontis de Brembate Ordinis Predicatorum, qui hoc opus [cioè lo statuto] composuit pro remedio anime sue et pro remisione peccatorum suorum et ut omnes teneantur et debeant orare pro ipso, cum ipse sit de ipsa congregatione et fidelis et favorabilis in omnibus factis huius congregationis." Maria Teresa Brolis, Giovanni Brembilla, and Micaela Corato, *La matricola femminile della Misericordia di Bergamo (1265–1339)* (Rome: École française de Rome, 2001), 68.

75. Luigi Giacometti, *San Francesco del Monte a Perugia* (Perugia: Fabrizio Fabbri, 2014), 23–32.

76. Di Meglio, *Gli ordini Mendicanti nella Napoli dei secoli XIII–XV*, 106–7.

and sometimes they had the prestigious and demanding job of being the manager of estates or treasurer (Perugia and Pistoia).[77] In southern Italy, the friars were employed at court as chaplains, confessors, advisors, and almoners, and that they highly valued their employment in the service of the monarchy is attested by sermons in which the sovereigns were directly or indirectly exalted.[78]

Last but not least, the relation between the mendicants and cities finds confirmation in the emergence of holy friars—at times with a local background and therefore with a civic identity—as emblems of the city. Anthony of Padua is the ultimate example of this phenomenon. For the Augustinian Hermits in the Marches of Ancona, the case of Saint Nicola da Tolentino stands out in the early fourteenth century.

The integration of the mendicants into the social and religious fabric unfolded along with the affirmation of cults for new Umbrian saints linked to the mendicants. Siena is an emblematic case of cults that arose as civic religion: a few examples of such holy cults in Siena are Ambrogio Sansedoni, a Dominican preacher; Pietro Pettinaio, a Franciscan tertiary; Gioacchino, a member of the Order of Servites; and Agostino Novello, a man venerated by the Augustinians.[79] This amply demonstrates the capacity of the mendicant orders to cultivate the religious milieu to their own ends, not only at the level of the mass of the faithful but also at the public level of civic power. If Siena and Padua offer relevant examples here, there are many others such as Cortona and Santa Margherita; Sansepolcro and the Blessed Rainerius; Spoleto and Simone da Collazzone, OFM; and Orvieto and Ambrogio da Massa, OFM.

## The Order of Penitence: A Case Study

The Order of Penitence with its own *forma vitae* appeared in the first decades of the 1200s during which the mendicants (Franciscans and Dominicans) were forming and beginning to spread. We are speaking

---

77. Antonio Rigon, "Frati Minori e società locali," in *Francesco d'Assisi e il primo scolo di storia francescana* (Turin: Einaudi, 1997), 27–275; Frances Andrews, ed., with Maria Agata Pincelli, *Churchman and Urban Government in Late Medieval Italy, c.1200–c.1450: Cases and Contexts* (Cambridge: Cambridge University Press, 2013), 166–200.
78. Di Meglio, *Gli ordini Mendicanti nella Napoli dei secoli XIII–XV*, 108–18.
79. Vauchez, *Ordini Mendicanti e società italiana*, 186–205.

of the *Memoriale prepositi* (1221/28),[80] a legal document aimed at dictating a way of life for laypeople shaped by precise norms. Who were the propagators of such a text? Hugo/Hugolino—Pope Gregory IX? An entourage of jurists? The attributions are often problematic, even if the interest of Gregory IX in the Penitents is an established fact, given the notable number of papal letters that he sent in their defense and for their protection.[81]

By and large, these were the prescriptions set forth by the *Memoriale*: wear modest dress, avoid celebrations and public spectacles, avoid eating meat and eat with moderation, pray at meals, fast, recite the canonical hours, confess and take communion three times a year, be reconciled with your neighbor, pay the tithe, do not carry weapons, and refrain from swearing oaths; also required were monthly meetings of individual brotherhoods, mutual support within the brotherhood in life and in death, peace among brothers and with outsiders, and correction in case of wrongdoing committed by brothers.

These are norms of behavior that structure the life of the penitent, allowing them to lead a religious life without abandoning the world. Devoid of an orientation toward poverty, the *Memoriale* is open to men and women of different conditions. The Penitents of the Order of Penitence appear to have been freed from any connection to other religious orders. Initially, it gives the impression of an autonomous order for which the relevant authority is the diocesan bishop. On the basis of this Rule for living, Brothers and Sisters of Penance—*fratres et sorores de poenitentia*—which was also known as the *ordo Continentium*, spread throughout central and northern Italy at least.

While the *Memoriale* is a "rule" for all of the Penitents belonging to the Order of Penitence, *Supra montem* of 1289, issued by Pope Nicholas IV, fixed what would remain for centuries the Franciscan Third Order, the first third order linked to a mendicant order. With it, laypeople in the full sense of the word were encompassed within a real religious order, giving life to the lay-religious with a mixed legal nature. Between the *Memoriale* and *Supra montem*, certainly some groups and/

---

80. Lino Temperini, ed., *Testi e documenti sul Terzo ordine Francescano (sec. XIII–XV): Originale latino e versione italiana* (Rome: Editrice Franciscanum, 1991), 83–109. For the full text of this document, see Giles Gérard Meersseman, ed., *Dossier de l'ordre de la pénitence au XIII$^e$ siècle* (Fribourg: Editions Universitaires, 1961), 91–112.

81. Meersseman, *Dossier de l'ordre de la pénitence au XIIIe siècle*, 43–55.

or brotherhoods turned toward the Minors or, in any case, were drawn into the sphere of the Minorites. Whether and on precisely what terms Francis may have founded the order or his own Order of Penitence/Third Order is a question that has not been answered in a definite way. Nonetheless, it is certain that within the context of the Friars Minor the idea of forming an Order of Penitence/Third Order matured very quickly, anchored once again in the charisma of Francis himself.[82] The Franciscan Third Order was, in fact, open to a vast, articulated set of possible forms of religious life, ranging from the secular life, that is, a life led in one's own house, to the regular life, which was led in communal settings. The regular Penitents emerged as a valid alternative within the world of men as much as, it is worth noting, that of women, without excluding eremitic forms of life. The members of the Order of Penitence constituted in their turn a *novitas*. They engendered a new kind of *homo religiosus* who rested upon a plausible reconciliation between the possibility of living as a Christian and being saved, on the one hand, and the nonnecessity of abandoning the affairs and effects of the world, on the other.

The official birth of the Franciscan Third Order, therefore, is connected with the bull *Supra montem*. This rule encapsulated the *Memoriale* but also brought several interventions of its own:[83] there was more attention to the correct Catholic faith of the aspiring penitent; the use of arms was allowed for the defense of the Church, the faith, and one's own land; and the visitator absolutely had to be a Friar Minor. But who really were the Penitent Tertiaries? Aside from celebrated tertiaries who became saints and blessed ones,[84] such as Angela da Foligno, Margherita da Cortona, and Pietro Pettinaio, the group included men and women of various conditions and statuses. The concreteness of the documents allows us to see a world of common Christians who were not forced to abandon property, family, work, and other activities.

Many brotherhoods of Penitents engaged in the creation and operation of hospitals, attracted by that works-oriented charity characteristic of the High and late Middle Ages, and this in cities like Vicenza, Verona, Brescia, Ferrara, Bologna, Florence, Spoleto, Todi, and others. Since

---

82. Jacques Dalarun, "Tommaso da Celano: La vita del beato padre nostro Francesco," *Frate Francesco* 81, no. 2 (2015): 310.

83. Temperini, *Testi e documenti sul Terzo ordine francescano*, 286–311.

84. Lino Temperini, ed., *Santi e santità nel movimento penitenziale francescano dal Duecento al Cinquecento* (Rome: Analecta TOR, 1998).

the penitential tertiaries enjoyed the canonical and juridical status of lay-religious, in many cities they were employed during the 1200s and 1300s as fiduciaries at the heart of communal magistracies, occupying a vast array of offices that required guarantees of honorable behavior. This was the case, for example, in Bologna, Ferrara, Imola, Perugia, Pisa, Siena, Arezzo, and Parma.

If the Franciscans were quick to take possession of the Order of Penitence, this did not mean that other friars were not desirable for lay men and women in other forms aside from confraternities. During the thirteenth and fourteenth centuries, for example, we know about groups of *vestitae* (who were close to the Dominicans) in Florence, Siena, Lucca, and Pisa, but penitent women oriented to the Dominicans also appear in Orvieto and Siena. For the penitents of Orvieto it was the same Master General Munio di Zamora who redacted the *Ordinationes* (1286), which was later considered as a rule for the Dominican Third Order in the context of the making of the *Tractatus* of Caffarini.[85] In 1321, another master general, Herveus da Nedellec, sent specific *ordinationes* to the penitents of Siena. The two cases reveal the Dominican interest in this phenomenon and a certain desire to keep it under control on the part of the Dominican order's hierarchy.[86] The hagiographical sources, for their part, focused on the figures of Margherita da Città di Castello and Vanna da Orvieto as Dominican penitent-tertiaries.[87]

The Augustinian Hermits, the Servants of Mary, and the Carmelites attracted male and female converts and oblates.[88] In the hands of the mendicants, oblation—an inheritance from monasticism—drew the devout laity into an orbit closer to the life of the conventual community. They are not framed as a kind of third order, but they are also not free like members of various confraternities. They are bound to

---

85. Maiju Lehmijoki-Gardner, "Le penitenti domenicane tra Duecento e Trecento," in Zarri-Giovanni Festa, *Il velo, la penna e la parola*, 113–23.

86. Pierantonio Piatti, "All'ombra dei Padri: La 'memoria di Caterina' e il processo di istituzionalizzazione delle *Sorores de Poenitentia Sancti Dominici* fra Tre e Quattrocento," in *Virgo digna Coelo* (Vatican City: Libreria Editrice Vaticana, 2013), 379–406.

87. For Margherita from Città di Castello, see the entry of Giovanna Casagrande, in *Dizionario biografico degli Italiani*, vol. 70 (Rome: Istituto della Enciclopedia Italiana, 2008), 132–34; for Vanna from Orvieto, see Emore Paoli and Luigi G. G. Ricci, *La Legenda di Vanna da Orvieto* (Spoleto: Centro italiano di studi sull'alto medioevo, 1996).

88. Andrews, *The Other Friars*, 138–39; Andrea Czortek, "L'oblazione dei laici presso i frati Eremiti di Sant'Agostino nei secoli XIII e XIV," *Analecta Augustiniana* 65 (2002): 5–40; Andrea Czortek, "Frati e laici: Dagli oblati al Terz'Ordine," *Studi storici dell'Ordine dei servi di Maria* 59 (2009): 417–55.

communities of reference with a promise: they can be framed within the fluid state of the so-called lay-religious.

## Selected Bibliography

Alberzoni, Maria Pia. *Francescanesimo a Milano nel Duecento*. Milan: Edizioni Biblioteca francescana, 1991.
Andrews, Frances. *The Other Friars: Carmelite, Augustinian, Sack and Pied Friars in the Middle Ages*. Woodbridge: Boydell, 2006.
Andrews, Frances, ed., with Maria Agata Pincelli. *Churchmen and Urban Government in Late Medieval Italy, c.1200–c.1450: Cases and Contexts*. Cambridge: Cambridge University Press, 2013.
Bacci, Michele. *Investimenti per l'aldilà: Arte e raccomandazione dell'anima nel Medioevo*. Bari: Editori Laterza, 2003.
Brentano, Robert. *A New World in a Small Place: Church and Religion in the Diocese of Rieti, 1188–1378*. Berkeley: University of California Press, 1994.
Brolis, Maria Teresa, Giovanni Brembilla, and Micaela Corato. *La matricola femminile della Misericordia di Bergamo (1265–1339)*. Rome: École française de Rome, 2001.
Casagrande, Giovanna. "Monaci e Ordini Mendicanti nell'Umbria del secolo XIII." In *L'Umbria nel XIII secolo*, edited by Enrico Menestò, 45–72. Spoleto: Centro italiano di studi sull'alto medioevo, 2011.
——. *Religiosità penitenziale e città al tempo dei comuni*. Rome: Istituto Storico dei Cappuccini, 1995.
Czortek, Andrea. *A servizio dell'altissimo Creatore: Aspetti di vita eremitica tra Umbria e Toscana nei secoli XIII–XIV*. Assisi: Edizioni Porziuncola, 2010.
——. *Eremo, convento, città*. Assisi: Edizioni Porziuncola, 2007.
Dal Pino, Franco Andrea. *I frati Servi di S. Maria dalle origini all'approvazione (1233 ca.–1304)*. Louvain: UCL Presses, Universitaires de Louvain, 1972.
De Sandre Gasparini, Giuseppina. *Statuti di confraternite religiose di Padova nel Medioevo*. Padua: Istituto per la storia ecclesiastica padovana, 1974.
Di Meglio, Rosalba. *Gli ordini Mendicanti nella Napoli dei secoli XIII–XV*. Naples: ECI, 2005.
*Francescanesimo e cultura in Sicilia*. Palermo: Officina di Studi Medievali, 1987.
*Francescanesimo e vita religiosa dei laici nel '200*. Assisi: Università degli Studi di Perugia, 1981.
*Francesco d'Assisi e il primo secolo di storia francescana*. Turin: Einaudi, 1997.
*Francesco d'Assisi: Storia e Arte*. Milan: Electa, 1982.
*I Frati Minori e il Terzo Ordine: Problemi e discussioni storiografiche*. Todi: Accademia Tudertina, 1985.
Gazzini, Marina. *Confraternite e società cittadina nel Medioevo italiano*. Bologna: Clueb, 2006.
Lawrence, Clifford Hugh. *I Mendicanti: I nuovi ordini religiosi nella società medievale*. Cinisello Balsamo (Milan): San Paolo, 1998.
——. *Il monachesimo medievale*. Cinisello Balsamo (Milan): San Paolo, 1993.

Meersseman, Gilles Gérard, ed. *Dossier de l'ordre de la pénitence au XIII$^e$ siècle*. Fribourg: Editions Universitaires, 1961.

Meersseman, Gilles Gérard, in collaboration with Gian Piero Pacini. *Ordo fraternitatis: Confraternite e pietà dei laici nel Medioevo*. 3 vols. Rome: Herder, 1977.

Nico Ottaviani, Maria Grazia. *Francesco d'Assisi e francescanesimo nel territorio aretino (secc. XIII–XIV)*. Arezzo: Biblioteca della città di Arezzo, 1983.

*Nolens intestatus decedere*. Perugia: Regione dell'Umbria, 1985.

Pacaut, Marcel. *Monaci e religiosi nel Medioevo*. Bologna: Il Mulino, 1989.

Pellegrini, Luigi. *Insediamenti francescani nell'Italia del Duecento*. Rome: Laurentianum, 1984.

Rava, Eleonora. *"Volens intestatus vivere": Testamenti a Pisa, 1240–1320*. Rome: Istituto Storico Italiano per il Medio Evo, 2016.

Rusconi, Roberto. "La vita religiosa nel tardo Medioevo fra istituzione e devozione." In *Chiesa, chiese, movimenti religiosi*, edited by Glauco Maria Cantarella, Valeria Polonio, and Roberto Rusconi, 192–254. Bari: Editori Laterza, 2001.

Temperini, Lino, ed. *Santi e santità nel movimento penitenziale francescano dal Duecento al Cinquecento*. Rome: Analecta TOR, 1998.

———, ed. *Testi e documenti sul Terzo ordine Francescano (sec. XIII–XV): Originale latino e versione italiana*. Rome: Editrice Franciscanum, 1991.

Vauchez, André. *Ordini Mendicanti e società italiana*. Milan: Mondadori, 1990.

*Virgo digna Coelo*. Vatican City: Libreria Editrice Vaticana, 2013.

Zarri-Giovanni Festa, Gabriella, ed. *Il velo, la penna e la parola*. Florence: Nerbini, 2009.

CHAPTER 9

# Saints

*Antonella Degl'Innocenti*

The panorama of the sanctity in Italy between the eleventh and fourteenth centuries is extremely diverse and complex, as we can see through the historical, religious, and cultural events of this long period. This chapter follows a chronological order to make more visible the evolution of the concepts and manifestations of the sanctity within this temporal arc, presenting the most noticeable phenomena and most important figures in a historical context based on surviving hagiographical testimonies. Along with the essential biographical details, I aim to illuminate the specific features of saints' religious choices, the novelty of their religious experience, and the reception they enjoyed. My purpose is essentially to reconstruct and summarize a history of sanctity in Italy, not only of single individuals, but also of the ideals, forms of devotion, spirituality, and religious culture expressed in the hagiographical tradition in Italy between the eleventh and fourteenth centuries.

## The Eleventh Century

The eleventh century represented a time of crucial importance for Western religious history. In fact, the great process of rethinking and

---

This chapter was translated by Greco Muratori.

reorganizing the Church, known as the Gregorian Reform (after Pope Gregory VII, 1073-85), took place in this very century.

The reform's actions occurred on different levels with a variety of effects. On the one hand, the concept of *libertas ecclesiae*, which guided the thought and action of Gregory VII, allowed the affirmation of papal sovereignty and established the complete independence of religious authority from political authority, leading to a serious conflict between the Church and Empire, lasting until the Concordat of Worms in 1122. On the other hand, the need for moral and spiritual renovation led to a search for new solutions, in an attempt to end detrimental practices within the Church (simony, Nicolaism) and to restore the *ecclesiae primitivae forma*—that is to say, the conditions of purity and poverty of the first Christian communities.

Although at this time some ancient monastic centers still maintained their authority and prestige (e.g., Montecassino reached its pinnacle of glory under Abbot Desiderio, 1058-86), it can be said that the downfall of traditional monasticism had already begun, as the signs of an irreversible moral deterioration were becoming more evident.[1] However, the monastic path had not exhausted its historic role. Both eremitism, which can be understood as a radical alternative to debased monasticism, and the newer forms of cenobitic monasticism, which were generally characterized by a greater interest in the world and history, offered concrete answers to the demands for perfection coming from the *societas Christiana* and were therefore greatly appealing. Even the priestly lifestyle, which had also been criticized by the reformers, was renovated through the implementation of tougher regulations based on those of monastic orders (such as leading a common life and giving up individual possessions).

Within this framework, a further, deeper change began, which concerned not only specific behaviors, but also how faith was experienced. In fact, a new understanding of the relationship between man and God came about, which suggested a different image of God, as well as a different understanding of Christians' prerogatives and duties. While it is true that the Church that resulted from the reform was an essentially clerical Church—that is, dependent on clerical authority—it is also true that at this time the laity took on a more active role as they offered their

---

1. On the complex problem of the crisis of monasticism and on the historiographical debate around this theme, see Cristina Sereno, "La 'crisi del cenobitismo': Un problema storiografico," *Bullettino dell'Istituto storico italiano per il Medio Evo e Archivio Muratoriano* 104 (2002): 31-83.

own contribution to Church reform. In fact, the change in conscience produced by the reform interacted with social and political transformations taking place at the same time. Sofia Boesch Gajano describes this process very well: "At its first stage, the reform surely had an accelerating effect on favoring the autonomy of urban communities from episcopal and feudal authority, as well as inviting the laity to participate in Church life within their communities. It could be said that it served as a catalyst for social forces and emerging religious needs."[2]

To understand the phenomenon of sanctity within Italian society of the eleventh century, it is essential not to neglect the framework that has been described up to this point. However, it must be specified that not every expression of holiness, devotion, and hagiographic memory occurring within the eleventh century should automatically be referred to the unrest of the Gregorian era. Many of the people mentioned in the subsequent paragraphs were affected by these characteristics, but other individuals have also contributed to outlining the scenario of holiness during this time: together with contemporary saints, hermits, monks, and bishops participating in the reform process (praised by hagiographies usually written shortly after their death), many ancient saints, martyrs, apostles, confessors, and glorious proponents of a distant past also received considerable attention and strengthened the devotion of that time. In the eleventh century, as well as in succeeding centuries, the society of the perfect was presented as extremely rich and composite. From the early Middle Ages onward, the saint, both ancient and contemporary, represented an example of Christian lifestyle to believers, but the functions assigned to sanctity were different compared to the past. Despite being limited within a traditional role, the contemporary saints generally expressed an innovation, a change of perspective, that was more pronounced when they were monks or hermits. Even when they took the path of withdrawal from the social world, medieval saints did not alienate themselves from the world, but rather acted within their environment to bring about change whenever it was needed. Having seen the evil deeds in the Church clearly, they saw the necessity for a historic commitment and were highly motivated to intervene in order to put right corruption in the Church. The hagiographies dedicated to medieval saints generally derived from a milieu in favor of the reform, addressing its specific needs. The ancient saint, on the other

---

2. Sofia Boesch Gajano, "La strutturazione della cristianità occidentale," in Anna Benvenuti et al., *Storia della santità nel cristianesimo occidentale* (Rome: Viella, 2005), 137.

hand, represented and served other interests and purposes: their commemoration was generally related to procedures of remembrance aimed at the establishment or confirmation of a place of worship, the sanctioning of the possession of relics, and the accreditation of an authority, ecclesiastical institution, or monastic center. Such procedures were generally described through rewritings of more ancient texts, or in the genre of *inventiones* or *translationes* in which miracles were the prevailing theme—that is, the most evident sign of an active presence within the saint's remains. In the first half of the eleventh century, the number of ancient saints was still greater than that of contemporary saints. This is a clear example of how well established such figures were within the people's devotion. However, already in the second half of the century, an opposite trend emerged, consolidating during the following period.[3]

However, the clear dominance of men over women—which had characterized the history of sanctity since its very beginning—did not change. A recovery of the female element would only occur later, during a further time of change in the thirteenth century, when the message of Francis of Assisi and Dominic of Guzman—which was also addressed to women—allowed them to be partly emancipated from the unfavorable bias derived from a strongly hostile tradition.

### Hermitic-Monastic Sanctity

Eremitism is a phenomenon that has always characterized the history of Christianity. Since its origins, it has represented an absolutely radical experience, based on asceticism and contemplation, and has satisfied the need for dedicating oneself completely to God through a lifestyle of absolute rigor, away from the social world and from any earthly ties. Initiated in the East, where it was made famous by many ascetics living in the deserts of Egypt and Palestine, the phenomenon of eremitism spread to the Western world, but only in the eleventh and twelfth centuries did it become a generalized phenomenon, presenting itself as an alternative to the monastic lifestyle.[4]

---

3. Paolo Tomea, "L'agiografia dell'Italia settentrionale (950–1130)," in *Hagiographies: Histoire internationale de la littérature hagiographique latine et vernaculaire en Occident des origines à 1550*, ed. Guy Philippart, vol. 3 (Turnhout: Brepols, 2001), 141.

4. André Vauchez, *La spiritualità dell'Occidente medioevale, secoli VIII–XII* (Milan: Vita e Pensiero, 1978), 101; Derek Baker, "'The Whole World a Hermitage': Ascetic Renewal and the Crisis of Western Monasticism," in *The Culture of Christendom: Essays in Medieval History in Memory of Denis L. T. Bethell*, ed. Marc Antony Meyer (London: Hambledon, 1993), 207–23.

There is evidence of the presence of hermits and groups of hermits in various areas of Italy (the Po delta, the Tuscan-Emilian Apennines, and the southern regions) already in the second half of the tenth century, an important sign of the religious upheaval that would occur in the following century.[5] In a time of crisis for the Church and of decadence in traditional monasticism, the path of eremitism—seldom associated with cenobitic forms—appeared to be the most suitable solution for leading an authentically Christian lifestyle, and for distancing oneself from a reality that was judged unfavorably.

Within the hermitic field, there are figures that have contributed to the very image of sanctity itself in the eleventh century. First of all, Romuald of Ravenna (d. 1027) must be mentioned.[6] He was the founder and reformer of retreats and monasteries in central Italy (such as the Camaldoli retreat, established around 1023 in the Tuscan-Romagnolo Apennines). His life, as told by Peter Damian, seemed to be characterized by a search for "increasingly perfect experiences of solitary life, which were nonetheless not separate from a concrete intervention in the ecclesiastical lifestyle—and in particular, in the monastic-hermitic lifestyle—of his time."[7] In fact, Romuald managed to combine different dimensions in a difficult balance: the personal desire for solitude, the incentive to establish new retreats (as if he wanted "totum mundum in heremum ... convertere"),[8] and the constant attention to monasticism in his time that he attempted to reform—although not always successfully. In short, Romuald represented a "rational eremitism"—Bruno of Querfurt (d. 1009) defined him as "pater rationabilium heremitarum"[9]—that

---

5. Giovanni Miccoli, "La storia religiosa," in *Storia d'Italia*, vol. 2, *Dalla caduta dell'Impero romano al secolo XVIII*, edited by Ruggero Romano and Corrado Vivanti (Turin: Einaudi, 1974), bk. 1:471-72.

6. For biographical and bibliographical information on the saints mentioned here, see *Bibliotheca Sanctorum* (Rome: Istituto Giovanni XXIII della Pontificia Università Lateranense, 1961-); *Dizionario biografico degli Italiani* (Rome: Istituto della Enciclopedia Italiana, 1961-); Claudio Leonardi, Andrea Riccardi, and Gabriella Zarri, eds., *Il grande libro dei santi: Dizionario enciclopedico* (Cinisello Balsamo [Milan]: Edizioni San Paolo, 1998). For an updated bibliography, see the database *Mirabile: Archivio digitale della cultura medievale. Digital Archives for Medieval Culture*, http://www.mirabileweb.it.

7. Giuseppe Fornasari, "Romualdo," in Leonardi, Riccardi, and Zarri, *Il grande libro dei santi*, 732.

8. Petri Damiani, *Vita beati Romualdi*, ed. Giovanni Tabacco (Rome: Istituto Storico Italiano per il Medio Evo, 1957), c. 37.

9. Bruno di Querfurt, *Vita quinque fratrum*, ed. Reinhard Kade, c. 2, in Monumenta Germaniae Historica, Scriptores 15.2 (Hannover: Monumenta Germaniae Historica, 1888), 718. Among the most relevant studies, see Giuseppe Fornasari, *Medioevo riformato del secolo XI: Pier Damiani e Gregorio VII* (Naples: Liguori, 1996), 203-66.

maintained its connection to the noble tradition of the "fathers of the desert," while at the same time being aware of the importance of the present and not refraining from taking action.

Peter Damian (d. 1072), spiritual disciple of Romuald and author of his *vita*, was an exponent of this type of eremitism.[10] Born in Ravenna, having been a hermit at Fonte Avellana (of which he became prior in 1043), Damian inherited Romuald's love for retreats, and like him, he applied himself to the organization of eremitic life. However, he dedicated himself to the task of working for Church reform more than his master, accepting the title of cardinal bishop of Ostia (1057) and collaborating closely with Pope Nicholas I and Pope Alexander II. His hagiographer, Giovanni of Lodi,[11] relates what was presumably a painful time of his life—that is, moving from his hermitic phase to serving the Church. Yet, giving up the *solitaria quies* was compensated with an awareness of his new duties and the merits he would derive before God.

San Domenico Loricato (Loricatus) (d. 1060) and san Rodolfo di Gubbio (d. 1061) were figures tied to Peter Damian and to the retreat of Fonte Avellana. Having first entered the retreat of Ponterezzoli in Umbria, Domenico then moved to Fonte Avellana— run by Peter Damian— and he seemed to incarnate the eremitic ideal in its purest form: his hagiographer (none other than Peter Damian himself) describes in detail the harshness of his asceticism (the Latin epithet *loricatus* derives from the practice of carrying a *lorica*— iron armor—on his body as a means of penitence). Rodolfo di Gubbio was also a hermit at Fonte Avellana, under the guidance of Peter Damian (who would write his life). He represented a more articulate form of sanctity: he was elected as bishop of Gubbio and, as such, while still conducting ascetic practices, he applied himself to preaching and fighting against simony. From the hagiographic point of view, Domenico and Rodolfo represented two different ways of interpreting the hermitic condition, in which the complex personality of their common biographer can be recognized. Although Peter Damian himself was probably more oriented toward a purer form of eremitism, he was forced by necessity to move toward a form of eremitism that combined with ecclesiastical commitments.

---

10. On hagiographic works of Peter Damian, see Umberto Longo, *Come angeli in terra: Pier Damiani, la santità e la riforma del secolo XI* (Rome: Viella, 2012).

11. Pierluigi Licciardello, "Agiografia latina dell'Italia centrale, 950-1130," in *Hagiographies: Histoire internationale de la littérature hagiographique latine et vernaculaire en Occident des origines à 1550*, ed. Guy Philippart, vol. 5 (Turnhout: Brepols, 2010), 487-93.

The different forms of eremitism were also highlighted by another saint of this time, Saint Dominic of Sora (d. 1031), who continuously shifted from the position of hermit to that of a church builder and monastery founder, of abbot and preacher, working in an area ranging from Foligno (Perugia), his birthplace, to Sora (Frosinone), where he would die.[12] This saint clearly showed how hermits in the pre-Gregorian era were already able to be present in historical reality and to bring their moral thrust into it, taking into account the specific sociopolitical situations of the time. As a matter of fact, in his work as a founder of monasteries (such as san Pietro Avellana, san Bartolomeo in Trisulti, Santa Maria in Sora), Dominic knew perfectly how to move in a politically strategic way, establishing contacts with the local landowners or with the *castra*, who would support his establishments in many ways.

### Cenobitic-Monastic Sanctity

Since its birth, monasticism had presented itself as the only possible school of Christian perfection. From the Carolingian era onward, mostly thanks to the large-scale implementation of the *Rule of Saint Benedict*, it had reached both an impressive dissemination and compactness. In the first decades of the eleventh century, Benedictine monasticism generally still presented itself as a stable institution under a religious, cultural, and economic profile—due to the Cluniac Reform, which was widespread in Italy. However, initial displays of a crisis of monasticism would soon appear, essentially determined by external conditioning, corruption, and the loss of values. Consequently, this type of monasticism would soon cease to be able to satisfy the expectations of those who wanted to dedicate themselves to God with no compromise, by renovating themselves profoundly and retrieving the more authentic Benedictine spirit.[13]

In the first half of the eleventh century in northern Italy, the Benedictine monastery of Pomposa still presented an image of prosperity. One of the people responsible for this positive representation was Abbot Guido (1008–46) who was praised as a holy man by his peers, including Peter Damian who had stayed in Pomposa for two years.[14] With

---

12. Licciardello, "Agiografia latina dell'Italia centrale," 502–3.
13. Claudio Leonardi, "Eremo e cenobio," in Leonardi, *Medioevo latino: La cultura dell'Europa cristiana* (Florence: SISMEL-Edizioni del Galluzzo, 2004), 815–18.
14. Tomea, "L'agiografia dell'Italia settentrionale (950–1130)," 131.

the support of popes and emperors, and thanks to his good relations with the archbishop of Ravenna who had been in conflict with the community in the past, and with the powerful family of Canossa, Guido managed to boost his monastery, both materially (the expansion and restoration works of the abbey complex) and spiritually. The distinctive traits of his monastic dedication appeared to be, on the one hand, the reconciliation of the twin aspects of Pomposian monasticism, the hermitic spirit (inspired by Romuald) and the cenobitic one, and on the other hand, the unique political stability that the abbey had reached under his guidance. Both of these elements ensured that Pomposa had a position of great relevance within the Italian monastic landscape of the time.

Another important figure who was active in northern Italy was san Guglielmo da Volpiano (d. 1031), who was born on the island of san Giulio at Lake Orta (Novara), yet lived mostly in France where he followed Abbot Maiolo, becoming a monk at Cluny in 987. He is especially remembered as a severe monastic reformer, earning him the nickname of *ultra regulam*. During one of his journeys in Italy, he founded the monastery of Fruttuaria (diocese of Ivrea), where he implemented a very harsh protocol, a life vowed to penitence; but other monasteries in Italy were also influenced by his work, which was inspired by the most elevated monastic ideals and by the desire for absolute independence from any bishop, monastery, or secular authority.

In southern Italy, a monastery that was affected by the Cluniac Reform was the abbey of Holy Trinity in Cava (Cava dei Tirreni, Salerno), established by Sant'Alferio (d. 1050)—after his experience of eremitism—who had been a disciple of Odilone in Cluny. Alferio and the three abbots who succeeded him (Leone, Pietro, and Constabile) were venerated as saints, all officially canonized in 1893. Their lives were narrated by Hugh, a monk at Cava and later abbot of Venosa, in a single hagiographical work written around 1140, which probably began with the intent of celebrating the greatness of the monastery—as well as of the four abbots—and following its history in a time of splendor.[15]

Once the push for the Cluniac Reform had ended, monasticism, both in Italy and elsewhere, slowly entered a period of decadence, which

---

15. Amalia Galdi, "Le *Vitae* dei santi abati Cavensi tra memoria e autorappresentazione," in *Riforma della chiesa, esperienze monastiche e poteri locali: La Badia di Cava nei secoli XI–XII. Atti del Convegno internazionale di studi Badia di Cava, 15–17 settembre 2011*, ed. Maria Galante, Giovanni Vitolo, and Giuseppa Z. Zanichelli (Florence: SISMEL-Edizioni del Galluzzo, 2014), 77–95.

would only end with the birth of new religious orders. The person who above all represented the crisis of traditional cenobitism in Italy and the attempt to overcome it was san Giovanni Gualberto (d. 1073), who can be included within the protagonists of the Gregorian era.[16] He was able to combine his commitment to the renewal of monastic life—with the consequent establishment of the Vallombrosa monastery, in the Tuscan-Emilian Apennines—with the battle against ecclesiastical corruption (his condemnation of Pietro Mezzabarba, simoniac bishop of Florence, was vigorous).

Other figures in this period were inspired by the *Rule of Saint Benedict* and recovered its effective value. In particular, the abbots of the monastery of San Michele della Chiusa in the Susa Valley, Benedict I (d. before 1046) and Benedict II (d. 1091), come to mind as they stood out for their efforts in defending their monasteries' independence from any external interference.[17] Moreover, Benedict II, although he could count on the support of Gregory VII, for a long time had to cope with the hostility of the bishop of Turin, Cuniberto, who was opposed to the autonomy of the monastery and sided with the excommunicated Henry IV. Benedict II was also forced into a period of exile by the bishop, at a time when the Gregorian Reform had already been long in place.

### Sanctity of the Clergy

While the hermit-monks who had access to sanctity were numerous, those who were part of the secular clergy (priests, bishops, deacons) seem to have enjoyed this privilege less at this time. The clericalization process of the Church was probably still too new to have an effect on the construction of models of sanctity. The scenery, as will be seen shortly, would change in the following century, when there would be a clear recovery of the episcopal model.

Despite this, at least two figures should be remembered: the deacon sant'Arialdo (d. 1066), and sant'Anselmo da Baggio, bishop of Lucca (d. 1086).[18] Arialdo was leader of the Pataria movement, working actively

---

16. For an overview of hagiographies of Giovanni Gualberto, see Antonella Degl'Innocenti, ed., *Vallombrosa: Memorie agiografiche e culto delle reliquie* (Rome: Viella, 2012), 15–140 (essays of Sofia Boesch Gajano and Antonella Degl'Innocenti).

17. Antonio Placanica, *Le storie di San Michele della Chiusa* (Florence: SISMEL–Edizioni del Galluzzo, 2015).

18. On Arialdo, see Giovanni Miccoli, *Chiesa Gregoriana: Ricerche sulla Riforma del secolo XI* (Florence: La Nuova Italia, 1966), 101–60. On Anselmo, see Paolo Golinelli, "*Indiscreta*

to report the clergy's vices—Nicolaism and simony—and opposing the simoniac archbishop Guido da Velate, who ordered his murder. Anselmo displayed an exceptional personality: he supported the reform of the clergy's lifestyle, siding in favor of Gregory VII in the battle against the emperor. Together with Giovanni Gualberto, from a monastic point of view and despite the diversity of their roles, Arialdo and Anselmo appeared to be worthy proponents of a historically and socially active sanctity, which perfectly reflected the turmoil and agitation of the Gregorian era.

A different story is that of the figure of the holy pope.[19] It is well known that Gregory VII showed a significant interest in the concept of pontifical sanctity, and—in light of the assertion of the Petrine primacy—in his *Dictatus papae*, he theorized a "functional" sanctity of the pope, that is, a sanctity that was tied to the practice of the roles of *vicarius Petri*, common to every legitimately elected pope.[20] Some popes were particularly venerated and celebrated in the eleventh century (Leo IX, Gregory VII, Victor III, Urban II).[21] However, as Vauchez has argued, only in the thirteenth century would a pope be venerated as a saint for his own individual worth.[22]

## The Twelfth Century

From the point of view of the history of sanctity, the twelfth century displayed elements of continuity from the previous century, but also introduced significant developments. While the influence exerted by cenobitic monasticism appeared to be strongly declining, and the new forms of renewed monasticism that arose at the end of the eleventh century (Carthusians, Cistercians) did not seem to affect the construction of new images of perfection as much as outside of Italy, the hermitic

---

*sanctitas": Studi sui rapporti tra culti, poteri e società nel pieno Medioevo* (Rome: Istituto Storico Italiano per il Medio Evo, 1988), 117-55. On the hagiographies of Arialdo and Anselmo, see Kathleen G. Cushing, "Events that Led to Sainthood: Sanctity and the Reformers in the Eleventh Century," in *Belief and Culture in the Middle Ages: Studies Presented to Henry Mayr-Harting*, ed. Richard Gameson and Henrietta Leyser (Oxford: Oxford University Press, 2001), 187-96.

19. Roberto Rusconi, *Santo Padre: La santità del papa da san Pietro a Giovanni Paolo II* (Rome: Viella, 2010), 15-18; André Vauchez, *La santità nel Medioevo*, trans. Alfonso Prandi (Bologna: Il Mulino, 1989), 291-300.

20. *Dictatus papae*, 23 (= Gregorii VII *Registrum* II, 55 a), in *Das Register Gregors VII.*, ed. Erich Caspar, Monumenta Germaniae Historica, Epistolae selectae 2 (Berlin: Weidmannsche Buchhandlung, 1920), 1:207.

21. Licciardello, "Agiografia latina dell'Italia centrale," 593-98.

22. Vauchez, *La santità nel Medioevo*, 293.

solution—in all its different forms (pure eremitism, eremitism combined with cenobitic monasticism, etc.)—found its momentum during the twelfth century, often leading to experiences of sanctity.

Moreover, compared to the previous century, what asserts itself more was the model of episcopal sanctity—which was obviously already very different from that of the early Middle Ages, due to the difference of the historical conditions. Especially in the heart of central Italy (Lazio), where the pope's control was exerted the most strongly, the bishop vouched for the reform ideals and became a close ally and collaborator of the pope. Because of this, bishops found themselves working in difficult situations, facing opposition within the clerical milieu itself or clashing with the representatives of the local political powers.

However, the most different factor regarding sanctity at this time was probably another one. In the context of transformations that affected the social and political system, of critiques and demands that had come from within and from outside the Church (in the twelfth century there were numerous heretical movements), what was gradually put forward was an idea of sanctity that would satisfy different needs. While the most traditional models did not lose their relevance, perfection became open—for the first time—to a variety of conditions, becoming accessible to seculars.

The phenomenon of "modernization" of sanctity, which could already be observed in the previous century, was in this way significantly advanced, although, in the context of local cults and of patron saints, the presence of ancient saints (and especially martyrs) showed no sign of decreasing. In many locations—for various reasons—there was an attempt to reinstall the cult of ancient patron saints, or to add new patrons to the ancient ones, as well as taking advantage of events such as the *inventio* or *translatio* of relics. To this purpose, new hagiographical texts—often reelaborations of ancient texts—were written. In some cases, the relics of certain saints were contested, and some were claimed back through the composition of hagiographies: for example, in the case of san Prospero di Reggio Emilia, whose remains were contested, as Paolo Golinelli explained, between two urban institutions—the rectory of San Prospero and the monastery of the same name.[23] The transfer of

---

23. Paolo Golinelli, "Italia settentrionale (1130–1220)," in *Hagiographies: Histoire internationale de la littérature hagiographique latine et vernaculaire en Occident des origines à 1550*, ed. Guy Philippart, vol. 1 (Turnhout: Brepols, 1994), 137.

the relics of the apostle Saint James the Great to Pistoia (1144-45) and of the apostle Saint Philip to Florence (1205), which the local clergy and bishops desired strongly, accounted for the composition of celebrative writings (in the case of Pistoia, it was an actual liturgical and hagiographical dossier, assembled by Bishop Attone) revealing the interests and preoccupations of ecclesiastical politics, which emerged in situations of crisis for the episcopal authority (e.g., Pistoia), or in situations of concern due to heretic threats (e.g., Florence).[24]

Compared to the past, the context in which sanctity was recognized and celebrated generally changed. In central and northern Italy cities, which had seen great transformations starting from the end of the eleventh century, became in many cases the main areas of construction and reelaboration of hagiographic memories. It is in this context that a clear definition of the concept and roles of patron saints was reached. As Anna Benvenuti has written, "Despite having their origin during late antiquity and the early Middle Ages, it was essentially within the particular political and ideological contexts that were determined by the establishment of the Gregorian Reform in the eleventh century and by the episcopal 'renaissance' of the twelfth century that the patronage of saints returned to being inextricably integrated within the urban system, becoming one of the focal points of its communal conscience."[25]

Another important change in this period occurred in terms of the control of sanctity: while until that moment the Roman Curia had felt no need to verify and authorize the cult of saints, from the end of the twelfth century onward it began to "hold the turbulent waves of sanctity back (that is, the constant turbulent emergence of new saints), by verifying the authenticity of the miracles attributed to the servants of God."[26] It was at this time that the process of canonization was born—and the most ancient one remaining to us is that regarding the Tuscan hermit Galgano da Chiusdino, who shall be mentioned again below.

Having been initiated by the impetus of the Gregorian Reform, the renewal of sanctity then proceeded throughout the twelfth century, paving the way for further developments. Women—except in certain cases—were still excluded from this process, unlike what was happening

---

24. Antonella Degl'Innocenti, "Agiografia latina dell'Italia centrale, 1130-1220, 950-1130," in Philippart, *Hagiographies*, 5:768-70.

25. Anna Benvenuti Papi, "La civiltà urbana," in Benvenuti Papi et al., *Storia della santità nel cristianesimo occidentale*, 161.

26. Vauchez, *La santità nel Medioevo*, 41.

outside of Italy at this time in regions where the rise of the mystical phenomenon offered them chances for sanctification.

## Sanctity between Hermitage and Cloister

The Benedictine monastic model retained its vitality to important centers such as Montecassino, Subiaco, and Cava, which maintained their prestige during this period.[27] At the same time, the hermitic model became very successful.

Two hermit saints of central Italy were san Galgano da Chiusdino (d. 1181) and Saint William of Maleval (d. 1157).[28] Associated with clearly mythical traits and described by hagiographies strongly influenced by the chivalric romance genre, Galgano gave up his life as a knight (performing the symbolic act of sticking his sword into the ground as if it were a religious cross) and retreated to a hermitage on the hill of Montesiepi, not far from his hometown.[29] He would spend his whole life here, leaving only to visit Rome to see Pope Alexander III. After his death, he quickly benefited from papal recognition (1185) following an *inquisitio in partibus*, the documents of which are available to us and provide an important testimony of a process of canonization that was still in its initial phase.

William of Maleval had a different historical impact, although also in his case the hagiography altered his profile with invented mythical contaminations. Of French descent, after a series of pilgrimages and eremitical experiences he settled definitively in a desolate valley near Castiglione della Pescaia (Grosseto), known as *Stabulum Rodis*. The hermit community that had formed around him would spread widely after his death, reaching northern Europe, gradually attaining a well-defined

---

27. In this time in Montecassino Pietro Diacono, author of several hagiographic works, is active. In particular, his *Ortus et vita iustorum cenobii Casinensis* is a great portrayal of the sanctity of Montecassino from the monastery's origin to the eleventh century. See Oronzo Limone, "Italia meridionale (950–1220)," in *Hagiographies: Histoire internationale de la littérature hagiographique latine et vernaculaire en Occident des origines à 1550*, ed. Guy Philippart, vol. 2 (Turnhout: Brepols, 1996), 30–32.

28. On Galgano, see Vauchez, *La santità nel Medioevo*, 41; Degl'Innocenti, "Agiografia latina dell'Italia centrale," 762–63. On Guglielmo, see Degl'Innocenti, "Agiografia latina dell'Italia centrale," 760–62.

29. Anna Benvenuti Papi, ed., *La spada nella roccia: San Galgano e l'epopea eremitica di Montesiepi. Atti del Convegno di studi (Chiusdino 20–21 sett. 2001)* (Florence: Mandragora, 2004).

structure until it became the Hermit Order of Saint William (or "Williamites"), recognized in 1249 by Innocent IV as an *ordo monasticus*.[30]

In central Italy at this time, there was a woman hermit named Chelidonia (d. 1151 or 1152).[31] Not much about her is known to us, and what we do know has been conveyed through a late hagiography, probably composed in the female monastery of Morra Feronia (Subiaco), established before 1183 near the saint's tomb and controlled by the monastery of Subiaco.

In southern Italy—in an area where the Italo-Greek hermitic monastic tradition had always been active—we can find san Guglielmo da Vercelli (d. 1142) and san Giovanni da Matera (d. 1139).[32] Guglielmo was first and foremost a penitent and a pilgrim. Following a pilgrimage to Santiago de Compostela, he decided to travel to the Holy Land, and for this reason he went to southern Italy, where he met Giovanni da Matera. Forced to abandon the pilgrimage by an unfortunate event and—perhaps even more so—by Giovanni's advice, he settled, together with some of his disciples, on the Partenio mountains (near Avellino). Here, in two years they formed a mixed community of men and women that also included priests, and embraced a hermitic lifestyle. Together they founded the monastery of Montevergine. Disagreements with the priests regarding the community management and the application of the principles of poverty led Guglielmo to leave Montevergine together with a few followers. Subsequently, he founded in the plain of Goleto, in Campania, a new mixed hermitic community (prevalently female). Meanwhile, the community of Montevergine continued to exist, later adopting a well-defined monastic structure following the *Rule of Saint Benedict*. Supported by a unique ascetic force, Guglielmo never ceased to follow his hermitic vocation. However, the effort he put into providing a stable organization to hermits and the attention he gave to the women's religious vocation made him stand out. As Giancarlo Andenna wrote, such factors have certainly earned him the title of one "of the most open-minded monastic reformers of the twelfth century."[33]

---

30. Kaspar Elm, *Beiträge zur Geschichte des Wilhelmitenordens* (Cologne: Bohlau, 1962).
31. Sofia Boesch Gajano, *Chelidonia: Storia di un'eremita medievale* (Rome: Viella, 2010).
32. For an overview of hagiographic sources relating to southern Italy and Sicily between the eleventh and twelfth centuries, see Paul Oldfield, *Sanctity and Pilgrimage in Medieval Southern Italy, 1000–1200* (Cambridge: Cambridge University Press, 2014).
33. Giancarlo Andenna, "Guglielmo da Vercelli," in *Dizionario biografico degli Italiani*, 61:42–46.

A different profile is that of Giovanni da Matera,[34] who nonetheless shows some similarities to Guglielmo. Giovanni was also animated by a very strong desire for solitude, which early in life led him to leave his family and to retreat in various locations—Puglia, Calabria, Sicily, and finally, Ginosa near Matera. But he also felt the urge to dedicate himself to the apostolate, and therefore became an itinerant hermit-preacher in the same way as the *Wanderpredigers*, who operated in other European regions during this period. Apparently, however, his actions met with criticism from ecclesiastical circles (in Bari he risked being sentenced as "evil and heretic" for his criticisms of the clergy's behavior). During his wanderings, Giovanni founded in Gargano (Puglia) the monastery of Pulsano with a thriving congregation, which had a fair amount of success in Italy up until the fourteenth century. The adoption of the Benedictine Rule, ordered by the saint, would ensure a cenobitic organization to this monasticism, which had originated from a clearly hermitic impulse with the aim to preserve (including through hagiographic testimonies) the lessons of its founder's ascetic and moral rigor.

Lastly, the figure of Joachim of Fiore (d. 1202), in Calabria, is noteworthy. He was a hermit, Cistercian monk, and founder of a monastic order (known as *Florense*). In particular, he is well known for his original theological reflections, which would have a strong theoretical impact in the following centuries.

## Episcopal Sanctity

The sanctity of bishops was consecrated in the numerous hagiographies composed during this period that updated its traditional image, based on the old topoi of the patron bishop and adapted to express new moral values within the various local contexts, in a relationship of dialogue/conflict with the new political institutions.

Common characteristics can be recognized in the figures of certain bishops of central Italy (and in particular, the area of Lazio), such as those of Pietro di Anagni (or Pietro da Salerno) (d. 1105), Bruno of Segni (d. 1123), and Berardo dei Marsi (d. 1130).[35] Loyal to the pope,

---

34. Antonio Vuolo, "Monachesimo riformato o predicazione: La 'Vita' di san Giovanni da Matera (sec. XII)," *Studi medievali*, 3rd series, 27 (1986): 69–121.

35. On the saints in the Lazio area, see Pierre Toubert, *Les structures du Latium medieval: Le Latium méridional et la Sabine du IX$^e$ siècle à la fin du XII$^e$ siècle* (Rome: École française de Rome, 1973), in particular 807–40; and Degl'Innocenti, "Agiografia latina dell'Italia centrale," 740–45.

actively participating in the material reorganization and moral reform of their churches, these bishops—who often found themselves clashing with local political figures and sometimes even with the clergy (as in the case of Pietro di Anagni)—best represented the Gregorian episcopal model. In such a model, the traditional role of "patron bishop" was implemented with adherence to the reformist actions that highlighted the institutional and political role of the episcopal ministry, exerted through the control and the influence of the apostolic seat.

Out of the three abovementioned bishop-saints, Bruno of Segni, author of numerous writings and biographer of Pietro di Anagni, was the most complex figure.[36] He was persecuted by the local political authorities and even imprisoned by Count Ainulfo, supporter of Emperor Henry IV. Once released, however, he decided—with the approval of the pope—to retreat to Montecassino, motivated by a desire for peace and contemplation, which he would only partly be allowed to satisfy. Forced to become an abbot, he faced the hostility of the monks who would eventually order him to leave the monastery, supported by Paschal II who disliked Bruno of Segni because of his criticisms of the Sutri pact (the February 9, 1111, agreement between Henry V and Pope Paschal II). He then had no choice but to return to Segni, where he undertook his mandate again, comforted by the approval of his people. The political prophecy attributed to him before his death (that the city of Segni would no longer be governed by tyrants, and its people would always live in freedom) symbolically sealed the image of this bishop as "guarantor of urban freedom, champion of cities' rights against the masters living in their proximity,"[37] who was able to ensure his protection over the urban community even after his own death. Bruno was canonized in 1181 or 1183.

In a different geographical area, a clear Gregorian connotation is also found in the bishop of Parma, Bernardo degli Uberti (d. 1133),[38] a Vallombrosian who occupied important roles in the service of the pope (before being elected bishop, he had been nominated cardinal and had served as papal legate) and supported Pope Paschal II at an extremely

---

36. On Bruno's literary work, see Ian Stuart Robinson, "Political Allegory in the Biblical Exegesis of Bruno of Segni," *Recherches de théologie ancienne et médiévale* 50 (1983): 69–98; and Leidulf Melve, "Intentional Ethics and Hermeneutics in the *Libellus de symoniacis*: Bruno of Segni as a Papal Polemicist," *Journal of Medieval History* 35 (2009): 77–96.
37. Anna Benvenuti Papi, *Pastori di popolo: Storie e leggende di vescovi e di città nell'Italia medievale* (Florence: Arnaud, 1988), 188.
38. Degl'Innocenti, "Agiografia latina dell'Italia centrale," 749–51.

delicate moment during the battle for investitures, and was persecuted for this reason. He would also prove to be an alert and diligent bishop, true *defensor civitatis* in the wars between Parma and its rival cities. In 1139, his successor, Bishop Lanfranco, proceeded with the canonization, carrying out—according to the practice of the time—the solemn elevation of the relics.

A commitment to the reform was also found in sant'Ubaldo da Gubbio (d. 1160),[39] but he was predominantly interested in the city, which he expressed by restoring its internal peace and defending it from external enemies. As well, Ubaldo embodied the traditional role of *defensor civitatis*, but in his case, his function reflected the balance that had been reached between the bishop's authority and that of the new urban institutions. Ubaldo was canonized by Pope Celestine III in 1192.

On the other hand, a bishop who openly clashed with his city was Lanfranco da Pavia (d. 1198), fierce defender of the rights of his church against the demands of the new political subjects—and for this reason he would be exiled. His hagiography (written by Bishop Bernardo da Pavia) "consciously inserts itself within the battle of the urban Church in defense of its possessions and prerogatives, and clearly reflects the historical time in which the *libero comune*—which had won the war against Barbarossa, and which had reached its highest power—takes possession of the city, undermining the bishops' properties."[40]

The bishops mentioned here played a highly active role in the history of the Church of this period thanks to their unique personalities and their moral and political authority. Their cults were often promoted by the successive bishops and their monastic orders, but their acts that usually took place inside cities, accompanied by miracles, engendered a popular devotion and led to their recognition as patron saints of those cities.

## Secular Sanctity

The twelfth century was also the time in which the secular saint came to the fore, in response to the need for perfection in a society that was changing, in which new political and economic balances were being established, and profound changes of spiritual and religious life began to take place. The secular saint was a "citizen" saint, penitent and ascetic

---

39. Degl'Innocenti, "Agiografia latina dell'Italia centrale," 747–49.
40. Golinelli, "Italia settentrionale," 142–43.

(but of a moderate asceticism), ready to intervene for the common good, and close to the poor and those in the margins of the society.[41] At a time of major mobility, such as the twelfth century, they could also be travelers and pilgrims.

As Vauchez has noted, the presence of secular saints is higher in intensely urbanized areas of Italy: western Tuscany, in particular the area of the Po valley, with a maximum concentration around Milan.[42] Although generally these saints did not receive the honor of canonization, they were nevertheless celebrated and venerated locally.

One of the first secular saints was Allucio da Pescia (d. 1134), restorer and builder of churches and hospitals in Valdinievole (Tuscany), father of the poor, comforter of orphans and widows. He was also able to restore peace between rival cities (Ravenna and Faenza), convert brigands, and perform miracles.

San Ranieri da Pisa (d. 1160), son of a wealthy merchant, embraced a life of penitence following a business trip in the East and thus departed for the Holy Land, where he remained for many years.[43] Returning later to Pisa, following a vision that entrusted him with the safety of his fellow citizens, he settled in the monastery of Sant'Andrea in Chinzica and subsequently in the monastery of San Vito, spending the rest of his life persuading sinners to convert and helping the ill and the possessed. Buried in the cathedral of Pisa, he quickly came to be worshipped by the population.

In northern Italy, two secular saints were sant'Omobono da Cremona (d. 1197) and san Raimondo Palmerio da Piacenza (d. 1200). Omobono—son of a cloth merchant, and a husband and family man himself—also wore the cassock of penitence (a dark cloth, fitted with a *cilice*) and dedicated himself to charity, employing his own earnings. According to the hagiographic tradition, he would also conduct a "pacifying and antiheretical role within the city, which was then tormented by

---

41. Vauchez thoroughly researched the model of secular sanctity. See André Vauchez, *Esperienze religiose nel Medioevo* (Rome: Viella, 2003), 15-50; Vauchez, *La santità nel Medioevo*, 337-59, for the references on the saints mentioned in this section. See also André Vauchez, "Lay People's Sanctity in Western Europe: Evolution of a Pattern (Twelfth and Thirteenth Centuries)," in *Images of Sainthood in Medieval Europe*, ed. Renate Blumenfeld-Kosinski and Timea Szell (Ithaca, NY: Cornell University Press, 1991), 21-32.
42. Vauchez, *Esperienze religiose*, 32.
43. Gabriele Zaccagnini, *La "Vita" di san Ranieri (secolo XII): Analisi storica, agiografica e filologica del testo di Benincasa. Edizione critica dal codice C 181 dell'Archivio Capitolare di Pisa* (Pisa: GISEM-ETS, 2008); Colin Morris, "San Ranieri of Pisa: The Power and Limitations of Sanctity in Twelfth-Century Italy," *Journal of Ecclesiastical History* 45 (1994): 588-99.

religious and urban discords,"⁴⁴ supporting Bishop Sicardo. It was this very bishop who, following the death of Omobono, went to Innocent III in Rome and asked him to recognize his fellow citizen's sanctity, obtaining the canonization from the pope in 1199. Innocent's bull is an interesting document not only because it was the first one directed to a secular saint, but also because—as Vauchez has observed—it implied that "Omobono did not deserve to be glorified by the Church as a worker, a husband, or a father, but rather as a penitent who had remained faithful to orthodoxy and compliant to the clergy's authority."⁴⁵

Raimondo Palmerio was a shoemaker, married and with children. He undertook a pilgrimage to the Holy Land when he was still a child (the nickname "Palmerio" is due to the palm branch he brought back from the pilgrimage) then, as a widower, to Santiago de Compostela and to Rome. After a vision in which Christ called him to help the poor people of the city, he gave up his further planned travels and dedicated himself to charity work and to defending the weak from injustice. Furthermore, he tried to mitigate the internal city conflicts and to stop the outbreak of war between Piacenza and Cremona, but he was then imprisoned by the people of Cremona. After his death, numerous miracles occurred at his place of burial.

Among all the Italian secular saints of the twelfth century and the beginning of the thirteenth century, there were only two women. These were Ubaldesca (d. 1206-07) and Bona (d. 1207), both from Pisa.⁴⁶ The first was an oblate in the hospital of San Giovanni in Pisa and in charge of collecting alms; the latter—a more interesting profile—was also an oblate of San Martino in Kinzica, but first and foremost was a tireless pilgrim, as well as founder of a monastery-hospice near Pisa.

These two blessed women signal the beginning of a phenomenon that would, in a few decades, become well established when conditions would exist for a broader entry of women into sanctity. Secular woman

---

44. Adelaide Ricci, "Omobono da Cremona," in *Dizionario biografico degli Italiani*, vol. 79 (Rome: Istituto della Enciclopedia Italiana, 2013), https://www.treccani.it/enciclopedia/omobono-da-cremona_(Dizionario-Biografico)/. See also André Vauchez et al., *Saint Homebon de Crémone, "père des pauvres" et patron des tailleurs: Vies médiévales et histoire du culte* (Brussels: Société des Bollandistes, 2018).

45. Vauchez, *La santità nel Medioevo*, 341.

46. Gabriele Zaccagnini, *Ubaldesca, una santa laica nella Pisa dei secoli XII–XIII* (Pisa: GISEM-ETS, 1995). Gabriele Zaccagnini, *La tradizione agiografica medievale di santa Bona da Pisa* (Pisa: GISEM-ETS, 2004).

saints would become the protagonists of one of the most intense periods of the religious history of Italy.

## The Thirteenth Century

In the previous sections I have stressed, on the one hand, the elements of continuity, and on the other, the change and innovation that have characterized the development of sanctity, of its historical manifestations, and of its representations, within the eleventh and twelfth centuries.

When taking the thirteenth century into consideration, it must be especially highlighted that the change that had started during the Gregorian era began to accelerate. This had both short- and long-term effects. This acceleration was caused by the influence exerted on people's religious and spiritual life by two great saints—Saint Dominic of Guzman (d. 1221) and Saint Francis of Assisi (d. 1226).[47] They had very different life experiences, and each founded an order with different characteristics from the other (respectively, the Order of Preachers, and the Order of Friars Minor), yet they both understood the radical need for poverty, testimony of faith, and a different relationship with God in a world that was becoming more and more afflicted by religious tension and turmoil, which often gave rise to heretical phenomena. They quickly became charismatic leaders as the head of orders that were recognized and supported by the Church, and as role models for a Christian life, able to change the representation of sanctity radically. Hand in hand with the success of the lifestyles they were proposing, figures of other saints and blessed stood out (for instance, the Dominicans Peter Martyr, Benvenuta Boianni, and later, Catherine of Siena; and the Franciscans Anthony of Padua, Clare of Assisi, Umiliana de' Cerchi, Margherita Colonna). Among these figures there were also men and women of secular backgrounds, who often—but not always—were part of a third branch of these orders, expressing a zeal and desire for God that was perceived as fully legitimate, as Francis's teachings had influenced people's consciences and revealed the possibility for a secular

---

47. The bibliography on Dominic is very extensive; see at least *Domenico di Caleruega e la nascita dell'ordine dei frati predicatori: Atti del XLI Convegno storico internazionale. Todi, 10–12 ottobre 2004* (Spoleto: Centro italiano di studi sull'alto medioevo, 2005). Among the many studies on Francis, see André Vauchez, *Francis of Assisi: The Life and Afterlife of a Medieval Saint*, trans. Michael F. Cusato (New Haven, CT: Yale University Press, 2012).

individual to have an experience of God that would have previously been inconceivable.[48]

Due to all these developments, male sanctity certainly changed its image: as the figure of the mendicant friar became more popular, the more traditional models became rarer, that is to say the bishop-saint—except in its ancient variant, to which many still turned in order to offer prestige and authority to a particular location by reconstructing and renewing its hagiographic memory—and the Benedictine monk-saint.

The process of renewal also greatly affected women's condition. For the first time, women stepped into the limelight and became the subject of a new era for sanctity, between the thirteenth and fourteenth centuries: women of various descents and social backgrounds, motivated by a desire for a life of prayer, penitence, and contemplation, either opted for an individual solution (hermitage) or for a communal one. Many were either married or widowed. When they chose to begin a cloistered life, they generally preferred the new forms of monasticism over the traditional kinds. Many remained lay, not becoming tied to any religious order, or entering a third order; for some, the monastic phase followed other forms of religious life. Mostly concentrated in central Italy, between Umbria and Tuscany, they exerted political authority within different urban realities.[49] In some cases, they stood out for the mystical phenomena that were associated with their religious life.

The Church's attitude toward them—particularly where mystical experiences were present—was generally characterized by cautious control, exerted through confessors or spiritual directors. The only one to benefit from an early official recognition of sanctity was Clare of Assisi (canonized in 1255 by Alexander IV, only two years after her death), who moreover can be considered particularly important in this context, due to her close tie to Francis (canonized by Gregory IX in 1228, also two years after his death).

---

48. Thomas Head, *The Mendicant Orders and Sanctity in the Thirteenth Century: A Bibliography*, https://the-orb.arlima.net/encyclop/religion/hagiography/bfriars.htm; Michael E. Goodich, *Vita perfecta: The Ideal of Sainthood in the Thirteenth Century* (Stuttgart: Hiersemann, 1982); Sally J. Cornelison, Nirit Ben-Aryeh Debby, and Peter Francis Howard, eds., *Mendicant Cultures in the Medieval and Early Modern World: Word, Deed and Image*, Europa Sacra 19 (Turnhout: Brepols, 2016); Donald S. Prudlo, ed., *The Origin, Development, and Refinement of Medieval Religious Mendicancies*, Brill's Companions to the Christian Tradition 24 (Leiden: Brill, 2011).

49. Vauchez, *Esperienze religiose*, 107.

## 9. SAINTS

Together with the innovations that affected the models of sanctity, developments within the writing of hagiographies also took place. Outside Italy, women's mysticism had been generating hagiographic texts for some time; in Italy, the first mystical autobiography was the *Memoriale* of Angela of Foligno, written in the final years of the thirteenth century, dictated by the saint herself.[50] Among the female hagiographies, one of the most interesting is the *Legenda* of Margaret of Cortona, composed between the end of the thirteenth century and the beginning of the fourteenth century by her spiritual director, friar Giunta Bevegnati, who seemed to portray the woman's mystical experience with substantial accuracy.[51]

Overall, the hagiographic production of this time appeared to be varied and rich.[52] More than before, it seemed to reflect the new ideals of sanctity and, therefore, to give space to the contemporary saints. Yet—except in certain cases—it did not become widespread, as the conservatism that presided over the organization of the hagiographic collections, both of traditional and abbreviated form (called *legendae novae* and intended for preachers, which started to be produced at this very time),[53] ensured that more ancient and traditional hagiographies were still preferred over these. Nonetheless, the act of preaching, which the mendicant orders were mostly carrying out, brought laity closer to the hagiographic subject and to the dissemination of role models that were not always imitable, yet that influenced their worship. And in fact, the new saints gradually gained ground within the hearts of believers and increasingly tended to replace the ancient saints, inheriting the role of support that those had exerted.

---

50. See the most recent edition: Angela da Foligno, *Memoriale*, ed. Enrico Menestò (Florence: SISMEL-Edizioni del Galluzzo, 2013).

51. Iunctae Bevegnatis, *Legenda de vita et miraculis beatae Margaritae de Cortona*, ed. Fortunato Iozzelli (Grottaferrata: Editiones Collegii S. Bonaventurae ad Claras Aquas, 1997). On the relationship between holy women and their spiritual directors, see John Wayland Coakley, *Women, Men, and Spiritual Power: Female Saints and Their Male Collaborators* (New York: Columbia University Press, 2006).

52. For a review of the hagiographic production in Umbria, see Edoardo D'Angelo, "Bibliotheca Hagiographica Umbriae (1130–1500)," in *Hagiographies: Histoire internationale de la littérature hagiographique latine et vernaculaire en Occident des origines à 1550*, ed. Guy Philippart, vol. 6 (Turnhout: Brepols, 2014), 142–90.

53. Antonella Degl'Innocenti, "I leggendari agiografici latini," in *Forme e modelli della santità in Occidente dal tardo antico al medioevo*, ed. Massimiliano Bassetti, Antonella Degl'Innocenti, and Enrico Menestò (Spoleto: Centro italiano di studi sull'alto medioevo, 2012), 137–58.

## Dominic of Guzman, Francis and Clare of Assisi

Dominic of Guzman was in fact not an Italian saint, but Portuguese, born around 1172 in Caleregua, in the diocese of Osma, yet he lived and worked long in Italy. Following his studies in Palencia, Dominic entered the chapter house of the cathedral of Osma—recently reformed—and was made a minister. Beside Bishop Diego, he soon got to know the heretical movements of the Waldensians and Cathars, which were particularly widespread in southern France at that time. He then decided to dedicate himself to the conversion of heretics by preaching and providing the example of a poor and austere lifestyle. He obtained the pope's authorization to preach. It was the beginning of a growing commitment, which would mark his whole life. His order was founded in 1215 in Toulouse and was immediately approved by Innocent III who suggested the adoption of an existing rule (the choice would be the Rule of Saint Augustine, combined with canonical constitutions). In 1217 it received confirmation from Honorius III who officially recognized its historic mission, conferring the title of "preachers" to the friars. When Dominic died (in Bologna, in 1221), the order had almost definitively reaffirmed its founding principles and had assumed a clear territorial organization.

Despite the uncertain beginning,[54] the cult of Dominic became largely widespread, as did his order, and Dominic also had a great influence on the formation of a new Christian awareness—thanks to the proposal of ideals such as poverty, an austere lifestyle, a commitment to preaching, or the adoration of the Virgin Mary, which were all taken up and interpreted in different ways by those who took inspiration from him. Dominic's focus on the women's world led to a large adhesion of women to his order, as well as to the elaboration of a hagiographic model that—despite referring to values that were common to other religious statuses—had a stronger ascetic connotation.[55]

Francis of Assisi was—together with Dominic—the other great architect of the religious and spiritual change that marked the thirteenth century.[56] Son of a merchant, after converting himself in public, he

---

54. Luigi Canetti, *Il culto e l'immagine di Domenico nella storia dei primi frati Predicatori* (Spoleto: Centro italiano di studi sull'Alto Medioevo, 1996).

55. Antonella Degl'Innocenti, "Mistica e agiografia," in *Il "Liber" di Angela da Foligno e la mistica dei secoli XIII–XIV in rapporto alle nuove culture* (Spoleto: Centro italiano di studi sull'alto medioevo, 2009), 374–78.

56. Claudio Leonardi, ed., *La letteratura francescana*, vol. 1, *Francesco e Chiara d'Assisi* (Milan: Fondazione Lorenzo Valla-Mondadori, 2004).

embraced—as a layman—a life as a penitent and hermit and dedicated himself to rebuilding churches and assisting lepers (in his *Testamento*, Francis remembers meeting a leper as the decisive episode that led him to make his religious choice). By 1209, a group of disciples had formed around him. They shared his ideals of poverty, fraternity, and examining the Gospel, and Francis felt the need to put his purpose of life in writing. Innocent III gave his approval in 1210 and allowed him to preach. Francis and his friars (whom he called *minores*) could then dedicate themselves more strongly to the apostolate, both within and outside Italy (in 1219, Francis personally went to Egypt and preached before the sultan). Later, in the face of the huge development of the first community, which also caused the first internal disagreements, Francis adopted an actual set of rules and subsequently amended it (the first Rule, known as *non bullata* since it had not been formally approved by Honorius III, dates from 1221; the second Rule, approved by Honorius III, dates from 1223), keeping in mind his people's various needs, but without giving up the values that were essential to him—which can be summed up in the formula of "living according to the holy Gospel," which had always been his priority.[57]

Francis died on October 4, 1226, and was canonized in 1228 by Gregory IX. The order's mood had significantly changed compared to its early days. Disagreements between opposite tendencies (the Spirituals and the Conventuals) soon came to undermine the cohesion of the order. Such tendencies were divided on the basis of two different interpretations of the principle of poverty.[58] Nevertheless, the Friars Minor immediately celebrated their founder's memory with a variety of hagiographical writings—starting with the first biography (*Vita prima*), written by Tommaso of Celano, requested by Gregory IX following Francis's canonization—which also reflected the diversity of thought within the order.[59] In 1266, the chapter of Paris pointlessly tried to provide a unitary

---

57. Francesco d'Assisi, "Testamentum," in *Fontes Franciscani*, ed. E. Menestò et al. (Assisi: Porziuncola, 1995), 227–32.

58. David Burr, *Olivi and Franciscan Poverty: The Origins of the "Usus Pauper" Controversy* (Philadelphia: University of Pennsylvania Press, 1989) and David Burr, *The Spiritual Franciscans: From Protest to Persecution in the Century after Saint Francis* (University Park: Pennsylvania State University Press, 2001).

59. Claudio Leonardi, ed., *La letteratura francescana*, vol. 2, *Le Vite antiche di san Francesco* (Milan: Fondazione Lorenzo Valla-Mondadori, 2005); Claudio Leonardi, ed., *La letteratura francescana*, vol. 4, *Bonaventura: La leggenda di Francesco* (Milan: Fondazione Lorenzo Valla-Mondadori, 2013). An abridged and updated version of the *Vita prima* by Tommaso of Celano has recently been discovered: see Jacques Dalarun, "Thome Celanensis Vita beati patris nostri

image, establishing that the *vita* of the saint written shortly after the middle of the century by the order's minister general, Bonaventure of Bagnoregio, known as *Legenda Maior*, was to be considered the only official biography of the founder and that all the previous *vitae* were to be destroyed. Such a decision definitely had serious consequences but did not cause a concealment of the first biographies, nor did it cause the end of hagiographical initiatives, which, instead, continued in great numbers amid recurring conflicts about the order's tendencies.

Historiographies have been divided on the interpretation of Francis's religious experience, as well as on the interpretation of the hagiographical literature about him. However, it seems that on one matter there is a substantial general agreement: the saint of Assisi represented a turning point, since he brought the historical crisis of Benedictine monasticism to its extreme consequences, starting a different form of monasticism, in which the greatest innovation was the apostolic mission, preaching to all (not only to an intramonastic audience, as in the Benedictine tradition). Another relevant innovation introduced by Francis was the secularity of his understanding of God, which led him to believe that it was possible to reach a direct relationship between man and God within any kind of life, without having to resort to a clerical or monastic mediation. This spiritual secularity was favorable to the manifestation of female sanctity, especially in its mystic variant.[60]

Moreover, a female figure soon stood beside Francis, showing how his proposed lifestyle could also be embraced by women: the young Clare of Assisi,[61] who, against the will of her family, turned to Francis and strove to live under his guidance according to the perfection of the holy Gospel in complete poverty. She was immediately followed by other women. Thus, the Damianite community was born, taking its name

---

*Francisci* (*Vita brevior*): Présentation et édition critique," *Analecta Bollandiana* 133 (2015): 23–86; Jacques Dalarun, "The New Francis in the Rediscovered Life (*Vita brevior*) of Thomas of Celano," in *"Ordo et Sanctitas": The Franciscan Spiritual Journey in Theology and Hagiography. Essays in Honor of J. A. Wayne Hellmann, O.F.M. Conv.*, ed. Michael F. Cusato, Timothy J. Johnson, and Steven J. McMichael, The Medieval Franciscans 15 (Leiden: Brill, 2017), 32–46.

60. See in particular Claudio Leonardi, "L'esperienza del divino in Francesco d'Assisi," in Leonardi, *Agiografie medievali*, ed. Antonella Degl'Innocenti and Francesco Santi (Florence: SISMEL-Edizioni del Galluzzo, 2011), 383–92; Claudio Leonardi, "La santità delle donne," in Leonardi, *Agiografie medievali*, 455–69.

61. Among the many studies on Clare, see Leonardi, *La letteratura francescana*, 1:cxxxvii–lxxvii; Catherine Mooney, *Clare of Assisi and the Thirteenth-Century Church: Religious Women, Rules, and Resistance* (Philadelphia: University of Pennsylvania Press, 2016); Lezlie Knox, *Creating Clare of Assisi: Female Franciscan Identities in Later Medieval Italy*, The Medieval Franciscans 5 (Leiden: Brill, 2008).

from the church of San Damiano, where they had gone to live on the advice of Francis. Their name was later changed to the Clarisses. Adapting to the Curia's regulations (in 1215, the Fourth Lateran Council had established that the new religious communities must adopt an existing set of rules), they would adopt a Benedictine organization (in which Clare was the abbess), based on a rule of strict seclusion. But Clare was nonetheless able to maintain—at least while she was alive—"an original spirituality, which was not merged with that of Benedictines,"[62] and protected the specific characteristics of her inspiration in the Rule she had written, in which she had stressed the importance of poverty and of faith in the Gospel. On the other hand, her hagiography manipulated this profile: a different image—based on her monastic dimension—was attributed to her by her main biographer (Tommaso of Celano, apparently) who, "in order to indulge the papal commission's need to regulate the liveliness and multiplicity of the female religious life,"[63] diminished her extremely Franciscan spirit.

### The Mendicant Saints

After Dominic and Francis, the sanctity scene was quickly filled by *fratres* of the two orders, who tried to follow the example of their masters' lives.[64] Although only two such friars, the Franciscan Anthony of Padua (d. 1231) and the Dominican Peter of Verona (also known as Peter Martyr, d. 1252), were canonized, many more were greatly worshipped.

The characteristics of sanctity largely coincide within the two orders, since "the imitation of the God-man Christ is . . . at the center of a new model, which both Dominic and Francis proposed, individually, in the same years."[65] In terms of male saints, the apostolate represented an essential aspect, as can be deduced by the events concerning the two most famous saints, mentioned above, Anthony of Padua and Peter of Verona, who nonetheless appeared to be very different from each another. Anthony—canon, minister, and Franciscan friar—was a mystic

---

62. Vauchez, *La santità nel Medioevo*, 330-31.
63. Stefano Brufani, "Chiara d'Assisi," in Leonardi, Riccardi, and Zarri, *Il grande libro dei santi*, 427.
64. Claudio Leonardi, "Il modello di santità negli Ordini Mendicanti," in Leonardi, *Agiografie medievali*, 215-23; Stefano Brufani, "I santi mendicanti," in Bassetti, Degl'Innocenti, and Menestò, *Forme e modelli della santità in Occidente*, 57-96; D'Angelo, "Bibliotheca Hagiographica Umbriae," 142-75.
65. Leonardi, "Il modello di santità negli Ordini Mendicanti," 220.

and a preacher, whereas Peter was exclusively a preacher and his work focused entirely on fighting heresy, also due to the role of inquisitor he had undertaken. His violent death attested the radicalism of his work.

As for female sanctity, the mystical aspect—which had been one of the basic characteristics of Francis[66]—became more common and, together with other elements (asceticism, poverty, charity), became an essential part of the model of sanctity that was establishing itself at this time. Many laywomen made a contribution to the definition of this very model of sanctity.

## Female Saints

As mentioned above, in the thirteenth century, female sanctity presented itself as having a much more dynamic and articulate character, compared to the past. The phenomenon appeared to be tied mostly to the widespread dissemination of the mendicant orders through the cities of central and northern Italy. Their presence was inspiring and, at the same time, controlling new forms of religious lifestyles, suitable for different sections of society. In this context, a new sanctity was formed, which was primarily represented by secular women.

Santa Verdiana da Castelfiorentino (d. 1242) was a virgin who, having worked as a servant in the home of one of her relatives, withdrew from social life and closed herself in a cell where she remained until her death, dedicating herself to prayer and asceticism.[67] Beata Umiliana de' Cerchi (d. 1246) from Florence, whose life would be held up as an example by the Friars Minor to the urban seculars, married a local lord, but—after only one month of marriage—she began mostly to dedicate herself to charity work, neglecting her family life.[68] Having

---

66. Francesco Santi, "L'eredità di Francesco d'Assisi nella mistica fra XIII e XIV secolo," in *La letteratura francescana*, vol. 5, *La mistica*, ed. Francesco Santi (Milan: Fondazione Lorenzo Valla-Mondadori, 2016), xvii–xxxv.

67. On Verdiana and the other abovementioned woman saints, see Michael E. Goodich, "'Ancilla Dei': The Servant as Saint in the Late Middle Ages," in *Women of the Medieval World: Essays in Honor of John H. Mundy*, ed. Julius Kirshner and Suzanne Fonay Wemple (Oxford: Blackwell, 1985), 119-36; Anna Benvenuti Papi, *"In castro poenitentiae": Santità e società femminile nell'Italia medievale* (Rome: Herder, 1990); Leonardi, *Agiografie medievali*, 455ff.; Alessandra Bartolomei Romagnoli, *Santità e mistica femminile nel Medioevo* (Spoleto: Centro italiano di studi sull'Alto Medioevo, 2013), in particular 67-101. On Verdiana, see Silvia Nocentini, ed., *Verdiana da Castelfiorentino: Contesto storico, tradizione agiografica e iconografia* (Florence: SISMEL-Edizioni del Galluzzo, 2011).

68. Anne M. Schuchman, "The Lives of Umiliana de' Cerchi: Representations of Female Sainthood in Thirteenth-Century Florence," in *Essays in Medieval Studies: Proceedings of the*

become a widow, she retreated to an isolated cell in a domestic tower, where she increasingly focused on contemplation. Santa Rosa da Viterbo (d. 1251), while still very young, wore the penitent's robes and conducted an apostolate in her city, also preaching against heretics, until she was exiled by the chief magistrate of Viterbo.[69] Beata Gherardesca da Pisa (d. ca. 1269), following her married life, retreated to a cell in the Camaldolese monastery of San Savino in Pisa, where she experienced visions and revelations.[70] Saint Margaret of Cortona (d. 1297) fled her home at the age of sixteen, together with a youth from Montepulciano, with whom she had a son.[71] After her partner's death, disowned by her father, she approached the Friars Minor and became a tertiary, retreating into a cell where she practiced severe asceticism. Beata Giovanna da Orvieto (d. 1306), orphaned and trained as a seamstress (thus supporting herself her whole life), refused to marry and became a Dominican tertiary.

These women often balanced asceticism and charitable practices. Furthermore, they were the subjects of mystical phenomena. Umiliana de' Cerchi was one of the first woman saints in Italy, with whom many raptures and visions were associated.

Hagiographies promptly acknowledged the plurality and significance of the contents of such experiences. As a matter of fact, numerous women's biographies were composed between the thirteenth and fourteenth centuries—and usually not long after the death of the subject. While the Church struggled to recognize their sanctity officially (a typical example is that of santa Chiara da Montefalco, whose canonization process, begun shortly after her death, would only be completed in modern times), these *vitae*—despite being written by men—allowed women to emerge from the shadows, exposing the various forms of their perfection.

---

*Illinois Medieval Association* 14 (1997), 15-28; Anne M. Schuchman, "'Within the Walls of Paradise': Space and Community in the 'Vita' of Umiliana de' Cerchi (1219-1246)," in *Negotiating Community and Difference in Medieval Europe: Gender, Power, Patronage and the Authority of Religion in Latin Christendom*, ed. Katherine Allen Smith and Scott Wells (Leiden: Brill, 2009), 49-64.

69. Darleen N. Pryds, "Proclaiming Sanctity through Proscribed Acts: The Case of Rose of Viterbo," in *Women Preachers and Prophets through Two Millennia of Christianity*, ed. Beverly Mayne Kienzle and Pamela J. Walker (Berkeley: University of California Press 1998), 159-72.

70. Cécile Caby, "La sainteté féminine au moyen âge: Autour de la b. Gherardesca de Pise," *Hagiographica* 1 (1994): 235-69.

71. Beverly Mayne Kienzle, "Margherita of Cortona: Women, Preaching and the Writing of Hagiography," *Medieval Sermon Studies* 54 (2010): 38-50.

## Other Models of Sanctity

While the great success of the orders founded by Dominic and Francis was clearly followed by the growing presence of saints tied to them, there were also other examples of Christian life that stood out during the thirteenth century. We find lay saints, whose experiences sometimes took place autonomously and sometimes with the protection of mendicants (always attentive in nurturing and managing the various forms of religious lifestyle that developed in their local area, as has also been seen in relation to the phenomenon of female sanctity), hermit saints (who in some cases became the founders of communities), and exponents of the new religious communities that arose beside the two major orders.

The model of the lay saint—which first appeared in the twelfth century, with specific characteristics such as poverty, work, and charity—was further found in figures such as Gerardo dei Tintori (Monza) (d. 1207), Gualtiero da Lodi (d. 1224), and Pietro Pettinaio (d. 1289).[72]

The hermitic lifestyle continued to be popular and produced exemplary figures such as Lorenzo Loricato (d. 1243), ascetic and penitent who lived in the woods of Subiaco, and Giovanni Bono (d. 1249), who retreated to live in isolation close to Cesena in Romagna—founder of a community of hermits (known as Giambonites) that in 1256 would merge into the Augustinian Friars (Order of the Hermit Friars of Saint Augustine), the third largest mendicant order after the Dominicans and the Franciscans.[73] San Pietro da Morrone (d. 1296) also gained a great reputation as a hermit and an ascetic.[74] After retreating to the mountains of Abruzzo, he was then elected pope under the name of Celestine V in 1294. A controversial figure, who is well known for resigning the pontificate only a few months after being elected, Pietro embodied the hope of a renewal of the Church in a time of strong conflicts and discord within the Curia. However, when he was canonized by Clement V in 1313, the image that was offered of him was

---

72. On these saints, see Vauchez, *La santità nel Medioevo*, 161, 163–64, 212.

73. On hermit sanctity, including the abovementioned figures, see Vauchez, *La santità nel Medioevo*, 307–15.

74. Alessandra Bartolomei Romagnoli, *Una memoria controversa: Celestino V e le sue fonti* (Florence: SISMEL–Edizioni del Galluzzo, 2013); George P. Ferzoco, "Church and Sanctity: The Hagiographical Dossier of Peter of Morrone," in *Normes et pouvoir à la fin du moyen âge: Actes du colloque "La recherche en études médiévales au Québec et en Ontario," 16–17 mai 1989*, ed. Marie-Claude Déprez-Masson (Montreal: Ceres, 1990), 53–69.

exclusively that of hermit saint. Choosing life in a hermitage was also at the core of the religious experience of san Nicola da Tolentino (d. 1305), one of the first hermit saints, who nonetheless managed to combine asceticism and contemplation with a strong apostolic and priestly vocation.

Other religious communities, of more recent formation, were graced by their own saints. This includes, for example, san Filippo Benizi (d. 1285), a major figure in the Friar Servants of Mary (or Servites). This was an order created in the 1230s on Mount Senario close to Florence, set up by seven seculars—known as the seven founding saints—who had come together, motivated by ideals of contemplation, poverty, charity, and a strong devotion to the Virgin Mary.

To conclude, it can be said that the thirteenth century was one of the most fruitful times in the history of sanctity. However, the importance and variety of the experiences that characterized it were the product of the religious enthusiasm that can be observed in the previous centuries, starting from the Gregorian era when a new understanding of the role of the Church toward the Empire had been established. This was coupled with the need to control the moral crisis of the ecclesiastical and religious institutions through a return to more authentic values of Christianity. During this phase, eremitism and the new forms of monasticism represented two effective solutions to the need for reform, and in fact it was within them that the most representative figures of the new ideals of sanctity arose. In the twelfth century, in conjunction with the social and political transformation of the time, the process of change strengthened itself, and what could be identified as the outcome was the proposal—together with the more traditional models—of a model of sanctity that was finally accessible to seculars. These innovations, however, imposed themselves in a context in which the legacy of traditionalism still remained strong—on both a cultural and a hagiographic level—even for the impetus that was given, especially in urban environments, to the emergence of patronal figures, drawn from the most ancient tradition of sanctity (the apostles and martyrs). Despite the persistence of such traditions, the thirteenth century marked the beginning of a new era: the affirmation of the mendicant orders' saints, the development of a lay and of a female sanctity, and the appearance of mystical phenomena effectively revolutionized the images and language of Christian perfection, leaving a great legacy to the subsequent centuries.

## Selected Bibliography

Baker, Derek. "'The Whole World a Hermitage': Ascetic Renewal and the Crisis of Western Monasticism." In *The Culture of Christendom: Essays in Medieval History in Memory of Denis L. T. Bethell*, edited by Marc Antony Meyer, 207-23. London: Hambledon, 1993.

Bartolomei Romagnoli, Alessandra. *Una memoria controversa: Celestino V e le sue fonti*. Florence: SISMEL-Edizioni del Galluzzo, 2013.

——. *Santità e mistica femminile nel Medioevo*. Spoleto: Centro italiano di studi sull'alto medioevo, 2013.

Bassetti, Massimiliano, Antonella Degl'Innocenti, and Enrico Menestò, eds. *Forme e modelli della santità in Occidente dal tardo antico al medioevo*. Spoleto: Centro italiano di studi sull'alto medioevo, 2012.

Benvenuti Papi, Anna. *"In castro poenitentiae": Santità e società femminile nell'Italia medievale*. Rome: Herder, 1990.

——. *Pastori di popolo: Storie e leggende di vescovi e di città nell'Italia medievale*. Florence: Arnaud, 1988.

——, ed. *La spada nella roccia: San Galgano e l'epopea eremitica di Montesiepi. Atti del Convegno di studi (Chiusdino 20-21 sett. 2001)*. Florence: Mandragora, 2004.

Benvenuti Papi, Anna, et al. *Storia della santità nel cristianesimo occidentale*. Rome: Viella, 2005.

*Bibliotheca Sanctorum*. Rome: Istituto Giovanni XXIII della Pontificia Università Lateranense, 1961-.

Boesch Gajano, Sofia. *Chelidonia: Storia di un'eremita medievale*. Rome: Viella, 2010.

Burr, David. *Olivi and Franciscan Poverty: The Origins of the "Usus Pauper" Controversy*. Philadelphia: University of Pennsylvania Press, 1989.

——. *The Spiritual Franciscans: From Protest to Persecution in the Century after Saint Francis*. University Park: Pennsylvania State University Press, 2001.

Caby, Cécile. "La sainteté féminine au moyen âge: Autour de la b. Gherardesca de Pise." *Hagiographica* 1 (1994): 235-69.

Canetti, Luigi. *Il culto e l'immagine di Domenico nella storia dei primi frati Predicatori*. Spoleto: Centro italiano di studi sull'alto medioevo, 1996.

Coakley, John Wayland. *Women, Men, and Spiritual Power: Female Saints and Their Male Collaborators*. New York: Columbia University Press, 2006.

Cornelison, Sally J., Nirit Ben-Aryeh Debby, and Peter Francis Howard, eds. *Mendicant Cultures in the Medieval and Early Modern World: Word, Deed, and Image*. Europa Sacra 19. Turnhout: Brepols, 2016.

Cushing, Kathleen G. "Events that Led to Sainthood: Sanctity and the Reformers in the Eleventh Century." In *Belief and Culture in the Middle Ages: Studies Presented to Henry Mayr-Harting*, edited by Richard Gameson and Henrietta Leyser, 187-96. Oxford: Oxford University Press, 2001.

D'Angelo, Edoardo. "Bibliotheca Hagiographica Umbriae (1130-1500)." In *Hagiographies: Histoire internationale de la littérature hagiographique latine et vernaculaire en Occident des origines à 1550*, edited by Guy Philippart, 6:107-234. Turnhout: Brepols, 2014.

## 9. SAINTS

Dalarun, Jacques. "The New Francis in the Rediscovered Life (*Vita brevior*) of Thomas of Celano." In *"Ordo et Sanctitas": The Franciscan Spiritual Journey in Theology and Hagiography. Essays in Honor of J. A. Wayne Hellmann, O.F.M. Conv.*, edited by Michael F. Cusato, Timothy J. Johnson, and Steven J. McMichael, 32–46. The Medieval Franciscans 15. Leiden: Brill, 2017.

———. "Thome Celanensis *Vita beati patris nostri Francisci* (*Vita brevior*): Présentation et édition critique." *Analecta Bollandiana* 133 (2015): 23–86.

Degl'Innocenti, Antonella. "Agiografia latina dell'Italia centrale, 1130–1220." In *Hagiographies: Histoire internationale de la littérature hagiographique latine et vernaculaire en Occident des origines à 1550*, edited by Guy Philippart, 5:731–98. Turnhout: Brepols, 2010.

———, ed. *Vallombrosa: Memorie agiografiche e culto delle reliquie*. Rome: Viella, 2012.

*Dizionario biografico degli Italiani*. Rome: Istituto della Enciclopedia Italiana, 1961–.

*Domenico di Caleruega e la nascita dell'ordine dei frati predicatori: Atti del XLI Convegno storico internazionale. Todi, 10–12 ottobre 2004*. Spoleto: Centro italiano di studi sull'alto medioevo, 2005.

Elm, Kaspar. *Beiträge zur Geschichte des Wilhelmitenordens*. Cologne: Bohlau, 1962.

Ferzoco, George P. "Church and Sanctity: The Hagiographical Dossier of Peter of Morrone." In *Normes et pouvoir à la fin du moyen âge: Actes du colloque "La recherche en études médiévales au Québec et en Ontario," 16–17 mai 1989*, edited by Marie-Claude Déprez-Masson, 53–69. Montreal: Ceres, 1990.

Fornasari, Giuseppe. *Medioevo riformato del secolo XI: Pier Damiani e Gregorio VII*. Naples: Liguori, 1996.

Galante, Maria, Giovanni Vitolo, and Giuseppa Z. Zanichelli, eds. *Riforma della chiesa, esperienze monastiche e poteri locali: La Badia di Cava nei secoli XI–XII. Atti del Convegno internazionale di studi Badia di Cava, 15–17 settembre 2011*. Florence: SISMEL-Edizioni del Galluzzo, 2014.

Golinelli, Paolo. *"Indiscreta sanctitas": Studi sui rapporti tra culti, poteri e società nel pieno Medioevo*. Rome: Istituto Storico Italiano per il Medio Evo, 1988.

———. "Italia settentrionale (1130–1220)." In *Hagiographies: Histoire internationale de la littérature hagiographique latine et vernaculaire en Occident des origines à 1550*, edited by Guy Philippart, 1:125–53. Turnhout: Brepols, 1994.

Goodich, Michael E. "'Ancilla Dei': The Servant as Saint in the Late Middle Ages." In *Women of the Medieval World: Essays in Honor of John H. Mundy*, edited by Julius Kirshner and Suzanne Fonay Wemple, 119–36. Oxford: Blackwell 1985.

———. *Vita perfecta: The Ideal of Sainthood in the Thirteenth Century*. Stuttgart: Hiersemann, 1982.

Head, Thomas. *The Mendicant Orders and Sanctity in the Thirteenth Century: A Bibliography*. https://the-orb.arlima.net/encyclop/religion/hagiography/bfriars.htm.

Knox, Lezlie. *Creating Clare of Assisi: Female Franciscan Identities in Later Medieval Italy*. The Medieval Franciscans 5. Leiden: Brill, 2008.

Leonardi, Claudio. *Agiografie medievali*. Edited by Antonella Degl'Innocenti and Francesco Santi. Florence: SISMEL-Edizioni del Galluzzo, 2011.

———, ed. *La letteratura francescana*. Vols. 1–4. Milan: Fondazione Lorenzo Valla-Mondadori, 2004–13.

———. *Medioevo latino: La cultura dell'Europa cristiana*. Florence: SISMEL-Edizioni del Galluzzo, 2004.

Leonardi, Claudio, Andrea Riccardi, and Gabriella Zarri, eds. *Il grande libro dei santi: Dizionario enciclopedico*. Cinisello Balsamo (Milan): Edizioni San Paolo, 1998.

*Il "Liber" di Angela da Foligno e la mistica dei secoli XIII–XIV in rapporto alle nuove culture*. Spoleto: Centro italiano di studi sull'Alto Medioevo, 2009.

Licciardello, Pierluigi. "Agiografia latina dell'Italia centrale, 950–1130." In *Hagiographies: Histoire internationale de la littérature hagiographique latine et vernaculaire en Occident des origines à 1550*, edited by Guy Philippart, 5:447–727. Turnhout: Brepols, 2010.

Limone, Oronzo. "Italia meridionale (950–1220)." In *Hagiographies: Histoire internationale de la littérature hagiographique latine et vernaculaire en Occident des origines à 1550*, edited by Guy Philippart, 2:11–60. Turnhout: Brepols, 1996.

Longo, Umberto. *Come angeli in terra: Pier Damiani, la santità e la riforma del secolo XI*. Rome: Viella, 2012.

Mayne Kienzle, Beverly. "Margherita of Cortona: Women, Preaching and the Writing of Hagiography." *Medieval Sermon Studies* 54 (2010): 38–50.

Melve, Leidulf. "Intentional Ethics and Hermeneutics in the *Libellus de symoniacis*: Bruno of Segni as a Papal Polemicist." *Journal of Medieval History* 35 (2009): 77–96.

Miccoli, Giovanni. *Chiesa Gregoriana: Ricerche sulla Riforma del secolo XI*. Florence: La Nuova Italia, 1966.

———. "La storia religiosa." In *Storia d'Italia*, vol. 2, *Dalla caduta dell'Impero romano al secolo XVIII*, edited by Ruggero Romano and Corrado Vivanti, bk. 1:431–1079. Turin: Einaudi, 1974.

*Mirabile: Archivio digitale della cultura medievale. Digital Archives for Medieval Culture*. http://www.mirabileweb.it.

Mooney, Catherine. *Clare of Assisi and the Thirteenth-Century Church: Religious Women, Rules, and Resistance*. Philadelphia: University of Pennsylvania Press, 2016.

Morris, Colin. "San Ranieri of Pisa: The Power and Limitations of Sanctity in Twelfth-Century Italy." *Journal of Ecclesiastical History* 45 (1994): 588–99.

Nocentini, Silvia, ed. *Verdiana da Castelfiorentino: Contesto storico, tradizione agiografica e iconografia*. Florence: SISMEL-Edizioni del Galluzzo, 2011.

Oldfield, Paul. *Sanctity and Pilgrimage in Medieval Southern Italy, 1000–1200*. Cambridge: Cambridge University Press, 2014.

Placanica, Antonio. *Le storie di San Michele della Chiusa*. Florence: SISMEL-Edizioni del Galluzzo, 2015.

Prudlo, Donald S., ed. *The Origin, Development, and Refinement of Medieval Religious Mendicancies*. Brill's Companions to the Christian Tradition 24. Leiden: Brill, 2011.

Pryds, Darleen N. "Proclaiming Sanctity through Proscribed Acts: The Case of Rose of Viterbo." In *Women Preachers and Prophets through Two Millennia of*

*Christianity*, edited by Beverly Mayne Kienzle and Pamela J. Walker, 159-72. Berkeley: University of California Press, 1998.

Robinson, Ian Stuart. "Political Allegory in the Biblical Exegesis of Bruno of Segni." *Recherches de théologie ancienne et médiévale* 50 (1983): 69-98.

Rusconi, Roberto. "Un popolo di santi." In *Cristiani d'Italia*. Rome: Istituto della Enciclopedia Italiana, 2011. http://www.treccani.it/enciclopedia/un-popolo-di-santi_%28Cristiani-d%27Italia%29/.

———. *Santo Padre: La santità del papa da san Pietro a Giovanni Paolo II*. Rome: Viella, 2010.

Santi, Francesco, ed. *La letteratura francescana*. Vol. 5, *La mistica*. Milan: Fondazione Lorenzo Valla-Mondadori, 2016.

Schuchman, Anne M. "The Lives of Umiliana de' Cerchi: Representations of Female Sainthood in Thirteenth-Century Florence." *Essays in Medieval Studies: Proceedings of the Illinois Medieval Association* 14 (1997): 15-28.

———. "'Within the Walls of Paradise': Space and Community in the 'Vita' of Umiliana de' Cerchi (1219-1246)." In *Negotiating Community and Difference in Medieval Europe: Gender, Power, Patronage and the Authority of Religion in Latin Christendom*, edited by Katherine Allen Smith and Scott Wells, 49-64. Leiden: Brill, 2009.

Sereno, Cristina. "La 'crisi del cenobitismo': Un problema storiografico." *Bullettino dell'Istituto storico italiano per il Medio Evo e Archivio Muratoriano* 104 (2002): 31-83.

Tomea, Paolo. "L'agiografia dell'Italia settentrionale (950-1130)." In *Hagiographies: Histoire internationale de la littérature hagiographique latine et vernaculaire en Occident des origines à 1550*, edited by Guy Philippart, 3:99-178. Turnhout: Brepols, 2001.

Toubert, Pierre. *Les structures du Latium médiéval: Le Latium méridional et la Sabine du IXe à la fin du XIIe siècle*. 2 vols. Rome: École française de Rome, 1973 (rist. anast. 1993).

Vauchez, André. *Esperienze religiose nel Medioevo*. Rome: Viella, 2003.

———. *Francis of Assisi: The Life and Afterlife of a Medieval Saint*. Translated by Michael F. Cusato. New Haven, CT: Yale University Press, 2012.

———. "Lay People's Sanctity in Western Europe: Evolution of a Pattern (Twelfth and Thirteenth Centuries)." In *Images of Sainthood in Medieval Europe*, edited by Renate Blumenfeld-Kosinski and Timea Szell, 21-32. Ithaca, NY: Cornell University Press, 1991.

———. *La santità nel Medioevo*. Translated by Alfonso Prandi. Bologna: Il Mulino, 1989 (*La sainteté en Occident aux derniers siècles du Moyen Âge d'après les proces de canonisation et les documents hagiographiques*. Rome: École française de Rome, 1981; *Sainthood in the Later Middle Ages*. Translated by Jean Birrell. New York: Cambridge University Press, 1997).

———. *La spiritualità dell'Occidente medioevale, secoli VIII-XII*. Milan: Vita e Pensiero, 1978 (*La spiritualité du Moyen Âge occidental*. Paris: Presses Universitaires de France, 1975; *The Spirituality of the Medieval West: From the Eighth to the Twelfth Century*. Translated by Colette Friedlander. Piscataway, NJ: Gorgias Press, 2010).

Vauchez, André, with the collaboration of Umberto Longo, Laura Albiero, and Véronique Hazebrouck-Souche. *Saint Homebon de Crémone, "père des pauvres" et patron des tailleurs: Vies médiévales et histoire du culte*. Brussels: Société des Bollandistes, 2018.

Vuolo, Antonio. "Monachesimo riformato e predicazione: La 'Vita' di san Giovanni da Matera (sec. XII)." *Studi medievali*, 3rd series, 27 (1986): 69–121.

Zaccagnini, Gabriele. *La tradizione agiografica medievale di santa Bona da Pisa*. Pisa: GISEM-ETS, 2004.

———. *Ubaldesca, una santa laica nella Pisa dei secoli XII–XIII*. Pisa: GISEM-ETS, 1995.

———. *La "Vita" di san Ranieri (secolo XII): Analisi storica, agiografica e filologica del testo di Benincasa. Edizione critica dal codice C 181 dell'Archivio Capitolare di Pisa*. Pisa: GISEM-ETS, 2008.

CHAPTER 10

# Heresy
*Maria Pia Alberzoni*

"Oportet et haereses esse" ("For there must be also heresies among you," 1 Corinthians 11:19). Saint Paul's words, chosen by Herbert Grundmann as the title of his landmark 1963 article, have made for a disturbing reference point since the beginning of the medieval period, inasmuch as the apostle had actually intended to use them to confirm the need for divisions within the Church, divisions that would be useful in formulating correct doctrine.[1] If Saint Paul's position was accepted, its meaning was deepened when the Council of Nicaea of 325 condemned the teachings of Arius of Alexandria as heretical. As a result, heresy took on a specific doctrinal content, and heterodoxy was no longer considered simply as an internal division of the Church but a doctrinal error, a departure from tradition considered as an expression of orthodoxy. Afterwards it was the influence of

---

This chapter was translated by George Ferzoco.

1. Herbert Grundmann, "Oportet et haereses esse: Das Problem der Ketzerei im Spiegel der mittelalterlichen Bibelexegese," *Archiv für Kulturgeschichte* 45 (1963): 129-64; Italian translation: "Oportet et haereses esse: Il problema dell'eresia rispecchiato nell'esegesi biblica medievale," in *Medioevo ereticale*, ed. Ovidio Capitani (Bologna: Il Mulino, 1977), 29-66.

a Greek-rooted philosophical culture that would confer a more certain doctrinal dimension onto the concept of orthodoxy.[2]

In the path leading to a more precise definition of heresy, the point of departure were the writings of the Church Fathers, especially those of Augustine of Hippo (354–430) who in 427–28 wrote the fundamental *Liber de haeresibus* that provided the base for the understanding and interpretation of heterodox doctrines. From the political point of view, another important transition began with Constantine the Great (280–337), who set an example whereby the defense of the correct faith was considered to lie within the competence of the public authority. The emperor, responsible for the well-being of his subjects and the state, had to guarantee that orthodoxy was followed as an indispensable condition for the prayers of priests to obtain the protection of the Omnipotent for the empire and its leader.

The role of the defender of the correct faith was again taken up by Charlemagne who, with the support of the learned clerics in his court (particularly Alcuin of York), wanted to show himself capable of assuming the role of guarantor of orthodoxy, a role recognized (albeit with some reservations) by Pope Hadrian I (772–95). The pope, in fact, presented a canonical collection (the Dionysius-Hadrian collection) to Charlemagne as a model of legislation for the Frankish realm that Charlemagne with the help of the clergy in his court transformed into a "law": the *Admonitio generalis* (789).

An important part of the vast cultural project undertaken by Charlemagne, consecrated on Christmas Day 800 with his imperial coronation by the pope, was ensuring the full orthodoxy of the sovereign and the uniformity of the Catholic faith among all the empire's subjects.[3]

---

2. In outlining this introduction I have relied mainly on Lorenzo Paolini, "La concezione dell'eresia e dell'eretico nella sua evoluzione storica," in Lorenzo Paolini, *Le piccole volpi: Chiesa ed eretici nel medioevo*, ed. Riccardo Parmeggiani (Bologna: Bononia University Press, 2013), 19–52.

3. Stefan Weinfurter, *Carlo Magno: Il barbaro santo* (Bologna: Il Mulino, 2015), 187–204; originally published as *Karl der Grosse: Der heilige Barbar* (Munich: Piper, 2013), 205–24. For the recent edition of one of the most important documents of the religious politics of Charlemagne, see *Die Admonitio generalis Karls des Großen*, ed. Hubert Mordek, Klaus Zechiel-Eckes, and Michael Glatthaar, Monumenta Germaniae Historica, Fontes iuris Germanici antiqui in usum scholarum separatim editi 16 (Hannover: Hahnsche Buchhandlung, 2012), 1–40; see also Thomas Martin Buck, *Admonitio und Praedicatio: Zur religiös-pastoralen Dimension von Kapitularien und kapitulariennahen Texten (507–814)*, Freiburger Beiträge zur mittelalterlichen Geschichte 9 (Frankfurt am Main: Lang, 1997), Nikolas Staubach, "'Populum Dei ad pasqua vitae aeternae ducere studeatis': Aspekte der karolingische Pastoralreform," in *La pastorale della Chiesa in Occidente dall'età ottoniana al concilio lateranense IV: Atti della quindicesima Settimana*

## Reform Tensions and Religious Dissidence

By the ninth century in Constantinople, debates surrounding theological issues and iconoclasm had ended. In the West, thanks to the understanding between the Apostolic See and the reborn Roman Empire, heresy seemed to fade into the background. This was possibly because the episcopate's main concern was the need to reinforce lifestyles inspired by the Gospels in order to Christianize all aspects of society, and so it did not concern itself with—or was not sufficiently alert to—the presence of doctrinal errors among the flocks of their respective dioceses. With the West's economic and social recovery beginning early in the tenth century, there emerged examples of Church reform that fueled scattered expressions of dissent. It is worth noting that from the first decades of the eleventh century, contemporary sources—mainly monastic chronicles—emerge, along with synodal acts and legal documents, that give useful information regarding the world of dissidence, perhaps because it was the moment when it emerged into public view with force.

Up until the thirteenth-century developments in scholasticism and canon law, the ecclesiastical authors who sought to characterize groups they believed to be heterodox continued to refer to doctrines that Saint Augustine had condemned, using terminology from his writings to identify new heretics, thus making it difficult to grasp the content of eleventh-century heresies. A convincing example of this tendency is the famous decretal *Ad abolendam*, issued in Verona by Pope Lucius III with the approval of Emperor Frederick Barbarossa in November 1184. The document, sanctioning the renewed desire to proceed in unison to persecute heretics, offers, however, only generic indications. References to "those who falsely call themselves poor" are fairly easy to identify as the Poor of Lyon (or Waldensians) and the Humiliati, but it is more difficult to know who the pope is condemning as "Cathars and Patarines," the Passagini, the Giosefini, and the Arnaldists (though the last term may refer to followers of Arnald of Brescia).[4] In fact, the Patarines, far from being considered heretics, had been in the service of the reforming

---

*internazionale di studio (Mendola, 27–31 agosto 2001)* (Milan: Vita e Pensiero, 2004), 27–54, and Maria Pia Alberzoni, "La cura animarum," in *Città e campagna nei secoli altomedievali*, Settimane di studio della Fondazione Centro italiano di studi sull'alto medioevo 56 (Spoleto: Centro italiano di studi sull'alto medioevo, 2009), 151–90.

    4. X 5.7.9 = Aemilius Friedberg, *Corpus iuris canonici*, vol. 2, *Decretalium collections* (Lipsiae, 1922), cols. 780–82: "Ad abolendam diversam haeresium pravitatem, quae in plerisque mundi partibus modernis coepit temporibus pullulare ... et omnem haeresim, quocumque nomine censeatur, per huius constitutionis seriem auctoritate apostolica condemnamus. Imprimis

papacy in several areas of the Italian peninsula with the explicit support of Popes Alexander II and Gregory VII. Perhaps it did not help that the terms "Catari" and "Patari" sounded similar, or it may be that the papal condemnation referred to an extremist branch of such a group with ill-defined borders (we may recall that some sources clearly refer to the Humiliati as Patarines).[5] Such terminological confusion reveals a lack of interest in understanding the content of the beliefs held by those condemned as heretics, ultimately taking the deciding factor to be the extent to which they obeyed the Apostolic See's dispositions.[6]

Despite the lack of terminological clarity, there is no doubt that some dissent did exist in some organized way, spurring efforts in canon law to define such matters with greater clarity. Not until the inquisition instituted by Innocent IV would heterodox doctrines be closely examined, in part through the testimony of converted heretics. Yet, as the sources we possess come from ecclesiastical authorities or from the chanceries of public authorities, the voices of the protagonists, even when reported, are mediated in some way by the culture of those writing their testimony. Thus, in attempting better to define the characteristics of heresy, we can do no more than make hypotheses.

### Italy, Home of All Heresies

The recovery witnessed in various aspects of society and the Church from the early eleventh century onward favored social mobility and communication on a broader scale than previously. Ideas circulated with greater speed and intensity, requiring some mechanisms to control public opinion. One result was that when there were cases of religious dissent, these were considered to be heresies. These seemed to develop in two distinct environments. On the one hand there were the learned heresies, formulated by clerics and theologians with theological arguments; on the other, there were incidents of a more popular dissent, by laypeople capable of proselytizing simply through literal Gospel teachings.

---

ergo Catharos et Patarinos et eos, qui se Humiliatos vel Pauperes de Ludguno falso nomine mentiuntur, Passaginos, Iosephinos, Arnaldistas perpetuo decernimus anathemati subiacere."

5. See below, note 75, and the corresponding text.

6. Othmar Hageneder, "Il concetto di eresia nei giuristi dei secoli XII e XIII," and "La ierocrazia pontificia e l'eresia della disobbedienza," in Othmar Hageneder, *Il sole e la luna: Papato, impero e regni nella teoria e nella prassi dei secoli XII e XIII*, ed. Maria Pia Alberzoni (Milan: Vita e Pensiero, 2000), 69-130 and 213-34.

## 10. HERESY

The chronicler Raoul Glaber (ca. 985–ca. 1050) was a restless monk who, thanks to his travels from one Burgundian monastery to another, came to know many events in the surrounding areas. In his so-called "Chronicles of the Year One Thousand" he recounts that around that year, several hotbeds of heresy became visible. The case of a layman of Ravenna named Vilgardo is worth noting in particular. This man was well educated, having studied Latin classics such as Virgil, Horace, and Juvenal as well as the grammarians Donatus and Priscian. His heresy consisted in putting his passion for classical literature before Christian doctrine. Here we find a case that was not infrequent in the Italian peninsula, as the cult of classical authors remained vibrant in certain lay and urban circles, above all among schoolteachers. Raoul Glaber himself affirmed that the study of grammar "was always the habit of Italians who so applied themselves to this that they put aside all other endeavors."[7] Vilgardo was judged to be a heretic, and possibly condemned to death, by the archbishop of Ravenna, Pietro (d. 971).

Heretics hailing from the Italian peninsula were thought to be dangerous because they were equipped with a solid cultural education and thus may have been better able to spread their heterodox doctrines in other lands. Indeed, Raoul Glaber continued by saying: "There were discovered in Italy others who sustained these pernicious theories, and they too were put to death by the sword or at the stake. Even from Sardinia, an island where heretics abound, some at that time went out to corrupt part of the population of Spain and ended up being killed by the Catholics there."[8] The words of this monk in his chronicle show how by the beginning of the eleventh century Italy acquired a certain reputation as the "home of heresies."

Alongside such cases of heterodox doctrines formulated by literate laypeople, in the early decades of the eleventh century there were also episodes involving suspect doctrines put forth by clerics, as occurred in Orléans in 1022. Here, two canons of the cathedral, together with a group of their followers, were excommunicated by an assembly of bishops. Accordingly, King Robert the Pious condemned them to death, but the local population did not wait for the judgment to be carried out

---

7. Rodolfo il Glabro, *Cronache dell'anno Mille (Storie)*, ed. Guglielmo Cavallo and Giovanni Orlandi (Milan: Mondadori-Fondazione Lorenzo Valla, 1989), 2:106-9, n. 23: "Quidam Vilgardus dictus, studio artis gramatice magis assiduus quam frequens—sicut Italicis mos semper fuit artes negligere ceteras, illam sectari."

8. Rodolfo il Glabro, *Cronache*, 2:109.

and burned the heretics at the stake themselves. This was the first case in which heretics died at the stake.

The canons of Orléans taught doctrines of a gnostic dualist nature, generally held to be Manichaean, and denied the principal dogmas of the Christian faith such as the Trinity, the incarnation of Christ, and the maternity of Mary. They refused the sacraments (including marriage) and abstained from eating meat. It is notable that, according to Raoul Glaber, even this heresy had been imported by a woman who hailed from the Italian peninsula.[9] In this regard it is interesting to note the testimony of Gerard of Csanád (or Gerardo Sagredo, d. 1046), who had spent time as a monk at San Giorgio in Venice. Before going to Hungary on an evangelization mission, he wrote: "the children of the demon, with their shadowy power, reign and conquer everywhere: Italy did not normally nurture heresies, but presently one hears that in some regions fermentation abounds. Gaul is truly lucky as it is said to be immune. . . . Verona, the most noble of Italian cities is said to be full of them. Illustrious Ravenna and peaceful Venice, which used not to put up with God's enemies, now tolerate them."[10]

In another case it is possible to witness the circulation of heretical doctrines in the kingdom of France, where indication that they came from the Italian peninsula seems to underline that this belief was effectively a commonplace. In 1025, Bishop Gerard of Arras and Cambrai was informed that some preachers from Italy had recently arrived in Arras. He spoke to each of them there and interrogated them regarding the doctrines they held. "They replied saying they were followers of a certain Gundulo, an Italian from whom they had learned evangelical and apostolic precepts; they were not to accept any other scripture than this, and to comply with it through words and deeds." Their adhesion to this preaching led to the rejection of the sacraments, the Church hierarchy, and the cult of the saints. This was a "lay and ascetic Christianity," an expression of the will to follow the New Testament to the letter and, thus, to devote their entire life to it. The bishop refuted their

---

9. Rodolfo il Glabro, *Cronache*, 3:158, n. 26: "Fertur namque a muliere quadam ex Italia procedente hec insanissima heresis in Galliis habuisse exordiumm que, ut erat diabolo plena, seducebat quoscumque valebat, non solum idiotas ac simplices, verum etiam plerosque qui videbantur doctiores in clericorum ordine."

10. Gerardo Sagredo, *Deliberatio*, from Malcolm D. Lambert, *Medieval Heresy: Popular Movements from Bogomil to Hus* (London: Edward Arnold, 1977), appendix A, 347 cited in Lorenzo Paolini, *Eretici del Medioevo: L'albero selvatico*, Il mondo medievale: Sezione di storia delle istituzioni, della spiritualità e delle idee 20 (Bologna: Pàtron Editore, 1989), 19–20.

claims point by point in a convincing manner, and everyone abjured their false doctrine and, since they were illiterate, affirmed their profession of the faith with a simple sign of the cross.[11]

## Heresies of the Italian Peninsula

An early case emerged in Monforte, a *castrum* located near Alba in present-day Piedmont. The *Historia Mediolanensis*, written by a Milanese Churchman in the second half of the eleventh century, gives considerable space to celebrating the administrative gifts of Archbishop Ariberto d'Intimano (d. 1045), and it relates that in 1028 during a pastoral visit to Turin, he was informed of the presence of a heretical group in the area.[12] He immediately sought to learn their teachings and called upon their most authoritative representative, named Gerardo, to interrogate him regarding the articles of faith they professed. A disturbing picture emerged. They practiced an austere lifestyle, assiduously read the Scriptures, and prayed ceaselessly, but they held a singular interpretation of the Trinity: the Father was the eternal God, creator of all things; "the Son was the soul of the man born of the Virgin and loved by God, the soul of the Sacred Scripture, through the work of the Holy Spirit, which is the intelligence of the divine of knowledge."[13] They had their own hierarchy, distinct from that of the Church, with a "pontiff" who visited the brothers daily and absolved them of their sins—perhaps they understood this to be the Holy Spirit. They did not recognize the sacraments, and the remission of sins was assured via the ceaseless prayers of the elders. They, moreover, believed they could be liberated from carnal sins by practicing absolute chastity, refusing private property, and abstaining from eating meat. These closely echo if not the doctrine, then surely the practices of Catharism. It has rightly been noted that the learned beliefs of this sect closely reflect what was taught in those years by some masters of theology in northern France. This could allow us to reconsider the topos of the Italian origin of heresies—the inspiration could emanate from Paris.[14] One final and disturbing note to close the

---

11. Paolini, *Eretici del Medioevo*, 29-33.
12. *Landulfi Historia Mediolanensis*, ed. Ludwig Konrad Bethmann and Wilhelm Wattenbach, in Monumenta Germaniae Historica, Scriptores 8 (Hannover: Hahnsche Buchhandlung, 1848), 65-66.
13. Paolini, *Eretici del Medioevo*, 39.
14. Huguette Taviani, "Naissance d'une hérésie en Italie du Nord au XI$^e$ siècle," *Annales E.S.C.* 29 (1974): 1124-52; Alfredo Lucioni, "Eretici a Monforte d'Alba," in *Alba medievale:*

description of this group: all of its members were convinced that they would die a violent death, whether at their own hand or that of another, because those who were dying were being killed by their confrères.

Gerardo's confession convinced Archbishop Ariberto of the need to disperse the group. He went with his knights to where they lived and ordered everyone he found there to be arrested and led to Milan. It would seem that he hoped to convince them to abandon their faith, but as soon as word spread of the presence of the group in Milan, many rushed from the countryside to meet them and become their followers. To keep the false doctrines from spreading, the vassals of the archbishop set fire to an enormous stake, and they erected a cross next to it. "Then, against Ariberto's will, they led them all there and gave them the option of returning to orthodoxy, adoring the cross, and professing the orthodox faith, in which case they would save their lives; otherwise, they would have to go into the flames and be burned alive. And it was the case that some approached the Lord's Cross, professed the Catholic faith, and were saved; many, however, covering their faces with their hands, threw themselves into the flames and died horribly."[15]

## Church Reform and Heresies

With the eleventh-century reform of the Church and the progressive affirmation of Roman primacy, the boundaries of heresy became clearer. If, on the one hand, simony became a heresy—a revealing motive to discourage the appointment of unworthy clerics—on the other there was a greater insistence on the fact that disobedience to the Apostolic See was heterodoxy. One of the declarations of Gregory VII's *Dictatus papae* (1075) is based on this understanding: "whoever is not in agreement with the Roman Church is not to be considered Catholic."[16] At the same time, and in relation to the developments of canon law, the conviction grew that a heretic was less one who professed an error, and more one who obstinately continued to profess this error, even after the error itself had been confuted by ecclesiastical authorities. This

---

*Dall'alto Medioevo alla fine della dominazione angioina, VI–XIV secolo*, ed. Rinaldo Comba (Alba: Famija albèisa, 2010), 331–32.

15. *Landulfi Historia Mediolanensis*, 65–66; translated in Paolini, *Eretici del Medioevo*, 40–43.

16. *Das Register Gregors VII.*, ed. Erich Caspar, Monumenta Germaniae Historica, Epistolae selectae 2 (Berlin: Weidmannsche Buchhandlung, 1955), 207, n. 26: "Quod catholicus non habeatur, qui non concordat Romane Ecclesie."

definition has remained in force up to the most recent Code of Canon Law, in 1983.[17]

In particular, Church reform favored the emergence of new interpretations, usually formulated on the basis of a *sine glossa* reading of Scripture and aimed at combating the sometimes debatable behavior of Churchmen. The fact that a cleric or a religious could be invested in ecclesiastical office by a layperson (such as an emperor or king) gave rise to the suspicion that the office (such as a bishopric or abbacy) had been obtained through a cash payment or an exchange of benefices and this, beginning with deliberations of the Roman synods of the mid-eleventh century, came to be considered a heresy. In fighting this and other clerical vices, especially Nicolaism (relating to priests who married or had concubines), the papacy was supported by organized religious groups, which twentieth-century historiography inaccurately defined as "movements."[18]

## Patarines

Among these groups, the Pataria have a privileged place: a unique expression of popular religion, the Pataria emerged in Milan around 1056 through the work of several clerics—notably the deacon Arialdo and the priest Landolfo—who found many followers within the laity who supported a reform in clerical living. Why discuss the Pataria in a study of heresies? Before presenting this group's characteristics, it is necessary to note the similarity in the meanings of the terms "heretic" and "reformer" that marked the experiences of the renewal of religious life. According to a careful definition by Lorenzo Paolini, "the points of contact between heretics and reformers multiplied, and many religious needs of the first group found an institutional home through the work of the second."[19] In fact, when dissent took on the language of the institutions, it appeared credible and hence had a good chance of being

---

17. *Codex iuris canonici auctoritate Ioannis Pauli PP. II promulgatus* (Vatican City: Libreria Editrice Vaticana, 1983), Can. 751: "Heresy is the obstinate negation of a truth or obstinate doubt about that truth that one, after having received baptism, has to believe for the divine and catholic faith. Apostasy is the total repudiation of the Christian faith; schism is to refute to submit to the pope and the communion with the members of the Church subject to him."

18. Martina Wehrli-Johns, "Voraussetzungen und Perspektiven mittelalterlicher Laienfrömmigkeit seit Innozenz III: Eine Auseinandersetzung mit Herbert Grundmanns 'Religiösen Bewegungen,'" *Mitteilungen des Instituts für Österreichische Geschichtsforschung* 104 (1996): 286–309.

19. Paolini, *Eretici del Medioevo*, p. 43.

accepted.[20] The Pataria was born to respond to the need for reform of Churchmen who seemed to be living in open contrast to evangelical teachings; such needs were taken on by the reform papacy, starting with Alexander II (the Milanese Anselmo da Baggio), as part of a move to guarantee that the Apostolic See could intervene in the affairs of all churches.

The Patarines even engaged in military action to fight an archbishop and clergy held to be unworthy. At the head of the militia they appointed Erlembaldo, a noble belonging to the feudal episcopal network, who obtained from Alexander II the right to use the banner of Saint Peter in battle, signifying the complete support of the Apostolic See. On the basis of such papal recognition, Patarine ideals spread into other north-central Italian cities such as Florence, Brescia, Cremona, and Piacenza, and even reached as far afield as Flanders.

To obtain clerical reform, the Patarines engaged in some audacious undertakings. They practiced a sort of "liturgical strike," refusing sacraments from unworthy priests because they were judged to be invalid. They imposed chastity on the entire clergy, even against the consolidated customs of the Milanese Church. Notwithstanding the fact that the group consisted mainly of laypeople, they went so far as to try clerics who were already subject to episcopal jurisdiction.[21] Such rigor was imposed on clerical life that Alfredo Lucioni, one of the greatest scholars of the movement, hypothesized that the deacon Arialdo had been among the men from the surrounding countryside who came to Milan in order to face the heretics of Monforte and their doctrine when they were taken to the city to await judgment.[22] In any case, it is certain that the Patarines acted with determination, to the point of subverting the established order with a disorder that shook Milan for more than two decades and had as its tragic outcome the wounding and death of Landolfo and, above all, the murder of Arialdo in 1066, probably at the hands of hired killers sent by the archbishop of Milan, Guido da Velate. Arialdo's body was found the following year in the environs of Lago Maggiore, and following the miraculous events that were then

---

20. Enrico Faini, review of *Disciplined Dissent: Strategies of Non-Confrontational Protest in Europe from the Twelfth to the Early Sixteenth Century*, ed. Fabrizio Titone, *Nuova Rivista Storica* 104 (2020): 849: "La critica al potere, scritta seguendo le regole dettate dal potere stesso, poteva talvolta dare scacco matto all'ordine costituito."

21. Alfredo Lucioni, "L'età della Pataria," in *Diocesi di Milano*, ed. Adriano Caprioli et al., Storia religiosa della Lombardia 2 (Brescia: La Scuola, 1989), 167–94.

22. Lucioni, "Eretici a Monforte."

deemed to occur on its account, it was solemnly transferred to Milan for entombment.

The *miles* Erlembaldo, who had been at the head of the Patarine militia, made many enemies on account of the extreme rigidity of his positions regarding the Milanese clergy, and paid for his zeal for reform with his life because he so destabilized the established order. Both Arialdo and Erlembardo were quickly canonized by Popes Alexander II (1167) and Urban II (1195) respectively. In the Patarines and their leading representatives, these popes had found formidable support. Yet, with the death of their leaders, the Pataria gradually lost strength and cohesion, and the return of full communion between Rome and Milan in 1088 initiated a process that would bring the most devoted of the remaining Patarines to line up openly against the Apostolic See. Thus, in the early years of the twelfth century a Patarine phase we can label as "heretical" began: it took a critical attitude toward the Church of Rome, which under Urban II had preferred to work with local hierarchies, and so "for the following centuries the term 'Patarine' became automatically and fully associated with the term 'heretic.'"[23]

## Arnaldists

The papal decree *Ad abolendam* (1184) completes the list of condemned heretics by mentioning the "Arnaldistae."[24] We have no other independent evidence that corroborates the existence of an organized sect bearing this name, but this decree allows us to understand the persistence of the preaching of Arnaldo da Brescia (d. 1155).

Arnaldo was born in Brescia around the end of the eleventh century. He began a clerical career but only reached the level of *lector* in the Holy Orders, before studying theology in Paris under Peter Abelard. Returning to Brescia, he gained attention as a preacher against the corruption of the Church, and the local bishop banished him, after which he went back to Paris. In 1141 he took part in the Council of Sens, where Bernard of Clairvaux succeeded in having Abelard condemned. Arnaldo remained faithful to Abelard and succeeded him in teaching theology to poor students, who would gather on the hill of Saint-Geneviève in

---

23. Lucioni, "L'età della Pataria," 189, and Paolini, *Eretici del Medioevo*, 44.
24. "Imprimis ergo Catharos et Patarinos et eos, qui se Humiliatos vel Pauperes de Ludguno falso nomine mentiuntur, Passaginos, Iosephinos, Arnaldistas perpetuo decernimus anathemati subiacere" (see the complete text at note 4, above).

Paris, until he was expelled from the kingdom of France. Afterward, Arnaldo went to Zurich and Konstanz where his preaching continued to be well received.[25]

In 1145 near Viterbo, he was reconciled with Pope Eugene and undertook a penitential pilgrimage to Rome. He arrived there in the midst of terrible strife linked to the birth of the commune (or, the "senatus" as it was then called) and put aside his good intentions to relaunch his preaching with great vigor, no longer aimed solely at the moral rejuvenation of the Church but also at the creation of an alternative Church, free from all earthly powers and fallen lifestyles. "He, a man from a Lombard commune, who had grown up within the tradition of the Patarine movements, was handed the unique opportunity of finding himself within the heart of the earthly Church, to see it injured and almost conquered."[26] The success he enjoyed among much of the lower clergy, the common people, and especially among women led people to denounce him for being dangerous: in the agreements stipulated with the Commune of Rome and Frederick Barbarossa in 1154 in light of the imperial coronation, Pope Hadrian IV included the stipulation that Arnaldo be exiled. He was captured while fleeing northward; he was first hanged, then his body burned, and his ashes dispersed in the Tiber (1155). After his death his followers, the Arnaldists, spread throughout the Po valley and later joined with the Waldensians or Cathars.[27]

The cases of the Patarines and Arnaldo da Brescia show the extent to which the links between Parisian theological schools and northern Italy aided the spread of positions that were critical toward the hierarchical Church. Religious dissent relied on a greater knowledge of scripture by laypeople and on their desire to follow them to the letter. But present along with these positions of radical evangelism were learned interpretations inspired by what was taught in the schools, as we have seen in the case of the heretics of Monforte and Arnaldo.

## Cathars

"We alone are the true followers of Christ and the apostles, because we do not only preach words but we also put them into practice": these

---

25. Arsenio Frugoni, *Arnaldo da Brescia nelle fonti del secolo XII*, Studi Storici 8-9 (Rome: Istituto Storico Italiano per il Medio Evo, 1954), esp. 15-39 and 175-91.
26. Arsenio Frugoni, "Arnaldo da Brescia," in *Dizionario biografico degli Italiani*, vol. 4 (Rome: Istituto della Enciclopedia italiana, 1962), 248.
27. Paolini, *Eretici del Medioevo*, 75.

words, quoted in a letter to Bernard of Clairvaux by Eberwin of Steinfeld, a Premonstratensian canon in the diocese of Cologne, in 1144, express the self-consciousness of the Cathars as true followers of Christ and the Apostles.[28] They justified the use of terms like "good Christians" and "good men" on the basis of their ascetically exemplary behavior and the desire to create an alternative to the other, less positive, name in use. The name "Cathars" referred to the word's Greek etymology: they were the pure ones. Heretics, defined as such because they were condemned by the ecclesiastical authorities, considered themselves to be reformers of a corrupted Church, far from the evangelical ideal, and thus defined themselves with titles such as "good Christians" to legitimize themselves. This helps us to understand the fluctuating aspect of heresies that are often difficult to define or describe unambiguously.[29]

Historiography has repeatedly tried to deal with Catharism, seeking to understand its origins and teachings.[30] In recent years, historiographical positions described as "deconstructivist" have been successful in casting doubt over the existence of Catharism before the early decades of the thirteenth century. This approach has hypothesized an "invention" of Catharism by inquisitors seeking to justify their work, or even by nineteenth-century historians who simplified a complex reality.[31] These are positions often based on mere clues that reveal a sociological approach. One must not overlook the fact that those who held that Catharism did not exist until the early 1200s are Francophone or Anglophone scholars.[32] Among the latter, Pegg and Moore,

---

28. Eberwin of Steinfeld, *Epistula ad Bernardum "De haeretici sui temporis,"* ed. J. P. Migne, Patrologia Latina 182 (Paris: Migne, 1854), cols. 676-80: "Haec est haeresis illorum. Dicunt apud se tantam Ecclesiam esse, eo quod ipsi soli vestigiis Christi inhaereant; et apostolicae vitae veri sectatores permaneant, ea quae mundi sunt non quaerentes . . . . Vos autem, dicunt nobis, domum . . . et quae mundi sunt huius quaeretis. . . . De se dicunt: Nos pauperes Christi, instabiles, de civitate in civitatem fugientes. . . . Nos hoc sustinemus, quia de mundo non sumus: vos autem mundi amatores, cum <de> mundo estis."
29. Paolini, *Le piccole volpi*, 22-28: "Concetto fluttuante di eresia."
30. Raoul Manselli, *L'eresia del male*, 2nd ed. (Naples: Morano, 1980).
31. This current of historiography has met with consent as well as with well-founded criticism. For opinions on both sides, see Antonio Sennis, "Questions about the Cathars," in *Cathars in Question*, ed. Antonio Sennis, Heresy and Inquisitions in the Middle Ages 4 (York: York Medieval Press, 2016), 1-20, and recently also the synthesis of Marina Montesano, *Ai margini del Medioevo: Storia culturale dell'alterità*, Frecce 323 (Rome: Carocci, 2021), 87-125.
32. Jean-Louis Biget, *Église, dissidences et société dans l'Occitanie médiévale* (Lyon: CIHAM Editions, 2020); Julien Théry, "L'érésie des bons hommes: Comment nommer la dissidence religieuse non vaudoise ni béguine en Languedoc (XII$^e$-début du XIV$^e$ siècle)?" *Heresis* 36-37 (2002): 75-117; Uwe Brunn, *Des contestataires aux "Cathares": Discours de réforme et propaganda antihérétique dans les pays du Rhin e de la Meuse avant l'Inquisition*, Collection des études

in particular, largely ignore the heresies in medieval Italy and do not sufficiently consider the Italian historiography, which has dealt with Catharism for a very long time. They concentrate exclusively on the region of Albi and on the crusade launched by Innocent III.[33] However, debates allow for new tests and developments. For example, let us look at the acts of a council that took place in Saint-Félix-de-Caraman in May 1167 called by the churches of Toulouse and Carcassonne, where many women and men gathered. Before bishops and advisors from churches in France, Lombardy, Albi, Carcassonne, and Aran, Niquinta, a dualist bishop of the radical Dragovitza Church (*ordo Drugonthie*), conferred the order and *consolamentum* on new bishops. He spoke to them about fixing the borders of their churches as they did in Asia (which was considered a model) in order to minimize conflict.[34] As there is no extant manuscript tradition of the document (which has reached us through a seventeenth-century publication), its authenticity has been questioned, and some have considered it a forgery created by Catholic apologists. As one would expect, this document does not use terms such as "Cathar" or "heretic," given that the writer would have been convinced of the orthodoxy of the people mentioned therein. Must it be that Cathars did not exist because they did not describe themselves as such? A way to describe the participants at this council must be found. Moreover, a recent and thorough study under the aegis of the Institut de recherche et d'histoire des textes in Paris has established that the text that has come down to us can be considered neither a forgery nor a thirteenth-century reworking.[35]

---

augustiniennes, Série Moyen-Âge et temps modernes 41 (Turnhout: Brepols, 2006). Mark Gregory Pegg, "On Cathars, Albigenses and Good Men of Languedoc," *Journal of Medieval History* 27 (2001): 181–95; Mark Gregory Pegg, *The Corruption of Angels: The Great Inquisition of 1245–1246* (Princeton, NJ: Princeton University Press, 2001); Robert Ian Moore, *The War on Heresy* (Cambridge, MA: Harvard Belknap Press, 2012), trans. into French as *Hérétiques: Résistances et repression dans l'Occident médiévale*, trans. Julien Théry (Paris: Belin, 2017).

33. It will suffice to refer to Lorenzo Paolini, "Prefazione," in Pseudo Giacomo de Capellis, *Summa contra hereticos*, ed. Paola Romagnoli and Maurizio Ulturale, Ordines: Studi su istituzioni e società nel medioevo europeo 7 (Milan: Vita e Pensiero, 2018), vii–xi, and to Maurizio Ulturale, "Introduzione," in the same volume, 3–39.

34. "Compte rendu des interventions de Monique Zerner, Jean-Louis Biget et Jacques Chiffoleau," in *L'histoire du catharisme en discussion: Le "concile" de Saint-Félix (1167)*, ed. Monique Zerner, Collection du Centre d'études médiévales de Nice 3 (Nice: Centre d'études médiévales, 2001), 37–43.

35. David Zbíral, "La charte de Niquinta et les récits sur les commencements des Églises cathares en Italie et dans le Midi," *Heresis* 44–45 (2006): 135–62; David Zbíral, "La charte de Niquinta et le rassemblement de Saint-Félix, état de la question," in *1209–2009, cathares: Une histoire à pacifier?*, ed. Anne Brenon (Portet-sur-Garonne: Loubatières, 2010), 31–44; Jacques

Catharism—as we shall continue to call this alternative church—spread widely especially in areas that were economically and culturally advanced. Ecclesiastical authorities, in the period up to the developments in scholasticism and canon law of the early thirteenth century, had been more concerned with identifying heretics through their behavior rather than through the study of the doctrines they professed. Consequently, the names given to these people and their teachings were often imprecise. This does not prevent us from noting a common background, compatible with the inspirations of Cathar preaching since the twelfth century.

The first useful evidence relative to the existence and spread of these doctrines in the West is in the abovementioned letter of Eberwin of Steinfeld to Bernard of Clairvaux, informing him of a worrying development. Eberwin referred to a public debate at Cologne in front of many clerics (including the archbishop), where the dualist teachings of presumed heretics as well as their belief they were representing the true Church, of which they held themselves to be the new apostles, became obvious. The clerics (including Eberwin) present at this debate repeatedly exhorted the heretics to mend their ways and to renounce their teachings. These exhortations had no effect and instead reached a tragic conclusion. The people in attendance were horrified by the obstinacy of the heretics and became "steeped in an excess of zeal." Against the will of the clerics, they took the heretics and burned them at the stake. A stupefied Eberwin concluded by saying those who died "entered the flames and underwent the torture of the fire not only patiently but even joyfully."[36]

From the mid-twelfth century, accounts of Catharism grew. Catharism initially spread as an expression of popular religiosity, tied to an awakening of evangelism and polemics against the clergy and the Roman Church. In what we might call the "evangelical phase" of Catharism, the few written texts concerned preaching, such as the Cathar

---

Dalarun, "La charte de Niquinta: Débats heuristiques, enjeux herméneutiques," *Aevum* 86 (2012): 535–48. The position of Montesano makes a lot of sense: Montesano, *Ai margini del Medioevo*, 111-12: "While the accurate analysis of the controversial texts, the scrutiny not to adopt uncritically the point of view of the Catholic exponents, and the sensible invitation not to consider the movements of the eleventh and twelfth centuries in the light of what has come after are methodologically correct premises, the negation of every reality of the Cathar experience seems to take these premises to the extreme, to the point of refuting some of the evidence. Also, if we admit the existence of Catharism in the thirteenth century we have to give it also a history, insofar as it is impossible that it appeared out of nowhere."

36. Paolini, *Eretici del Medioevo*, 123–25.

Treatise, reported by Durand of Huesca in his *Liber contra Manicheos*, written around 1220 to offer the Catholic preachers a point-by-point refutation of Cathar doctrine—thereby showing that the Cathar's doctrinal treatise was already circulating at the end of the twelfth century in the regions of the French Midi.[37] In the second half of the twelfth century, due to the influence of preachers from the Balkans, some mythological elements were added that justify the antithesis between the principle of good and the principle of evil relative to the creation of the world. Initially there prevailed a moderate dualism, inspired by the Bulgarian priest Bogomil. Here, the only creator was the good God; Satan, cast out of paradise down into the world with the rebel angels, created lifeless human beings, in which the rebel angels resided and thus became prisoners in physical matter. Jesus Christ, considered an angel sent by God to save humankind, demonstrated to people through his asceticism and penitence how to free themselves from the weight of matter. The most radical dualistic position—elaborated perhaps as a result of contact with other currents from the East—sustained that at the origin of the world there were two different principles: Satan, the evil creator and the lord of matter; and God, the good creator of the heavens to which the spirit was linked.[38]

Itinerant preachers—laymen in possession of a certain level of education—spread Cathar doctrines in the various regions of Europe. These men were prepared to hold debates with clergymen, who at that time possessed a similar cultural education. When faced with exponents from the hierarchy or theologians, however, the Cathars were disadvantaged by their lack of a scholastic training. They soon caught up in this area, however, motivated by their desire to present themselves as the true exegetes of the Gospel, that is, as *sapientes*.[39] Preaching dualist

---

37. Christine Thouzellier, *Un traité cathare inédit du début du XIII<sup>e</sup> siècle*, d'après le "Liber contra Manicheos" de Durand de Huesca, Bibliothèque de la Revue d'histoire ecclésiastique 37 (Leuven: Bibliothèque de l'Université, Bureaux de la Revue, 1961); Christine Thouzellier, *Une somme anti-cathare: Le "Liber contra Manicheos" de Durand de Huesca*, Spicilegium sacrum Lovaniense 32 (Leuven: Spicilegium sacrum Lovaniense Administration, 1964); Kurt-Victor Selge, *Die ersten Waldenser mit Edition des "Liber antiheresis" des Durandus von Osca*, 2 vols., Arbeiten zur Kirchengeschichte 37 (Berlin: de Gruyter, 1967).

38. In addition to reconstruction of Manselli, *L'eresia del male*, see also Grado Giovanni Merlo, *Eretici ed eresie medievali*, Universale Paperbacks Il Mulino 230 (Bologna: Il Mulino, 1989), 39–48 and 85–98; Paolini, *Eretici del Medioevo*, 119–50; and Francesco Zambon, "Dissimulation, secret et allégorie dans le dualism chrétien du Moyen Âge: Paulicianisme, bogomilisme, catharisme," *Annali di Scienze religiose* 4 (2011): 157–89.

39. Lorenzo Paolini, "Italian Catharism and Written Culture," in *Heresy and Literacy, 1000–1530*, ed. Peter Biller and Anne Hudson (Cambridge: Cambridge University Press, 1994), 83–103.

doctrines resulted in a transition from teaching of a mainly ethical and practical nature to one of a theological character. Dualism, in this way, both moderate and radical, emerged in the wider culture, whereas previously it had consisted of teachings, referred to as the *Secretum*, known only to a few.

The work of "pope" Niquinta, present at the aforementioned council of Saint-Félix-de-Caraman (1167), favored the affirmation of radical dualism in the West.[40] In the 1160s he sojourned in the Po valley, visiting the region's Cathars and leading them to accept his teachings: Lombardy's Cathar bishop Marco followed these doctrines, and many in turn followed him. When the Cathars of Toulouse asked Niquinta to visit them as well, he similarly convinced many there to follow the absolute, or radical-diarchic, dualism that posited the existence of two eternal and uncreated principles, the good-spirit and the evil-matter.[41]

The council fully revealed the Cathar Church's organization. In it, "pope" Niquinta imparted the only "sacrament" recognized by the Cathars, the *consolamentum*, primarily to bishops, thus instituting a hierarchy dependent on him, distinct from the preceding one. This created divisions that remained unresolved and became a cause of weakness. During the council, Cathar dioceses were organized, copying the Roman Church's boundaries and putting bishops at their heads as points of reference and a guarantee for the salvation of the faithful. Catharism was thus the only heretical current to give itself a hierarchical structure, which for two centuries, even in a fragmentary form and in the absence of a unifying leader, guaranteed a certain cohesion and wide diffusion.

The most important churches were in France and Italy. Those of southern France—Albi, Toulouse, and Carcassonne—all adhered to radical dualism, while northern French Cathars were mainly moderate dualists. Italy's Po valley saw adherents of radical dualism at Desenzano on Lake Garda, and a more moderate dualism in places like Concorezzo near Milan, Bagnolo near Mantua, and Vicenza. Similar moderate views were shared by more relatively southern groups, like those of Florence and the Spoleto valley. The communes constituted a favorable terrain for the spread of Catharism, because the absence of a strong central power permitted it to escape easily from the control of the authorities and to find support among urban dwellers; moreover, the world of the communes was culturally active, as judges, notaries, and merchants

---

40. See above, notes 34–35 and corresponding text.
41. Merlo, *Eretici ed eresie medievali*, 40–45; Paolini, *Eretici del Medioevo*, 122–23.

knew Latin and could read and write, and had access to higher learning as well as to sacred scripture.[42]

Some treatises written in the thirteenth century by Catholic controversialists or converts from Catharism allow for the reconstruction of the history of its hierarchy and its doctrinal divisions. It is not possible to examine these changes for the twelfth century here; one need but recall the *Ad abolendam* of 1184 that placed the Cathars/Patarines at the head of the heretical sects to be condemned and persecuted. The Cathars became "the quintessential heretics. . . . The Church feared only them, and feared them greatly, for the entire thirteenth century."[43] The Church promoted systematic repression, perfected with the birth of the Inquisition as a permanent organ of control and judgment of orthodoxy. Cathars, especially the *perfecti*, had to adapt to new conditions and chose a clandestine state of constant itinerance in order to ensure ties among the faithful and to keep their faith alive.[44]

A convert from Catharism, the Dominican Raniero da Piacenza was active as an inquisitor between 1250 and 1262. His *Summa de Catharis* provides a lively and detailed overview of the Catharism of his times. He states that there were then four thousand Cathars (presumably referring to the number of *perfecti*). He provides rough indications of their presence in the Po valley and the Italian peninsula. For example, the church of Concorezzo had more than 1,500 Cathars; Desenzano, 500; Mantua, 200; Vicenza, 100. Escaping violent persecutions in France were 150 *perfecti* who were given shelter in Verona and other places. The churches of Florence and the Spoleto valley had about 100 *perfecti*, while there were 200 in the churches of Albi, Carcassonne, and Toulouse. The list continues with the church of the Latins in Constantinople and the churches of the Greeks, Bulgarians, and Dragovitza, that together numbered 500. As one can ascertain from these figures, most Cathars were in northern Italy: here among the Good Christians freedom of action remained possible for a longer period.[45]

---

42. Merlo, *Eretici ed eresie medievali*, 63–67; Maria Pia Alberzoni, "Ugo Speroni e i suoi epigoni: Tra eresia e critica all'istituzione chiesa," in *"Sapiens, ut loquatur, multa prius considerat": Studi di storia medievale offerti a Lorenzo Paolini*, ed. Caterina Bruschi and Riccardo Parmeggiani, Uomini e mondi medievali 64 (Spoleto: Centro italiano di studi sull'alto medioevo, 2019), 3–25.

43. Paolini, *Eretici del Medioevo*, 120–21.

44. Marina Benedetti, "Eresia e Inquisizione," in *Storia del cristianesimo*, vol. 2, *L'età medievale (secoli VIII–XV)*, ed. Marina Benedetti (Rome: Carocci, 2015), 315–41.

45. Merlo, *Eretici ed eresie medievali*, 85–89.

Things changed, at least in central and northern Italy, from the 1230s onward, especially with the 1233 preaching campaign of the Alleluia. Here, Dominicans and Franciscans showed their willingness to support the Apostolic See—in this case, to get the communes to use the antiheretical legislation that had been approved by Emperor Frederick II when he received the imperial crown on November 22, 1220, and was then adapted by Pope Gregory IX. Possibly profiting from the ties between the Apostolic See and the communes that were allied against Frederick II in the war that went from 1239 to the emperor's death in 1250, the mendicants succeeded in applying antiheretical measures.[46] Thus, in this part of Italy, the Cathars were contested actively, well before the Inquisition was officially instituted.

A recent important contribution by Giovanni Vitolo sheds light on the interesting analogies between the situation in the period just after the mid-thirteenth century in some parts of southern Italy and the diffusion of Catharism in the south of France. The evidence points to the circulation of heresies and heretics in the Angevin Empire, some of which originated in the Occitan and northern Italy.[47]

## Waldensians

The Waldensians like the Humiliati were living expressions of evangelical poverty that grew strongly in the second half of the twelfth century. Their experience marked an important stage in the evolution that—through papal recognition of their form of life—would lead to the foundation of the mendicant orders and to the institutionalization of the ideal of literally following Christ.

The Waldensians, named after their founder Waldo or Waldesius of Lyon (d. 1206/7), called themselves the Poor of Lyon, in keeping with their place of origin. Waldo, a rich merchant who was also the financial administrator of the cathedral chapter of Lyon, decided in the year 1170 to respond as literally as possible to the Gospel's invitation: "If you want to be perfect, go, sell what you have and give to the poor, and you will have a treasure in the kingdom of heaven" (Matthew 19:21). He

---

46. Riccardo Parmeggiani, "Papato, Impero e Comuni nella lotta contro gli eretici di 'Lombardia' (1198-1233)," in *Maggio 1218: Il Colloquio di Bergamo. Un dibattito all'inizio della storia valdese*, ed. Francesca Tasca (Turin: Claudiana, 2020), 161-74.

47. Giovanni Vitolo, "Gli eretici di Roccamandolfi (1269-1270): Una Montaillou molisana?" in Bruschi and Parmeggiani, *"Sapiens, ut loquatur, multa prius considerat,"* 119-48.

radically changed his way of life, quitting work and leaving his earthly possessions to his wife and their two daughters (providing them the dowry required to enter the monastery of Fontevraud). He returned the profit he had made from lending money (as before banks were widely established, it was normal for merchants to be involved in lending money to those who needed or wanted to borrow), gave his money to the poor, and became truly poor. He became an itinerant preacher in the hope of supporting the Church in its efforts to suppress the Cathars of southern France. Earlier, he had paid for translations of the New Testament into his vernacular, so that he could use these texts in his sermons. He aimed to preach to support the faith and to offer his lifestyle as an example of poverty and the evangelical life within the boundaries of orthodoxy. He had no desire to oppose the Church or its teaching. His example drew a number of laypeople to him, fascinated by the possibility of imitating the example of the apostolic community, but lay preaching had always been considered suspect by Churchmen.[48]

To eliminate any suspicion of heresy, Waldo and some followers went to Rome in 1179, when the Third Lateran Council was in progress. He was able to speak with Alexander III and ask him for recognition of his lifestyle and his itinerant preaching. The pope embraced Waldo, praised his lifestyle and that of his followers, and said he would need to ask his bishop's permission to continue his itinerant preaching.[49] Notwithstanding this oral approval, and notwithstanding the solemn profession of faith made by Waldo and his companions at the diocesan synod of 1180 in the presence of the cardinal bishop of Albano and the papal legate Henry of Marcy, there were problems: due perhaps to the overly polemical tones used by lay preachers concerning the corrupt clergy, the archbishop of Lyon not only forbade them from preaching, but in 1182/83 he expelled them from the diocese and excommunicated them.[50] These decisions were probably dictated by a fear that the preaching of the Poor of Lyon could favor the positions held by Cathar preachers in their drastic condemnations of the Catholic clergy.

Instead of obeying and abstaining from preaching, Waldo and his followers decided to obey the task assigned to them by the Lord. Their

---

48. Besides Selge, *Die ersten Waldenser*, 1:227–303, see also the concise systhesis in Merlo, *Eretici ed eresie medievali*, 51–52, and in Paolini, *Eretici del Medioevo*, 80–95 (with the translation of most important documents).

49. Alexander Cartellieri and Wolf Stechele, eds., *Chronicon universale Anonymi Laudunensis* (Leipzig: Dyksche Buchhandlung, 1909), 29–30.

50. Paolini, *Eretici del Medioevo*, 80–81.

disobeying the archbishop was the cause of their being accused of heresy, and the Poor of Lyon were included in the list of heretics condemned by Lucius III and Frederick Barbarossa in the *Ad abolendam* (1184). "Waldensianism . . . came to be a heresy because of its disobedience and its rebellion against the Catholic hierarchy; this came to be as a result of local circumstances in a heretical area."[51] The Roman Church was not yet able to assess and direct new forms of lay religiosity, even when these groups wanted to support its struggles against the greatest of heretics, the Cathars. Waldo sought to keep his disciples from abandoning orthodoxy, "possibly maintaining the hope of overcoming the misunderstandings and tensions" of the Church.[52]

Until Waldo's death, sometime between 1205 and 1207, the desired reconciliation with the Roman Church was not reached. Indeed, the group radicalized, rejecting the jurisdictional power of the pope and his bishops; considering prayers for the dead and consequently the doctrine of purgatory to be useless; assigning sacramental duties to worthy laypeople and ultimately denying the sacrament of Holy Orders; and narrowing the sacraments only to baptism, confession, and the Eucharist (called "Waldensian supper") administered by laypeople. In this way the Waldensians increasingly came to establish themselves as "anti-Church." Waldo did not agree with such developments, as can be seen in his reaction when, in 1205, Giovanni di Ronco, a native of Piacenza, created the Poor of Lombardy, a group very critical toward the Church; Waldo immediately excommunicated him but failed to avoid a schism.[53]

Despite papal condemnation, the Waldensians spread especially in southern France but also in the north of Iberia, northern France, the lands of Germany and Bohemia, some valleys of present-day Piedmont, the Po valley, and central Italy as far south as Spoleto. They set themselves up secretly, and this allowed them to remain alive, unlike other coeval heretical groups; they were to find a new vitality, in Italy and in Europe, especially during the Protestant Reformation of the sixteenth century.

The divisions within Waldensianism began to appear before Waldo's death, after which a desire to avoid naming a successor prevailed. Rather, local communities would refer matters to established and respected elders from within, who would visit and comfort fellow brothers and

---

51. Paolini, *Eretici del Medioevo*, 82.
52. Merlo, *Eretici ed eresie medievali*, 52.
53. Paolini, *Eretici del Medioevo*, 82.

sisters with their words and demeanor. An attempt was made to unify the Italian Waldensians with those north of the Alps in May 1218, when their representatives met in Bergamo.[54] They failed to settle on a doctrinal agreement, as the Lombards did not wish to cease to work, while the ultramontanists (those from north of Alps) wished to remain faithful to Waldo's example and dedicate themselves totally to preaching. Other points of disagreement were linked to how the sacraments should be practiced, and also the ways in which the elders would be selected. All this made their divisions insoluble.

After Waldo's death some of his followers reconciled with the Roman Church. The election of Innocent III (1198–1216) marked a turning point. The pope and some of his closest collaborators, the cardinals, had studied together in Paris at the time of Peter the Chanter (d. 1197), where they had discussed the lawfulness of lay preaching. The circle of Peter the Chanter formulated the important distinction between the *exhortatio*, characterized by its edifying moral content, and the *praedicatio*, focused on theological and doctrinal questions. This second mode of preaching was reserved for members of the *ordo doctorum* or *praedicatorum*—or in other words, theologians.[55] We possess excellent studies on this by John Baldwin, Philippe Buc, and above all Nicole Bériou.[56] Innocent III, in fact, was the first to bring together canon law and theology in this regard, with an orientation open to the laity's demands concerning poverty and the evangelical life.[57]

The reconciliation of the Poor Catholics with the Roman Church constitutes an interesting point from which to observe the origins and the development of the Waldensians on the one hand, and the choices made on the other by Innocent III and his Curia in the face of requests by groups that in the past had been condemned as heretical. As early as 1201, the Humiliati had received full recognition by the Roman Church

---

54. Lothar Vogel, "Il Rescriptum sul colloquio di Bergamo: Una fonte per la cultura e la spiritualità del primo valdismo," in Tasca, *Maggio 1218*, 17–40.

55. Martina Wehrli-Johns, "Das mittelalterliche Beginentum: Religiöse Frauenbewegung oder Sozialidee der Scholastik? Ein Beitrag zur Revision des Begriffes 'religiösen Bewegungen,'" in *"Zahlreich wie die Sterne des Himmels": Beginen am Niederrhein zwischen Mythos und Wirklichkeit* (Bergisch: Thomas-Morus-Akad. Bensberg, 1992), 21–28.

56. John W. Baldwin, *Masters, Princes and Merchants: The Social Views of Peter the Chanter and His Circle*, 2 vols. (Princeton, NJ: Princeton University Press, 1970); Philippe Buc, "Vox clamantis in deserto? Pierre le Chantre et la prédication laïque," *Revue Mabillon*, n.s., 4 (1993): 5–47; Nicole Bériou, *L'avènement des maîtres de la Parole: La prédication à Paris au XIII$^e$ siècle* (Paris: Institut d'études augustiniennes, 1998), 1:15–71.

57. Wehrli-Johns, "Voraussetzungen und Perspektiven," 294.

and thus showed the possibility of accepting experiences that earlier had been seen as suspect.

In September 1207 there was a debate in Pamiers in the diocese of Toulouse, in the presence of Bishop Foulques.[58] One of the leading exponents of the Waldensians ranging from the Languedoc to northeastern Spain, Durand of Huesca, debated with Bishop Diego of Osma who had in the previous year obtained from Innocent III a special mandate to combat heretical preaching in the south of France. The two men chose as their judge a lay cleric who was not hostile to the Waldensians, but Durand was nevertheless defeated. His response, and that of his followers, was to make peace with the Apostolic See. Diego's arguments had been better than those of his adversaries, who were also well versed in sacred scripture, but what really convinced them to reconcile with the papacy was the assurance that they would be able to attain papal authorization for their antiheretical preaching.[59]

Durand and his followers reached the Curia in mid-November 1208. On December 18, Innocent III received from them an oath of obedience, including one of full adhesion to the Roman Church and to the sacraments administered by canonically ordained clergymen. Thus the *propositum conversationis* was approved with regulations concerning the life and prayers of the newly reconciled men.[60] For the first time, papal documents referred to such men as Poor Catholics, a title that indicated recognition of their aspirations to a life of evangelical poverty in full communion with the Church. Durand's profession of faith repeated much of what was in the oath taken by Waldo in 1180 and contained a series of propositions that guaranteed his orthodoxy. The Poor Catholics did not constitute a religious order, since the *propositum* did not allow for a common life or fixed places of residence, but instead it permitted a life of absolute poverty and itinerance. It is not necessary to

---

58. Maria Pia Alberzoni, "Innocent III et les Pauvres Catholiques du Midi," in *Innocent III et le Midi*, ed. Michelle Fournié, Daniel Le Blévec, and Julien Théry-Astruc, Cahiers de Fanjeaux 50 (Toulouse: Privat, 2015), 311–36; on Folchetto di Tolosa, see Francesco Zambon, "Il poeta vescovo: Folchetto di Marsiglia," in *Nel Duecento di Dante: I personaggi*, ed. Franco Suitner (Florence: Le lettere, 2020), 39–58.

59. Marie-Humbert Vicaire, "Rencontre à Pamiers des courants vaudois et dominicain (1207)," in *Vaudois languedociens et Pauvres catholiques*, Cahiers de Fanjeaux 2 (Toulouse: Privat, 1967), esp. 183–85.

60. *Die Register Innocenz' III.*, vol. 11, *Pontifikatsjahr, 1208/1209: Texte und Indices*, ed. Othmar Hageneder et al. (Vienna: Verlag der Österreichischen Akademie der Wissenschaften, 2010), nos. 191 (196)–193 (198), 311–17.

underline the extent to which these reconciled Waldensians were similar to the *minores* of Francis of Assisi.[61]

Churchmen struggled to accept this reconciliation, so Innocent III himself communicated to the bishops of the dioceses in which these reconciled Waldensians lived of the recognition the Church of Rome had granted. He assured them of their oath of obedience made in his hands, and of the dedication promised in combating *disputando et exhortando* the heretics. An example of the papal interventions made in favor of Durand and his followers is a letter sent by the pope in April 1209 to the archbishop of Milan, Uberto da Pirovano (1206-11). When early in his pontificate (1198) Innocent III had upheld the antiheretical legislation laid out in *Ad abolendam*, Uberto's predecessor, Filippo da Lampugnano (1196-1206), had ordered the destruction of the place where Waldensians met.[62] Now, the pope praised Uberto for the way he kindly welcomed the Poor Catholics, and he charged the bishop to consider a bold request from Durand. The newly arrived leader of the Poor Catholics maintained that there were at least a hundred Waldensians in Milan who were ready to reconcile with the Church authorities, as long as their one-time meeting place—destroyed by Archbishop Filippo—could be restored to them. This is interesting evidence of the notable Waldensian presence in the city, and of the favor bestowed on these people by the administrative authorities who had given them a plot of land with a meeting place where they could study the Bible and sustain each other morally. The pope, while noting that Durand should not have laid down any conditions for reconciliation with the Apostolic See, asked Uberto to do the best he could in returning the land or another suitable place where the Poor Catholics could see and sustain each other.[63]

The reconciliation with the Poor Catholics achieved a positive outcome as they got what they requested: recognition of their orthodoxy and an essential *propositum conversationis*, guaranteed by the pope. Their followers who remained in the world were moreover recognized as a

---

61. Maria Pia Alberzoni, "Spunti per una rilettura del 'Testamentum' di Francesco d'Assisi," in *Zwischen Rom und Santiago: Festschrift für Klaus Herbers zum 65. Geburtstag. Beiträge seiner Freunde und Weggefährten, dargereicht von seinen Schülerinnen und Schülern*, ed. Claudia Alraum et al. (Bochum: Verlag Dr. Dieter Winkler, 2016), 261-72.

62. Luigi Zanoni, "Valdesi a Milano nel secolo XIII," *Archivio storico lombardo* 39 (1912): 5-22; Alberzoni, "Innocent III et les Pauvres," 320-22.

63. *Die Register Innocenz' III.*, vol. 12, *Pontifikatsjahr, 1209/1210: Texte und Indices*, ed. Andrea Sommerlechner et al. (Vienna: Verlag der Österreichischen Akademie der Wissenschaften, 2012), 34-36, n. 17.

sort of semireligious group. In addition to Bishop Foulques de Toulouse, they also received the support of several cardinals, including Leo of Santa Croce (named "corrector/protector" of the Poor Catholics), Nicholas of Tusculum, and Pelagius of Santa Lucia, noted as special friends in the prologue of the *Liber contra Manicheos*, written ca. 1220 by Durand himself.[64]

The status obtained by the followers of Durand from Innocent III favored a return to broader communion with Bernard Prim as well. Bernard and some of his followers went to the papal Curia and on June 4, 1210, they received a sort of letter patent that informed all archbishops and bishops of their readmission to full communion with the Church.[65]

## Humiliati

In the *Ad abolendam* (1184), the Humiliati, like the Poor of Lyon, were accused of heresy because they were not truly poor; their "outlaw" status, however, proved to be "a brief heretical episode."[66]

Very little information about their origin is known, and it often contains falsehoods invented to glorify them. For example, Bernard of Clairvaux allegedly created them in Milan in 1135; other sources speak of Milanese nobles led to Germany in the early twelfth century by Emperor Henry V.[67] There are, however, only two certain facts. One is the lack of a named individual as the founder or leader, even though in the fifteenth century a story circulated that they had come into being thanks to an otherwise unknown saint, John of Meda.[68] The second one

---

64. This discussion regarding the relations between these cardinals and Durand of Huesca is in Thouzellier, *Une somme anti-cathare*, 36-38, and in Selge, *Die ersten Waldenser*, 1:218.

65. *Die Register Innocenz' III.*, vol. 13, *Pontifikatsjahr, 1210–1211: Texte und Indices*, ed. Andrea Sommerlechner et al. (Vienna: Verlag der Österreichischen Akademie der Wissenschaften, 2015), 164-68, n. 94.

66. Merlo, *Eretici ed eresie medievali*, 57.

67. Maria Pia Alberzoni, "Gli inizi degli Umiliati: Una riconsiderazione," in *La conversione alla povertà nell'Italia dei secoli XII–XIV: Atti del XXVII Convegno storico internazionale, Todi, 14-17 ottobre 1990*, Atti dei Convegni dell'Accademia Tudertina e del Centro di studi sulla spiritualità medievale 27 (Spoleto: Centro italiano di studi sull'alto medioevo, 1991), 187-237; Maria Pia Alberzoni, "San Bernardo e gli Umiliati," in *San Bernardo e l'Italia: Atti del Convegno di studi (Milano, 24–26 maggio 1990)*, ed. Pietro Zerbi, Bibliotheca erudita 8 (Milan: Vita e Pensiero, 1993), 101-29; for an overall reconstruction of the beginnings of the Humiliati, with indication of the available sources, see Frances Andrews, *The Early Humiliati* (Cambridge: Cambridge University Press, 1999), esp. 1-98.

68. Maria Pia Alberzoni, "Giacomo di Rondineto: Contributo per una biografia," in *Sulle tracce degli Umiliati*, ed. Maria Pia Alberzoni, Annamaria Ambrosioni, and Alfredo Lucioni,

is that from the start the Humiliati were a composite group: there were married laypeople living in a community with religious, brought together by the desire to live following the example of the early Church.[69]

Was it therefore an error to include them in the list of heretics that the Church condemned and excommunicated? It is likely that the condemnation in *Ad abolendam* had to do with the laity, married or living in a community, who like the Waldensians devoted themselves to antiheretical preaching. This is confirmed by the chronicle of Laon, written in the first decade of the thirteenth century. After narrating the meeting of Waldo with Alexander III during the Third Lateran Council (1179), the anonymous author added: "There were then several citizens, living in the cities of Lombardy, who while living with their families in their own homes chose a particular manner of religious living. . . . They were happy with their simple clothes and fought for the catholic faith against heresy." These people also went to the pope and "asked for confirmation of their religious request. The pope permitted them to do anything with humility and honesty, but he explicitly forbade them from meeting privately and he did not applaud their having dared to preach in public. But they went against this apostolic command and thus drew excommunication upon themselves."[70] As with the Waldensians, preaching carried out by laypeople was the decisive factor in their condemnation.

From the start of his pontificate on February 22, 1198, Innocent III invited bishops to observe the antiheretical legislation, albeit with some important distinctions aimed at avoiding condemning people who were not heretics. Thus, for example, the archpriest of Verona had renewed the excommunication of the Humiliati of his city, without distinguishing between those who were stubborn in their error and those who instead had sworn to obey the Church's orders.[71] As a result, the Humiliati turned to the Apostolic See in December 1199. The pope accepted their complaints and agreed to open negotiations so as to grant

---

Bibliotheca erudita: Studi e documenti di storia e filologia 13 (Milan: Vita e Pensiero, 1997), 117-62.

69. Maria Pia Alberzoni, "'Sub eadem clausura sequestrati': Uomini e donne nelle prime comunità umiliate lombarde," in *Uomini e donne in comunità*, Quaderni di storia religiosa 1 (Verona: Cierre Edizioni, 1994), 69-110.

70. Cartellieri and Stechele, *Chronicon universale Anonymi Laudunensis*, 29-30; Paolini, *Eretici del Medioevo*, 98 (the translation).

71. *Die Register Innocenz' III.*, vol. 2, *Pontifikatsjahr: Texte*, ed. Othmar Hageneder, Werner Maleczek, and Alfred A. Strnad (Vienna: Verlag der Österreichischen Akademie der Wissenschaften, 1979), no. 219 (228), 424-25.

them a unitary rule that was recognized by the Apostolic See. By December 1200, the leaders of the various groups within the Humiliati were asked to gather information about their customs and to use this to create normative texts to be submitted to the Apostolic See for final revision and approval. Since it proved impossible to compile a unified set of canonical rules for the various components of the Humiliati, Innocent III approved three different rules in June 1201. The first was for laypeople, whether married or not, who lived within a family and who dedicated themselves to their work; the second was for laypeople of both sexes who lived a common life and practiced traditional trades (such as the making of woolen clothes), or who worked in agriculture or as merchants;[72] and the third was for followers of a more rigid religious life, whether men or women, who lived in common and were organized according to quasi-monastic norms. Thus were born the three orders of the Humiliati in an arrangement created by the pope and the Roman Curia that probably mirrored their preexistent organization.

With these three approvals the brief and uncertain heretical phase of the Humiliati came to an end. As with the reconciled Waldensians, local hierarchies continued to run into some resistance, especially relative to the laypeople (or Third Order), whose *propositum* called for weekly meetings in their *convenia* in order to hear the exhortations of brethren of undisputed faith. This was not preaching but exhortation, the same condition that was laid down in 1209 for Francis and his (lay) brothers by Innocent III.[73] A few years later Jacques de Vitry travelled to Perugia to be made bishop of Acre (Accon) by Innocent III, who had probably been in Paris alongside Jacques as a student of Peter the Chanter. Jacques was a preacher renowned for his sermons against heresy and for the crusading movement, and he was sensitive to new forms of religious life. It happened that Jacques arrived in Perugia sometime after July 16, 1216, the day Innocent III died, so he received his episcopal consecration from the new pope, Honorius III.[74] Traveling from the north of

---

72. Maria Pia Alberzoni, "Die Humiliaten zwischen Legende und Wirklichkeit," *Mitteilungen des Instituts für Österreichische Geschichtsforschung* 107 (1999): 324–53 (with the edition of documents addressed to the First and Second Orders).

73. Buc, "Vox clamantis in deserto?," 18–24.

74. Agostino Paravicini Bagliani, *Cardinali di Curia e "familiae" cardinalizie dal 1227 al 1254*, Italia sacra: Studi e documenti di storia ecclesiastica 18 (Padua: Antenore, 1972), 1:99–109; see also a short biography in John Frederick Hinnebusch, *The Historia Occidentalis of Jacques de Vitry: A Critical Edition*, Spicilegium Friburgense 17 (Fribourg: University Press Fribourg Switzerland, 1972), 3–15.

Europe through the Italian peninsula, he noted several new elements in the life of the Church and wrote of them to his friends in Flanders. He told of how he met Humiliati in the region of Milan, and near Perugia he had known *fratres* and *sorores minores*. His description of the Humiliati is noteworthy. Not long after crossing the Alps he reached the Milan area, which he called a *fovea hereticorum* (lair of heretics); here he stopped for a few days, preaching. His experience must have been dramatic, as he wrote:

> I hardly found in all of Milan anyone who opposed the heretics except for some holy men and religious women, called by worldly and malicious laypeople "Patarines." The supreme pontiff, however, authorized them to preach and fight heretics and approved their way of religious life; he referred to them as "Humiliati." Renouncing everything for Christ, they have come together in different meeting places. They live by the fruit of their labor, frequently preaching the Divine Word and listening to it. They are perfect and unshakeable in the faith, and efficacious in their good works. This *religio* has spread so far in the Milan diocese that there are a good 150 conventual communities, men in some and women others, not counting those who have remained in their own homes.[75]

This is an extremely interesting piece of evidence, which, apart from demonstrating the spread of the Humiliati in the region, allows us to understand that calling them "Patarines" did not correspond to an actual accusation of heresy, but to the desire of some to discredit them in the eyes of the faithful.

## Heretics or Rebels?

With the approval of the Waldensians and the Humiliati, the phase in which the Apostolic See was on the defensive when faced with new forms of religious life, whether orthodox or heretical, came to an end. If Innocent III had already changed the orientation of the Roman Curia, Gregory IX and above all Innocent IV definitively took away from bishops the duty of identifying and persecuting heretics, and they established the papal Inquisition that they delegated to the mendicant orders. The friars, in fact, had demonstrated with their choice of life

---

75. *Lettres de Jacques de Vitry, évêque de Saint-Jean-d'Acre: Edition critique*, ed. Robert Burchard Constantijn Huygens (Leiden: Brill, 1960), 72–73.

the possibility of reconciling evangelicalism and orthodoxy; they built upon a solid theological culture, often acquired in a university milieu; this was fundamental in permitting them to effectively take on the heretics. Catharism was severely persecuted by the Inquisition and, also because of internal divisions, disappeared. The Waldensians, on the other hand, survived because, even though they were spread out, they managed to maintain contact with one another.[76]

New heresies also arose, but they had a more circumscribed spread, both geographically and over time. In northern Italy their origin was tied to the lively cultural climate of the communes, favored by the active urban presence of laypeople with a good cultural education: judges, notaries, and schoolteachers. I will limit myself to mentioning a heresy that arose in Piacenza, which took its name from Ugo Speroni, an expert in civil law who between 1177 and 1185 gathered his theories into one work. This work is known to us both through an attack written by *magister* Vacario, another civil lawyer and a classmate of Speroni, and through the writings of Salvo Burci, a Piacenza layman belonging to the communal elite. In 1235 Burci wrote the *Liber supra Stella* in which he denounced, along with the errors of different Cathar churches in the north of Italy, the doctrines of Speroni, which, he says, became known around 1185. Ugo proposed a spiritual interpretation of Christianity that led him to refute the hierarchy and the administration of the sacraments by the ordained clergy. Influenced above all by the Pauline Epistles, he held the primacy of divine grace undisputable, contrasting it to teachings that men had superimposed on the Christian message in order to justify the desire of the hierarchical Church for dominion.[77] Unlike the Waldensians, Ugo Speroni advanced a learned interpretation rather than a direct approach to scripture.

In the first half of the thirteenth century, thanks to widespread interventions by the Apostolic See that could now count on mendicant orders such as the Dominicans and Franciscans, the presence of heretics was very clearly reduced in the Po valley and especially that *fovea hereticorum* (to use Jacques de Vitry's words), Milan. The papacy asked Frederick II, in view of his imperial coronation of November 1220, to approve harsh antiheretical legislation (the *Constitutio in basilica Petri*) that was

---

76. Paolini, *Le piccole volpi*, 43–52.
77. Ilarino da Milano, *L'eresia di Ugo Speroni nella confutazione del maestro Vacario: Testo inedito del secolo XII con studio storico e dottrinale*, Studi e testi 115 (Vatican City: Biblioteca Apostolica Vaticana, 1945); see also Merlo, *Eretici ed eresie medievali*, 63–67.

made a part of communal statutes above all from 1229, when a solid alliance developed between the communes of the Lombard League and the Apostolic See against Frederick.[78] As Stephan the Spaniard, the provincial prior of the Dominican friars of Lombardy, declared in the 1233 process of canonization of Saint Dominic, "in the cities of Lombardy many heretics were burned and more than one hundred thousand men, who did not know if they should adhere to Rome or the heretics, sincerely converted to the catholic faith of the Roman Church thanks to the preaching of the Dominican friars. . . . And almost all the cities of Lombardy and the Marches entrusted to the friars their questions and their statutes so that they might eliminate, add to, reduce, and change them in whatever way may seem better to them."[79]

It will suffice to observe that the *podestà* of Milan in 1233, Oldrado da Tresseno from Lodi, was praised in an inscription at the base of the equestrian statue representing him on the façade of the Palazzo della Ragione in Milan for more than simply having completed the construction of the town hall: Oldrado was praised for having defended the faith and for having burned heretics at the stake, "as it was his duty as his position demanded."[80]

## The Apostles

In the years that followed we do not find any new heresies. This leads us to deduce that the collaboration between the Roman Church and the communal governments created an effective force for repression.

---

78. Maria Pia Alberzoni, "Minori e Predicatori fino alla metà del Duecento," in *Martire per la fede: San Pietro da Verona domenicano e inquisitore. Atti del Convegno (Milano, 24–26 ottobre 2002)*, ed. Gianni Festa (Bologna: Edizioni Studio Domenicano, 2007), 51–119; Maria Pia Alberzoni, "I Frati Minori nello scontro tra Federico II e il papato," in *Francescani e politica nelle autonomie cittadine dell'Italia basso-medievale: Atti del convegno (Ascoli Piceno, 27–29 novembre 2014)*, ed. Isa Lori Sanfilippo and Roberto Lambertini (Rome: Istituto Storico Italiano per il Medio Evo, 2017), 35–58.

79. "Acta canonizationis s. Dominici," ed. Angelus Walz, in *Monumenta Historica Sancti Patris nostri Dominici* (Rome: Institutum Historicum FF. Praedicatorum, 1935), 2:158–59.

80. I find it very significant that this reference to Cathars comes from an epigraph, a publicly exposed inscription, not from a literary or doctrinal source. "Civis Laudensis fidei tutoris et ensis // Qui soliu<m> struxit catharos ut debuit uxit." On this epigraph, see Saverio Lomartire, "'Iustitia, maiestas, curialitas': Oldrado da Tresseno e il suo ritratto equestre nel Broletto di Milano," *Arte medievale*, 4th series, no. 5 (2015): 101–36; Maria Pia Alberzoni, "Legittimazione personale e costruzione del consenso: La statua equestre di Oldrado da Tresseno (1233)," in *Costruire il consenso: Modelli, pratiche, linguaggi (secoli XI–XV)*, ed. Maria Pia Alberzoni and Roberto Lambertini (Milan: Vita e Pensiero, 2019), 181–98.

Afterward, in fact, heretical doctrines were not persecuted, but rather "heresies of disobedience."

Let us consider the case of the Apostolics or, better, the Apostles. This was, and was seen to be, a mendicant religious order that arose in Parma in 1260 following the conversion and penitential preaching of Gerardo Segarelli.[81] This man was an illiterate layman who, not admitted to the Friars Minor, had nonetheless decided to indulge his religious vocation. He gave his goods to the poor and gave himself over to itinerant penitential preaching. Since his Latin was not very good, he would exhort the faithful to change their ways by repeating the word "penitençiagite," as ironically recalled by the chronicler Salimbene of Parma (who was an eyewitness with a hostile prejudice against Gerardo and his followers).[82] These men presented themselves as the new Apostles. They did not possess goods unless they were held in common; they devoted themselves fully to exhortation and to the service of the needy in hospices. They could be seen as a new realization of the ideal of Francis of Assisi and his first companions. The Apostles, following the example of the apostolic community of Jerusalem, also had a female component. The sisters followed and served the friars and were active with them in the hospices and in helping the needy. Segarelli enjoyed the favor of important prelates, particularly Obizzo Sanvitale, the bishop of Parma and a nephew of Innocent IV who often made known his esteem for the new order. To receive further indications of approval of their lifestyle, the Apostles also turned to the Apostolic See where Albert of Parma, a papal notary and probably an acquaintance given their shared city of origin, advised them to seek out the abbot of the Cistercian monastery of Fontevivo, near Parma. He effectively approved the Apostles' rules and the regulations that had been followed up to then, and he advised them to remain faithful to them.[83]

The condemnation of Gerardo and the Apostles was not for doctrinal matters but for disobeying the Church's commands. During the Second Council of Lyon in 1274 there were complaints from bishops about

---

81. Merlo, *Eretici ed eresie medievali*, 99–105; Marina Benedetti, "Segarelli, Gherardo," in *Dizionario biografico degli Italiani*, vol. 91 (Rome: Istituto della Enciclopedia Italiana, 2018), 736–39.

82. Grado Giovanni Merlo, "Salimbene e gli apostolici," in *Salimbeniana: Atti del Convegno per il VII Centena-rio di fra Salimbene (Parma 1987–1989)* (Bologna: Radio Tau, 1991), 144–57.

83. Giancarlo Andenna, "Il carisma negato: Gerardo Segarelli," in *Charisma und religiöse Gemeinschaften im Mittelalter (Dresden, 10.–12. Juni 2004)*, ed. Giancarlo Andenna, Mirko Breitenstein, and Gert Melville (Münster: LIT, 2005), 415–42.

the ever-growing number of mendicant orders within their respective areas.[84] And that was not all. Tensions between the various mendicant orders—the Preachers, Minors, Hermits of Saint Augustine or Augustinians, the Sack Friars (or Brothers of Penitence of Jesus Christ), Carmelites, Servites—were frequent, as each of them lived off donations, and more orders meant fewer donations per order. The council declared that only the two oldest orders, the Friars Preachers and Friars Minor, would continue to exist. It suspended judgment on the Augustinians, Carmelites, and Servites (who were all eventually recognized close to thirty years later by Popes Boniface VIII and Benedict XI), and decreed that the other mendicant orders would be made no longer to exist.[85]

In particular, the Sack Friars and the Apostles were immediately forbidden to accept new recruits. The Sack Friars, despite having a notable presence in France and the Italian peninsula, obeyed, and their history ended as they became part of the Servite order. The Apostles, however, paid little heed to the council's decree, until Popes Honorius IV in 1286 and Nicholas IV (the first pope from a mendicant order—in his case, the Friars Minor) in 1290 forced them to accept the judgment of the recent Lyon council. Thus in 1294 in Parma four Apostles—two men and two women—died at the stake, accused of heresy as they had disobeyed papal dispositions, while Segarelli, thanks to the intercession of Obizzo Sanvitale, was imprisoned and before long set free again. When, however, Sanvitale became archbishop of Ravenna in 1295, Segarelli was again imprisoned and put on trial. He died at the stake in July 1300.[86]

After this, brother Dolcino of Novara became head of the Apostles. His religious message, inspired by the teachings of Joachim of Fiore, featured a strong eschatological element. He preached the imminent arrival of a fourth age, inaugurated by Gerardo Segarelli, that was to follow the age of Church decline that had begun with the emperor

---

84. Jacques Le Goff, "Le dossier des Mendiants," in *1274 Année charnière: Mutation et continuité (Lyon-Paris, 30 septembre–5 octobre 1974)*, Colloques internationaux du Centre National de la Recherche Scientifique 558 (Paris: Centre National de la Recherche Scientifique, 1977), 211-22, and Micheline de Fontette, "Religionum diversitatem et la suppression des Ordres Mendiants," in the same volume, 223-29.

85. "Concilium Lugdunense II (1274)," ed. Burkhard Roberg, in *Conciliorum oecumenicarum generaliumque decreta. Editio critica*, vol. 2, bk. 1, *The General Councils of Latin Christendom: From Constantinople IV to Pavia-Siena (869–1424)*, gen. ed. Giuseppe Alberigo and Alberto Melloni, Corpus Christianorum (Turnhout: Brepols, 2013), 247-358; const. XXVIII at 354-57.

86. Franco Andrea Dal Pino, "Papato e Ordini mendicanti apostolici 'minori' nel Duecento," in *Il papato duecentesco e gli Ordini mendicanti, Atti del XXV Convegno internazionale (Assisi, 13–14 febbraio 1998)* (Spoleto: Centro italiano di studi sull'alto medioevo, 1998), 105-59.

Constantine and the progressive enrichment of ecclesiastics. The renewal of the Church was meant to begin with an angelic pope who would eliminate all the evil prelates, with the help of the emperor (possibly identified as Frederick of Aragon). The Inquisition had ample grounds to charge Dolcino with heresy. He was, nonetheless, able to preach for a few years: he was known to be in Bologna in 1300, and in 1302–3 he was in Trent and around Lake Garda; around 1303 he moved to Piemonte, and in 1304 he was in Vercelli. It was there that he was discovered, causing him to flee to Val Sesia before escaping with his followers to other mountainous areas until Holy Week in 1307 when he had to surrender to the forces that besieged the mountain where he had taken refuge. He was taken alive, and after suffering terrible torture, he was burned at the stake on June 1, 1307. The Apostles, deprived of their leader, dispersed.[87]

### From Heresy to Dissent

From the mid-thirteenth century, forms of religious (and sometimes political and religious) dissent rather than heresy continued to be manifest. Heresy had by then largely diminished due to the effective repression exerted by the Roman Church, and this religious dissent often took the form of disobedience toward the ecclesiastical authorities. During the clashes between Frederick II and Gregory IX (1227–41), these political enemies accused each other of heresy. The papal Curia unleashed a violent ideological war against Frederick II, even accusing him of being the precursor of the Antichrist, if not the Antichrist himself.[88]

It was Cardinal Raniero da Viterbo and his entourage who elaborated short pamphlet-like diatribes aimed at denying the empire any role in supporting the Church in its struggle against heresy and against external forces (the Saracens and the Tartars) who seemed to foreshadow scenes of the apocalypse. This favored moves by the more extremist of the mendicants, based on pseudo-Joachimite texts, thanks to which the friars held themselves to be the sole defenders of the Church in

---

87. Giovanni Miccoli, "Dolcino," in *Dizionario biografico degli Italiani*, vol. 40 (Rome: Istituto della Enciclopedia italiana, 1991), 440–44.

88. Dieter Berg, "Staufische Herrschaftsideologie und Mendikantenspiritualität: Studien zum Verhältnis Kaiser Friedrichs II. zu den Bettelorden," *Wissenschaft und Weisheit* 51 (1988): 26–51; Giancarlo Andenna, "Federico II ed i Mendicanti di Lombardia: Dalla collaborazione allo scontro," *Tabulae del Centro di studi federiciani* 11, no. 1 (1998): 48–67.

the imminent struggle against the Antichrist.[89] To understand this, one must recall the mid-thirteenth-century dispute at the University of Paris, largely between the mendicants and the secular masters but also involving the episcopate, that shows to what an extent such a doctrine came to be rooted in the leadership of the mendicant orders, leading even to heterodox positions.[90] The Franciscan Gerard of Borgo San Donnino, a master of theology, published the *Concordia Novi et Veteris Testamenti* of Joachim of Fiore in Paris in 1254, preceded by a *Liber introductorius in evangelium aeternum*, in which Gerard presented Joachim's work as the gospel of the age of the Holy Spirit, almost a new addition to the biblical Gospel, reconsidering the meaning of the Incarnation and Trinitarian dogma. Gerard's *Liber* was examined by a commission of cardinals who judged it to be heretical, and in 1255 it was burned. Soon afterward the minister general of the Friars Minor, John of Parma, had to resign for not having limited the spread of Joachimite ideas within the order. His successor, Bonaventure of Bagnoregio (in office from 1257 to 1274), tried Gerard in Paris for his obstinacy in following Joachimite teachings, excommunicated him, and sentenced him to prison for life. A similar fate also befell John of Parma, exiled to the hermitage of Greccio (but in this case without excommunication).[91]

Within the realm of the political use of accusations of heresy, mention must be made of the crusade launched by Boniface VIII against the Colonna, followed by the 1297 expulsion from the college of cardinals of Cardinals James and Peter, who took shelter in the court of the great enemy of the pope, the king of France. The Colonna brothers, in response, did not miss the opportunity to spread terrible accusations

---

89. Marco Rainini, *Il profeta del papa: Vita e memoria di Raniero da Ponza, eremita di curia* (Milan: Vita e Pensiero, 2016); Matthias Thumser, "Kardinal Rainer von Viterbo (+ 1250) und seine Propaganda gegen Friedrich II," in *Die Kardinäle des Mittelalters und der frühen Renaissance*, ed. Jürgen Dendorfer and Ralf Lützelschwab (Florence: SISMEL-Edizioni del Galluzzo, 2013), 187–200.

90. For what follows, see Roberto Lambertini, "Momenti della formazione dell'identità francescana nel contesto della disputa con i secolari (1255–1279)," in *Dalla "sequela Christi" di Francesco d'Assisi all'apologia della povertà: Atti del XVIII Convegno internazionale della Società internazionale di Studi francescani (Assisi, 18–20 ottobre 1990)* (Spoleto: Centro italiano di studi sull'alto medioevo, 1992), 123–72.

91. In addition to Gratien de Paris, *Histoire de la fondation et de l'évolution des Frères Mineurs aux XIIIᵉ siècle* (Paris, 1928), reprint with a bibliographic update ed. Mariano d'Alatri and S. Gieben, Bibliotheca seraphico-capuccina 29 (Rome: Istituto storico dei Cappuccini, 1982), 579-91, see Josef Ratzinger, *Die Geschichtstheologie des heiligen Bonaventura* (Munich: Schnell & Steiner, 1959); Italian trans.: *San Bonaventura: La teologia della storia* (Florence: Nardini Editore, 1991), exp. 59–75; and Gian Luca Podestà, *I Francescani e la Bibbia nel '200*, Aleph 1 (Milan: Edizioni Biblioteca Francescana, 1994).

against Boniface VIII, presenting him as a heretic who gave himself to necromancy and other practices of magic.[92]

Toward the end of the thirteenth century, there were eschatological expectations, which had already been raised concerning to the year 1260—the year that supposedly marked the return of Christ in relation to the 1,260 days allocated to the domination by the great red dragon as narrated in the book of the Apocalypse (12:6). Such expectations manifested themselves at the popular level, when Boniface VIII called for a jubilee on February 22, 1300, when a large number of pilgrims were already visiting Rome.

Among these extreme positions, a heresy should be recalled that was present solely in Milan in the last decades of the thirteenth century. It was built around Guglielma, a woman commonly referred to as the Bohemian, who died with a reputation for sanctity in 1281 or 1282 and was buried in the cemetery of the Cistercian monastery of Chiaravalle Milanese.[93] Guglielma was one of a substantial group of female mystics who, in the second half of the thirteenth century, attracted a number of devotees who gave themselves up to the guidance of such women. Guglielma and her devotees had two reference points in the city's ecclesiastical institutions. One was the monastery of Chiaravalle: Guglielma was very close to the Cistercians as she lived in a shelter owned by these monks. The other was a house of the Humiliati for their religious women in Milan called the *domus de Biassono*, where there lived sister Maifreda da Pirovano, a woman held to be the "special daughter" of Guglielma. After Guglielma's death and inspired by the miracles that fed her cult (such as the belief among her devotees that she had received the stigmata), a group of devotees led by Andrea Saramita developed a doctrine that held Guglielma to be the incarnation of the Holy Spirit. In reality, she had always told her followers she was a woman, born of a father and a mother; she was not an uncreated being. Guglielma's words and deeds were considered by the Inquisition and others to be orthodox. Her cult was celebrated openly at Chiaravalle, and several churches possessed her relics.[94]

---

92. Agostino Paravicini Bagliani, *Bonifacio VIII*, Biblioteca di cultura storica 245 (Turin: Einaudi, 2003), 137–205; 313–44.

93. Marina Benedetti, "Guglielma di Milano, detta la Boema," in *Dizionario biografico degli Italiani*, vol. 60 (Rome: Istituto della Enciclopedia italiana, 2003), 704–8.

94. Marina Benedetti, *Io non sono Dio: Guglielma di Milano e i Figli dello Spirito Santo* (Milan: Edizioni Biblioteca francescana, 1998).

The Dominicans, leading the Inquisition, interrogated several devotees of Guglielma between 1284 and 1296 and recorded their sworn testimony that Guglielma was the incarnation of the Holy Spirit and that after her death, this divine prerogative had passed to sister Maifreda da Pirovano. If, on the one hand, such a doctrine reflected Joachimite and pseudo-Joachimite theories that held the final age of the world, the age of the Spirit, to be imminent or indeed already under way, the heresy of the Guglielmites presented the novel element of the absolute centrality of a woman—first Guglielma, then Maifreda—as the incarnation on earth of the Holy Spirit. This conviction led to what was perhaps the most audacious act, which was decisive in the condemnation of Guglielma's followers: in the church of the sisters of the Humiliati of Biassono on May 29, 1300—the feast of Pentecost—Maifreda, assisted by Saramita and other followers, celebrated a pontifical High Mass. When news of this became known to the inquisitors, they again took up their examination of the devotees of Guglielma and Maifreda, condemning the leaders of the group. In September 1300, to keep the cult of Guglielma from continuing near the monastery of Chiaravalle Milanese, the remains of the woman were exhumed and destroyed. Thus a religious experience inspired by a deep devotion for a holy woman came to an end. Over the course of the fourteenth century there arose other groups of devotees around women considered to be holy and who were often counsellors or sources of inspiration to Churchmen—one need only think of Angela of Foligno, Clare of Montefalco, and Catherine of Siena. Even in cases such as these, the inquisition often kept an eye on possible subversions of ecclesiastical order and hierarchy. In this way, heresy came to be considered the expression of widespread spiritual dissatisfaction rather than new doctrinal developments.

At the end of this overview, we have come to the point where we must ask ourselves whether it is possible to identify any peculiarities of heresy in the Italian peninsula. If, for various reasons, it is impossible to separate the history of heresy as it manifested itself in the territories of present-day Italy from that of the analogous experience on the other side of the Alps, it is also true that some elements allow us to highlight forms of originality.

We must not underestimate the fact, in the first place, that the pope was the only bishop of a see of apostolic foundation in the West, and increasingly aware of this authority, he aimed to extend his jurisdiction starting with those regions that bordered on the Apostolic See. In 1059

Nicholas II became the feudal lord of the incipient Norman polities of southern Italy; Alexander III (1159-81) and then Gregory IX and Innocent IV (1243-54) had the Lombard League as their fundamental ally in countering the policy of the emperor and preventing the *Patrimonium beati Petri*—nominally controlled by the Byzantines but in which the popes were increasingly interested—from being completely surrounded by the empire.

Up until the pontificate of Innocent III (1198-1216), the Apostolic See developed a policy that aimed at creating a stronger link with the regions of central Italy, and the most effective tools of this policy were control over the appointments of bishops and their actions on one hand, and repression of religious dissent on the other, sometimes confused or identified with political dissent. We could perhaps hypothesize that in the Italian peninsula there were no phenomena on a vast scale, like the spread of Catharism in the Midi, thanks to the greater level of control exercised by the Apostolic See.

Another peculiarity of heresy in Italy is its undeniable link with the world of the city: if, for example, in the Midi heretics were found mostly in small towns and were linked, above all, to local centers of power, such as the counts of Toulouse, in central and northern Italy, after a period that we could define as one of initial proselytism, which took place in the countryside, heresy also became rooted in the city, where it had its greatest spread. Heresy then returned to the countryside, or to the area around the cities (it is enough to think of the position of the principal Cathar churches, those of Desenzano and Concorezzo) or to the minor cities (Mantua or Vicenza), in order to escape repression.[95]

The city remained the privileged place for the spread of religious novelties, sometimes considered heresies. It is enough to think of the case of the Waldensians and, above all, the Humiliati in Lombardy. This was the region of greatest cultural elaboration, with schools also for the laity, which trained experts in law and notaries, in such a way that the laity involved in the legal professions could often compete as equals with the clerics who were experts in canon law or theology, as we have seen in the case of Ugo Speroni. The accusation aimed at Italy for being the home of all heresies is rooted in the suspicion aroused by these learned laymen, who claimed to interpret the scriptures regardless of

---

95. Cinzio Violante, "Eresie nelle città e nel contado in Italia dall'XI al XIII secolo," in Cinzio Violante, *Studi sulla cristianità medioevale: Società, istituzioni, spiritualità*, ed. Piero Zerbi (Milan: Vita e Pensiero, 1975), 349-79.

the ecclesiastical authority or who could allow themselves to criticize the life of the prelates and express the desire for a renewal of the Church, at times according to complex gnostic principles.

We can thus come to understand an Italian peculiarity: most of the heresies that we have considered in this review, too, were born in the city and spread principally from there. Only in the extreme case of the repression organized by the ecclesiastical authorities, as happened from the beginning of the thirteenth century onward with the Waldensians and at the end of the century with the Apostles, and Fra Dolcino in particular, do we see it flee from towns and cities in order to organize resistance.

Only the agreement between the papacy and local political powers and, above all, the presence of the mendicant orders made it possible for the ecclesiastical authorities to intervene in a more effective way. We could say that the mendicants were the right answer at the right moment: their centralized constitution gave the Apostolic See a ready tool of control within Christendom. They were also given the task of the Inquisition from the mid-thirteenth century onward, a new institution that was to be decisive in containing and eliminating religious dissent in the Italian peninsula too.

## Selected Bibliography

### Primary Sources

Pseudo Giacomo de Capellis. *Summa contra hereticos*. Edited by Paola Romagnoli and Maurizio Ulturale. Ordines: Studi su istituzioni e società nel medioevo europeo 7. Milan: Vita e Pensiero, 2018.

Tiraboschi, Gerolamo. *Vetera Humiliatorum Monumenta*. Vol. 2. Mediolani, 1759.

### Secondary Sources

Alberzoni, Maria Pia. "Il concilio dopo il concilio: Gli interventi normativi nella vita religiosa fino al pontificato di Gregorio IX." In *The Fourth Lateran Council: Institutional Reform and Spiritual Renewal. Proceedings of the Conference Marking the Eight Hundredth Anniversary of the Council Organized by the Pontificio Comitato di Scienze Storiche (Rome, 15–17 October 2015)*, edited by Gert Melville and Johannes Helmrath, 289–318. Affalterbach: Didymos-Verlag, 2017.

———. "Giacomo di Rondineto: Contributo per una biografia." In *Sulle tracce degli Umiliati*, edited by Maria Pia Alberzoni, Annamaria Ambrosioni, and

Alfredo Lucioni, 117-62. Bibliotheca erudita: Studi e documenti di storia e filologia 13. Milan: Vita e Pensiero, 1997.

———. "Die Humiliaten zwischen Legende und Wirklichkeit." *Mitteilungen des Instituts für Österreichische Geschichtsforschung* 107 (1999): 324-53.

———. "Gli inizi degli Umiliati: Una riconsiderazione." In *La conversione alla povertà nell'Italia dei secoli XII–XIV: Atti del XXVII Convegno storico internazionale, Todi, 14-17 ottobre 1990*, 187-237. Atti dei Convegni dell'Accademia Tudertina e del Centro di studi sulla spiritualità medievale, n.s., 4. Spoleto: Centro italiano di studi sull'alto medioevo, 1991.

———. "Innocent III et les Pauvres Catholiques du Midi." In *Innocent III et le Midi*, edited by Michelle Fournié, Daniel Le Blévec, and Julien Théry-Astruc, 311-36. Cahiers de Fanjeaux 50. Toulouse: Privat, 2015.

———. "'Sub eadem clausura sequestrati': Uomini e donne nelle prime comunità umiliate lombarde." In *Uomini e donne in comunità*, 69-110. Quaderni di storia religiosa 1. Verona: Cierre Edizioni, 1994.

———. "Ugo Speroni e i suoi epigoni: Tra eresia e critica all'istituzione chiesa." In *"Sapiens, ut loquatur, multa prius considerat": Studi di storia medievale offerti a Lorenzo Paolini*, edited by Caterina Bruschi and Riccardo Parmeggiani, 3-25. Uomini e mondi medievali 64. Spoleto: Centro italiano di studi sull'alto medioevo, 2019.

Andrews, Frances. *The Early Humiliati*. Cambridge: Cambridge University Press, 1999.

Benedetti, Marina. "Eresia e Inquisizione." In *Storia del cristianesimo*, vol. 2, *L'età medievale (secoli VIII–XV)*, edited by Marina Benedetti, 315-41. Rome: Carocci, 2015.

———. *Io non sono Dio: Guglielma di Milano e i Figli dello Spirito Santo*. Tau 8. Milan: Edizioni Biblioteca francescana, 1998.

Biget, Jean-Louis. *Église, dissidences et société dans l'Occitanie médiévale*. Lyon: CIHAM Editions, 2020.

Brunn, Uwe. *Des contestataires aux "Cathares": Discours de réforme et propaganda antihérétique dans les pays du Rhin e de la Meuse avant l'Inquisition*. Collection des études augustiniennes, Série Moyen-Âge et temps modernes 41. Turnhout: Brepols, 2006.

Dalarun, Jacques. "La charte de Niquinta: Débats heuristiques, enjeux herméneutiques." *Aevum* 86 (2012): 535-48.

Frugoni, Arsenio, *Arnaldo da Brescia nelle fonti del secolo XII*. Studi Storici 8-9. Rome: Istituto Storico Italiano per il Medio Evo, 1954.

Grundmann, Herbert. "Oportet et haereses esse: Das Problem der Ketzerei im Spiegel der mittelalterlichen Bibelexegese." *Archiv für Kulturgeschichte* 45 (1963): 129-64. (Italian Translation: "Oportet et haereses esse: Il problema dell'eresia rispecchiato nell'esegesi biblica medievale." In *Medioevo ereticale*, edited by Ovidio Capitani, 29-66. Bologna: Il Mulino, 1977.)

Ilarino da Milano, *L'eresia di Ugo Speroni nella confutazione del maestro Vacario: Testo inedito del secolo XII con studio storico e dottrinale*. Studi e testi 115. Vatican City: Biblioteca Apostolica Vaticana, 1945.

Lucioni, Alfredo. "Eretici a Monforte d'Alba." In *Alba medievale: Dall'alto Medioevo alla fine della dominazione angioina, VI–XIV secolo*, edited by Rinaldo Comba, 323-37. Alba: Famija albèisa, 2010.

———. "L'età della Pataria." In *Diocesi di Milano*, edited by Adriano Caprioli et al., 167-94. Storia religiosa della Lombardia 2. Brescia: La Scuola, 1989.

Manselli, Raoul. *L'eresia del male*. 2nd ed. Naples: Morano, 1980.

Merlo, Grado Giovanni. *Eretici ed eresie medievali*. Universale Paperbacks Il Mulino 230. Bologna: Il Mulino, 1989.

———. "Salimbene e gli apostolici." In *Salimbeniana: Atti del Convegno per il VII Centenario di fra Salimbene (Parma 1987–1989)*, 144-57. Bologna: Radio Tau, 1991.

Miccoli, Giovanni. "Dolcino." In *Dizionario biografico degli Italiani*, 40:440-44. Rome: Istituto della Enciclopedia italiana, 1991.

Montesano, Marina. *Ai margini del Medioevo: Storia culturale dell'alterità*. Frecce 323. Rome: Carocci, 2021.

Moore, Robert Ian. *The War On Heresy*. Cambridge, MA: Harvard Belknap Press, 2012.

Paolini, Lorenzo. "L'eresia e l'inquisizione: Per una complessiva riconsiderazione del problema." In *Lo spazio letterario del Medioevo*, vol. 1, *Il Medioevo latino*, bk. 2, *La circolazione del testo*, edited by Guglielmo Cavallo, Claudio Leonardi, and Enrico Menestò, 361-405. Rome: Salerno, 1994.

———. *Eretici del Medioevo: L'albero selvatico*. Il mondo medievale: Sezione di storia delle istituzioni, della spiritualità e delle idee 20. Bologna: Pàtron Editore, 1989.

———. "Italian Catharism and Written Culture." In *Heresy and Literacy, 1000–1530*, edited by Peter Biller and Anne Hudson, 83-103. Cambridge: Cambridge University Press, 1994.

———. *Le piccole volpi: Chiesa ed eretici nel medioevo*. Edited by Riccardo Parmeggiani. Bologna: Bononia University Press, 2013.

Parmeggiani, Riccardo. "Papato, Impero e Comuni nella lotta contro gli eretici di 'Lombardia' (1198-1233)." In *Maggio 1218: Il Colloquio di Bergamo. Un dibattito all'inizio della storia valdese*, edited by Francesca Tasca, 161-74. Turin: Claudiana, 2020.

Pegg, Mark Gregory. *The Corruption of Angels: The Great Inquisition of 1245–1246*. Princeton, NJ: Princeton University Press, 2001.

———. "On Cathars, Albigenses and Good Men of Languedoc." *Journal of Medieval History* 27 (2001): 181-95.

Selge, Kurt-Victor. *Die ersten Waldenser mit Edition des "Liber antiheresis" des Durandus von Osca*. 2 vols. Arbeiten zur Kirchengeschichte 37. Berlin: de Gruyter, 1967.

Sennis, Antonio. "Questions about the Cathars." In *Cathars in Question*, edited by Antonio Sennis, 1-20. Heresy and Inquisitions in the Middle Ages 4. York: York Medieval Press, 2016.

Théry, Julien. "L'érésie des bons hommes: Comment nommer la dissidence religieuse non vaudoise ni béguine en Languedoc (XII$^e$-début du XIV$^e$ siècle)?" *Heresis* 36-37 (2002): 75-117.

Thouzellier, Christine. *Une somme anti-cathare: Le "Liber contra Manicheos" de Durand de Huesca*. Spicilegium sacrum Lovaniense 32. Leuven: Spicilegium sacrum Lovaniense Administration, 1964.

———. *Un traité cathare inédit du début du XIII<sup>e</sup> siècle, d'après le "Liber contra Manicheos" de Durand de Huesca*. Bibliothèque de la Revue d'histoire ecclésiastique 37. Leuven: Bibliothèque de l'Université, Bureaux de la Revue, 1961.

Vicaire, Marie-Humbert. "Rencontre à Pamiers des courants vaudois et dominicain (1207)." In *Vaudois languedociens et Pauvres catholiques*, 163-94. Cahiers de Fanjeaux 2. Toulouse: Privat, 1967.

Violante, Cinzio. "Eresie nelle città e nel contado in Italia dall'XI al XIII secolo." In Cinzio Violante, *Studi sulla cristianità medioevale: Società, istituzioni, spiritualità*, ed. Piero Zerbi, 349-79. Milan: Vita e Pensiero, 1975.

Vitolo, Giovanni. "Gli eretici di Roccamandolfi (1269-1270): Una Montaillou molisana?" In *"Sapiens, ut loquatur, multa prius considerat": Studi di storia medievale offerti a Lorenzo Paolini*, edited by Caterina Bruschi and Riccardo Parmeggiani, 119-48. Uomini e mondi medievali 64. Spoleto: Centro italiano di studi sull'alto medioevo, 2019.

Vogel, Lothar. "Il Rescriptum sul colloquio di Bergamo: Una fonte per la cultura e la spiritualità del primo valdismo." In *Maggio 1218: Il Colloquio di Bergamo. Un dibattito all'inizio della storia valdese*, edited by Francesca Tasca, 17-40. Turin: Claudiana, 2020.

Zambon, Francesco. "Dissimulation, secret et allégorie dans le dualism chrétien du Moyen Âge: Paulicianisme, bogomilisme, catharisme." *Annali di Scienze religiose* 4 (2011): 157-89.

Zanoni, Luigi. "Valdesi a Milano nel secolo XIII." *Archivio storico lombardo* 39 (1912): 5-22.

Zbìral, David. "La charte de Niquinta et le rassemblement de Saint-Félix, état de la question." In *1209–2009, cathares: Une histoire à pacifier?*, edited by Anne Brenon, 31-44. Portet-sur-Garonne: Loubatières, 2010.

———. "La charte de Niquinta et les récits sur les commencements des Églises cathares en Italie et dans le Midi." *Heresis* 44-45 (2006): 135-62.

Zerner, Monique, ed. *L'histoire du catharisme en discussion: Le "concile" de Saint-Félix (1167)*. Collection du Centre d'études médiévales de Nice 3. Nice: Centre d'études médiévales, 2001.

CHAPTER 11

# Urban Religion

*Frances Andrews*

            The present discussion works from two
premises. The first is that to comprehend urban religious practice in
medieval Italy ca. 1050–ca. 1300, a primary focus on the activities of
Latin Christians is justified by the long-standing and deepening political and cultural dominance of Christian ruling elites. In a volume
dedicated to Italy and Christianity this may seem obvious. What is perhaps less self-evident is that understanding medieval Italian Christianity also requires us to come to grips with the experience and perspective
of religious minorities on their own terms. Unlike northern Europe
in these centuries, Greek Christianity and Islam were significant presences alongside Judaism on the peninsula and its islands, particularly
in the south. No outline of religious practices can ignore them or their
interactions with Latin Christians. A second presupposition is that
the complex interweaving of religious experience across almost two

---

I would like to thank the audience of the School of History Seminar at the University of Durham who responded with useful feedback to an early version of the arguments presented here, and also five valiant colleagues, Eleonora Rava, Edward Coleman, David Ditchburn, Emily Michelson, and John Arnold, who each generously read and responded to earlier drafts. I am also grateful to the editors who conceived of this volume and who kindly invited me to contribute, and to Holger Kaasik who spotted a couple of slips at the last minute. Those that remain are entirely my own.

centuries, in a land of multiple, overlapping, and sometimes contrasting social and political ways of being, must be taken as a given, as must the impossibility of doing this complexity justice. The aim here is to exemplify a perspective, not to perfect it.

The entry point I have chosen, "urban religion," is initially offered as a more capacious framework than "civic religion," an evocative concept that is nonetheless insufficient for our purposes. To explain the logic behind this approach, we first need to understand the historiographical implications of writing about "civic" as against "urban religion." Of the two, civic religion, though much debated, has acquired near-normative status in writing about later medieval Italy. In most cases, it is used to indicate religious activities such as major processions, lay confraternities, or the burgeoning cults of patron saints, as sanctioned and promoted by civic leaders, who found in the Christian religion a means to amplify their authority and power.[1] For late medieval governmental powers lacking a monopoly on either force or legitimacy, religious language and behaviors might serve to validate secular practices and growing civic consciousness.[2]

The concept of "civic religion," which originated in studies of the ancient world, was first widely debated among late medieval Italianists in the 1970s and 1980s, following the pioneering work of, among others, David Herlihy, who had adopted the earlier coinage of "civic Christianity" for a study of Pistoia.[3] For more recent historians of the

---

1. For example, Trevor Dean, *The Towns of Italy in the Later Middle Ages: Selected Sources Translated and Annotated* (Manchester: Manchester University Press, 2000), 63–108. Nicholas Terpstra, "Civic Religion," in *The Oxford Handbook of Medieval Christianity*, ed. John H. Arnold (Oxford: Oxford University Press, 2014), 148–65.

2. For the lack of state monopoly and the persistence of intrigue, resistance, and conflict, see Andrea Gamberini, *The Clash of Legitimacies: The State-Building Process in Late Medieval Lombardy* (Oxford: Oxford University Press, 2018), originally published as *La legittimità contesa: Costruzione statale e culture politiche (Lombardia, secoli XII–XV)* (Rome: Viella, 2016).

3. David Herlihy, *Medieval and Renaissance Pistoia: The Social History of an Italian Town, 1200–1430* (New Haven, CT: Yale University Press, 1967), 241–58. This terminology is discussed and refined, for example, by David M. D'Andrea, *Civic Christianity in Renaissance Italy: The Hospital of Treviso, 1400–1530* (Rochester: University of Rochester Press, 2007), 3–5. For historiographical reviews of the debates, see, among many others, Andrew Brown, "Civic Religion in Late Medieval Europe," *Journal of Medieval History* 42 (2016): 338–56. See also Mauro Ronzani, "La 'chiesa del Comune' nelle città dell'Italia centro-settentrionale (secoli XII–XIV)," *Società e storia* 6, no. 21 (1983): 499–534. In the following years Ronzani preferred terminology based on "city/citizen": Mauro Ronzani, "La chiesa cittadina pisana tra Due e Trecento," in *Genova, Pisa e il Mediterraneo tra due e trecento: Per il VII centenario della battaglia della Meloria, Genova, 24–27 ottobre 1984*, Atti della società ligure di storia patria 24 (Genoa: Società Ligure di storia patria, 1984), 283–348; Mauro Ronzani, "Un aspetto della 'Chiesa di Città' a Pisa nel Due e Trecento: ecclesiastici e laici nella scelta del clero parrocchiale," in *Spazio, società e potere*

period the key contribution remains a conference dedicated to "la religion civique" organized by André Vauchez in 1993 and published by the École française de Rome. The printed papers range across north-central Italy and France (fifteen and nine respectively) along with five studies centered on other Christian locations and four on non-Christian realities.[4] The prominence of Christian Italy in the volume matches the perception of northern and central Italian religious life as quintessentially and precociously civic.

"Civic religion" has continued to be adopted, and contested, for other regions and particularly for the towns of Flanders, where the evidence is later.[5] But north-central Italy can claim to be the locus classicus. There are good reasons for this and for its continued use. "Civic religion" is a handy explanatory model that accommodates multiple divergences, as elites in different towns and cities varyingly strove to build or sustain civic-religious cults, deploying religious language and behaviors to legitimate lay practices and, with them, distinct communities of power. Although usually associated with the end of the Middle Ages, these practices can be seen taking shape in the center and north of the peninsula from the twelfth or early thirteenth centuries, during the period of interest here. They came in the wake of the relatively autonomous communal institutions that were transforming the political landscape and slowly, ever more profoundly, intervening in the functioning of daily life. In the south too, where early urban dynamism was once deemed to have been dismantled by Norman, Hohenstaufen, and Angevin rulers, recent research has done much to undermine that view, proving many

---

*nell'Italia dei Comuni*, ed. Gabriella Rossetti (Pisa: Gisem, 1986), 143–94. Others used Herlihy's "civic Christianity"; see for example Alba Maria Orselli, "Vita religiosa nella città medievale italiana tra dimensione ecclesiastica e 'cristianesimo civico': Una esemplificazione," *Annali del'Istituto storico italo-germanico in Trento* 7 (1981): 361–68.

4. André Vauchez, ed., *La religion civique à l'époque médiévale et moderne (chrétienté et islam): Actes du colloque de Nanterre (21–23 juin 1993)* (Rome: École française de Rome, 1995) has been described as giving "civic religion" its "program": Gabriella Signori, "Religion civique–Patriotisme urbain: Concepts au banc d'essai," *Histoire Urbaine* 27 (2010): 12. The other locations featured in *La religion civique* are Morocco (two essays), Syria, Egypt, colonial Mexico, Constantinople, Poland, Catalonia, and Nuremberg.

5. See Andrew Brown, *Civic Ceremony and Religion in Medieval Bruges, c.1300–1520* (Cambridge: Cambridge University Press, 2011), 15. Brown, "Civic Religion in Late Medieval Europe."

southern cities and towns to have been vigorous communities, where "civic religion" can also be found to apply.⁶

Civic religion has never claimed the whole picture, and previous historians have pointed out the limitations, including an undue focus on social and political elites.⁷ Indeed the allied attention to building projects and social good can acquire something of a nineteenth-century "civic" resonance. A possible equation of civic religion with secular, lay *control* of religion is perhaps one reason why Augustine Thompson used "civic religion" just once in his extended account of what he cheerfully identified as the "homely holiness" of the Italian cities, though he encompassed much that might go by the name.⁸ It is also "obvious," as Trevor Dean has written, "that not all religion in towns was 'civic' and that the impact of 'civic religion' over the countryside could be marginal."⁹ On the other hand, many religious practices we might want to identify with towns did spill into rural hinterlands (often roughly coterminous with dioceses), if they did not begin there.¹⁰

These and other ambiguities have led to ever greater precision in using "civic religion." Nicholas Terpstra has recently suggested that it best describes "the rituals, institutions and practices of religious belief as

---

6. On southern urban dynamism, see Paul Oldfield, *City and Community in Norman Italy* (Cambridge: Cambridge University Press, 2009) and also below.

7. As well as those named above, see Cécile Caby, "Religion urbaine et religion civique en Italie au Moyen Âge: Lieux, acteurs, pratiques," in *Villes de Flandre et d'Italie (XIIIᵉ–XVIᵉ siècle): Les enseignements d'une comparaison*, ed. Élisabeth Crouzet Pavan and Elodie Lecuppre-Desjardin, Studies in European Urban History (1100–1800) 12 (Turnhout: Brepols, 2008), 115–30; Pierre Monnet, "Pour en finir avec la religion civique?," *Histoire Urbaine* 27 (2010): 107–20 (who notes the very different understanding of civic religion in German historiography); Jörg Oberste, "Gibt es eine urbane Religiosität des Mittelalters?," in *Städtische Kulte im Mittelalter*, ed. Susanne Ehrich and Jörg Oberste, Forum Mitteralter, Studien 6 (Regensburg: Schnell und Steiner, 2010), 15–34; Patrick Boucheron, "Religion civique, religion civile, religion séculière: L'ombre d'un doute," *Revue de Synthèse* 134, no. 2 (2013): 161–83. None of these identify "urban religion" in the inclusive sense adopted in the present discussion.

8. Augustine Thompson, *Cities of God: The Religion of the Italian Communes, 1125–1325* (University Park: Pennsylvania State University Press, 2005), 11.

9. Dean, *Towns of Italy*, 63.

10. See Giorgio Chittolini, "Civic Religion and the Countryside in Late Medieval Italy," in *City and Countryside in Late Medieval and Renaissance Italy: Essays Presented to Philip Jones*, ed. Trevor Dean and Chris Wickham (London: Hambledon, 1990), 69–80. The idea that religious practices may have originated in the countryside was debated from the early 1960s onwards, particularly in the context of heresy: see Cinzio Violante, "Hérésies urbaines et hérésies rurales en Italie du XIᵉ au XIIIᵉ siècle," in *Hérésies et sociétés dans l'Europe pré-industrielle, 11ᵉ–18ᵉ siècles*, Communications et débats du Colloque de Royaumont [27–30 Mai 1962], ed. Jacques Le Goff (Paris: Mouton, 1968), 171–98.

these were shaped around the circumstances and goals of towns, cities and their inhabitants."[11] Admirably neutral, avoiding undue attribution of agency, this definition opens civic religious practice to all social classes, and yet provides clear contours. Civic religion encompasses the goal-driven, Christian religious practices of lay and cleric working together.[12]

Terpstra's refinements are well targeted and do much to answer the concerns of those who consider the idea of civic religion too secular, or too narrow. Yet as writers about "civic religion" might well agree, the term itself barely resonates with the complexity of urban religious experience in medieval Italy. Nor does it resolve the question of power. Where were the Jews, the Muslims, the migrants? What roles did women play? How was orthodoxy determined? What happened to doubt and unbelief? And where did urban clergy and regular religious fit when not engaged in goal-driven civic projects? In other words, where does the rest of ecclesiastical history or religious practice sit? In proposing that historians of the eleventh to fourteenth centuries focus on "urban" not just "civic" religion, I am taking my lead from a great deal of excellent research, as will become clear.[13] I am also pursuing my own longstanding interest in the way that the engagement of religious in public life was determined by factors that were local and political.[14] But I do

---

11. Terpstra, "Civic Religion," 148.

12. See also Guido Marnef and Anne-Laure Van Bruaene, "Civic Religion: Community, Identity and Religious Transformation," in *City and Society in the Low Countries, 1100–1600*, ed. Bruno Blondé, Marc Boone, and Anne-Laure Van Bruaene (Cambridge: Cambridge University Press, 2018), 128–61 (originally "Civic Religion: Gemeenschap, identiteit en religieuze vernieuwing," in *Gouden eeuwen: Stad en samenleving in de Lage Landen 1100–1600* [Ghent: Academia Press, 2016], 165–206), who underline the early role of religious orders (particularly the mendicants) and of semireligious communities, but also a broad swathe of the population in general, as against urban magistracies.

13. A study that adopts a regional rather than urban approach, but that encompasses the religious landscape with breadth and depth, demonstrating that "people of different faiths and different languages lived and died in close proximity," is Linda Safran, *The Medieval Salento: Art and Identity in Southern Italy* (Philadelphia: University of Pennsylvania Press, 2014), quote at 15.

14. Frances Andrews, "Regular Observance and Communal Life: Siena and the Employment of Religious," in *Pope, Church and City: Essays in Honour of Brenda M. Bolton*, ed. Frances Andrews, Christoph Egger, and Constance Rousseau, The Medieval Mediterranean 56 (Leiden: Brill, 2004), 357–83. Frances Andrews, "Living Like the Laity? The Negotiation of Religious Status in the Cities of Late Medieval Italy," *Transactions of the Royal Historical Society* 20 (2010) 27–55; Frances Andrews, ed., with Maria Agata Pincelli, *Churchmen and Urban Government in Late Medieval Italy, c.1200–c.1450: Cases and Contexts* (Cambridge: Cambridge University Press, 2013); Frances Andrews, "Como and Padua," in *Italy and Early Medieval Europe: Papers for Chris Wickham*, ed. Ross Balzaretti, Julia Barrow, and Patricia Skinner (Oxford: Oxford University Press, 2018), 533–37.

want to propose a corrective to the historiography, one that does justice to the differences to be found in these centuries and assigns diversity and multiplicity due space.

"Urban religion" is not a new coinage. In proposing its adoption for the twelfth to fourteenth centuries in Italy, I have in mind the definitions provided by Robert A. Orsi, a historian of religion in the modern American city. Orsi proposes that urban religion stands for

> the dynamic engagement of religious traditions (by which I mean constellations of practices, values, and beliefs, inherited and improvised, in ongoing exchanges among generations and in engagement with changing social, cultural, and intellectual contexts) with specific features of . . . cityscapes and with the social conditions of city life. The results are distinctly and specifically urban forms of religious practice, experience, and understanding.

Urban religion is, moreover,

> the site of converging and conflicting visions and voices, practices and orientations, which arise out of the complex desires, needs, and fears of many different people who have come to cities by choice or compulsion (or both) and who find themselves intersecting with unexpected others.[15]

Just as the city in modern America has been "cast as the necessary mirror of American civilization," so towns or, more often, episcopal cities are central to how historians characterize the Italian Middle Ages.[16] The different alignments of cathedrals, squares, walls, and markets shaped religious practices in the same way that the different topographies of Orsi's urban neighborhoods, schools, and recreational sites were fundamental to the kind of religious phenomena that emerged.[17]

Modern definitions and their implications for the modern imaginary cannot be swallowed whole and regurgitated to apply to the premodern. There is nothing in modern American religion to match the deepening authority of the twelfth- and thirteenth-century Roman Church, or the

---

15. Robert A. Orsi, "Crossing the City Line," in *Gods of the City: Religion and the American Urban Landscape*, ed. Robert A. Orsi (Bloomington: Indiana University Press, 1999), 43, 44.
16. Orsi, "Crossing the City Line," 5.
17. For the realignment of urban spaces, recent work in English includes Areli Marina, *The Italian Piazza Transformed: Parma in the Communal Age* (Philadelphia: University of Pennsylvania Press, 2012) and Dennis Romano, *Markets and Marketplaces in Medieval Italy, c. 1100 to c. 1440* (New Haven, CT: Yale University Press, 2014).

singular orientation of the Christian religion in the late medieval city. Orsi explores an open, more-or-less borderless space, unlike anything in the evidence for the Italian Middle Ages, where the ideal boundaries between a town and the hinterland, or a city and its *contado*, were clear-cut in social and political as well as legal terms, if more fluid in practice. As we will see, our medieval sources are multiple, eloquent, and sometimes to be found in unexpected places. Even so, had we all the texts, images, and objects ever produced in medieval Italy still extant, we still would not be able to match the pluralism of religious traditions, small and large, old and new, that Orsi's use of oral histories, novels, letters, images, and other documentation allowed him to trace in the streets of Italian Harlem or in the Bronx.[18] Nor is it feasible to engage here with the medieval evidence for identifying distinct urban subjectivities, though they certainly existed. When individual confession emerged as a social as well as a religious expectation in the course of the twelfth and thirteenth centuries, conceptions of sin and penance encouraged nuns dwelling in urban or suburban monasteries to shape a different perception of self to that of sex workers, for example, whether inside or outside the walls.[19] Yet thinking about urban religion is one way to avoid overprioritizing consensus, or the religious activities and values promoted and directed by secular and ecclesiastical elites, with orthodoxy somehow taken for granted, clearly delineated and practiced.

"Urban religion" too can be criticized: it is vague and draws no easy boundary between city and countryside, just as the urban hinterland might belong to a city in political terms and yet be sharply distinguished from it by legal and social practices. In this case, however, vagueness is a virtue. It comes closer to capturing the complicated, multiple practices, civic and non-civic, female and male, Christian and non-Christian, orthodox and nonorthodox, lay and clerical, of high medieval Italy. Thinking about urban religion allows space for the different scale of activities, from the intimately personal to the coordinated and communal, while also matching the relative abundance of our extant sources.

---

18. On Harlem, see Robert A. Orsi, *The Madonna of 115th Street: Faith and Community in Italian Harlem, 1880–1950*, 3rd ed. (New Haven, CT: Yale University Press, 2010); originally published 1985.

19. On confession, see Nicole Bériou, "Autour du Latran IV (1215): La naissance de la confession moderne et sa diffusion," in *Pratiques de la confession, des Pères du desert au Vatican II*, ed. Groupe de la Bussière (Paris: Les Éditions du Cerf, 1983), 73–93, and Peter Biller and A. J. Minnis, eds., *Handling Sin: Confession in the Middle Ages*, York Studies in Medieval Theology 2 (York: York Medieval Press, 1998).

Alongside (and also within) emerging larger, goal-driven civic initiatives, there was spontaneity, uncertainty, and changeability, as well as activities characteristic of the urban cityscape, but not aligned with the goals of the civic and Christian. "Urban religion" thus contains but is not restricted to "civic religion." Paying attention to it sharpens the silhouette of Roman, Christian orthodoxy.

The possibilities of this approach are explored below in a series of microstudies. Each has been selected because of the questions it raises, and where necessary is followed by a brief discussion of further implications and of change. There can be no attempt at comprehensive coverage, but each miniature is intended to engage with the boundaries of "civic religion" and where "urban religion" may find its uses.

## The *Mariegola* of San Giovanni Evangelista, Venice: Civic Religion Defined?

A powerful trace—almost a caricature—of what we might understand by "civic religion" can be captured in a single page from a *Mariegola* or Rule book produced for members of the Scuola di San Giovanni Evangelista in Venice. The explicit aim of the Scuola, founded in March 1261 as a fraternity of penitential flagellants or *disciplinati*, was "to do things that are pleasing to *messer* the Doge, the commune of Venice, and every faithful Christian."[20] These things, the regulations reveal, included acts of self-punishment by flagellation and in particular of charity toward both the other members of the Scuola and, more generally, the poor, a commonplace of "civic religion." The illumination on the first page of a copy of the *Mariegola* made in the 1360s (figure 1) shows a group of brothers making their promise before the altar.[21]

The new brothers' right hands are placed on the open copy of the *Mariegola* itself, an illustration of chapter 9 in the text:

> our warden, with his companions shall go before the altar of Saint John the Evangelist, each of them having his own mantle (*cappa*). And there he must receive them [the new brothers], holding the

---

20. Gian Andrea Simeone, ed., *La mariegola della Scuola Grande di San Giovanni Evangelista a Venezia (1261–1457)* (Venice: Scuola Grande di San Giovanni Evangelista, 2003), 37 (chap. 3).

21. Lyle Humphrey, *La miniatura per le confraternite e le arti Veneziane: Mariegole dal 1260 al 1460* (Verona: Cierre Edizioni, 2015), 240–45. For a later, equally clergy-free image from the same confraternity, see Boston, Public Library, MS Med., fol. 147r, reproduced in Humphrey, *La miniatura*, plate XXXIB.

**FIGURE 1.** Promise of new *Confradelli*: Opening Leaf of the Mariegola of the Scuola di San Giovanni Evangelista, Venice, detail. Workshop of the Venetian Miniaturist known as Giustino del fu Gherardino da Forlì, ca. 1366 (Venice Cini, MS 2041, fol. 1r).

*Mariegola* open in his hand and having [the new brother] put his hand on it, and telling him to promise to God, the Virgin Mary, and Saint John the Evangelist, to observe what is contained in it, making him kiss it and also kissing [the new brother] on the mouth, giving him peace.[22]

In the illumination, one of the leaders of the confraternity, painted in red, holds open the book of the *Mariegola*; another holds a cross. To the right, a banner of the confraternity shows John the Evangelist between two red crosiers.

The Scuola Grande di San Giovanni Evangelista was not an average confraternity. While its beginnings lie in a much wider wave of flagellant, revivalist, and penitential enthusiasm, in Venice the confraternity was also to become an alternative source of power and identity for those excluded from government councils by the *Serrata* (closure) of 1297 that made membership of the *Maggior Consiglio* hereditary.[23] Membership of the Scuola was restricted to 550, and the right to wear or to own the *cappa* was jealously guarded.[24] For historians, the Scuola Grande di San Giovanni has become emblematic of the political and spatial significance of a confraternity, famously captured by Giovanni Bellini in

---

22. Simeone, *La mariegola della Scuola Grande di San Giovanni Evangelista*, 44 (chap. 9).
23. On the flagellant movement, see Gary Dickson, "The Flagellants of 1260 and the Crusades," *Journal of Medieval History* 15 (1989): 227–67, and Giovanna Casagrande, *Religiosità penitenziale e città al tempo dei comuni* (Rome: Istituto Storico dei Cappuccini, 1995), 353–438.
24. Simeone, *La mariegola della Scuola Grande di San Giovanni Evangelista*, 39, 45 (chaps. 5 and 9). Chapter 5 refers to an informal waiting list for membership.

his 1496 painting of a confraternal procession circulating in Piazza San Marco now in the Galleria dell'Accademia, Venice.

The *Mariegola* image does not slavishly mimic the text, choosing to represent its promise as a collective action—the new brothers shown as a group placing their hands together on the open *Mariegola*—thereby encompassing the communal, shared yet exclusive intention of confraternal activity. But what makes the *Mariegola* an extreme case of "civic religion," understood as religious language and behaviors deployed to legitimate lay practices, is the use of a Christian altar and altarpiece together with liturgical modes (the promise to God and the Virgin, the kiss of peace), with a layman officiating. It is not that this or other confraternities precluded clerical involvement. Many such thirteenth-century flagellant bodies were aligned, willy-nilly, with the mendicant orders, whose centripetal powers have been well studied.[25] And elsewhere in the *Mariegola* of San Giovanni, we learn that at its three chapter meetings each year, a talented friar was to preach ("un valente frar se debia predicar").[26] But like most of its activities, the ritual of joining, of becoming a *confradello*, a religiously framed transition, did not involve the clergy. Christ blesses the moment from the figurated initial at the top of the manuscript page, but neither the illuminator nor the drafters of the text it accompanies considered inclusion of the clergy necessary to the construction of meaning. Membership was a religious undertaking that gave prominence and autonomy to the laity, a point further underscored by the vernacular language of the *Mariegola*.[27]

## The Fontana Maggiore Perugia: Converging Values and Beliefs

Completed in 1278, the spectacular Fontana Maggiore of the Commune of Perugia (figure 2) marks the terminus of an impressive engineering

---

25. See also the chapter by Giovanna Casagrande in this volume. On confraternities, see for example, Roisin Cossar, "The Quality of Mercy: Confraternities and Public Power in Medieval Bergamo," *Journal of Medieval History* 27 (2001): 139–57; Marina Gazzini, *Studi confraternali: Orientamenti, problemi, testimonianze* (Florence: Firenze University Press, 2009). See also Jacques Chiffoleau, "Note sur le polycentrisme religieux urbaine à la fin du moyen âge," in *Religion et société urbaine au Moyen Âge: Études offertes à J. Biget*, ed. Patrick Boucheron and Jacques Chiffoleau (Paris: Éditions de la Sorbonne, 2000), 227–52.

26. Simeone, *La mariegola della Scuola Grande di San Giovanni Evangelista*, 42 (chap. 7).

27. See also the chapter by Marina Gazzini on confraternities in this volume.

FIGURE 2.   Fontana Maggiore, Perugia. Photo courtesy of Abbey Taylor.

project, bringing water uphill over three miles, from Monte Pacciano to the center of this foremost Umbrian city.

Located in the main square between the cathedral of San Lorenzo, the episcopal residence, and the public buildings of the commune, the fountain's complex decorative program eloquently conveys a combination of messages. The lowest tier of the water basins features panels with familiar Old Testament pairings: Adam and Eve, David and Goliath, Samson and Delilah. On the upper level stand local and less local saints: Lawrence and Ercolano, patrons of cathedral and commune; Peter and Paul, patrons of the papacy, which was frequently resident in thirteenth-century Perugia; John the Baptist, communal saint par excellence; and Benedict, patron, among others, of the Silvestrine (Benedictine) congregation of Brother Bevignate, who designed and oversaw the fountain's stone design and construction, on behalf of the *popolo*-led commune.[28] The imagery thus embodies a combination of

---

28. See Attilio Bartoli Langeli, *Notai: scrivere documenti nell'Italia medievale* (Rome: Viella, 2006), 223. On John the Baptist as a communal saint, see Frances Andrews, "Doubting John?," in *Doubting Christianity: The Church and Doubt*, ed. Frances Andrews, Charlotte Methuen, and Andrew Spicer, Studies in Church History 52 (Cambridge: Cambridge University Press, 2016),

the communal, the papal, and—if we allow Bevignate any role in the choice of saints portrayed—the personal.

The multilayered Old Testament and saintly iconography of Perugia's Fontana is not the whole design. Other panels on the lower basin show the Labors of the Months, the Liberal Arts, scenes from Aesop's Fables, and the symbols of the commune, the Griffin and the Lion. Further standing figures on the upper basin include the *podestà*, Matteo da Correggio, and classicizing personifications of the cities of Rome and Perugia. The leading sculptural workshop of the moment, that of Nicola and Giovanni Pisano, carved the statuary and the extensive metrical inscription running around the rim of the upper stone basin, probably devised by a prominent local notary that in its praise of the city also incorporated praise of Fra Bevignate.[29] A Perugian atelier completed the bronze nymphs and third basin at the top. The multiple messages combined in this one object typify the complex juxtaposition of different discourses in late medieval Italian religion. Christian biblical and saintly narratives were embedded with non-Christian and the Christianized. The religious, secular, and political worlds of Perugia intertwined to express pride, abundance, and manifold personal and institutional ties. Similar discourses could be traced in the cathedrals of episcopal cities, joint building projects between laity and clergy, whose interests combined both in the fabric of the new buildings and in the *Opere*, the organizations that oversaw their construction, in which the laity often took the lead, increasingly aware of what they could do, as was becoming the case in Pisa already in the late eleventh century.[30] Sponsored by the commune, the Fontana Maggiore began perhaps as medieval civic religion at its most creative and, through the pumping of water, literally bound city and countryside together. It is also, however,

---

22 and references provided there. Holger Kaasik completed a PhD dissertation at the University of St Andrews in 2022 that articulates the divergent cults of saints in the liturgical calendars of three Umbrian centers: "Patterns of Commemoration in Central Italy: Manuscript Calendars and Social Time in Perugia, Assisi and Gubbio, c. 1100-1500."

29. For the inscription and the meaning of a "plausible" attribution to the notary Bovicello, see Bartoli Langeli, *Notai*, 225-32.

30. See Mauro Ronzani, "Dall' 'edificatio ecclesiae' all' 'Opera di S. Maria': Nascita e primi sviluppi di un'istituzione nella Pisa dei secoli xi e xii," in *Opera, carattere e ruolo delle fabbriche cittadine fino all'inizio dell'età moderna: Atti della Tavola rotonda, Villa i Tatti, Firenze, 3 aprile 1991*, ed. Margaret Haines and Lucio Riccetti (Florence: Olschki, 1996), 1-70. On the financing of cathedrals shared between bishops, chapters, lords, and the faithful, though mostly focused on the more abundant evidence surviving from the later Middle Ages, see Wim Vroom, *Financing Cathedral Building in the Middle Ages: The Generosity of the Faithful* (Amsterdam: Amsterdam University Press, 2010).

a powerful example of *urban* religion, not constrained to a single Christian and biblical discourse.

## The *Ordinarius* of Padua: Ongoing Engagement with Cityscapes

The surviving *Ordinarius* of the cathedral of Padua, an "Ordinal" or guide to the performance of the liturgy completed in the late thirteenth century, describes the bishop passing from church to church, blessing and praying at each location as he itinerated around the city on the three Rogation Days before Ascension. Preceded by boys and clerics carrying crosses, an image of a dragon, and barefoot acolytes carrying the relics of saints in a "very beautiful chest" (pulcherrimam cassam), the bishop was to be followed by other clergy and scholars carrying the necessary liturgical books and holy water, and—since the *Ordinarius* describes the bishop setting out "with clergy and people"— presumably by the laity. At the front of the procession, the first of the crosses was identified with the boys ("parva crux que vocatur crux puerorum"). Two other crosses were specifically identified: that of the clergy (carried upright on day one, sloping on day two, and flat on day three) and, after the bishop, the cross "for the people" (pro populo) for which no lay bearers were mentioned. The itineraries encompassed *capellae* ([incipient] parishes), monastic, and hospital buildings. At the door of each church the procession was met by its own clergy and by the ringing of bells, miniature *adventus* or "reception" ceremonies.[31] At each new building the assembled company sang an antiphon before the door, recited prayers both on entry and inside, and placed the relics on the altar for the length of a penitential psalm. On each occasion the bishop asperged any men and women present with holy water. He also blessed the waters of the river, presumably at the (fairly numerous) bridges the processions crossed.[32]

---

31. On the collaborative legitimation embedded in the clerical *adventus*, see now Emil Lauge Christensen, "Visits from Rome: Papal Legates and the *Adventus* in English Accounts, c. 1170–1250" (PhD dissertation, Aalborg University, 2019). This is forthcoming as a monograph with Boydell Press.

32. Giulio Cattin and Anna Vildera, eds., *Il "Liber ordinarius" della Chiesa di Padova: Padova Biblioteca Capitolare, ms. E 57, sec. XIII* (Padua: Istituto per la storia ecclesiastica padovana, 2002), 140–45. See also Antonio Lovato, "Le processioni della Cattedrale di Padova nei secoli XIII–XV," in Cattin and Vildera, *Il "Liber ordinarius" della Chiesa di Padova*, cxxiv.

The Padua *Ordinarius* ordained Rogation Day processions that would be complex to set in train, involving carefully coordinated performances (and with lunches provided for all the clerical participants). Moreover, though the route always started at the cathedral, it differed for each of the three days, encompassing in total more than fifty churches, a clue to the density of the ecclesiastical presence, without considering the shrines, wayside crosses, and painted religious images that would have existed on almost every street corner.[33] On day one they headed first to the female Benedictine monastery of San Prosdocimo, continued through the northwest of the city visiting monasteries of nuns and monks, canonesses and canons, a hospital of the Crucifers, and at least six churches identifiable as *capellae* before returning to the cathedral. On day two, the procession extended to twenty-three churches in the center and east of the city, of which at least seven were *capellae*. The final day covered the longest distance, visiting fifteen churches to the south of the center, including another five *capellae*.[34]

Antonio Lovato has suggested that the different itineraries around Padua marked the distinct sociopolitical layers of the city, moving from the tenth- and eleventh-century chapels and churches closest to episcopal and feudal power on day one, to settlements associated with the commune on day two, and then to the outer suburbs, areas of expansion including the churches of the mendicants and a leper hospital, on day three.[35] Whether this was the result of haphazard accretion or conscious planning, the itineraries could therefore be understood as mapping a landscape of urban religion in social and political as well as religious terms. In practice, however, the scheme and chronology are not so clear-cut: routes crossed each other, and the churches visited on day one included monasteries of the local congregation of White Benedictines (the *ordo Sancti Benedicti de Padua*) founded only in the early thirteenth century, whereas on day three, alongside the mendicants, the procession visited the sixth-century basilica of Santa Giustina, as also four churches datable to the tenth or eleventh century (two of which would become *capellae* in 1170: Santa Giuliana and San Michele). The distinctions were probably not as manifest as Lovato imagined, but

---

33. See George Bent, *Public Painting and Visual Culture in Early Republican Florence* (New York: Cambridge University Press, 2016).
34. Lovato, "Le processioni della Cattedrale di Padova," cxlviii–clvi and figs. 9–12.
35. Lovato, "Le processioni della Cattedrale di Padova," cxlvi–cxlvii. See also Giulio Cattin, "L'edizione di un 'Liber Ordinarius,'" in Cattin and Vildera, *Il "Liber ordinarius" della Chiesa di Padova*, xxvii.

he is right to assume that churches were anchored in socially and politically distinct communities and that those experiencing the procession could have spotted the differences. If those watching did so from "their" *capellae*, we can be confident that the numbers of immigrants encountered on day one would have been fewer than those found near the edges of the city on day three.

Major processions similar to those on the Rogation Days in Padua took place in every cathedral city, and by the time of the *Ordinarius*, routes and routines were well developed, each taking account of specific cityscapes and their clerical and lay communities. In Salerno, south of Naples, the archiepiscopal procession on May 6, the feast of the Translation of Saint Matthew, followed an elaborate format already by the late twelfth century. The front of the Salerno procession was, like the Rogation Day processions in Padua, led by a boy carrying a cross, followed by other boys in age order, the clergy of the *choro*, the *primicerius*, archdeacon, acolytes carrying candelabra, thuribles, and a cross, the chaplains of dependent abbots and of suffragan bishops, and then the abbots themselves of the eight abbeys subject to the jurisdiction of the archbishop of Salerno. Next came the chapter of the cathedral (in order), the suffragan bishops of Sarno, Acerno, Nusco, and Marsico, and finally, the archbishop, preceded by a subdeacon carrying a golden cross, the bishops of Capaccio and Policastro to his right and left. In the cathedral itself the representatives (*filiani*) of the fifteen urban parishes were each to offer the archbishop a flowering branch decorated with roses, flowers, and lighted candles. The thirteen baptismal churches (*pievi*) of the diocese were also involved.[36] Participation in this spectacularly designed event articulated the ecclesiastical hierarchy centered on the archbishop.

Writing about civic processions thirty years ago, Giorgio Chittolini proposed that "in such ceremonies the elements of civil celebration are obvious and easily distinguishable from those ceremonies with a more specifically religious content."[37] The central elements of the processions on Rogation Days in Padua or on the feast of the Translation of Saint Matthew in Salerno would presumably fall into Chittolini's second category. Neither sequence explicitly involved the secular elite, except insofar as they may have been linked to one of the churches

---

36. Giovanni Vitolo, "Città e Chiesa nel Mezzogiorno medievale: La processione del santo patrono a Salerno (secolo XII)," *Studi Storici* 41 (2000): 978–79.

37. Chittolini, "Civic Religion and the Countryside," 72.

visited, or the kin of those processing. In Padua on Rogation Days, the *Ordinarius* constructed the laity as followers, a perspective that is hardly surprising in a book instructing the clergy on how to perform: the laity just needed to know what to do when a procession arrived at a church, perhaps at most to be asperged with holy water. Lay men and women seem to have been largely absent from the Salerno procession too (unless perhaps as representatives of the parishes). Yet in neither case is it likely that the procession's articulation of the hierarchy of the city or archdiocese was conceived in exclusively religious or ecclesiastical terms.

There is, of course, plenty of evidence for Chittolini's "more specifically religious" elements in other urban processions, many of which involved the laity. The Padua *Ordinarius* provides details of several sequences that remained in the liturgical heartland of baptistery and cathedral. During High Mass on the Sundays from Septuagesima to Easter the bishop was required to process out of the cathedral to "asperge men and women with holy water" in the baptistery before returning.[38] The laity also participated in processions on the fairly restricted Paduan list of solemn feasts in the *Ordinarius*: the Purification of the Virgin on February 2, Palm Sunday, Good Friday (as penitents seeking reconciliation), Easter, and Pentecost.

The active contribution of the laity was undoubtedly more evident in some set-piece civic processions, such as those for the August vigil and feast of the Assumption of the Virgin in Modena, Siena, and Verona, among others. Of these, most famously, the Sienese procession in the middle of August was dominated by the commune and by civic concerns. Citizens and residents of the countryside enacted their political relations through the size, quality, and weight of candles carried by guilds, *contrade* (quarters), and subject communities, the minutiae regulated by communal decree.[39] Their candles were brought to the

---

38. Cattin and Vildera, *Il "Liber ordinarius" della Chiesa di Padova*, 89.

39. For the feast of the Assumption in Siena, see "Constitutum Comunis Senarum," ed. Ludovico Zdekauer, *Il constituto del comune di Siena dell'anno 1262* (Milan: U. Hoepli, 1897), 80, 276, 288, 384 (distinction 1, rubric 95; distinction 3, rubrics 3 [addition], 45, and 356). The evidence becomes clearer in the later vernacular version: Mahmoud Salem Elsheikh, ed., *Il costituto del Comune di Siena volgarizzato nel MCCCIX-MCCCX*, 4 vols. (Siena: Fondazione Monte dei Paschi di Siena, 2002), 1:47-52, 185, 404-7, 411-12; 2:23, 584-85 (distinction 1, rubrics 36, 212, 583, 586; distinction 3, rubric 51; and distinction 6, rubric 84). For discussions in English, see Diana Norman, "Civic Rituals and Images," in Diana Norman, *Siena and the Virgin: Art and Politics in a Late Medieval City State* (New Haven, CT: Yale University Press, 1999), 1-5, and Daniel Waley, *Siena and the Sienese in the Thirteenth Century* (Cambridge: Cambridge

cathedral, just as they were, for example, in the much smaller town of Cortona.[40] Yet in Pisa under the Popolo, whereas most offerings of candles were again brought to the cathedral, the "large candles" required from Sardinia, a politically sensitive lordship, were to be brought to the office of the *podestà* and *capitano*, hubs of secular government.[41] More or less explicit political signaling of this sort is easily identified in relation to Assumption festivities elsewhere: in Messina, for example, Latin Christian celebration of the feast of the Assumption is traditionally dated to 1282 and the Sicilian Vespers when, according to Bartolomeo di Neocastro—a Messinese judge writing a decade later—a vision of Mary was seen during fighting as the Angevins were ejected from the island, to be replaced by the Aragonese.[42]

For the Christian laity, living in an episcopal city necessarily brought awareness of, if not keen involvement in, both processions that were more obviously civil or civic in organization and intent and those with mostly religious elements, dominated by the clergy. The great Assumption processions drew in large numbers. "More specifically religious" undertakings could also be substantial. Something of this can be gauged in extant account books of the cathedral chapter of Padua toward the end of our period (1305). These record numerous related payments, covering not just the cost of the meals for clerical participants on Rogation Days, or the five hundred hosts for the celebration of Mass, but also essential maintenance, such as the three *grossi* spent on cleaning up the church after it had been left in a mess (*turpefacta*) with olive leaves on Palm Sunday.[43] Both civic and more obviously religious processions implicated large swathes of the population, lay and clerical: their meaning is best captured by thinking in terms of "urban religion."

As well as offering a straightforward way to show how urban religious practices engaged with "cityscapes," sources for processional liturgies

---

University Press, 1991). Thompson, *Cities of God*, 166–74, gives an account of the festivities for the Assumption pooled from sources for various cities.

40. See Simone Allegria and Valeria Capelli, eds., *Statuto del Comune di Cortona (1325–1380)* (Florence: Leo S. Olschki, 2014), 434 (book 4, rubric 75).

41. Antonella Ghignoli, ed., *I brevi del Comune e del Popolo di Pisa dell'anno 1287* (Rome: Istituto Storico Italiano per il Medio Evo, 1998), 248 (rubric CLIIII).

42. Bartholomaei de Neocastro, "Historia Sicula, AA 1250–1293," ed. Giuseppe Paladino, *Rerum Italicarum Scriptores*, new ed., vol. 13, bk. 3 (Bologna: Nicola Zanichelli, 1921–22), 26–27 (chap. XL [1282]).

43. Claudio Bellinati, "Specimen expensarum et reddituum, 1305 BcapP, Diversa X (41)," in *Nuovi studi sulla cappella di Giotto all'Arena di Padova (25 marzo 1303–2003)* (Padua: Il Poligrafo, 2003), Appendice documentaria, 50.

allow us to trace something of Orsi's "inherited and improvised" practices that, while not exposed in these sources in "ongoing *exchanges*" between generations, can certainly be seen transforming between them and in engagement with changing contexts. In thirteenth-century Padua, alongside inherited practices, a new generation added a procession on April 13 for the feast of Saint Anthony (d. 1231, canonized 1232), whose basilica was in construction from 1265. Later liturgical books track the way subsequent generations continued to innovate and improvise, inserting new churches into the route of the Padua Rogation Day processions, or adding a procession for *Corpus Domini*, for example.[44] The combination of inherited practices and local changes brought with it the multiplication of local distinctiveness. Lovato notes that in late thirteenth-century Padua, responsories involving soloists, or soloists and a choir, were more common than antiphons involving two choirs, whereas the latter were preferred in relatively nearby Aquileia and Cividale.[45] Sound worlds differed. Religious practice was a local and distinct dialect of a single language, in this case, that of Latin Christianity.

Set-piece civic processions not only contained evident religious elements but were also part of a clerically determined liturgical year. But this sort of logic also works in the other direction. The "more specifically religious" processions of the clergy involved sociopolitical, not just religious choices, including the sequence of churches to be visited. They implicated the laity, even if in passive roles. And once the laity were involved, processions of all types surely acquired something like the multilayered devotional activities of the *Festa della Madonna* in Italian Harlem described by Orsi. The debris of olive leaves in Padua cathedral implies crowds coming together in attendance. A question nonetheless remains: Where were the laity when the cathedral's clergy and boys sat down to their lunch on procession days? Urban religion, too, made social and community demarcations evident.

## Recluses in Pisa and Siena: Distinctly and Specifically Urban Forms?

A practice that fits the urban label without always aligning with the civic is that of urban voluntary reclusion. Dedicated to prayer and

---

44. For the additions to the Padua Rogation Day processions, see Lovato, "Le processioni della Cattedrale di Padova," cxlvii–clvi.
45. Lovato, "Le processioni della Cattedrale di Padova," cxiv.

asceticism, often dependent on the goodwill of others to support them, urban recluses sought out the toughest form of rejection of self and the body advocated in medieval Christian teaching. These were not tertiaries, or the beguines of the southern Low Countries, who gathered in beguinages from the 1230s onward, some of which grew to number hundreds of women working in local industries such as cloth production, living in houses arranged within convent-like enclosures, including perhaps a chapel, bakery, and infirmary.[46] Recluses instead remained enclosed in a cell for extended periods, sometimes until death, and lived alone, if with a servant to assist nearby. Their form of life broke with the household-based social norms of either monastic or secular kin.

The scale and the retrievable details of the presence of recluses vary greatly by location. In the south of the peninsula recluses have been identified in Naples, in Palermo, in Benevento, and in a few minor centers, but not yet in large numbers anywhere, though this is likely to be the combined effect of research priorities and source loss. Recent research shows that recluses were also to be found in good numbers north of the Apennines—in both major and minor settlements.[47] It remains the case, however, that most of what we know comes from central Italy.

In Pisa, studied by Eleonora Rava, recluses are now most visible in the pious legacies of locals, receiving gifts from testators who were mainly women and mostly from artisan and mercantile families.[48] The evidence begins in the mid-thirteenth century, when making a will first became a widespread practice, and largely peters out by the second half of the fourteenth century. Initially located in groups of cells along the main roads some way out of the city (and therefore relatively rural), in the early fourteenth century the cells and their occupants, mostly female, moved into the urban streets of Pisa, it would seem, for reasons of security. This put them close to the foci of public life and to a larger

---

46. Walter Simons, *Cities of Ladies: Beguine Communities in the Medieval Low Countries, 1200–1565* (Philadelphia: University of Pennsylvania Press, 2001).

47. Frances Andrews and Eleonora Rava, eds., "Ripensare la reclusione volontaria nell'Europa mediterranea (XIII–XVI secolo)," 2 vols., *Quaderni di storia religiosa medievale* 24, nos. 1 and 2 (2021).

48. Eleonora Rava, "Le testatrici e le recluse: Il fenomeno della reclusione urbana nei testamenti delle donne pisane (secoli XIII–XIV)," in *Margini di libertà: Testamenti femminili nel medioevo*, ed. Maria Clara Rossi, Biblioteca dei Quaderni di storia religiosa 7 (Caselle di Sommacampagna [VR]: Cierre edizioni, 2010), pp. 313–14; Eleonora Rava, "Eremite in città: Il fenomeno della reclusione urbana femminile nell'età comunale. Il caso di Pisa," *Revue Mabillon*, n.s., 21 (2010), 139–62.

range of ecclesiastical institutions, including monasteries, hospitals, and parish churches. The pinnacle of Pisan legacies was in the early 1300s, which also saw a peak in will making, and indeed the two can be linked, insofar as both offer evidence for choices being made on a personal scale while conditioned by social and notarial norms. By contrast, in 1348 and 1362, when plague struck, large numbers of wills were still being drawn up, but recluses more or less disappeared as beneficiaries.

In Siena, studied by Alison Clark Thurber, the main evidence for recluses is to be found in the records of regular pious donations paid out by the treasurers of the commune.[49] More often situated at or inside the city gates than in Pisa, Sienese recluses can first be documented in the 1230s, but by the mid-fourteenth century they were located close to female monastic houses and very rarely to parish churches. In the early 1340s, for instance, there were over sixty women living as recluses near the house of Clare nuns at Santa Petronilla. So reclusion need not be as isolated, or as "individual" as it might at first appear. It was also strongly determined by social imperatives: becoming a recluse who was accepted by the wider community required at least some familial and ecclesiastical backing.[50]

The twinned case-studies of Pisan and Sienese recluses go some way toward matching Orsi's "distinct and specifically urban forms of religious practice." It would be difficult to imagine such clusters of women surviving alone in cells without being in an urban population center, or on the roads nearby. How far was this "civic religion"? In Siena recluses could expect regular donations from the city government, agreed by the communal councils and incorporated into urban legislation, the payments recorded alongside other government expenses. In Pisa no such outgoings are documented, even though, like Siena, other religious institutions were recipients of regular alms. Did this make Pisan recluses

---

49. Alison Clark Thurber, "Female Urban Reclusion in Siena at the Time of Catherine of Siena," in *A Companion to Catherine of Siena*, ed. George Ferzoco, Beverley M. Kienzle, and Carolyn Muessig, Brill's Companions to the Christian Tradition 32 (Boston: Brill, 2012), 47–72.

50. See Eleonora Rava and Alison Clark Thurber, "Recluse: Due casi a confronto (Siena e Pisa)," in *Beata Civitas: Pubblica pietà e devozioni private nella Siena del '300*, ed. Anna Benvenuti and Pierantonio Piatti, Toscana sacra 5 (Florence: SISMEL-Edizioni del Galluzzo, 2016), 425–52. The authors provide extensive earlier bibliography. Alison Clark Thurber translated some wills with legacies for recluses in *Medieval Towns: A Reader*, ed. Maryanne Kowaleski (Peterborough, ON: Broadview Press, 2006; repr. Toronto: University of Toronto Press, 2008), 265–68. Eleonora Rava, a Marie Skłodowska-Curie Postdoctoral Fellow at the University of St. Andrews 2017–19, is pursuing a large-scale study of recluses in Italy that will update this outline. See also Andrews and Rava, "Ripensare la reclusione volontaria nell'Europa mediterranea."

less civic than those in Siena? It surely made the women more vulnerable and more reliant on the support and interest of urban neighbors.

## Benjamin of Tudela and the Jews in Italy: Dynamic Engagement of Religious Traditions

In the late twelfth century, a Spanish merchant and Sephardic Jew known to historians as Benjamin of Tudela journeyed through Italy on his way to and from the eastern Mediterranean, recording in Hebrew the Jewish communities he encountered. Benjamin's route did not include all the centers on the Italian peninsula and its islands where Jews were living in the 1160s and early 1170s. Even so, he counted over 4,830 families, of which just sixty-two were north of Rome. In the coastal port of Genoa he found two Jewish men, originally from Ceuta in North Africa: a rabbi and his brother, presumably living there with their families. As he traveled further south the numbers (and his admiration for the land) increased. In Pisa he recorded twenty Jewish heads of household and in Lucca forty, in Rome two hundred, in Capua three hundred, in Naples five hundred, and in Salerno six hundred, perhaps the largest Jewish community on the mainland (and surely witnesses to the Translation of Saint Matthew processions described above). On his way back from the East, Benjamin traversed the island of Sicily, estimating some 200 Jewish households in Messina and 1,500 in Palermo.[51]

As well as the numbers, Benjamin of Tudela also offers us glimpses of the activities of the Jews he encountered. In Rome, he wrote, Jews "occupy an honorable position and pay no tribute." One of them, Rabbi Jechiel, was working for Pope Alexander III (d. 1181) as "steward of his house and all that he has." Elsewhere Benjamin came across Jewish merchants and, in Brindisi, ten who were dyers. But he was most interested in the numerous deeply learned rabbis he met and their writings. The vast scope of this Jewish learning was certainly not a figment of Benjamin's imagination. Like manuscripts in any language, whether they fell out of use because of the arrival of print or were forced out of use by the activities of inquisitors, the parchment once used for Hebrew books was frequently put to new purpose in sixteenth- and seventeenth-century book covers and bindings. This presents us with innumerable fragments of eleventh- to fourteenth-century Hebrew

---

51. *The Itinerary of Benjamin of Tudela: Critical Text, Translation and Commentary*, ed. Marcus N. Adler (New York: Philipp Feldheim, 1907), 5–10, 78–79.

texts, dozens of copies of bibles, commentaries, rabbinic legal texts, and literature, together with smaller numbers of Hebrew dictionaries, medical or scientific texts, and liturgy. They include copies of the Talmud, much-contested by Christians in the thirteenth century and beyond (though the set-piece debates were not in Italy).[52]

Although always a tiny percentage of the total population, in many urban centers the Jews were a significant religious and learned presence ca. 1050–ca. 1300.[53] And despite Benjamin's southern focus, this included not just port cities like Salerno or Palermo, but many locations further north. In twelfth-century Rome, the heartland of the Roman Church, moreover, the Jewish community played an important and visible role in the *adventus* ceremony (later the *possesso*) for new popes entering Rome as lords, at least in 1145, 1165, 1191, and 1198, when they presented a copy of the Torah and, it may be, sang the pope's praises in Hebrew.[54]

Within little more than a generation, like Jews everywhere in Latin Europe, the families Benjamin encountered would be instructed through the legislation of the Fourth Lateran Council (1215) to wear a badge distinguishing them from Christians. Bishops, ecclesiastical synods, and secular rulers often ignored or modified papal directives, and indeed evidence for the enforcement of this measure, like others

---

52. See Mauro Perani and Enrica Sagradini, *Talmudic and Midrashic Fragments from the Italian Genizah: Reunification of the Manuscripts and Catalogue* (Florence: La Giuntina, 2004), one result of a much larger research project led by Mauro Perani of the University of Bologna. The numbers later expand: of 495 manuscripts identified in 803 fragments from the Archivio di Stato in Bologna, one can be dated to the eleventh century, five to the twelfth, eighteen to the twelfth-thirteenth centuries, thirty-four to the thirteenth, ninety-one to the thirteenth-fourteenth centuries, 157 to the fourteenth, fifty-eight to the fifteenth, and two to the fifteenth-sixteenth centuries. See Mauro Perani, "La '*Genizah* italiana': Caratteri generali e stato della ricerca," *Morashà*, https://www.morasha.it/zehut/mp02_ghenizaitaliana.html, accessed March 15, 2019. On the disputations, see most recently, Alexander Fidora and Görge K. Hasselhoff, eds., *The Talmud in Dispute in the High Middle Ages* (Bellaterra: Universitat Autònoma de Barcelona, 2019).

53. There are numerous city-based studies of Jews in Italy. See, for example, Aldo Saccaro, *Gli Ebrei di Palermo, dalle origini al 1492* (Florence: Giuntina, 2008). For more general studies consult the volumes of *Italia Judaica*.

54. On the complex relations between popes and Jews in Rome and interpretation of these encounters that bore Easter-like messages, see Marie Thérèse Champagne, "The Relationship between the Papacy and the Jews in Twelfth-Century Rome" (PhD diss., Louisiana State University, 2005); Marie Thérèse Champagne, "Celestine III and the Jews," in *Pope Celestine III (1191–1198): Diplomat and Pastor*, ed. John Doran and Damian J. Smith (Aldershot: Ashgate, 2008), 271–86; Marie Thérèse Champagne, "Walking through the Shadows of the Past: The Jewish Experience of Rome in the Twelfth Century," *Medieval Encounters: Jewish, Christian, and Muslim Cultures in Confluence and Dialogue* 17 (2011): 464–94.

designed to prevent contact, is hard to come by. As Jeffrey Wayno has observed, "the process of disseminating the [1215] reform decrees was much messier and more complicated" than we might imagine.[55] But under the Angevin and Aragonese rulers in the south at the end of the 1200s, the pressure to convert was to be backed up with threats, or actual violence, comparable to that found in France or England in these decades. The status of Jews as "servants of the royal chamber" that had provided protection now made them vulnerable to exploitation. Even so, Jewish communities continue to be widely documented, both in the south of the peninsula and in towns much further north, where immigration seems to have been relatively frequent. In early fourteenth-century Assisi, for example, a number of newly arrived Jews could be found moneylending, and one created a brief partnership with a Christian to trade in almonds.[56] This small group of migrants acquired citizenship and with it the need to build a house, soon followed by the construction of two buildings of white stone, checked by messengers sent by the *podestà* of the commune, the elegant detailing copied as per contract from the houses of neighbors. Relations with these mostly Roman Christian neighbors were not always smooth: there are individual cases of fines and controversies in the following decades. At the same time the Assisi commune and the local clergy, including the canons of the cathedral, frequently relied on money borrowed from the Jews of Assisi, ignoring any ecclesiastical sanction.[57] It is not easy to identify Jewish devotional practice in such records, but the experience of these Jews living in a Christian commune aligns as closely with the diversity and creativity described by Benjamin of Tudela (or Robert Orsi) as it does with the more familiar, though nonetheless painful, narratives of exclusion and persecution.

In these years around 1300, the end of our period, the efforts to marginalize Jews become more visible. A reforming synod called by the patriarch of Ravenna issued a decree that reiterated the conventional,

---

55. See Jeffrey M. Wayno, "Rethinking the Fourth Lateran Council of 1215," *Speculum* 93 (2018): 611–37, with notes to earlier bibliography on the subject; quote at 616.

56. On the multifaceted nature of Jewish economic life, see Anna Sapir Abulafia, *Christian–Jewish Relations, 1000–1300: Jews in the Service of Medieval Christendom* (Harlow: Longman, 2010). And on the Jews as integral to the Italian Middle Ages, Giacomo Todeschini, *Gli Ebrei nell'Italia Medievale* (Rome: Frecce, 2018).

57. On Assisi, see Ariel Toaff, *Gli Ebrei nell'Assisi Medievale 1305–1487: Storia sociale ed economica di una piccola comunità ebrea in Italia* (Assisi: Accademia Properziana del Subasio, 2001), 12–31.

papally supported teaching that the Roman Christian faithful must tolerate Jewish rites as an act of mercy and a witness to their unbelief (*incredulitas*). At the same time the synod now sought to enforce the 1215 badge requirement. To avoid scandal Jewish men must wear a round yellow badge on their chests, women wearing it on their heads.[58] In 1313 in Pisa an apparently ineffectual provision included in the commune's statute compilation was intended to require Jews to reside in a single, agreed location within one district of the city and nowhere else.[59] A later addition in Pisa required the wearing of a badge, to be colored vermilion. Once again, legislation is certainly not evidence for implementation. Yet similar thinking may have lain behind the early fourteenth-century Assisi *podestà*'s decision to check and record details of the houses of local Jews.

Much more could be said about Jewish life and religious activity. For present purposes it is enough to observe that it was probably more mobile than that of most Christians, increasingly circumscribed by canonical prohibition, and continually overwritten by Christian narratives.[60] Persecution and oppression cannot be ignored: the central Middle Ages were the centuries when Jews acquired minority status in the peninsula. These centuries set precedents for practices that were to continue into the early modern period, such as badge-wearing. Yet rabbis were also producing and using Hebrew religious books in large numbers. "Urban religion" encompasses this significant minority both on its own terms and in its changing relations to the Christian majority.

## Ibn Jubayr and Muslim Italy: Conflicting Orientations

A decade or so after Benjamin of Tudela, in 1183–85, a Muslim from Valencia, Ibn Jubayr, secretary to an Almohad governor in Andalusia, passed through Sicily on his way to Mecca for the Ḥajj, the first of

---

58. Joannes Dominicus Mansi, ed., *Sacrorum conciliorum nova et amplissima collectio* (Venice: apud Antonium Zatta, 1782), 25:462.

59. "Breve pisani communis," in *Statuti inediti della città di Pisa dal XII al XIV secolo*, ed. Francesco Bonaini (Florence: P. Vieusseux, 1870), 2:377–78 (book 3, rubric 89). Cited in Thompson, *Cities of God*, 139.

60. The argument for the relative mobility of Jews was forcefully promoted by Michele Luzzati. Though he focused on the end of the Middle Ages, the point seems applicable to the period discussed here. Michele Luzzati, "Again on the Mobility of the Italian Jews between the Middle Ages and the Renaissance," in *The Italia Judaica Jubilee Conference*, ed. Shlomo Simonsohn and Joseph Schatzmiller, Brill's Series in Jewish Studies 48 (Leiden: Brill, 2013), 97–106.

three such journeys, and wrote a travelogue in Arabic describing what he saw. Ibn Jubayr portrayed Palermo and Messina as bustling cities full of merchants but also observed a religious contrast between the two. Whereas there were now no Muslims resident in Messina, "except a few who are insignificant as their work has dried up," in Palermo he described Muslim residents filling numerous mosques, responding to the prayer call, and studying the Qur'ān, the sermon for Friday prayers having been proscribed. Muslims were also resident in the countryside, and some were employed by the king, William II (1166–89), who, Jubayr wrote, "puts a lot of trust in the Muslims, relying on them in his affairs and important matters of business to the extent that even the supervisor of his kitchen is a Muslim." According to Ibn Jubayr, William read and wrote in Arabic and, when news of an earthquake reached Palermo, allowed all those in his palace to "call upon [their] own God and in whomever [they] believe[d]." Ibn Jubayr also commented that Christian women in Palermo wore Muslim dress, spoke Arabic, and covered themselves with veils.[61] To use Orsi's language, according to this visitor urban religion in twelfth-century Palermo witnessed a convergence of voices and practices.

By the 1180s the Muslim population in Sicily had, however, long been under pressure. The Norman invasion and conquest of the island in the eleventh century slowly displaced a population that included indigenous converts to Islam as well as North African settlers. Their legal status was as slaves or servants of the king (*servi regis*), both protected by and vulnerable to direct royal power, fiscal and judicial. William II may have spoken Arabic, but he also sponsored the major monastic community of Monreale just outside Palermo, to which he gave vast tracts of land. Monreale became the second largest landholder after the king, and arguably this shift to monastic jurisdiction promoted conversion away from Islam (apparently at first not to Latin but to Greek Christianity, which had long roots in the region).[62] Four decades later,

---

61. For the excerpts discussed here see "Ibn Jubayr's Account of Messina and Palermo (1184–85)," translated from Arabic by Alex Metcalfe, with additional texts by Joshua Birk, in *Medieval Italy: Texts in Translation*, ed. Katherine L. Jansen, Joanna H. Drell, and Frances Andrews (Philadelphia: University of Pennsylvania Press, 2009), 234–40. A complete English translation is available in Ronald J. C. Broadhurst, *The Travels of Ibn Jubayr* (London: J. Cape, 1952), 335–63. See also Yann Dejugnat, "Ibn Jubayr," in *Encyclopaedia of Islam*, 3rd ed., ed. Kate Fleet et al. (Leiden: Brill, 2017), 129–32.

62. As observed by Jeremy Johns, "The Greek Church and the Conversion of Muslims in Sicily?," *Byzantinische Forschungen* 21 (1995): 144–53.

Frederick II (d. 1250), on his return to the south after his coronation as emperor, found the Muslim population in more or less open rebellion, and in the early 1220s he began transporting them to Lucera in northern Apulia.[63] The transfers continued over some twenty years and created a Muslim town of around fifteen to twenty thousand. In 1239 Frederick further decreed that all Muslims in the kingdom must reside in Lucera. The colony was useful, an urban community over which the emperor had direct control, which he could tax at will, and whose men he used as bodyguards. Many of the settlers were or became farmers, major suppliers of grain. As Julie Taylor has shown, there may have been a Qur'anic school or Madrasa in Lucera and there were certainly literate and educated Muslims, with *qadis* to settle internal disputes. The emperor's decision thus created a particular variety of urban religion. All the same, in 1300 Lucera was abruptly dismantled at the command of the Angevin king Charles II (1285–1309), the majority of its population killed or moved to "relocation centers" to be sold as slaves, their possessions and property confiscated. A scattering of Muslims continued to reside in the south over the next few decades, but the religious and financially driven decision of the Angevin king brought an end to any substantial, autonomous Islamic presence in the south.[64] In this, the Italian case preempts the expulsion of Muslims from the Spanish peninsula by nearly two centuries, the product of immediate vulnerability to royal power and closer in chronology to the treatment of Jews in England or, indeed, the French Crown, with which the Angevins were dynastically connected. Religious practice, whether urban or rural, could be starkly reliant on lay power.

## Armanno Pungilupo of Ferrara: Complex Desires, Needs, and Fears

On December 16, 1269,

> the man of God, blessed Armanno [Pungilupo] of Ferrara, having persevered for a long time before God and men in praiseworthy

---

63. For the view that the revolt was provoked and the move to Lucera did not encompass all Muslims, whose fate remains an enigma, see Graham Loud, "Communities, Cultures and Conflict in Southern Italy, from the Byzantines to the Angevins," *Al-Masāq: Journal of the Medieval Mediterranean* 28 (2016): 132–52.

64. See Julie Taylor, *Muslims in Medieval Italy* (Lanham, MD: Lexington Books, 2003) and Alex Metcalfe, *The Muslims of Medieval Italy* (Edinburgh: Edinburgh University Press, 2009).

penitence, in vigils, fasts, and prayers, faithful and chaste, humble, patient, merciful, benign, and simple, a true dove of simplicity, devoted to God and the glorious Virgin, as it pleases the Lord serving the cross of Christ, was miraculously called to him and died.[65]

On hearing this news, crowds of men and women immediately gathered at the cathedral where Armanno's lifeless body had been taken. Within three days of his funeral, a first miracle was reported. Nova, a local woman, swore before the bishop, the archpriest, a canon of the cathedral, three named laymen, and "many others" that she had that very day been cured of a tumor in her right eye, having gone in person and knelt three times in prayer before the tomb of Armanno, praying that God would cure her on account of Armanno's merits. Other women and men followed Nova later that month, and again until June 1271, witnessing to miraculous cures for themselves and their children, in statements given in person and on oath before the bishop and other Churchmen of Ferrara.

Armanno's cures were repeatedly described as the response to devout and insistent prayer or vigils before the tomb, offerings of wax candles equal to the length of the body (a large expense), of wax images of an affected body part, of lamps before the tomb, or vows to offer future prayers, vigils, and fasting. One miracle touched Dominicus in Capo d'Istria, condemned to death for a murder he said he had not committed. Having overheard a blind man near his prison window singing of the miracles of Armanno to a gathering crowd, Dominicus had dedicated himself to fasting and promised, were he to be freed through Armanno's merits, to visit the tomb. On the day before he was due to be executed, he had a vision of a pale and thin man who told him to get up and leave. He immediately found himself in the square outside, shackle-free (and vindicated).

In this closely connected urban world, neighbors, family, friends, and doctors who had treated patients later cured by Armanno came forward to swear to the truth of miracles received, which included freeing the possessed and healing the paralyzed. Some of the beneficiaries, like Dominicus, came from outside Ferrara, a clue to a successful and growing cult. The witnesses to the miracles included two Augustinian Hermit Friars, members of an order approved only in 1256 (and, from 1274,

---

65. Gabriele Zanella, ed., *Itinerari ereticali: Patari e catari tra Rimini e Verona* (Rome: Istituto Storico Italiano per il Medio Evo, 1986), p. 72.

endangered by conciliar action against new orders). The surviving text contains a selection of documented miracles, as required for the canonization of a saint.[66] There is furthermore a deposition from the clergy of Ferrara cathedral, dating to April 1272, recording their own and other local Churchmen's personal knowledge of Armanno's repeated, orthodox performance of confession and penance (including to Augustinian Hermit Friars). This was addressed to the pope, Gregory X.

The dossier for Armanno was copied by episcopal notaries in 1286, but he was never canonized. Other records, again compiled from witness statements, suggest a very different career and in doing so expose the conflicting visions of different urban religious entities and of different city dwellers. Summarizing accusations against him, the second set of witness statements comprises depositions before an inquisition tribunal in Ferrara that identified Armanno as a "believer of the heretics" (credens hereticorum). Among his many sins, he had spoken ill of the body of Christ, expressed skepticism about the Eucharist, criticized Churchmen, received and given the rite of Cathar heretics (the *consolamentum*), and avowed that the only way to salvation lay through Cathar beliefs. After examination by inquisition in 1254, he had abjured heresy, but had then relapsed. Other witnesses swore that Armanno had often been seen in the company of known heretics, supporting, receiving, and revering them. These were all activities frequently interrogated by inquisitors and identified in this sort of testimony as they tracked down and eliminated heretical associates.[67] Statements were made by officials of the inquisition, by friars of the Dominican and Franciscan orders, Penitent Brothers, and numerous men and women identified as

---

66. For the documents, most of which survive only in a fifteenth-century copy, and for the corrected dates used here, see Zanella, *Itinerari ereticali*, appendices 1 and 2, an edition of Modena, Archivio di Stato, Biblioteca, MS 132, fols. 11r-33v, the autograph of the *Historiae Ferrariae liber VIII* composed by Pellegrino Prisciani (d. 1518), who included transcriptions of the thirteenth-century texts. Zanella reprinted this with an appendix of corrections in Gabriele Zanella, *Hereticalia: Temi e discussioni* (Spoleto: Centro italiano di studi sull'alto medioevo, 1995), 225-29. See also Marco G. Bascapè, "In armariis officii inquisitoris Ferrariensis: Ricerche su un frammento inedito del processo Pungilupo," in "Le scritture e le opere degli inquisitori," *Quaderni di storia religiosa* 9 (2002): 31-110, and, briefly, Marina Benedetti, "I libri degli inquisitori," in *Libri, e altro: Nel passato e nel presente*, ed. Grado G. Merlo (Milan: Fondazione Mondadori, 2006), 28-30.

67. Model questions used by inquisitors across the Alps are discussed in Peter Biller, Caterina Bruschi, and Shelagh Sneddon, eds. and trans., *Inquisitors and Heretics in Thirteenth-Century Languedoc: Edition and Translation of Toulouse Inquisition Depositions, 1273-1282*, Studies in the History of Christian Traditions 147 (Leiden: Brill, 2011), 66-71. Zanella notes the link to inquisitors' manuals in Zanella, *Hereticalia*, 10.

(former) heretics often, in this last case, themselves on trial. As well as direct witness, many of the testimonies refer to Armanno's reputation or standing, to common knowledge or hearsay. In addition to criticizing Armanno himself, some witnesses attacked the cult. Gratius of Bergamo testified that at the time of Pungilupo's death, a heretic who had come from Bergamo to stay with him had pretended to be unable to speak and then miraculously cured, though Gratius swore that he had not been mute before. The first witness in date order, Friar Atasius of Bergamo, a Dominican, swore on January 7, 1270, that he had seen believers of the heretics, people who never went to church, bringing offerings to the tomb of Armanno and boasting that one of their own had been made a saint.[68]

It was the inquisitors' version of Armanno and his cult that was to prevail. The cathedral clergy resisted for three decades, refusing to accept the instructions of the inquisitors requiring them to exhume the body, despite excommunication and interdict. Attempts by the canons to appeal to the papacy were rebuffed, and in March 1301 Armanno was condemned as a relapsed heretic, his body to be exhumed, his tomb and any altars dedicated to him destroyed. The Dominicans had won. In 1304, moreover, it was the Dominican inquisitor Guido of Vicenza, one of those charged by Boniface VIII with resolving the Pungilupo case, who was nominated bishop of Ferrara, taking control of the building in which the shrine had once stood.[69]

Was Armanno Pungilupo's a "double life," as Malcolm Lambert once put it?[70] It need not have been. What is certain, as Trevor Dean has pointed out, is the difficulty contemporaries found in separating orthodox and heretic.[71] Both might live devoted, holy lives. Armanno was clearly interested in the afterlife but unsure who, how, or what to believe. If we accept all the testimonies in good faith, he improvised,

---

68. Useful short extracts are available in Dean, *Towns of Italy*, 83–88, but derive from the transcriptions of Muratori, now superseded by those in Zanella, *Itinerari ereticali*. A thirteenth-century loose leaf, originally from a register used at an earlier stage in the compilation of accusations against Pungilupo, has also been found and published by Bascapè, "In armariis officii inquisitoris Ferrariensis." In a version of this essay uploaded to academia.edu, Bascapè reports that the leaf, which includes extracts from depositions dated between 1270 and 1288, is now Milan, Archivio dei Luoghi Pii Elemosinieri: Comuni. Arti e scienze. Culto, 164.

69. See Marina Benedetti, *Inquisitori Lombardi del Duecento* (Rome: Edizioni di Storia e Letteratura, 2008), 91, 281, and 296–99.

70. Malcolm Lambert, *The Cathars* (Oxford: Blackwell, 1998), 281, also cited by Dean, *Towns of Italy*, 83.

71. Dean, *Towns of Italy*, 70.

frequently confessing to different clergy in Ferrara, talking to and about heretics, and making confession to the inquisitors. In the process he acquired a reputation for holiness in overlapping communities. There was a strong urge on the part of Churchmen to force the issue, to categorize in one direction or the other. And talk of miracles, however carefully documented, might be met with disbelief.

A Franciscan friar and chronicler, Salimbene de Adam, writing in the 1280s, offers an illuminating commentary on the Pungilupo episode. Accounting for cults that he deemed to be fake, Salimbene supplied multiple linked reasons for their appearance, in both general and specific terms. Most straightforwardly, he recognized that cults might arise from the longing of the sick to be cured, but he also targeted several different groups of which he disapproved. Fake cults might arise from the desire of the curious to see novelties (curiosity being a vice), or the jealousy of the clergy toward "modern religious," by which he meant his own mendicant brothers, whose success put that of other clergy under pressure. Warming to his subject he added that cults could be driven by the desire of bishops and canons for the profits they could acquire, citing in particular the great earnings made out of Armanno by the bishop and canons of Ferrara, a case not yet resolved when he was writing. Finally, expanding on the theme of conflicting voices, Salimbene tied fake cults to factionalism: new saints might spring from the desires of those who had been banished from their cities as promoters of the imperial cause (*pars imperii*). Exiles thereby hoped, he suggested, to have peace with their cocitizens on account of these miracles of new saints, to regain their (small) possessions, and no longer to have to travel the world as vagabonds.[72]

Salimbene's tone is patronizing if not derisive; it is also political and underscores the significance of different and competing urban factions, in which Churchmen like Salimbene were weighty participants. Were the bishop and canons of Ferrara (assisted by some Augustinian Hermit Friars) dealing with a spontaneous, devotional response to a holy life, or were they orchestrating a process to their own benefit? Both versions are plausible. Were other mendicant friars and Churchmen engaged in inquisition keen to oppose an episcopally promoted cult, or concerned by the dangerous influence of a false believer? Once more, our answers should not be mutually exclusive. What *is* certain is

---

72. Salimbene da Parma, *Cronica*, ed. Giuseppe Scalia, trans. Berardo Rossi (Parma: Monte Università Parma Editore, 2007), 1406 (para. 2368).

the contested nature of urban religious practice and urban political life in thirteenth-century Italy, as well as the potential for conflicting responses to the holy within the Roman Church. Belonging to a particular Christian community, whether as a mendicant friar, as an inquisitor, or in a chapter of canons, could generate strong and contrasting ties. Dissident groups were not as prominent in all Italian cities as they appear in Ferrara or its neighbors, but contrasting clerical and lay loyalties reverberated loudly in these relatively autonomous and tightly settled urban communities.

## Christodoulos: Dynamic Traditions and Engagement with Unexpected Others

Sometime before October 1194 Christodoulos, an aspiring monk, made a donation of a house he had inherited and a structure for producing wine to Onofrio, *proestos* (prior or abbot) of the Greek monastery of Santa Maria della Grotta, in the Albergaria quarter of Palermo. The neighbors to the property included the new monk's sister Olou, and qāʻid Sawdān, a Saracen (Muslim). The witnesses to Christodoulos's donation, drawn up by Giovanni, a priest and *taboularios* (notary) of Palermo, included several men who recorded their names in Greek, one in Latin. Such juxtapositions are typical of this multilingual city. The witnesses included a Greek cleric from a famous neighboring church, also dedicated to Mary, that had been founded by Admiral (*Amiras*) George of Antioch (d. 1151). Ioannes Maimoun, an official (ἄρχων) and himself a benefactor of the monastery, was also present, as was Stefano, son of Peter, head of the royal *duana de secretis* or *Sekreton*.[73] The church Christodoulos sought to join is traditionally associated with the eleventh-century Norman leader Robert Guiscard but can be documented only from December 1183. In that month, Eugenio "the Good" (τοῦ Καλοῦ), also

---

73. Termini Imerese, Biblioteca Liciniana A 2, as discussed (and dated) in Vera Von Falkenhausen, "I documenti greci di S. Maria della Grotta rinvenuti a Termini Imerese," in *Byzantino—Sicula VI: La Sicilia e Bisanzio nei secoli XI e XII. Atti delle X giornate di studio della Associazione italiana di studi bizantini (Palermo, 27–28 Maggio 2011)*, ed. Renata Lavagnini and Cristina Rognoni (Palermo: Istituto Siciliano di Studi Bizantini e Neoellenici "Bruno Lavagnini," 2014), 224–25 and appendix 4. I am very grateful to the author for drawing my attention to these documents and to Julian Gardner for putting us in touch. A convenient summary of royal offices is provided by Hiroshi Takayama, "Law and Monarchy in the South," in *Italy in the Central Middle Ages 1000–1300*, ed. David Abulafia (Oxford: Oxford University Press, 2004), 66–68.

known as Abū l-Ṭayyib, a senior Arab-Greek official in the royal administration, having been healed from a serious illness by an image of the Virgin in Santa Maria, donated a garden to be used to contribute to the costs of the lighting.[74] The church, built over some sort of cave or rock church, was a significant cult center, attracting numerous donations from the Palermo elite. In autumn 1194 for example, Stefano, head of the *Sekreton*, made a large donation of a vineyard, with seven thousand plants he had acquired for seven hundred *tarì*. The income from the vineyard was to be used to support a hieromonk (priest-monk) to celebrate the liturgy in the lower church.[75] Other gifts of land came from members of the royal family, one of many royal donations made to both Greek and Latin monastic houses.

The ties that Norman and Angevin rulers maintained with Greek as well as Latin Christianity have been well studied. That Greek saints and holy sites less close to the court than Santa Maria della Grotta also attracted active and intimate devotion can, however, also be documented. A series of incised and painted graffiti in the early Christian church of Santa Maria della Croce, on the edge of Casaranello in the Salento, southeast of Gallipoli, includes several Greek devotional inscriptions recording named individuals. One group of three on an image of Saint Barbara may or may not be linked to a single couple: "Remember, Lord, your servant John and his wife . . ."; "The servant of God John died in 1094/95"; "The servant of God Maria died in 1098/99."[76] As Linda Safran has argued, such personal graffiti were intended to be legible, to make known things that mattered to the individual. They often also attracted later viewers to add their own.[77] As such they are witness to an expectation of continued, shared devotion. Slightly further north, in the rock-cut church of Santa Cristina in Carpignano there are again numerous graffiti and painted inscriptions, this time dating from the late tenth to the late eleventh century. Several record the patrons or painters of the different frescoes; others may be either coetaneous with the fresco or subsequent accretions located to connect with a saint: on an image of the Virgin and Child and Saint Vincent, "Remember Lord, the soul of your servant John and your servant Vincent and assign them to the place of light"; on a fresco of Saint Anne and the Virgin,

---

74. Von Falkenhausen, "I documenti greci di S. Maria della Grotta," 218.
75. Von Falkenhausen, "I documenti greci di S. Maria della Grotta," 219.
76. Safran, *The Medieval Salento*, 267–68.
77. Safran, *The Medieval Salento*, 15.

"Remember Lord, your servant Anna and her child, Amen."[78] There are other, repeated evocations of family and children. Those entering the church were being invited to participate in prayer and commemoration. Comparable personal and shared devotion is legible in the visual and material culture of monastic houses all over the Italian peninsula, urban and rural, Greek and Latin.

In the center and north of the peninsula, the Greek rite was less frequent than in the south, but other forms of diversity were part of the religious landscape in numerous twelfth- and thirteenth-century urban centers. In Perugia on Sunday, July 2, 1273, the bishop was to be found consecrating a new Armenian monastery, dedicated to Saint Matthew, just outside Porta Sant'Angelo. One year earlier, brother Profeta, prior and custodian of the community (and prior of the Armenian brothers elsewhere in Italy), acting with the consent of a brother Gregorio, had donated the house to the canons of the cathedral of San Lorenzo, agreeing to pay an annual cense of six pennies on the feast of Saint Ercolano (a patron saint of Perugia, as we have seen). The brothers petitioned the commune for a contribution to the expenses of the consecration, receiving ten lire two days before the ceremony, a payment that was to be followed in later decades by several others designed to cover the costs either of clothing or of works on the church.[79] The community would also receive legacies from Perugian testators that as Giovanna Casagrande has demonstrated, confirms that San Matteo was integrated into the "devotional circuit" of the local faithful.[80] The church of San Matteo degli Armeni was soon frescoed, including a monumental portrayal on the counter façade of a saint on horseback, conceivably intended to be Saint Leonard, Saint George, or, as understood by a fifteenth-century graffito, Saint Sergius.[81] The saint looms

---

78. Safran, *The Medieval Salento*, 263–66.
79. See Giovanna Casagrande, "San Matteo degli Armeni nel contesto insediativo-religioso di Perugia (secc. XIII–XV)," in *Ad limina Italiae: In viaggio per l'Italia con mercanti e monaci armeni*, ed. Lewan Zekiyan (Zēk'ieǎn) (Padua: Editoriale programma, 1996), 118–23, and Lewan Zekiyan, "Le colonie Armene del Medio Evo in Italia," in *Atti del Primo Simposio Internazionale di Arte Armena (Bergamo, 28–30 Giugno 1975)* (San Lazzaro, Venice: Centro Studi di Documentazione della cultura Armena [Milan], 1978), 867.
80. Casagrande, "San Matteo degli Armeni," 120.
81. Giusto Traina, "Materiali sulla presenza Armena nella Perugia medievale," in Zekiyan, *Ad limina Italiae*, 102–7, notes that the fresco has a later graffito in Armenian. This reads: "I Łukianos priest of Kafa [Crimea] went to Rome [bor] in [the Armenian] era 872 [1422-23 CE]. I am pleading personally to you Saint Sargis [Saint Sergius], Amen and Amen." I am very grateful to my colleague Tim Greenwood for assistance with checking and translating the inscription.

over a bearded devotee in a black habit, perhaps the patron and presumably one of the monks, shown along with three other tiny figures, former prisoners holding shackles, symbols of their liberation.

The community of San Matteo was never large and was to be slowly Italianized at the end of the Middle Ages. But in the thirteenth century it was one small piece in a larger urban landscape of diversity, including Armenian language and liturgy. The books the Armenian brothers produced or acquired were written in their own language, including a lectionary penned in 1230 and sent to the monastery in 1279 by Levon III of Cilicia.[82]

San Matteo was one piece in an expansion of Armenian religious houses in the Italian peninsula that had begun in the twelfth century.[83] In the thirteenth century new houses were founded in Rome (1226/42), Rimini (1254), Ancona (1261), Siena (1263), Perugia (as above, 1272), Salerno (1283), and Orvieto (1288).[84] But Armenian communities and religious houses had long existed: Armenians came to Puglia and Calabria with the Byzantine reconquests of the early Middle Ages, and San Giorgio degli Armeni in Bari, for example, was established in the tenth century.[85] Armenians later continued to travel to the peninsula as merchants and traders from the Kingdom of Cilicia; still others were perhaps refugees.

The presence of the Armenian brothers in Perugia is one small fragment of the Christian religious landscape of Perugia in the thirteenth century that, as in other cities, encompassed divergences. In the thirteenth century the brothers of San Matteo were using the Armenian language for their liturgy, and if the devotee of the Saint Sergius fresco is any witness, they wore long beards, following the custom for Greek Christian monks. They were supported by urban charity both communal and personal. And San Matteo was part of an extended network of Armenian religious houses across central and northern Italy. For modern historians if not for medieval Italians, they bear comparison with Orsi's "unexpected others," with whom urban visitors and residents necessarily interacted.

---

82. Traina, "Materiali sulla presenza Armena," 97; see also 112n.
83. See Zekiyan, "Le colonie Armene del Medio Evo," 806, 852.
84. Zekiyan, "Le colonie Armene del Medio Evo," 851–71.
85. Cosimo Damiano Fonseca, "Tra gli Armeni dell'Italia meridionale," in Zekiyan, *Ad limina Italiae*, 181.

What is offered here is a template for a fuller understanding of urban religion in Italy ca. 1050–ca. 1350. A complete account would need to encompass more than these microstudies: the patterns of Latin Christian baptisms in cathedrals, *pievi*, or, in a crisis, at the bedside; of burials in local cemeteries; and of the polycentrism of the *cura animarum*, the care of souls that was shaped by the development of the parish. It would engage with the rapidly expanding role of the mendicant friars, whose urban mission was accompanied by professionalized preaching, as well as by inquisition, confraternities, and new urban places, their churches and squares opening new spaces between the conventual buildings of canons, military orders, and urban monastics.[86] There would be more on the different generations involved, passing on and modifying shared religious practices; more on what was going on inside the household, on the lives of laywomen, on the families of urban clergy, and on the political and cultural contexts that saw urban recluses moving inside the city, or *signori* replacing communes with courtly cultures and court chaplains; more on the noise involved in worship, whether chants, bells, or muezzins, and on the smells of the city, placing incense alongside urine and tanners' dyes. Socioeconomic differences also require greater attention than is possible here.

A full account of urban religion would also need to say more about the stories that adherents of one belief system told themselves about others: Greek criticism of Latin Christians (and vice versa), Christian denigration of Muslim "Ishmaelites," or Christians and Jews encountering each other in juxtaposed lives but in increasing conflict. Orthodoxies on all sides were pushed and pulled by changing intellectual and practical disputes. A full account of urban religion in these centuries would necessarily have more to say about repression, and the silencing of divergent voices through inquisitions like that directed at Armanno and his dissenting neighbors, part of mechanisms of power that gave strength to civic religion in later decades.

If I have multiplied the urban centers here rather than concentrating on one location in the way that Orsi and his collaborators did for

---

86. Examples of the squares, walls, and new roads built or taken over to accommodate the mendicants and their vast "hall" churches are in Frances Andrews, *The Other Friars: Carmelite, Augustinian, Sack and Pied Friars in the Middle Ages* (Woodbridge: Boydell, 2006), 31, 37–41, 107–19, and, for Italy in particular, Cécile Caby, "Les implantations urbaines des ordres religieux dans l'Italie médiévale: Bilan et propositions de recherche," *Rivista di storia e letteratura religiosa* 35 (1999): 151–79.

Harlem or the Bronx, it is to demonstrate the strength of intersections and convergences, of constellations of practices. I have done so purposefully, as the history of the Italian peninsula is most frequently written in city-size intaglios. The need to move across political difference and to acknowledge diversity within the Latin Christian experience (which it is all too easy to standardize) requires a different approach. Looking to the south highlights diversity, which encourages questions about diversity further north.

There is more work to do. But enough has been said to make the case for thinking about the religion of medieval Italy in the eleventh to early fourteenth centuries modified in Orsi's urban terms. Religion on the ground was the multiple relations to the holy of Jews, Muslims, and Christians, of clergy and laity, women and men, heretics and orthodox, incorporating conflicting and changing desires, beliefs, and contexts. Ecclesiastical history was integral to the social fabric. "Civic religion" stands, but as a useful descriptor of a body of practices that emerged slowly within a broad and divergent religious landscape. To paint a picture of medieval Christianity in Italy, that larger vision of urban religion requires to be colored in.

## Selected Bibliography

Andrews, Frances. *The Other Friars: Carmelite, Augustinian, Sack and Pied Friars in the Middle Ages*. Woodbridge: Boydell, 2006.

Andrews, Frances, ed., with Maria Agata Pincelli. *Churchmen and Urban Government in Late Medieval Italy, c.1200–c.1450: Cases and Contexts*. Cambridge: Cambridge University Press, 2013.

Brown, Andrew. *Civic Ceremony and Religion in Medieval Bruges, c.1300–1520*. Cambridge: Cambridge University Press, 2011.

Cossar, Roisin. *Clerical Households in Late Medieval Italy*. Cambridge, MA: Harvard University Press, 2017.

Gazzini, Marina, ed. *Studi confraternali: Orientamenti, problemi, testimonianze*. Florence: Firenze University Press, 2009. http://www.rmoa.unina.it/2332/.

Gentile, Marco, ed. *Guelfi e ghibellini nell'Italia del Rinascimento*. Rome: Viella, 2005.

Haines, Margaret, and Lucio Riccetti, eds. *Opera, carattere e ruolo delle fabbriche cittadine fino all'inizio dell'età moderna: Atti della Tavola rotonda, Villa i Tatti, Firenze, 3 aprile 1991*. Florence: Olschki, 1996.

*Italia Judaica: Atti del I Convegno internazionale Bari 18–22 maggio 1981*. Rome: Ministero per i Beni Culturali e Ambientali, Pubblicazioni degli Archivi di Stato, 1983 (the first of a series of 4 conference volumes).

Jansen, Katherine L., Joanna H. Drell, and Frances Andrews, eds. *Medieval Italy: Texts in Translation*. Philadelphia: University of Pennsylvania Press, 2009.

Metcalfe, Alex. *The Muslims of Medieval Italy*. Edinburgh: Edinburgh University Press, 2009.

Oldfield, Paul. *Sanctity and Pilgrimage in Medieval Southern Italy, 1000–1200*. Cambridge: Cambridge University Press, 2014.

Orsi, Robert A. "Crossing the City Line." In *Gods of the City: Religion and the American Urban Landscape*, edited by Robert A. Orsi, 1–78. Bloomington: Indiana University Press, 1999.

——. *The Madonna of 115th Street: Faith and Community in Italian Harlem, 1880–1950*. 3rd ed. New Haven, CT: Yale University Press, 2010.

Presciutti, Diana Bullen, ed., *Space, Place and Motion: Locating Confraternities in the Late Medieval and Early Modern City*. Art and Medieval Culture in Medieval and Renaissance Europe 8. Leiden: Brill, 2017.

Ramseyer, Valerie. "Religious Life in Eleventh-Century Salerno: The Church of Santa Lucia in Balnearia." *Haskins Society Journal* 13 (2002): 39–56.

——. *The Transformation of a Religious Landscape: Medieval Southern Italy, 850–1150*. Ithaca, NY: Cornell University Press, 2006.

Safran, Linda. *The Medieval Salento: Art and Identity in Southern Italy*. Philadelphia: University of Pennsylvania Press, 2014.

Sapir Abulafia, Anna. *Christian–Jewish Relations, 1000–1300: Jews in the Service of Medieval Christendom*. Harlow: Longman, 2010.

Stow, Kenneth R. *Alienated Minority: The Jews of Medieval Latin Europe*. Cambridge, MA: Harvard University Press, 1992.

Taylor, Julie. *Muslims in Medieval Italy*. Lanham, MD: Lexington Books, 2003.

Terpstra, Nicholas. "Civic Religion." In *The Oxford Handbook of Medieval Christianity*, edited by John H. Arnold, 148–65. Oxford: Oxford University Press, 2014.

Thompson, Augustine. *Cities of God: The Religion of the Italian Communes, 1125–1325*. University Park: Pennsylvania State University Press, 2005.

Todeschini, Giacomo. *Gli Ebrei nell'Italia Medievale*. Rome: Frecce, 2018.

CHAPTER 12

# Case Study I
*Florence*

George Dameron

Any room with a view in Florence of Brunelleschi's dome and the Piazzale Michelangelo allows one to see two of the most important ecclesiastical structures in Florence today: the cathedral complex of Santa Maria del Fiore and the basilica and monastery of San Miniato al Monte. The timing of the construction of these two structures frames the time period that is the subject of this essay (ca. 1000–ca. 1300). When Bishop Hildebrand founded San Miniato al Monte in 1018, he chose a site high on the ridge overlooking the Arno and the city below. At the same time, he established a new cult center for the veneration of Saint Minias, a former third-century Roman soldier who was supposedly the first Christian martyr of the city, and he placed into its endowment under the protection of the saint many of the properties of the bishopric. Florence at that time was small in population and size, far from the vital artery of the Via Francigena linking Rome with the north, and considerably less import…tant economically and politically than Lucca or Pisa at that time. When Bishop Francesco Monaldeschi presided over the initial steps to rebuild the cathedral (then named Santa Reparata) in 1296, however, Florence was no longer the small and economically marginal city it had been in the early eleventh century. By the last decade of the thirteenth century, it had become one of the most populated cities in Europe, one of the most economically powerful communes in Tuscany, and a major *popolo*-dominated city-state linking Florentine bankers and merchants, on the one hand, with the papacy and the Angevin kingdom in southern Italy (the *Regno*), on the other.[1] The Florentine Church both helped to facilitate this remarkable transformation and was in turn shaped by it. To understand how the Florentine Church helped to enable this transformation, a brief overview of Florentine thirteenth-century history is appropriate.

The second half of the thirteenth century was indeed a period of decisive and transformative change for the city of Florence. It marked the rise to political power of a new social and economic elite, the *popolo*, and the marginalization of the Ghibelline political faction by the Guelfs. Members of the *popolo* were prosperous, nonnoble, and urban, enriched by the quickening pace of the commercial revolution of the later Middle Ages. They achieved initial success when they dominated the principal levers of power in Florence between 1250 and 1260 (the Primo Popolo). Their rise to power mirrored developments in other communes throughout central and northern Italy in the thirteenth century. At roughly the same time, roiling tensions between Guelf and Ghibelline political factions were intensifying. These conflicts peaked in Florence and elsewhere around the middle of the century. The Guelfs in Florence tended to be those anti-imperialist members of the elite,

---

1. This essay updates some of the conclusions in my book, *Florence and Its Church in the Age of Dante* (Philadelphia: University of Pennsylvania Press, 2005), and in my later essay, "Church and Orthodoxy," in *Dante in Context*, ed. Zygmunt G. Barański and Lino Pertile (Cambridge: Cambridge University Press, 2015), in the light of recent research. For a general history of Florence at this time, see John M. Najemy, *A History of Florence, 1200–1575* (Oxford: Blackwell, 2006), chaps. 1-5, including useful treatments on the Church: "Culture and Religion" (27-34) and "Religion" (50-56). For the building of the cathedral (Duomo) of Florence and documents, see David Friedman, Julian Gardner, and Margaret Haines, eds., *Arnolfo's Moment: Acts of an International Conference, Florence, Villa I Tatti, May 26–27, 2005* (Florence: Olschki, 2009); Timothy Verdon and Annalisa Innocenti, eds., *Atti del VII centenario del Duomo di Firenze*, 3 vols. in 5 (Florence: EDIFIR, 2001); Cesare Guasti, *Santa Maria del Fiore: La costruzione della chiesa e del campanile* (Florence: M. Ricci, 1887); Enrica Neri Lusanna, "Arnolfo e Firenze," in *Arnolfo: Alle origini del Rinascimento fiorentino*, ed. Enrica Neri Lusanna (Florence: Polistampa, 2005), esp. 43. For San Miniato al Monte, see George W. Dameron, "The Cult of Saint Minias and the Struggle for Power in the Diocese of Florence, 1011–24," *Journal of Medieval History* 13 (June 1987): 125–41. For more recent overviews of the cult of Saint Minias and the foundation in 1018 of San Miniato al Monte, see Benjamin Brand, *Holy Treasure and Sacred Song: Relic Cults and Their Liturgies in Medieval Tuscany* (New York: Oxford University Press, 2014), 61–68, and Francesco Salvestrini, ed., *La Basilica di San Miniato al Monte di Firenze (1018–2018): Storia e documentazione* (Florence: Firenze University Press, 2021), especially the essay by Mauro Ronzani, "Vescovi e monasteri in Tuscia nel secolo XI (1018–1120 circa)," 17–48.

primarily though not exclusively bankers and cloth merchants, who assumed that their local interests were best served by aligning themselves with the broader political agendas of the papacy in Italy. Ghibellines, primarily though not exclusively knights and members of the traditional Florentine noble aristocracy, however, tended to assume that their own local concerns were best served by identifying with the broader interests of the German emperor in Italy. Initially, the government of the Primo Popolo (1250-60) tried to remain neutral in the factional conflict between Guelf and Ghibelline. However, increasingly, the regime found itself aligning with the Guelfs against Ghibellines. This alliance deepened after the collapse of the Primo Popolo in 1260 and the establishment of a Ghibelline regime. However, in 1266 and 1267 in northern and central Italy the proimperial Ghibellines suffered a series of severe setbacks when Charles of Anjou, the younger brother of the propapal French king, Louis IX, successfully invaded Italy with a Guelf-backed army to seize the Kingdom of Sicily. His victorious army marched into Florence in April 1267.

After the spring of 1267 the pro-Angevin, Guelf elite in Florence therefore found itself in a position to consolidate its hold over the major magistracies, ecclesiastical institutions, and guilds of the city. New political regimes in the later Middle Ages, like that of the *popolo*-dominated Guelf Party (Parte Guelfa) in Florence, once taking power from former rulers, normally had to establish their legitimacy. That is to say, they had to demonstrate that the previous regime was illegitimate, that the acquisition of power by the new one was justified by tradition and law, and that the new rulers were acting in accord with Christian morality and God's will. The process of political consolidation and legitimization at Florence was political, cultural, and religious. Politically, antimagnate legislation, common in communes throughout northern Italy in the 1280s and 1290s, contributed to the final and ultimate success of the wealthiest Guelfs, the *popolo grasso*. Magnates were those members of the traditional, predominately landowning aristocracy who relied on knighthood (not guild membership) as the dominant path to elite status; they also had a reputation among members of the *popolo* for violence against nonmagnates. In the Ordinances of Justice in 1293, the priorate, the principal magistracy of the city, imposed severe penalties on the 140 magnate lineages in countryside and city regarding any future violence perpetrated against nonmagnates. The Ordinances also excluded magnates from eligibility to the priorate and to the guild consulates. As their political and economic power was peaking in the second half of the thirteenth century, Guelf families and major guilds associated with the Parte Guelfa were also supporting new religious initiatives like the Franciscan-promoted cult of Umiliana de' Cerchi (d. 1246), the construction of a new cathedral dedicated to the Virgin Mary (begun in 1294), and the cults of patron saints John and Zenobius. By so doing, the pro-Angevin, Florentine Guelf elite (the *popolo grasso*) claimed that only God's favor could explain the sudden economic and political rise of Florence and that they were his chosen instruments to create this "New Jerusalem" on earth. Patronage of the major cults of Florentine saints and the financial and political backing of the new cathedral project by the most powerful Guelf-controlled guilds therefore helped bring to fruition the final consolidation of a pro-Angevin, Guelf power in Florence, known after 1268 as the Secondo Popolo.[2]

This chapter will emphasize three major themes. First, Florentine ecclesiastical institutions, communities, and religious traditions played a formative role in the evolution of the commune and the elevation of Florence from minor to major status in Tuscany. Yet the relationships between Church and commune—and among ecclesiastical communities themselves—were complex and often vexed. There was cooperation, but there was also tension and conflict. Whereas the orchestration of the cults of civic saints helped underscore the legitimacy of the post-1267 Guelf commune, for example, growing papal influence and family rivalries actually helped stoke factional conflicts within ecclesiastical institutions like the cathedral chapter and contributed to splitting the Guelf elite into White and Black factions after 1300.

Second, the evolution of the medieval Florentine Church bears many similarities with ecclesiastical and religious developments elsewhere in medieval Italy and Europe. As in other localities, for example, we find in Florence, especially in the thirteenth century, the establishment of mendicant friaries and *studia*, the arrival of new types of male and female monastic communities, the growth of confraternities and hospitals, the expanding influence of the papal Curia with regard to the appointment to key offices, and the rise to prominence of civic saints to legitimize existing regimes. Yet there also existed significant differences

---

2. For the history of Guelfs and Ghibellines, the Primo Popolo, magnates, and the Ordinances of Justice in Florence, see Najemy, *A History of Florence*, chap. 3. For Guelfs, Ghibellines, the *popolo*, and magnates in the history of Italian communes as a whole, see Daniel Waley and Trevor Dean, *The Italian City-Republics*, 5th ed. (London: Routledge, 2022), chap. 7.

that helped set the Florentine Church apart from its peers. They include (but are not limited to) the social composition of its clergy (both magnate and nonmagnate mercantile and banking families), the economic and social importance of ecclesiastical institutions (especially the bishopric and cathedral chapter) as vital links connecting city with countryside before ca. 1120 and after ca. 1200, the explosive growth of new ecclesiastical foundations and communities in the thirteenth century, a vibrant tradition of lay and clerical confraternities that began quite early in both city and countryside, the particularly strong devotion of its religious culture to the concept of purgatory, a creative vernacular culture, and the uniquely close (yet vexed) ties to the papacy from at least the mid-thirteenth century.[3] Some of these features may help explain why and how after ca. 1250 the religious culture of Florence was able to nurture, inspire, and even infuriate some of the most important intellectuals, writers, and artists of the later Middle Ages, including Dante Alighieri (d. 1321), Ubertino da Casale (d. ca. 1329), Brunetto Latini (d. 1294), Giovanni Villani (d. 1348), Pietro di Giovanni Olivi (d. 1298), and Giotto di Bondone (d. 1337).

Third, a major turning point in Florentine Church history, as with the commune itself, occurred in the closing decades of the thirteenth century and the first decades of the fourteenth (ca. 1280-ca. 1340). The cultivation of ever closer connections between the papacy and Church and commune, the formal orchestration of cults of patron saints associated specifically with the commune (especially after 1310), and the impact of a flourishing vernacular culture on preaching and confraternities were increasingly evident after ca. 1250. In addition, the development of key constitutions for the clergy (1310 and 1327), the restructuring of the management of the properties of major ecclesiastical institutions, the erection of the major ecclesiastical structures in the city, and the increasing devotion to—if not obsession with—the doctrine of purgatory, all helped define the distinctive character of the Florentine Church during these same decades. This was the world described

---

3. Dameron, "Church and Orthodoxy"; Dameron, *Florence and Its Church*, chaps. 2 and 4; Maria Elena Cortese, *Signori, castelli, città: L'aristocrazia del territorio fiorentino tra X e XII secolo* (Florence: Olschki, 2007), 230, 252; Enrico Faini, *Firenze nell'età romanica (1000–1211): L'espansione urbana, lo sviluppo istituzionale, il rapporto con il territorio* (Florence: Olschki, 2010), 218. For a general, intellectual, and theological development of the idea of purgatory, see Alan Bernstein, "Heaven, Hell, and Purgatory: 1100-1500," in *The Cambridge History of Christianity*, ed. Miri Rubin and Walter Simons (Cambridge: Cambridge University Press, 2009), 4:200–216.

so well by the fourteenth-century chronicler Giovanni Villani, and these were the crucial decades that coincided with the emergence of Florence as the dominant power in Tuscany.[4] As Florence grew in population and expanded its circle of walls after 1284, especially in the course of the thirteenth century, confraternities and hospitals became more numerous, new religious communities for women like the *pinzochere* (female lay penitents) appeared, and public preaching in the newly cleared public spaces (*piazze*) became more and more a feature of urban, public religious life. The physical manifestations of these changes were the initiation of the cathedral project (mid-1290s) and rebuilding of the two mendicant friaries of Santa Croce (founded 1294/95) and Santa Maria Novella (begun by 1279) at the end of the thirteenth century.[5]

In the scholarship of some of the most influential historians of medieval communal Italy—Robert Brentano, Robert Davidsohn, Raoul Manselli, David Herlihy, Giovanni Miccoli, Philip Jones, Anna Benvenuti, and Augustine Thompson—Church and religion have certainly been at the center of the evolution of communal Italian society and politics. Davidsohn's treatment of Church and religion in his history of Florence is still the most comprehensive account in print, even if it was decidedly anticlerical in spirit. Politics (anti-Ghibellinism) could not be separated from accusations of heresy for Florence, according to Raoul Manselli. Similarly, Giovanni Miccoli's story of religion was one that is deeply embedded in social developments and movements. Robert Brentano avoided simple generalizations; instead, he emphasized the unique and localized nature of every ecclesiastical corner of Italy. Deep research in archival sources revealed for David Herlihy that church property played a key role in the development of local economies, including the countryside around Impruneta south of Florence. By the last decade of the last century Philip Jones, who had earlier in

---

4. Giovanni Villani, *Nuova Cronica*, ed. Giuseppe Porta, 3 vols. (Parma: Ugo Guanda, 1990–91); Paula Clarke, "The Villani Chronicles," in *Chronicling History: Chroniclers and Historians in Medieval and Renaissance Italy*, ed. Sharon Dale, Alison Williams Lewin, and Duane Osheim (University Park: Pennsylvania State Press, 2007), 113–43.

5. John White, *Art and Architecture in Italy, 1250–1400* (New Haven, CT: Yale University Press, 1993), 29–31; John M. Najemy, "The Beginnings of Florence Cathedral: A Political Interpretation," in Friedman, Gardner, and Haines, *Arnolfo's Moment*, 183–210. Pinzochere were female lay penitents associated with the mendicant orders, many of whom formed small communities in several houses near the friary of Santa Croce in Florence: see Anna Benvenuti Papi, "Mendicant Friars and Female Pinzochere in Tuscany: From Social Marginality to Models of Sanctity," in *Women and Religion in Medieval and Renaissance Italy*, ed. Daniel Bornstein and Roberto Rusconi (Chicago: University of Chicago Press, 1996), 85; Robert Davidsohn, *Storia di Firenze*, It. translation, various translators, 5 vols. in 8 (Florence: Sansoni, 1956–78), 7:66–67.

his career focused on the economic history of ecclesiastical institutions, was highlighting the importance of religion in the legitimizing claims by the ruling elites of the communes. Indeed, he observed, it was the clergy who often proclaimed their cities as "New Jerusalems." Arguing that the commune was "embedded in religion" and the clergy "embedded" in society, he noted, however, that as religion was increasingly "urbanized," there prevailed much conflict between secular (the laity) and "the established church." Anna Benvenuti's interdisciplinary work on the history of religion in Florence recovered the neglected religious history of Florentine women, highlighting in particular the complicated interplay of piety, gender, and politics in the evolution of the cults of saints, both rural and urban. Richard Trexler was a pioneer in the study of Florentine Church governance and ritual, documenting collaboration as well as conflict and tension between secular and religious authorities. Using Florence as a case study, he was also one of the first historians to write about the key role played in Florence by monks in the economic and fiscal governance of Italian cities.[6] In contrast to Jones however, Augustine Thompson, in his general survey of religion in the Italian communes, strongly downplayed divisive conflict between the laity (and communes) and the established Church. Where Jones often saw hostility, Thompson primarily saw solidarity of interests. In his view, in the history of orthodox religion in Italian medieval cities, the civic and the ecclesiastical were a "single communal organism." Indeed, in agreement with Jones, Thompson emphasized that established Church and orthodox traditions were indeed necessary to the legitimizing claims of secular elites for political legitimacy. Among more recent historians of the medieval Italian commune, however, Chris Wickham has left little if any room for religion in his interpretation of the origins and early formation of the commune. Nevertheless, even in his many works on the social and legal history of city and countryside in Tuscany before ca. 1200, ecclesiastical institutions often appear as economic and legal agents and entities with tangible legal and material interests. In addition, the attention given by Chris Wickham and David Herlihy to church property has certainly influenced the direction of recent scholarship by historians such as Enrico Faini and Maria Elena Cortese. Their work on the history of the early Florentine commune and its countryside has highlighted the central role of church property

---

6. On this subject, see the chapter by Frances Andrews in this volume.

and ecclesiastical patronage in the evolution of eleventh- and twelfth-century Tuscany.[7]

This chapter on Florence owes much to the work of these and other historians, but the evolution of this city also contains particularities that any reader of history should keep in mind. Florence is indeed a very unusual place with its own unique, local history, and that makes it difficult to extrapolate from the Florentine situation to other city-states. However, there is much that it shares with other city-states, such as the importance of church and clergy to the legitimizing strategies of the triumphant *popolo* after ca. 1267. Church property, especially the holdings of the bishopric and cathedral chapter, did indeed constitute significant social and economic links between city and countryside for the period of this essay. However, this ecclesiastical tie linking city and countryside was lost apparently for most of the twelfth century. Philip Jones stressed that the urban environment absorbed the religious culture of the city-state, but no story of the Florentine Church can ignore the existence of significant, separate traditions in the countryside. In addition, for Jones, there had been "a failure of ecclesiastical influence, an estrangement over much of society between laity and established

---

7. Davidsohn, *Storia di Firenze*; Raoul Manselli, "Per la storia dell'eresia catara nella Firenze del tempo di Dante," *Bullettino dell'Istituto storico italiano per il Medio Evo e Archivio Muratoriano* 62 (1950): 123–38; Giovanni Miccoli, "La storia religiosa," in *Storia d'Italia*, vol. 2, *Dalla caduta dell'Impero romano al secolo XVIII*, ed. Ruggiero Romano and Corrado Vivanti (Turin: Einaudi, 1974), bk. 1:431–1079; William North, "Introduction," in Robert Brentano, *Bishops, Saints, and Historians: Studies in Ecclesiastical History of Medieval Britain and Italy*, ed. William North (Aldershot: Ashgate, 2008), ix–xviii; David Herlihy, "Santa Maria Impruneta: A Rural Commune in the Late Middle Ages," in *Florentine Studies: Politics and Society in Renaissance Florence*, ed. Nicolai Rubinstein (Evanston, IL: Northwestern University Press, 1968), 242–76; Philip Jones, *The Italian City-State: From Commune to Signoria* (Oxford: Clarendon Press, 1997), 291–98; Anna Benvenuti Papi, *"In castro poenitentiae": Santità e società femminile nell'Italia medievale* (Rome: Herder, 1990); Augustine Thompson, *Cities of God: The Religion of the Italian Communes, 1125–1325* (University Park: Pennsylvania State University Press, 2005), esp. 1–11, with quote from 6; Richard Trexler, *Synodal Law in Florence and Fiesole, 1306–1518* (Vatican City: Biblioteca Apostolica Vaticana, 1971); Trexler, the chapter, "Honor among Thieves," in *Dependence in Context in Renaissance Florence* (Binghamton: SUNY Press, 1994), 17–34; Trexler, "Death and Testament in the Episcopal Constitutions of Florence (1327)," in *Renaissance Studies in Honor of Hans Baron*, ed. Anthony Molho and John Tedeschi (Dekalb: Northern Illinois University Press, 1971), 29–74; Trexler, *Public Life in Renaissance Florence* (Ithaca, NY: Cornell University Press, 1991); Chris Wickham, *Sleepwalking into a New World: The Emergence of Italian City Communes in the Twelfth Century* (Princeton, NJ: Princeton University Press, 2015); Wickham, *Legge, pratiche e conflitti: Tribunali e risoluzione delle dispute nella Toscana del XII secolo* (Rome: Viella, 2000), especially chap. 6; Herlihy, "Santa Maria Impruneta"; Faini, *Firenze nell'età romanica*; Cortese, *Signori, castelli, città*.

church." This does not seem, however, to have been the case at Florence. Instead, there was often significant cooperation, solidarity, and collaboration between commune and Church, clergy and laity, much as Thompson was emphasizing for Italian communes as a whole.[8] Nevertheless, there was also significant tension and conflict that we cannot ignore, and occasionally collaboration on one issue coexisted at the same time with conflict on another. No one word—cooperation or conflict—can alone describe in general the complicated relationship between clergy and laity, Church and commune. It was far more complex than any simple characterization or turn of phrase can convey.

## The Laity and the Church: Parish and Religious Practice

In the Florence of ca. 1300, the cathedral was the ritual and liturgical center for the celebration of major feast days and the promotion of the cults of patron saints. However, for the typical Florentine of that time, as was true for all residents of the major communes in Italy, the primary center of religious life was the local parish. One's local parish church in city or countryside was either a *pieve*, equipped with a baptismal font, led by an archpriest (*pievano*), and collegiate in nature (sheltering a community of clergy), or, alternatively, one of the numerous churches without baptismal fonts (*ecclesie*, *cappellae*, or oratories) within the district of the local *pieve*. In the diocese of Florence in ca. 1300 there was one urban *pieve* (San Giovanni) and sixty rural *pievi*. The diocese of Fiesole included thirty-five *pievi*. A good example of such a rural community was the *pieve* of Santa Maria Impruneta south of Florence, located in one of the most important towns in the *contado*, the center of a major cult to the Virgin Mary. Located within the earliest (Roman) circle of walls (pre-1284) was the *pieve* of San Giovanni, the many-sided white and black marble building constructed between the eleventh and thirteenth centuries. It was at the heart of the religious center of the city. Here, below the thirteenth-century mosaics depicting the end of time and the division of the saved and the damned, all Florentines, including the poet Dante Alighieri, the saintly recluse

---

8. Jones, *The Italian City-State*, 294; Thompson, *Cities of God*, introduction. Thompson does agree that "bishop and commune, clergy and laity, feuded occasionally," but the dominant environment however was still "the same culture" (6).

Umiliana de' Cerchi, and the chronicler Giovanni Villani, were baptized by their parents, most likely on the Saturday before Easter.⁹

The physical fabric of the Florentine Church (and that of Fiesole), from the urban *pieve* to the rural oratories or *ecclesie*, first and foremost functioned to nurture and administer to the spiritual needs of the population within the two dioceses. Our sources tend to be institutional or prescriptive in nature, and we have relatively less information about grassroots piety and religious practice. However, our understanding of the actual "lived and practiced" religious world of medieval Florentines has grown richer, even if it still remains primarily elusive as it does elsewhere in Italy.¹⁰ But there are a number of common experiences that Florentines would have shared at their local parish. An urban resident in 1300, like the thirty-five-year-old Dante Alighieri, or Covero del fu Corso, a rural resident in the countryside at Petrognano, would have been baptized as infants in the urban *pieve* of San Giovanni and in the local rural *pieve* of Sant'Appiano, respectively.¹¹ Salvation for fallen mankind was possible only through the administration of the sacraments by the priesthood. Baptism wiped away the stain of original sin, and the sacrament of penance was required for the remission of sins after baptism. The Fourth Lateran Council of 1215 mandated confession to a priest at least once a year, and that was supposed to occur at the parish level. For Florentines as well as for Christians elsewhere in Europe the principal worship service was the administration of the sacrament of the Eucharist. It commemorated, through the transubstantiation of the wine and bread into the body and blood of Christ, the sacrifice of Christ for the remission of the sins of mankind. The value of this ritual on the local level is evident from the fact that many Florentines left bequests in their testaments in both city and countryside—increasingly after the middle of the thirteenth century—for altar cloths, candles,

---

9. Dameron, "Church and Orthodoxy," 88–89; Peter Hawkins, "Religious Culture," in Barański and Pertile, *Dante in Context*, 319–24; Timothy Verdon, "Firenze e le sue chiese," in *Le chiese e la città*, ed. Timothy Verdon, vol. 1 of Alla riscoperta delle chiese di Firenze (Florence: Centro Di, 2002), 24. The earliest document on the baptistery at this location dates, however, from 897: Franklin Toker, *On Holy Ground: Liturgy, Architecture, and Urbanism in the Cathedral and Streets of Medieval Florence*, The Florence Duomo Project 1 (Turnhout: Brepols, 2009), 3.

10. Aside from Dameron, "Church and Orthodoxy," the following is heavily indebted to the works of Burr, Hawkins, Najemy, Tacconi, and Thompson that are cited in the bibliography.

11. For what follows, see Dameron, "Church and Orthodoxy," 85–87; Hawkins, "Religious Culture," 320–21; ASF *NA* 17577 (Ranieri da Cione, Petrognano, 1299–1300), fol. 17v.

and vestments (most often, chasubles).[12] Many testators stipulated that Masses continue to be celebrated and suffrages be said for themselves and their loved ones long after their deaths. This helps account for the popularity of the idea of purgatory and for the many chasubles in the bequests of many testators. Suffrages and Masses and charity figured highly in many testaments. In 1325, Fia del fu Salario, widow of Lamberto, requested in her testament that she should be buried in the parish of Santa Felicita in Piazza and that fifty *lire* be dispensed for her soul and for that of her dead son, Duccio ("pro anima ipsius testatricis et pro anima Duccii"). Her legacies included money set aside for Masses and for the hospital of Santa Maria Nuova, and one of the largest bequests was for clothing the poor.[13] At the close of their lives, Florentines like Covero or Fia expected to receive the sacrament of extreme unction (or the anointing of the sick), often from a local priest or friar they had chosen, to prepare them for the afterlife.

The number and frequency of testaments with legacies for postmortem anniversary Masses and suffrages increased significantly from the end of the thirteenth through the fourteenth century, in direct proportion with the growing diffusion of belief in purgatory.[14] From the earliest centuries of Christianity (Augustine, d. 430), Christians had worried about what happened to those who are not good enough to go to heaven immediately but are not sinful enough to deserve hell. The origins of belief in a third realm in the afterlife for those people, purgatory, are found in the New Testament (1 Corinthians 3:15). By ca. 1160 theologians such as Peter Lombard were agreeing that prayers (suffrages) could quicken the pace by which a soul would pass through purgatory. It finally found official Church acceptance in 1274 at the Second Council of Lyons, and seems to have been particularly well diffused among elites in those regions of Europe that were the most commercialized and economically advanced: Tuscany, southeast England, and the Mediterranean coast of France. In Florence alone, in both city and countryside, there are hundreds of testaments leaving legacies for suffrages and anniversary Masses for dead family members and for

---

12. The chasuble was a "poncho-like garment that is the outermost vestment worn by the priest to say Mass": Maureen C. Miller, *Clothing the Clergy: Virtue and Power in Medieval Europe, c. 800–1200* (Ithaca, NY: Cornell University Press, 2014), 248.

13. ASF *NA* 6169 (Dini di Lotto di Firenze, 1314-29), fol. 127r-v.

14. For what follows, see Bernstein, "Heaven, Hell, and Purgatory"; Dameron, *Florence and Its Church*, 171-72; Jacques Le Goff, *The Birth of Purgatory*, trans. Arthur Goldhammer (Chicago: University of Chicago Press, 1981), part 3.

the donor herself or himself. They become particularly more numerous after 1290, especially among those who benefited the most from credit at a time of rapid if not explosive economic growth. Entrusted to administer these legacies by the testators were friars and local priests, members of both the mendicant and secular clergy. For example, one of the two executors of the many legacies to several local churches and to the poor, left by a certain Rodolfo of the parish of the *pieve* of Settimo, was Presbyter Rodolfo of the *pieve* of Settimo.[15] No one, however, drew more attention to purgatory than a Florentine, Dante Alighieri, the author of *Purgatorio*.

There was certainly a difference between ideal religious practice, as set forth in some of the most important Church councils like the Fourth Lateran of 1215 and the First and Second Councils of Lyon (1245 and 1274), and what was probably actually happening on the ground. This is a world that for the most part eludes us. Most of the residents in this part of Tuscany who were subject to the spiritual guidance of the bishops of Florence and Fiesole were rural, not urban residents. As surprising as it may seem, a minority of the residents of the two dioceses in the *contado* of Florence actually lived in the city itself. Giovanni Villani estimated there were around 130,000 in the city of Florence around ca. 1300. However, there were probably another 200,000–300,000 living in the countryside, and here the local parish, the neighboring monastery, a friary, or perhaps a hospital were the dominant ecclesiastical presences in the immediate region. We are dealing, therefore, when describing the Florentine Church, with two separate and not always overlapping environments: the urban and the rural. The bishops of Florence and Fiesole only began to promote systematically the feast days of major civic saints in the countryside and city with the promulgation of the synodal constitution of 1310. However, the rural religious environment was never fully integrated into the urban church, absorbed by civic traditions and demands. The *contado* had its own confraternities, its own hospitals, its own local parish priests, and its own local saints' cults (such as Saint Verdiana). Contrary to canon law, concubinage among priests in the outer reaches of the diocese of Fiesole, for example, was not uncommon, and most likely, though it was perhaps worrisome to the bishop of Fiesole in the last decade of the thirteenth century, it was

---

15. ASF *NA* 12527 (Maffei da Settimo, 1300–1315), fol. 26v; Dameron, *Florence and Its Church*, 175–94.

probably tolerated by local residents.[16] In addition, some of the earliest associations of lay penitents or *conversi* began in the countryside, including Tuscany. They probably arrived in Florence between 1218 and 1221, primarily drawn from the most recently urbanized, and are first documented as being present in the city in 1224. They became strongly involved with hospitals and with care for the poor. In addition, what we know of heresy, persistent ideals and beliefs that ran counter to the canons of the principal church councils, probably originated in the countryside before appearing in the cities of central and northern Italy in the late twelfth and early thirteenth centuries.[17]

## The Laity and Its Church: The Emergence of a Penance Culture

Throughout Italy, following the era of Gregorian reform, the interaction between two separate but overlapping pathways to the ideal of spiritual purity—the traditional pursuit of monastic asceticism, on the one hand, and the newer embrace of the ideal of the apostolic life, on the other—helped generate in the twelfth century, in the words of Augustine Thompson, a lay "penance culture."[18] Like other communes in Italy from the late twelfth century, Florence had its own lay penitential traditions. These laymen and women, who sought to pursue the penitential life, wanted to "imitate Christ" in the world without having to enter a monastery. One could remain in one's own home, devoting oneself to a life of prayer, fasting, simplicity (though not usually absolute poverty), and charity. Many of the earliest associations of lay penitents or *conversi* in Italy were rural, such as the rural confraternity

---

16. Archivio Vescovile di Fiesole, Visite Pastorali V.1, fols. 8r-12r, 31v. For religion in the countryside, see the nine essays in Charles M. de La Roncière, *Religion paysanne et religion urbaine en Toscane (c. 1250–c. 1450)* (Aldershot: Ashgate Variorum, 1994). The life and cult of Saint Verdiana in the *contado* of Florence (Castelfiorentino) is discussed in Benvenuti Papi, "La serva-patrona," in *"In castro poenitentiae,"* 263-303.

17. Benvenuti Papi, "I Penitenti," in *"In castro Poenitentiae,"* 30-37; Carol Lansing, *Power and Purity: Cathar Heresy in Medieval Italy* (Oxford: Oxford University Press, 1998), 71 (Florentine Cathars in the 1240s "included petty elites and merchants, often of recent urban origins"); Cinzio Violante, "Eresie nelle città e nel contado in Italia dall'XI al XIII secolo," in Cinzio Violante, *Studi sulla cristianità medioevale: Società, istituzioni, spiritualità*, ed. Piero Zerbi (Milan: Vita e Pensiero, 1972), 355-66.

18. Thompson, *Cities of God*, 69; André Vauchez, "*'Ordo Fraternitatis'*: Confraternities and Lay Piety in the Middle Ages" and "Medieval Penitents," in Vauchez, *The Laity in the Middle Ages: Religious Beliefs and Devotional Practices*, ed. Daniel E. Bornstein, trans. Margery J. Schneider (Notre Dame, IN: University of Notre Dame Press, 1993), 107-17 and 119-27, respectively.

at San Cassiano d'Imola, ca. 1160, in northern Italy. Its members took care of their less fortunate associates, distributed charity to the poor, and met annually on the feast of their patron saint (Saint James). This was a prayer community founded by those who had made the pilgrimage to Santiago de Compostela. By 1227 penitential confraternities of lay men and women like this had functioned for decades, but in that year they also formally received official recognition by Pope Gregory IX as the Brothers and Sisters of Penance. These communities remained largely managed and directed by members of the laity until Pope Nicholas IV in *Supra montem* (1289) brought them under the control of the Franciscans.[19]

The development of this new post-1100 way of life was particularly strong and evident in Tuscany and in the countryside near the city of Florence. One of the major ways by which members of the Florentine laity were profoundly engaged in the spiritual life of the city and countryside was the confraternity.[20] In the countryside at least, from as early as the eleventh century, laity and clergy alike were contributing to the pastoral care of their community in one of the earliest confraternities in all of Italy. By 1311 the bishop of Florence, Antonio d'Orso, had given the confraternity of the clergy permission to build its own hospital in the parish of San Lorenzo.[21] Most of the confraternities in thirteenth- and fourteenth-century Florence, however, grew out of the lay penitential movement and benefited from the inspiration and support of the friars. For example, in the middle of the thirteenth century, the Dominicans favored the development of new lay confraternal associations in the city, at least partly as a hedge against the appeal of Ghibelline ideas. As at Imola, these were associations of the laity in both city and countryside, devoted to the veneration of a particular patron saint and dedicated to the mutual support and protection of its living and its dead members. Most of the confraternities in city and countryside

---

19. Thompson, *Cities of God*, 100–101; Neslihan Şenocak, "Twelfth-Century Italian Confraternities as Institutions of Pastoral Care," *Journal of Medieval History* 42 (2016), 206–8, http://dx.doi.org/10.1080/03044181.2016.1141702. I am grateful to Neslihan Şenocak for information about the Imola confraternity and the significance of *Supra montem*.

20. Much of the following regarding hospitals and confraternities relies on John Henderson, *Piety and Charity in Late Medieval Florence* (Oxford: Clarendon Press, 1994); Şenocak, "Twelfth-Century Italian Confraternities"; La Roncière, "Les Confréries," in *Religion paysanne et religion urbaine*, essay 8; Hawkins, "Religious Culture," 329–32; and Dameron, "Church and Orthodoxy," 100–101.

21. William Bowsky, *Le Chiesa di San Lorenzo a Firenze nel medioevo*, ed. Renzo Nelli (Florence: Meridiana, 1999), 200–205; Davidsohn, *Storia di Firenze*, 7:104–5.

## 12. CASE STUDY I: FLORENCE 349

in Florence in the fourteenth century had emerged in the course of the thirteenth and fourteenth. However, in Tuscany they were present in religious life as early as the eleventh and twelfth centuries and included clergy as well as women. Pastoral care (the "care of souls") was their primary function. Duties by both lay and clergy in these early confraternities like those at Sant'Appiano in Val d'Elsa included public confession, prayers for the dead by both clergy and laity, and visiting the sick and performing last rites (if required). The clergy and laity (men and women) of this community in the Val d'Elsa in the southern part of the diocese, for example, dated from the eleventh century and met at least three times a year for Mass, confession, and "refreshment" or meal. Close to Florence, the Val d'Elsa was one of the most economically advanced regions of the Tuscan countryside. It was agriculturally rich, supplying needed grain to local and regional markets, and its location in proximity to the Via Francigena placed it on one of the most important channels for communication and information in Europe. In this same river valley in the fourteenth century southwest of Florence (the Val d'Elsa), Charles de La Roncière found twenty-seven confraternities.[22] Economic ties connecting local residents, coupled with the arrival of innovative ideas about reform and the penitential life from the north and south along the Via Francigena, fostered the emergence of these early corporate associations.

Before ca. 1350 there were at least forty-three confraternities of various types in the city, and in the countryside there was at least a third of that number. Of those forty-three urban confraternities documented by John Henderson between ca. 1240 and ca. 1350, over a third (fifteen) were either founded in the four decades between ca. 1280 and ca. 1320 or mentioned for the first time during those decades. Inspired and promoted by the Franciscans after their first arrival in the city in 1208 or 1209 and also by the Dominicans (at Santa Maria Novella by 1221), these thirteenth- and fourteenth-century confraternities took on a variety of forms and missions. The *laudesi* lay confraternities were particularly devoted to singing the praises of the Virgin Mary. The earliest *laudesi* hymns appeared in Tuscany and Umbria in the 1230s and quickly diffused throughout central and northern Italy. Sant'Agnese e

---

22. The number of fourteenth-century confraternities in the Val d'Elsa is cited in Vauchez, "'*Ordo Fraternitatis*,'" 116; Şenocak, "Twelfth-Century Italian Confraternities," 207–21; La Roncière, "La place des confréries dans l'encadrement religieux du contado florentin: L'exemple de la Val d'Elsa au XIV siècle," in *Religion paysanne et religion urbaine*, essay 1.

Santa Maria delle Laude, founded in 1249, met in the Carmelite convent of Santa Maria del Carmine on the south side of the Arno River (the Oltrarno). They often gathered monthly. The *laudesi* fraternity of Sant'Eustachio, established in the early fourteenth century, gathered in the collegiate church of Sant'Ambrogio near the eastern gate. Most of the *laudesi* confraternities were, however, founded in those crucial decades of Florentine growth between ca. 1280 and ca. 1340. A good example is the confraternity of Saint Zenobius, a principal patron saint of the city, founded in 1281. There was *lauda* singing every evening and feast day, and every month members of the company (two by two) would process into the cathedral and light candles. In 1310 the bishop stipulated that Zenobius's cult was to be venerated throughout the diocese, especially on May 25 (his feast day). Like so many urban confraternities, statutes established the governance structure for the company of Saint Zenobius. In 1326 the company issued a new set of statutes.[23] Members of flagellant confraternities, like that of San Lorenzo in Palco (founded in 1279 and meeting in the Dominican friary of Santa Maria Novella), subjected themselves to self-mortification to imitate the sufferings of Christ and do penance. A third major type of association was the charitable confraternity, and some of these were the largest distributors of charity in the city. The fraternity of the Madonna of Orsanmichele, both *laudesi* and charitable, established in 1291, and the company of the Misericordia (Oratory of the Misericordia) were perhaps the most important charitable institutions. For example, during the catastrophic grain shortage of 1329, the leaders of the commune designated the confraternity of Orsanmichele in October of that year as the major distributor of poor relief (a two thousand *lire* annual subsidy).[24]

Not all confraternities were fraternities, as some associations continued to include both genders. However, by the middle of the thirteenth century, the division of men and women into separate confraternities or companies had become common in the communes. The first reference to the female company of San Lorenzo delle Donne (*societas mulierum S. Laurentii*), for example, was 1303. Augustine Thompson has argued that

---

23. Henderson, *Piety and Charity*, 444–74; Blake Wilson, "Music, Art, Devotion: The Cult of Saint Zenobius at the Florentine Cathedral during the Early Renaissance," in Verdon and Innocenti, *Atti del VII centenario*, 3:17–27; Blake Wilson, *Music and Merchants: The Laudesi Companies of Republican Florence* (Oxford: Clarendon Press, 1992), 1–4; Rona Goffen, *Spirituality in Conflict: Saint Francis and Giotto's Bardi Chapel* (University Park: Pennsylvania State Press, 1988), 1.

24. Henderson, *Piety and Charity*, 273–79, 460–61; Dameron, *Florence and Its Church*, 146.

women penitents outnumbered their male counterparts everywhere in communal Italy. Those who chose not to take the veil had a variety of options to pursue as they sought to imitate Christ and live a life of penance. Among the most important of such communities were those women, mostly widowed, who chose to live the penitential life close to one another and in proximity to the two mendicant friaries of Santa Maria Novella (Dominican) and Santa Croce (Franciscan). These were the *pinzochere*, associated with the friars of Santa Croce, and the *mantellate* (with ties to the Dominicans at Santa Maria Novella). According to their principal historian, Anna Benvenuti Papi, these women penitents began to gather around both Santa Croce and Santa Maria Novella in the middle of the century (ca. 1250–ca. 1260), pooling their resources. Gradually, like so many of these bottom-up, grassroots penitential associations of men and women, they were brought under the control of the mendicant orders and pressured to adopt a monastic model of governance by the end of the thirteenth century. By 1299 there was an abbess supervising this loose community. Clustered around these friaries in private homes, they dedicated the final chapter of their lives to a life of penance, charity, and prayer. What is most unusual about these Florentine *pinzochere* is the large number of testaments (187, by my estimate) drawn up and notarized between 1297 and 1300. The vast majority of the legacies left by these propertied widows went to the friars, whom, no doubt, they knew personally and for whom they had great affection.[25]

The Franciscan friars encouraged this sort of enduring connection. An example is the short life of Umiliana de' Cerchi (1219–46), a penitent or *conversa* who followed an unusual path and whose veneration received significant support from the local friars in the years immediately following her death. Our source of information on Umiliana is Vito da Cortona, a Franciscan who composed his account as early as a year after her death. She was the daughter of a prosperous banker from a well-connected family (the Cerchi). At sixteen she was married to another banker, and their marriage produced two children (daughters). After six years of marriage, her husband died, and her paternal family pressured her to marry again. She refused, rejecting the demands of

---

25. Benvenuti Papi, "Forme communitarie," in *"In castro Poenitentiae,"* 582–83; Benvenuti Papi, "Mendicant Friars and Female Pinzochere in Tuscany," 91–92; Dameron, *Florence and Its Church*, 47–48; ASF NA 15527 (Opizzo da Pontremoli, 1296–1304); Thompson, *Cities of God*, 97.

her paternal household and the prosperous quality of life available to young women of her class in Florence at the time. Instead, she devoted herself to charity to the poor, often distributing food and clothing to the less fortunate. Perhaps mindful of the choices made by Clare of Assisi (d. 1253), who was still alive at the time and also from a prosperous (noble) lineage, Umiliana resisted the demands of her patrilineage and thereby faced the wrath of her father. He sent Umiliana's two daughters away (to the household of their father) and tricked her into signing over to him her dowry (her only means of economic support). Umiliana lived out the rest of her days in a small room in the Cerchi tower (just a block north of the present-day Piazza della Signoria), dependent on whatever her father was willing to give her. Under the influence and guidance of two male spiritual directors (one of whom was Franciscan), she became a recluse within the family tower and increasingly devoted herself to a life of prayer and contemplation. As Anna Benvenuti Papi and André Vauchez have argued, her cult became a Franciscan model of spirituality for women: excluded from the public sphere behind walls, she had dedicated herself to the penitential life, devoting herself to prayer, charity, and contemplation. A member of a prosperous family who had benefited greatly from the expanding banking and manufacturing sectors in early thirteenth-century Florence, Umiliana had, like Clare, rejected worldly comfort and wealth to pursue a life of penitence, embracing poverty, charity, and increasingly, prayer and contemplation. Not all women seeking to live lives in imitation of Christ would or could follow her example. However, she became a model for the Florentine women who were gathering as tertiaries around the two friaries of the Franciscans and the Dominicans in the course of the thirteenth century. They were still living in private homes, guided spiritually by the friars, and devoted to a life of austerity and prayer. Like Umiliana, many of these women were widows from some of the most economically prosperous families of the city.[26]

Charity and care for the poor and sick were key goals of the life that Umiliana de' Cerchi and other enthusiasts for the penitential life chose

---

26. Vito da Cortona, *Vita beatae Humilianae de Cerchis, Acta Sanctorum*, Maii IV (Antwerp, 1685), cols. 385–402; André Vauchez, "Female Sanctity in the Franciscan Movement," in Vauchez, *The Laity in the Middle Ages*, 171–83; Benvenuti Papi, *"In castro poenitentiae,"* 59–98; Dameron, *Florence and Its Church*, 192–94; Carol Lansing, *The Florentine Magnates: Lineage and Faction in a Medieval Commune* (Princeton, NJ: Princeton University Press, 1991), 109–24.

for themselves, but these were also the primary functions of another major ecclesiastical institution in both the city and countryside of Florence: the hospital. The recipients of their care and attention tended to be people permanently or temporarily outside of or excluded from the community because of a special status: the ill, the poor and indigent, travelers, and even (probably) rural, immigrant, or itinerant laborers in the cloth industry. However, hospitals were also significantly important dispensers of other forms of charity, including grain, especially during food shortages (as in 1329). Tracking the growth of population, most hospitals existing in the middle of the fourteenth century had emerged primarily after the closing decades of the thirteenth, post ca. 1280. The chronicler Giovanni Villani estimated there were thirty hospitals in the city in 1338, equipped with about a thousand beds for their residents. There were probably many more hospitals in the city, however, as a recent estimate has put the number at fifty-eight. Among the most important of these institutions in the city were Santa Maria Nuova, San Paolo (which could accommodate over seven hundred people in the early fourteenth century), San Gallo (one of the largest institutions for the ill), and Santa Maria della Scala (which served orphan children). Santa Maria Nuova is a good example of growth. Founded in 1288 by Folco Portinari, the father of the Beatrice beloved by Dante, Santa Maria Nuova emerged close to the church of Sant'Egidio in central Florence. It is still there and remains one of the major hospitals of the city. It began with just seventeen beds to care for travelers and for the poor, but by the eve of the Black Death it had over two hundred beds for the ill and the poor. In the rural areas of the two dioceses of Florence and Fiesole, hospitals also had a special role to play to take care of travelers and pilgrims along the major roads who were making their way to or from Florence. For the countryside, between ca. 1280 and ca. 1350, Charles de La Roncière documented at least 136 hospitals, most of which, however, were very small. Many of these, no doubt, served the needs of laborers moving from one job to another.[27]

---

27. Dameron, "Church and Orthodoxy," 100-102; Dameron, *Florence and Its Church*, 51-57; John Henderson, "The Hospitals of Late Medieval and Renaissance Florence: A Preliminary Survey," in *The Hospital in History*, ed. Lindsay Granshaw and Roy Porter (London: Routledge, 1989), 63-92; La Roncière, "Dans la campagne Florentine au XIV siècle: Les communautés chrétiennes et leurs curés," in *Religion paysanne et religion urbaine*, essay 3, 285.

## The Monastic Tradition and Regular Clergy

The major orders of the regular clergy were represented before ca. 1350 in the city and countryside within the two dioceses of Florence and Fiesole, and they varied greatly in size. We usually find the most ancient monastic institutions in the city center or just outside the first (Roman) circle of city walls. Two of the oldest were the Badia, founded in the late tenth century (967-69) by the widow of the Tuscan marquis (Willa), and San Miniato al Monte, created in the early eleventh century by Bishop Ildebrando. Benedictine establishments retained consistent and traditional presences both inside and outside the walls throughout the three centuries that are the subject of this chapter. Indeed, both the Badia and San Miniato al Monte continue to dominate the Florentine skyline today. Among the most important of the rural Benedictine monasteries were San Michele di Passignano, located in the southern reaches of the diocese, and Vallombrosa, founded in the eleventh century by the former monk at San Miniato al Monte, Giovanni Gualberto. Later monastic establishments, and many of them associated with communities of women, were smaller and were concentrated in particular between the second and third circle of walls (construction from 1284). These were communities created and established during the era of greatest population expansion in the city (thirteenth century). Villani estimated that in the 1330s there were about five hundred nuns in urban convents. There were probably many more than those, however, living in a wide variety of communities that varied in size (or alone as *recluse*). Most of these convents, unlike the earliest monasteries for males, were located far from the city center. In 1333 there were seventeen major female convents within the third (latest) circle of walls. As a growing number of hospitals helped support rural immigrants who were entering the city seeking work, many originally rural female religious communities were coming to the city for safety and security during periods of unrest and insecurity in the countryside (late thirteenth and early fourteenth century). This coincided with the apparent economic decline in the countryside of many of the families who had first endowed them.[28] As the city saw its population expand and its economic

---

28. Saundra Weddle, "Identity and Alliance: Urban Presence, Spatial Privilege, and Florentine Renaissance Convents," in *Renaissance Florence: A Social History*, ed. Roger J. Crum and John T. Paoletti (Cambridge: Cambridge University Press, 2006), 394-96; Dameron, "Church and Orthodoxy," 94-100; Davidsohn, *Storia di Firenze*, 1:174-75, 242-52. Comprehensive overviews of mendicants and religious communities exist in Benvenuti Papi, "Donne religiose

and political prominence rise in the course of the thirteenth and early fourteenth centuries, Florence increasingly attracted and then hosted new religious institutions of regular clergy, many of them mendicant. The Franciscans were at Santa Croce by 1221 and the Dominicans at the opposite end of the city by 1221 as well. These were located in areas of greatest economic growth, increasingly populated with rural immigrants and artisans. The Carmelites settled in the Oltrarno in 1268, and the Humiliati were at San Donato a Torri outside the city by 1239–40 and in the city by 1251. In the late thirteenth and early fourteenth centuries, emblematic of the growth in population and the elevation of the economic and political profile of the city itself, the mendicant convents hosted major schools of study: Santa Maria Novella became a *studium generale* by 1309 and Santa Croce by 1287. At the same time, the commune increasingly depended on the economic expertise of major monastic orders (the Humiliati and the Cistercians) to manage some of its most important public funds.[29]

## Florence and Its Church: Cooperation and Conflict

The relationships between Florentine ecclesiastical communities—especially the bishopric—and its clergy, on the one hand, and the city (and from the late twelfth century, the commune), on the other, were often cooperative, but occasional conflict was common. In the eleventh century ecclesiastical institutions were deeply embedded in the economic, cultural, and social fabric of both the city and its countryside. The breakup of the Kingdom of Italy in the tenth and eleventh centuries left the marquis of Tuscany, the major abbeys (the Badia and Marturi) and bishoprics, and the cathedral chapters (Florence and Fiesole) among the most powerful property-holders in the two dioceses. New family, proprietary (Benedictine) monasteries appeared at this

---

nella Firenze del Due-Trecento," in *"In castro Poenitentiae,"* 593–634, and especially 601–22; parts 1 and 6 provide detailed overviews of religious communities. For Passignano, see Paolo Pirillo and Italo Moretti, eds., *Passignano in Val di Pesa: Un monastero e la sua storia*, 2 vols. (Florence: Olschki, 2009–14).

29. Dameron, "Church and Orthodoxy," 96–99; Frances Andrews, *The Early Humiliati* (Cambridge: Cambridge University Press, 1999), 140–43, 277; Trexler, "Honor among Thieves." For the role of regular clergy in urban governance in medieval Italy as a whole, see Frances Andrews, ed., with Maria Agata Pincelli, *Churchmen and Urban Government in Late Medieval Italy, c.1200–c.1450: Cases and Contexts* (Cambridge: Cambridge University Press, 2013), and (in particular for Florence and Siena) see William Day's essay, "The Cistercian Monk and the Casting Counter," 251–67.

time at places like Settimo, Strumi, and Coltibuono to safeguard and preserve the patrimonies of the elite families in the region from threats of appropriation from other families or members of the elite. Some of these establishments were centers of reform, with the exception of the urban San Pier Maggiore (founded by Gisla dei Firidolfi, ca. 1067). Before the early twelfth century, they were among the very same families who easily moved between city and countryside, possessing interests in both. They were members of the clienteles of both marquis and bishop. Through the marquis and the bishop of Florence, major landholding families in the countryside had strong ties to the city. Beginning on an infrequent basis as early as 931 (and becoming more frequent over time), the bishopric required its tenants to pay their rents on the octave of the feast of San Giovanni, and the ritualistic offerings of *ceri* by leaseholders on the actual feast day was also becoming increasingly common (but was not an actual obligation until at least 1127). Evidence for feudo-vassalic relations linking the bishops of Florence and Fiesole with aristocratic clients is weak and rare, however, with the exception of the early twelfth-century bishop Goffredo degli Alberti (1113–42). By the end of the eleventh century, a number of ecclesiastical institutions were even taking the lead in the economic development of the region around Florence. In 1084 we first find documentary evidence for mills, significantly first on church properties, especially those of major monasteries. The expanding economic growth of the Florentine region from the late eleventh and twelfth centuries obviously increasingly benefited ecclesiastical institutions, but it also contributed to creating the conditions for intraecclesiastical conflict. One very well documented legal case in the second half of the twelfth century at Figline in the Arno valley, for example, shows how neighboring ecclesiastical institutions were using litigation to resolve their conflict over access to various mills.[30]

---

30. Cortese, *Signori, castelli, città*, 50, 110, 138, 227; Faini, *Firenze nell'età romanica*, 71, 180, 275; Davidsohn, *Storia di Firenze*, 1:338–39, 498; Trexler, "Death and Testament"; Chris Wickham, "Ecclesiastical Dispute and Lay Community: Figline Valdarno in the Twelfth Century," *Mélanges de l'École française de Rome: Moyen Âge* 108, no. 1 (1996): esp. 8; Mauro Ronzani, "Dalla regione romana alla Marca di Tuscia," in *Storia della Toscana*, ed. Pietro Pezzino, Elena Fasano Guarini, and Giuseppe Petralia (Rome: Laterza, 2004), 72–90. In "Church and Community," in *A Florentine Church*, ed. Robert W. Gaston and Louis A. Waldman (Florence: Villa I Tatti, the Harvard University Center for Italian Renaissance Studies, 2017), 43, I argue that the canons of San Lorenzo might have played an indirect role in the development of the commune (42–43). We find consuls (*consules*) at Florence in 1125 and 1138, often seen by some scholars as marking the beginning of a commune. There is a significant debate, however, about when we can actually document the origin of any commune. For some historians, like Chris Wickham and Enrico Faini, the mere existence of consuls is not sufficient (Wickham, *Sleepwalking*

## 12. CASE STUDY I: FLORENCE

In contrast to many other bishops in central and northern Italy (such as at Arezzo), with the exception of the failed attempt by Bishop Goffredo degli Alberti, no bishops of Florence in the eleventh or twelfth centuries attempted to control the city. They possessed no army (with the exception of Goffredo), and the social ties with their rural and urban clienteles were weak. In the early twelfth century, the dominant political figure in Tuscany was the Countess or Marquise Matilda, of the house of Canossa. She ruled over the march of Tuscany, a coherent and autonomous region with Lucca as its capital that dated back to the third quarter of the ninth century. Her power base in Tuscany was, however, in her vast rural estates (not cities), though most of her holdings were north of the march. When Marquise Matilda died in 1115, we find that the ties linking midlevel rural patrilineages to the city were rapidly fraying. Most of the twelfth century, particularly the period between ca. 1126 and ca. 1150, was marked by a sharp separation between city and countryside, characterized by the loss of ties by these major rural families to the city and its bishop. As Maria Elena Cortese has argued, the bishop of Florence was no longer a "sufficient pole of attraction" for these lineages. Nevertheless, even during this era of city/country "rupture," ecclesiastical communities were often at the forefront of new economic and social developments. Early immigration into the city by nonelite rural residents seeking employment in the nascent cloth industry was facilitated through ties to those churches in the countryside that also had an urban presence. Ecclesiastical institutions functioned as sources of credit in both countryside and city. The rural aristocracy obtained credit from local monasteries and churches, and rural churches (*cappelle*) often served as economic supports for local residents. The urban Visdomini lineage, traditionally charged with administering the episcopal estate during vacancies, relied on the bishopric for credit, essentially looting the episcopal estate during vacancies. To benefit from the growing markets for grain to feed an expanding population, major

---

*into a New World*, chap. 1, esp. 15–21, 182–84). Enrico Faini has argued that the Florentine commune emerged no later than the late twelfth century (1170s and 1180s), though it could have been sooner (*Firenze nell'età romanica*, chap. 4, esp. 243–75). Documents are simply lacking. The argument in his 2010 book regarding the importance of the conflicts associated with Bishop Goffredo degli Alberti for the development of the Florentine commune seem, however, to support my own perspective on the topic, first presented in 2009 at the conference on San Lorenzo in Florence, that whether or not a commune was in existence in 1138 or the 1170s, the impact of these conflicts on its development was at least indirect and at most decisive.

ecclesiastical lords such as the cathedral chapter of Florence and the monastery at Vallombrosa were clearing land for wheat cultivation. In the second quarter of the twelfth century we also first have evidence that ecclesiastical institutions were investing in residential (and not just agricultural) properties. Simultaneously, and significantly, the bishopric of Florence was actively building *castelli* (fortified villages) throughout the countryside to organize and manage its estates more efficiently, create rent-collecting centers, and become more sensitive to local market demand and needs. By the late twelfth century, however, rural lords were again beginning to return to the city, attracted by the lucrative investments in its rapid economic growth (the expanding cloth industry) and opportunities for political advancement.[31] It was also precisely during this period near the end of the twelfth century—an era of rapid population growth, explosion of wealth, and expanding commercial ties throughout the Mediterranean—that we first have evidence that a commune of Florence had emerged and that Cathars had a presence there (ca. 1173).[32]

In the middle of the thirteenth century, conflict between communal officials and the bishop erupted over the handling of certain Cathar suspects. The relationship between Bishop Ardingo (1231-47) and the young commune was, however, essentially collaborative. The importation into Florence of the arm of Saint Philip was most likely an attempt to draw attention away from the lures of Catharism among urban Florentines. At the same time, later than at Lucca, Ardingo and the cathedral chapter were reorganizing their estates by encouraging the commutation of traditional rents (in money and kind) into rents purely in kind (grain). This suited major ecclesiastical lords (higher income

---

31. Faini, *Firenze nell'età romanica*, 36, 71, 92, 123, 157, 162-65, 205, 217-18, 247, 316; Cortese, *Signori, castelli, città*, 172, 227, 230 ("polo di aggregazione"); Dameron, *Florence and Its Church*, 85-86; George W. Dameron, *Episcopal Power and Florentine Society, 1000-1320* (Cambridge, MA: Harvard University Press, 1991), 16-18; Lansing, *The Florentine Magnates*, chap. 4 ("Ecclesiastical Rights as Joint Property"). For information on Matilda and the March of Tuscany, see Chris Wickham, *Early Medieval Italy: Central Power and Local Society, 400-1000* (Ann Arbor: University of Michigan Press, 1989), 60, 183. See also Ronzani, "Dalla regione romana alla Marca di Tuscia," 79-90.

32. What follows on heresy in the next paragraph relies largely on the following: David Burr, "Heresy and Dissidence," in Barański and Pertile, *Dante in Context*, 106-18; Manselli, "Per la storia dell'eresia catara nella Firenze del tempo di Dante"; Raoul Manselli, *L'Eresia del male*, 2nd ed. (Naples: Morano, 1980), 217-18, 262-63, 278-88, 331; Lansing, *Power and Purity*, 71-78; Dinora Corsi, "Aspetti dell'inquisizione fiorentina nel '200," in *Eretici e ribelli del XIII e XIV secolo: Saggi sullo spiritualismo francescano in Toscana*, ed. Domenico Maselli (Pistoia: Tellini, 1974), 65-90 (with documents).

from grain sales) and the city alike (more grain for a growing immigrant population). At the same time, the city consuls were helping the bishopric negotiate power-sharing arrangements with emerging rural communes in regions where the bishop had traditionally been the sole authority. Precisely as these changes were occurring on major ecclesiastical estates, the papacy was promoting a major effort to root out Cathars living in the city.

Catharism was primarily a rural phenomenon, but its presence in the city was both a religious threat (to orthodoxy) and a political menace for Guelfs (since it was closely associated with Ghibellines). In 1227 the pope called for a campaign in Florence against any suspected heretics, and in 1235 the Dominicans were entrusted with that responsibility (that burden would eventually fall to the Franciscans in 1254). In 1245 there erupted civil, faction-based unrest within the city as the bishop opposed the attempts of the *podestà* to protect Cathars and their noble Ghibelline sympathizers. After 1245 there is little evidence of heresy in the city, even though the Inquisition became active again in the 1280s. In some instances, however, bishop and commune found common cause against the papacy. A good case in point is the episode involving the rural, female convent of Sant'Ellero. In the mid-1250s the papacy had wanted to cede the convent, located near Ubaldini territory close to the Casentino, to the abbey of Vallombrosa. The commune resisted, knowing the location could become a major strategic location for the Ubaldini, a traditional enemy. Eventually, the papacy imposed an interdict on the city in 1256, and the bishop, *prepositus* of the cathedral chapter, and communal leaders all refused to recognize it. Clergy who wanted to observe the interdict had apparently been jailed by public authorities.[33]

Other interdicts imposed by the papacy followed in the second half of the thirteenth century: 1273-80 and 1285. For the most part, though conflicts occasionally erupted, the growing power of Florentine public authority in the thirteenth and early fourteenth centuries forced the clergy and its leaders into an uneasy tolerance of communal laws, based on what Richard Trexler has characterized as ad hoc settlements. Among those disputes was the conflict between the commune and the

---

33. Davidsohn, *Storia di Firenze*, 2:632-35; Benvenuti Papi, *"In castro Poenitentiae,"* 602-3. For Ardingo, see Anna Benvenuti Papi, "Un vescovo, una città: Ardingo nella Firenze del primo duecento," in Benvenuti Papi, *Pastori di popolo: Storie e leggende di vescovi e di città nell'Italia medievale* (Florence: Arnaud, 1988), 21-124; Dameron, *Episcopal Power*, chap. 3.

bishop between 1327 and 1330 over the complicated issue of the disposition of unspecified pious legacies (*indistincte*) left by the deceased. In this and other disputes with the bishop, the commune ultimately had the upper hand.[34]

Even though there were periodic disputes setting the papacy against the Florentine Church and commune, overall, the second half of the thirteenth century constituted a period in which the influence of the papacy over the major ecclesiastical institutions of the city was expanding. This is evident primarily through the ability of the papal Curia to make ecclesiastical appointments or provisions to the cathedral chapter and to shape the elections of new bishops, especially after 1286. Conflict between the bishop, papacy, and clergy on the one hand and the commune on the other also flared up in the 1280s, such as the clash over the issue of fictitious clerks. It even resulted in what was essentially a clerical strike in 1285.[35] Nothing was to split the city more into factions, however, than the policies of Pope Boniface VIII toward Tuscany, intended to further the interests of his office and his family. On the one hand, in cooperation with the ruling mercantile and commercial elite, the papacy was supporting the construction of a new cathedral to glorify Guelf hegemony. However, at the same time, the machinations of Pope Boniface VIII in internal Florentine politics were also contributing to the eventual rupture of the Guelf elite into separate Black (propapal) and White (proempire) factions. Those factional struggles exploded in 1300, and the poet Dante Alighieri was caught up in it in 1302. He was apparently in Rome on a diplomatic mission to the papacy to secure papal military assistance when he learned that he and his sons had been condemned by the Florentine (pro-Black) priorate for graft, extortion, and working against papal "peacemaking" initiatives. This marked the beginning of his exile.

Nevertheless, we should not conclude that public (communal) and ecclesiastical (papal and episcopal) relations were consistently conflictual at the end of the thirteenth century and beginning of the fourteenth. Indeed, at this time both commune and bishopric found common cause in the reacquisition of episcopal ownership of landed

---

34. Trexler, *Synodal Law*, 23–29; Trexler, "Death and Testament," 29–49.

35. Dameron, *Florence and Its Church*, 219–24; Richard Trexler, *The Spiritual Power: Republican Florence under Interdict*, Studies in Medieval and Reformation Thought 9 (Leiden: Brill, 1974), 22–23; Alessandro Gherardi, ed., *Le Consulte della repubblica fiorentina dell'anno MCLXXX al MCCXCVIII* (Florence: Sansoni, 1896), 1:284–337.

properties and estates in the strategically important location of Monte di Croce (near the mouth of the Sieve and Arno Rivers, east of the city).[36] There was indeed a continuous legacy of friction and conflict between commune and Church institutions in the second half of the thirteenth century, but there was also collaboration and a common set of interests between bishop and commune to promote Florence as one of the premier cities of Europe.

## The Commune and Its Church: Preaching and Saints in the City

In his comprehensive synthesis of the history of communal Italy, Philip Jones argued that "communal society was embedded in religion," so much so that the clergy served to resanctify the city. Italian cities of central and northern Italy such as Bologna, Verona, and Siena came to see themselves as holy, as a New Jerusalem. For Augustine Thompson and other historians, including Jones, in a similar vein, Italian city-states needed an aura of political legitimacy that only religion could provide, and devotion to the shrine of one or more patron saints also helped shape the direction and nature of civic identity and patriotism.[37]

Florence is an example of how a new (post-1266) Guelf regime of the *popolo* collaborated and cooperated with elements of the Florentine Church to claim a special, divine status for the city. This is certainly evident in the decades that witnessed the fullest maturation of Florentine economic and political power and the rebuilding of the city center—ca. 1280-ca. 1340. This was the period when the city solidified its alliances with the papacy, with other Guelf city-states, and with the Angevin monarchy in southern Italy. This is also when Florence was able to eclipse—economically, politically, and militarily—the two principal powers in Tuscany that had previously held sway before the middle of the thirteenth century: Pisa and Lucca. The reasons for the rebuilding of the cathedral complex and its piazza were therefore as political in intention as they were ecclesiastical and religious. A new social and political order in an expansionist Florence required nothing less than

---

36. Renzo Nelli, *Signoria ecclesiastica e proprietà cittadina: Monte di Croce tra XIII e XIV secolo* (Pontassieve: Comune di Pontassieve, 1985), 103-19; Najemy, *A History of Florence*, 92.

37. Thompson, *Cities of God*, 3-4; Jones, *The Italian City-State*, 291, 297-98 ("In growing numbers Italian cities asserted the identity of a New Jerusalem—Florence and Siena, Bologna and Verona, and also seemingly Venice and Milan," 298).

"spatial order" in its urban core, replicating the efforts of clergy and laity to bring liturgical consistency and coherence to this New Jerusalem and to encourage submission of the individual to the interests of the *popolo*-dominated commune.

Among the most fervent advocates of this last theme were the preachers, especially mendicant (Dominican) preachers and writers such as Giordano da Pisa (ca. 1255-1311) and Remigio dei Girolami (ca. 1235-1319). Perhaps nowhere else in communal Italy was the level and tradition of vernacular intellectual culture higher than it was at the end of the thirteenth and beginning of the fourteenth centuries than in Florence. Both men preached to an eager public to argue for the end of factionalism and vendetta at a time of intense social conflict. Both inveighed against the evils of usury, which was ironically the economic factor that actually made Florentine prosperity possible. Over seven hundred sermons by Giordano survive, and he pitched his extremely popular sermons to his *popolo* audience and to their specific spiritual needs. Among his many practically minded observations was the requirement to understand the necessity for sincere repentance at a time of intense economic change. Key themes in the sermons and writings of Remigio dei Girolami, the most important scholar at that time in the *studium* of Santa Maria Novella, were that factionalism constituted a mortal threat to the welfare of the commune and that true virtue required the individual to reject personal ambitions and submit to the common (pro-*popolo*) good. No Franciscan sermons survive from the thirteenth century, unfortunately, but two of the most important dissident Franciscan friars were lectors at Santa Croce between 1287and 1289: Ubertino da Casale (1259-ca. 1330) and Pietro Olivi (1248-98). Their critique of a materialistically focused established Church and Olivi's developing embrace of a stricter version of poverty ("poor use"), his views on evangelical perfection and obedience, and his apocalyptic writings were to have a lasting impact on later dissident Franciscans (the Spirituals) as well as members of the laity, including perhaps a young Dante Alighieri.[38]

---

38. Marvin Trachtenberg, *Dominion of the Eye: Urbanism, Art, and Power in Early Modern Florence* (Cambridge: Cambridge University Press, 1997), 6-7, 31-32 (for the rebuilding of the Piazza del Duomo), 260-72, esp. 267; Najemy, *A History of Florence*, 55-56; Dameron, *Florence and Its Church*, 207-16; Robert Black, "Education," in Barański and Pertile, *Dante in Context*, 273-74; Ronald G. Witt, *The Two Latin Cultures and the Foundation of Renaissance Humanism in Medieval Italy* (Cambridge: Cambridge University Press, 2012), 488-89; Hawkins, "Religious Culture," 336-39; David Burr, *The Spiritual Franciscans: From Protest to Persecution in the Century*

No aspects of Florentine history during this time exemplify these trends more clearly than the evolution of the cults of the principal patron saints of the city, culminating in the cathedral project (beginning in 1294), the synodal constitution of 1310, and the exhumation and translation of the relics of Saint Zenobius (in 1331). Collectively, these developments portrayed the commune of Florence as fulfilling a special, divine (Guelf) mission as a chosen city. At least until the ninth century, the principal church in Florence was not what we recognize today as Santa Maria del Fiore (previously called Santa Reparata). Rather, it was the extramural basilica of San Lorenzo, dedicated and consecrated with the assistance of Saint Ambrose in the fourth century. For almost half a millennium this was the primary center of worship and the seat of the bishop (the *domus episcopi*). In the ninth century, probably under the direction of Bishop Andrea (by tradition, an Irishman), the relics of Saint Zenobius were translated to the urban pieve of San Giovanni (basilica and detached baptistery complex) within the circle of (the originally Roman) walls. At the same time, as Anna Benvenuti Papi has argued, Bishop Andrea most likely brought relics of Saint Reparata to Florence (she was a Syrian saint who was a favorite of merchants). Simultaneously, a certain Pseudo-Simplician probably composed a life of Saint Zenobius in the same century. Of course, much of this is speculation and unproven, including a late twelfth-century ordinal (*Ritus in ecclesia servandi*) that records that Bishop Andrea dedicated a new altar to Saint Reparata in the ninth century around the same time as the translation of the relics of Zenobius. If correct, the altar dedication essentially elevated Saint Reparata to equal status with Saint John as the primary saints of the urban pieve complex. However, by the end of the tenth century, we find that the baptistery alone was exclusively dedicated to Saint John and that the basilica (now episcopal church) was separately affiliated with Saint Reparata.

The principal church of the bishop and city was now shifting from outside to inside the walls, from San Lorenzo to Santa Reparata. The latter, perhaps earlier and originally known as San Salvatore, was an

---

*after Saint Francis* (University Park: Pennsylvania State Press, 2001), 47, 51–62. According to Burr, although the term (Spirituals) is primarily a modern construct, he accepts that "we can speak of 'spiritual Franciscans' from the early fourteenth century on" (viii). For recent research on preaching and the cultural legacy of Dominicans in Florence, see the essays in Johannes Bartuschat, Elisa Brilli, and Delphine Carron, eds., *The Dominicans and the Making of Florentine Cultural Identity (13th–14th centuries) / I Domenicani e la costruzione dell'identità culturale fiorentina (secoli XIII–XIV)* (Florence: Firenze University Press, 2020).

early medieval church in the basilica plan originally built over a Roman house. By no later than the end of the tenth century the church had been renamed Santa Reparata (the first documented mention of it being called Santa Reparata is 987). It was now the principal center of worship for this very small city off the beaten track, at the time still dominated economically and demographically by Pisa and Lucca. Indeed, aside from Saints Lawrence and Zenobius, many of the principal saints venerated in the early medieval city had been primarily imported from Lucca. By the early eleventh century, a rebuilding program in the new Romanesque style had begun. A new life of Saint Zenobius also appeared about the same time (ca. 1039–ca. 1046), written by Lorenzo of Amalfi and probably timed to coincide with the completion of the building program. For the next 250 years, a period of extremely rapid demographic and economic growth for the city (including the emergence of the commune in the twelfth century), the Romanesque cathedral of Santa Reparata remained the dominant church of the city and its bishop. Until the very end of the thirteenth century the principal urban patron saints included Saint Minias (monastery dedicated in 1018), Saint Zenobius (first bishop whose relics were now in Santa Reparata), Saint Philip, and Saint John the Baptist (associated with the baptistery at least from the ninth century). From at least the end of the eleventh century, the cult of Saint John as the principal patron saint of the commune was growing in importance as the urban elite was expanding its control over the surrounding countryside.[39]

---

39. The summary relies on the following: Franklin Toker, "Excavations below the Cathedral of Florence, 1965-74," *Gesta* 14, no. 2 (1975): 17-36; Toker, "On Holy Ground: Architecture and Liturgy in the Cathedral and in the Streets of Late-Medieval Florence," in Verdon and Innocenti, *Atti del VII centenario*, vol. 2, bk. 2:544-59; Toker, *On Holy Ground*, 3, 10, 30, 35, 41, 56; Anna Benvenuti, "La Memoria di San Zanobi," in Verdon and Innocenti, *Atti del VII centenario*, vol. 1, bk. 1:107-36; Benvenuti, "San Lorenzo: la cattedrale negata," in *Le Radici cristiane di Firenze*, ed. Anna Benvenuti, Franco Cardini, and Elena Giannarelli (Florence: Alinea, 1994), 117-33; Benvenuti, "Stratigrafie della memoria: Scritture agiografiche e mutamenti architettonici nella vicenda del 'Complesso cattedrale' fiorentino," in *Il bel San Giovanni e Santa Maria del Fiore: Il centro religioso a Firenze dal tardo antico al Rinascimento*, ed. D. Cardini (Florence: le Lettere, 1996), 93-128; Benvenuti Papi, "San Zanobi: Memoria episcopale, tradizioni civiche e dignità familiari," in *Pastori di popolo*, 127-76; Dameron, *Florence and Its Church*, chap. 5; Marica Tacconi, *Cathedral and Civic Ritual in Late Medieval and Renaissance Florence: The Service Books of Santa Maria del Fiore* (Cambridge: Cambridge University Press, 2005), 2-25, 40-73; and Brand, *Holy Treasure and Sacred Song*, 23, 39-42, 61-68, 74-82, 109, 118, 132, 159, 196, and 213-20. For the excavations below the cathedral-baptistery complex, see Franklin Toker, *Archaeological Campaigns below the Florence Duomo and Baptistery, 1895–1980*, The Florence Duomo Project 2 (Turnhout: Brepols, 2013).

By the 1280s, however, it was evident to the ruling merchants and bankers of the city, the papacy, the Angevin Kingdom of Sicily, and other Guelf city-states that Florence was now becoming the most dominant economic and political power in Tuscany. It derived support and assistance in that regard from some of the principal ecclesiastical institutions of the city. The agents of the bishopric and cathedral chapter, with extensive grain-growing properties in the major river valleys of the two dioceses, brought their grain rents into the city to the market at Orsanmichele (1284), helping to feed a city swelling with new rural immigrants seeking work in the cloth industry. Some of the major urban confraternities such as the Misericordia were now major dispensers of charity. At times of severe food shortages, such as in 1329 and 1346, they helped maintain social stability. From 1254 the Franciscans had taken charge of the Inquisition from their friary at Santa Croce. Led by Salomone da Lucca in the 1280s, the Inquisition pursued only a few individuals suspected of Cathar sympathies. Evidently quite strong in the 1240s, the appeal of Catharism by the 1280s had largely been spent. There were nevertheless quite a few actions taken against various individuals by the Inquisition, including a certain Saraceno Paganelli. Apparently there were few to no Cathars left in Florence in the last quarter of the thirteenth century, and this may help explain why Dante never mentioned them in the *Inferno*. The worry of heresy, however, did not go away. For example, an inquisitor named Pace da Castelfiorentino traveled through isolated parts of the diocese of Fiesole looking for followers of Fra Dolcino in 1322, perhaps acting on rumors or a tip.[40]

After a new and stronger executive magistracy (the priorate) had emerged in Florence in 1282, the Pisans had lost at Meloria (1284), and the Florentines had defeated Arezzo at Campaldino in 1289, it was evident to Florentine secular and religious leaders alike that the commune deserved to have among its patrons and protectors the most prestigious and holiest of saints. After all, Florence did indeed appear to be a New Jerusalem, the center of the Tuscan world, and its rapid rise to regional supremacy could only be explained by divine favor. It was also a city on a mission to promote the Guelf tradition and alliance, to combat heresy and what remained of the Ghibellines, and to bring peace to Tuscany.

---

40. Manselli, "Per la storia dell'eresia catara nella Firenze del tempo di Dante," 124-33; Felice Tocco, *Quel che non c'è nella Divina Comedia o Dante o l'eresia* (Bologna: Nicola Zanichelli, 1899), 1-27, with documents; Burr, "Heresy and Dissidence," 107-8 (for Fra Dolcino); Dameron, *Florence and Its Church*, 232; Archivio Vescovile di Fiesole, Atti Civili XII.1, fol. 28r.

As such, it deserved nothing less than the saint with the highest status: the Virgin Mary herself, whom Dante placed next to God himself in his vision of heaven in *Paradiso*. For this reason the bishop and commune collaborated, with support from the papacy, and embarked on an ambitious cathedral-building project that would be appropriate in stature and grandeur for a commune so clearly chosen by God for a special purpose. So, in 1293, political and religious leaders of Florence decided formally not just to restore the by now two-hundred-year-old Romanesque structure, but to rebuild it entirely. This was a project that was primarily promoted by those members of the *popolo* who dominated government at the time, and it eventually garnered the support and cooperation of the bishopric (especially Francesco dei Monaldeschi) and the papacy (Boniface VIII). Bishop, commune, and pope all had a stake in the creation of a grand cathedral that proclaimed the divine status, power, and prestige of the Guelf commune of Florence. After all, Florence was now the centerpiece of the propapal Guelf alliance.

The dedication to the Virgin took place in 1296. Not only did it spur the initial stages of construction, but it also inspired the production of new, magnificent service books for the liturgy of the emerging cathedral. The new bishop, Francesco dei Monaldeschi (1295–1301), had previously enjoyed a strong relationship with the papacy during his service as bishop of Orvieto (where he also presided over a cathedral project), and he took a strong role in the new cathedral project for Florence. In the same year as the dedication, the Opera del Duomo was created to supervise the construction, and by 1330 it was under the supervision of the Arte della Lana (the Wool Guild). By 1300 Arnolfo di Cambio, the celebrated and prestigious sculptor and architect, was directing the project. As the new structure began to take shape within the shell of the former Romanesque church at the end of the thirteenth and early fourteenth centuries, a major shift in liturgical and hagiographical direction from Lucchese to Roman traditions was simultaneously under way. In 1310 the promulgation of the new synodal constitution confirmed the removal of twenty-nine feasts associated with the former church of Santa Reparata (many of them connected to early medieval cultural influences emanating from the previously dominant Lucca). In their place, the new constitution added twenty-nine Roman feasts. The tie to the papacy, a key player in the Guelf political and economic axis, was deepened and enhanced. This same constitution promoted liturgical unity and reform by bringing some order and cohesion to the celebration of the cults of the principal civic saints. The feast of the Annunciation (March 25) and the feast days of Saints Zenobius (May 25), Philip and James (May 1, celebrated from the early thirteenth century), and John (June 24) were among the most important.

As these changes in the liturgical direction of Florence were under way, the commune, papacy, and bishop collaborated to help pay for the cathedral project through subsidies (actually, taxes, direct and indirect). At the same time, the clergy was shouldering more and more financial burdens imposed by bishop, commune, and papacy. Apparently, the bishop of Fiesole was the first of the two bishops in the region of Florence to tax his own clergy to help pay for the new cathedral (1299). Since *Super cathedram* (1300), the papacy had declared taxation of ecclesiastical institutions canonically forbidden, unless the pope had specifically allowed it in certain cases. The cathedral project seems to have been one of those exceptions, and taxation of the clergy was permitted. This comes at the same time (1305) when both the bishops of Florence (1305) and Fiesole (1298) were imposing subsidy obligations on their clergies to help pay for the installation and ritual entry of a new prelate (this tradition had begun no later than 1286 in Florence).

The members of the clergy of Florence understandably balked at these growing pressures, which increased after 1318 as the secular clergy bore even greater fiscal burdens to help pay for the cathedral and after 1323 for the new walls (in addition). The clergy had already organized itself into an association of mutual support and protection from at least the early fourteenth century. No later than July 1311 there had emerged a confraternity of the Florentine clergy, and it requested permission from the bishop to build a hospital in the urban parish of San Lorenzo. The problem of the origins of this clerical confraternity is a vexed one. There are indications but no proof that it originated in 1131. Relevant documents were, however, lost in the flood of 1966. By 1326 they had formed their own corporate organization, chose a procurator to represent them ("procurator totius cleri civitatis et diocesis Florentinae"), and sought redress with the episcopal vicar. Partly because of clerical resistance to these subsidies, and also (as John Najemy has argued) because the *popolo* no longer dominated the government, the cathedral project essentially stalled during the 1320s. The new synodal constitution of 1327, however, put an end to the attempts by the clergy to become more powerfully engaged in the governance of the Florentine Church.

In 1330, in a bid to bring a higher quality of management to the cathedral project, the Arte della Lana took over the Opera del Duomo. A year later, the bishop of Florence, surrounded by prelates from neighboring city-states, exhumed the remains of Saint Zenobius from under the altar and placed the head in a new, magnificent silver reliquary. At the very least, this was a bid to revive the cult of a major, traditional saint, to jumpstart the financing process for the new cathedral, and to rally laity and clergy alike around the unifying figure of an ancient, native Florentine saint. Coming very soon after the devastating grain dearth of 1329, it was also probably an attempt to bring back the memory of the first protector saint of the city (Saint Zenobius) at a time of crisis. Later attempts to focus on the cult of Saint Reparata were unsuccessful (a plaster cast of her arm was brought to Florence in 1353), and her cult receded as the level of regard for Saints John, Zenobius, and the Virgin Mary increased. By 1375 the former Romanesque church of Santa Reparata had been completely demolished, and in its place there emerged the new cathedral of Santa Maria del Fiore, dedicated not to an obscure Syrian saint, but to the Queen of Heaven.[41] After all, it was she whose favor had transformed Florence from a small, second- or third-rank city located in a swamp, to become one of the most powerful and populated cities in the world, with a legacy of art, literature, and architecture that continues to dazzle us today.

## Selected Bibliography

### Primary Sources

ASF *NA* = Archivio di Stato di Firenze. *Notarile Antecosimiano*.
Gherardi, Alessandro, ed. *Le Consulte della repubblica fiorentina dell'anno MCCLXXX al MCCXCVIII*. Vol. 1. Florence: Sansoni, 1896.
Guasti, Cesare. *Santa Maria del Fiore: La costruzione della chiesa e del campanile*. Florence: M. Ricci, 1887.

---

41. For a review of this historical problem, see Bowsky, *La Chiesa di San Lorenzo*, 187–202; Davidsohn, *Storia di Firenze*, 7:102–4. For the cathedral, see Tacconi, *Cathedral and Civic Ritual*, 2–73; Lucio Ricetti, "Il Vescovo Francesco Monaldeschi e l'avvio del cantiere di S. Maria del Fiore (1295-1301)," in Verdon and Innocenti, *Atti del VII centenario*, 1:195–226; Najemy, "The Beginnings of Florence Cathedral"; George W. Dameron, "Cathedral, Clergy, and Commune in the Age of Arnolfo di Cambio," in Friedman, Gardner, and Haines, *Arnolfo's Moment*, 211–32; Anna Benvenuti, "Arnolfo e Reparata: Percorsi semantici nella dedicazione della cattedrale fiorentina," in Friedman, Gardner, and Haines, *Arnolfo's Moment*, 233–52. For the liturgical revolution that occurred in the early trecento, see Marica S. Tacconi, "Architecture, Liturgy, and Music in Arnolfo's Florence: The Case of Santa Maria del Fiore," in Friedman, Gardner, and Haines, *Arnolfo's Moment*, 253–64.

Villani, Giovanni. *Nuova Cronica*. Ed. Giuseppe Porta. 3 vols. Parma: Ugo Guanda, 1990–91.

Vito da Cortona, *Vita beatae Humilianae de Cerchis, Acta Sanctorum*, Maii IV (Antwerp, 1685), cols. 385–402.

## Secondary Sources

Barański, Zygmunt G., and Lino Pertile, eds. *Dante in Context*. Cambridge: Cambridge University Press, 2015.

Bartuschat, Johannes, Elisa Brilli, and Delphine Carron, eds. *The Dominicans and the Making of Florentine Cultural Identity (13th–14th centuries) / I Domenicani e la costruzione dell'identità culturale fiorentina (secoli XIII–XIV)*. Florence: Firenze University Press, 2020.

Benvenuti, Anna, Franco Cardini, and Elena Giannarelli, eds. *Le Radici cristiane di Firenze*. Florence: Alinea, 1994.

Benvenuti Papi, Anna. *"In castro poenitentiae": Santità e società feminile nell'Italia medievale*. Rome: Herder, 1990.

———. "Mendicant Friars and Female Pinzochere in Tuscany: From Social Marginality to Models of Sanctity." In *Women and Religion in Medieval and Renaissance Italy*, edited by Daniel Bornstein and Roberto Rusconi, 84–103. Chicago: University of Chicago Press, 1996.

Bornstein, Daniel, and Roberto Rusconi, eds. *Women and Religion in Medieval and Renaissance Italy*. Chicago: University of Chicago Press, 1996.

Bowsky, William. *Le Chiesa di San Lorenzo a Firenze nel medioevo*. Edited by Renzo Nelli. Florence: Meridiana, 1999.

Brand, Benjamin. *Holy Treasure and Sacred Song: Relics Cults and Their Liturgies in Medieval Tuscany*. New York: Oxford University Press, 2014.

Burr, David. "Heresy and Dissidence." In *Dante in Context*, edited by Zygmunt G. Barański and Lino Pertile, 106–18. Cambridge: Cambridge University Press, 2015.

Cortese, Maria Elena. *Signori, castelli, città: L'aristocrazia del territorio fiorentino tra X e XII secolo*. Florence: Olschki, 2007.

Dameron, George W. "Cathedral, Clergy, and Commune in the Age of Arnolfo di Cambio." In *Arnolfo's Moment: Acts of an International Conference, Florence, Villa I Tatti, May 26–27, 2005*, edited by David Friedman, Julian Gardner, and Margaret Haines, 211–32. Florence: Olschki, 2009.

———. "Church and Orthodoxy." In *Dante in Context*, edited by Zygmunt G. Barański and Lino Pertile, 83–105. Cambridge: Cambridge University Press, 2015.

———. *Episcopal Power and Florentine Society, 1000–1320*. Cambridge, MA: Harvard University Press, 1991.

———. *Florence and Its Church in the Age of Dante*. Philadelphia: University of Pennsylvania Press, 2005.

Davidsohn, Robert. *Storia di Firenze*. It. translation, various translators, 8 vols. Florence: Sansoni, 1956–68.

Dean, Trevor, and Daniel Waley. *The Italian City-Republics*. 5th ed. London: Routledge, 2022.

Faini, Enrico. *Firenze nell'età romanica (1000–1211): L'espansione urbana, lo sviluppo istituzionale, il rapporto con il territorio*. Florence: Olschki, 2010.

Friedman, David, Julian Gardner, and Margaret Haines, eds. *Arnolfo's Moment: Acts of an International Conference, Florence, Villa I Tatti, May 26–27, 2005*. Florence: Olschki, 2009.

Gaston, Robert W., and Louis A. Waldman, eds. *San Lorenzo: A Florentine Church*. Florence: Villa I Tatti, the Harvard University Center for Italian Renaissance Studies, 2017.

Hawkins, Peter. "Religious Culture." In *Dante in Context*, edited by Zygmunt G. Barański and Lino Pertile, 319–40. Cambridge: Cambridge University Press, 2015.

Henderson, John. *Piety and Charity in Late Medieval Florence*. Oxford: Clarendon Press, 1994.

Herlihy, David. "Santa Maria Impruneta: A Rural Commune in the Late Middle Ages." In *Florentine Studies: Politics and Society in Renaissance Florence*, edited by Nicolai Rubinstein, 242–76. Evanston, IL: Northwestern University Press, 1968.

Jones, Philip. *The Italian City-State: From Commune to Signoria*. Oxford: Clarendon Press, 1997.

La Roncière, Charles M. de. *Religion paysanne et religion urbaine en Toscane (c. 1250–c. 1450)*. Aldershot: Ashgate Variorum, 1994.

Manselli, Raoul. *L'Eresia del male*, 2nd ed. Naples: Morano, 1980.

——. "Per la storia dell'eresia catara nella Firenze del tempo di Dante." *Bullettino dell'Istituto storico italiano per il Medio Evo e Archivio Muratoriano* 62 (1950): 123–38.

Miccoli, Giovanni. "La storia religiosa." In *Storia d'Italia*, vol. 2, *Dalla caduta dell'Impero romano al secolo XVIII*, edited by Ruggiero Romano and Corrado Vivanti, bk. 1:431–1079. Turin: Einaudi, 1974.

Najemy, John M. "The Beginnings of Florence Cathedral: A Political Interpretation." In *Arnolfo's Moment: Acts of an International Conference, Florence, Villa I Tatti, May 26–27, 2005*, edited by David Friedman, Julian Gardner, and Margaret Haines, 183–210. Florence: Olschki, 2009.

——. *A History of Florence, 1200–1575*. Oxford: Blackwell, 2006.

Ronzani, Mauro. "Dalla regione romana alla Marca di Tuscia." In *Storia della Toscana*, edited by Pietro Pezzino, Elena Fasano Guarini, and Giuseppe Petralia, 72–90. Rome: Laterza, 2004.

Salvestrini, Francesco, ed. *La Basilica di San Miniato al Monte di Firenze (1018–2018): Storia e documentazione*. Florence: Firenze University Press, 2021.

Tacconi, Marica. *Cathedral and Civic Ritual in Late Medieval and Renaissance Florence: The Service Books of Santa Maria del Fiore*. Cambridge: Cambridge University Press, 2005.

Thompson, Augustine. *Cities of God: The Religion of the Italian Communes, 1125–1325*. University Park: Pennsylvania State University Press, 2005.

Toker, Franklin. *Archaeological Campaigns below the Florence Duomo and Baptistery, 1895–1980*. The Florence Duomo Project 2. Turnhout: Brepols, 2013.

———. *On Holy Ground: Liturgy, Architecture, and Urbanism in the Cathedral and Streets of Medieval Florence*. The Florence Duomo Project 1. Turnhout: Brepols, 2009.

Trexler, Richard. "Death and Testament in the Episcopal Constitutions of Florence (1327)." In *Renaissance Studies in Honor of Hans Baron*, edited by Anthony Molho and John Tedeschi, 29-74. Dekalb: Northern Illinois University Press, 1971.

———. *Dependence in Context in Renaissance Florence*. Binghamton: SUNY Press, 1994.

———. *Public Life in Renaissance Florence*. Ithaca, NY: Cornell University Press, 1991.

———. *Synodal Law in Florence and Fiesole, 1306–1518*. Vatican City: Biblioteca Apostolica Vaticana, 1971.

Verdon, Timothy, ed. *Le chiese e la città*. Vol. 1 of Alla riscoperta delle chiese di Firenze. Florence: Centro Di, 2002.

Verdon, Timothy, and Annalisa Innocenti, eds. *Atti del VII centenario del Duomo di Firenze*, 3 vols. in 5. Florence: EDIFIR, 2001.

Wickham, Chris. *Early Medieval Italy: Central Power and Local Society, 400–1000*. Ann Arbor: University of Michigan Press, 1989.

———. *Legge, pratiche e conflitti: Tribunali e risoluzione delle dispute nella Toscana del XII secolo*. Rome: Viella, 2000.

———. *Sleepwalking into a New World: The Emergence of Italian City Communes in the Twelfth Century*. Princeton, NJ: Princeton University Press, 2015.

Wilson, Blake. *Music and Merchants: The Laudesi Companies of Republican Florence*. Oxford: Clarendon Press, 1992.

CHAPTER 13

# Case Study II
## Naples

Giovanni Vitolo
*In memory of Gilles Gérard Meersseman*

At the dawn of the second millennium, southern Italy was still suspended between the East and the West despite various attempts by the German emperors to enforce the sovereign rights they claimed effective, by chasing out the Byzantines and inserting the Lombard principalities into their sphere of influence. In the course of the tenth century, these attempts had seemed on the point of success, first with Otto of Saxony, then with his son Otto II, and above all with his grandson Otto III, born from the marriage between Otto II and the Byzantine princess Theophane. In this context, Naples, "a frontier city" where the connections with the East were most visible, was not under direct Byzantine dominion, unlike Bari, Taranto, or Reggio (in Calabria). Rather, Naples, essentially a city-state, had been governed at this point for more than two centuries by dynasties of dukes from the local aristocracy, who dated their documents according to the regnal years of the Byzantine emperors. However, this fact has appropriately been used to highlight their cultural rather than political and constitutional significance.[1] Despite the resulting vain and repeated attempts

---

This chapter was translated by Carolyn Quijano.

1. Vera Von Falkenhausen, *La dominazione bizantina nell'Italia meridionale dal IX all'XI secolo* (Bari: Ecumenica, 1978), 12–13.

to impose the spiritual jurisdiction of the patriarch of Constantinople, the Greek imprint on the city did not manifest itself principally in scattered elements—each of which was also recognizable in the other centers mentioned above, as well as in those of North and Central Italy that had remained tied to Byzantium for a longer period of time, such as Rome, Venice, and Ravenna. Rather, it showed itself in the wholly original way in which these elements created a system. To use an expression now codified in the field of medieval urban historiography, they left an unmistakable impression both on the city of stone and on that of men.

## The Cult of Images

Naples, which one ninth-century writer had praised for the coexistence of Greek and Latin rites and where at the beginning of the thirteenth century, Greek and Latin clerics were present in the church of San Gennaro in Diaconia (today San Gennaro all'Olmo),[2] was clearly divided into four parishes (*ecclesiae catholicae maiores*), which had formed in the course of the fifth and sixth centuries. The space within the walls was divided between them, cut through by the *platee* and the *vici* (squares and neighborhoods) of the Greco-Romano period. In both the parochial and private churches—which were similar more to those founded on the basis of the Byzantine rite than lay *ecclesiae propriae* of Lombard Italy[3]—there were, as we will see later, forms of clerical associations, and they used a liturgy and forms of worship that despite the fact that they had begun a slow homogenization with the other Western churches between the eleventh and twelfth centuries, still maintained a peculiar characteristic. This was due to a stronger and more durable tie with the late antique and Eastern tradition where there was no confusion between the roles of civil and ecclesiastical institutions.

---

2. A. Vuolo, ed., *Vita et Translatio S. Athanasii Neapolitan episcopi (BHL 735 e 737): Sec IX*, Fonti per la storia dell'Italia medievale, Antiquitates 16 (Rome: Istituto Storico Italiano per il Medio Evo, 2001), 118. The *congregatio sacerdotum et clericorum graecorum et latinorum* is attested in the church of San Gennaro in Diaconia in the years 1105-1302: Bartolommeo Capasso, *Topografia della città di Napoli nell'XI secolo* (Naples: F. Giannini, 1895), 89; Rosaria Pilone, *Il Diplomatico di S. Gregorio Armeno conservato nell'Archivio di Stato di Napoli* (Naples: Laurenziana, 1989), 101, 115.

3. The analogy with another area strongly influenced by the Romano-Byzantine tradition, the Venetian lagoon, is not without significance. This area also lacked the private Church of Lombard Law, which allowed alienation and investiture, and was largely under Byzantine law, as Daniela Rando has highlighted in *Una chiesa di frontiera: Le istituzioni ecclesiastiche veneziane nei secoli VI-XII* (Bologna: Il Mulino, 1994), 92-93.

The stability of the parish structures and charitable organizations—connected to them and having close relations with the ruling class, but not subordinate to them—could explain the absence in the city of the tensions triggered between the eleventh and twelfth centuries in much of the Latin West. These reforms were aimed at restoring the common life of the clergy, bringing private churches under the control of the bishops, and ousting the laity and political authorities from the conferral of ecclesiastical benefices. Tensions caused by the reforms also affected other territories, first those of the Lombards and then those of the Normans of southern Italy, especially near Salerno. The opposite may also have occurred: the fact that the city was outside the Germanic imperial orbit and Carolingian public, which granted bishops and great abbots positions of power and functions of responsibility in the governance of men and territories, served to keep Naples outside the reach of reforms, which started with the need to redefine those roles as the premise for the renewal of religious life.

This attempt to identify which was the cause and which the effect in the relationship between the city's stronger connection with the late antique and the oriental religious tradition and the absence of the movement for the renewal of the Church would be pointless if the findings of the studies of the last decades aiming to reconsider Neapolitan Hellenism on the religious level as an expression of a type of Byzantine commonwealth were to turn out to be valid.[4] On the one hand, these studies traced this Hellenism back to a precise phase in the duchy's history, between the ninth and tenth centuries. On the other, they underestimated the value of individual material and immaterial elements, which, as I shall attempt to demonstrate, should instead be considered as original developments of widespread practices and institutions in the Byzantine East, and even earlier in the ancient world, both Christian and pagan (in all its manifestations, not only those of classical origin).

The most recent studies in the field of the history of art call attention to the phenomena of the cult of images and of the Cross. The latter was practiced from the seventh century throughout Christendom and focused on the two feasts of the Invention of the Cross (lat. *Inventio*) (May 7 in the East, May 3 in the West) and the Exaltation (lat. *Exaltatio*) (September 14), as well as the Adoration of the Cross during the Easter

---

4. Jean-Marie Martin, "Hellénisme politique, hellénisme religieux et pseudo-hellénisme à Naples (VII<sup>e</sup>–XII<sup>e</sup> siècle)," *Νέα Ῥώμη* 2 (2005): 65–66.

processions. The difference between the two cults, but always in the unitary context of high medieval Naples, is one of significance, which was mainly anthropological and religious in the first case, and institutional and social in the second. Regarding the cult of images, we need to consider the descent from funerary portraits and the representation of gods and emperors in antiquity (in Naples, as in the other cities of the empire, there were portraits in the forum of deified emperors, such as Trajan and Hadrian), which is by now well studied—although today our understanding of this phenomenon, viewed as one of many cases of the Christianization of paganism, could be much more complex. Supporting this idea, Luigi Canetti suggests "that it was the earlier belief that appropriated Christian tradition, which, in order to continue to survive had to in some way accept its own transformation into something it never thought it could become."[5]

This is not the place to tackle a problem that, concerning more generally what Canetti calls "new paradigms for the cultural and religious history of the high Middle Ages," goes far beyond the cult of images, even if the context of late antique and early medieval Naples could offer many opportunities for reflection in this regard. In fact, as can be seen from both the literary and documentary evidence, it presents particular traits attributable not only to the "humanization" of images, which, as in the East, resembled living people, but also and above all to the particular relationship that they had with the faithful, who cast aside all reverential fear and turned toward images, as Maria Rosaria Marchionibus explains, "as if they were their peers, as if they shared the same language: indeed the supplicant even comes to provoke them verbally to elicit their reaction . . . without fear of consequences, because, in some way, the bond of shared affection allows for the same confidentiality that one forms with a family member."[6] This closeness had remained unaltered over time and has been rightly seen to be at the root of the insolent language with which the faithful still today rebuke San Gennaro, when his blood is slow to liquefy.[7] However, what is even more significant here—because it leads directly back to antiquity and

---

5. Canetti Luigi, "Il bruco e l'arcobaleno: Nuovi paradigmi per la storia culturale e religiosa dell'alto Medioevo," *Storica* 66 (2016): 65.

6. Maria Rosaria Marchionibus, *Icone in Campania: Aspetti iconologici, liturgici e semantici* (Spoleto: Fondazione Centro italiano di studi sull'alto medioevo, 2011), 40.

7. The liquefaction of the blood of San Gennaro takes place three times a year (the Saturday before the first Sunday of May, September 19, the saint's feast day, and December 16). If the blood does not liquefy it is considered to be a bad omen.

to the cult of images of the deceased and the deified emperors—is the phenomenon of the appearance of the portrait of soccer player Maradona in the streets of the historic center. Evoking Roman and Byzantine emperors, this phenomenon both fosters the memory of a sort of golden age of Neapolitan soccer and makes him seem present, if not at the stadium, at least in the city and with an authority that is not at all diminished by the misadventures following his abandonment of the sport.

Between the tenth and eleventh centuries, the icons, which mostly represented the Virgin either alone or with the Child, must have been widely present in the city. They were imported from Byzantium or made locally according to Eastern models, and were kept in private homes or, more often, destined for churches. Here they were visible to all, but without this preventing a close relationship with the ancient owners or patrons, which seem especially to be women. In addition to creating a true dialogue with them, they considered the icons capable of accomplishing through their procurators, the custodians of the churches in which they were kept, legal actions, such as receiving donations and bequests, and making purchases or exchanges.[8] The oldest known example is the act in which a certain Maru promises, on July 26, 985, with the consent of her husband, to leave part of her goods to the abbot of the monastery of Santi Severino e Sossio and part to the hegumen (the Greek equivalent of the abbot in Latin monasteries), of the Italo-Greek monastery of Santi Sergio e Bacco, with the obligation for them and their successors to pay two golden *soldi* every year to the image of the Virgin she had commissioned to be painted on the door of the church of Santa Maria ad Albini. The location of the Virgin is clearly a throwback to the Virgin Mary Portaitissa (Keeper of the Gate), whose icon was placed at the entrance of the monastery of Iviron on Mount Athos to protect it.[9]

A document from August 31, 1132, is particularly interesting because it lends itself to a double interpretation of both the content of

---

8. Jean-Marie Martin, "Quelques remarques sur le culte des images en Italie méridionale pendant le Haut Moyen Âge," in *Cristianità ed Europa: Miscellanea di studi in onore di Luigi Prosdocimi*, ed. Cesare Alzati (Rome: Herder, 1994), vol. 1, bk. 1:223–36; Giovanni Vitolo, "San Gennaro e il culto delle immagini a Napoli: A proposito di alcune recenti pubblicazioni," in *"Acri Sanctorum Investigatori": Miscellanea di studi in memoria di Gennaro Luongo*, ed. L. Arcari (Rome: L'Erma di Bretschneider, 2019), 729–43.

9. Marchionibus, *Icone in Campania*, 6–7.

the image (as the simple shape of the cross, or as the representation of Christ?) and its material support (an icon or merely a wooden crucifix?). It deals with the act by which Pietro Scintilla gave an herb garden and two pieces of land to Gregorio Tribunopardo and his brother Sergio, which the brothers subsequently donated to the Holy Cross in the church of San Severino.[10] The double interpretation is founded upon the fact that the oldest wooden crucifixes of the Neapolitan churches were thought to date to around these years—even though art historians do not always agree in their analyses—among which is also the representation of the plain cross without Christ.

## The Cult of the Cross and the *Staurita*

The singularity of Naples in the context of the West is also seen in the cult of the Cross (in Greek, *stauròs*), but less so in the preeminence given to the feast of the Exaltation instead of the Invention of the Cross in conformity with the Byzantine tradition and Eastern liturgy in general. Rather, it shows in the significance that the Palm Sunday and Easter Vespers processions assumed in city life as early as the ninth century, if not even earlier. These processions started at the cathedral and stopped on street corners. Here, the cross was raised on altars prepared for the occasion, on which the faithful deposited their offerings, which the clergy and inhabitants of the neighborhood afterward distributed to the poor. Over the course of time, but in any case by the ninth and tenth centuries, the regularity of the rite caused the temporary altars to be transformed into permanent installations in the form of street shrines and chapels, the latter often constructed by adapting preexisting buildings and making use of designated spaces inside religious buildings (both parochial and otherwise). In this way the staurite was born, a term that initially indicated churches and chapels fashioned in connection with the procession of Palm Sunday and the devotion of the Holy Cross, where Christian charity was practiced through the giving of alms to the poor and the celebration of suffrage rites for the dead. Over time, these were followed by more demanding activities, such as

---

10. Bartolommeo Capasso, ed., *Monumenta ad Neapolitani ducatus historiam pertinentia*, re-edited by Rosaria Pilone (Salerno: Carlone, 2008; orig. ed. Neapoli: Giannini, 1881–92), vol. 2, bk. 1:475–77; Marchionibus, *Icone in Campania*, 9.

the foundation of hospitals and the establishment of dowries for impoverished girls.[11]

In some cases, all the inhabitants of a neighborhood were mobilized in the new enterprise of perpetuating those ancient traditions of local associationism that some historians date back to the Greek *fratríe*.[12] In other cases, the egoisms of class operated with greater force, and the *staurita* was created on the initiative of one or more noble families, who made it a sort of status symbol. The noble families founded and managed them like normal churches of lay patronage, and as such they functioned as instruments of familial cohesion and rootedness in the neighborhood in which they resided.

But more precisely, what did the life of the staurites consist of? It must be said first of all that they were not confraternities, even if they did end up becoming like them. Mutual assistance was not one of the original tasks of their members, but instead they focused on spreading the cult of the Cross and the exercise of charitable works.[13] These goals were gradually tempered, and two other factors eventually emerged to contribute to the vitality of the institution. On the one hand, as previously mentioned, the staurites were an instrument of cohesion among the families that were part of them. On the other hand, they stimulated the religious activism of the laity, who soon aimed to extend their control to the parish churches that hosted them, or to which they were in some way connected, attempting to participate in the choice of the clergy charged with the care of souls, thus provoking more than a few conflicts with the ecclesiastical authorities or with the religious bodies that had the patronage of the churches. However, this did not prevent the staurites from continuing to play an important role in the Holy Week processions, as is clearly seen in the 1337 constitutions of Archbishop Giovanni Orsini, who wanted to regulate them at a time when growing political and social tensions ended up by conditioning (sometimes heavily) the same religious sentiment. This is what happened with the processional paths, which turned into a true political struggle at certain times.

---

11. Giovanni Vitolo, *Tra Napoli e Salerno: La costruzione dell'identità cittadina nel Mezzogiorno medievale* (Salerno: Carlone, 2001), 89-131.

12. Ferdinando Ferrajoli, *Le fratrie della Napoli greco-romana* (Naples: Gallina, 1986).

13. Giovanni Vitolo, "Esperienze religiose nella Napoli dei secoli XII-XIV," in *Medioevo Mezzogiorno Mediterraneo: Studi in onore di Mario Del Treppo*, ed. Gabriella Rossetti and Giovanni Vitolo (Naples: GISEM-Liguori, 2000), 3-34.

The staurites are not present in the Eastern Church, so they are considered to have originated in Naples, from where they spread to the surrounding area over the course of time. This spread probably occurred in the wider context of the circulation of cultural, religious, and artistic models that the city was able to nurture, first within the Duchy of Naples and, once it became the capital of the Angevin Kingdom (1266), throughout the south. Nevertheless, the staurites should be considered within the context of the discourse surrounding the influence of the East on the religious life in Naples between late antiquity and the early Middle Ages. The connection with the East is justified not only by the use of the Greek term to indicate the Cross, but also by the particular intensity of this cult, which is at the root of two other practices: the offerings of votive candles by the faithful for the celebration of Mass with the *proprium* of the Cross (*proprium* is a section of the liturgy of the Mass that changes in relation to the particular feast day), but above all, the custom mentioned above, of donations and legacies made not to the churches in which the crucifixes were preserved, but directly to the crucifixes themselves. The crucifixes were considered to be endowed with juridical personality in all respects,[14] similar to the icons noted above. This practice was probably very old and appears to have been continually documented since the beginning of the eleventh century, when a piece of land was donated to the crucifix of the church of San Basilio de Nonnaria in the territory of Herculaneum, which was dependent on the Italo-Greek monastery of Santi Sergio e Bacco (March 9, 1027).[15] In this case, it is certainly a portable panel ("illum grucixfissum que ego pingere feci et illum positum abeo intus ecclesia vestra Sancti Basili"). However, a little later (December 20, 1063) there is another document, which this time refers to a wooden crucifix: it only talks of an artifact that the benefactress declares to be in the possession of the church of San Severo, without specifying that she had it painted ("crucifissum quem abeo intus memorata ecclesia").[16] If the hypothesis is correct, as the permanence of the form used by the Neapolitan notaries leads one to believe, it would be the oldest mention of a wooden crucifix. Its presence in Neapolitan churches is attested again not long afterward in any case by specimens still existing today in addition to the documents, although they are variously dated by art historians between the ends

---

14. Vitolo, *Tra Napoli e Salerno*, 109–23.
15. *RNAM*, 331; Martin, "Quelques remarques sur le culte des images," 229.
16. *RNAM*, 403; Martin, "Quelques remarques sur le culte des images," 229.

of the eleventh and twelfth centuries.[17] The donations made directly to the crucifixes were still widespread at the end of the Middle Ages, as seen in the will dictated by Franceschello Carafa on February 15, 1493. In intercession for the soul of his son Paul, he left a legacy of fifteen *tarì* and assigned an annual income of five ducats, paid for by a tavern he owned near the loggia of Genoa. He dedicated this legacy not to the convent of San Domenico, but to the crucifix in the church.[18]

## The *Diaconiae* and the Sanctorale

The *diaconia*, a church officiated by a deacon that gave subsidies to the poor, is another religious and charitable institution with indubitable Eastern origins. Indeed it is found in other Italian cities that remained in the Byzantine orbit for a longer period; but in Naples it had a particular significance and for many centuries left an imprint on the dedication of some churches. As many as seven have been attested starting from about 670, when the *diaconia* of San Gennaro (today San Gennaro all'Olmo) was founded. The church of San Gennaro was still officiated by a *congregatio sacerdotum et clericorum graecorum et latinorum* in 1238 and 1302, as mentioned above. However, as Bartolommeo Capasso hypothesizes, by then it is possible that the church of San Andrea already existed, where it is known for certain that in 713 the subdeacon Teodimo was rector. Shortly thereafter, in 721, the *diaconia* of Santi Giovanni e Paolo was founded by Theodore, the consul and duke of Naples, who was buried there and whose epitaph was inscribed in Greek. In the ninth century, the church of Santa Maria in Cosmedin had already been a *diaconia* for some time, but it was only documented as such in 1017 and was the seat of a staurite in 1116. The temporal succession between *diaconia* and *staurita* must be interpreted not only in terms of continuity with late antiquity, but also as a manifestation of the protagonism of the pious laity, who, in the name of the Cross, undertook charitable works that had previously been performed by deacons. There are other churches-*diaconie* documented between the tenth and eleventh centuries, but there are certainly older ones: San Pietro

---

17. Vitolo, *Tra Napoli e Salerno*, 109-19. It focuses on crucifixes in chronological order from the churches of San Giorgio Maggiore, San Giovanni Maggiore, Sant'Aniello a Caponapoli, the cathedral, and Saints Cosma and Damiano.
18. Archivio di Stato di Napoli, Corporazioni religiose soppresse, 447, fols. 95r-97v.

*de diaconia* (941), San Giorgio *ad forum* or *ad mercatum* (936), and Santa Maria Rotonda (1025).[19]

The connection of the institution of the *diaconia* with the Byzantine world and the liturgy of the Greek rite, taken for granted since the fourteenth century by Neapolitan chroniclers (the Chronicle of Partenope and the Chronicle of Santa Maria del Principio), is nevertheless reflected in the custom documented by the constitutions of Archbishop Orsini. According to the constitutions— even if at that time the *diaconie* no longer existed and their functions were performed by the staurites and confraternities— the *primiceri* (the priests who governed and supervised the minor clerics in divine service) of the churches were required, in accordance with very ancient traditions, to go to the cathedral on the morning of Holy Saturday and read one Greek lesson each. Additionally, on Easter Sunday they were obligated to sing the creed in Greek together with the *cimiliarca* (the canon custodian of the treasure and relics of the cathedral). Obviously, it is not possible to say whether and to what extent they understood what they read and sang. However, it seems very difficult to doubt that this part of the Easter Rite of the Neapolitan Church was a true historical relic, testimony of a distant past that was still alive in the imagination, if not of the entire community of the city, then at least of that small or large part of it that acted as guardian of the collective memory, even if probably with little awareness.

We should also note the tenacious resistance with which the Neapolitan sanctorale (the liturgy of the feast days of saints worshipped by the Neapolitan Church) opposed the penetration of new cults connected to the piety expressed by the laity of every social condition. This series of saints found its definitive form between late antiquity and the early Middle Ages and included many Eastern and African saints, as indeed happened elsewhere in Italy and the West. In the areas of central and northern Italy with the prevailing communal regime, such new cults found favor even if not always the support of the local authorities. In truth, the phenomenon was not completely absent in Naples. Apart from the delay, it should be noted that the city was very selective in opening up to new forms of devotion, which were successful above all when they existed in continuity with previously existing cults or when the new cult was similar to an old one. This happened in the case of

---

19. Capasso, *Topografia*, 88–96.

the cult of the Magdalene, which had a strong revival at the end of the thirteenth century, not only thanks to the first Angevin sovereigns but also because it superimposed itself onto the more deeply rooted cult of Saint Maria Egiziaca. Yet, the process failed in the case of Saint Catherine of Siena, a Dominican tertiary whose cult, despite its full adherence to the spirituality of the fourteenth century and the support of the Dominicans and Augustinians, could not supplant the much older cult of her namesake of Alexandria.[20]

But naturally, discussion of the Neapolitan sanctorale is based above all on its liturgical calendars, which, compared to other texts (such as hagiographies), allow us an overview of the cults practiced in a given period. These calendars may be either original redactions or copies, which suggests their enduring validity. Of fundamental importance to the present discussion is the so-called Marble Calendar (*Calendario marmoreo*), which was probably compiled in the second half of the eighth century and engraved in the following century on two large slabs of marble on the wall of the side entrance of the church of San Giovanni Maggiore. It was discovered in 1742, and today, after having been moved to various locations, is located in the four-sided portico of Stefania inside the Neapolitan episcopal palace. The calendar has generated debate ever since an edition of it appeared immediately after its discovery.[21] The debate initially attempted to grasp its political and ecclesiastical significance, based on the controversial identification of feasts considered of either Byzantine or Western origin, linking it to the iconoclastic crisis and to the conflicts between those who were open to the influences of the Roman Church and those who instead favored Byzantine influences. The investigation then moved to the liturgical level, which is the most pertinent to its nature. Was it the official calendar of the Church of Naples, or that used only in the church of San Giovanni? Was it destined for the clergy in charge of the liturgical office, or was it a text for the edification of the faithful, who would have found a saint to invoke every day? More recently, scholars' attention has focused on the importance of the text as a linguistic and cultural

---

20. Giovanni Vitolo, "Santità, culti e strutture socio-politiche," in *Pellegrinaggi e itinerari dei santi nel Mezzogiorno medievale*, ed. Giovanni Vitolo (Naples: GISEM-Liguori, 1999), 23–38.

21. Alessio Simmaco Mazzocchi, *In vetus marmoreum Sanctae Neapolitanae Ecclesiae Kalendarium Commentarius* (Neapoli: ex officina Novelli de Bonis typographi archiepiscopalis, 1744–55).

testimony of early medieval Naples, in which the spelling, morphology, and syntax of vernacular Latin were conditioned by the interference of Latin and Greek, operating at more levels than merely the liturgical.[22]

It is not possible to discuss the question at length here, though it may suffice to note that between the eighth and ninth centuries the preponderance of Eastern saints was an entirely natural fact, as it was primarily the East that had produced the kernel of saints in the early centuries of Christianity, starting with the apostles and disciples of Christ, followed by the martyrs, the doctors of the Church, and the Desert Fathers. This nucleus was further enlarged by figures from the ranks of monasticism, both hermetic and cenobitic, who enjoyed great prestige not only in the East, but throughout the empire. By comparison, Western monasticism, which developed later and in a context of economic and demographic depression, was not able at that time to do the same as in the East. Thus, the "factory of saints," to use an evocative expression coined in another context, was put into motion much later. It came about in the twelfth and thirteenth centuries, and at least initially, as will be discussed later, did not lead to the same results everywhere. If Naples is placed at a much lower level than the other great Italian cities of the middle and late Middle Ages in the production and reception of new saints within its liturgical calendars, it probably means that the cults that emerged and were practiced in late antiquity had planted firmer roots, despite the contribution of the marble calendar of San Giovanni Maggiore to their propagation. However, the fact remains that when Neapolitans in the later centuries of the Middle Ages began to feel the need to add other celestial patrons to the two who had previously protected them (namely Gennaro and Agrippino), they initially took in large part from the ancient and late antique sanctorale (Aspreno, Severo, Efebo, and Agnello). The most "modern" saint in this sanctorale was Bishop Atanasio who headed the Church of Naples from 849 to 872. To see the first signs of saints of the High Middle Ages, such as Thomas Aquinas (d. 1274) and Giacomo della Marca (d. 1475), one needs to wait until the beginning of the seventeenth century, thanks to maneuvering by the nobility of a political and ideological nature. Their maneuvers, however, were not followed by any promotion of the

---

22. Gennaro Luongo, "Il calendario marmoreo napoletano: Un approccio linguistico," *Bollettino linguistico campano* 13–14 (2008): 43–66.

cult itself, which in fact did not and still does not have any following among the people.[23]

## Monks and Hermits

At the beginning of the new millennium, the network of monasteries and hermitages that had marked the city territory both inside and outside the walls since the sixth century also bore the imprint of the Eastern model of Christian origins. This was characterized by neither a sharp distinction between eremitism and cenobitism nor an unsurmountable conflict between eremitism and the urban environment, given that eremitism was primarily a spiritual detachment and not a physical separation. The anchorites not only lived in the outskirts of the cities but did not hesitate to return to the center to preach or for other reasons. The choice of a solitary life was not definitive; rather it was lived as a harsher form of religious experience, to be faced only after adequate preparation in a community under the guidance of an abbot. Hence, a continuous exchange between inside and outside, which made hermits, or rather those who can be called "urban hermits," well-known characters to city dwellers distinct from those who lived in distant and inaccessible places. We will return later to discuss one such hermit who was killed at the beginning of the fourteenth century and was immediately honored with sainthood. Here it is necessary to outline, albeit in a rapid manner, the panorama of urban and peri-urban male and female monasteries. This contributes to making Naples, like Rome, a case of great interest for the large number of such monasteries, for the variety of liturgical ordinances and practices that punctuated the life, and for the times and ways through which the overall picture was simplified between the end of the thirteenth and early decades of the fourteenth centuries.

With respect to the number of monasteries in Naples, the epistolary of Gregory the Great gives us a starting point. There we learn of the existence of ten monasteries, three or four of them female,[24] at the end

---

23. Giuseppe Galasso, "Ideologia e sociologia del patronato di san Tommaso d'Aquino su Napoli (1605)," in *Per la storia sociale e religiosa del Mezzogiorno d'italia*, ed. Giuseppe Galasso and Carla Russo (Naples: Guida, 1982), 2:213–49.

24. San Martino, Santi Erasmo, Massimo e Giuliana, San Arcangelo, the monastery ruled by the abbot Barbatianus, Santi Severino and Sossio, Santi Teodoro and Sebastiano, the Monastery of Graterense, Santa Maria in vico Lampadi, Santa Maria in domo Felicis scholastici, the monastery ruled by the abbess Giuliana: *Gregorii I papae registrum epistolarum*,

of the sixth century. By the end of the twelfth century, there were thirty-one within the city (twelve for men, to which four were added outside the walls, and nineteen for women). It is not possible to know what form of life they actually lived, except in a very approximate way: in the absence of customs and statutes, simple reference to the Rules of Saints Basil or Benedict is not enough. It must be added that in Naples there was most probably nothing known of the Rule of Saint Benedict of Aniane (who had integrated the Benedictine *Rule*), which the Synods of Aachen in 816 and 817 had ordered to be adopted throughout the Carolingian Empire. Moreover, there are no decisive elements for identifying the nationality of the monks or the figure of the hegumen given that some of them undoubtedly had Latin names (Benedetto, Sergio, etc.), nor are there inscriptions of the monks in Greek characters, which are more often in Latin. Everything suggests that Jean-Marie Martin and Thomas Granier, who denied the continuity of a "solid Greek monasticism" in Naples from the seventh to the twelfth century, are correct. These two scholars hypothesized, with good foundations, that the general chronology of Eastern influence on Naples can be reconstructed as follows. The monasteries were probably founded in the seventh century, when they were documented in Rome, followed by a long phase of "latent Hellenism," represented by a small minority of Greek-speaking monks in the context of communities formed by the local religious. Again, a phase of "visible and dynamic hellenism" between the tenth and eleventh centuries coincides with the arrival of Greek monks from Calabria, not only in Naples but also in other parts of the south.[25] To this it must be added that Greek monasticism was not a monolithic reality and that terms such as "Basilian rule" and "Basilian order" were formed and used only in the Latin environment to indicate the Greek monks.[26] This meant that in culturally open contexts such as Rome,

---

ed. Paul Ewald and Ludo Moritz Hartmann, 2 vols., Monumenta Germaniae Historica, Epistolae 1–2 (Berlin: Monumenta Germaniae Historica, 1957); Giovanni Vitolo, "Caratteri del monachesimo nel Mezzogiorno altomedievale (secoli VI–IX)," in *Montecassino: Dalla prima alla seconda distruzione. Momenti e aspetti di storia cassinese (secc. VI–IX). Atti del II convegno di studi sul Medioevo meridionale (Cassino-Montecassino, 27–31 maggio 1984)* (Montecassino: Pubblicazioni cassinesi, 1987), 34–35.

25. Martin, "Hellénisme politique"; Thomas Granier, "Les moines 'grecs' de Saints Serge-et-Bacchus et Saints-Théodore-et-Sébastien dans la société napolitaine des VII<sup>e</sup>–XII<sup>e</sup> siècles," in *Vivre en société au Moyen Âge: Occident chrétien VI<sup>e</sup>–XV<sup>e</sup> siècle*, ed. Claude Carozzi, Daniel Le Blévec, and Huguette Taviani-Carozzi (Aix-en-Provence: Publications de l'Université de Provence, 2008), 197–218.

26. Basil, bishop of Caesarea in Cappadocia (present-day Turkey) from 378, did not found a Basilian order but merely promoted the foundation of monasteries, both in remote places

Naples, and Venice, and in a historical phase characterized by the variety of monastic orders adopted in a local area, it was not difficult to refer (not only ideally but also on the organization level) to the Rules dictated by both Benedict of Nursia and Basil of Cappadocia. They were not considered incompatible with each other, as is explicitly stated at the end of the Benedictine *Rule*.

Moreover, for the Naples of the early Middle Ages, there is not enough evidence to be able to specifically discuss the "culture of the monks" that would allow us to verify differences among the various communities and between them and the world of secular clerics. We can only hypothesize. However, it is evident from a cultural perspective that Naples is without a doubt one of the most vital centers of the peninsula, with an abundant production of hagiographic texts, both original and, above all, translated from Greek. Yet the authors are not Latin or Greek monks, but the episcopal clergy. We must attribute a text from the end of the ninth century, the *Life of the Bishop Athanasius*, probably to a cleric (and not to a certain monk Guarimpoto as was thought in the past). This text is of great importance in showing us not only the level of maturity of the civic consciousness of the city, but also the peculiarity of its cultural and religious environment, characterized, as the author makes evident, by the coexistence of the Greek and Latin rites.

While keeping all this in mind, it is important to note that between the eleventh and twelfth centuries the Benedictine *Rule* was increasingly mentioned in the documents concerning monasteries. This does not necessarily mean a change of observance, and it can also be attributed to a reduced influx of Greeks into the city—both monks and laypeople—from Calabria following the Norman conquest and the end of the Saracen raids, which had made all (not only coastal) areas south of Salerno particularly unsafe. Over time, this made the presence of the Greek component in both male and female monasteries ever smaller. Significant in this regard is the case of the women's monastery of Santi Marcellino e Pietro (later Saints Marcellino and Festo) in the area of the present-day church of San Marcellino. This monastery was created by the union of two contiguous monasteries, the first documented since 763 when it was ruled by the deacon and abbess Eufrosina, and the second from the following century. In 1041 it followed the Benedictine

---

and in cities. He gave them his "Rules," which did not constitute a true body of law (as the *Rule of Saint Benedict* was to do), but was, rather, a series of suggestions and teachings for Christians who lived in a community, which he frequently visited.

*Rule*, but there were also Greek nuns or at least nuns who knew Greek, probably continuators of the older community. These nuns were to be buried in the male monastery of Santi Teodoro e Sebastiano, which evidently was then still of Basilian observance ("omnes monache grece seu que sciunt licteras grecas sepeliantur in monasterio Sancti Sebastiani secundum quod fuit consuetudo").[27] This testimony is important because it gives us three pieces of information: that at that time, Greek and Latin nuns lived together in San Marcellino, and were destined to be separated only at the moment of burial; that their nationality did not necessarily coincide with their linguistic and literary education; and that knowledge of Greek was probably an element of social distinction, since it is legitimate to conjecture that the aristocratic families placed their daughters in the most important monasteries of the city—and the monastery of Santi Marcellino e Pietro was certainly important, as it was located near the ducal palace.

If we add to this the fact that the Greek signatures present in the documents from the tenth and eleventh centuries were also connected to the ducal milieu, the monasteries, and the high levels of society, and that Greek was and would long continue to be employed in the liturgy, even if it was incomprehensible to the common faithful (much like Latin), then one can only conclude that in eleventh- and twelfth-century Naples there were still many elements of an institutional and cultural nature that made, if not the whole city, then its middle- and upper-class citizens feel not too far away from the Greek-Byzantine world.

At the same time, the growing influence of the papacy should not be underestimated. In the mid-twelfth century, despite continuing tensions with rulers and princes, among which the Norman kings of Sicily held first place, the papacy was already armed with all the tools it needed to exercise greater control over local churches. It recruited cardinals within them, conferring on them ecclesiastical benefices and encouraging the penetration of new orders that had been linked to the Apostolic See since their creation. In 1150 in Naples we see the arrival of monks of the Badia di Cava (with two monasteries in San Arcangelo agli Armieri and San Pietro di Regionario, both in the most economically and socially vibrant areas of the city), and a few years later the foundation in that same area of the canon regulars of San Pietro in Aram as well, at

---

27. Capasso, *Topografia*, 160-63.

the instigation of the Neapolitan cardinal Giovanni de Pizutis, who was once prior of the canonry of Saint-Victor in Paris.[28] For various reasons, both innovations were attributable, if not to the spirit of ecclesiastical reform (which in the middle of the twelfth century was considered to be over), then to its more lasting results, the canons regular. Canon regulars had managed to create a symbiosis between pastoral commitment and the common life of the clergy. Moreover, various reforms aimed not only at renewing monasticism on the spiritual and cultural level, but also, thanks to their exemption from episcopal jurisdiction, at making them a useful resource to the papacy, which would have drawn heavily on the canon regulars for the recruitment of bishops. The Benedictine monks of Montevergine (Verginiani) and the Carthusians (Certosini), who arrived in Naples much later at the end of the twelfth century and in the first decades of the fourteenth century respectively, were somehow connected to that period of reforms.[29] Of the religious orders that could be placed in the category of New Monasticism, the only ones not to establish a seat in Naples were the Cistercians, who evidently did not consider Naples an environment compatible with their style of life as it was already too crowded with monastic institutions.

In effect, it was the case. The thirty-one Benedictine or Basilian-inspired monasteries of the eleventh and twelfth centuries, mentioned above, which had shown themselves capable of taking on the new challenges of the times—albeit with changes of observance and occasionally

---

28. Gennaro Aspreno Galante, *Guida sacra della città di Napoli* (Naples: Stamperia del Fibreno, 1872), 275.

29. Domenico Ambrasi, "La vita religiosa," in *Storia di Napoli* (Naples: Edizioni Scientifiche Italiane, 1969), 3:514–17. The congregation of Monte Vergine was founded from the second half of the twelfth century by the hermit monks who gathered on Mount Partenio (today in the Comune of Mercogliano in the province of Avellino) around Guglielmo da Vercelli, who had withdrawn there around 1118. The original inspiration for hermitic life gradually waned following the spread of the new congregation through much of the south of Italy, but this did not prevent the monks of Monte Vergine from preserving their identity right through the Modern Age thanks to pilgrimages to the Madonna of Monte Vergine and the network of hospitals serving the pilgrims and the poor. Giovanni Araldi, "Verginiani," in *Federico II: Enciclopedia fridericiana* (Rome: Istituto della Enciclopedia Italiana, 2005), 2:879–85. The Carthusian order originated in France, around Grenoble, at the end of the eleventh century, created by the hermit monks who gathered around Bruno of Cologne before he moved to Calabria. It took its name from the Grande Chartreuse, where the first community arose in 1084, which also gave its name to the dependent monasteries, known as charterhouses. In southern Italy, besides Campania (Naples, Capri, Padula), they were also present in Molise (Guglionesi), Basilicata (Chiaromonte), Calabria (Serra San Bruno), and Sicily (Catania). Giovanni Vitolo, "Aspetti e problemi della storia delle certose nel Mezzogiorno medievale: Gli esempi di Napoli e Padula," *Napoli Nobilissima*, 5th series, 2 (2001): 5–14.

even of headquarters—were still in existence in the thirteenth century. The mendicant orders, which, as will be discussed, constituted an absolute novelty in the religious panorama of the city, had only two friaries in the city. The Dominicans settled in the Benedictine monastery of Sant'Arcangelo a Morfisa in 1231, and the Augustinians in the Basilian monastery of San Vincenzo in 1259.

Returning to the hermits who lived in the immediate vicinity of the city, the story of the Lombardian hermit Nicolò offers a real glimpse of the dynamics underway in the Neapolitan religious society at the end of the thirteenth and beginning of the fourteenth century. Of this Nicolò, we know not only his name and place of residence (the hill of Pizzofalcone, in front of the Castel dell'Ovo), but also the date (May 11, 1310) and manner of his death, because it raised a vast echo in the city, agitating even the local ecclesiastical institutions at a time when a great and delicate architectural intervention was in progress, destined to have a strong impact on the city's topographical structure. This was the construction of a new and impressive cathedral, begun in 1294. It was not difficult to identify and arrest the guilty party, a Provençal named Pierottino, who occasionally brought him food and alms on behalf of Queen Maria, wife of Charles II of Anjou because, as a hagiographical text recounts, after killing him with a sword, Pierottino remained immobilized beside the corpse until he was apprehended by the captain of the city, who hurried to the site along with a great multitude of people and the canons of the cathedral. They immediately took the corpse of the hermit to the old Basilica of Santa Restituta, which was under direct management of the canons.

At the time of the murder of Nicolò, Archbishop Umberto d'Ormont was not in the city. However, upon his return, he not only gave his full support to the work of the canons, but also brought about a sort of canonization of the hermit, sponsoring the translation of his remains to a marble tomb placed in a small chapel carved inside the great chapel-sanctuary of Santa Maria del Principio, which was the most sacred part of the Santa Restituta complex.[30] The front slab of the tomb, where miracles soon began to occur, is still preserved. It is not known when

---

30. The legend of the blessed hermit Nicolò was written several years after his death by master Giacomo da Pisa, a member of the Angevin court: Gennaro Aspreno Galante, *Memorie della vita e del culto del beato Nicolò eremita di S. Maria a Circolo in Napoli* (Naples, 1875-77), offprint from *La Scienza e la Fede*; Vitolo, "Esperienze religiose nella Napoli dei secoli XII-XIV," 15-16.

the thirteen columns that supported it were replaced by a base, as they were still documented in a pastoral visit in 1582–83.

The Lombard hermit was not the only hermit who lived on the periphery of Naples and of whom the inhabitants had news. His presence in Naples is not very surprising because the south had for centuries been considered in the religious imagination of Christians of the West as the promised land of hermits, as it was thought to be the most suitable place to have religious experiences of particular intensity (it suffices here to recall the arrival between the eleventh and twelfth centuries of Bruno of Cologne in Calabria, Conrad of Bavaria in Puglia, and Guglielmo da Vercelli in Campania). That Neapolitans knew the hermits well is proven by the fact that they left them bequests, usually small sums of money that the executors of the wills were evidently able to give to the beneficiaries because they knew who they were and where to find them. The surviving testimonies also refer to those of the early fourteenth century, but everything suggests that the phenomenon had a long tradition behind it, most likely linked to the insular eremitism of the fifth and sixth centuries. The best-documented locations of hermits in the lower Tyrrhenian were in the gulf of Naples, on the islet of Megaride, then separated from the mainland where the Castel dell'Ovo now stands, and further north on the island of Ponza. "To the brothers and hermits residing on the Island of Ponza" (fratribus seu eremitis morantibus in insula Pontii), whose fame must have spread far beyond the local area, the Neapolitan noblewoman Maria Mostacia left an *oncia* of gold in 1357.[31] Their presence on the island is documented at the beginning of the ninth century, thanks to a letter from September 25, 813, by which the pope informed Charlemagne of the ransacking perpetrated by the Saracens. We know that those who had settled on the islet off the coast of Naples adhered to a particular form of monastic life, alternating between moments of solitary life and cenobitic life over the course of the day, which would later be realized more fully in Carthusian monasticism. This experience was interrupted when the Neapolitans, strengthening the city's defenses from Roger II's attacks, decided shortly before 1127 to fortify the island. The monks were forced to move to the hill facing Pizzofalcone, which in turn held a strong eremitical presence and was as such a sacred space in defense of the city. A similar function as a hermitage and sacred space in the city's

---

31. *Oncia* was the conventional money equivalent to five florins of gold.

defense probably also developed on the north side of the Capodimonte Hill. On its slopes the presence of two poor hermits (*pauperes heremitae*) are documented in the 1420s, the names of whom are known: *frater* Domenico de Pontiaco and *frater* Nicola de Lafercha, originally from Palena in Abruzzo.[32] Compared to the well-documented hermitages of Pizzofalcone and Capodimonte, it may seem difficult to believe that there was yet another hermitage on the hill (today it does not seem like a hill, after the elevation of the area of the current Piazza Municipio and the surrounding streets, following the deposit of alluvial material from Capodimonte during the Middle Ages and the Early Modern era), on which Charles of Anjou built the Castelnuovo in 1270. However, it cannot be doubted that, although closer to the city walls than the other two, the hermitage had a substantially similar function. It was certainly not accidental that the first Friars Minor to arrive in the city settled there between the end of the 1220s and the beginning of the 1230s.

Only in recent years has this event been given the correct emphasis in the history of the Franciscan settlement in southern Italy. Other than being chronologically significant, this is the perfect example of how the first communities of the Friars Minor, characterized by extreme precariousness and freedom of movement from their origins, were only able to use the ruins of an ancient Roman villa that they adapted into a chapel dedicated to the Virgin. From there, the friars went to the city every day for alms and their work of religious revival, though preaching was not yet the most important tool in those early years. However, in the meantime, their settlement on the hill of Santa Maria a Palazzo, as it was immediately called, had much in common with that of the older monk-hermits on the islet of Megaride, and the situation developed in the same way a little more than a century later. The friars were removed to create space for a new fortified building, this time not only for the defense of the city but also as the residence of the court. The first monk-hermits settled in a territory that was suitable for both a proper cenobitic community (what would soon become the monastery of San Pietro a Castello) and the settlements of hermits dependent on this community or in some way connected to it, as was perhaps the case with Nicolò Lombardo's hermitage. The friars, on the other hand, had everywhere (not just in Naples) reinterpreted the characteristic elements of their original inspiration, namely their marginality and their

---

32. Riccardo Bevere, "Suffragi, espiazioni postume, riti e cerimonie funebri dei secoli XII, XIII e XIV nelle provincie napoletane," *Archivio Storico per le Province Napoletane* 21 (1896): 122.

*minoritas*. They deeply integrated themselves into the urban environment by moving just a few hundred meters to build a proper convent close to—and inside of—the western walls of the city. This convent was linked to their original settlement, at least in name, as it was called Santa Maria la Nova.

We will return to the developments of the presence of the Friars Minor and other mendicant orders in Naples later. Here, it is exigent to take a step backward to complete the panorama of the religious experiences of the most noteworthy fringes of the lay faithful, which did not result in their entry into either the clergy or monastic communities that were more or less linked to the organizational practices of their cenobitic origins. It concerns the penitential life, chosen by various people, both men and women, and usually mentioned in the historiography as "penitents," whom the Church had been trying to channel since the early Middle Ages into an intermediate order between that of the religious and the laity. The laity entered into this order through a ceremony regulated by a special ritual placed under the control of the bishops, before it was given definitive organization by Pope Nicholas IV in 1289, who entrusted its direction to the Franciscan order.

The variety of lifestyles and commitments undertaken by the penitents is similarly characterized by a multiplicity of terms to define them. This terminological variety is in itself not without significance for the historian because it is proof of the different ways of perceiving the phenomenon. As has been noted, functionalism is not a decisive element for explaining the behavior of human beings as individuals and as a society, but one cannot deny the natural tendency of the narrators to avoid complicating the language by introducing new terms, even when such terms would have been necessary to indicate things that did not previously exist. As Marc Bloch has stated: "To the despair of historians, men fail to change their vocabulary every time they change their customs."[33] Therefore, if in a given historical and geographical context we have a variety of terms to indicate a lifestyle that is not easily framed in a codified model, while in another we have only one, it will always signify something, and in any case, we cannot be exempt from the duty of trying to explain it. The terms that interest us here are *monacus/monaca*, *heremita* and *poenitens* (used as masculine and feminine), *reclusus/a*, *bizoca*, *incarcerata*, and *reincarcerate*. Now, of these terms

---

33. Marc Bloch, *Apologia della storia o mestiere di storico*, ed. Girolamo Arnaldi (Turin: Einaudi, 1960), 47.

that are variously attested in the south, in Naples we find *monacus/a* in the tenth and eleventh centuries and *heremita* in the twelfth to qualify some people involved in legal actions. How do we explain this more limited range of terms, and what is meant by *monacus/a*? The answer to the second question is fairly clear from the documents, which use the term *monacus/a* for three different meanings:

- *Monacus/a*, someone who lives in a monastery, in which it is sometimes expressly said that the Benedictine or Basilian Rule is followed.
- A deceased monk, *postmodum (vero) monacus*, mentioned as already a husband or father of someone who performs a legal action, where the status of monk is referred to more than anything else as a further element of identification. In this case, the term signifies an individual who entered into the monastery at a later age, or after becoming a widower, or perhaps even at the end of his days, wanting to die wearing the monastic habit. This use, as is known, was not uncommon, especially among the wealthy, who were in a position to leave the monks generous bequests.[34]
- Living *monacus/a*, whose monastery is not indicated, but who appears not to live under the authority of an abbot or abbess, since he freely disposes of his possessions.[35]

It is this last meaning that is particularly interesting here. The men and women in this category are, in fact, referred to as monks, and are sometimes themselves children or grandchildren of monks, who act as

---

34. Only some examples are treated in Capasso, *Monumenta*: "dominus Iohannes filius quondam domini Stephani Longobardi, post modum veri monachi" (vol. 2, bk. 1:323, October 10, 1033); "Anna honesta femina filia quondam Gregorii Cofinelli, iugalis Gregorii Ipato, post modum vero monachi" (vol. 2, bk. 1:424, January 11, 1112); "Anna honesta femina filia quondam Iohannis de Sicula postmodum vero monachi et quondam domine Purpure honeste femine iugalium personarum" (vol. 2, bk. 1:475-76, August 31, 1132).

35. Capasso, *Monumenta*: "Anna honesta femina filia quondam domini Algierni monachi cui supra nomen Pictuli, relicta quondam domini Gregorii" (vol. 2, bk. 1:159-60, August 30, 978; among the witnesses, Marino son of Cesario the monk); "Sergius filius quondam domini Gregorii monachi et quondam domine Eufimie honeste femine iugalium" (vol. 2, bk. 1:173, May 15, 982); "domina Anna gloriosa femina iugalis Petri monachi" (vol. 2, bk. 1:177, March 11, 983); "domina Anna filia quondam domini Marini monachi et quondam domine Maru honeste femine iugalium" (vol. 2, bk. 1:193, February 12, 990); "domina Anna venerabilis monaca filia quidem Iohannis Varvocia nunc monachi" (vol. 2, bk. 1:323, October 1, 1033); "Purpura et Iohannes filii domini Leonis Amalfitani et domine Drose monache, iugalium personarum" (vol. 2, bk. 1:344, July 2, 1050).

private lay individuals and are considered household monks/nuns (it: *monaci/che di casa*). It is important to note that these are laypeople with a certain economic privilege, who have decided to live in a secluded and moderate manner, had their choice of life approved by the bishop, and assumed the relative obligations including the guidance of a spiritual father and the regular participation in Mass and other religious functions of the parish church. Yet, despite all this, they chose to remain in their own homes. It would not be wrong to relate this experience to domestic monasticism prevalent in Rome in late antiquity, even if for Naples—which was closely linked to the ancient capital of the empire on the basis of their common, though strictly formal dependence on Byzantium—there is no direct evidence of buildings whose owners practiced monasticism together with their servants.

Household monks and nuns are found in other places too between the tenth and twelfth centuries, as in Salerno and its immediate surroundings, where between 1070 and 1188 fourteen nuns "who live not in a monastery but at home" (que non degent in monasterio sed domi) are documented.[36] This is certainly not a random phrase, as the notaries who drafted the acts in which it appears deemed it opportune to insert it both because it must have been a practice that was not universally known (as it would have been in Naples in the tenth century) and to ensure the legitimacy of the acts carried out by their clients, who could freely dispose of their property as they were not subject to the authority of an abbess. In other words, what may seem to be an equally widespread practice in a different context from a political and cultural point of view reveals elements more appropriately related to the anthropological and religious sphere, notwithstanding the conservative nature of the notary formulas and thanks to the high standard of professionalism of the Salerno notaries. The anthropological and religious sphere in Naples was perceived as a condition—that of the household nun or monk—that was part of the normal institutional and religious landscape of the city, and had to be explicitly explained in Salerno to avoid possible disputes concerning the validity of deeds.

One aspect of this situation was to be clarified, but another aspect was to complicate itself between the thirteenth and fourteenth centuries under the pressure of two opposing phenomena. The first was

---

36. Rosalba Di Meglio, "*Esperienze religiose femminili nell'Italia meridionale (sec. XIII–XIV),*" in *Vita religiosa al femminile (secoli XIII–XIV): Atti del Ventiseiesimo Convegno Internazionale di Studi del Centro italiano di studi di storia e d'arte (Pistoia, 19–21 maggio 2017)* (Rome: Viella, 2019), 181–82.

the growing religious protagonism of women, impatient to experiment with forms of religious life distinct from the cloistered monastic tradition, not only on an organizational but also on a linguistic level, with the rejection of the term *monaca* (nun), which felt indelibly connected to a condition that could not be accepted even as an ideal reference. The second was the increasingly firm desire of the papacy to channel the erupting demands for religious renewal into institutions that were more reassuring, not only for ecclesiastical but also for political and social authorities. From these institutions in the south, no less than elsewhere, an exponential growth of female monasteries emerged, which were linked to both the old and new Benedictine monasticism and to the mendicant orders, with a consequent further decrease in the phenomenon of household monasticism.

Household monasticism did not disappear, but it became increasingly controlled by the mendicant orders and the parish clergy throughout Italy (not only in the south). The terms most used to describe that composite movement were penitents and *bizzoche*, with the latter divided into recluses and nonrecluses. We see an example of this in Trani, while in fourteenth-century Naples we have evidence of hermits residing in the "ecclesia Sancte Restitute sita intus maiorem ecclesiam Neapolitanam"—that is to say, they were in what was a lateral part of the cathedral and free to move about in it, rather than being walled in isolated cells. However, the possibility that they may have lived in cells inside the church and communicated through a grate or a wheel cannot be entirely excluded, as it was still the case during the sixteenth century in the cathedral of Ferrara and Saint Peter's Basilica in the Vatican, as is documented in Benevento. These cells might have been located in the space now occupied by the courtyard that divides Santa Restituta from the buildings of the diocesan curia. However, after 1385 we hear no more about them, so it must have been that in Naples, as in the rest of Italy, the phenomenon of voluntary imprisonment had come to an end by the beginning of the fifteenth century.[37]

## The Associationism of the Clergy and the Laity

The religious associationism of the clergy and laity, which we have already touched upon when speaking about the cult of the Cross and the staurite, was destined not only to maintain itself over time, but

---

37. Vitolo, "Esperienze religiose nella Napoli dei secoli XII–XIV," 20–25.

actually to assume increasingly noticeable dimensions, leaving a mark on the urban fabric of the historical center. Although this phenomenon is present in all of Western Christianity, in Naples it is expressed with traits of a certain originality that also emerged from the attempt to experiment with new forms of coexistence between the two types of associationism: that of the clergy and of the laity. This can be seen very well in the case of the *congregatio et fraternitas* of priests and the laity, which in 1179 moved from its original headquarters outside the city, near the church of Santa Venere in the area of Pizzofalcone, to inside the walls near the church of San Giovanni Maggiore, settling in the nearby chapel of San Bartolomeo. This chapel was dependent on the monastery of San Pietro a Castello, which was then, as we have said, in the area of Pizzofalcone, to which the confreres gave their former headquarters in exchange.[38]

A mixed confraternity was not a novelty in the south or elsewhere in Italy, but the one in Naples appears very original in its configuration. The novelty consisted mainly of the fact that priests and laymen constituted two distinct groups, each with its own *primicerius*, even if they were operating with a single aim. In 1179, there were fourteen priests, with many more laymen. In the document in which they exchanged their original seat for the new one, as many as forty-four laypersons participated, declaring that they also acted on behalf of other *fratres et sorores*. The unity of the two components was ensured by the existence of a superior authority, that of the abbot of the monastery of San Pietro a Castello, who appointed the *primicerius* of both the priests and laity. The deed of the 1179 exchange also contains a sort of statute for the confraternity, defining the rights and duties of the two groups both on the occasion of the death of a member and the use of their income, and in the domain of charitable activities, which consisted mainly of giving alms to the poor on Tuesdays and Saturdays, when the priests and laity gathered in the church.

It is not known what happened to this association in the following years. What is certain is that by 1374 it had become a very different thing, as it was then a simple college of clerics, even if they continued to call themselves confreres.[39] In addition, the original number of twelve clerics had been reduced to ten, as the church's income could not maintain more. To understand the character of the new institution, it is

---

38. Vitolo, "Esperienze religiose nella Napoli dei secoli XII–XIV," 4–7.
39. Archivio di Stato di Napoli, *Monasteri soppressi*, no. 1396, fol. 46.

necessary to keep in mind the situation of Naples in reference to both the forms of organization of the clergy and the terminology used for them. The terms that generate the most misunderstandings are those of *confrater* and *confratantia*, which in the late Middle Ages could indicate, respectively, a member of a lay association or the association itself, or a layman linked to a monastic community through a relationship of spiritual brotherhood. However, it could also mean a cleric or priest working in a church who is part of a college without being invested with pastoral duties, and who simply was required to attend the funeral and liturgical celebrations linked to particular holidays, mostly the feast of the saint to whom the church was dedicated. In addition to these *confratres*, at the head of whom there was always a *primicerius* or a *cellelarius*, there was another college in the parish churches, that of the *ebdomadari*. The latter were equipped with individual prebends and were required to celebrate a Mass once a week, and to participate in weekly shifts for the celebration of the Divine Office in the choir. The *ebdomadari* and the *confratres* formed the *congregatio ebdomadariorum et confratrum* of a given church, but, as we have said, they were two distinct organisms with separate roles and incomes.

    The *ebdomadari* essentially constituted the aristocracy of the clergy and belonged mostly to the families of the city's ruling class. The *confratres* were the intermediate segment, formed by those ecclesiastics without prebends who, waiting to procure them, tried to secure an income by being welcomed into one or more *confratantiae*. Still further down were those clerics who formed a sort of underclass, deprived of any prebend. They lent their work here and there, not infrequently as a substitute for those with prebends who, because of the accumulation of benefices and other tasks that kept them away from their church, needed to be replaced by others in the fulfillment of their pastoral duties. The *confratres* of San Bartolomeo in the mid-fourteenth century, therefore, were not the lay members of a confraternity, but the priests and clerics who formed the college assigned to the church's office. Every available post in the college was called precisely this, a *confratantia*, a term also used to indicate the entire college or *congregatio*, reduced in 1541 at the time of the pastoral visit of Archbishop Francesco Carafa to only four members: the *primicerius*, two priests, and a cleric.[40]

---

40. Vitolo, "Esperienze religiose nella Napoli dei secoli XII–XIV," 4–13.

To complete the complex picture of the associationism of the clergy, two particular bodies operating in the cathedral should be mentioned: the chapter of canons, whose members enjoyed individual prebends and often united them to become, as mentioned, the rectories of the parish churches for many of the clergy in the city, and the college of the *ebdomadari*, who ensured the liturgical service of the cathedral in weekly shifts and who not infrequently came into conflict with the chapter of the canons.

## The Confraternities

The time has now come to return to the lay confraternities, which we have already distinguished from the staurite, even if the staurites came to progressively resemble confraternities, often keeping their former names. This serves as historical testimony, as the confraternal associations of the laity that are still called staurites in the late Middle Ages should probably be considered as having early medieval origins.

One of the elements that characterized the confraternities was their range of action, which exceeded the boundaries of the neighborhood in which they emerged and in principle covered the entire city. They were often linked to local contexts because of the obligations that their members assumed, which could be carried out more easily if the members lived nearby. However, this did not preclude a wider recruitment, nor did it involve a reduction in the scope of activity, which, having increasingly focused on charity and assistance for both the confreres and the poor, had all the residents of the city as its recipients. This focus is best demonstrated by the confraternity of Sant'Eligio, built in 1270 in the area of the Mercato, which was in full expansion on an urban and economic level. The promoters of the movement were representatives of the French colony, especially those from Provençal and Marseilles, who were working as merchants and artisans, but were also largely residents. At the beginning, the confraternity was destined to welcome its compatriots only, but soon it was opened to everyone. No preclusion of national or social order was implemented for the reception of the poor and sick in the hospital, which the confraternity founded and patronized thanks to the support of the Angevin dynasty. These were the years in which the so-called "religiosity of works" flourished in Italy and elsewhere in the West, which saw the religious associations of the laity involved not only in the practice of faith and the promotion of old and new cults, but also and above all in the exercise of charity and assistance for the poor and pilgrims.[41]

Until then, charity and poor relief had been considered the responsibility of bishops—whose description as the fathers of the poor was not accidental—and of ecclesiastical institutions in general (monasteries, cathedral chapters, and canonical orders). All were particularly active in Naples, judging by the large number of hospitals documented continuously from at least 680. It was a tradition that could not fail to impose itself on the staurites as well, in whose culture the exercise of charity was fundamental within the sphere of their neighborhood. We have evidence of their foundations, but everything leads us to believe that they were small and had primarily a symbolic character until 1248 when the members of a *staurita* based in the church of San Giovanni Maggiore decided to build a hospital. However, there are no remains of this hospital, which was located at the top of the steps accessing the church today.[42]

Some of the hospitals founded by bishops and monasteries were maintained throughout the Middle Ages. Particular mention should be made of those hospitals that are documented as being in full operation by at least the twelfth century, such as Sant'Atanasio (the name of its founder toward the middle of the ninth century) in the atrium of the cathedral. There were also Santa Maria di Piedigrotta near the sanctuary of the same name, San Severino at the monastery of Santi Severino e Sossio, Santa Maria a Campagnano near the area of the future Piazza del Mercato, and San Giovanni a Mare, which was run by the Order of San Giovanni di Gerusalemme.[43]

With the Hospital of Sant'Eligio we enter a completely new dimension at the institutional and organizational levels. Its model was replicated a few decades later by the Hospital of Ss. Annunziata and was then adopted in many other cities of the Regno, becoming one of the many channels through which the capital city was able to exercise its hegemony over the provinces even outside the political sphere.[44]

---

41. Gilles Gérard Meersseman, in collaboration with Gian Piero Pacini, *Ordo fraternitatis: Confraternite e pietà dei laici nel Medioevo*, 3 vols. (Rome: Herder, 1977); Grado Giovanni Merlo, ed., *Esperienze religiose e opere assistenziali nei secoli XII e XIII* (Turin: Il Segnalibro, 1987); Giovanni Vitolo, "Religiosità delle opere e monachesimo verginiano nell'età di Federico II," *Benedictina* 43 (1996): 135-50.

42. Giovanni Vitolo, "L'ospedale di S. Eligio e la piazza del Mercato," in Giovanni Vitolo and Rosalba Di Meglio, *Napoli angioino-aragonese: Confraternite, ospedali, dinamiche politico-sociali*, Immagini del Medioevo 7 (Salerno: Carlone, 2003), 83.

43. Vitolo, "L'ospedale di S. Eligio," 72-86.

44. Vitolo, "L'ospedale di S. Eligio."

The constituent elements of the Sant'Eligio-Ss.Annunziata model can be summarized as follows: prioritizing the religious and symbolic character of the hospital, which was often equipped with twelve beds—inspired by the example of the twelve apostles—where the sick were provided essentially with only food and religious assistance; recruitment of doctors and nurses, even though the staff mainly consisted of pious laypeople, sometimes even married couples, who served as penitents and had a communal life with the patients; connection with the monarchy and the political authorities in general for protection and economic aid, beginning by locating the land for construction of the hospital itself, its church, and its cemetery; search for new income not only through donations and bequests, but also by the management of its real estate assets and its financial transactions, including the purchase of public debt securities, the management of private deposits, and the creation of its own banks (from which the modern Bank of Naples grew); and separation of welfare from management activities, with the consequent insertion of confreres from the world of commerce and freelance professionals into the governing bodies, as they were the only ones considered to have the technical skills to handle the accounts of increasingly complex institutions.[45]

The confreres of Sant'Eligio and of the Ss. Annunziata were engaged above all in the work of hospital assistance and the reception of abandoned children, while not neglecting other charitable practices, including the provision of dowries for impoverished girls and aiding confreres who had difficulties. The members of the confraternity of Disciplina della Croce, founded in the second half of the thirteenth century and still active today, were concerned with assisting prisoners and the burial arrangements of those who had died in prison or on the gallows, regardless of where these prisoners or the dead were once resident and where they were to be buried.[46]

Another important element that characterized the new associations was their mix of social classes. Even when they were founded on the initiative of members of a certain social class, they made room in their

---

45. Vitolo, "L'ospedale di S. Eligio," 97–122; Rosalba Di Meglio, "Before the Public Banks: Innovation and Resilience by Charities in Fifteenth-Century Naples," in *Financial Innovation and Resilience*, ed. Lilia Costabile and Larry Neal, Palgrave Studies in the History of Finance (Basingstoke: Palgrave Macmillan: 2018), 55–70, https://doi.org/10.1007/978-3-319-90248-7_3.

46. Giovanni Vitolo, "Confraternite e dinamiche politico-sociali a Napoli nel Medioevo: La Disciplina della Santa Croce," in *Compagnia della Santa Croce: Sette secoli di storia a Napoli*, ed. M. Pisani Massamormile (Naples: Electa Napoli, 2007), 59–70.

governing bodies for people of different backgrounds. The confraternities of Sant'Eligio and Ss. Annunziata managed systematically, effectively, and enduringly to connect the area in which they were rooted with the rest of the community, and even appeared from the outside as representative institutions of the city. They also involved the two great social and political groupings, the nobility and the *popolo*. Their governing bodies were mostly formed of members of the mercantile bourgeoisie and professionals, but they were presided over by members of the noble families of Portanova and Capuana respectively. The confraternity hospital of La Maddalena, built near the bridge of the same name in 1330 or a few years earlier, did not have an analogous organization, but until at least the early decades of the fifteenth century it was also administered by members of noble, bourgeois, and mercantile factions. The latter were increasingly represented at the head of the institution.

The forms of oligarchic closure, when they existed, took place in the sixteenth century in the context of a generalized phenomenon affirming the aristocratic lifestyle. On the one hand, they aimed to connote in an aristocratic sense some associations that had earlier been open to all (such as the confraternity hospital of the Maddalena and Disciplina della Croce). On the other hand, it sought to ennoble the origins of those institutions that were formed on the initiative of the members of the bourgeois class, such as the confraternity hospital of Sant'Eligio al Mercato and the Disciplina di Santa Marta.[47]

## Heretics

The strong presence of male and female monastic communities and the even more concentrated network of associations of clergy and laity were not enough to provide a response to the religious anxieties that had spread even in a city like Naples, as they did in much of the medieval West between the twelfth and thirteenth centuries. The city had always been a point of convergence for people coming not only from the surrounding areas, but also from the East. The surviving evidence does not allow us to hypothesize a consistent number of heretics, but it is also not without interest. Dominican Anselmo di Alessandria in his *Tractatus de hereticis*, written around 1267, mentions a journey to Naples around 1165 taken by a Milanese man named Marco and three of his

---

47. Rosalba Di Meglio, "La Disciplina di S. Marta: Mito e realtà di una confraternita popolare," in Vitolo and Di Meglio, *Napoli angioino-aragonese*, 147–234.

friends. They stayed there for almost a year to deepen their knowledge of dualistic doctrines under the guidance of a Cathar bishop.[48] After his residence in Naples, Marco became a deacon and established himself as a skilled preacher and a tireless missionary.

The activism of Archbishop Pietro, responsible for the arrival of Dominicans in Naples, shows that there must have been a large group of heretics in Naples, not just fugitive Cathars in transit through the city. Pietro asked the Dominicans for assistance in 1231 specifically to cope with the danger presented by heretics. Moreover, a campaign of proselytism was underway in the *Regno* as Frederick II himself states under Title I of the Constitutions of Melfi, where, referring precisely to the Cathars, he declares, "From the borders of Italy, especially from the lands of Lombardy, where we know that their iniquity is more serious, and they bring rivulets of their perfidy to our *Regno* of Sicily."[49] Nor was this the first time that this matter had been raised. As early as 1213, he had promised Innocent III to take action to eradicate "the error of heretical depravity" (*Promissio egrensis*);[50] in 1220 he applied the third canon of the Fourth Lateran Council against the heretical movements;[51] and in 1224 he first introduced the use of the stake.[52] Certainly, however, the presence of heretics from the area around Milan in the south is demonstrated by the case of Andrea di Vimercate, a town very close to Concorezzo, home of the main Cathar church in Italy adhering to the moderate dualism of the Church of Bulgaria (*ordo Bulgariae*), burned down in Benevento in 1276.[53] We cannot exclude the fact

---

48. Giovanni Brancaccio, "Movimenti ereticali e correnti eterodosse," in *Storia del Mezzogiono* (Naples: Edizioni del Sole, 1991), 9:280.

49. *Die Konstitutionen Friedrichs II. für das Königreich Sizilien*, ed. Wolfgang Stürner, Monumenta Germaniae Historica, Constitutiones et acta publica imperatorum et regum 2 (Hannover: Monumenta Germaniae Historica, 1996), 150; Grado Giovanni Merlo, *Contro gli eretici: La coercizione all'ortodossia prima dell'Inquisizione* (Bologna: Il Mulino, 1996), 106–8; Giovanni Vitolo, "Gli eretici di Roccamandolfi (1269–1270): una Montaillou molisana?," in *"Sapiens, ut loquatur, multa prius considerat": Studi di storia medievale offerti a Lorenzo Paolini*, ed. Caterina Bruschi and Riccardo Parmeggiani, Uomini e mondi medievali 64 (Spoleto: Centro italiano di studi sull'Alto Medioevo, 2019), 139–41.

50. Jean-Louis-Alphonse Huillard-Bréholles, ed., *Historia diplomatica Friderici secundi* (Paris: Plon, 1852–61), 1:268–71.

51. Huillard-Bréholles, *Historia diplomatica*, vol. 2, bk. 1:2–6; Riccardi de Sancto Germano notarii, *Chronica*, ed. Carlo Alberto Garufi (Bologna: Zanichelli, 1938), 85–86.

52. Huillard-Bréholles, *Historia diplomatica*, vol. 2, bk. 1:421–23.

53. Camillo Minieri Riccio, *Saggio di Codice diplomatico formato sulle antiche scritture dell'Archivio di Stato di Napoli* (Naples: Rinaldi e Sellitto, 1878–83), 1:117; *I registri della cancelleria angioina ricostruiti da Riccardo Filangieri con la collaborazione degli archivisti napoletani*, 50 vols. (Naples: Accademia Pontaniana, 1963–2010), 14:21.

that the intervention of the archbishop of Benevento had been solicited by Gregory IX, as he warned the sovereign not to go too far in the application of antiheretical laws and to distinguish between the heretics and the errant, that it to say, between those who are against the Church and those who had nothing to do with heretical movements, but were merely rebels against the sovereign.[54] In Naples in 1230, Lando, archbishop of Reggio, and Riccardo di Principato, marshal of the *Regno*, were operating as inquisitors. However, it seems that the royal officers proceeded with absolute freedom, arresting those suspected of heresy, confiscating their assets, and submitting them only subsequently to ecclesiastical judges. They did not even hesitate to inflict death sentences when they thought it appropriate, a procedure that alarmed the Roman Curia because it appeared as an undue and dangerous interference of the monarchical authority in ecclesiastical matters. Riccardo di San Germano speaks of various condemnations to the stake carried out in 1231, but he gives no indication of names or locations.[55] In those years, the situation in the rest of Italy was different, where the Tribunal of the Inquisition took its first steps. This was an autonomous institution entrusted to the Dominicans and Franciscans, who worked with a staff and their own financial resources, which came from fines and the confiscation of the goods of the convicted, within a well-defined legal system on the basis of which the sentences were issued and the political authorities were obliged to execute them.

The situation changed to some extent with the arrival of Charles of Anjou, when the *Regno*, which constituted one of the two inquisitorial provinces entrusted to the Dominicans (the other being Lombardy), was divided into four districts entrusted to as many Dominican inquisitors. However, not even then was there a complete homogenization of the south compared to the rest of Italy, where the Tribunal of the Inquisition acquired a centrality that was not only religious, but also political and social.[56] The Angevin monarchy, despite being ready to accept the requests that came from the Holy See in other spheres, never allowed it in South Italy, and it was the royal officers who made confiscations, kept the heretics' assets, and remitted to the inquisitors only the salary

---

54. Huillard-Bréholles, *Historia diplomatica*, vol. 4, bk. 1:444–45.
55. Riccardi de Sancto Germano notarii, *Cronica*, 173–74.
56. Riccardo Parmeggiani, "Frati Predicatori e Inquisizione nel Medioevo," in *L'Ordine dei Predicatori: I Domenicani. Storia, figure e istituzioni (1216–2016)*, ed. G. Festa and M. Rainini (Bari: Editori Laterza, 2016), 325–50.

that had been decided by the sovereign. For this reason, we do not have the accounts of the Inquisition tribunals, as we do for the communal governments elsewhere in Italy. However, although Gregory IX's suspicions about the antiheretical zeal of Frederick II were amply justified, there is no doubt that there really were heretics moving throughout the city. One cannot imagine that they suddenly made their appearance with the arrival of the Angevins, whose very close bond with the papacy was well known. In this regard, the evidence is quite fragmented due to the loss of documents produced by the Inquisitional courts, which were generally preserved in the friaries in which they were based (in Naples, at the convent of San Domenico). The archives of these friaries have all suffered serious dispersion, though to an unequal extent. As a result, the scant evidence that we have comes to us from administrative sources, that is, from the registers of the Angevin chancery. As it is known, these were destroyed during World War II in 1943, but some scholars had previously managed to derive useful information to draw an (albeit sketchy) picture of the situation concerning the presence of heretics in the city and the procedures put in place to combat them. We know that in 1276 three Cathars were identified, while in 1291–92 the assets of four indicted persons were confiscated after their deaths.[57] However in the Angevin era, heresy in Naples no longer seems to have been a problem for either the religious or the political authorities.

## The Mendicant Orders

The mendicants contributed above all to depriving heresy of any possibility of taking root and spreading. They represented an absolute novelty in the panorama of religious orders present in the city, catalyzing the religious fervor of the laity at all levels of the social scale, but also acting as a strong stimulus for the ecclesiastical institutions and for the plethora of clergy in the city. It is possible that the construction of the new cathedral was a response to the impressive work of renovating the churches by all four mendicant orders. The renovation was complex and expensive and required great economic resources and long years of work, so that in 1308 it was still in full swing. It is easy to imagine the visual but also invasive impact that all these construction sites had on the daily life of the Neapolitans, as four of them were only a few

---

57. *I registri della cancelleria angioina*, 15:270; 16:36; Vitolo, "Gli eretici di Roccamandolfi," 123.

hundred meters apart. In other words, Naples had become a real "città cantiere," as the historian Rosalba Di Meglio has put it. In a will dated February 14, 1308, a wealthy, but not noble, widow made bequests to all of the construction projects, designated as *opera*, a term that was then widely used in the cities of central and northern Italy, even if in reference to quite different situations.[58] In Naples, the word *opera* did not indicate institutions run by laypeople and under the control of the commune, destined to last, fully operational, up to the present times; rather it was a matter of simple construction projects managed directly by the archiepiscopal curia and convents through their lay procurators whose function was terminated once the work was completed.[59]

The will of 1308 constitutes further evidence of a phenomenon widely present in this type of historical record: the perception that the faithful viewed the four mendicant orders as a unitary phenomenon. In the majority of wills, although one could clearly grasp the predilection of the testator for an order or convent in particular, all four orders are remembered according to a standardized sequence, which must have been well known to the Neapolitan notaries and curia scribes. The sequence was San Domenico, San Lorenzo (Franciscans), Sant'Agostino, and Santa Maria del Carmine. There could be possible inversions of place among the first three according to the devotional choices of the testator. Two other mendicant convents followed the first four, that is, the convents of San Pietro Martire (Dominicans) and Santa Maria la Nova (Franciscans).

However, the most remarkable thing concerning the intensity of the mendicant presence in the city is the very close connection that the friars managed to establish with all the articulations of political power and society: from the monarchy to the city administration, and from the nobility to the urban merchants and artisans and the humblest classes. These connections also manifested themselves at the territorial level, given that according to an orientation not entirely coinciding with what is generally observed elsewhere in Italy, the mendicant settlements sometimes emanated from the ancient center (San Domenico, Sant' Agostino) toward areas outside the walls (Santa Maria del Carmine, San Pietro Martire, San Giovanni a Carbonara), to the development of

---

58. Rosalba Di Meglio, "Napoli 1308: Una città cantiere," *Archivio Storico per le Province Napoletane* 123 (2005): 93–113.

59. Mario Gaglione, "La cattedrale e la città: Monarchia, episcopato, comunità cittadina nella Napoli angioina," *Studi Storici* 52 (2011): 195–227.

which they significantly contributed. The very first Franciscan *locus* that was on the hill where Castelnuovo was to rise as a defensive structure and royal residence does not fit this scheme. In exchange for this *locus*, Charles of Anjou granted to the order the area within the wall for the construction of Santa Maria la Nova in 1279. However, it should be said that practically nothing is known of this original Minorite community, so it cannot be ruled out that it soon moved to the small church of San Lorenzo, which was donated in the 1230s by the bishop of Aversa. It is not known what title this church possessed (a private church?), but the Franciscans probably kept their place on the hill outside the city as a hermitage until 1279. To exchange the hermitage in 1279 was probably not very traumatic, since Franciscans had by then firmly inserted themselves into the city, and their mission of religious revival of the laity was well defined, especially through preaching and confession.

Regardless of all this, it is this social and political entrenchment of the mendicants that determined the capacity for religious revival unparalleled in other parts of Italy and Europe. A first important advantage was their very close connection with the Angevin monarchy that although it oscillated in favor of this or that religious order, supported them all. This royal connection provided an effective support not only at the ideological level, but also for the development of diplomatic missions and for the realization of public works in various parts of the *Regno*, for which it was necessary to guarantee the highest managerial efficiency. No less strict, and indeed destined to challenge the centuries and periodic dynastic changes, was the link with the city administration and with the social classes that had control of it. This bond has thus far not been adequately understood due to the original political-administrative structure of the city, which was still governed through the modern age by a municipal council of six members (the Six). Originally, there were five seats filled with members of the nobility. After the minireform instituted in 1494 by King Charles VIII of France, the council included a sixth position, a representative of the *popolo*, drawn from the merchants, luxury artisans, professional men, and men of the royal bureaucracy.

The most original element of this political and administrative arrangement was that the Six were not elected by a council or by a parliament of citizens, which did not exist in Naples unlike other cities in the *Regno*. Furthermore, each elected person managed, with a certain freedom, the sector of the public administration that traditionally fell to that seat. He usually governed from his own seat where the relative documentation was kept, or even from his own home. Nor did this particular political and administrative structure change with the entry of the sixth person elected by the *popolo*, given that this seat was assigned the sector of public assistance. However, if we consider that of the five noble seats, three (Nido, Montagna, and Porto) were very attached to the mendicant convents (those of Nido even met in the chapter hall of San Domenico), whose procurators they appointed, and had burial spots in their churches, and that the seat of the *popolo* was located in the convent of Sant'Agostino, then we can well understand how the link between the mendicants, the ruling noble class, and the bourgeois class went far beyond individual and class relationships to become fully involved in the municipal organization as well.[60]

These bonds were a source of prestige for the friars and certainly facilitated pastoral activity. They provided them with the economic resources that made possible their assistance to the poor, but sometimes also created difficulties due to the interference of the procurators appointed by the seat, when they tended to go beyond their prerogatives. They would attempt to interfere in granting burial spaces inside churches, to preclude them from families who were not in the jurisdiction of their seat. However, this did not prevent the friars from penetrating deeply into all folds of Neapolitan society, thanks primarily to their intense pastoral activity. Their pastoral activity specialized in two closely connected areas, for which the urban clergy proved to be poorly equipped, better to say entirely inadequate—that is to say, preaching and confession, which often arose precisely from the contrition caused by the relatively fiery preaching of the friars. No less effective was the work of religious revival carried out by the confraternities, which were promoted by the friars or had their headquarters in their churches, among which most famously were the Crucifix in the church of San Domenico and Sant' Antonio in San Lorenzo.[61]

## The Foundation of Santa Chiara

The church that was the symbol of the many links between friars, society, and politics, even though it was founded in the context of a project

---

60. Giovanni Vitolo, *L'Italia delle altre città: Un'immagine del Mezzogiorno medievale* (Naples: Liguori 2014), 285–300.
61. Rosalba Di Meglio, *Ordini Mendicanti, monarchia e dinamiche politico-sociali nella Napoli dei secoli XIII–XV* (Raleigh, NC: Aonia, 2013), 121–36.

that seemed to privilege one order in particular, was the church of Santa Chiara, which had a double Franciscan convent of both friars and nuns. There is now much written about it on both its history and history of art. In the past, there has not always been adequate conversation between these studies. Today, however, the situation has much improved, and this church is the subject of research conducted also by foreign scholars, individually or in teams and with very advanced technology, from which one expects new and interesting discoveries regarding its construction.[62] On a more strictly historical level, the picture that emerges seems to be defined broadly enough. It was a grandiose project that brought together political planning and religious ideals, created by two sovereigns. The royal couple Robert of Anjou (1309–43) and Sancia di Maiorca have no equal in the history of Naples (and not only in Naples) for activism, determination, effective distribution of roles, and strong awareness of both their political and religious responsibilities, all despite their not inconsiderable differences of temperament. The spiritual predilections of the members of the Angevin dynasty were decisively on the Franciscan side, if only for their foundations in both Naples and Provence and for their commitment in the promotion of the beatification of their relative Ludovico da Tolosa, and then of his cult. In my view, however, attention must focus foremost on what their almost forty-year reign represented as a point of arrival on the path of the social and religious history of Naples from the beginning of the eleventh century.[63] The death of Robert, followed by Sancia's retreat into the convent of Santa Croce in 1343, marked the beginning of a convulsive phase in Neapolitan history, culminating in the 1382 murder of their heir Giovanna I and characterized, among other things, by the heavy interference of the papacy in the life of the *Regno* on the basis of the pope's sovereignty over it as a feudal lord. This did not impede the Neapolitan Church, despite the ever-increasing pace that forced it to assimilate to the Latin Church, firstly with the mendicant orders and then in the sixteenth century by the Council of Trent, from

---

62. Caroline Bruzelius, *The Stones of Naples: Church Building in Angevin Italy, 1266–1343* (New Haven, CT: Yale University Press, 2004), 1:85–208.

63. Mario Gaglione, "Dai primordi del francescanesimo femminile a Napoli fino agli Statuti per il monastero di S. Chiara", in *La chiesa e il convento di Santa Chiara*, ed. Francesco Aceto, Stefano d'Ovidio, and Elisabetta Scirocco (Battipaglia: Laveglia & Carlone, 2014), 27–128; Caroline Bruzelius, Alessandra Perriccioli Saggese, and Paola Vitolo, "Santa Chiara", in *Architettura e arti figurative di età gotica in Campania*, ed. Francesco Aceto and Paola Vitolo (Battipaglia: Laveglia & Carlone, 2017), 185–208.

maintaining its unmistakable profile, thanks to the enduring vitality of elements dating back to late antiquity, and the unique way in which they had come together, endogenous or of external origin, in the following centuries.

## Selected Bibliography

### Primary Sources

Capasso, Bartolommeo, ed. *Monumenta ad Neapolitani ducatus historiam pertinentia*. Reedited by Rosaria Pilone. Salerno: Carlone, 2008; orig. ed. Neapoli: Giannini, 1881-92.

Frederick II. *Die Konstitutionen Friedrichs II. für das Königreich Sizilien*. Edited by Wolfgang Stürner. Monumenta Germaniae Historica, Constitutiones et acta publica imperatorum et regum 2. Hannover: Monumenta Germaniae Historica, 1996.

Galante, Gennaro Aspreno. *Memorie della vita e del culto del beato Nicolò eremita di S. Maria a Circolo in Napoli*. Naples, 1875-77, off-print from *La Scienza e la Fede*.

Gregory I. *Gregorii I papae registrum epistolarum*. Edited by Paul Ewald and Ludo Moritz Hartmann. 2 vols. Monumenta Germaniae Historica, Epistolae 1-2. Berlin: Monumenta Germaniae Historica, 1957.

Huillard-Bréholles, Jean-Louis-Alphonse, ed. *Historia diplomatica Friderici secundi*. Paris: Plon, 1852-61.

Minieri Riccio, Camillo. *Saggio di Codice diplomatico formato sulle antiche scritture dell'Archivio di Stato di Napoli*. Naples: Rinaldi e Sellitto, 1878-83.

Pilone, Rosaria. *Il Diplomatico di S. Gregorio Armeno conservato nell'Archivio di Stato di Napoli*. Naples: Laurenziana, 1989.

*I registri della cancelleria angioina ricostruiti da Riccardo Filangieri con la collaborazione degli archivisti napoletani*, 50 vols. Naples: Accademia Pontaniana, 1963-2010.

Riccardi de Sancto Germano notarii. *Chronica*. Edited by Carlo Alberto Garufi. Bologna: Zanichelli, 1938.

RNAM = *Regii Neapolitani Archivii Monumenta edita ac illustrata*. Edited by Antonio Spinelli. Naples: Regia typographia, 1845-57.

Vuolo, Antonio, ed. *Vita et Translatio S. Athanasii Neapolitani episcopi (BHL 735 e 737): Sec IX*. Fonti per la storia dell'Italia medievale, Antiquitates 16. Rome: Istituto Storico Italiano per il Medio Evo, 2001.

### Secondary Sources

Aceto, Francesco, Stefano d'Ovidio, and Elisabetta Scirocco, eds. *La chiesa e il convento di Santa Chiara*. Battipaglia: Laveglia & Carlone, 2014.

Aceto, Francesco, and Paola Vitolo, eds. *Architettura e arti figurative di età gotica in Campania*. Battipaglia: Laveglia & Carlone, 2017.

Ambrasi, Domenico. "La vita religiosa." In *Storia di Napoli*, 3:439–573. Naples: Edizioni Scientifiche Italiane, 1969.

Araldi, Giovanni. "Verginiani." In *Federico II: Enciclopedia fridericiana*, 2:879–85. Rome: Istituto della Enciclopedia Italiana, 2005.

Bevere, Riccardo. "Suffragi, espiazioni postume, riti e cerimonie funebri dei secoli XII, XIII e XIV nelle provincie napoletane." *Archivio Storico per le Province Napoletane* 21 (1896): 119–32.

Bloch, Marc. *Apologia della storia o mestiere di storico*. Edited by Girolamo Arnaldi. Turin: Einaudi, 1960.

Brancaccio, Giovanni. "Movimenti ereticali e correnti eterodosse." In *Storia del Mezzogiorno*, 9:277–310. Naples: Edizioni del Sole, 1991.

Bruzelius, Caroline. *The Stones of Naples: Church Building in Angevin Italy, 1266–1343*. New Haven, CT: Yale University Press, 2004.

Bruzelius, Caroline, Alessandra Perriccioli Saggese, and Paola Vitolo. "Santa Chiara". In *Architettura e arti figurative di età gotica in Campania*, edited by Francesco Aceto and Paola Vitolo, 185–208. Battipaglia: Laveglia & Carlone, 2017.

Canetti, Luigi. "Il bruco e l'arcobaleno: Nuovi paradigmi per la storia culturale e religiosa dell'alto Medioevo." *Storica* 66 (2016): 45–71.

Capasso, Bartolommeo. *Topografia della città di Napoli nell'XI secolo*. Naples: F. Giannini, 1895.

Colesanti, Gemma, and Salvatore Marino. "L'economia dell'assistenza a Napoli nel tardo Medioevo." In "L'ospedale, il denaro e altre ricchezze: Scritture e pratiche economiche dell'assistenza in Italia nel tardo Medioevo," edited by Marina Gazzini and Antonio Olivieri, monographic section in *Reti Medievali Rivista* 17, no. 1 (2016): 309–44. https://doi.org/10.6092/1593-2214/503.

Di Meglio, Rosalba. "Before the Public Banks: Innovation and Resilience by Charities in Fifteenth-Century Naples." In *Financial Innovation and Resilience*, edited by Lilia Costabile and Larry Neal, 55–70. Palgrave Studies in the History of Finance. Basingstoke: Palgrave Macmillan, 2018. https://doi.org/10.1007/978-3-319-90248-7_3.

——. "La Disciplina di S. Marta: Mito e realtà di una confraternita popolare." In Giovanni Vitolo and Rosalba Di Meglio, *Napoli angioino-aragonese: Confraternite, ospedali, dinamiche politico-sociali*, 147–234. Immagini del Medioevo 7. Salerno: Carlone, 2003.

——. "Esperienze religiose femminili nell'Italia meridionale (sec. XIII–XIV)." In *Vita religiosa al femminile (secoli XIII–XIV): Atti del ventiseiesimo Convegno Internazionale di Studi del Centro italiano di studi di storia e d'arte (Pistoia, 19–21 maggio 2017)*, 175–87. Rome: Viella, 2019.

——. "Napoli 1308: Una città cantiere." *Archivio Storico per le Province Napoletane* 123 (2005): 93–113.

——. *Ordini Mendicanti, monarchia e dinamiche politico-sociali nella Napoli dei secoli XIII–XV*. Raleigh, NC: Aonia, 2013.

Ferrajoli, Ferdinando. *Le fratrie della Napoli greco-romana*. Naples: Gallina, 1986.

Gaglione, Mario. "La cattedrale e la città: Monarchia, episcopato, comunità cittadina nella Napoli angioina." *Studi Storici* 52 (2011): 195–227.

———. "Dai primordi del francescanesimo femminile a Napoli fino agli Statuti per il monastero di S. Chiara." In *La chiesa e il convento di Santa Chiara*, edited by Francesco Aceto, Stefano d'Ovidio, and Elisabetta Scirocco, 27-128. Battipaglia: Laveglia & Carlone, 2014.

Galante, Gennaro Aspreno. *Guida sacra della città di Napoli*. Naples: Stamperia del Fibreno, 1872.

Galasso, Giuseppe. "Ideologia e sociologia del patronato di san Tommaso d'Aquino su Napoli (1605)." In *Per la storia sociale e religiosa del Mezzogiorno d'Italia*, edited by Giuseppe Galasso and Carla Russo, 2:213-49. Naples: Guida, 1982.

Granier, Thomas. "Les moines 'grecs' de Saints Serge-et-Bacchus et Saints-Théodore-et-Sébastien dans la société napolitaine des VII$^e$-XII$^e$ siècles." In *Vivre en société au Moyen Âge: Occident chrétien VI$^e$-XV$^e$ siècle*, edited by Claude Carozzi, Daniel Le Blévec, and Huguette Taviani-Carozzi, 197-218. Aix-en-Provence: Publications de l'Université de Provence, 2008.

Luongo, Gennaro. "Il calendario marmoreo napoletano: Un approccio linguistico." *Bollettino linguistico campano* 13-14 (2008): 43-66.

Marchionibus, Maria Rosaria. *Icone in Campania: Aspetti iconologici, liturgici e semantici*. Spoleto: Fondazione Centro italiano di studi sull'alto medioevo, 2011.

Martin, Jean-Marie. "Hellénisme politique, hellénisme religieux et pseudo-hellénisme à Naples (VII$^e$-XII$^e$ siècle)." *Νέα Ρώμη* 2 (2005): 59-77.

———. "Quelques remarques sur le culte des images en Italie méridionale pendant le Haut Moyen Âge." In *Cristianità ed Europa: Miscellanea di studi in onore di Luigi Prosdocimi*, edited by Cesare Alzati, vol. 1, bk. 1:223-36. Rome: Herder, 1994.

Mazzocchi, Alessio Simmaco. *In vetus marmoreum Sanctae Neapolitanae Ecclesiae Kalendarium Commentarius*. Neapoli: ex officina Novelli de Bonis typographi archiepiscopalis, 1744-55.

Meersseman, Gilles Gérard, in collaboration with Gian Piero Pacini. *Ordo fraternitatis: Confraternite e pietà dei laici nel Medioevo*. 3 vols. Rome: Herder, 1977.

Merlo, Grado Giovanni. *Contro gli eretici: La coercizione all'ortodossia prima dell'Inquisizione*. Bologna: Il Mulino, 1996.

———, ed. *Esperienze religiose e opere assistenziali nei secoli XII e XIII*. Turin: Il Segnalibro, 1987.

Parmeggiani, Riccardo. "Frati Predicatori e Inquisizione nel Medioevo." In *L'Ordine dei Predicatori: I Domenicani. Storia, figure e istituzioni (1216-2016)*, edited by G. Festa and M. Rainini, 325-50. Bari: Editori Laterza, 2016.

Rando, Daniela. *Una chiesa di frontiera: Le istituzioni ecclesiastiche veneziane nei secoli VI-XII*. Bologna: Il Mulino, 1994.

Vitolo, Giovanni. "Aspetti e problemi della storia delle certose nel Mezzogiorno medievale: Gli esempi di Napoli e Padula." *Napoli Nobilissima*, 5th series, 2 (2001): 5-14.

———. "Caratteri del monachesimo nel Mezzogiorno altomedievale (secoli VI-IX)." In *Montecassino: Dalla prima alla seconda distruzione. Momenti e aspetti di storia cassinese (secc. VI-IX). Atti del II convegno di studi sul Medioevo *meridionale (Cassino-Montecassino, 27–31 maggio 1984)*, 31–54. Montecassino: Pubblicazioni cassinesi, 1987.

———. "Confraternite e dinamiche politico-sociali a Napoli nel Medioevo: La Disciplina della Santa Croce." In *Compagnia della Santa Croce: Sette secoli di storia a Napoli*, edited by M. Pisani Massamormile, 59–70. Naples: Electa Napoli, 2007.

———. "Gli eretici di Roccamandolfi (1269–1270): Una Montaillou molisana?" In *"Sapiens, ut loquatur, multa prius considerat": Studi di storia medievale offerti a Lorenzo Paolini*, edited by Caterina Bruschi and Riccardo Parmeggiani, 119–50. Uomini e mondi medievali 64. Spoleto: Centro italiano di studi sull'Alto Medioevo, 2019.

———. "Esperienze religiose nella Napoli dei secoli XII–XIV." In *Medioevo Mezzogiorno Mediterraneo: Studi in onore di Mario Del Treppo*, edited by Gabriella Rossetti and Giovanni Vitolo, 3–34. Naples: GISEM-Liguori, 2000.

———. *L'Italia delle altre città: Un'immagine del Mezzogiorno medievale*. Naples: Liguori, 2014.

———. "L'ospedale di S. Eligio e la piazza del Mercato." In Giovanni Vitolo and Rosalba Di Meglio, *Napoli angioino-aragonese: Confraternite, ospedali, dinamiche politico-sociali*, 39–145. Immagine del Medioevo 7. Salerno: Carlone, 2003.

———. "Religiosità delle opere e monachesimo verginiano nell'età di Federico II." *Benedictina* 43 (1996): 135–50.

———. "San Gennaro e il culto delle immagini a Napoli: A proposito di alcune recenti pubblicazioni." In *"Acri Sanctorum Investigatori": Miscellanea di studi in memoria di Gennaro Luongo*, edited by L. Arcari, 729–43. Rome: L'Erma di Bretschneider, 2019.

———. "Santità, culti e strutture socio-politiche." In *Pellegrinaggi e itinerari dei santi nel Mezzogiornomedievale*, edited by Giovanni Vitolo, 23–38. Naples: GISEM-Liguori, 1999.

———. *Tra Napoli e Salerno: La costruzione dell'identità cittadina nel Mezzogiorno medievale*. Salerno: Carlone, 2001.

Vitolo, Giovanni, and Rosalba Di Meglio. *Napoli angioino-aragonese: Confraternite, ospedali, dinamiche politico-sociali*. Immagini del Medioevo 7. Salerno: Carlone, 2003.

Von Falkenhausen, Vera. *La dominazione bizantina nell'Italia meridionale dal IX all'XI secolo*. Bari: Ecumenica, 1978.

# Contributors

**Maria Pia Alberzoni** is professor of medieval history at the Università Cattolica del Sacro Cuore in Milan. Her research interests are primarily the institutional history of the Order of Friars Minor in the thirteenth and fourteenth centuries and its relationship with the Apostolic See; the various religious movements of the early thirteenth century such as the Poor Clares, Humiliati, Vallombrosians, and Carthusians; and the history of the communes in thirteenth-century Italy and their interactions with the papacy and the bishops. Among her major publications are *Città, vescovi e papato nella Lombardia dei Comuni* (Novara, 2001); *Clare and the Poor Sisters in the 13th Century* (St. Bonaventure, NY, 2004); *Santa povertà e beata semplicità: Francesco d'Assisi e la Chiesa Romana* (Milan, 2015).

**Frances Andrews** is professor of medieval history at the University of St. Andrews, Scotland. She specializes in the history of medieval Christianity, religious orders, and the Italian cities. She is the author of *The Early Humiliati* (Cambridge, 1999) and *The Other Friars: Carmelite, Augustinian, Sack and Pied Friars in the Middle Ages* (Woodbridge, 2006), and has edited several volumes, including, most recently, *Churchmen and Urban Government in Late Medieval Italy, c.1200–c.1450: Cases and Contexts*, with M. A. Pincelli (Cambridge, 2013); *Doubting Christianity: The Church and Doubt*, with C. Methuen and A. Spicer (Cambridge, 2016), and *Ripensare la reclusione volontaria nell'Europa Medievale*, with E. Rava (Bologna, 2021-22). She is currently preparing a follow-up to *Churchmen and Urban Government*.

**Cécile Caby** is professor of medieval history at Sorbonne University (Paris). Her publications focus on eremitism and monasticism in the late Middle Ages, particularly in Italy. She is currently working on preaching by the late medieval religious orders. She is author of *De l'érémitisme rural au monachisme urbain: Les Camaldules en Italie à la fin du Moyen Âge* (Rome, 1999), and coeditor of *L'histoire des moines, chanoines et religieux au Moyen Âge: Guide de recherche et documents*, with A. Vauchez

(Turnhout, 2003), *Congregazione Camaldolese dell'Ordine di San Benedetto*, with S. Megli (Vatican City, 2014), and *Camaldoli e l'ordine camaldolese dalle origini alla fine del XV secolo*, with P. Licciardello (Cesena, 2014).

**Giovanna Casagrande** was until recently the professor of medieval history at the University of Perugia. Her research interests center on the religious life of medieval Italy, in particular mendicant orders, religious movements, the history of Perugia, and the history of women. She has published extensively on these subjects. Among her publications are *Intorno a Chiara: Il tempo della svolta. Le compagne, i monasteri, la devozione* (Assisi [PG], 2011); *Religiosità penitenziale e città al tempo dei comuni* (Rome, 1995). She also edited *Donne tra Medioevo ed Età Moderna in Italia: Ricerche* (Perugia, 2004).

**George Dameron** is professor emeritus of history, Saint Michael's College (Colchester, Vermont). His research interests include economic and social history, medieval Florence and Tuscany, Church history, and the medieval history of Italy. Among his publications are *Florence and Its Church in the Age of Dante* (Philadelphia, 2005) and *Episcopal Power and Florentine Society, 1000–1320* (Cambridge, MA, 1991). He is currently working on a new monograph titled *Feeding the Medieval Italian Commune: Grain, Political Legitimacy, and War in Medieval Tuscany, c. 1100–c. 1350*.

**Antonella Degl'Innocenti** is professor of medieval and humanistic Latin in the Department of Humanities at the University of Trento. Her primary research interests are medieval Latin philology, hagiography, hagiographic manuscripts of the Trentino region, female sanctity, and mystical literature. She has published extensively on these subjects. She is the editor of *Vita beati Roberti* (Florence, 1995); coeditor of *Gregorio Magno e l'agiografia fra IV e VII secolo: Atti dell'Incontro di studio delle Università degli studi di Verona e Trento, Verona, 10–11 dicembre 2004* (Verona, 2004) and of *Manoscritti agiografici latini di Trento e Rovereto* (Florence, 2005).

**Marina Gazzini** is professor of medieval history at the University of Milan. Her research interests include medieval institutions, communities, and religious orders dedicated to charitable activities; accounting in public and welfare institutions; closed spaces (cloisters, hospitals, prisons); theoretical and judicial aspects of human–animal interaction in the Middle Ages; declinations of forgery in historical research;

and Albertano da Brescia, politician and writer of didactic and moral treatises and sermons. Among her publications are *Confraternite e società cittadina nel Medioevo italiano* (Bologna, 2006); "Guides for a Good Life: Instructions for Citizens and Believers in Italian Medieval Confraternities," in *A Companion to Medieval and Early Modern Confraternities*, ed. K. Eisenbichler (Leiden, 2019), pp. 157–75; and (as editor) *Il falso e la storia: Invenzioni, errori, imposture dal medioevo alla società digitale* (Milan, 2020).

**Maureen C. Miller** is professor of history at the University of California, Berkeley. She is a historian of medieval Europe with a particular interest in Italy. The author of three prize-winning monographs, she has utilized various forms of material culture—surviving rural churches, ecclesiastical and secular palaces, as well as liturgical vestments—to illuminate changes in the Western Church and the culture of the secular clergy across the Middle Ages. Most notably, she is the author of *The Bishop's Palace: Architecture and Authority in Medieval Italy* (Ithaca, NY, 2000), *Clothing the Clergy: Virtue and Power in Medieval Europe, c. 800–1200* (Ithaca, NY, 2014), and the editor of a special centennial issue of the *Catholic Historical Review* (101, no. 1, 2017) dedicated to Catholic material culture. She is currently working on ecclesiastical registers and the "documentary revolution" in medieval Italy with special attention to material aspects of new documentary forms and administrative systems.

**Agostino Paravicini Bagliani** was scriptor of the Vatican Library (1969–81) and professor of medieval history at the University of Lausanne. Fellow of the Medieval Academy of America, he has been president of the Società internazionale per lo studio del Medioevo latino (SISMEL, International Society for the Study of the Latin Middle Ages) since 2008. His interests are centered on the history of the medieval papacy. He is the author of *Il Corpo del papa* (Turin, 1994; trans. Chicago, 2000) and of a biography of Pope Boniface VIII (Turin, 2003). Recently he published the first complete anthology of all texts concerning the medieval legend of Pope Joan: *La Papessa Giovanna: I testi della leggenda, 1250–1500* (Florence, 2021). Since 1993 he has been the director of the journal *Micrologus: Nature, Sciences and Medieval Societies*, and since 2008, of the *Rivista di storia della Chiesa in Italia*.

**Antonio Rigon** is emeritus professor of medieval history at the University of Padua. His research interests are the ecclesiastical institutions, mendicant orders, medieval political and religious life, monasticism, and clerical confraternities of medieval Italy. He is a member of the executive committee of the Istituto storico italiano per il Medio Evo. Together with Giuseppina De Sandre Gasparini and Giovanni Grado Merlo he founded and edited the journal *Quaderni di storia religiosa* and is also editing the foremost series on Italian religious history, Italia Sacra. Among his publications is *Clero e città: "Fratalea cappellanorum," parroci, cura d'anime in Padova dal XII al XV secolo* (Padua, 1988), which paved the way for studies on clerical confraternities in Italy. Among his other publications are *Dal Libro alla folla: Antonio di Padova e il francescanesimo medievale* (Rome, 2002); *Antonio di Padova: Ordini mendicanti e società locali nell'Italia dei secoli XIII–XV* (Spoleto, 2016); *Gente d'arme e uomini di Chiesa: I Carraresi tra Stato pontificio e regno di Napoli (XIV–XV secolo)* (Rome, 2017); and *La vita che si fa storia: Studiosi e letture di storia medievale* (Rome, 2022).

**Neslihan Şenocak** is an associate professor of history at Columbia University. Her research interests are centered around the religious life in medieval Europe, confraternities, medieval Italy, political theology, pastoral power, and the Franciscan order. She is the author of *The Poor and the Perfect: The Rise of Learning in the Franciscan Order, 1209–1310* (Ithaca, NY, 2012), and coeditor of *Lateran IV: Theology and Care of Souls*, with C. Monagle (Turnhout, 2023). She is now working on a history of the emergence and rise of pastoral power in western Europe.

**Pietro Silanos** is assistant professor at the University of Bari Aldo Moro. He teaches medieval history, medieval Mediterranean history, and the exegesis of medieval historical sources. He is interested in the history of the papacy and the papal court, the symbolic communication of political institutions, religious orders, and universities. He is the author of *Gerardo Bianchi da Parma († 1302): La biografia di un cardinale-legato duecentesco* (Rome, 2010) and editor of *La distruzione di Milano (1162): Un luogo di memorie*, with K.-M. Sprenger (Milan, 2015).

**Giovanni Vitolo** is professor emeritus of medieval history at the Università di Napoli Federico II. His research interests include the social history of medieval Europe and the political and religious history of South Italy. He is particularly interested in the dynamics between political-social history and the religious life. Among his books are *Istituzioni ecclesiastiche e vita religiosa dei laici nel Mezzogiorno medievale: Il codice della confraternita di S. Maria di Montefusco (sec. XII)* (Rome, 1982); *Medioevo: I caratteri originali di un'età di transizione* (Milan, 2000); *L'Italia delle altre città: Un'immagine del Mezzogiorno medievale* (Naples, 2014).

# Index

Aachen, 385; Rule of, 165
Acuto, Giovanni, 150
Agostino Novello, Augustinian, 216
Agrippino, saint, 383
Albert of Morra, 37
Albert of Parma, papal notary, 287
Albert the Great (Albertus Magnus), 14
Alberto, archbishop of Siponto, 60
Alberto, bishop of Montecorvino, 64
Alberto da Vercelli, Latin patriarch of Jerusalem, 193
Albi, 270, 273–74
Alcuin of York, 258
Alessandria, 49
Alessandro, bishop of Forli, 119
Alexander II, pope (Anselmo I da Baggio, bishop of Lucca), 25, 62, 66, 95, 227, 260, 266–67
Alexander III, pope (Rolando Bandinelli), 32, 37, 68, 166, 234, 276, 283, 293, 318; schism, 33–34
Alexander IV, pope (Reginaldo di Jenne), 43, 194–95, 203, 24
Alexandria, saint, 382
Alfanus I, archbishop of Salerno, 62
Alferio, saint, abbot of Cava, 97, 229
Allucio da Pescia, saint, 239
Alvaro Pais, OFM, 214
Amalfi, 56–57, 206
Amato, saint, bishop of Nusco, 64
Ambrogio da Massa, OFM, 216
Ambrogio Sansedoni, 216
Ambrose, saint, 363

Anacletus II, antipope, 31, 106
Anagni, 12, 34, 110
Anastasius IV, pope, 75
Ancona, 99, 206, 331
Andrea, bishop of Florence, 363
Andrea da Strumi, 102
Andrea del fu Teuperto, 83
Andrea di Vimercate, 402
Andrea Saramita, 291–92
Angelo de Bencivenne, 209
Angela of Foligno, saint, 218, 243, 292
Anselmo I da Baggio. *See* Alexander II
Anselmo II, saint, bishop of Lucca, 64, 230–31
Anselmo di Alessandria, 401–2
Anthony of Padua, saint, 204, 214, 216, 241, 247, 315
Antonio d'Orso, bishop of Florence, 348
Aosta, 143
Aquileia, 49, 54–56, 315
Aquinas, Thomas, 196, 383
Ardingo, bishop of Florence, 358
Arezzo, 58, 76, 99, 105, 112, 118, 143, 211, 357, 365; mendicants, 202–3, 211, 219
Arialdo, saint, 25, 32, 230–1, 265–67
Ariberto d'Intimano, archbishop of Milan, 263–64
Arius of Alexandria, 257
Armanno di Mignardo, pievano of Fosciana, 87

# INDEX

Armanno Pungilupo of Ferrara, 323–28, 332
Arnaldo da Brescia, 31–32, 259, 267–68
Arnolfo di Cambio, sculptor, 366
Assisi, 150, 200, 320–21
Asti, 10, 58
Atanasio, saint, bishop of Naples, 383
Atasius of Bergamo, Dominican, 326
Attone, bishop of Florence, 100
Attone, bishop of Milan, 27
Attone, bishop of Pisa, 233
Augustine of Hippo, saint, 176, 258–59, 345
Augustinians (Friars/Hermits), 109, 193–96, 219, 250, 288, 324–25, 327, 382, 389; bequests, 209–10; in cities, 196–97, 201–7, 216; diffusion, 199–201
Aversa, 49, 51, 165, 406

Badia Florentina, 118
Bagnocavallo, 61
Bagnolo, 273
Balduino, abbot of Montecassino, 96
Baliante, 87
Bandino del fu Ammannato, 79
Bari, 50, 55, 57, 67, 236, 331, 372
Bartolomeo da Braganze, 212
Bartolomeo di Neocastro, 314
Basel, Council of (1431–37), 183
Basil of Caesarea, saint, 103, 385–86, 393
Bassano del Gruappa, 148
Bellini, Giovanni, 306, *306*
Bellino, saint, 165
Benedict I and II, abbots of San Michele della Chiusa, 230
Benedict X, antipope, 23
Benedict XI, pope, 195, 288
Benedict of Aniane, saint, 385
Benedictines, 62–63, 113, 123, 146, 228, 234, 242, 246–47, 308, 311, 354–55, 388–89, 395; Rule, 93, 100, 103, 109–10, 112, 228, 230, 235–36, 385–87, 393; mendicants, 189, 192
Benevento, 32, 53, 55, 60, 206–7; 402–3; confraternities, 134, 167–71, 179–81; recluses, 316, 395; synods, 53–54, 67
Benigno, abbot of Vallombrosa, 111–12
Benjamin of Tudela, 318–21
Benvenuta Boianni, saint, 241
Berardo, saint, bishop of Marsi, 64, 236
Bergamo, 19, 144, 211, 214–15, 278
Bernard of Clairvaux, saint, 106–7, 267, 267, 269–70, 281
Bernardo, apostolic legate, 27, 32
Bernardo, bishop of Verona, 54
Bernardo degli Uberti, bishop of Parma, 64, 103, 237–38
Bernardo Prim, 281
Bernardo Tolomei, 123
Besançon, diet of (1157), 32
Bevagna, 200
Bevignate, Brother, 308–9
Biandrate, 90
Biassono, 152, 292
bishops and dioceses (general), 9–13, 54–55; administration, 51–53, 180; appointment, 59–63 (*see also* Investiture Controversy); Holy See, proximity, 48, 66–69; numbers, 47–55, 69; prosopography, 10, 12, 59, 62–63; saints, 63–64, 232, 236–38; status, 47–48, 55–65
Bitetto, 50
Bogomil, dualist priest, 272
Bologna, 13, 15–16, 42, 68, 114, 120–21, 198, 212, 244, 361; Apostles, 289; confraternities, 136, 142, 144, 150, 182, 211; mendicants, 198, 211–12, 218–19

INDEX    419

Bona, saint, 240
Bonaventure of Bagnoregio, OFM minister general, 196, 211, 246, 290
Bonaventure, saint, 213
Boniface III, marquis of Canossa, 22, 63
Boniface VIII, pope, 288, 290–91, 360, 366; *Super cathedram*, 367
Bonvesin de la Riva, 205, 210
Brescello, 49
Brescia, 49, 121, 168, 205, 210, 215, 218, 266–67
Brettinesi, 194, 201, 203–4
Brettino, 194, 203
Brindisi, 53, 207, 318
Brunetto Latini, 339
Bruno, abbot of San Pietro in Cerreto, 107
Bruno of Cologne, saint, 122, 390
Bruno of Querfert, saint, 99, 226
Bruno of Segni, saint, 64, 164, 236–37
Buffino di Bertoloto, 209
Burchard of Ursperg, *Chronicon*, 191

Cadalo, bishop of Parma. *See* Honorius II, antipope
Caetani, Pietro, bishop of Todi and Anagni, 12
Calixtus II, pope, 30, 37
Calvi, 50
Camaldoli, 99, 102–6, 110–12, 114, 116, 118, 120, 122, 226, 249
Canossa, 29
Capua, 55, 60, 206, 318
Carafa, Franceschello, 379
Carcassonne, 269, 273–74
Carmelites, 193–6, 199–200, 202–7, 209–10, 250, 288, 350, 355
Carpignano, 329–30
Carthusians, 122–23, 231, 388, 390
Casanova, 107
Casaranello, 329

Castaglion della Pescaia, 234
Catania, 207
Catherine of Alexandria, saint, 152
Catherine of Siena, saint, 241, 292, 382
Cava dei Tirreni, 55, 62, 97, 229, 234
Celestine III, pope, 109, 238
Celestine IV, pope (Goffredo Castiglioni), 43
Celestine V, pope, saint (Pietro da Morrone), 113, 250
Celle, 116, 202
Cerreto, 107
Cesana, 194, 250
Charlemagne, Frankish emperor, 93, 258, 390
Charles VIII, king of France, 406
Charles II, king of Naples, 323
Charles I of Anjou, king of Sicily, count of Provence, 43, 207, 337, 391, 403, 406
Chelidonia, saint, 235
Chiara da Montefalco, saint, 249, 292
Chiaravalla della Columba, 107
Chiaravalle di Fiastra, 107
Chiaravalle Milanese, 107, 291–92
Cistercians, 69, 75, 97, 106–10; 118, 121, 152, 236, 287, 291, 355; laypersons, 115–16; spread in Italy, 106–8, 111, 22, 231, 388; women, 113, 115, 291
Città del Castello, 13, 51–52, 111, 200–1
Cividale, 315
Clare of Assisi, saint, 198, 241–42, 247, 352
Clement III, antipope, 67
Clement III, pope, 37
Clement IV, pope, 43, 60
Clement VIII, pope, 131
Clement of Osimo, prior general of Hermits of Saint Augustine, 212–13

Cluny, 95–98, 228–29
Colignòla, 78
Colombano, 90
communes (general), 33–34, 117, 119, 173, 142–43, 166–67, 183, 215, 309, 340–43; advance, 31–32, 68, 268, 336, 355–61; Catharism, 273–74, 358–59
Como, 33, 58, 60, 68, 138
Concordia, 75, 85
Concorezzo, 273–74, 293
confraternities, clerical, 13–16, 332, 395–98; activities, 169–71, 173, 175–80; care of souls, 170–71, 173, 175–80, 185–86; characteristics, 162–64; city society, 173–75; expansion, 165–69; income, 172–73; late medieval, 182–86; laypeople, 171, 178–79, 185–86; Marian-*laudesi*, 210–13, 349–50; origins, 163–66; restrictions, 180–82; sources, 161–64; statutes, 169–71
confraternites, lay, 13–15, 142–43, 166–67, 183, 332; heresy, 136, 145, 151–52; legal profile, 130–32; local variants, 132–36, 398–401; models, 136–37; penitential, 348–51; post-medieval, 153–54; public functions, 149–53, 398–401; *scholae*, 130, 139–42, 147, 151, 305–7; solidarity, 143–48; sources, 137–39; terms, 128–31, 139–40; women, 15, 128, 144–45, 152, 350–52
Conrad II, Holy Roman Emperor, 60
Conrad III, Holy Roman Emperor, 34
Conrad IV, Holy Roman Emperor, 67
Conrad of Bavaria, saint, 390
Conrad of Wittelsbach, 37
Conradin, king of Sicily & Jerusalem, 67
Constabile, abbot of Cava, 229
Constance, 34, 49

Constantine the Great, Roman emperor, 258, 289; Donation of, 35, 38–39
Constantinople, 26, 102, 259, 274, 373
*Constitutiones Clementinae*, 119
Corazzo, 109
Cortona, 202–3, 216, 314
Cosenza, 53
Covero del fu Corso, 344–45
Cremona, 33, 41–42, 47, 50, 56, 135, 211, 240, 266
crusades, 30, 35, 168, 269
Cuniberto, bishop of Turin, 230

Daimberto, bishop of Pisa, 103
Dante Alighieri, 339, 343–44, 346, 360, 362, 365–66
*Descriptio Marchiae*, 206
Desenzano, 274, 293
Desiderius of Motecassino. *See* Victor III
Diego, bishop of Osma, 244, 279
Dolce, primicerius of Lucca, 79
Dolcino of Novara, 2, 288–89, 294, 365
Domenico de Pontiaco, hermit, 391
Domenico Loricato (Loricatus), saint, 227
Dominic of Guzman, saint, 41, 193, 225, 241, 244, 247, 250, 286
Dominic of Sora, saint, 228
Dominicans (Friars Preachers), 41, 195–97, 153, 211–14, 288, 325, 389; bequests, 209–10; in cities, 196–97, 200–7, 348–51, 355, 362, 402, 405; confraternites, 211–15, 219; diffusion, 199–201, 216; disruption, 190–91; heresy, 193, 196, 205, 207, 244, 285, 291, 359, 402–3; Holy Rosary, 153; women, 198, 244, 352, 382

# INDEX   421

Dominicus of Capo d'Istria, 324
Durando of Huesca, 272, 279-81

Eberwin of Steinfeld, 269-70
Egidio di Albornoz, cardinal, 206
Egidius, companion of St Francis, 215
Elias of Cortona, 203
Erbord, bishop of Bergamo, 214
Erlembaldo, saint, 266-67
Eufrosina, abbess of Santi Marcellino e Pietro, 386
Eugene III, pope, 31, 268
Eugene IV, pope, 183
Eugenio the Good (Abū l-Ṭayyib), 328-29
Ezzelino da Romano, 41, 61, 120

Faenza, 23, 163, 174, 179, 184, 239
Farfa, 93-96, 111
Favale, 203
Federico Visconti, bishop of Pisa, 202
Fenestrella, 80
Ferrara, 54, 180, 218-19, 323-28, 395
Fia del fu Salario, 345
Fieschi, Sinibaldo. *See* Innocent IV
Fiesole, 343-44, 346, 353-56, 365, 367
Figline, 356
Filippo da Lampugnano, archbishop of Milan, 280
Filippo Benizi, saint, 251
Fiore, 109
Florence, 10, 16, 18, 42, 63, 100, 102, 111, 118, 122, 233, 248, 273, 336-43, 348; bequests, 344-46, 351, 360, 367; confraternities, 134-35, 142, 144-45, 148-49, 151, 182-83, 211, 213-14, 338, 340, 348-51, 365, 367; economics and Church, 355-59, 367; heresy, 266, 274, 340, 358-59, 365; hospitals, 338, 340, 345, 346-48, 353, 367; mendicants, 195, 202-3, 211, 213-14, 218-19, 251, 338, 340, 348-51, 355; monasteries, 117-19, 121, 251, 335, 338, 354-56; New Jerusalem, 361-62, 365-66; penance culture, 347-53; pievi, 75-76, 343-44, 346; rural area, 346-47, 353; saints' cults, 338-39, 343, 346, 352, 358, 363-64, 366-68; San Miniato al Monte, 100, 335, 354; Santa Maria del Fiore cathedral, 335, 338, 343, 363, 366-68; wealth, 58, 355-59; women, 340-41, 350-52, 354
Foligno, 201, 228
Fondaco dei Tedeschi, 141
Fonte Avellana, 23, 99, 102-4, 227
Fontevivo, 287
Forli, 119
Fornovo, 50
Fortunatianus, bishop of Aquileia, 48
Fosciana, 79, 87-88
Foulques, bishop of Toulouse, 281
Francesco Carafa, archbishop of Naples, 397
Francesco Monaldeschi, bishop of Florence, 335, 366
Francis of Assisi, saint, 2, 13, 41, 201, 203, 213-15, 218, 245-47, 250, 280, 283, 287; foundation of Franciscans, 192-93, 241, 244-5; *Rules*, 192, 245; *Testament*, 193, 245; women, 198, 225, 242, 246, 248
Franciscans (Friars Minor; OFM), 123, 192-3, 196, 211, 250, 280, 285, 288, 325, 348; bequests, 209-10; in cities, 196-97, 200-7, 349, 351, 355, 359, 362, 391-92, 405-6, 408; confraternities, 211, 213, 215; diffusion, 199-201, 216; eremitism, 195-96; female, 198, 241-42, 247-49, 352, 408; heresy, 196, 359, 365, 403; Observant, 197;

Franciscans (*continued*)
   Poor Clares, 198, 317; preaching, 283, 362, 406; Spiritual (*Fraticelli*), 123, 193, 197, 362; Third Order, 146, 217–19, 340, 351
Frederick II, duke of Swabia, 31–32
Frederick I Barbarossa, Holy Roman Emperor, 31, 33–4, 38, 268
Frederick II, Holy Roman Emperor, 41–43, 57–58, 61, 67–68, 101, 107–8, 207, 275, 323; heresy, 259, 277, 285–86, 289, 402
Frederick of Aragon, 289
Frederick of Lorraine. *See* Stephen IX
Friars Minor. *See* Franciscans
Friars Preachers. *See* Dominicans
Fruttuaria, 97, 105, 229

Gaeta, 206–7
Galdino della Sala, saint, archbishop of Milan, 64
Galgano da Chiusdino, saint, 233–34
Gennaro, saint, 375, 380, 383
Genoa, 16–17, 37, 42–43, 49, 53, 56, 121, 380; Jews, 318; pievi, 90
George of Antioch, admiral, 328
Gerard, archbishop of Siponto, 62
Gerard, bishop of Arras and Cambrai, 262
Gerard of Borgo San Donnino, 290
Gerard Offreducci, bishop of Padua, 166
Gerardo, saint, bishop of Potenza, 64
Gerardo dei Tintori (Monza), saint, 250
Gerardo of Csanád (Gerardo Sagredo), 262
Gherardesca da Pisa, blessed, 249
Giacomo Benfatti, bishop of Mantua, 213
Giacomo, bishop of Orvieto, 67
Giacomo Corrado, bishop of Padua, 61
Giacomo della Marca, saint, 383

Giamboniti, 194, 203–4, 250
Giordano, bishop of Padua, 61
Giordano da Pisa, 362
Giovanna I, queen of Naples, 408
Giovanna da Orvieto, blessed, 249
Giovanni Cacciafronte, bishop of Vicenza, 64
Giovanni Forzatè, bishop of Padua, 61
Giovanni de Pizutis, cardinal, 388
Giovanni, saint, bishop of Montemarano, 64
Giovanni Bono, saint, 194, 203, 250
Giovanni da Matera, saint, 110, 235–36
Giovanni Gualberto, saint, 100, 102–4, 115, 230–1
Giovanni de Ronco, 277
Giovanni of Lodi, 227
Giovanni Villani, 339
Gisla dei Firidolfi, 356
Giunta Bevegnati, 243
Godfrey of Castiglione, antibishop of Milan, 27
Godfrey the Bearded of Tuscany, 22–23
Goffredo Castiglioni. *See* Celestine IV
Goffredo degli Alberti, bishop of Florence, 356–57
Gozzano, 83, 88–89, 133
Grado, 49
Gratian, *Decretum Gratiani*, 35, 73
Gratius of Bergamo, 326
Gregorio da Catino, *Liber Floriger*, 95
Gregory I the Great, pope, 10, 384
Gregory VI, pope, 23
Gregory VII, pope (Hildebrand of Sovana), 2, 22–23, 25, 27–29, 66, 231, 260, 264; Gregorian Reform, 3, 28, 35, 96, 98, 164, 223, 230, 233
Gregory IX, pope, 12, 41–43, 61, 67, 110, 207, 217–18, 242, 245, 293, 348; heresy, 284, 289, 403–4

# INDEX    423

Gregory X, pope, 43, 113, 325
Gregory XI, pope, 58
Grifo, bishop of Ferrara, 54
Gruaro, 75
Gualtiero da Lodi, saint, 250
Gubbio, 145, 201
Guglielma (Boema), 152, 291–92
Guglielmiti, 109, 203–4, 292
Guglielmo da Vercelli, 110, 235–36, 390
Guglielmo da Volpiano, saint, 97, 229
Gui, Bernard, inquisitor, 199
Guido, abbot of Pomposa, 228–29
Guido da Velate, archbishop of Milan, 26, 231, 266
Guido of Vicenza, inquisitor, 326
Guido, prior of Camaldoli, 112

Hadrian I, pope, 258
Hadrian IV, pope, 32, 37, 68, 268
Hadrian, Roman emperor, 375
Henry II, Holy Roman Emperor, 98
Henry III, Holy Roman Emperor, 22, 24, 29, 60, 99
Henry IV, Holy Roman Emperor, 22, 25, 27–30, 230, 237
Henry V, Holy Roman Emperor, 30, 237, 281
Henry VI, Holy Roman Emperor, 41
Henry of Marcy, papal legate, 37, 276
Herculaneum, 379
heresy, 2, 19–20, 192, 205, 207, 212, 233, 236, 248–49, 289–90, 347, 401–4; Apostles, 286–89; Arians, 257; Arnaldists, 259, 267–68; Cathars, 19, 193, 210, 244, 259–60, 263, 285, 293, 358–59, 365, 402, 404; confraternities, 136, 145, 151–52, 211; definition, 257–58; Dragovitza, 269, 274; Free Spirit, 152; Giosefini, 259; Guglielma, 291–92; Humiliati, 259, 275, 278, 281–4, 291–3; Inquisition, 196, 260, 275, 284–85, 289, 291–92, 294, 325–27, 325–27, 332, 359, 365, 403–4; Italy as home of heresies, 260–64; Manichaeism, 262; Passagini, 259; Patarines, 259–60, 265–68, 272, 284; Pungilupo, 325–28; Ugo Speroni, 285; Waldensians, 244, 275–81, 283–85, 293–94
Herveus da Nedellec, Dominican master general, 219
Hildebrand, bishop of Florence, 335
Hildebrand of Sovana. *See* Gregory VII
historiography of Italian Church, 1–20
Honorius II, antipope (Cadalo, bishop of Parma), 25, 27, 62
Honorius II, pope, 37
Honorius III, pope, 41, 43, 168, 193, 244–45, 283
Honorius IV, pope, 288
Hubert, archbishop of Siponto, 62
Hugh, abbot of Cluny, 97
Hugh, abbot of Venosa, 229
Hugh of Arles, king of Italy, 96
Hugh, margrave of Tuscany, 118
Humbert of Silva Candida, cardinal bishop, 23–24
Humbert of Romans, master general of Dominicans, 190
Humiliati, 19, 41, 152, 191–92, 198–99, 205, 210, 355; as heretics, 259, 275, 278, 281–84

Ibn Jubayr, 321–23
Ildebrando, bishop of Florence, 354
Ildibrando, bishop of Orvieto, 54
Imola, 133, 219, 348
Innocent II, pope, 31, 74–75, 95, 104, 106–7

INDEX

Innocent III, pope (Lothar of Segni), 5, 15, 36–39, 41, 43, 107, 240, 278–83, 293; Albigensians, 269; Fourth Lateran Council, 36, 40, 402; mendicants, 191–92, 199, 244–45; monastic reform, 109–12
Innocent IV, pope, 12, 41–42, 112, 131, 193–94, 235, 260, 284, 287, 293
Investiture Controversy, 27–29, 60, 231

Jacques de Vitry, 190–91, 283–85
Jews, 57, 298; Hebrew texts, 318–19, 321; urban, 302, 318–21, 332–33
Joachim, Servite, 216
Joachim of Fiore, saint, 109–10, 236, 288, 290, 292
John of Parma, OFM minister general, 290
John of Meda, saint, 281

La Ferté, 107
Lando, archbishop of Reggio, 403
Landolfo, priest, 265–66
Landulfo, bishop of Ferrara, 68
Lanfranco, bishop of Parma, 238
Lanfranco, saint, bishop of Pavia, 64, 238
Lateran Councils, 66; First, 165; Third, 86, 276, 282; Fourth, 36, 40–41, 101, 111, 113, 118, 181, 247, 319, 344, 346, 402
Legnano, Battle of (1176), 34
Leo of Santa Croce, cardinal, 281
Leo I the Great, pope, 36
Leo IX, pope, 22–24, 231
Leone, abbot of Cava, 229
Levon III, king of Cilicia, 331
*Liber eremitice regule*, 105
Litifredo, bishop of Novara, 74, 88
Lodi, 33, 107, 169
Lombard League, 33–34, 41, 57, 68

Lorenzo Loricato, saint, 250
Lorenzo of Amalfi, 364
Lothar II, king of Italy, 96
Lothar of Supplingenburg, Holy Roman Emperor, 31
Lothar of Segni. *See* Innocent III
Lottieri Tosinghi, bishop of Florence, 63
Louis IX, king of France, 337
Lucca, 10, 16, 18, 77, 110–11, 335, 358, 361, 364, 366; confraternities, 148, 164, 166–67, 173–74, 177–78, 182, 211; Jews, 318; mendicants, 202–3, 211, 215, 219; pievi, 77, 79, 83, 87, 89
Lucedio, 97, 107
Lucera, 323
Lucius, bishop of Verona, 48
Lucius III, pope, 37, 166; *Ad abolendam*, 259, 267, 274, 277, 280–82
Luco, San Pietro di, 114
Ludovica da Tolosa, saint, 408
Lyon, 13, 275–76; councils: First, 346; Second, 113, 195–96, 287–88, 345–46

Maconeto, 80
Maguzzano, 94
Maiella, 113
Maifreda da Pirovano, 291–92
Maiolus, saint, abbot of Cluny, 97, 229
Manfred, king of Sicily, 67
Manfredino, rector of Ottava, 79
Mantua, 151, 211, 213, 273–74, 293
Margaret of Antioch, saint, 152
Margherita Colonna, saint, 241
Margherita da Città di Castello, saint, 219
Margherita da Cortona, saint, 216, 218, 243, 249
Maria, wife of Charles II of Anjou, 389

# INDEX  425

Marseilles, 98, 142, 398
Martin IV, pope, *Ad fructus uberes*, 196
Martino II, prior of Camaldoli, 112
Martino III, prior of Camaldoli, 112, 114
Matilda of Canossa, 29, 63, 68, 97, 357
Matteo, bishop of Città di Castello, 51–52
Matteo da Correggio, 309
Melfi, 49, 57; Constitutions of, 402; synod (1059), 24, 26; synod (1089), 30, 60, 67
mendicants (general), 212, 311; in cities, 196–216, 404–7; diffusion, 199–200, 216; *disciplinati*, 212–14; disruptive quality, 190–92, 256; foundation, 189–96; preaching, 192, 194–96, 243–44; women, 217–19, 246–47; *see also individual orders*
Messina, 30, 53, 101, 199, 207, 314, 318, 322
Michael Cerularius, patriarch of Constantinople, 24
Milan, 12, 33, 41, 42–43, 49, 53–54, 59, 107, 239; confraternities, 131, 135, 146, 148, 150–51, 166–67, 214; heresy, 151–52, 263–67, 273, 280–81, 284–86, 291, 401; mendicants, 205–6, 210, 214; Patarines, 25–27, 102, 230
Mileto, 49
Minias, saint, 335, 364
Modena, 16, 212, 313
Molfetta, 50
monasticism (general); cenobitism, 97–99, 101–2, 104–6, 110, 195, 223, 226, 228–32, 236, 383–84, 390–92; Cluniac Reform, 95–98, 228–29; eremetism, 98–103, 106, 110, 122, 194–95, 223, 225–28, 232, 234, 236, 250–51; Italo-Greek, 100–2; laypeople, 115–17, 122; networks, 104–6, 110–11; new Italian, 102–4, 110–13; papacy & institutionalization, 110–13; pre-tenth century, 93–94; reorganization, 94–96; urban centers, 117–21; women, status of, 113–15, 118–19, 225, 386–87, 393–94; *see also under* saints; *individual orders*
Monforte, 263, 266, 268
Monopoli, 57
Monreale, 53, 322
Montecassino, 37, 62, 93–94, 223, 234, 237; reform, 95–96, 111
Montefano, 112
Montefusco, 133
Monteoliveto, 123
Montevergine, 110, 113, 235, 388
Morbegno, 138
Mostacia, Maria, 390
Mount Catria, 104
Mozzi, Andrea de', bishop of Florence, 63
Munio di Zamora, Dominican master general, 219
Muslims, 298, 302, 321–23, 328, 332–33

Naples, 55, 318, 380–81, 392; Byzantium, 372–74, 382, 385–87, 406–7; clergy & laity, 395–98, 401; confraternities, 133–34, 136, 378, 398–401; cult of Cross & *staurita*, 374–75, 377–80, 395, 398–99; cult of images, 373–80; eremitism & cenobitism, 384, 389–91, 393, 406; heretics, 401–4; hospitals, 398–401; mendicants, 206–7, 215, 391–92, 395, 401, 404–7; monasteries, 384–89, 391–93, 396, 401, 408; monasticism, household, 393–95; recluses, 316, 384, 395; sanctorale, 381–84; Santa Chiara, 407–9

INDEX

Napoleon Bonaparte, French emperor, 154
Narni, 200
Nicholas of Tusculum, cardinal, 281
Nicholas Gallo, Carmelite general, 194
Nicholas I, pope, 227
Nicholas II, pope, 23–25, 293
Nicholas IV, pope, 217–18, 288, 348, 392
Nicholas Breakspear. *See* Hadrian IV
Nicola, abbot of Sassovivo, 111
Nicola de Lafercha, hermit, 391
Nicola da Tolentino, saint, 216, 251
Nicholaism, 223, 231, 265, 346
Nicolò Lombardo, hermit, 389–01
Nil of Rossano, 101
Niquinta, Dragovitzan bishop, 269, 273
Nocera, 201
Nonantola, 94, 117
Norandino, bishop of Verona, 172
Novara, 16, 56, 75, 83, 88

Oberto, bishop of Cremona, 51
Obizzo Sanvitale, bishop of Parma, 287–88
Odilo, abbot of Cluny, 97
Odo, abbot of Cluny, 96
Odo of Ourscamp, 37
Oldrado, da Tresseno, 286
Omobona da Cremona, saint, 239–40
Order of Penitence, 216–20
Orsi, Antonio degli, bishop of France, 63
Orsini, Giovanni, archbishop of Naples, 378, 381
Orso, subdeacon of Fosciana, 79
Orvieto, 10, 54, 67, 331, 366; mendicants, 200–1, 211, 216, 219
Osimo, 67, 206
Osma, 193, 244
Ostiglia, 50, 54

Ottavo, 79
Otto I, Holy Roman Emperor, 372
Otto II, Holy Roman Emperor, 372
Otto III, Holy Roman Emperor, 98, 372

Pace da Castelfiorentino, inquisitor, 365
Padua, 9, 60–61, 117–19; confraternities, 165–68, 170–72, 174–75, 180, 182, 185, 211; *Liber ordinarius*, 13, 310–15; mendicants, 204, 209, 211, 215–16
Padule, 77
Palermo, 57, 147, 207, 316, 318–19, 322, 328–29
Paolo, pievano of Fosciana, 87
Paolo d'Angelo, 209
Paolo da Venezia, 199
Paolo Traversari, *signore* of Ravenna, 61
papacy and politics, 21–22, 30–36, 223, 232; *libertas ecclesiastica*, 42; Normans, 31–32; *patria* of Italy, 36–37; patrimony, apostolic, 38–41; reform of, 23–27; schisms, 23–26, 31–33, 37. *See also* Investiture Controversy; Lateran Councils
Paris, 13, 41, 245, 267, 283, 290, 388; heresy, 152, 263, 268
Parma, 23, 42, 56, 62, 238; Apostles, 287–88; confraternities, 142, 144–46, 213; mendicants, 212–13, 219
Paschal II, pope, 30, 66–67, 105, 237
Patarines. *See under* heresy; Milan
Paul, saint, 21, 257
Pavia, 42, 60, 68, 93, 123, 238; council (850), 79, 85; council (1160), 33
Paxius de Ossona, 210
Pelagius of Santa Lucia, cardinal, 281
Perugia, 111, 200–3, 209, 211, 215–16, 219, 228, 283;

confraternities, 136, 151, 165, 169, 181, 211; Fontana Maggiore, 307–10, *308*; San Matteo, 330–31
Pescia, 77, 89, 133
Peter, archbishop of Naples, 62
Peter, bishop of Anagni, 64
Peter Abelard, 31, 267
Peter Damian, cardinal bishop of Ostia, 63, 99, 103, 226–28; reform, 23–25, 97, 99–100, 102–4, 106, 227
Peter Lombard, 345
Peter of Verona, saint (Peter Martyr), 13, 151, 211, 214, 241, 247–48
Peter the Chanter, 278, 283
Philip, saint, 233, 364, 367
Piacenza, 16, 43, 56, 60, 62, 111, 142, 144–45, 163, 166, 239–40, 266, 277, 285
Piazza Armerina, 207
Piedmont, 277
Piemonte, 10, 289
Pietro Pappacarbone, abbot of Cava, 97, 229
Pietro, archbishop of Naples, 402
Pietro, archbishop of Ravenna, 261
Pietro III, bishop of Novara, 75
Pietro Mezzabarba, bishop of Florence, 63, 100, 230
Pietro di Anagni (Pietro da Salerno), saint, 236–37
Pietro Pettinaio, saint, 216, 218, 250
Pietro da Morrone. *See* Celestine V
Pietro di Giovanni Olivi, 339, 362
pieve (baptismal churches; *plebs*), 52–54, 88, 189; baptism, 72–73, 84, 88–90, 332, 343–44; as collegiate churches, 82–84; dependent churches, 77–82; erosion of, 89–91; Florence, 76–76, 343–44, 346; jurisdiction, 73–76, 88, 90; pastoral functions, 72–73, 84–89; processions, 312; terminology, 71–72; tithes, 76–78, 90

Pisa, 10, 12–13, 53, 118, 213, 239–40, 249, 309, 314, 335, 361, 364; Jews, 318, 321; mendicants, 202, 209, 213, 219; pievi, 75–76, 78, 82–83; recluses, 316–17
Pisano, Nocola and Giovanni, sculptors, 309
Pistoia, 17, 79–80, 216, 233, 299
Placido, prior of Camaldoli, 106
*plebs. See* pieve
Polirone, 96–97
Pompossa, 228–29
Porete, Marguerite, 152
Prato (Pratolungo), 51, 80
Prospero di Reggio Emilia, saint, 232
Protasius, bishop of Milan, 48
Pulsano, 110, 236

Raimondo Goffredi, OFM minister general, 213
Raimondo Palmerio da Piacenza, saint, 239–40
Rainerio da Genova, 213
Rainerio of Ponza, 109
Rainerius, blessed, 216
Rangerio, bishop of Lucca, 166
Ranieri, bishop of Forcona, 64
Ranieri da Pisa, saint, 239
Raniero da Piacenza, 274
Raniero da Viterbo, cardinal, 289
Raoul Glaber, 261–62
Raterio, bishop of Verona, 94
*Rationes Decimarum Italiae*, 75–77
Ravenna, 23, 53, 56, 60–61, 98–99, 229, 239, 320–21, 373; heresy, 261–62
Raymond of Peñafort, 131
recluses, 315–18, 332, 352
Reggio, 56, 212
Reggio Calabria, 60, 372
Reginaldo di Jenne. *See* Alexander IV
Remigio dei Girolami, 362
Reparata, saint, 363–64, 368

## INDEX

Riccardo di Principato, 403
Riccardo di San Germano, 403
Richard of Aversa, 24
Rieti, 10, 63, 203
Rimini, 111, 331
Riperbella, 76
Robert, bishop of Aversa, 51
Robert II the Pious, king of France, 261
Robert of Anjou, king of Naples, 408
Robert Guiscard, 24, 26, 30, 328
Robert Pullus, 37
Rodolfo, presbyter of Settimo, 346
Rodolfo I, prior of Camaldoli, 105
Rodolfo di Gubbio, saint, 63–64, 227
Roffredo, bishop of Benevento, 55
Roger, duke of Puglia and Calabria, 30
Roger II, king of Sicily, 60, 107, 390
Roger I of Altavilla, 26
Rolandino, *Chronicle of the Facts of the March of Treviso*, 120
Rolando Bandinelli. *See* Alexander, III
Rome, 16, 21, 23, 36, 43, 48, 53, 96, 111, 134, 198, 240, 268, 331, 373, 384; confraternities, 136, 142, 147, 149; 163–64, 167, 181, 184–85; council (826), 86; dioceses, proximity, 66–69, 335; iconography, 309; Jews, 319
Romuald of Ravenna, saint, 98–99, 102–4, 226–27, 229
Rosa da Viterbo, saint, 249
Rossano, 55
Ruffino Gorgone da Piacenza, 212
Ruggero, archbishop of Pisa, 76
Ruggero da Torre, bishop of Split, 12

Sack Friars (Brethren of Penitence of Jesus Christ), 195–96, 201–2, 204; 209–10; 288
Saint-Félix-de-Caraman, council, 269, 273
saints; eleventh century, 222–31; twelfth century, 231–241; thirteenth century, 241–44; cenobitic-monastic, 228–30; clerical, 230–31; episcopal, 232, 236–38; female, 225, 241–43, 248–50; hermetic-monastic, 225–28, 234–36; mendicant, 244–48; other models, 250–51; secular, 238–41, 250; *see also individual saints*
Salerno, 29, 55, 60, 97, 206, 331, 374, 386, 394; Jews, 318–19; processions, 312–13
Salimbene de Adam, OFM, 287, 327
Salomone da Lucca, 365
Salvo Burci, *Liber super Stella*, 285
San Felice di Vada, 76
San Galgano, 118, 121
San Lorenzo, 88–89
San Martino al Cimino, 111
San Michele della Chiusa, 230
San Michele in Borgo, 78
San Salvatore di Goleto, 113
San Vincenzo al Volturno, 93–94
San Zeno, 94
Sancia di Maiorca, queen of Naples, 408
Sansepolcro, 195, 200, 214, 216
Sant'Apollinare in Classe, 98
Sant'Appaino in Valdelsa, 133
Sant'Eufemia, 62
Santa Cristina de Quinto al Tiveron, 114
Santa Fiora, 118
Santa Maria a Fine, 75, 83
Santa Maria de *Turri* (or *de Heremo*), 122
Santa Maria di Betleem, 114
Santa Maria di Follina, 107
Santa Maria di Mirtelo, 75
Santa Maria in Biandrate, 90
Santa Maria in Vezzolano, 80

# INDEX 429

Santiago de Compostela, 145, 235, 240, 348
Santissimo Salvatore, 101
Saraceno Paganelli, 365
Sassovivo, 95, 111
Savona, 54
Segarelli, Gerardo, Apostolic Brethren of, 195–96, 287–88
Segni, 55, 237
Sens, 12; Council of (1141), 267
Serdica, Council of (343), 48
Servants of Blessed Mary Mother of God (Brothers of Valley Verde), 195–96
Servites (Servants of Mary), 195–96, 211, 251, 288, 356; bequests, 209–10; in cities, 202–4; diffusion, 199–200
Severus, bishop of Ravenna, 48
Sicardo, bishop of Piacenza, 240
Siena, 16–18, 42, 118, 121, 123, 313, 331, 361; confraternities, 182, 211; mendicants, 203, 211, 215–16, 219; recluses, 317–18
Sigifredo, bishop of Piacenza, 166
Silvester I, pope, 35, 38
Silvestro Guzzolini, 112
Simeone, archbishop of Ravenna, 61
Simon da Collazzone, OFM, 216
simony, 24–25, 29, 32, 102, 223, 227, 230–31, 264
Sinibaldo da Alma, Dominican prior, 211
Siponto, 53, 60
Spoleto, 201, 211, 216, 218, 274, 277
Staffarda, 107
Stefano, head of Palermo *Sekreton*, 328–29
Stephan the Spaniard, Dominican prior, 286
Stephen IX, pope (Frederick of Lorraine), 22–23
Stephen of Tournai, 73
Stifonte, 114
Subiaco, 111, 234–35

Taranto, 53, 65, 372
Tebaldus, bishop of Verona, 50
Tedaldo, bishop of Arezzo, 63, 103
Tedaldo, marquis of Canossa, 63
Tederico, archbishop of Ravenna, 61
Teobaldo, abbot of Montecassino, 95
Teodimo, rector of San Andrea, 380
Terni, 201
Teuzone, Florentine hermit, 102
Theodore, duke and consul of Naples, 381
Tiso, bishop of Treviso, 58
Todi, 12, 201, 218
Tommaso of Celano, 245, 247
Toulouse, 244, 269, 273–74, 279, 293
Trani, 53, 55, 57, 207, 395
Trapani, 207
Tre Fontane, 107–8
Trent, 148, 289; Council of, 2, 141, 154, 408
Treviso, 3, 58, 163, 168–69, 204
Tricesimo, 86–87
Trisulti, 123, 228
Troia, 55, 62; synod (1093), 67

Ubaldesca, saint, 240
Ubaldo, canon of Fosciana, 79
Ubaldo, saint, bishop of Gubbio, 64, 238
Ubertino da Casale, 339, 362
Uberto da Pirovano, archbishop of Milan, 280
Ugo, *Biccherna* of Siena, 121
Ugo, bishop of Vercelli, 80
Ugo Speroni, 285, 293
Ugolino, archpriest of Montone, 52
Ugolino of Ostia, cardinal, 205
Umberto Crivelli. *See* Urban III
Umberto d'Ormont, archbishop of Naples, 389

Umiliana de'Cerchi, saint, 241, 248–49, 338, 344, 351–52
Urban I, pope, 122
Urban II, pope, 29–30, 43, 55, 60, 66–67, 103, 105, 231, 267
Urban III, pope (Umberto Crivelli, archbishop of Milan), 66, 166
Urban IV, pope, 43, 67, 113
urban religion, 298; Armanno Pungilupo, 323–28, 332; Armenian Church, 330–31; "civic religion," 299–303, 305–7; Greek Church, 298, 328–31; iconography of Fontana Maggiore, 307–10, *308*; Jews, 298, 302, 318–21, 332–33; *Mariegola*, 305–5, *306*; Muslims, 298, 302, 321–23, 328, 332–33; *Ordinarius* of Padua, 310–15; processions, 310–15; recluses, 315–18, 332; as term, 303–5; women, 302, 304, 311, 317, 321, 332–33
Ursacius, bishop of Brescia, 48

Valdicastro, 99, 104
Valdinievole, 239
Vallombrosa, 100, 102–3, 105–6, 110–12, 115–19, 230, 237, 358–59
Vanna da Orvieto, blessed, 219
Venice, 9, 16, 37, 56, 121–22, 262, 373, 386; confraternities, 134, 140–41, 145–48, 151, 163, 171, 183, 211, 305–7; heresy, 262; mendicants, 202–4, 211, 215; Scuola di San Giovanni Evangelista, 305–7
Venosa, 229

Vercelli, 16, 56, 80–81, 85, 90, 107, 211, 289
Verdiana da Castelfiorentino, saint, 248
Verona, 3, 17, 50, 53, 56, 65, 94, 204, 218; confraternities, 149, 162, 166, 168, 170–72, 184; heresy, 262, 274, 282; as New Jerusalem, 361; processions, 313
Vicenza, 184, 204, 218, 273–74, 293
Victor II, pope, 22–23
Victor III, pope (Desiderius, abbot of Montecassino), 29, 95, 223, 231
Victor IV, antipope, 32–34
Vienna, Council of, 119
Villani, Giovanni, 340, 344, 353–54
Villano, archbishop of Pisa, 78
Visconti, Ambrogio, 150
Visconti, Federico, archbishop of Pisa, 12
Visconti, Otto, archbishop of Milan, 12
Viterbo, 169, 211, 249, 268

Waldensians (Poor of Lyon), 41, 191–92, 244, 259, 275–81, 283–85, 293–94
Waldo (Waldesius) of Lyon, 275–79, 282
Walter, archbishop of Troia, 62
William, archbishop of Siponto, 62
William I of Altavilla of Sicily, 32
William II of Altavilla of Sicily, 34, 322
William of Maleval, saint, 109, 234–35

Zenobius, saint, 350, 363–64, 367–68

www.ingramcontent.com/pod-product-compliance
Lightning Source LLC
Chambersburg PA
CBHW020030200126
38435CB00027B/470